A COMMENTARY ON
THE EPISTLE TO THE HEBREWS

OTHER BOOKS BY PHILIP E. HUGHES

Commentary on the Second Epistle to the Corinthians (NICNT)
Interpreting Prophecy
But for the Grace of God

A COMMENTARY
ON THE
EPISTLE TO THE HEBREWS

by
PHILIP EDGCUMBE HUGHES

William B. Eerdmans Publishing Company

Reprinted September 1979

Library of Congress Cataloging in Publication Data

Hughes, Philip Edgcumbe.
    A commentary on the Epistle to the Hebrews.

    Includes indexes.
    1. Bible.   N.T.   Hebrews—Commentaries.
I. Title.
BS2775.3.H84   227'.87'077   76-49104
ISBN 0-8028-3495-7

The Scripture quotations in this publication are from the Revised Standard Version of the Bible, copyrighted 1946, 1952, © 1971, 1973 by the Division of Christian Education of the National Council of the Churches of Christ in the U.S.A., and used by permission.

Excursus III, "The Blood of Jesus and His Heavenly High Priesthood," was initially published in *Bibliotheca Sacra* 130 (1973), 99–109, 195–212, 305–314, and 131 (1974), 26–33; Excursus IV, "The Doctrine of Creation in Hebrews 11:3," first appeared in *Biblical Theology Bulletin* 2 (1972), 64–77; and the section "Hebrews 6:4–6 and the Peril of Apostasy" was published originally in *Westminster Theological Journal* 35 (1973), 137–155. They are republished by permission of the publishers of these journals.

For
MARTYN LLOYD-JONES
speaker of the word of God
in gratitude
for the constancy of his friendship
during more than thirty-five years

PREFACE

Living on close terms with the Epistle to the Hebrews for a half-dozen years has immensely deepened my appreciation of the rich strength and compassion of the Christian gospel and increased my own personal grasp of the faith won for us and delivered to us by him who is the Apostle and High Priest of our confession.

The author of Hebrews has a superb perspective on Christ's transcendental supremacy, on the uniqueness of his priestly mediation, and on the total "once-for-all" efficacy of his sacrifice of himself for us sinners. His understanding of the logic of the incarnation as the means both to the Son's self-identification with mankind and also to his self-offering, Man for man, in our place on the cross is penetrating. He perceives that the exaltation of the risen Savior means the exaltation also of our humanity, which he united to himself in order that he might redeem it, with the result that the way is now open for us into the heavenly sanctuary of the presence of God himself. He apprehends that the glorious destiny for which man was created, and which was lost through man's disobedience, has been restored through the perfection of the faithfulness, obedience, and suffering of this one true Man. Without wavering he insists on the immutability of the word and the promises of God; consequently, he says, we are required to be constant in faith, hope, and perseverance as we run the Christian race, no matter how menacing the hostile forces that surround us may appear to be. Along with these insights, the author's pastoral concern, earnest warnings, sympathetic encouragement for those tempted to compromise or even give up the struggle, and his appeal to them to take their stand with Christ "outside the camp"—all combine to make this writing indeed a tract for the times, and not only for the author's times, but for *all* times.

The serious study of the Epistle to the Hebrews cannot fail to have a powerfully beneficial effect on the personal life of the individual Christian and on the corporate well-being of the church. It is my desire and prayer that this commentary, even with its deficiencies, may be of service to fellow pilgrims who wish to lay hold of the important instruction communicated in this writing by an author who must have been a truly remarkable person.

There are many to whom I would like to express my gratitude, but I must content myself by mentioning in particular my friends Mr. William B. Eerdmans, Jr., for the willingness with which he took on the publication of this volume and the care with which he and his staff have produced it; Mr. Arthur W. Kuschke, Jr., for his genial cooperation in placing the facilities of the library of Westminster Theological Seminary (Philadelphia) at my disposal; Professor C. Spicq, O.P., of the University of Fribourg, Switzerland, whose own work on the Epistle to the Hebrews is a monument of dedicated piety and erudition, for his cordial encouragement in conversation and correspondence; and Mr. Dan G. McCartney for valued assistance in the preparation of the indices for this volume. My indebtedness to many others, past and present, is apparent in the pages that follow.

PHILIP EDGCUMBE HUGHES
Rydal, Pennsylvania

CONTENTS

ABBREVIATIONS

ASV	American Standard Version (1901).
Blass-Debrunner	*A Greek Grammar of the New Testament and Other Early Christian Literature* by F. Blass and A. Debrunner, trans. and rev. by Robert W. Funk (1961).
Goodspeed	*The New Testament: An American Translation* by Edgar J. Goodspeed (1923).
JB	The Jerusalem Bible (1966).
JBL	*Journal of Biblical Literature*.
JTS	*Journal of Theological Studies*.
KJV	King James Version = Authorized Version (1611).
Kittel, TDNT	*Theological Dictionary of the New Testament,* ed. by Gerhard Kittel, trans. by Geoffrey W. Bromiley (9 vols., 1964–1974).
Knox	*The New Testament of our Lord and Saviour Jesus Christ,* trans. by Ronald Knox (1945).
Liddell and Scott	*A Greek-English Lexicon,* comp. by Henry George Liddell and Robert Scott (1883 edn.).
LXX	The Septuagint (Greek) version of the Old Testament.
Migne, PG	*Patrologia Graeca,* ed. by J. P. Migne (162 vols., 1857–1866).
Migne, PL	*Patrologia Latina,* ed. by J. P. Migne (217 vols., 1844–1855).
Moffatt	*The New Testament: A New Translation* by James Moffatt (1922).
Moulton and Milligan	*The Vocabulary of the Greek Testament illustrated from the papyri and other non-literary sources* by James Hope Moulton and George Milligan (1949).
NEB	The New English Bible (1961).
NTS	*New Testament Studies*.
NTTE	The New Testament in Today's English Version (1966).
Phillips	*The New Testament in Modern English,* trans. by J. B. Phillips (1958).
RSV	The Revised Standard Version (1952).
RV	The Revised Version (1881).

Strack-Billerbeck

Vg

Weymouth

ZNTW

Kommentar zum Neuen Testament aus Talmud und Midrasch by H. L. Strack and P. Billerbeck (1922–1961).
The Vulgate (Latin) Version.
The New Testament in Modern Speech, trans. by Richard Francis Weymouth (1902).
Zeitschrift für neutestamentliche Wissenschaft.

COMMENTARIES

The following is a select list of commentaries. A comprehensive bibliography of commentaries and other writings on the Epistle to the Hebrews is available in C. Spicq, *L'Epître aux Hébreux* (Etudes Bibliques), I, pp. 379ff., "Hébreux (Epître aux)," in *Supplément au Dictionnaire de la Bible*, VII, col. 272ff., and *Epître aux Hébreux* (Sources Bibliques), pp. 44ff., covering the periods up to 1950, 1951 to 1961, and 1962 to 1976 respectively.

4th century:
Chrysostom (Migne, PG, 63; ET, London, 1893).
5th century:
Theodoret (Migne, PG, 82).
6th century:
Ecumenius (Migne, PG, 119).
8th century:
Alcuin (Migne, PL, 100).[1]
11th century:
Theophylact (Migne, PG, 125).
12th century:
Peter Lombard (Migne, PL, 192).
Herveus (Migne, PL, 181).
13th century:
Thomas Aquinas (*Super Epistolam ad Hebraeos Lectura*, Rome, 1953).
16th century:
Jacques Lefèvre d'Etaples [Faber Stapulensis] (*Commentariorum in Epistolas Beatissimi Pauli Apostoli Liber Quartusdecimus*, Paris, 2nd edn. 1515).
Erasmus (*Opera Omnia*, Vol. VI, *Adnotationes*, Lyon, 1705).

1. The text I have used for Alcuin is found in Vol. III of the *Opera Ambrosii* published in Paris in 1586. This volume contains commentaries on Luke's Gospel (which is a genuine work of Ambrose), and on the Epistles of Paul (the first thirteen of which are the work of the fourth-century and as yet unidentified author known as Ambrosiaster, and the fourteenth of which is on Hebrews), together with some other exegetical writings. The work on Hebrews covers the first ten chapters of that epistle only. I am indebted to Professor F. F. Bruce for bringing to my attention E. Riggenbach's *Die ältesten lateinischen Kommentare zum Hebräerbrief*, which is *Forschungen zur Geschichte des neutestamentlichen Kanons und der altkirchlichen Literatur*, viii, 1, ed. by T. Zahn (Leipzig, 1907), pp. 18ff., where proof is offered that it is in fact the work of Alcuin. The commentary, which is of considerable worth and which clearly has roots in the fourth century, is available, as stated above, in Migne, PL, Vol. 100 (cols. 1031ff.).

Luther (*Opera*, Weimarer Ausgabe, Vol. 57, Pt. 3, 1883; ET by James Atkinson, *Lectures on the Epistle to the Hebrews 1517–1518*, in *Luther: Early Theological Works*, London, 1962).

Cajetan (*Epistolae Pauli et aliorum Apostolorum, etc.*, Venice, 1531).

Calvin (*Opera Omnia*, Vol. VII, 1567, Amsterdam; ET by John Owen, Edinburgh, 1853).

Beza (*Jesu Christi Domini nostri Novum Testamentum*, Geneva, 1582).

17th century:

Cornelius à Lapide (*Commentarii in Scripturam Sacram*, Tom. IX, Paris, 1864).

Estius (*In Epistolam Beati Pauli Apostoli ad Hebraeos Commentarius*, Cologne, 1631).

H. Grotius (*Annotationes in Acta Apostolorum et in Epistolas Catholicas*, Paris, 1646).

W. Gouge (*Commentary on the Whole Epistle to the Hebriews*, Edinburgh, 1866).

J. Owen (*Exercitations on the Epistle to the Hebrews*, Edinburgh, 1855).

18th century:

J. A. Bengel (*Gnomon Novi Testamenti*, Stuttgart, 1860).

19th century:

F. Bleek (*Der Brief an die Hebräer*, Berlin, 1828–40).

H. Alford (*The Greek Testament*, Vol. IV, London, 1861).

J. Brown (*An Exposition of the Epistle to the Hebrews*, Edinburgh, 1862).

W. Lindsay (*Lectures on Hebrews*, 2 vols., Edinburgh, 1867).

F. Delitzsch (*Commentary on the Epistle to the Hebrews*, 2 vols., Edinburgh, 1872).

A. B. Davidson (*The Epistle to the Hebrews*, Edinburgh, 1882).

C. Wordsworth (*The New Testament of our Lord and Saviour Jesus Christ*, Vol. II, London, 1882, pp. 361–426).

C. F. Keil (*Kommentar über den Brief an die Hebräer*, Leipzig, 1885).

G. Lünemann (*Commentary on the Epistle to the Hebrews*, New York, 1885).

B. Weiss (*Handbuch über den Brief an die Hebräer* [Meyer Kommentar], Göttingen, 1888).

B. F. Westcott (*The Epistle to the Hebrews*, London, 1889).

F. W. Farrar (*The Epistle of Paul the Apostle to the Hebrews*, Cambridge, 1891).

20th century:

A. Schlatter (*Der Brief an die Hebräer*, in *Erläuterungen zum Neuen Testament*, Vol. III, Stuttgart, 1910).

E. C. Wickham (*The Epistle to the Hebrews*, London, 1910).

A. Nairne (*The Epistle of Priesthood: Studies in the Epistle to the Hebrews*, Edinburgh, 1913).

E. Riggenbach (*Der Brief an die Hebräer*, Leipzig, 1913).

A. Nairne (*The Epistle to the Hebrews*, Cambridge, 1921).

J. Moffatt (*A Critical and Exegetical Commentary on the Epistle to the Hebrews*, Edinburgh, 1924).

H. Windisch (*Der Hebräerbrief*, Tübingen, 1931).

O. Michel (*Der Brief an die Hebräer*, Göttingen, 1936, rev. 1949).

J. Bonsirven (*Epître aux Hébreux*, Paris, 1943).

R. C. H. Lenski (*The Interpretation of the Epistle to the Hebrews*, Columbus, Ohio, 1946).

C. Spicq (*L'Epître aux Hébreux*, 2 vols., Paris, 1952/53).

P. Teodorico da Castel S. Pietro (*L'Epistola agli Ebrei*, Rome, 1952).

COMMENTARIES

J. Héring (*L'Epître aux Hébreux*, Paris and Neuchâtel, 1954).

F. W. Grosheide (*De Brief aan de Hebreën en de Brief van Jakobus*, Kampen, 1955).

T. Hewitt (*The Epistle to the Hebrews*, London, 1960).

F. F. Bruce (*The Epistle to the Hebrews*, London and Grand Rapids, 1964).

H. Montefiore (*A Commentary on the Epistle to the Hebrews*, New York and Evanston, 1964).

G. W. Buchanan (*To the Hebrews*, New York, 1972).

When authors are cited in this volume by name only, without the titles and page numbers of their works, the references are to commentaries in the list above, at the place dealing with the verse(s) under discussion.

INTRODUCTION

If there is a widespread unfamiliarity with the Epistle to the Hebrews and its teaching, it is because so many adherents of the church
have settled for an undemanding and superficial association with the
Christian faith. Yet it was to arouse just such persons from the lethargic
state of compromise and complacency into which they had sunk, and to
incite them to persevere wholeheartedly in the Christian conflict, that
this letter was originally written. It is a tonic for the spiritually debili-
tated. The study of this epistle leads us beneath the surface of things to
the profound depths of our evangelical faith, and enriches and establishes our understanding of the grace of God manifested on our behalf in
the incarnation, self-offering, and exaltation of him who is the Apostle
and High Priest of our confession. "There is, indeed, no book in Holy
Scripture," says Calvin in the foreword to his commentary on Hebrews,
"which speaks so clearly of the priesthood of Christ, so splendidly extols
the power and worth of that unique sacrifice which he offered by his
death, deals more adequately with the use and also the abrogation of
ceremonies, and, in short, explains more fully that Christ is the end of
the Law." We neglect such a book to our own impoverishment.

It is true that the Epistle to the Hebrews has been the battleground
of discordant opinion and conjecture: its author is unknown, its occasion
unstated, and its destination disputed. But these are matters at the
periphery, not the heart of the book's importance. All are agreed on the
intrinsic nobility of its doctrine. The writer's mastery of Greek is unmatched elsewhere in the New Testament and his powerfully argued
development of fundamental theological themes indicates the exceptional quality of his intellect. His language, in Westcott's judgment, is
"both in vocabulary and style purer and more vigorous than that of any
other book of the New Testament";[1] and Moffatt writes admiringly: "He
has a sense of literary nicety, which enters into his earnest religious
argument without rendering it artificial or over-elaborate. He has an art

1. B. F. Westcott, p. xliv.

of words, which is more than an unconscious sense of rhythm. He has the style of a trained speaker; it is style, yet style at the command of a devout genius."[2] Stylishness is indeed far from being synonymous with artificiality in the case of our author. Like all the other parts of the New Testament, the Epistle to the Hebrews is a writing with a purpose. Seriousness is the tone by which it is dignified throughout, and the language is as free from superficiality as is the subject matter. Addressed as it is with the utmost earnestness to a specific situation which calls for compassion and correction, it is no mere literary essay or theoretical treatise. The doctrines, warnings, and appeals of the letter are compelling, not primarily because they are presented with linguistic artistry, but because their concern is with matters of eternal consequence. Moffatt rightly counsels against the unreality of explaining away the most striking passages as "rhetorical abstractions" or treating the epistolary form as "a piece of literary fiction."[3] The spirit of zeal and urgency which pervades the letter from beginning to end is eloquent evidence of the deep concern by which the writer is motivated.

THEME AND STRUCTURE

The comprehensive theme of the Epistle to the Hebrews is that of the absolute supremacy of Christ—a supremacy which allows no challenge, whether from human or angelic beings. As this is not an essay in academic speculation, it is apparent that those whom the writer is addressing, attracted by the teachings of some contemporary movement, are being tempted to assign to certain personages a prominence which would detract from the unique authority of Christ and thus have the effect of subverting the gospel of their salvation. It is of vital importance, for their eternal destiny is at stake, that they should not lose hold of this salvation which they have professed to receive, and to this end they must see clearly that Christ is without rival or equal. The unchallengeable supremacy of Christ is established by the demonstrations, through the logic of Scripture, of his superiority to the great leaders and instructors of God's people in the past, namely, prophets and patriarchs in

2. James Moffatt, p. lxiv. The Jesuit scholar Albert Vanhoye writes: "One recognizes in this epistle the work of a true man of letters whose extraordinary talent is enhanced by excellent powers of organization. In these pages nothing seems left to chance; on the contrary, the choice of words, the rhythm and construction of phrases, the arrangement of different themes, all appear to be controlled by the pursuit of a harmonious balance in which subtle variations contribute to a wisely calculated symmetry" (*La Structure Littéraire de l'Epître aux Hébreux*, 1963, p. 11). Vanhoye in his detailed study seems to me to err on the side of overstatement and to tend to find more stylistic symmetries and literary subtleties than are really present.
3. Moffatt, p. xxx.

general and Moses and Aaron in particular, and also to spiritual angelic creatures. The superiority of Christ, moreover, is identical with the superiority of the new covenant, of which he is both the fulfilment and the mediator, to the old covenant, which was conveyed by the agency of angels and administered by prophets, priests, and rulers of former times, and which by its very nature was imperfect and temporary. In Christ the new order, which is perfect and eternal and by which therefore the old is done away, has been inaugurated.

The analysis which follows will help to show the structure of the epistle's content.

Theme: THE SUPREMACY OF CHRIST

I. *Christ superior to the prophets:* his absolute uniqueness as Divine Son, Incarnate Redeemer, and Exalted Lord (1:1–3).

II. *Christ superior to the angels* (1:4–2:18)
Proved from the Old Testament: 1:4–13.
First warning: the peril of neglecting such a great salvation: 2:1–4.
Christ the true Man exalted above the angels: 2:5–9.
The purpose and consequence of the Incarnation: 2:10–18.

III. *Christ superior to Moses* (3:1–4:13).
Moses and Christ compared: 3:1–6a.
Second warning: the peril of copying the example of the Israelites in the wilderness: 3:6b–4:2.
Necessity of faith and obedience for entry into God's rest: 4:3–11.
The sharp and penetrating discernment of God's word: 4:12–13.

IV. *Christ superior to Aaron* (4:14–10:18).
Our compassionate High Priest: 4:14–16 (resuming the subject already introduced in 2:17–3:1).
High priesthood: general qualifications: 5:1–4.
Christ's qualifications: 5:5–10.
Third warning: the peril of stagnation and apostasy: 5:11–6:8.
Encouragement to persevere: 6:9–20.
The order of Melchizedek: 6:20b–7:28 (already mentioned in 5:6, 10; cf. 2:17; 4:14f.).
Significance of Melchizedek: 7:1–10.
Imperfection of the levitical priesthood contrasted with the perfection of Christ's priesthood: 7:11–28.
The shadows of the old covenant superseded by the realities of the new covenant: 8:1–9:10.
The redemption procured by Christ's sacrifice all-sufficient and eternal: 9:11–10:18.

V. *Christ superior as the new and living way* (10:19–12:29).
Encouragement to enter boldly into the true sanctuary: 10:19–25 (cf. 4:14–16).
Fourth warning: the peril of despising the gospel: 10:26–31.

Encouragement to endure: 10:32–39.
The triumph of faith and perseverance illustrated by the example of the
    believers of the former age: 11:1–39.
The supreme example of Christ: 12:1–4.
The significance and value of discipline: 12:5–11.
Encouragement to resume the struggle: 12:12–14.
Fifth warning: the peril of following the example of Esau: 12:15–17.
Mount Sinai and Mount Zion compared: 12:18–24.
Sixth warning: the peril of refusing him who speaks from heaven: 12:25–29.

VI. *Concluding exhortations, requests, and greetings* (13:1–25).

SYNOPSIS

The superiority of Christ to the prophets of old is suggested in the
opening verses of the epistle by the declaration that God's final word
has been spoken in the person of him who is a Son. This final word
fulfils and transcends all previous words spoken by God through the
prophets, so that there is no place for venerating the ancient prophets in
a manner that would challenge the supremacy of him who himself is
uniquely the Word, consubstantial with the Father, the agent of creation, the sustainer of the universe, the heir of all things, and the exalted
Redeemer of the world (1:1–3).

As Son, moreover, Christ is superior to the angels, as quotations
adduced from the Old Testament scriptures show. There can be no
question of a parity, let alone a superiority, of the angels to the sovereign
Son. Angels are but creatures, ministering spirits in the service of the
Creator, sent forth to serve for the sake of those who, thanks to the Son,
are to inherit salvation (1:4–14).

This leads to the first warning. To assign to angels a position of
undue prominence can only mean that the recipients of the epistle are
drifting away from the evangelical truth in which they have rejoiced. It is
true that the message declared through angels when the law was given
at Sinai was important and carried condign penalties for those who
transgressed its commandments; but much more important is the message declared through the Lord himself, for it is the message of God's
great salvation—for us law-breakers!—in and through the Son: much
less can those who spurn such incomparable grace expect to escape
divine judgment (2:1–4).

Nowhere do the Scriptures suggest that the world to come is to be
subjected to the authority of angels—a belief which the readers are being
enticed to accept. On the contrary, it is under the feet *of man* that everything is to be placed in subjection, as Psalm 8 teaches—not, of course,
sinful and fallen man who has perverted the order of creation, but again

4

the Son, who through his incarnation fulfils the perfection of manhood, who by his redeeming death, Man for man, deals with the radical problem of sin and restores the harmony between man and God and between man and creation, and who in his exaltation raises our redeemed humanity united to him by faith to a destiny higher than that of the angels. For the Son, who to procure our salvation made himself for a little while lower than the angels, is even now crowned with glory and honor, far above all angels (2:5–9).

It is Jesus, therefore, the incarnate Son, our true brother, and not an unincarnate angelic creature incapable of self-identification with man and his plight, who is the pioneer and prince of our salvation. It is he who has broken the power of that hostile angel the devil and has brought us from death and bondage to life and freedom. And his incarnation means the assumption of the nature not of angels but of the covenant seed of Abraham. The covenant made by God with Abraham, which is the root of the new covenant, finds its fulfilment in him whose work as a merciful and faithful high priest making propitiation for the sins of mankind depends on his identification with us. Such a high priest—God indeed, but also by reason of the incarnation our compassionate fellow man who knows and understands our temptations—is uniquely qualified to help us in our trials in a way that no angel or any other creature possibly can (2:10–18).

Certainly, under the old order Moses and Aaron were prominent as apostle and high priest respectively; but in the new and eternal order the two offices of apostleship and high priesthood are combined in the one person of Jesus Christ. To attempt to put the clock back by a return to the Mosaic pattern and the disciplines of the wilderness experience of the Israelites betrays a serious misconception of the Christian situation. Moses, it is true, was commended for his faithfulness, and in this he prefigured Christ and his faithfulness; but there is this important difference, that Moses was faithful *in* God's house *as a servant*, whereas Christ was faithful *as a son* who is *over* God's house: the superiority of a son to a servant needs no demonstration (3:1–6).

The period of forty years in the wilderness, moreover, was far from being a glorious chapter in the history of Israel. Indeed, centuries later the Holy Spirit, speaking through the Psalmist (Ps. 95), held up the hard-heartedness of that generation, whose rebellious disobedience precluded them from entering into the rest of the promised land, as an example to be avoided. A return to the wilderness régime, even with the intention of scrupulously observing the conditions of the Mosaic covenant, must involve the imitation of the disobedience of that generation, only to a more serious degree, since those to whom this epistle is addressed are contemplating an action which would render them disobedient to him who is God's final word to man (cf. 1:1f.) and in whom the old order has been replaced by the new (3:7–19).

A failure of faith will mean, too, a failure to reach the promised rest, not now, however, a transient earthly respite, but the abiding rest of God's eternity. In any case, the entry into Palestine under Joshua was not the attainment of the true rest, for otherwise there would have been no point in speaking, as God did through David so long afterwards, of a day of opportunity for avoiding the judgment which overtook the wilderness generation. Accordingly, the readers are exhorted, in view of the penetrating and infallible judgment of God's word, to concentrate every energy on entering into that true rest which still remains for the people of God (4:1–13).

The author now proposes to demonstrate that Christ is superior, not only to angels and Moses, but also to Aaron. Christ has become "the source of eternal salvation to all who obey him"—which cannot be said of angels or Moses or Aaron! The main premise of his argument is that Christ's priesthood is of a different order from that of Aaron, a priesthood, namely, as announced in Psalm 110, of the order of Melchizedek, who is designated a priest forever. Having broached the subject, however, he interrupts his theme in order to issue a further solemn warning to his readers. Their progress as Christians has been arrested to such a degree that they are scarcely competent to receive the careful teaching he wishes to give them; indeed, there is even a danger of their lapsing into a state of apostasy from which it would be impossible for them to recover. Yet he is confident that a true work of God has taken place in their midst and that he will be able to stir them up to renewed zeal and perseverance in the Christian contest (4:14–6:12).

They must appreciate that their spiritual roots go back not to Moses but to Abraham; for the word of God's covenant promise to Abraham was confirmed with an oath—something, again, which cannot be said of the intermediate covenant given through Moses. Moreover, the blessings of the Abrahamic covenant have come to fulfilment in Christ and have been made available to us by virtue of the redemptive work of him who is our high priest forever after the order of Melchizedek, and who has led the way as our forerunner into the heavenly sanctuary (6:13–20).

Now at length the theme of the nature and purpose of Christ's high priesthood receives full development. The significance of Melchizedek as prefiguring Christ is drawn from the two places in the Old Testament where he is mentioned, that is, Genesis 14:18ff. and Psalm 110:4, and his superiority to Abraham and thence Levi is argued—and thus the superiority of his priesthood to that of the levitical order. There would, furthermore, have been no point in the mention by the Psalmist, in the midstream of Jewish history, of another order of priesthood if under the order of Aaron then in operation perfection had been attainable: the mere reference to a different order implies the imperfection and inadequacy of the existing order. It was only to be expected, then, that Christ, our high priest after the order of Melchizedek, should not have belonged to the priestly line of Aaron. His descent, in fact, on the human side, was from Judah, not Levi. Here, too, the adding of a divine oath ("The Lord has sworn. . . ," Ps. 110:4) indicates the superiority of the priesthood of Christ to that of the Levites, who were appointed to office without the swearing of an oath (7:1–22).

There are other considerations which confirm the superiority of the order of Melchizedek. The Aaronic order had many priests in a long succession because each in turn was carried away by death, whereas the order of Melchizedek has but one priest whose priesthood is permanent because he continues forever. The former priests were sinful as well as mortal men and therefore had to offer sacrifices for their own sins before they offered sacrifices for the sins of the people, whereas the sole priest of the latter order was entirely without sin and therefore had no need to make an offering on his own behalf. The fact that in the former system there was a multiplicity not only of priests but also of sacrifices, day after day and year after year, is eloquent of the imperfection and ineffectiveness of that system to bring about a radical reconciliation between man and God, whereas the fact that our High Priest of the order of Melchizedek offered only one sacrifice forever indicates the absolute perfection and efficacy of that one all-availing offering. The unblemished sacrifice offered by the incarnate Son provided, indeed, the perfect substitution, Man for man, because it was the willing sacrifice *of himself*, unlike the sacrifices of irrational and uncomprehending brute beasts offered by the levitical priesthood (7:23–28).

It would be vain to imagine that advantage could result from any kind of restoration of the wilderness tabernacle and its ceremonies, for these were no more than a copy and shadow of the true heavenly sanctuary and its ministry. Bound up as the earthly sanctuary was with the former, Mosaic, covenant, there would have been no point in speaking, as the prophet Jeremiah does (31:31ff.), of God's intention to establish a new covenant if the former covenant had been without fault (the argument is parallel to that already used in connection with the mention of a different order of priesthood in Ps. 110, at 7:11ff.). The mere announcement of a new covenant implies both the faultiness and the obsolescence of the covenant in existence when Jeremiah uttered his prophecy (8:1–13).

Far from needing restoration, the observances belonging to the tabernacle of the Israelites were of a superficial and temporary character, "until the time of reformation," for they were incapable of cleansing and making perfect the conscience of the worshipper. This is symbolized by the consideration that under the former system the people were actually excluded from entry into the inner sanctuary (the holy of holies) of God's presence, which the high priest alone was permitted to enter, and then only once a year on the Day of Atonement. But Christ by shedding his own blood—human blood, not the blood of goats and bulls—has secured an eternal redemption for us, and by his entry into heaven itself has opened the way for us all into the true sanctuary of God's presence; for the radical effect of his blood-shedding has been the cleansing of our conscience from dead works so that we may serve the living God, and the sanctuary he has entered is no copy or shadow but that sanctuary which is authentic and eternal. In view of these great truths, there is and can be no repetition of his one perfect and final sacrifice (9:1–28).

Had the levitical sacrifices made perfect those on whose behalf they were offered, they would have ceased to be offered; but, continually repeated as they were, they served only to remind the people of their sinfulness and to point to the need for a sacrifice that would once and for all take away sin. In the nature of the case, this is something the blood of bulls and goats could not do. What the former system lacked, however, the Son has provided by coming into the world to fulfil the divine will for the world's redemption by the offering of himself. The levitical priests *stand* daily in the performance of their never completed sacerdotal work, offering sacrifices that can never take away sins; but Christ, after offering a single sacrifice for sins, *sat down* at God's right hand: there is no more "standing" for him as a sacrificing priest because "by a single offering he has perfected for all time those who are sanctified." In fulfilment of Jeremiah's promise of the new covenant God has in this way removed the sins of his people; and where there is forgiveness of sins, that is to say, a truly radical justification of the sinner, there is no longer any offering for sin (10:1–18).

Through Christ's blood-shedding the way into the presence of God himself, hitherto closed to the people, has been laid open. Christ himself, and none other, is this "new and living way." On the basis, then, of the Son's perfect high-priestly offering the readers are urged to draw near with confidence and boldness, to hold fast their confession without wavering, and to encourage one another in their trials and struggles as the day of the Lord's return comes ever closer. This exhortation is followed by another solemn warning of the extreme peril of sinning against the light: those who violated the law of Moses were duly and severely punished; much more severe will be the judgment that overtakes those who trample underfoot the sacred blood of the covenant of grace. They are entreated, however, to recall the days when they first responded to the message of the gospel, and especially the joyful manner in which they had then endured suffering and shame and the plundering of their property, and the mutual love and compassion which had bound them together. They are begged not to throw away their confidence, but to persevere in the conflict, remembering that the people of God are to live by faith and that God has no pleasure in those who shrink back (10:19–39).

Faith which overcomes every obstacle and triumphs in the darkest situations and even in the hour of death has always been the glory of all true men and women of God. To illustrate this there follows an encomium of the dauntless faith and unquenchable hope of believers who lived and died in the time of promise but not yet of fulfilment, from Abel to the heroes of the Maccabean resistance, patriarchs and prophets, pilgrims and martyrs, persons both well known and little known, "of whom the world was not worthy," and whose gaze was fixed not on earthly shadows but on the heavenly reality. They with us, and we with them, are made perfect in Christ. This is the noble company we join in running the race of faith. The readers are encouraged, therefore, to run the Christian race with dedication, concentrating their attention, not on their fellow contestants, past or present, but on Jesus, who alone is the pioneer and perfecter of our faith, who in his single-minded endurance of the cross endured infinitely more than any follower of his will ever endure, and whose patient suffering has been crowned with glory. How can they lose heart with his supreme example before them (11:1–12:4)!

Have they forgotten the wise admonition that "the Lord disciplines him whom he loves"? Affliction endured for Christ's sake is a mark of that discipline which God, like any loving father, uses for the benefit of his children. Undisciplined children are not genuine sons. Such discipline, accordingly, should assure us of our sonship, and its beneficial purpose is that we may partake of the divine holiness. Painful though chastisement is for the time being, it produces an eternal and joyful harvest. Thus the readers are incited to brace themselves for the hardships of the struggle, being warned at the same time by the evil example of Esau, who for the ease of the moment bartered and irretrievably lost his birthright (12:5–17).

They must abandon all hankering after the Mosaic era, for the terrors of the law and the exclusion of the people from the glory of God's presence are, in Christ, things of the past. In coming to Christ it is not to Mount Sinai that they have come, but to Mount Zion, the heavenly Jerusalem, the realm of the new covenant in which all rejoice together in the gracious presence of God. A final warning is given, that to reject God when he speaks from heaven (in the person of his Son, cf. 1:2) is to invite judgment more dreadful even than that which came upon those

Israelites who rejected him when he spoke on earth in Moses' day (12:18–29).

In the concluding section there is yet one more appeal to the readers to turn their backs decisively on the old Mosaic/Aaronic order of things, with its impermanent city and sanctuary, and to concentrate on that true and lasting city which is to come, by going forth to Jesus "outside the camp" and taking their stand with him on the ground hallowed by his suffering, that is to say, by willingly bearing abuse for his sake (13:1–15).

* * * * *

It is evident, therefore, that the whole practical thrust of the epistle is to persuade those to whom it is addressed to resist the strong temptation to seek an easing of the hardships attendant on their Christian confession by accommodating it to the régime of the former covenant, which they had professed to leave behind when they were baptized in the name of him who is the Mediator of the new covenant, and which in any case has been rendered obsolete by the advent of Christ and the inauguration of the new and eternal order of priesthood. This practical purpose is pursued by demonstrating that the former system was inherently imperfect and therefore impermanent and that the period of forty years in the wilderness under Moses was no "golden age" to be recovered or emulated, and by insisting on the absolute supremacy of Christ and the sole and complete sufficiency of the redemption that is ours through him. To compromise this unique gospel is to lose it; and losing this is to lose everything.

OCCASION

What was the occasion that called forth this document? Because of the silence of the epistle itself and the absence of any external information or tradition which might provide a solution to this question, the only alternative to an incurious agnosticism is to attempt to construct a conjectural answer that takes account both of the internal implications of the epistle and of the contemporary circumstances of its composition. Leaving aside for the moment inquiries concerning the identity and locality of those who are being addressed, it is apparent that a situation has arisen in which a particular community of Christians is contemplating a compromise of disastrous consequences since it would mean in effect the abandonment of the gospel. On the one hand, faced with daily indignities and the prospect of persecution of a more severe nature, they are sorely tempted to withdraw from the good fight of faith; on the other, enticed by teachings which threaten the uniqueness of Christ, they are in danger of squandering their birthright in order to purchase temporary relief. More specifically, they are showing a disposition to assign to angels a dignity above that of Christ, and to treat the Mosaic system with its levitical priesthood as an institution of abiding value and efficacy.

The strong temptation to effect a compromise with idealistic Judaism points to the conclusion that the opposition being encountered by the recipients of the epistle was Jewish rather than Gentile. Accommodation to judaistic beliefs and practices was the price that would purchase ease and acceptance. It is clear from Luke's account of the fortunes of the early church that the first fierce opposition to the gospel came from the Jews, and that this hostility was intense because the original Christians were their compatriots whom they regarded as traitors to their ancestral religion. Peter and John, for example, were summoned before the Sanhedrin to be reprimanded and threatened (Acts 3 and 4); the apostles were imprisoned by the high-priestly party (Acts 5:17ff.); Stephen, the first of the martyrs, was stoned to death by the Jews (Acts 7:54ff.); the Pharisee Saul of Tarsus led the savage and systematic persecution of the apostolic church in Jerusalem and beyond (Acts 8:3; 9:1f.); and subsequently he himself, as Paul the apostle, met with violence from Jewish opponents of the gospel as he traveled from city to city (Acts 13:45ff.; 14:2, 19ff.; 17:5ff.; 21:30ff.; 22:22ff.; 23:12ff.). Congeneric antipathy must have been largely responsible also for the chronic poverty of the mother-church in Jerusalem (cf. Acts 11:29f.; 24:17; 1 Cor. 16:1ff.; 2 Cor. 8:1ff.; Gal. 2:10).

This consideration, together with the frequent indications that the temple priesthood was still in operation (see below, pp. 30ff.), would tell in favor of locating the recipients of Hebrews in Jerusalem or, more generally, on Palestinian soil. The earliest tradition of which we have knowledge, that recorded by Chrysostom in the introduction to his homilies on Hebrews, places the readers "in Jerusalem and Palestine"; and a Palestinian destination has become all the more probable since the discovery of the Dead Sea Scrolls—a discovery which raised afresh the question of the relationship of Christianity to Essenism in the first century.

In 1955 Oscar Cullmann called attention to the remarkable fact that in the New Testament there is no mention of the Essenes,[4] though Philo and Josephus speak of them as one of the three main religious groups in the Judaism of their day; whereas the other two sects, the Pharisees and the Sadducees, are repeatedly mentioned, especially the former, against

---

4. O. Cullmann, "The Significance of the Qumran Texts for Research into the Beginnings of Christianity," JBL, 74 (1955), pp. 213ff.

whose sophistry and traditionalism the severest denunciations of Jesus were directed. Since it is scarcely conceivable that Jesus and his followers had no contact with the Essenes, the suggestion has been made that the silence of the New Testament indicates that there was no conflict between them. F. M. Braun, also writing in 1955,[5] accepted Spicq's hypothesis[6] that the Epistle to the Hebrews was addressed to a group of converted Jewish priests (cf. Acts 6:7) who in the persecution following the martyrdom of Stephen had fled from Jerusalem, but he envisaged an additional and contributory dispersion of Jews, including priests, belonging to the Qumran community when this was disrupted by the upheavals leading up to A.D. 70, who supposedly carried with them into Asia the rule of their community.

Spicq himself extended his original perspective to include the influence of Qumranian beliefs as an important factor lying behind the writing of Hebrews.[7] Like others before him, he sees close affinities between this epistle and the thrust of Stephen's "defense" in Acts 7, and regards Stephen as the main cause of the conversion to the Christian faith of the great number of priests mentioned in Acts 6:7—though this connection is not indicated in Luke's account. At the same time Spicq remarks that the Qumran sect originated from a secession of priests from the temple of Jerusalem. He points out, among other things, that it is difficult not to see "a firm, almost aggressive, rejoinder to Qumranian speculations" in the assertion of Hebrews 7:13f.: "The one of whom these things are spoken belonged to another tribe [than that of Levi], from which no one has ever served at the altar; for it is evident that our Lord was descended from Judah, and in connection with that tribe Moses said nothing about priests." Spicq observes that the announcement of the new covenant by Jeremiah (31:31ff.), which the author of Hebrews cites (8:8ff.) as evidence of the obsolescence of the Mosaic covenant, held a place of primary importance in the speculations of the Qumran community, who of course interpreted the new covenant in terms of a recovery of the Mosaic/Aaronic ideal; and that "the moral predilections and preoccupations of Hebrews offer striking analogies" with those of Qumran. Altogether the best explanation, he concludes, is that the epistle "was addressed to Esseno-Christians, to certain Jewish priests—among whom a number of ex-Qumranians could be found—whose doctrinal and biblical training, spiritual presuppositions, and religious 'prejudices' he knew."

5. F. M. Braun, "L'Arrière-Fond Judaïque du Quatrième Evangile et la Communauté de l'Alliance," *Revue Biblique*, 62 (1955), pp. 5ff.
6. C. Spicq, I, pp. 242ff.
7. C. Spicq, "L'Epître aux Hébreux, Apollos, Jean-Baptiste, les Hellénistes et Qumrân," *Revue de Qumrân*, 1 (1958–59), pp. 365ff.

Jean Daniélou is another scholar who favors the opinion that the recipients of the Epistle to the Hebrews were a company of converted priests. He takes the silence of John the Baptist regarding the Essenes as an indication that he himself was deeply influenced by Essenism. The information that John the Baptist had been "in the wilderness till the day of his manifestation to Israel" (Lk. 1:80) is regarded as significant by Daniélou, who suggests also that John named only those sects to which he was opposed.[8] The fact that members of the Zadokite-Essene sect were exiled to Damascus about 60 B.C. is reason to suppose that they maintained their identity in that city in the succeeding decades. The "startling similarities," which Cullmann pointed out, between the speech of Stephen and the Essenian MS known as the Damascus Document lead Daniélou to suppose that the "Hellenists" of the early Jerusalem church were in fact converted Essenes, and that when they were driven from Jerusalem by persecution (Acts 8:1ff.), those who found their way to Damascus encountered the Zadokite remnant there and won some converts among them. Daniélou even entertains the possibility that Paul, whose first days as a Christian were spent in Damascus, may have been instructed there by these converted Essenes.[9] In this and much else Daniélou displays his penchant for building hypothesis on hypothesis. More substantial is the connection he proposes between "the extraordinary cult of angels" fostered by the Zadokites and the insistence in the opening section of the Epistle to the Hebrews on the superiority of Christ to angels, and between the Zadokite expectation of two messianic personages, one Aaronic and priestly and the other Davidic and kingly,[10] and the teaching of Hebrews that in the person of the incarnate Son the priestly, but Melchizedekian, and kingly offices are combined.[11]

In an important essay on "The Dead Sea Scrolls and the Epistle to the Hebrews,"[12] which was published in 1958 but the theme of which had previously been presented in lectures in different cities, the Jewish scholar Yigael Yadin, of the Hebrew University in Jerusalem, reminds us that "the fact that up to very recently we did not possess

---

8. J. Daniélou, *The Dead Sea Scrolls and Primitive Christianity* (1958), pp. 18ff.
9. *Ibid.*, pp. 94ff.
10. A. J. B. Higgins argues that contemporary Judaism expected only one messiah, of the royal line of Judah, and that the eschatological high priest, whose coming was also awaited, was not a messianic figure; "The Priestly Messiah," NTS, 13 (1967), pp. 211ff. Cf. R. B. Laurin, "The Problem of Two Messiahs in the Qumran Scrolls," *Revue de Qumrân*, 4 (1963), pp. 39ff.; Morton Smith, "What is implied by the variety of Messianic figures?", JBL, 78 (1959), pp. 66ff.; also J. Liver, "The Doctrine of the Two Messiahs," *Harvard Theological Review*, 52 (1959), pp. 149ff.; G. R. Beasley-Murray, "The Two Messiahs in the Testaments of the Twelve Patriarchs," JTS, 48 (1947), pp. 1ff.
11. Daniélou, *op. cit.*, pp. 112f.
12. *Scripta Hierosolymitana*, IV (1958), pp. 36ff.

sufficient data concerning the practices and beliefs of sectarian Judaism with which to compare the arguments of *Hebrews*, led some scholars to admit frankly their despair of ascertaining the identity of the 'addressees', or to remark subsequently in a rather axiomatic manner that this remarkable piece of primitive Christian thought 'had nothing to do with any movement in contemporary Judaism' (Moffatt)"; and he offers the thesis that the epistle is specifically directed against the beliefs of the Qumran community, holding that "the 'addressees' themselves must have been a group of Jews originally belonging to the DSS Sect who were converted to Christianity, carrying with them some of their previous beliefs." Yadin explains that the members of the Dead Sea Sect were awaiting the advent of two messianic figures, of whom the kingly would be subordinate to the priestly, but both of whom would be subordinate to the supreme figure of the archangel Michael, thus subjecting the world to come to angelic authority (cf. 2:5). They expected, also, the appearance of a prophet who would be another leading personage, in fact a second Moses in fulfilment of the promise of Deuteronomy 18:18, and the resumption, under an authentic (Zadokite) high priesthood, of the whole sacrificial system prescribed in the Mosaic law. With this consummation in view, they patterned their manner of life closely on the idealized model of the children of Israel under Moses in the wilderness during the forty years prior to their entry into the promised land. Their withdrawal from the corrupt ministry of the temple to the wilderness near the Dead Sea was for the purpose of preparing themselves for re-entry into Jerusalem when in due course the hour for the overthrow of the false leaders and the vindication of God's true covenant people arrived. A situation in which members of a Christian group were finding such beliefs attractive would fully explain the necessity for sending a letter insisting on the absolute and unique supremacy of Christ, and therefore his superiority to all others, with particular reference to prophets and angels, Moses and Aaron.

This is undoubtedly the best theory yet advanced to explain the occasion and purpose of the Epistle to the Hebrews. It is a key which seems quite remarkably to fit the lock and open a door that has for so long remained closed. I have used it as a working hypothesis in the course of the commentary on the text of the epistle, but with a broader view of the situation than is taken by Yadin. It is unnecessary to postulate, as Yadin does, that the recipients of Hebrews had themselves originally been members of the Qumran community. This, of course, is a possibility, but it is equally possible that the Hebrew Christians to whom the letter is addressed had in one way or another encountered and felt the attraction of the teachings of this sect. Indeed, it is not even necessary to limit the scope of reference to this particular settlement near the Dead Sea. This was not a very large group and it seems preferable to regard it as but one representative (by no means unimportant) of the much larger and more widely spread movement of Essenism. Qumran, no doubt, was an example of the movement in its most dedicated aspect, and as such may have enjoyed a reputation as proof of the practicability of the ideal. Pliny the Elder apparently had this settlement in mind when he wrote of "the solitary tribe of the Essenes" located on the west side of the Dead Sea;[13] but his Jewish contemporary Philo says that the Essenes lived "in many cities of Judea and in many villages" as well as in separate communities.[14]

The discovery of the Dead Sea Scrolls has given us much information, hitherto unavailable, concerning the precise doctrines and eschatological expectations of a particular group whose beliefs may be taken as representative in the main of Essenism in general, which, as we have noticed, was one of the three chief sects in first-century Judaism. Now quite unexpectedly we have knowledge of an important movement in Palestine contemporary with the composition of the Epistle to the Hebrews and showing close correspondences to the religious outlook which this epistle was designed to counteract. Indeed, the papyrus fragments found more recently in Cave 11 at Qumran provide evidence that Melchizedek, so significant a figure in the eyes of the author, was assigned a prominent role in the eschatological perspective of the Dead Sea Sect. Thus another link is forged, and we can now better understand the necessity for the careful instruction that is given these Hebrew Christians regarding the proper place and relevance of Melchizedek. The hypothesis we have been considering at least rests on definite evidence concerning beliefs and practices that were being advocated in contemporary Palestine and that have a close resemblance to the situation reflected in the Epistle to the Hebrews, unlike other hypotheses which have almost inevitably been imaginative and often fanciful attempts at reconstruction in the absence of materials for first laying a reasonably solid foundation. Unless further knowledge comes to light it is unlikely to find itself challenged by another hypothesis of comparable worth. A hypothesis it remains, however, and as such it cannot be allowed to determine questions of exegesis, though at many points it may seem to throw a suggestive and helpful light on the text.

PLACE OF ORIGIN AND DESTINATION

Speculations concerning the places from which and to which the Epistle to the Hebrews was written have been no less varied and inventive. The only possible indication in the epistle itself is the salutation at

---

13. Pliny the Elder, *Natural History* ii.73.
14. Philo, *Hypothetica* ii.1; cf. *Every Good Man Is Free* 75; Josephus, *Bell. Jud.* ii.119ff.

the end: "Those who are from Italy send you greetings" (13:24). Unfortunately, however, the designation "those who are from Italy"[15] is ambiguous. If it means Italian Christians who were *away from* Italy, that is, in some country other than Italy, this would exclude Italy as the place of the epistle's origin. But if it means those who are *from* or *of Italy*, in the sense that Italy was their homeland and implying that these were Italian as distinct from non-Italian Christians in Italy—a distinction to be expected in a cosmopolitan city like Rome—, the letter would then have been written from some place in the Italian peninsula. In favor of the latter interpretation is the only strand of external tradition known to us, namely, the subscription found in some manuscripts to the effect that Hebrews was written from Rome or from Italy.[16] This subscription is not original but is a later scribal or editorial addition, and as such it carries no authority; but it does indicate the existence of a tradition or belief that Rome or, more generally, Italy, was the place of the epistle's origin. It is impossible to determine the strength of this tradition. The probability is that it rests on no more than a scribal gloss on the phrase "those who are from Italy." There is no firm evidence that the letter was written from Rome.

The theory that the letter's recipients were located in or near Rome has gained wide acceptance in recent times. Its advocates, understandably, take the designation "those who are from Italy" as a reference to certain Italian believers in the author's company who were sending salutations back to friends in their homeland which, for one reason or another, they had left. To meet the objection that, if the recipients had been through the Neronian persecution, the author could hardly have written, "in your struggle against sin you have not yet resisted to the point of shedding your blood" (12:4), it becomes necessary to argue, either that they were not actually located in Rome, where this persecution was concentrated, and so escaped the emperor's fury, or that the letter was written prior to A.D. 64. In the latter event, the suggestion is offered that their "hard struggle with sufferings," involving public abuse, the plundering of their property, and imprisonment for some of their number (10:32ff.), may have been connected with the expulsion of the Jews from Rome in A.D. 49, on the assumption that Christians were at that time regarded as a Jewish sect and were a major cause of unrest in the Jewish community of the capital.[17] If, however, the letter is dated

15. Οἱ ἀπὸ τῆς Ἰταλίας.
16. Ἐγράφη ἀπὸ Ῥώμης is found in the fifth-century Codex Alexandrinus (A), and ἀπὸ Ἰταλίας in the sixth-century Codex Euthalianus (H) and in the Coptic and Peshitta versions. Both occur in a few still later manuscripts.
17. According to the Roman historian Suetonius (*Claudius* xxv.4), the Jews were expelled from Rome because "they were constantly indulging in riots at the instigation of Chrestus"—taking "Chrestus" to be a mishearing of the name of Christ. Among those forced to leave were Aquila and Priscilla, who subsequently settled in Corinth (Acts 18:2, 26).

after A.D. 64, a defense of the Roman destination has been based on the consideration that ordinarily Judaism was one of the religions approved in the Roman empire, which leads to the supposition that those to whom Hebrews was addressed were disinclined, situated as they were, *ex hypothesi*, at the heart of the empire, to make a clean break from the relative protection enjoyed by Judaism and invite opposition as adherents of a new and officially unrecognized religion. The suggestion is, accordingly, that these particular Christians in Rome had avoided martyrdom in the Neronian persecution of A.D. 64 by associating themselves closely with the Jews and their synagogue worship. But a reconstruction along these lines begs the question whether at this stage, more than thirty years after Pentecost, there would have been a welcome and a refuge for any group of Christians among Jews who would have been strongly antipathetic to the gospel of Jesus Christ. Moreover, as William Manson has observed, it is inconceivable that "such dissembling under the colour of the Jewish religion" should not have been plainly denounced by the writer of Hebrews: "we should have expected the infamy to resound through every page of his letter."[18]

The theory of a Roman destination goes back at least as far as Wettstein in the middle of the eighteenth century. Among its later advocates mention may be made of Alford, Milligan, Zahn, Windisch, Lenski, William Manson, and Neil.[19] It is tendentious to assert, as Neil does, that "the epistle was known and quoted in Rome earlier than anywhere else," for this conclusion is forced from the solitary fact that Clement of Rome, in his letter to the Corinthians, was demonstrably familiar with the Epistle to the Hebrews, which was written some thirty years earlier. It is hardly wise to make so sweeping an assertion on the basis of such a meager piece of evidence. But in any case the arguments in favor of a Roman destination are far from solid, and in view of the great increase of our knowledge and understanding of the contemporary scene in first-century Palestine which has resulted from the study of the documents discovered at Qumran Spicq has good reason for declaring that "the Roman destination of Hebrews is becoming more and more improbable."[20]

Many others have presented a case for Rome as the place from

---

18. W. Manson, *The Epistle to the Hebrews* (1951), p. 165.
19. J.-J. Wettstein, *Novum Testamentum Graece*, ii (1752), pp. 386f.; H. Alford, pp. 62ff.; G. Milligan, *The Theology of the Epistle to the Hebrews* (1899), pp. 49f.; see also *The Expositor*, IV (1901), pp. 437ff. (Milligan supposes that the group addressed had originally been composed of Jews from Rome visiting Jerusalem on the Day of Pentecost and converted on that occasion); A. von Harnack, ZNTW, 1 (1900), p. 19; A. S. Peake, *Hebrews* (1902), pp. 25ff.; T. Zahn, *Introduction to the New Testament*, ii (1909), pp. 341ff.; H. Windisch, pp. 127ff.; R. C. H. Lenski, *The Interpretation of the Epistle to the Hebrews* (1946); W. Manson, *ut supra*; W. Neil, *The Epistle to the Hebrews* (1955), pp. 16f.
20. C. Spicq, *Revue de Qumrân, ut supra*.

which the Epistle to the Hebrews was dispatched. W. F. Howard, for example, argued in a manner more fanciful than firm that it was addressed from Rome to Ephesus.[21] A. Ehrhardt adopted the view of Overbeek[22] that Hebrews was "a message of consolation from the Church at Rome to Christians in the Holy Land after the fall of Jerusalem."[23] A great many other places, virtually covering the Mediterranean world from Spain to Galatia, have been proposed both for the epistle's origin and for its destination. The earliest available tradition, as we have seen, locates the recipients in Palestine, or, more particularly, in Jerusalem. Certainly, if Rome had been the epistle's place of origin or destination, it is difficult to understand why it should for so long have been refused acknowledgment there; or if Alexandria (favored by many), where it did find acceptance, it is strange that the Christians there should not have told the world that they had a special association with it.

There is general agreement that those to whom the epistle was addressed, wherever they were located, did not constitute the worshipping community there in its entirety. This is suggested particularly by the request that they should convey the writer's greetings to all their leaders and to all the saints (13:24), implying, it seems, that there were leaders other than their own and saints other than themselves in that neighborhood.[24] Zahn and others have supposed that the recipients belonged to a house-church, similar perhaps to the congregation which used to assemble in the home of Aquila and Priscilla when they lived in Rome (Rom. 16:5; 1 Cor. 16:19). Be that as it may, theirs was a group which was seriously considering the advisability of devising a concordat or reconciliation with the Mosaic covenant and its levitical priesthood. Spicq's suggestion that the group was composed of former priests converted to the Christian faith, who would have been more susceptible than others to such a temptation, is not unattractive. The temptation to effect a compromise with an idealistic form of Judaism, however, would have been felt by Hebrew Christians, whether formerly priests or not, living in a Jewish environment, who thought that by this means they would be able to obviate the hardship and hatred which awaited those who professed Jesus as Christ and Lord. We may be sure that it was their "Hebrewness," possibly some specific background that as He-

---

21. W. F. Howard, "The Epistle to the Hebrews," *Interpretation*, 5 (1951), pp. 84ff.
22. F. Overbeek, *Zur Geschichte des Kanons* (1880), pp. 3f.
23. A. Ehrhardt, *The Framework of the New Testament Stories* (1951), pp. 84ff. Zahn (*ut supra*) is another who favors a date after the fall of Jerusalem.
24. The significance of the term ἐπισυναγωγή (10:25), which some have interpreted to mean a distinct congregation within the larger church community, is discussed in the note on pp. 417f. below.

brews they had in common, that bound them together into a distinct community and that made it necessary for the writer of the epistle to instruct them so carefully on the transient imperfection of the old order compared with the unique and abiding perfection of the redemption achieved by him who is our great High Priest. Where this group of Hebrew Christians was living we do not know, though the probabilities increasingly favor a location somewhere in Palestine. The obscurity surrounding the place from which the epistle was sent continues to be impenetrable.

AUTHORSHIP

The absence both of solid testimony, internal or external, and of any firm traditions means that, as things are, the riddle of the authorship of Hebrews is incapable of solution. Nonetheless many solutions have been proposed with varying degrees of dogmatism. Failing the discovery of fresh and positive evidence, however, we must be content with our ignorance. To say this is not to imply that the offering of conjectures is out of place; indeed, the history of the speculations concerning the identity of the epistle's author is of considerable interest and merits some attention.

In the epistle of Clement of Rome to the Corinthians, written before the close of the first century, echoes and imitations of the Epistle to the Hebrews are clearly discernible. Evidently, therefore, Hebrews was in his time known and received as an authoritative Christian writing in the church at Rome. This consideration makes it surprising that in the two following centuries it was neither used nor acknowledged in the Western Church. Clement gives no clue to the author's identity; but as he does mention Paul by name as the author of a letter the Corinthians had received—plainly, as the context shows, a reference to our canonical 1 Corinthians—his silence regarding the writer of Hebrews may at least indicate that he did not consider Paul its author. Certain affinities between Clement's letter and Hebrews have, as a matter of fact, induced some to suppose that the author was Clement. This, however, can scarcely be so, since there is an interval of some thirty years between the two compositions, and in any case it does not require an expert to see that as a stylist and theologian Clement is not to be compared with the writer of Hebrews.

The period of eclipse which Hebrews suffered in the West is attributable, as far as we can judge, to doubts concerning its apostolic origin and to the manner in which passages like 6:4–6 and 10:26–31 were used to bolster a rigorist doctrine of church discipline, expressed particularly in the denial of any possibility of repentance to those who sinned after baptism. The signs of a developing polemic are discernible as early as the first half of the second century in Hermas, who contends, in opposition to "teachers who maintain that there is no other repentance than that which takes place when we descend into the water and receive remission of our former sins," that the person who sins after baptism has one further opportunity of repentance.[25] Subsequently, the misappropriation of such passages by severely ascetic sects, such as those named after Montanus and Novatian, gave rise to unjustifiable prejudices against this epistle; and even in the fourth century, when Hebrews won general acceptance, the interpretation of orthodox commentators was influenced by the fear of seeming in any way to condone the rigorist exegesis, with the result that they too failed to comprehend the proper significance of the passages in question.[26] The fact that, for example, in the writings of Cyprian there is no reference to and no quotation from Hebrews indicates how little regarded this epistle had come to be in the West during the third century. Had Cyprian acknowledged its authenticity and studied its teaching, he would surely have reached very different conclusions regarding the nature of the Christian ministry from those he propounded, for it would then hardly have been possible for him to treat "all the passages of the Old Testament which refer to the privileges, the sanctions, the duties, and the responsibilities of the Aaronic priesthood as applying to the officers of the Christian Church."[27]

In the fourth century we find Eusebius asserting that "Paul's fourteen epistles are well known and undisputed" (by which he means the thirteen canonical epistles that bear Paul's name and the Epistle to the Hebrews); but Eusebius adds that "it is not right to overlook the fact that some have rejected the Epistle to the Hebrews, saying that it is disputed by the church of Rome on the ground that it was not written by Paul."[28] He informs us, moreover, that there were some even in his own day among the Romans who did not consider Hebrews a work of the apostle.[29] In Alexandria, however, comparable doubts concerning the genuineness of the epistle do not seem to have been entertained. Clement of Alexandria (d. ca. 215) held that Hebrews was the work of Paul, that it was written to the Hebrews in the Hebrew language, and that Luke subsequently translated it for the benefit of the Greeks. This, according to Clement, explains the similarities of style between Hebrews

---

25. Hermas, *Shepherd*, Commandment iv.3.
26. For fuller discussion see pp. 214f. below.
27. J. B. Lightfoot, "The Christian Ministry," in *St. Paul's Epistle to the Philippians* (1868), pp. 256f.
28. Eusebius, *Historia Ecclesiastica* iii.3.
29. *Hist. Eccl.* vi.20.

and Acts. He pointed out, further, that to avoid arousing a hostile attitude, because the Hebrews viewed him with prejudice and suspicion, Paul did not affix his name to the letter.[30] Clement claims the support of his own master and predecessor in the school of Alexandria, Pantenus (d. ca. 200), who had given the further quaint explanation that since the Lord had been sent to the Hebrews and Paul to the Gentiles, Paul modestly and through respect for the Lord suppressed his name as the author of this writing.[31]

Origen (d. 255), Clement's successor in Alexandria, expressed doubts concerning the Pauline authorship of Hebrews, drawing attention to the more polished style and purer Greek of Hebrews, though admitting that "the thoughts of the epistle are admirable and not inferior to the acknowledged apostolic writings, as anyone who carefully examines the apostolic text will admit." In his opinion, "the thoughts are those of the apostle, but the diction and phraseology are those of someone who remembered the apostolic teachings and wrote down at his leisure what had been said by his teacher." "Therefore," he adds, "if any church holds that this epistle is by Paul, let it be commended for this; for not without reason have the ancients handed it down as Paul's." Nonetheless, Origen continued an agnostic on this matter, for he continues, in words much quoted: "The truth God alone knows." He also mentions that previously some had ascribed the epistle to Clement of Rome and others to Luke.[32] Eusebius, who records these things, regarded Hebrews as a Pauline composition, originally written in Hebrew, but then translated, he says, in the view of some by Luke and in the view of others by Clement of Rome, whom he prefers.[33]

The continuing hesitancy of the Latin Church over the Pauline authorship of Hebrews is reflected in the writings of Jerome, who, toward the close of the fourth century, affirms that Paul sent letters to seven churches, whereas the letter to the eighth, that is, to the Hebrews, was excluded by most from the Pauline collection.[34] Jerome himself seems to have accepted the work as coming from Paul, for on another occasion he writes: "The epistle which is known as the Epistle to the Hebrews is not considered Paul's because it differs from the others in style and language, but is reckoned according to Tertullian to be the work of Barnabas, or according to others to be by Luke the Evangelist or Clement

---

30. Recorded in *Hist. Eccl.* vi.14.
31. Recorded in *Hist. Eccl.* vi.14. Pantenus is not mentioned by name in this passage, but it is virtually certain that the designation "the blessed presbyter" which Clement uses is a reference to Pantenus.
32. Recorded in *Hist. Eccl.* vi.25.
33. *Hist. Eccl.* iii.38.
34. Jerome, Letter 53, to Paulinus.

afterwards bishop of the church at Rome, who, they say, arranged and adorned the ideas of Paul in his own language, though, presumably, since Paul was writing to Hebrews and was in disrepute among them, he may have omitted his name from the salutations for this reason. Being a Hebrew he wrote Hebrew, his own language, most fluently, while the things which were eloquently written in Hebrew were more eloquently turned into Greek, and this explains why it seems to differ from Paul's other epistles."[35] In a letter to Dardanus, moreover, Jerome insists that, despite disagreements between East and West over the identity of the author, what is important is that the epistle is approved by all as the work of "a man of the Church" and "is daily honoured in the public reading of the churches."[36] Augustine speaks of "the many and great things" that are written about Melchizedek "in the epistle addressed to the Hebrews, which most say is by the apostle Paul, though some deny this,"[37] and he affirms his confidence in quoting from this book because of "the authority of the Eastern churches which expressly place it among the canonical scriptures."[38] Jerome must be held mainly responsible for the entrenchment of the belief that Hebrews was a writing of the apostle Paul because of the title "The Epistle of Paul to the Hebrews" (Epistola Pauli ad Hebraeos) which was placed at the head of the Vulgate version of this book. Certainly, from the time of Jerome on, misgivings about the Pauline authorship of Hebrews seem to have been set aside, so that for some eleven centuries the epistle was received without question as the work of Paul.

The attitude of Thomas Aquinas may be taken as characteristic of the medieval centuries. He observes (in the Prologue to his commentary on Hebrews) that prior to the Council of Nicea there had been some who doubted the Pauline authorship of Hebrews and that the epistle had been attributed variously to Luke, Barnabas, and Clement of Rome. But he reminds his readers that ancient doctors, including (Pseudo-) Dionysius and Jerome, accepted Hebrews as a genuine work of Paul. With this judgment he concurs, and for three main reasons: first, because Paul was the apostle not of the Jews but of the Gentiles and therefore suppressed his name, not wishing to impose his apostleship where officially it did not belong; secondly, because his name was hateful to the Jews, who regarded him as subversive of their system of law,

---

35. Jerome, De Viris Illustribus 5; cf. also Letter 140, to Cyprian, and his comment on Matthew 4:26, where he straightforwardly attributes Hebrews to Paul. Much of what Jerome says about Hebrews is lifted from Eusebius, with some slight variations; cf., for example, De Vir. Illus. 59.
36. Jerome, Letter 129.
37. Augustine, De Civitate Dei xvi.22.
38. Augustine, De Peccatorum Remissione et Meritis i.50; cf. also De Doctrina Christiana ii.8, where he lists Hebrews as belonging to "the fourteen epistles of the apostle Paul."

and his anonymity was intended to forestall their rejection of this epistle's most salutary teaching; and thirdly, because he himself was a Jew, and members of the same household do not readily acknowledge excellence among their fellows (cf. Mt. 13:57). The more elegant style of Hebrews is attributed to the fact that Paul was an accomplished linguist (which may be true, but Aquinas bases this judgment on a misunderstanding of 1 Cor. 14:18), and in fact wrote the letter in Hebrew, the language that came most naturally to him and in which, consequently, he was able to express himself most idiomatically. The translation into Greek, Aquinas holds, was done by Luke, who had a special proficiency in that language. This, of course, is essentially the same position as that propounded by Clement of Alexandria, with echoes also of Jerome and others.

With the dawn of the Reformation, which coincided with the distribution, thanks to the invention of printing, of many of the patristic writings, we find doubts concerning the Pauline authorship of Hebrews reappearing. Erasmus, for example, at the end of his annotations on Hebrews, writes that "as it differs considerably, where the phraseology is concerned, from the style of Paul, so it most definitely accords with the spirit and sentiment of Paul" (which is in effect a restatement of the judgment of Origen). After remarking that "for a great number of years, right up to the time of Jerome, it was not received by the Latins," and discussing a variety of opinions concerning the epistle, he comes to this conclusion, in characteristically Erasmian fashion: "If the Church in fact defines it as Paul's, I willingly submit my intellect to the obedience of faith, though as far as I can judge it does not seem to be his. . . . And even if I knew for a fact that it was not Paul's, the matter is not worth fighting over."

Luther, though at first, apparently, accepting the ascription of Hebrews to Paul, soon rejected the possibility of Pauline authorship. He perceived the incompatibility of Hebrews 2:3, where the writer says that the gospel "was attested to us by those who heard the Lord," with Paul's affirmation in the first chapter of Galatians that he did not receive the gospel from man but through a revelation of Jesus Christ, and that he "did not confer with flesh and blood" (Gal. 1:11f., 16f.). This, Luther says in a gloss on Hebrews 2:3, is "a very strong argument against Pauline authorship"; and he repeats this opinion in the preface to the 1522 edition of his lectures on Hebrews. In 1537 he put forward the name of Apollos, in a sermon on 1 Corinthians 3:4ff.: "This Apollos," he says, "is a man of high intelligence. The Epistle to the Hebrews is certainly from him." And he affirms this conviction again in his lectures on Genesis, when commenting on Genesis 48:20, in 1545, the last year of his life.

Calvin, in the introduction to his commentary, which appeared in 1549, places Hebrews "without hesitation among the apostolical writings" and attributes the fact that many had been led to dispute its authority to the craft of Satan. After mentioning various opinions assigning the epistle to Paul or Luke or Barnabas or Clement, he declares his own inability to accept it as Pauline in origin: "I can adduce no reason to show that Paul was its author," he states; "for those who say that he designedly suppressed his name because it was hateful to the Jews allege nothing to the point. . . . The manner of teaching and the style sufficiently witness that someone other than Paul was the author, and the writer himself asserts in the second chapter that he was one of the disciples of the apostles, and this is far removed from the manner in which Paul speaks of himself." This conclusion is repeated in his exegesis of 2:3; and in his comments on 13:23 Calvin expresses his preference for either Luke or Clement as the writer of the epistle.

Luke and Clement, it will be remembered, are among the earliest of candidates, for they are mentioned by Origen as having had their advocates. To their names must be added that of Barnabas, since Tertullian (d. ca. 220) refers approvingly to "an epistle to the Hebrews under the name of Barnabas." The quotations he gives from it make it certain that he is speaking of our present canonical book.[39] Neither Luke, who was a historian rather than a theologian, nor Clement, whose suitability has already been discussed, would seem to have had the particular competence required for the writing of Hebrews. Barnabas, however, is in many respects an attractive candidate. Unfortunately, unlike Luke and Clement, we possess no authentic writings of his with which to compare the epistle. Originally called Joseph, the name Barnabas, which Luke explains as meaning "son of encouragement," was given him by the apostles, and it may be understood accordingly as reflecting their estimate of his character and qualities. (The suggestion that the description of the epistle as a "word of encouragement," 13:22, is a pointer to Barnabas, the "son of encouragement," as the author is specious and paltry.[40]) A native of Cyprus, with Greek as his first language, Barnabas was a Jew. Of particular interest and perhaps significance is the information that he was a Levite (Acts 4:36). It was Barnabas who befriended Paul after his conversion and allayed the suspicions of the apostles regarding the genuineness of his Christian profession (Acts 9:26ff.). Sent by the apostles to Antioch, he showed himself an enthusiastic supporter of the evangelization of the Gentiles, and he subsequently spent a full year, together with Paul, in that city instructing the numerous converts

---

39. Tertullian, *De Pudicitia* 20.
40. See, for example, B. Weiss, p. 18.

in the faith. Thereafter the Antiochene church sent him and Paul to Jerusalem with contributions for the relief of their fellow Christians in Judea (Acts 11:20–30). On returning to Antioch Barnabas and Paul were commissioned by the church there for the work of evangelism and Barnabas accompanied Paul on his first missionary journey. John Mark, his cousin from Jerusalem, went with them as far as Perga in Pamphylia, where he turned back (Acts 12:25; 13:1ff., 13; Col. 4:10). Barnabas is described as "a good man, full of the Holy Spirit and of faith" (Acts 11:24), and was held in the highest regard as a leader in the apostolic church; indeed, in Acts 14:14 he is designated an apostle. Altogether, then, because of his acceptance among the leaders of the church in Jerusalem and farther afield, his close collaboration with the apostle Paul, his gifts as a teacher and evangelist, and his upbringing as a Levite, he possessed some excellent qualifications for writing the Epistle to the Hebrews. Moreover, as Weiss observes, Tertullian's identification of Barnabas as the author of Hebrews is "the sole positive tradition to be found in ecclesiastical antiquity";[41] for, as Salmon says, "when he speaks of Barnabas as the author he is plainly not making a private guess, but expressing the received opinion of the circle in which he moved."[42] In the fourth century, in addition to Jerome,[43] reference to this tradition is found in Filaster[44] and Gregory of Elvira.[45] Among the numerous modern scholars who favor Barnabas mention may be made of Wieseler,[46] Ritschl,[47] Keil,[48] Blass,[49] Bartlet,[50] Wickham,[51] Dibelius,[52] Cadoux,[53] Riggenbach,[54] and Bornhaüser.[55]

Of the various other names that have been proposed the most curious is that of Priscilla, who—in association, it is true, with her husband

---

41. Weiss, *loc. cit.*
42. G. Salmon, *Introduction to the New Testament*[6] (1892), p. 425.
43. Jerome, *De Viris Illustribus* 5.
44. Filaster, *De Haeresibus* 89.
45. Gregory of Elvira, *Tractatus Origenis*, ed. by Batiffol-Wilmart (1900), p. 108: "The most holy Barnabas says, 'Through him we offer to God the sacrifice of lips that acknowledge his name'" (see 13:15).
46. K. Wieseler, *Chronologie des apostolische Zeitalters* (1848), pp. 504ff.
47. A. Ritschl, *Studien und Kritiken* (1866), p. 89.
48. C. F. Keil, *Kommentar über den Brief an die Hebräer* (1885).
49. F. Blass, *Die Brief an die Hebräer* (1903).
50. J. V. Bartlet, "Barnabas and his Genuine Epistle," *The Expositor*, Sixth Series, 5 (1902), pp. 409ff.; 6 (1902), pp. 28ff.; "The Epistle to the Hebrews as the Work of Barnabas," *ibid.*, 8 (1903), pp. 381ff.; 11 (1905), pp. 431ff.; Eighth Series, 5 (1913), pp. 548ff. Subsequently, however, Bartlet abandoned Barnabas for Apollos.
51. E. C. Wickham, p. xii.
52. F. Dibelius, *Der Verfasser des Hebräerbriefes* (1910).
53. C. J. Cadoux, "The Early Christian Church in Egypt," *Expository Times*, 33 (1922), pp. 536ff.
54. E. Riggenbach, pp. xlff.
55. K. Bornhaüser, *Empfänger und Verfasser des Briefes an die Hebräer* (1932), pp. 75ff.

Aquila, but with the wife in the leading role—was Harnack's choice.[56] The arguments he deployed need not detain us here. There is, however, one place in the epistle, 11:32, where the masculine gender of a participle reveals the author to have been a man, not a woman.[57] This, at least, is a sound and reasonable conclusion to draw; though the possibility cannot be denied that an authoress might have been clever enough to conceal her femininity by putting the participle here in the masculine gender. But it is better seen as confirming the overwhelming probability that Hebrews was written by a man.

After being either called in question or forthrightly rejected by such leading figures as Erasmus, Luther, and Calvin in the sixteenth century, the advocacy of the Pauline authorship enjoyed an Indian summer in the next two centuries. Owen in the seventeenth and Bengel in the eighteenth century, for example, maintain that Peter is referring to the Epistle to the Hebrews when he says to his readers, in his second epistle: "So also our beloved brother Paul wrote to you according to the wisdom given to him" (2 Pet. 3:15). The argument is that the readers addressed are the same as those to whom the first epistle was sent (cf. 3:1, "This is now the second letter that I have written to you") and that, designated there as "the exiles of the Dispersion in Pontus, Galatia, Cappadocia, Asia, and Bithynia" (1 Pet. 1:1), they were in fact Hebrew Christians, identical with the recipients of our epistle. Apart from the consideration, however, that those to whom the Epistle to the Hebrews was sent were apparently a compact group in a particular locality rather than a scattering of Christians over an extensive geographical area, the likelihood is that the "Dispersion" addressed by Peter was a dispersion of Christians generally, comprising Gentile as well as Jewish believers. The letter of Paul to which Peter refers could well be his Epistle to the Galatians (especially if the North Galatian theory of its destination is correct). Supporting arguments based on doctrinal affinities between Hebrews and the Pauline writings, which no one denies, are little to the point once the main premise has fallen away.

More recently, there has been a surge of support for the candidacy of Apollos, whom Luther, as we have seen, held to be the writer of Hebrews, though without setting down the reasons which led him to this conclusion (except for asserting that Apollos was "a man of high

---

56. A. Harnack, "Probabilia über die Adresse und den Verfasser des Hebräerbriefs," ZNTW, 1 (1900), pp. 16ff.
57. In 11:32 the writer asks: "And what more shall I say? For time would fail me to tell. . . ." Here the pronoun με (which could be either masculine or feminine) is qualified by the participle διηγούμενον (which accordingly defines the pronoun as masculine). Harnack dismisses it as a neutral usage. Cf., however, J. Rendel Harris, Side-Lights on New Testament Research (1908), pp. 148ff.

intelligence"). Spicq, for instance, has developed and presented the case for Apollos with much enthusiasm. Few would wish to dispute that the author must have been a Jewish Christian, intellectually distinguished, with special competence in the Old Testament and a profound understanding of the Christian faith and its uniqueness, for this is demanded by the thrust and content of the epistle throughout. Coincidences of style and expression between Hebrews and the writings of Philo lend color to the supposition that the author had connections with Alexandria. These Apollos undoubtedly possessed; for in a brief biographical sketch Luke states that he was "a Jew . . . a native of Alexandria . . . an eloquent man, well versed in the scriptures . . . instructed in the way of the Lord," that "being fervent in spirit, he spoke and taught accurately the things concerning Jesus," and that, having arrived in Achaia, "he powerfully confuted the Jews in public, showing by the scriptures that the Christ was Jesus" (Acts 18:24ff.).

Of these qualifications, Spicq regards as decisive the fact that Apollos was an Alexandrian by birth, assuming as he does that he must have come under the influence of Philo, the philosopher Jew of Alexandria, to a degree that was formative of his thought. The unwillingness of the writer of Hebrews to disclose his name is explained by Spicq as due to his fear of arousing unworthy rivalries in the locality to which it was sent, and similarly the failure of Clement of Rome to mention Apollos by name in his letter to the Corinthians is attributed to concern lest the old contentions in that city might be rekindled by doing so. These arguments fail to carry conviction, however, for obviously the recipients of the Epistle to the Hebrews must have known very well who was writing to them (otherwise the requests, greetings, and plans of the concluding section would have been meaningless, not to mention the question of the authority of the epistle as a whole); moreover, if Clement was careful not to mention the name of Apollos to the Corinthians, why did he mention the name of Paul, which no less than the name of Apollos had been a focus of contentiousness among them (cf. 1 Cor. 1:12)?

Furthermore, to argue that the paucity of teaching on the Holy Spirit in Hebrews tells against Paul and in favor of Apollos as the author has the nature of special pleading.[58] There is no more teaching concerning the Holy Spirit in 2 Corinthians, a writing of comparable size, than there is in Hebrews: is 2 Corinthians therefore not Pauline? Even if the position of the dozen disciples at Ephesus, who had received only the baptism of John and were uninstructed concerning the Holy Spirit (Acts 19:1ff.), was comparable to that of Apollos, who also had known only John's baptism (Acts 18:25)—but of whom it is not in fact said that he

---

58. Spicq, I, pp. 209ff.

was ignorant concerning the Holy Spirit—it does not follow that this defect remained unremedied. On the contrary, Luke tells us that Priscilla and Aquila "took him and expounded to him the way of God more accurately" (Acts 18:26). If 1 Corinthians, so rich in the doctrine of the Holy Spirit, had been written after 2 Corinthians, which has so little to say on the subject, it could perhaps have been argued that Paul advanced from weakness to strength in this area of knowledge; but it was not so, and there is no reason to believe that the writer of Hebrews was inferior to the writer of 2 Corinthians in his understanding of the doctrine of the Holy Spirit.

It should be obvious, too, that a Jew of culture and education did not need to be from Alexandria in order to be familiar with the thought of Philo. In this connection, incidentally, it is interesting that, according to an early tradition, Barnabas preached in Alexandria shortly after the ascension of Jesus.[59] Clement's silence regarding the writer of Hebrews, despite his knowledge and use of the epistle, may indicate, as William Manson thinks, either that he was ignorant of the author's identity or that the name of the author was unfamiliar to the Christians in Corinth toward the end of the first century. A still more likely explanation is that the writer's name was well known both to Clement and to his Corinthian readers, so that there was no need for him to mention it. In Manson's opinion, "Apollos would admirably fill the part in point of his Jewish-Alexandrian origin"; but he finds this supposition outweighed by the consideration that, "if Apollos had been the author, it is difficult to think that the Alexandrian Church would not have preserved some knowledge of the fact in view of the distinguished role of this son of Alexandria in the world-mission, and that Clement would not have mentioned him in writing to the Corinthians in whose history Apollos had played a notable part."[60] Montefiore, who strongly supports Apollos as the writer of Hebrews, supposes that "the generation who knew the name of its author had died out by the time Clement wrote his Epistle in A.D. 95," and adds that "until the lucky guess of Luther, the secret was lost."[61]

In the search for the author of Hebrews the extent of his indebtedness to Philo of Alexandria has become a major issue. If this dependence can be demonstrated, the case for Apollos, the native of Alexandria, is improved. Spicq is one of the many modern scholars who believe that this dependence is demonstrable. Hebrews, he contends, is "completely

---

59. *The (Pseudo-) Clementine Homilies* i.9. The historical value of this document is of course questionable. The passage cited may, however, reflect an actual association of Barnabas with Alexandria.
60. W. Manson, *op. cit.*, pp. 171f.
61. H. Montefiore, p. 30.

interpenetrated with Philonic concepts assimilated by a Christian think-er."[62] Indeed, he judges that the author of the epistle was a Philonist converted to Christianity.[63] He does, however, make the large conces-sion that the exegesis of Hebrews is far removed from that of Philo and that, if the author "has borrowed from him this or that biblical theme or hermeneutical procedure, he has resolutely repudiated his allegorical method, with its subjectiveness and superficiality, in favour of an understanding which is profoundly religious and singularly more pene-trating."[64]

It is indeed possible that Philo and the author of Hebrews came from the same or a similar cultural background. But terminological and conceptual similarities do not at all necessarily point to a common philosophical origin; for when two writers whose systems are radically incompatible are expounding the same material, in this case the Old Testament institutions, it is only to be expected that there will be coinci-dences. It is important to stress, therefore, that the differences between Philo and Hebrews are as fundamental as the affinities are peripheral. Nairne, properly cautioning that coincidences are not always agreements, gives it as his judgment that "it is doubtful whether our author had read Philo."[65] A detailed and exhaustive comparative study has brought Ronald Williamson to the conclusion not only that on "fun-damental subjects" "the thoughts of Philo and the Writer of Hebrews are poles apart" (a judgment with which Spicq would agree), but also that "the Writer of Hebrews had never been a Philonist, had never read Philo's works, had never come under the influence of Philo directly or indirectly."[66]

The insolubility of the problem is only emphasized when scholarly minds, working with the same material, reach diametrically opposed conclusions; and this at least says to us that we must be content not to know and willing to shun dogmatic declarations when the authorship of the Epistle to the Hebrews is being discussed. If Barnabas and Apollos are now the front contenders for the honor, the balance of probability, taking into account such slender evidence as is available to us, would seem to be in favor of the former. Spicq's later article, referred to above, in which while still holding to the authorship of Apollos he joins the company of those who discern important points of contact between Hebrews and contemporary Palestinian Judaism, particularly of the Qumran/Essene variety (which, for example, provides a hitherto un-

62. Spicq, I, p. 49.
63. Spicq, I, p. 91.
64. Spicq, I, pp. 63f.
65. A. Nairne, *The Epistle to the Hebrews* (1957), pp. cix, cx.
66. R. Williamson, *Philo and the Epistle to the Hebrews* (1970), pp. 576f., 579.

known and judasitically less eccentric perspective of first-century speculation regarding the significance of Melchizedek), betokens a considerable shift of focus from Alexandria to Palestine, that is to say, if one
judges rightly, from less to more solid ground.

DATE

The clear evidence of the familiarity of Clement of Rome with the
Epistle to the Hebrews places it firmly within the first century. Other
evidence, of an internal nature, in particular the author's consistent use
of the present tense when speaking of the ministry of the levitical priesthood, points to a date for the writing of Hebrews prior to the destruction
of Jerusalem in A.D. 70; for these present tenses signify that the levitical
priesthood was still functioning, even though the coming of Christ and
his offering of himself denoted the inauguration of the eternal priesthood of Melchizedek. Had the Jerusalem temple been in ruins and its
ministry abruptly ended, the use of the past tense would have been
expected throughout. Moreover, it would be incredible that the author
should not then insistently have drawn his readers' attention to the
striking fact that both temple and priesthood now belonged to past
history, since this would have clinched his argument with visible proof
that the former covenant had given way to the new, the Aaronic order to
that of Melchizedek.

The rebuke in 5:11ff., that "by this time" they ought to be teachers,
instead of dull of hearing and immature, shows that the recipients had
been Christians for some years, as also does the writer's appeal to them
in 10:32 to "recall the former days." The assertion that the gospel "was
attested to us by those who heard the Lord" (2:3) means that the author
and the Hebrew Christians to whom he is writing had been evangelized
by persons, possibly apostles, who had received instruction from Christ
himself. To describe them as "second-generation Christians," as F. F.
Bruce, Spicq, and others do, is misleading, at least in the ordinary sense
of the expression. They were simply believers at one remove from direct
contact with the Lord. Their conversion could have taken place at any
time after Pentecost—quite soon after that event, if Spicq's hypothesis is
correct which links them to the great number of priests who were obedient to the faith in the days preceding the martyrdom of Stephen (Acts
6:7).

More than this cannot be said, unless, as some have judged, the
note of urgency that sounds through the epistle is indicative that the
author foresaw that the judgment which Christ predicted would come
upon Judaism and its temple was close at hand (cf. Mk. 13:14ff.; Mt.
24:15ff.; Lk. 21:5ff.). The date of the composition of Hebrews would then

be shortly before A.D. 70. At any rate, sometime in the sixties would seem best to accord with the few pointers mentioned above.

The present tenses which indicate that the levitical priesthood was still operative when the epistle was written are as follows.

5:1–4. "For every high priest who is chosen from among men is appointed . . . to offer . . . he can deal gently . . . he himself is beset with weakness . . . he is bound to offer . . . one does not take . . . but he is called."[67]

7:21 (7:20 Gk.). "They have become priests. . . ."[68]

7:23. "They are many in number who have become priests, because they are prevented by death from continuing in office."[69]

7:27. "He has no need, like those high priests, to offer sacrifices daily."[70]

7:28. "The law appoints men in their weakness as high priests."[71]

8:3. "For every high priest is appointed to offer. . . ."[72]

8:4f. ". . . since there are priests who offer gifts according to the law, who serve a copy and shadow. . . ."[73]

8:13. "What is becoming obsolete and growing old is ready to vanish away."[74]

9:6f. ". . . the priests go continually into the outer tent, performing their ritual duties, but into the second only the high priest goes . . . not without blood, which he offers. . . ."[75]

9:9. ". . . gifts and sacrifices are offered which cannot perfect the conscience of the worshipper."[76]

9:13. "For if the sprinkling . . . with blood . . . and ashes . . . sanctifies. . . ."[77]

---

67. Πᾶς γὰρ ἀρχιερεὺς ἐξ ἀνθρώπων λαμβανόμενος . . . καθίσταται . . . ἵνα προσφέρῃ . . . μετριοπαθεῖν δυνάμενος . . . καὶ αὐτὸς περίκειται ἀσθένειαν . . . ὀφείλει . . . προσφέρειν . . . οὐχ ἑαυτῷ τις λαμβάνει . . . ἀλλὰ καλούμενος. . . .
68. Οἱ μὲν . . . εἰσὶν ἱερεῖς γεγονότες. The periphrastic use of the present tense of the verb "to be" with the perfect participle defines a state that is still in existence (here and in the next example).
69. Οἱ μὲν πλείονές εἰσιν γεγονότες ἱερεῖς διὰ τὸ θανάτῳ κωλύεσθαι παραμένειν.
70. Οὐκ ἔχει καθ' ἡμέραν ἀνάγκην, ὥσπερ οἱ ἀρχιερεῖς . . . θυσίας ἀναφέρειν.
71. Ὁ νόμος γὰρ ἀνθρώπους καθίστησιν ἀρχιερεῖς ἔχοντας ἀσθένειαν.
72. Πᾶς γὰρ ἀρχιερεὺς εἰς τὸ προσφέρειν . . . καθίσταται.
73. . . . ὄντων τῶν προσφερόντων κατὰ νόμον τὰ δῶρα, οἵτινες ὑποδείγματι καὶ σκιᾷ λατρεύουσιν. . . .
74. Τὸ δὲ παλαιούμενον καὶ γηράσκον ἐγγὺς ἀφανισμοῦ. The present tense of the two participles implies a main verb, which has to be supplied, in the same tense. There is a question, however, as to whether the present is that of the prophet Jeremiah, who has just been quoted, or of the author of Hebrews; if the latter, then it follows that the former covenant with its ceremonies was still in operation when the epistle was written.
75. . . . εἰς μὲν τὴν πρώτην σκηνὴν διὰ παντὸς εἰσίασιν οἱ ἱερεῖς τὰς λατρείας ἐπιτελοῦντες, εἰς δὲ τὴν δευτέραν . . . ἡόνος ὁ ἀρχιερεύς, οὐ χωρὶς αἵματος, ὃ προσφέρει. . . .
76. . . . δῶρά τε καὶ θυσίαι προσφέρονται μὴ δυνάμεναι κατὰ συνείδησιν τελειῶσαι τὸν λατρεύοντα.
77. Εἰ γὰρ τὸ αἷμα . . . καὶ σποδὸς . . . ῥαντίζουσα . . . ἁγιάζει. . . .

9:25. "... the high priest enters the sanctuary yearly...."[78]

10:1. "... the law... can never, by the same sacrifices which are continually offered year after year, make perfect those who draw near."[79]

10:3f. "... in these sacrifices there is a reminder of sin year after year. For it is impossible that the blood of bulls and goats should take away sins."[80]

10:8. "... these are offered according to the law."[81]

10:11. "... every priest stands daily at his service, offering repeatedly the same sacrifices, which can never take away sins."[82]

13:10. "We have an altar from which those who serve the tent have no right to eat."[83]

13:11. "... the bodies of those animals whose blood is brought into the sanctuary by the high priest... are burned outside the camp."[84]

If J. A. T. Robinson, persuaded by the arguments offered by George Edmundson in his Bampton Lectures for 1913,[85] is right in his conclusion that the Epistle of Clement of Rome to the Corinthians should be dated early in A.D. 70, just before the destruction of Jerusalem, rather than in the last decade of the century,[86] this would only serve to confirm the plain indication of the internal evidence that the Epistle to the Hebrews was written prior to the catastrophe of A.D. 70, because of the unmistakable manner in which Clement quotes from this Epistle. The fact that Clement, like the author of Hebrews, speaks of the levitical ritual of the temple in the present tense—"Not in every place, brethren, are the continual daily offerings offered, or the free will offerings, or the sin offerings and the trespass offerings, but in Jerusalem alone..."—certainly gives the impression that the Jewish priesthood was still in operation. However, the internal evidence afforded by our epistle is by itself sufficient to justify the conclusion we have reached regarding the date of its composition, namely, that A.D. 70 is a *terminus ante quem*.

78. ... ὁ ἀρχιερεὺς εἰσέρχεται εἰς τὰ ἅγια κατ᾽ ἐνιαυτὸν....
79. ... ὁ νόμος... κατ᾽ ἐνιαυτὸν ταῖς αὐταῖς θυσίαις ἃς προσφέρουσιν εἰς τὸ διηνεκὲς οὐδέποτε δύναται τοὺς προσερχομένους τελειῶσαι.
80. ... ἐν αὐταῖς ἀνάμνησις ἁμαρτιῶν κατ᾽ ἐνιαυτόν, ἀδύνατον γὰρ αἷμα ταύρων καὶ τράγων ἀφαιρεῖν ἁμαρτίας. Although there is no verb in the Greek here, the present tense is implicit in the context (see immediately preceding excerpt).
81. ... αἵτινες κατὰ νόμον προσφέρονται.
82. ... πᾶς μὲν ἱερεὺς ἕστηκεν καθ᾽ ἡμέραν λειτουργῶν καὶ τὰς αὐτὰς πολλάκις προσφέρων θυσίας, αἵτινες οὐδέποτε δύνανται περιελεῖν ἁμαρτίας. As usual, the sense of ἕστηκεν is present, though its tense is perfect.
83. Ἔχομεν θυσιαστήριον ἐξ οὗ φαγεῖν οὐκ ἔχουσιν ἐξουσίαν οἱ τῇ σκηνῇ λατρεύοντες.
84. ... ὧν γὰρ εἰσφέρεται ζῴων τὸ αἷμα... εἰς τὰ ἅγια διὰ τοῦ ἀρχιερέως, τούτων τὰ σώματα κατακαίεται ἔξω τῆς παρεμβολῆς.
85. G. Edmundson, *The Church in Rome in the First Century* (London, 1913), pp. 188ff.
86. J. A. T. Robinson, *Redating the New Testament* (London and Philadelphia, 1976), pp. 327ff.
87. Clement of Rome, *Ep. ad Cor.* 41 (Lightfoot's translation).

COMMENTARY

I. CHRIST SUPERIOR TO THE PROPHETS (1:1–3)

1:1, 2a. *In many and various ways God spoke of old to our fathers by the prophets; but in these last days he has spoken to us by a Son.*

The abrupt manner in which this writing opens—without mention of either author or destination and without the salutation customarily associated with the epistolary form—suggests that it may be not so much a letter as an admonitory treatise addressed to a particular group or class of persons.[1] The fact that in 13:22 the author describes what he has written as a "word of exhortation" may perhaps support this conclusion. The same expression is used in Acts 13:15 where Paul and Barnabas, who had joined the worshippers in the synagogue in Pisidian Antioch, are invited to deliver a "word of exhortation" and Paul responds with an impressive homily. At the same time, however, there is no reason why a writer should not describe a letter as a "word of exhortation" if that is an appropriate designation of its content; and even if this document does not start like a letter, it certainly ends like one. Thus the author immediately adds, "I have written to you briefly," using language which in the original Greek would seem to indicate that he thought of his composition as a letter;[2] and he concludes the composition with some brief personal news and with greetings and a benediction. The work may be described, then, as both an epistle and a treatise, indeed, the most extensively developed and logically sustained piece of theological argumentation in the whole of the New Testament. In accordance with its traditional title, however, it will be spoken of as a letter or epistle throughout this commentary.

The author plunges straight into the exposition of the grand theme

---

1. For a discussion of the questions of authorship and destination see the Introduction, pp. 15ff.

2. See the commentary on 13:22 below. It should not be overlooked that this is not the only writing among the New Testament epistles that starts abruptly without any introductory salutation or identification of himself by the author, for the First Epistle of John provides a close parallel in this respect.

the truth of which he is intent on communicating to his readers, namely, the uniqueness and finality of the revelation of God in his Son Jesus Christ. This revelation stands both in fulfilment of and in contrast to the old order of things. Thus Christ, the Son through whom God has spoken his ultimate word, and indeed who is himself that word, is the Prophet *par excellence,* whose coming is the culmination of all the prophecies and promises of the past (2 Cor. 1:20). Like the former prophets he spoke the word of God; but unlike them he is the Eternal Word who became the Word Incarnate (Jn. 1:1–14). *God spoke* both *by the prophets* and by him; but his uniqueness is seen in that he is *a Son,*[3] which is something that cannot be said of any of the prophets. This designation declares him to be greater than and in a different category from all the prophets that preceded him. The distinction is given further point by the consideration that there were *many* prophets, whereas there is but *one* Son. (This contrast between the many and the one is of great importance later on in this epistle when the priesthood of Christ is compared with that of the levitical succession; see 7:15ff.) Accordingly, God's utterance through the prophets is described as having come *in many and various ways.* "In times past," as Luther explains, "God apportioned to many the spirit of prophecy, and through such apportionment caused Christ to be preached in many different ways." Of equal importance with and implicit in the contrast between the many and the one is the contrast between the fragmentary and incomplete character of ancient prophecy on the one hand (cf. NEB, "in fragmentary and varied fashion"[4]) and, on the other, the finality and completeness of the word spoken by God in Christ. "That which is communicated in parts, sections, fragments," writes Westcott, "must of necessity be imperfect; and so also a representation which is made in many modes cannot be other than provisional. The supreme element of unity is wanting in each case. But the Revelation in Christ, the Son, is perfect both in substance and in form."

---

3. *By a Son* is the RSV rendering of ἐν υἱῷ: the anarthrous noun serves to emphasize the absolute change of category to that of sonship—all the more so as the article is present in the contrasting phrase ἐν τοῖς προφήταις. The medium of God's communication is no longer the prophets but the *Son.* The absolute intensification of the relationship implied by the transition from "prophets" to "Son" indicates also the absolute intensification of the solemnity of God's speaking, for *Son* is the ultimate category of relationship and the ultimate medium of communication. Similar occurrences of υἱός without the article are found in 3:6, 5:8, and 7:28 below.

4. Greek: πολυμερῶς καὶ πολυτρόπως. Luther understood πολυμερῶς to refer to "the distribution of the prophetic gifts among the many" and πολυτρόπως to indicate "the varied and repeated use every prophet whoever he may be makes of this one and the same gift." The NEB rendering brings out well the distinction between πολυμερῶς, "in many different parts," and πολυτρόπως, "in many different ways." It is unlikely that the two adverbs are intended as a hendiadys, as, e.g., Chrysostom and Moffatt suppose.

The contrast is further emphasized by the assertion that it was *in former times* that God spoke through the prophets, whereas it is *in this final age*[5] that he has spoken through his Son. That quite distinct ages or dispensations are involved—the one marked by incompleteness and anticipation, the other by completeness and fulfilment, the one preliminary, the other ultimate—shows how fundamental the contrast is. This contrast, too, plays a prominent part in the structure of the epistle as our author demonstrates that the old order of patriarchal expectation, prophetic utterance, Mosaic covenant, and levitical priesthood has given way to the new order of messianic reality which, unlike the old, is final and permanent because its leadership, its priesthood, and its kingdom belong uniquely to him who is the eternal Son.

But while there is this aspect of discontinuity there is at the same time a strong line of continuity. This is evident from the affirmation, made both of the old order and of the new, that *God spoke*. The authoritative character of the word previously spoken through the prophets *to our fathers* and of the word now spoken *to us* through the Son is established by the fact that in both cases it was none other than God who was speaking. Hence the consistency with which the whole is pervaded: the new covenant in Christ is the realization of the promises, prophecies, and figures which form the heart of the old order. The past tense of the verb *spoke* indicates, further, that God's speaking is complete: this is true not only of the past era of the Old Testament prophets but also of the present age of messianic fulfilment.[6] God's word in Christ has been spoken, fully and finally. It is his ultimate word of grace, and therefore also of judgment. Christ is God's eschatological Word. "If the word of the prophets is accepted," writes Luther, "how much more ought we to seize the gospel of Christ, since it is not a prophet speaking to us but the Lord of the prophets, not a servant but a son, not an angel but God. And further, it is not our forefathers he is addressing, but us. Quite clearly the Apostle argues in this way so that every excuse of unbelief is excluded." Athanasius recounts that Antony, whose reputation was such that even the Roman emperors wrote him letters, called the monks to him and said: "Do not be astonished if an emperor writes to us, for he is a man; but rather wonder that God wrote the Law for men and has spoken to us through his own Son."[7]

---

5. The expression ἐπ᾽ ἐσχάτου τῶν ἡμερῶν τούτων matches ἐπ᾽ ἐσχάτου τῶν ἡμερῶν, "at the extremity of the days (of history)," which occurs a dozen times in the LXX (Hebrew, בְּאַחֲרִית הַיָּמִים) and designates the eschatological time of the Messiah. The addition of τούτων by our author indicates that the messianic age has arrived.
6. The aorist tense, used both of God's speaking by the prophets (λαλήσας) and also of his speaking by Christ (ἐλάλησεν), indicates that God has finished speaking in both cases.
7. Athanasius, *Life of St. Antony* 81.

The opening statement, then, sets the tone and introduces the main theme of the whole epistle, namely, the uniqueness and supremacy of Christ in comparison with the transitory and incomplete character of all that preceded his coming. It has a bearing also on the apostolic doctrine of Scripture according to which the Old Testament writings, representing as they do the summation of the prophetic message, are held to be God-breathed (2 Tim. 3:16): it is God who "spake by the mouth of his holy prophets which have been since the world began" (Lk. 1:70 RV). Indeed, Paul explicitly links the prophets with the Old Testament scriptures when he describes himself as an apostle "specially chosen to preach the Good News that God promised long ago through his prophets in the scriptures" (Rom. 1:1f. JB; cf. Lk. 18:31; 24:25; Acts 3:18; 24:14; 26:22, 27; 1 Pet. 1:10f.; 2 Pet. 1:19ff.). Then, too, our author's affirmation that "God has spoken to us by a Son" crystallizes in a single sentence the message and the meaning of the New Testament, not only because the New Testament is the witness to the redeeming act of God in Christ but also because it is the summation of the teaching of him who himself is the authentic Word of God (Jn. 1:1ff.). "While the revelations of the Old and New Covenants are thus sharply distinguished," comments Westcott, "God is the One Author of both. He spoke in old time, and He spoke in the last time. In the former case His speaking was *upon earth* and in the latter case *from heaven* (cf. 12:25), but in both cases the words are alike His words. Not one word therefore can *pass away*, though such as were fragmentary, prospective, typical, required to be fulfilled by Christ's presence (Mt. 5:18)."

1:2b. *Whom he appointed the heir of all things, through whom also he created the world.*

Since Christ is the Son, and more particularly the *only* Son, of God, He is also the Heir, the *sole* Heir, of all things. The concept of heirship is involved in that of sonship, and accordingly the transition here is quite natural. This, however, is not a statement concerning divine ontology. It does not imply that God the Father, like a man, must die before God the Son can enter into his inheritance any more than it implies that because God the Father is eternally existent God the Son will never enter into his inheritance. The distinction between Father and Son in the Godhead is a deep mystery of revelation; but God is one and we must always beware of sundering the divine unity by attempting to make the divine persons conform to the limitations of our human situation. The statement that the Son was *appointed the heir of all things* is a statement, rather, concerning the mediatorial office of Christ. In this connection, it is worth noting that the patristic authors and their medieval followers associated the statement with the words of the messianic second psalm: "Ask of me, and I will make the nations your heritage, and the ends of the earth your possession" (Ps. 2:8)—words which come immediately after and belong to the declaration: "You are my son, today I have begotten you," a text which in the teaching of the apostles was seen as bearing a particular relation to the mediatorial work of Christ (see also the commentary below on v. 5). The heirship of Christ, then, is established within the perspective of redemption: his inheritance is the innumerable company of the redeemed and the universe renewed by virtue of his triumphant work of reconciliation. "The name 'heir' is attributed to Christ as manifest in the flesh," says Calvin; "for in being made man and putting on the same nature as us, he took on himself this heirship, in order to restore to us what we had lost in Adam."

Christ is the heir of *all* things precisely because God has only *one* Son and *one* Heir. Christians, it is true, are also called sons and heirs of God, but they are so not in their own right but solely by virtue of their incorporation into the only-begotten Son with whom alone God is well pleased (Mt. 3:17; 17:5; Rom. 8:14–17; Gal. 4:4–7; 1 Pet. 1:3f.). In short, apart from Christ there is no sonship and heirship. Those therefore who desire to enjoy the privileges of the sons and heirs of God can do so only as by faith they are found *in Christ*. Thus the author of our epistle, when he says that it is God's purpose to bring many sons to glory, makes it plain that this is achieved through him who is the Author and Pioneer of their salvation (2:10). Again, it is because Christ, and Christ alone as the only Son, is the heir of all things that Paul is able to assure the believers in Corinth that, since they are Christ's, and Christ is God's, all things are theirs (1 Cor. 3:21–23). Truly Christ is the door that opens the whole universe to us!

The declaration that it is the Son *through whom also he created the world* is in effect an affirmation that creation no less than redemption is the work of the God and Father of our Lord Jesus Christ; and this in itself can be regarded as a corrective of current Pythagorean dualistic notions of reality according to which the material universe was held to be inherently evil. And it is, further, an affirmation of the dynamic agency of the Son in the accomplishment of creation, which in turn is consonant with both the Johannine and the Pauline teaching that "not one thing had its being but through him" who is the eternal Word (Jn. 1:3 JB) and that in him and through him all things without exception were created (Col. 1:16; 1 Cor. 8:6). Later in our epistle the superiority of

39

Jesus over Moses is effectively conveyed by the description of Jesus as "the one who built the house," whereas Moses was no more than a faithful steward in the house (3:2f.).

The implication of this doctrine, here and elsewhere, is the priority of Christ to the whole created order, and therefore his pre-existence and co-existence with the Father. Thus Athanasius explains that "when the sacred writers say that 'he is before all ages' and that 'through him he created the world', they proclaim the eternal and everlasting being of the Son and thereby designate him as God."[8] In the light of this teaching it is not surprising that the title "Son" itself implies the consubstantiality of Christ with the Father. As Cullmann observes, "Hebrews understands 'Son of God' to mean 'one with God,'" so that "'Son of God' means complete participation in the Father's deity."[9] For this reason our author does not hesitate to apply to the Son the words addressed to the Lord (Yahweh), the eternally sovereign Creator of all things, in Psalm 102: "Thou, Lord, didst found the earth in the beginning, and the heavens are the work of thy hands..." (see the commentary below on v. 10), thereby reinforcing and making still more explicit the christological significance of the assertions here of verse 2, that it was through the Son that God created the world.[10]

1:3a. *He reflects the glory of God and bears the very stamp of his nature.*

On first sight it might seem that the description of the Son as "the radiant light of God's glory and the perfect copy of his nature" (JB) implies some kind of essential inferiority of the Son to the Father. Does not the concept of radiance or effulgence suggest a mere emanation, an effluence of light? And is not a copy, however perfect, something other than the real thing? In the fourth century, when the church was torn by christological conflict, we find, for example, Chrysostom warning against "some who derive certain strange things from this illustration," affirming that "the brightness is not substantial but has its being in another." He admonishes his readers not to be "sick of the disease of Marcellus and Photinus," whose doctrines were among those con-

---

8. Athanasius, *Orationes contra Arianos* i.12.
9. O. Cullmann, *The Christology of the New Testament* (London, 1959), p. 305.
10. Literally, "the ages," τοὺς αἰῶνας, i.e., the world in its historical perspective. It is common for αἰών to be virtually synonymous with κόσμος, hence the rendering "world" in RSV, though the force of the plural is better brought out by NEB, "all orders of existence." Hermann Sasse suggests that the αἰῶνες here and in 11:3 "are to be understood spatially as 'worlds' or 'spheres'" (Kittel, TDNT, I, p. 204).

demned by the Council of Constantinople (Canon I). [11] The real problem, as Chrysostom discerns, is that of terminology: human language is inadequate to describe transcendental truth with precision. "Since language is incapable of speaking worthily of God and the intellect unable to comprehend him," comments Alcuin, "for that very reason, when speech and understanding fail in the description of God, then all the more ought we to glorify God, for we have such a God as transcends both intellect and perception." So too Calvin observes that "we must allow that there is a measure of impropriety in what is taken from earthly things and applied to the hidden majesty of God." Moreover, phrases and sentences should not be isolated and interpreted without regard to the teaching of the epistle as a whole.

It is perfectly possible, without doing violence to the text, to interpret the language of this verse in a manner which is consonant with the classical doctrine of the person of Christ as it was formulated by the patristic scholars who were involved in the christological controversies of the early centuries. In fact, this verse is repeatedly cited by them as affording a refutation of the false teaching of the heretics. [12] If, in the figurative language used by our author, "the radiant light of God's glory" suggests the oneness of the Son with the Father, "the perfect copy of his nature" suggests the distinctness of the Son from the Father; though, as we shall see, both oneness and distinctness are implicit in each. Thus to some extent the two figures serve to balance and correct each other; what the one does not stress the other does. These complementary descriptions of the Son must now be examined in greater detail.

He reflects the glory of God. The idea of "reflection," favored by our version, would apply particularly to the Son as incarnate and would fit well with the statement in the prologue to John's Gospel: "We have beheld his glory, glory as of the only Son from the Father" (Jn. 1:14), and with Paul's teaching concerning "the light of the knowledge of the glory of God in the face of Christ" (2 Cor. 4:6). The concept, then, on this interpretation, is not so much that of the glory of the Son's deity shining

---

11. In his comments on this passage Chrysostom goes on to mention other heresiarchs—Sabellius, Paul of Samosata, Arius, and Marcion—as well as Marcellus and Photinus, against whose errors, he maintains, our author is fighting throughout this epistle.

12. "Any over-all consideration of the use of Hebrews in the Fathers would draw particular attention to their constant reference to Heb. i.3: ὃς ὢν ἀπαύγασμα τῆς δόξης καὶ χαρακτὴρ τῆς ὑποστάσεως αὐτοῦ as a proof text against the Arians. Athanasius' writings are saturated with references to it. It is interesting to note that Theodoret says in his commentary that the Arians rejected the Epistle from the canon because of this text. All the commentators use chapter 1 to prove against the Arians that Christ is greater than the angels and is in fact ὁμοούσιος τῷ Πατρί." Frances M. Young, "Christological Ideas in the Greek Commentaries on the Epistle to the Hebrews," JTS, Vol. XX, Part 1 (April 1969), p. 151.

through his humanity, but that of the glory of God being manifested in the perfection of his manhood, completely attuned as it was to the will of the Father (cf. 10:7, 9). It is preferable, however, to translate the Greek as "he is the radiant light of God's glory" (JB; cf. NEB, "the effulgence of God's splendour"), understanding the author to be speaking here of the essential glory of the Son's eternal person.[13] This is nothing less than the essential glory of God himself, corresponding to the *shekinah* glory which in the Old Testament signified the very presence of God in the midst of his people. It was the radiant glory of Yahweh's presence which settled as a luminous cloud on Mount Sinai when Moses went up to meet with God (Ex. 24:15ff.), and which was seen at the door of the tabernacle when Yahweh "used to speak with Moses face to face, as a man speaks to his friend" (Ex. 33:9ff.). It was, moreover, the glory manifested on the occasion of Christ's transfiguration, again accompanied by the resplendent cloud of the *shekinah* (Mk. 9:2ff., par.), an event which demonstrated that this glory belongs to the Son and was not just a reflection of a glory not his own: the apostles who were present were witnesses for a brief while of the glory which the Son had with the Father before the world was made (Jn. 17:5). The brilliant light, brighter than the midday sun, seen by Paul at his encounter with the Risen Jesus on the road to Damascus (Acts 9:3; 22:6; 26:13) was the same radiant glory of the divine presence.

"Who does not see," asks Athanasius, "that the brightness cannot be separated from the light, but that it is by nature proper to it and co-existent with it, and is not produced after it?"[14] "Think not," Ambrose admonishes, "that there was ever a moment of time when God was without wisdom, any more than that there was ever a time when light was without radiance." For "where there is light there is radiance, and where there is radiance there is also light; and thus we cannot have a light without radiance nor radiance without light, because both the light is in the radiance and the radiance in the light. Thus the Apostle has taught us to call the Son 'the Radiance of the Father's glory', for the Son is the Radiance of his Father's light, co-eternal because of eternity of

---

13. In the expression ἀπαύγασμα τῆς δόξης the noun ἀπαύγασμα is properly the light or radiance of a luminous body (the uncompounded noun αὐγή is the light of the sun). The term seems also to have been used in the sense of "reflection" in literature contemporary with our epistle. The latter sense, however, would make the expression virtually tautologous with the immediately following expression, "the very stamp of his nature," leaving us with two different ways of saying the same thing, namely, that the Son is a true manifestation of God. It is better, therefore, to take ἀπαύγασμα in the sense of "radiance" here, and it is certainly a consideration of some significance that the Greek fathers of the early centuries understood the term in this sense. Cf. the rendering of the Vulgate, *splendor gloriae*, and the parallel description of the Son as "Light of Light" in the Nicene Creed, both brought together in the comment of Herveus: *"splendor gloriae quasi lumen de lumine."*
14. Athanasius, Encyclical Epistle to the Bishops of Egypt and Libya (A.D. 356) ii.4.

power, inseparable by unity of brightness."[15] Similarly Herveus explains that "the Son is co-eternal with the Father, just as brightness is co-eval with the sun . . . and just as brightness displays that of which it is the brightness, so the Son manifests the Father whose wisdom he is; and just as brightness exists essentially[16] in the sun and the sun in brightness, so the Son exists essentially in the Father and the Father in the Son." If the writers of the fourth century are over-concerned, understandably in view of the theological controversy of their day, to derive the unity of essence between Father and Son from this passage, Calvin would seem to go to the other extreme in denying that our author intended to teach this here; though his emphasis that it is in Christ alone that the glory of God is manifested to man provides a salutary counterbalance to the patristic interpretation. Thus he insists: "When you hear that the Son is the glory of the Father's glory, bear in mind that the glory of the Father is invisible to you until it shines forth in Christ, and that he is called the very image of his substance because the majesty of the Father is hidden, until it shows itself as impressed on his image." The two interpretations belong together, however (and are in fact combined in the passage quoted above from Herveus), and there is no question of the one being antithetical to the other. But to isolate the person of Christ from the work of Christ can only lead to distortion and error. That is why Athanasius and those who stood with him in the fourth century so clearly perceived that a false doctrine of the person of Christ must inevitably result in a false doctrine of the work of Christ and consequently undermine the whole system of the gospel.

And bears the very stamp of his nature. The Greek word translated "the very stamp" here[17] means an engraved character or the impress made by a die or a seal, as, for example, on a coin; and the Greek word translated "nature"[18] denotes the very essence of God. The principal idea intended is that of exact correspondence. This correspondence involves not only an identity of the essence of the Son with that of the Father, but more particularly a true and trustworthy revelation or representation of the Father by the Son. Herveus insists that the Son is the

---

15. Ambrose, *De Fide* i.13; iv.9. Cf. Basil, *De Spiritu Sancto 7,* and *Adversus Eunomium* ii.17: "How utterly absurd to deny the glory of God to have had brightness, to deny the wisdom of God to have been ever with God."

16. *Substantialiter,* i.e., hypostatically.

17. Χαϱακτήϱ, a term found only here in the New Testament.

18. Ὑπόστασις. Calvin, like many earlier and later commentators, takes the term to mean "not the *esse* or essence of the Father, but the person." Westcott, however, objects that "this use of the word is much later than the apostolic age" and is "distinctly inappropriate in this connexion. The Son," he continues, "is not the image, the expression of the 'Person' of God. On the other hand, He is the expression of the 'essence' of God. He brings the Divine before us at once perfectly and definitely according to the measure of our powers." Spicq comments to the same effect.

express likeness of the Father "not in an external sense but in substance," and links this truth with the declaration of the Incarnate Son: "He who has seen me has seen the Father" (Jn. 14:9). In a similar manner Paul teaches that Christ is the image or likeness of God (2 Cor. 4:4; Col. 1:15). It is according to this image that man was created (Gen. 1:27); and that same image, which was marred by the fall and is perverted by sin, is restored in Christ, the True Image, so that the believer is "being changed into his likeness from one degree of glory to another" (2 Cor. 3:18), and the new nature which is his "is being renewed in knowledge after the image of its creator" (Col. 3:10).

The patristic understanding of this passage is well summarized in the following comment of Gregory of Nyssa, who says: "The heir of all things, the maker of the ages, he who shines with the Father's glory and expresses in himself the Father's person, has all things that the Father himself has, and is possessor of all his power; not that the right is transferred from the Father to the Son, but that it at once remains in the Father and resides in the Son. For he who is in the Father is manifestly in the Father with all his might, and he who has the Father in himself includes all the power and might of the Father."[19] Of the two expressions, "the radiance of his glory" and "the very stamp of his nature," the former, which implies the consubstantiality of the Son with the Father, is balanced by the latter, which implies the distinctness of the person of the Son from that of the Father, and both designate the function of the Incarnate Son who, as the Light and the Truth (Jn. 8:12; 9:5; 14:6), is the Revealer of God to mankind.

This interpretation, whereby the description of the Son as "the radiance of God's glory" is understood as implying the Son's consubstantiality with the Father, while the expression "the very stamp of his nature" is taken to imply the distinction between the First and Second Persons of the Godhead, is found as early as Origen.[20] Theodore of Mopsuestia makes an interesting connection with John 1:1, where he sees the statement "the Word was with God" as the equivalent of "the very stamp of his nature," indicating distinctness, and "the Word was God" as the equivalent of "the radiance of his glory," indicating identity.[21] Chrysostom is saying the same thing when he points out that in the verse before us our author is following "two paths, by the one leading us away from Sabellius, and by the other from Arius." Sabellius denied a true trinitarian distinction in the Godhead, and Arius the consubstantiality of Father and Son. Origen, it should be added, also at-

---

19. Gregory of Nyssa, *Contra Eunomium* ii.6.
20. Origen, *De Principiis* I.ii.7f.
21. Theodore of Mopsuestia, *Commentary on John, ad loc.*

tempted to find support for his characteristic doctrine of subordinationism in the designation of the Son as "the very stamp of God's nature."

1:3b. *Upholding the universe by his word of power.*

The concept expressed here is dynamic, not static: the Son's work of *upholding* involves not only support but movement,[22] the carrying forward and onward of all things to the predestined consummation which is also implicit in their beginning. God creates the world in accordance with his will and purpose, and what he has created he sustains and directs toward the fulfilment of that purpose. Nor does the fall of man into sin, with its dire effects on the created order (Gen. 3), frustrate the will of the Creator; for the new creation, or the renewal of creation, in Christ is precisely the undoing of the fall and the bringing to fruition of all God's purposes in the original creation. Moreover, throughout the period that separates the beginning from the fulfilment the world is dependent on God for the continuance of its existence: were it not for the sustaining providence and government of God, all would relapse into non-existence. This emphasis is common in the patristic and medieval commentators. Alcuin, for example, observes that "it is no less to govern the world than to create it; for in creating, the substances of things were produced from nothing, while in governing, the things that have been made are sustained, lest they should return to nothing"; and

---

22. The verb φέρειν used here implies the motion of carrying something from one place to another. As Westcott points out, it is "not to be understood simply of the passive support of a burden," as though the Son were "an Atlas sustaining the dead weight of the world," but includes the notion of "movement, progress, towards an end." The present participle φέρων indicates that this is a continuous work of the Son. Cf. NEB mg., "bears along." Moffatt follows a different line, suggesting that "it would certainly carry on the thought of δι' οὗ ... αἰῶνας ['through whom also he created the world'] if φέρειν here could be taken in its regular Philonic sense of 'bring into existence' (e.g., *quis rer. div. haer.* 7, ὁ τὰ μὴ ὄντα φέρων καὶ τὰ πάντα γεννῶν; *de mutat. nom.* 44, πάντα φέρων σπουδαῖα ὁ θεός)"; adding that "this was the interpretation of Gregory of Nyssa (MPG xlvi.265), and it would give a better sense to 'word of power' as the fiat of creative authority." Spicq combines the notions of "continuous creation" and "providential action." "To create" or "bring into existence" is, however, uncommon as a sense of φέρειν, even in Philo (*pace* Moffatt), and to give it this meaning here would, as Montefiore remarks, only repeat the thought of verse 2; whereas "what is here being ascribed to the Son is the providential government of the universe, which is the function of God himself." "In my judgment," writes Erasmus, "φέρων here does not mean the same as 'bearing' (*portans*) or 'upholding' (*bajulans*), but rather 'acting' (*agens*) or 'moving' (*movens*) and 'guiding' (*moderans*), for in Greek things are described as φερόμενα which are acted upon by some impulse; and ἄγειν καὶ φέρειν is descriptive of one who governs someone under his authority. For Paul, or whoever was the author of the epistle, means not only that this world was fashioned by the Son, as he has just said, 'per quem fecit et secula', but that what has been fashioned is ruled and administered; and that not with the application and care and industry such as men exercise when they administer, but with his word, that is with the nod of his power."

45

Aquinas points out that as the absence of the sun means the withdrawal of light from the sky so "the removal of the divine power would mean the cessation of the being and the coming into being and the continuing in being of every creature."

Not only, then, did the universe come into existence through the Son (v. 2), but the whole created order is sustained in being and carried on to its appointed destiny by *his word of power*. The Son, so to speak, is the nucleus of creation: "in him all things hold together" (Col. 1:17); and the purposeful coherence of the whole is achieved by his word. This word, which is the expression of his will, is essentially a *dynamic* word;[23] that is to say, it is always and inevitably a word which effects its intended purpose. The word of the Son is not other or less than the word of the Father, for he who himself is the Word is the perfect and harmonious expression of the mind and will of God. The word of the Word is infallibly effective precisely because it is one with the word of the Father. And that word with which the Son sustains the universe is dynamic and efficacious because it is at the same time the word of judgment against all that is opposed to the divine will and the word of promise and restoration to the response of faith. The significance of the first half of this third verse of Hebrews 1 is to a large extent brought together in the proclamation of the Incarnate Son recorded in John 12:44–50, where he says: "He who believes in me, believes not in me but in him who sent me. And he who sees me sees him who sent me. I have come as light into the world, that whoever believes in me may not remain in darkness. If any one hears my sayings and does not keep them, I do not judge him; for I did not come to judge the world but to save the world. He who rejects me and does not receive my sayings has a judge: the word that I have spoken will be his judge in the last day. For I have not spoken on my own authority; the Father who sent me has himself given me commandment what to say and what to speak. And I know that his commandment is eternal life. What I say, therefore, I say as the Father has bidden me."

1:3c. *When he had made purification for sins, he sat down at the right hand of the Majesty on high.*

While the Son ceaselessly is "the radiant light of God's glory" and "the perfect copy of his nature" (JB) and continuously "upholds the universe by his word of power," there is also something which he did once for all, namely, *he made purification for sins*. This he did within the course of human history when, as Aquinas says, "he offered himself on

23. As the descriptive genitive τῆς δυνάμεως shows. "The word of his power" may well be a semitism, the equivalent of "his powerful word."

the altar of the cross as a sacrifice to God in satisfaction of the punishment to which man, because of his guilt, was subject."[24] This done, *he sat down at the right hand of the Majesty on high.* The description of the Son as being now seated signifies the completion of the work of purification, conveying the notion of rest after the fulfilment of a mission. But more than that, his position "at the right hand" of God ("the Majesty" being a periphrasis for God) indicates that his is the place of highest honor, that he is not merely on a seat but on a throne, and that he is not just "sitting" but ruling. Thus 12:2 below declares that, having endured the cross, he "is seated at the right hand of the throne of God": he is our sovereign Lord (cf. 8:1; 10:12; Acts 2:33ff.; Eph. 1:20ff.; Phil. 2:9ff.; Col. 3:1). His session, moreover, is "on high": his exaltation, which started with his resurrection from the grave and continued with his ascension into heaven, is completed by his session. This is the seal of the divine acceptance of his work of purification, for he now is received back to the height from which he descended for our redemption. He who humbled himself for our sakes is now supremely honored.

To picture Christ as seated in glory is not of course to suggest that he is now inactive. The work of purification which was the purpose of his coming to earth is completed, but otherwise the heavenly existence of the exalted Savior may be described as one of ceaseless activity. He is active, as the present verse has reminded us, constantly sustaining the universe by his dynamic word. He is active as, enthroned on high, he rules over history until every enemy has been subdued (1 Cor. 15:25). He is active on behalf of his chosen people as he dispenses mercy, grace, and help to them in the hour of their testing (Heb. 2:18; 4:14–16; cf. Acts 7:55f.) and as in heaven, whither he "has gone as a forerunner on our behalf" (Heb. 6:20), "he always lives to make intercession for them" (7:25), where, too, he is preparing a place for them (Jn. 14:2f.).

---

24. As Spicq points out, the rendering of καθαρισμόν τῶν ἁμαρτιῶν ποιησάμενος in the Vulgate by *purgationem peccatorum faciens* is defective, since "it substitutes a present participle for the aorist participle which our author without doubt deliberately chose for the purpose of showing both that this purification was accomplished by a single act in the past, once for all, and also that a transition is now being made from the eternal life of the Son to the consideration of his life in time which is terminated by his exaltation to heaven." F. F. Bruce explains that "the absence of a perfect participle active in Latin (except for deponent verbs) has led to the use of the present participle here in the Vulgate as the equivalent of the Greek aorist participle," and warns that "this rendering, reflected in most translations based on the Vulgate (*e.g.* R. A. Knox, 'making atonement for our sins'), has facilitated the view that during His present heavenly session Christ continues to make purification for sin." It should be added that Jerome was not obliged to translate a participle by a participle, and indeed that he should not have done so where, as in this case, the result would not plainly convey the sense of the original. Lefèvre d'Etaples may be right when he says that "when the old interpreter says *'faciens'* he intends the past tense"; but Lefèvre himself has given us an accurate Latin translation of καθαρισμόν τῶν ἁμαρτιῶν ποιησάμενος in his own rendering: *qui cum per seipsum purgationem peccatorum nostrorum fecit.*

Nor should it be imagined that the author of our epistle intended such expressions as "sat down," "on the right hand," and "on high" in a crassly literalistic sense. "That no literal location is intended," F. F. Bruce comments, "was as well understood by Christians in the apostolic age as it is by us." The patristic writers insist that what is being taught here is not the enclosing of Christ in a particular place but his absolute transcendence; and this has the concurrence of the medieval scholars. Herveus, for example, explains that "he sat down" denotes that he is resting and reigning and judging supremely, that "on the right hand" denotes a position of equality and honor, and that "on high" denotes above every creature.

Yet in defending the full deity of the Son in opposition to the false constructions of heterodox teachers the ancient authors insisted too much that the phrase "at the right hand" indicates the complete equality of the Son with the Father.[25] This is certainly true with reference to the eternally divine Son; but it is the glorification of the *incarnate* Son that is in question here, and this distinction should be taken into account, even though, dealing as we are with a category of existence that transcends our comprehension and experience, a distinction of this kind is difficult if not impossible to define: we are dealing with the mystery of him who is now the divine-human Son. Further, while the position "at the right hand" implies the place of highest honor and authority, it also implies, as ordinarily understood, a degree of subordination below the one who is supreme. Thus in requesting to be seated on either side of Jesus in his kingdom the sons of Zebedee were not challenging the supreme authority of their Master but were seeking the places of highest privilege under him (Mk. 10:37). Jesus told the high priest that he would see the Son of man, that is, the theanthropic Lord, sitting at the right hand of power (Mk. 14:62). It is Jesus, the Incarnate Son, whom "God has exalted at his right hand as Leader and Savior" and whom Stephen sees standing at the right hand of God (Acts 5:31; 7:55f.; cf. Rom. 8:34; Eph. 1:20; Col. 3:1; 1 Pet. 3:22). As Mediator, he subjects himself to the Father's will until his work of restoration has been brought to fulfilment (1 Cor. 15:24–28). But this Jesus is also the Eternal One, King of kings and Lord of lords, at whose name every knee shall bow and whose lordship every tongue shall confess to the glory of God the Father (Rev. 19:16; Phil. 2:11). Meanwhile we must acknowledge with Paul that we know at best in part and that our understanding of these things will not be complete until we ourselves share in the glory that is Christ's.

Luther in his day had to learn the lesson that if Christ has indeed

---

25. Basil, to give an example, is intent on refuting the doctrine of the Macedonians or pneumatomachi when he contends that "the expression 'right hand' does not, as they maintain, indicate the lower place, but equality of relation" (*De Spiritu Sancto* 6).

made purification for sins there is no room for self-cleansing or self-justification on the part of man. "By these words," he says, "he forthwith makes short work of all notions of righteousness and every idea of penances which the natural man holds. It is the supreme mercy of God he commends. . . . Therefore we must despair of our own penances and our own purging of our sins, because before we even begin to confess, our sins have already been forgiven. I would even go on to say, that it is not till then (i.e., until we despair of our own penance and purging), that Christ's own purging becomes operative, and produces true penitence in us. It is in this way that his righteousness works our righteousness." In the nature of the case, by self-righteousness a person excludes himself from the purging and the righteousness which are appropriated through faith in Christ and the atonement he has procured for us (Phil. 3:7–9).

Finally, it has well been observed that in these opening verses of the epistle we have the Son set before us in the threefold character of his messianic office: (1) as the *Prophet* through whom God's final word has been spoken to us; (2) as the *Priest* who made purification for our sins; and (3) as the *King* who is enthroned at the right hand of the Majesty on high.[26]

---

26. The doctrine of Christ's threefold messianic office is found in Eusebius, *Historia Ecclesiastica* I.iii; cf. *Demonstratio Evangelica* IV.xv; cf. also Chrysostom, Homily III on 2 Corinthians (1:21); Thomas Aquinas, *Summa Theologica* 3a.22.1. The doctrine was taken up and developed by Calvin (*Institutes* II.xv) and appears in many subsequent works on theology.

If, as is probable, the structure of verses 2b–3 is chiastic, the christological scheme of this passage can be clarified as follows:

Summary definition of him who is the Son:
  A. Whom he appointed the heir of all things
    B. through whom also he created the world
    B. who being the radiant light of God's glory
      and the very stamp of his nature
      and upholding the universe by his word of power
  A. after he had made purification for sins
    he sat down at the right hand of the Majesty on high.
The chiastic structure of these clauses is then represented thus:

The two A clauses speak of the incarnate Son and the two B clauses of the Son in his eternal existence, a distinction of the utmost importance as the Christology of this epistle unfolds in the following verses and chapters. For an interesting discussion see D. W. B. Robinson, "The Literary Structure of Hebrews 1:1–4" in the *Australian Journal of Biblical Archaeology*, 2 (1972), pp. 178ff. Bishop Robinson also suggests the possibility of an extension of the chiasmus to include as two outer clauses verses 1-2a and 4, which would be linked to each other as both teaching the superiority of the Son, the former to the prophets and the latter to angels. For another example of chiastic construction see the commentary below on 2:9 (p. 90).

II. CHRIST SUPERIOR TO THE ANGELS (1:4–2:18)

1:4. *Having become as much superior to angels as the name he has obtained is more excellent than theirs.*

The superiority[1] of the Son to the angels, which has already been suggested by the position of honor to which he has been exalted (v. 3), is indicated also in the name which he has inherited.[2] The Son who was described above (v. 2) as having been appointed "the heir of all things" is here spoken of as the inheritor of a name which in itself attests his supremacy. It is true, of course, that by virtue of his eternal Sonship he has an eternal inheritance and possesses a name which is eternally supreme—*the name* signifying, particularly for the Hebrew mind, the essential character of a person in himself and in his work. But our author at this point is speaking of something other than this: the Son who for our redemption humbled himself for a little while to a position lower than the angels has by his ensuing exaltation *become*[3] superior to the angels (2:9 below), and in doing so has achieved and retains the inheritance[4] of a name which is *more excellent than theirs*. Once more,

---

1. The comparative adjective κρείττων ("superior," "better") is a key-word in this epistle, occurring no less than 13 times: 1:4, a superior name; 6:9, superior things (this occurrence, however, is of an incidental character); 7:7, a superior priest; 7:19, a superior hope; 7:22, a superior covenant; 8:6, a superior covenant and superior promises; 9:23, a superior sacrifice; 10:34, a superior possession; 11:16, a superior country; 11:35, a superior resurrection; 11:40, a superior privilege; 12:24, superior blood-shedding. To these may be added 9:11, a superior sanctuary, where the Greek, instead of κρείττων, reads μείζων καὶ τελειότερα σκηνή.
2. Κεκληρονόμηκεν, "he has inherited" (NEB, JB), rather than the more vague "he has obtained" of RSV; cf. KJV, "he hath by inheritance obtained." It is a resumption of the concept of Christ as κληρονόμος, "heir," in verse 2.
3. The aorist participle γενόμενος, "having become," refers, as Spicq points out, to "a dated event of history"; it "designates a superiority which was achieved and clearly indicates that the theme here is not the Son in his eternal existence but Christ with his glorified human nature."
4. This is the force of the perfect κεκληρονόμηκεν, which implies that the name Christ inherited was gained as a permanent possession.

then, the reference is to the Son as Mediator and to the sequence of his humiliation and glorification as, so to speak, historic events.

The teaching here is, in fact, identical with that which Paul gives in Ephesians 1:19ff., where he speaks of "the immeasurable greatness of God's power in us who believe, according to the working of his great might which he accomplished in Christ when he raised him from the dead and made him sit at his right hand in the heavenly places, far above all rule and authority and power and dominion, and above every name that is named, not only in this age but also in that which is to come," and in Philippians 2:9f., where he says that God has highly exalted Christ Jesus and "bestowed on him the name which is above every name, that at the name of Jesus every knee should bow, in heaven and on earth and under the earth." The supreme name bespeaks the supreme honor and dignity to which Christ has been elevated. Those who seek for some specific designation to be attached to Christ betray a misconception of what is intended here. In Revelation 19:11–16, for example, the conquering Redeemer is identified by three "names": "Faithful and True," "The Word of God," "King of kings and Lord of lords," which describe the character of his person and position.

The "name" which distinguishes Christ from the angels and elevates him above them, in the comparison introduced by this fourth verse, is that of "Son," for, as our author goes on to show, the son inherits the position of privilege and authority, whereas angels are no more than ministers or servants in the realm of God's creation. "Both here and throughout the epistle," observes Athanasius, "the term 'better' is ascribed to the Lord, thus distinguishing him as better and other than mere created beings; for his sacrifice of himself, the hope that we have in him, and the promises which are ours through him are all better, not only as a matter of degree but as being of a quite different order, since he who has made these things available to us is better than all created beings."[5]

But why the comparison between Christ and angels? Why is our author so concerned to demonstrate at some length, as he is now about to do, the superiority of the risen and glorified Redeemer to angels, as though, in the thinking at least of his readers, angels posed a threat to the lordship of Christ? Clearly, he does so not because it might be a matter of general interest, but because the situation he is addressing demands it. The question is one of special relevance and urgency. It is important that the supremacy of Christ in this as in all other connections should be unequivocally established. It follows, then, that those to whom this letter was sent were entertaining, or being encouraged to

5. Athanasius, *Orationes contra Arianos* i.59.

entertain, teaching which elevated angels, or particular angels, to a position which rivalled that of Christ himself. To what degree is it possible for us to recover the nature of this teaching which our author so evidently regarded as false and dangerous?

At the time when Paul wrote his letter to the Christians in Colossae they were being troubled by certain persons who were insisting, among other things, on the worship of angels (Col. 2:18). This consideration, involving, it would seem, belief in the powers of "the elemental spirits" (Col. 2:8, 20), and coupled with stipulations concerning "questions of food and drink" (Col. 2:16), which appeared to find an answering chord in 13:9 of our epistle where the admonition is given that the heart is strengthened by grace, not by foods, caused T. W. Manson to conclude that the Epistle to the Hebrews was addressed to the churches of the Lycus Valley, which included that of Colossae. Indeed, he held that it constituted a complete refutation of the Colossian heresy, written, he suggested, prior to Paul's letter to the Colossians and perhaps a stimulus to the composition of that letter.[6] But, as F. F. Bruce has observed, there is nothing in our epistle to suggest that its recipients were addicted to angel-worship.[7] The Colossian situation points to influences of a gnostic and oriental rather than a judaistic type, and it is unlikely that those to whom this letter was sent, inclined as they evidently were to revert to the cultus of the Old Testament, were at all disposed to engage in the worship of angels. "Aversion to Gnosticism," G. Kittel explains with reference to Judaism, "has its basis in the fact that this can lead to the theory of a second god. The doctrine of angels is recognized to be a legitimate development of OT ideas because it never entails the independent divinization of angels, nor even seems to show tendencies in this direction. . . . Even in the most developed angelology the angels only serve to execute and reveal the power and deity of Yahweh; they are His court, and train, and ambassadors. . . . Rabbinic teaching always sees to it that they do not detract from God and His rule."[8]

Accepting, as we do, that those to whom this letter was addressed were, in accordance with its traditional title, "Hebrew" converts to Christianity who were in danger, as the letter's content repeatedly indicates, of relapsing into a refined type of judaistic Christianity, which in fact would be more than Jewish and less than Christian, it is far more satisfactory to suppose that the author's concern to establish, on biblical grounds, the superiority of the Son to angels was prompted by a ten-

---

6. T. W. Manson, *Studies in the Gospels and Epistles* (Manchester, 1962), ch. 13, "The Problem of the Epistle to the Hebrews," pp. 242ff. See also the commentary below on 13:9.
7. F. F. Bruce, " 'To the Hebrews' or 'To the Essenes'?", NTS, 9 (1963), p. 218.
8. Kittel, TDNT, I, pp. 81f.

dency on the part of these "Hebrew" Christians to view with favor teachings similar to those held by the Dead Sea Sect at that time. The eschatological perspective of the latter envisaged the introduction of a hierarchical structure with two messianic figures, of whom the kingly would be subordinate to the priestly messiah, and both of whom would be subordinate to the archangel Michael, thus assigning supremacy to an angelic being in the expected kingdom. Against such a background the necessity for our author to affirm and demonstrate the supremacy of Christ over all angelic beings is obvious, and his insistence that "it was not to angels that God subjected the world to come" (2:5) becomes full of meaning.[9]

1:5a. *For to what angel did God ever say, "Thou art my Son, today I have begotten thee"?*

The superiority of Christ to angels is now confirmed by a sequence of seven quotations from the Old Testament scriptures which attest his Sonship and his sovereignty. The marshalling of this chain of biblical testimonies makes it apparent that the recipients of the letter acknowledged the authority of the Old Testament and were open to persuasion from its pages. This, again, points to their being Christians from a Jewish background. It is important to notice that it is the divine Sonship *of Jesus* that is affirmed. "Jesus' deity," remarks Oscar Cullmann with this section of the epistle particularly in mind, "is more powerfully asserted in Hebrews than in any other New Testament writing, with the exception of the Gospel of John.... The Old Testament psalms (for example, Pss. 45:6f.; 102:25ff.) are applied to Jesus so that he can be addressed directly as 'God' (Heb. 1:8f.), and the creation of the world ascribed to him (Heb. 1:10ff.)."[10]

The first of the seven quotations comes from Psalm 2:7. The second psalm was well known, in Judaism as well as in the apostolic church, as one of the messianic psalms, and the declaration *"Thou art my Son,"* the application of which to the messianic figure was not in dispute, was never spoken of any angel. Hence our author's effective use of a rhetorical question here. The authoritative attestation of Jesus as the divine Son applies to the earthly sojourn of the incarnate Son in its entirety and at every moment of that entirety. Thus at his conception the annunciation is made to the Virgin Mary that the child to be born of her would be

---

9. See Introduction, pp. 11ff.
10. O. Cullmann, *The Christology of the New Testament*, p. 305.

called "the Son of the Most High" (Lk. 1:32); at his baptism, signalling the inauguration of his ministry, the voice from heaven proclaims, "Thou art my Son" (Mk. 1:11 NEB);[11] at his transfiguration the utterance from the cloud declares, "This is my Son" (Lk. 9:35; cf. Mt. 17:5); and at his resurrection he is "designated the Son of God in power" (Rom. 1:4). The perfection of his life and the innocence of his death mark him out as truly the Son of God and the Redeemer of mankind.

But what is the significance of the additional assertion, *"Today I have begotten thee"*? At what point of history is this "day" of his begetting to be fixed? In the early and medieval centuries it was frequently, in fact, taken to mean the "day" of God's eternity. Thus Augustine explains it as a reference to "the day of an unchangeable eternity, in order to show that this man was one in person with the Only-Begotten."[12] Aquinas likewise holds that "this begetting is not temporal but eternal." As Westcott observes, however, to interpret it as a declaration of the Son's eternal generation is foreign to the context. As early as the second century we find Justin Martyr associating the assertion with the occasion of Christ's baptism, as Hilary does two centuries later.[13] Both Theodore of Mopsuestia and Chrysostom understand it as a reference to the incarnation. F. F. Bruce prefers to apply it to the occasion of Christ's exaltation and enthronement, "the day when He was vested with His royal dignity as Son of God," relating it forward to the exaltation mentioned in 5:5f., where Psalm 2:7 is quoted again together with the acclamation of the king-priest of Psalm 110:4.

But in the apostolic perspective the day of the resurrection of Jesus is the chief focal point in the interpretation of the Psalmist's words, "Today I have begotten thee." It is by that event, as already mentioned above, that Jesus was "designated the Son of God in power" (Rom. 1:4). Significantly, the Risen Lord is described as "the first-born from the dead" (Col. 1:18; Rev. 1:5). The apostle Paul specifically proclaims the resurrection as the fulfilment of Psalm 2:7 when he tells his audience in Pisidian Antioch: "We bring you the good news that what God promised to the fathers, this he has fulfilled to us their children by raising Jesus; as also it is written in the second psalm, 'Thou art my Son, today I have begotten thee'" (Acts 13:32f.). Herveus, in a manner reminiscent of

11. Similarly JB; cf. Matthew 3:17; Luke 3:22; John 1:34. In the Greek the statement Σὺ εἶ ὁ υἱός μου is followed by ὁ ἀγαπητός, ἐν σοὶ εὐδόκησα, "my Beloved, on thee my favour rests" (NEB). An interesting and early "Western" variant in the Lucan account of the baptism actually reproduces the words of Psalm 2:9, υἱός μου εἶ σύ, ἐγὼ σήμερον γεγέννηκα σε (Lk. 3:22). This reading seems to be reflected in the middle of the second century in Justin Martyr, *Dialogue with Trypho* 88, and in the fourth century in Hilary, *De Trinitate* viii.25.
12. Augustine, *Enchiridion* 49.
13. See footnote 11 above.

Augustine's comment on Psalm 2:7,[14] interprets *today* as meaning "in the day of eternity, which has neither beginning nor end, and, eternally present, has neither past nor future"; but he qualifies this by remarking that "if we consider Paul's words in the Acts of the Apostles we see that he related this statement to the Lord's resurrection," concluding that "Christ according to his humanity who, while he was mortal, was the Son of man, clothed himself in the resurrection with immortality and became the Son of God, in such a way, however, that he did not cease to be the Son of man, because he remained true man." He adds the interesting observation that "so also our resurrection is called regeneration" (alluding, it would seem, to Mt. 19:28).

To sum up, we may say that at every moment of his earthly mission the incarnate Messiah is the Son beloved and accepted by the Father, but that the "day" spoken of here, on which he is said to have been begotten by God, is the day of his glorious victory and vindication, the day also which, for the purposes of our author's argument here, establishes for all to see his absolute superiority to all angels. This "day" belongs, in the first place, to the event of the resurrection, but it extends also to the ascension of Christ and his glorification at the right hand of the divine majesty. In other words, resurrection, ascension, and glorification should be viewed as forming a unity, each one contributing to the exaltation of the Son to transcendental heights of power and dignity.

It is important to recognize that there is only one to whom God says, "Thou art my Son," that God has but one son with whom he is well pleased, and that this son is Jesus Christ. All sonship before God is concentrated in the person of Christ, and Christian believers are designated sons only by virtue of the fact that they are incorporated into Christ and made one with him. They are accepted by God because they are united with Christ, with whom alone God is well pleased. Their acceptance is acceptance *in Christ* (a theme which is particularly prominent in Paul's theology). The Christian is precisely the man-in-Christ (2 Cor. 5:17). The uniqueness of Christ's Sonship is implied, as Aquinas points out, by the use of the singular in the statement, "Thou art my Son"—"as much as to say: Although many others are called sons, yet to be the natural son belongs to him alone; whereas others are called sons of God because they participate in the Word of God."

The "begetting," then, is the begetting of the *incarnate* Son—not the eternal begetting of the divine Son "before all worlds"—and it marks the completion and the acceptance of his redeeming mission to our world; but, importantly, it is at the same time the "begetting" in and with him, our true and fellow Man, of our fallen humanity, because this moment of his

14. Cf. Augustine, *Enarrationes in Psalmos, ad loc.*

begetting is also the moment of the begetting, in the sense of regeneration and rehabilitation, of mankind: his Sonship is now our sonship, his inheritance is now our inheritance, his exaltation is now our exaltation.

1:5b. Or again, "I will be to him a father, and he shall be to me a son"?

The second of the quotations adduced as evidence of the Son's superiority to angels is derived from the words spoken by the prophet Nathan to David, promising him that in the line of his posterity one would be raised up who would build a house for God's name and the throne of whose kingdom would be established forever (2 Sam. 7:14; cf. 1 Chr. 17:13; 28:6). God's promise that he would be a father to the son who was to succeed David, and that this son would be a son to him, was a promise of special blessing, which had its immediate or proximate fulfilment in the magnificence of the reign of David's son Solomon under whom the temple in Jerusalem was constructed. But both as a person and as a king Solomon was far from perfect and, mortal man that he was, by the very nature of things his could not possibly be described as an everlasting kingdom. Indeed, the corruption and dissoluteness of the latter days of Solomon's reign, and the subsequent overthrow of the kingdom of Judah and destruction of the Jerusalem temple, indicate clearly enough that the fulfilment of the promise in its ultimate sense was not yet.

Faith in the reliability of this remarkable promise did not die, however, for prophets and people confidently looked and longed for its fulfilment in the establishment of a truly everlasting kingdom which would be the kingdom of the messianic son of David. Thus, for example, Isaiah prophesied the birth from a virgin of a son whose name would be Immanuel, "God with us" (7:14), the gift of one who would rule forevermore on the throne of David (9:6ff.), and the appearance of him who would be a shoot from the stump of Jesse and a branch from this root of David and upon whom the Spirit of Yahweh would rest (11:1ff.). Jeremiah and Ezekiel foretold the restoration of the kingdom in accordance with the terms of the new covenant appointed by God (Jer. 31:1ff.; Ezek. 11:14ff.), and Micah the coming forth from Bethlehem of Judah of one "who is to be ruler in Israel, whose origin is from of old, from ancient days," and under whom God's people would dwell securely (5:2ff.). Jeremiah, indeed, despite the disastrous days in which he prophesied, repeated, as Isaiah had done before him, the promise first made through Nathan. "Behold," he proclaimed, "the days are coming, saith the Lord, when I will raise up for David a righteous Branch, and he shall reign as a king and deal wisely, and shall execute justice and righteousness in the land" (23:5; cf. 33:14f.).

That this Hebrew expectation based on the promise of 2 Samuel 7:12ff. was still alive at the end of the four-hundred-year intertestamental period is evident, apart from the persistent messianic longing of a subjugated people, from the midrash on the passage discovered among the Dead Sea Scrolls which explicitly interprets it as relating to the messianic "Branch of David" who is to arise at the end of time,[15] and, more pointedly still (as with the preceding quotation from Ps. 2), from the specific terms of the annunciation to the Virgin Mary: "He shall be great, and will be called the Son of the Most High, and the Lord God will give to him the throne of his father David, and he will reign over the house of Jacob for ever, and of his kingdom there will be no end" (Lk. 1:32f., cf. 68ff.). Our author is saying, then, that this ancient promise finds its fulfilment in the coming of Jesus, who is both Son of God and son of David (Rom. 1:3), truly God and, through the incarnation, truly man, and that never was any such promise made with reference to an angel. His Sonship, once again, is unique; all other sonship is by virtue of incorporation into him who is the only one to whom God has said, "I will be to him a father, and he will be to me a son." And his Sonship within this context is not simply ontological, in terms of his deity, but mediatorial, in terms of his incarnation, which enables him (as our epistle so clearly teaches) to offer himself on our behalf and through the perfection of his obedience to secure his, and in him our, filial acceptance with God.

1:6. *And again, when he brings the first-born into the world, he says, "Let all God's angels worship him."*

Our understanding of the precise meaning of this, the third in the chain of passages cited to prove the superiority of Christ to the angels, depends to a considerable degree on the manner in which we interpret the adverb *again* in the introductory formula. The main question to be determined is whether "again" goes with the verb *says* ("he says again") or with the verb *brings* ("when he brings again"). If the former, then it serves simply to introduce a fresh quotation, as in the preceding verse (1:5) and also in 2:13, 4:5, and 10:30 (and similarly in Jn. 19:37; Rom. 15:10, 11, 13; and 1 Cor. 3:20, and of course frequently in extrabiblical

15. See T. H. Gaster, *The Scriptures of the Dead Sea Sect* (London, 1957), pp. 351f.; G. Vermes, *The Dead Sea Scrolls in English* (London, 1962), p. 244.

literature). If the latter, then the quotation is associated with a second coming of the Son into the world, whereas the former, which is favored by the majority of translators and commentators, would imply that the reference of the quotation is to the coming of Christ at his incarnation. Westcott, indeed, contends that even if "again" is taken with the verb "says" the grammatical structure of the clause *when he brings the first-born into the world* in the original Greek must be taken to refer to a future event. [16] Even if this be granted, however, the reference is not at all necessarily to the event of Christ's future coming in glory, for the future reference of the words is from the point of view, not of the author of the Epistle to the Hebrews, but of the author of the verse he quotes. Within this perspective, the incarnation or first advent could equally well have been intended.

Among the fathers, Chrysostom and Alcuin interpret this verse in terms of the incarnation, while Jerome[17] and Gregory of Nyssa relate it to the second advent. Thus Gregory affirms that "the addition of 'again' asserts that manifestation of the Lord of all which shall take place at the last day."[18] Ronald Knox, who follows Jerome's Vulgate version, is uncertain whether "again" (or, to be precise, "anew" in his translation) "contrasts the Incarnation of our Lord with his activity in Creation (cf. verse 2 above), or his Resurrection with his Incarnation, or his second Coming with his first."[19] That either of the first two of the three contrasts he suggests could have been in mind is, however, improbable. But Knox exaggerates when he claims that "the general sense of the Fathers" is against the interpretation of this verse as a reference to Christ's first advent.[20] Montefiore suggests that an allusion is intended here to the praises of the angelic host at the nativity of Christ (Lk. 2:13f.) and that our author uses this quotation "as a proof text that the Son is so far superior to the angels that they worshipped him." This is an attractive connec-

---

16. This judgment is based not only on the order of the words in the Greek—ὅταν δὲ πάλιν εἰσαγάγῃ—which, as F. F. Bruce observes, is not conclusive, but also and primarily on the construction ὅταν with the aorist subjunctive, which, Westcott insists, cannot describe an event already completed in the past, but "must look forward to an event (or events) in the future regarded as fulfilled at a time (or times) as yet undetermined." Moffatt, however, while holding that "linguistically either the incarnation or the second advent might be intended," maintains that "neither the tense of εἰσαγάγῃ (unless it be taken strictly as futuristic = ubi introduxerit) nor the proximity of πάλιν is decisive in favour of the latter," adding, perceptively, that "ὅταν εἰσαγάγῃ might, by a well-known Greek idiom, be equivalent to 'when he speaks of introducing, or describes the introduction of.'"

17. As reflected in the Latin of his Vulgate version: *Et cum iterum introducit primogenitum in orbem terrae, dicit....*

18. Gregory of Nyssa, *Contra Eunomium* ii.8; cf. iv.3 where this verse is more fully discussed.

19. Ronald Knox, in an annotation to Hebrews 1:6 in his English translation from the Vulgate (London, 1944).

20. *Ibid.*

tion, though it could no doubt be argued that angels are also associated with the Son at his second advent and in the new creation (cf., e.g., Mt. 16:27; 24:30f.; 25:31; Mk. 13:27; Rev. 5:11f.).

The passage quoted corresponds verbatim with the Greek of the Septuagint version of Deuteronomy 32:43 (the Song of Moses).[21] It is missing, however, from the Massoretic Hebrew text and has commonly been regarded as a noncanonical addition. A more reasonable supposition would have been that the Septuagint here reflects a Hebrew text which was in the hands of the Ptolemaic translators in the third century B.C. That such was indeed the case is now virtually confirmed by the discovery of a fragment in Hebrew from Cave 4 at Qumran which includes the clause in question and thus provides a very early witness to its authenticity. The only difference is that the Hebrew reads "sons of God"; but this in the Septuagint is a synonymous variant (Codex Alexandrinus) for "angels of God" (Codex Vaticanus). A very similar exhortation is found in the Septuagint version of Psalm 97(96):7, "All you his angels, worship him."[22]

Our author's designation of the Son as *the first-born* carries important doctrinal implications. To begin with, it carries on the thought of the immediately preceding verse in which the Mediator is assigned the dignity of the divinely begotten Son: as the unique Son he is also the first-born, and as the first-born he has precedence over all others who, in a secondary and non-essential sense, may at times be addressed as sons, whether angels or men. As the first-born, moreover, he is the heir (as he has already been described in v. 2 above), to whom the birthright, "the right of the first-born," with all its privilege and prestige, belongs (Gen. 43:33; Dt. 21:17; Ps. 89:27). To be called the first-born is to be in a special sense sacred, since the first-born of God's people were demarcated as consecrated to the Lord (Ex. 13:2; 22:29; Num. 3:12f.); so Jesus was wholly dedicated to the will and the service of the Father (cf. Jn. 4:34; 6:38).

In the New Testament, apart from the nativity narratives in Matthew and Luke, the term "first-born" is used specifically of Christ on four other occasions. Two of these relate directly to the resurrection, namely, Colossians 1:18, "the first-born from the dead," and Revelation 1:5, "the first-born of the dead," where the significance of the term is equivalent to the affirmation of 1 Corinthians 15:20, that "Christ has been raised from the dead, the first fruits of those who have fallen asleep," or, as the NEB renders it, "the firstfruits of the harvest of the dead." This is one important respect in which Christ, through whom

21. Καὶ προσκυνησάτωσαν αὐτῷ πάντες ἄγγελοι θεοῦ.
22. Προσκυνήσατε αὐτῷ πάντες ἄγγελοι αὐτοῦ.

God "brings many sons to glory," is constituted "the pioneer of our salvation" (Heb. 2:10). The thrust is precisely the same in Romans 8:29, where he is described as "the first-born among many brethren" who are predestined to be conformed to his image. In Colossians 1:15, however, the statement that Christ is "the first-born of all creation" has a different connotation. Here the term indicates either the Son's priority to all creation as the one who is eternally begotten (an interpretation which is reflected in the clause, "begotten of his Father before all worlds," of the Nicene Creed and in Phillips' paraphrase, "he existed before creation began"), or his supremacy over all creation on the basis of his primogeniture, since, as first-born, his is the place of highest honor (an understanding of the expression which is reflected in the NEB rendering, "his is the primacy over all created things").[23] Our verse is the only place in the New Testament where the title "first-born" is used absolutely. As a title of superiority, and particularly, as the context requires, of superiority to the angels, the designation "first-born" belongs to Christ both as the eternal Son and also as the incarnate Redeemer who, after humbling himself for our salvation, has been exalted to the place of highest honor. To him the angels pay homage. The primary reference here, however, is to the incarnate Son who is brought into the world to accomplish our redemption. The astute comment of Herveus holds good, then, for the present passage, even though it may not be universally defensible: "With reference to his divinity, in which he has no brothers, the Son is called 'only-begotten' (unigenitus), but with reference to his humanity, in which he is qualified to have brothers, he is called 'first-begotten' (primogenitus)."

It should be noticed that in Deuteronomy 32:43 the pronoun "him" refers to the Lord God (Yahweh); there is no mention of any other person to whom worship is to be given. But when transferred to our present context the one ("him") whom God's angels are to worship is clearly the first-born Son. This consideration demonstrates, once again, that in the apostolic faith the fulness of deity is inherent in the Son, with the consequence that there is no hesitation in assigning to him what in the Old Testament is assigned to Yahweh.[24]

---

23. See Bishop Lightfoot's discussion of the term πρωτότοκος in Saint Paul's Epistles to the Colossians and to Philemon (London, 1892 edn.), pp. 144ff.

24. "The principle on which the writer proceeds," says Delitzsch, "is a general one, namely this: that wherever the Old Testament speaks of a final and decisive advent and manifestation of Jehovah in the power and glory of the final judgment and salvation; wherever it speaks of a revelation of Jehovah which shall be the antitype and fulfilment of that typical one in the Mosaic time, of a self-presentation of Jehovah as the manifested King over His own kingdom, there Jehovah = Jesus Christ; for Christ is 'Jehovah manifested in the flesh',—Jehovah Himself entering into fellowship with humankind, and taking part in our historical developments,—Jehovah rising as the Sun of righteousness,

1:7. Of the angels he says, "Who makes his angels winds, and his servants flames of fire."

The fourth in the sequence of quotations from the Old Testament adduces Psalm 104:4, which, in its original setting, is generally taken to mean that God employs winds as his messengers and flames as his servants. This would seem to accord with the immediate context, which speaks of God stretching the heavens out like a tent, building his palace on the waters above, using the clouds as his chariot, and riding on the wings of the wind. Psalm 104 is, in fact, an encomium of the wonders of God's creation and his sovereign control of all things. One problem that presents itself is that the Psalmist says "flaming fire" in the singular,[25] not "flames of fire" as in our version and JB (the singular is preserved in KJV and NEB), and it is not natural to combine a singular object with a plural predicate, that is: "he makes a flame of fire his servants." Ordinarily, one would expect a singular to be matched with a singular, or a plural with a plural; though, if "flame of fire" is taken as the predicate, there is not the same degree of awkwardness in saying, "he makes his servants a flame of fire." The problem probably arises, however, from the fact that the Hebrew noun for "fire"[26] is used only in the singular and that this singular has been retained in the Greek both of the Septuagint and of the quotation before us. The plural, "flames of fire," may well convey the legitimate sense of the original, in which case the translation, "who makes winds his messengers and flames of fire his servants," would certainly be possible—the word *angels*[27] being taken in its basic and nonspecific sense of "messengers." But our context, which is concerned with the contrast between Christ and the angels, demands that the term be rendered specifically as "angels."

Another problem of interpretation belongs to the word *winds*, which in both the Hebrew of the Old Testament[28] and the Greek of the New[29] may equally well be translated "spirits." Thus the rendering of the KJV, "who maketh his angels spirits," that is, spiritual, incorporeal creatures, which reflects a long-entrenched interpretation.[30] The rendering

---

and shining on His own people. This principle is irrefragibly true; it constitutes the innermost bond between the two Testaments. All writers of the New Testament are fully conscious of it. . . . The final glory of the theocracy is in God's plan of redemption no other than a Christocracy; the kingdom of Jehovah and the kingdom of Christ are one."

25. Hebrew אֵשׁ לֹהֵט (מְשָׁרְתָיו), "flaming fire," which the LXX renders πῦρ φλέγον, while Hebrews 1:7 has πυρὸς φλόγα, "flame of fire."

26. אֵשׁ, *esh.*

27. Ἄγγελοι.

28. רוּחוֹת.

29. Πνεύματα.

30. Cf. Vg *spiritus.*

"winds" rather than "spirits" is contextually required, however; for, if the latter were correct, then a consistently parallel interpretation should be sought for the description of God's servants as fiery flames. Herveus, like others before and after him (Alcuin and Aquinas, for example), does in fact offer such an interpretation: angels, he says, "are always spirits, but they are not always angels, for they are angels only when they are messengers," and he relates the mention of fire to their designation as *seraphim*, "which," he explains, "means 'burning ones', because they are totally inflamed with the fire of divine love." But, as has already been observed, Psalm 104 is speaking of the elemental forces of creation rather than of the constitution of angels.

Psalm 104:4, then, is susceptible of a double meaning. As Delitzsch points out, the verse "may either affirm that God makes wind and fire serviceable to Him for special missions (cf. cxlviii.8), or that He gives wind and fire to His angels as the material of their manifestation and, as it were, their assumption of a corporeal form, for the purpose of His activity within the world, which is mediated by means of them."[31] What, then, is the main point of contrast intended by our author's introduction of this quotation? Hardly, as Moffatt proposes, "that God can reduce angels to the elemental forces of wind and fire, so unstable is their nature, whereas the person and authority of the Son are above all change and decay"; for quasi-rabbinical speculation[32] respecting the constitution, stable or unstable, of angelic beings is out of place here. The contrast is rather between, on the one hand, the status of angels, which is that of *servants* (see the comparison between Moses as servant and Christ as son in 3:5f. below), and their function, which is effective but intermittent as are the elements of wind and fire through which their activities may be displayed, and, on the other hand, the status and authority of Christ, which are resident in the abiding glory and supremacy of his royal and eternal Sonship—as the next quotation shows. It is,

31. F. Delitzsch, *Biblical Commentary on the Psalms*, III (London, 1889), pp. 98f.
32. Cf. IV Ezra 8:21, "before whom heaven's hosts stand trembling, and at thy word change to wind and fire" (Latin version: "*cui adstat exercitus angelorum cum tremore, quorum servatio in vento et igni convertitur*"). The Qumran hymns speak of God as having appointed "the mighty winds according to their laws before they became angels [of holiness]" (1QH i.10f., G. Vermes' translation). F. F. Bruce cites also *Hagigah* 14a, "every day ministering angels are created from the fiery stream, and utter song, and cease to be," and *Yalqut Shim'oni* ii.11.3, where the angel says to Manoah, "God changes us hour by hour;... sometimes he makes us fire, and sometimes wind," from the Babylonian Talmud. Delitzsch follows Böhme in suggesting that the author of Hebrews may "have altered the πῦρ φλέγον of the Septuagint into πυρὸς φλόγα, and perhaps have had the appearance of the angel at Ex. iii.2, ἐν φλογὶ πυρὸς ἐκ τοῦ βάτου, in his mind, as an instance of what the psalmist was speaking of." A more satisfactory interpretation is found in the midrashic rendering of the Targum: "who makes his messengers speedy as the wind, his ministers strong as a flaming fire."

in short, the contrast between him who is the Son and Heir and them who are the servants under his command in the royal household of God's kingdom.

1:8, 9. *But of the Son he says, "Thy throne, O God, is for ever and ever, the righteous sceptre is the sceptre of thy kingdom. Thou hast loved righteousness and hated lawlessness; therefore God, thy God, has anointed thee with the oil of gladness beyond thy comrades."*

The fourth quotation, in the preceding verse, and this the fifth in the chain of passages cited from the Old Testament are in strong contradistinction to each other, as is plain both from their content and from the formulas which introduce them ("Of the angels he says . . . But of the Son he says").[33] The former describes the subservient position of the angels, whereas here the everlasting sovereignty of the Son is declared in words taken from Psalm 45:6f. The psalm itself is an epithalamium or marriage-ode written to celebrate a royal wedding. The exact historical occasion is unknown and is not a matter of importance in the exegesis of these verses.[34] It is clear, however, that the language of the Psalmist's encomium applies with particular appropriateness to one who belongs to the royal messianic line of David. Compare, for example, the promise given to David through Nathan: "Your house and your kingdom shall be made sure for ever before me; your throne shall be established for ever" (2 Sam. 7:16); and the affirmations of another psalm: "I have sworn to David my servant: 'I will establish your descendants for ever, and build your throne for David, my servant; with my holy oil I have anointed him'" (Ps. 89:3f., 20). The Davidic throne is eternally distinguished by justice and righteousness, and of the messianic Son of David it is said that "with righteousness he shall judge the poor, and decide with equity for the meek of the earth" (Isa. 9:7; 11:4). Plainly, the perspective of messianic expectation envisaged not merely an approximation to but an identification of the kingdom of Christ with the kingdom of God, for to God the Psalmist declares: "Righteousness and justice are the foundation of thy throne" (Ps. 89:14).

33. Λέγει, which occurs in the introductory formula of verse 7 but is not repeated, though it is understood, in that of verse 8, may mean either "it (i.e. Scripture) says" or "he (i.e. God) says." For the mind of both Hebrew and Christian there was no essential difference, since it was accepted that what Scripture said God said.
34. Among the conjectures that have been offered mention may be made of the following: that it was the marriage of Jehoram, king of Judah, to Athaliah of Israel; that it was the marriage of Ahab, king of Israel, to Jezebel of Tyre; that it was the marriage of Solomon to the daughter of Hiram or to the daughter of a pharaoh.

It is within this perspective that a king of the Davidic line can be addressed in the otherwise surprising terms: *"Thy throne, O God, is for ever and ever,"* since he prefigures the divine and eternal King, and that our author can assert that it is *of the Son* that these words are spoken, since, as the eternal Son who humbled himself to become man and endure the cross and who has been raised from the dead and exalted to the place of supreme authority, he is the fulfilment of every messianic hope. In him, as the incarnate Son, the divine and the human meet and the Davidic kingdom becomes truly the kingdom of God.

An alternative translation of the opening clause of the quotation, namely, "God is thy throne for ever and ever" instead of "Thy throne, O God, is for ever and ever," appears to have been in existence since the early centuries[35] (in more modern times it has been favored by Wycliffe, Tyndale, Moffatt, Westcott, Goodspeed, and others, and is mentioned as an alternative rendering in the margins of the RSV and NEB). But it would be an awkward and uncharacteristic mode of expression, and as an alternative it is dismissed by F. F. Bruce as "quite unconvincing" and by Nigel Turner as a "grotesque interpretation."[36] To address the royal messianic personage as God is not without parallel in the Old Testament. Isaiah, for example, proclaims that the coming one who will rule on the throne of David will be called "Mighty God" (Isa. 9:6), a designation used elsewhere of the Most High (cf. Dt. 10:17; Neh. 9:32; Ps. 24:8; Jer. 32:18); and Jeremiah prophesies that the "righteous Branch" who is to be raised up for David, who will reign as king, and who will execute justice and righteousness, will be called by the name "The Lord [Yahweh] is our righteousness" (Jer. 23:5f.).

These and the other messianic passages that we have cited indicate also how appropriately the declaration, *the righteous sceptre is the sceptre of thy kingdom,* is applied to the incarnate and exalted Son. The everlasting rule of the Son is marked by absolute justice and equity, whereas even in the best of human dominions there is some admixture of injustice and discrimination. It might well have been expected, in view of the frequency with which Psalm 110 is quoted or alluded to elsewhere in this epistle, that our author would have added verse 2 of that psalm, which states, "The Lord sends forth from Zion your mighty sceptre," to this chain of texts. Luther offers the explanation that the sceptre spoken of here is nothing else than "the Gospel of Christ or the Word of God," for

---

35. Moffatt is probably right in supposing that the interpretation "God is thy throne..." was responsible for the change of σου after βασιλείας into αὐτοῦ, so that the sentence then reads: "God is thy throne for ever and ever, and a righteous sceptre is the sceptre of his kingdom." The witnesses in which the reading αὐτοῦ is found, namely, p⁴⁶, ℵ, and B, are few but impressive.

36. *Grammatical Insights into the New Testament* (Edinburgh, 1965), p. 15.

"by no power other than the Word does Christ rule the Church." True though this may be, the main reason for the introduction of this quotation here is to underline the contrast between the royal and eternal office of the divine Son and the subservient function of the angels.

The affirmation, *Thou hast loved righteousness and hated lawlessness*, applies not just to the eternal holiness of the Son as divine but in particular to the life and ministry of the incarnate Son on earth. His love of righteousness and hatred of lawlessness was the essential preliminary to his atoning death on the cross, where he "died for sins once for all, the righteous for the unrighteous" (1 Pet. 3:18). The perfection of his obedience, which culminated in the ordeal of the cross, was the measure of his love of righteousness and hatred of lawlessness and at the same time of God's compassion for mankind (cf. Heb. 5:8f.).

He is, moreover, the one whom *God has anointed*. The very designation "Christ," which is the Greek equivalent of the Hebrew "Messiah," means the "Anointed One." The king of Judah whom the Psalmist honors had, like David before him (2 Sam. 2:4), been anointed with oil on assuming his high office. As such, he was a "christ," pointing on from himself to the coming of *"The Christ"* whom God would anoint with the oil of his Holy Spirit. The age-old understanding of the oil of anointing as a symbol of the Holy Spirit (thus, for example, Aquinas who says that the Psalmist's words cited here "have to do with spiritual unction, since Christ was filled with the Holy Spirit") is based on the original anointing of David by Samuel, following which "the Spirit of the Lord came mightily upon David" (1 Sam. 16:13), the prototype of the messianic King, and on Isaiah's messianic prophecy: "The Spirit of the Lord God is upon me, because the Lord has anointed me..." (Isa. 61:1; cf. 11:2)—words which Christ applied specifically to himself (Lk. 4:18ff.) following the descent of the Holy Spirit upon him at his baptism (Mk. 1:10) and his repulse of the tempter in the wilderness (Lk. 4:1ff.). The incarnate Son is uniquely God's Anointed One.

But the anointing *with the oil of gladness* refers neither to Christ's baptism nor to the perfection of his life and sacrifice, but to the triumphant entry of Jesus into the heavenly glory. It is the logical consequence (*therefore*) of the completion of his earthly mission. The achievement of eternal redemption for mankind and the world is the cause of gladness and rejoicing in the presence of God. The anointing with the oil of gladness which he then received is also the anointing with the oil of gladness which he thereafter bestows in the transforming experience of Pentecost when, in words taken from the passage in Isaiah already cited, he grants "the oil of gladness instead of mourning" (Isa. 61:3). As Peter explains on the day of Pentecost, the utterance of Psalm 16:11, "thou wilt make me full of gladness with thy presence," found its fulfilment in the resurrec-

65

tion and glorification of Jesus, as the victorious Savior rejoices to receive from the Father the gift of the Holy Spirit promised long ago through the prophet Joel—a gift which he exultantly pours upon all flesh. This is the oil of gladness. "Being therefore exalted at the right hand of God," Peter declares, "and having received from the Father the promise of the Holy Spirit, he has poured out this which you see and hear" (Acts 2:33; cf. 1:4f., 8; 2:1ff., 16ff.).

There is no necessity to seek particular significance in every part of a somewhat extended quotation for our immediate context. It has been suggested, however, that a further contrast between the Son and the angels is intended by the mention of his *comrades,* whose anointing with the oil of gladness is less than his own. This is the understanding of Lünemann, Moffatt, Windisch, and others. But it may properly be objected that angels are not elsewhere described as Christ's comrades and, further, that they are nowhere mentioned as the recipients of unction. More satisfactory is the identification of the "comrades" with all other anointed kings, favored by Delitzsch: Christ's exaltation is immeasurably superior to theirs. Another proposal equates the "comrades" here with those mentioned in 3:14 below,[37] that is, with Christian believers whom Christ, by virtue of his common humanity with them through the incarnation and their oneness with him through faith, is not ashamed to call "brethren" (Heb. 3:11). This is the interpretation of Chrysostom, Aquinas, Calvin, Westcott, F. F. Bruce, and others. The terminology of 3:14, however, occurs in a quite different setting and the notion there is of participation in Christ rather than that of comradeship. The truth which our author is intent on emphasizing here is that of the superiority and transcendence of the glorified Christ, in distinction particularly from the angels, and Teodorico wisely advises that we should not seek to impose on the term "comrades" in the quotation a too precise value.

The expression *thy God* in verse 9 seems to comport ill with the preceding verse in which the Son is addressed as *God;* but the apparent anomaly is resolved by the consideration that as the eternal Son, the Second Person of the Blessed Trinity, the Son is indeed God (cf. Jn. 1:1), while as the incarnate Son, and specifically in relation to his human nature, it is natural for him to speak of God as *his God* (cf. Jn. 20:17). This

---

37. The same noun, μέτοχοι, is used both here and in 3:14 (also in 3:1 and 6:4). In 3:14, however, the RSV rightly translates μέτοχοι τοῦ Χριστοῦ γεγόναμεν as "we share in Christ" rather than as "we have become Christ's comrades." The Arians explained this quotation from Psalm 45 in a manner agreeable to their contention that the Son was less than divine. Theodore of Mopsuestia sees the Psalmist as "marvellously separating the two natures for us," by understanding the Son's everlasting throne to refer to his divine nature and his anointing to refer to his human nature. It must be regarded, however, as a doubtful piece of exegesis.

is the explanation of the prayer-life of Jesus and of his cry of dereliction on the cross (cf. Jn. 17; Mk. 6:46; Lk. 9:28; Mk. 14:35ff.; 15:34).

> 1:10–12. And, "Thou, Lord, didst found the earth in the beginning, and the heavens are the work of thy hands; they will perish, but thou remainest; they will grow old like a garment, like a mantle thou wilt roll them up, and they will be changed. But thou art the same, and thy years will never end."

Number six in this series of quotations is a sublime passage from Psalm 102 (vv. 25–27), applied here to the Son, and extolling him as the one who brought into being the totality of heaven and earth and who, despite the change and dissolution of all created things, remains constant and unchanging. The force of this passage is enhanced by the consideration that the Psalmist had evidently witnessed the destruction of the city and temple of Jerusalem, which so many Jews had mistakenly imagined to be inviolable, and had suffered the desolating experience of bondage and exile. This was the stark setting of his faith in the Lord, not only as Creator and Judge, but also as Restorer. Moreover, if God is unchangeable, so also are the word of his promise and his oath, as our author explains later in the epistle (6:18); indeed, he teaches that there is to be one more cosmic shaking prior to the establishment of the unshakable kingdom of Christ extending over the renewed order of creation (12:26ff.).

In this opening section of the epistle our author has already declared that it was the Son through whom the world was created and by whose word of power the universe is sustained (1:2f.), and that it is the Son who is apostrophized by the Psalmist as God (Elohim, 1:8). He now applies to him words which another Psalmist addressed to the Lord (Yahweh)[38] in a manner fully consonant with the Christology of the New Testament. It is through apparently incidental and unlabored designations of this kind that the apostolic doctrine of the Trinity falls into place. Cullmann's assertion that the Old Testament text of Psalm 102 "obviously speaks of God the Father, the Creator" must be questioned, for it is not obvious that the First Person of the Trinity is being ad-

---

38. The vocative "Lord" is present in the LXX which our author ordinarily follows closely, but not in the Massoretic Hebrew text. Rather, however, than conclude that it was inserted into the text by the LXX translators, we prefer to assume that it was there in the Hebrew original with which they were working (see commentary on 1:6 above). Be that as it may, it is fully in harmony with the tenor of the psalm, which bears the title, "A prayer of one afflicted, when he is faint and pours out his complaint before the Lord [Yahweh]," and which opens with the appeal, "Hear my prayer, O Lord [Yahweh]" (v. 1) and includes another apostrophe to the Lord in verse 12.

dressed, but rather simply the eternal God without the specification of a trinitarian distinction. But he rightly observes that "as a result of the transfer of the name *Kyrios* to Jesus, the writer of Hebrews does not hesitate to address him with the words of the psalm, and thus to designate him the Creator of heaven and earth," adding that he does not believe discussions of New Testament Christology have given this passage in Hebrews the attention it demands. "We should generally give much more consideration," he says, "to the by no means self-evident fact that after the death of Jesus the first Christians without hesitation transferred to him what the Old Testament says about God."[39]

How inescapable, once again, is the contrast between the Son and the angels! He is the Lord God; they offer him worship and homage. He is the Creator; they are his creatures. He is infinite in being and power; they are finite and dependent. Though all else should pass away, he remains, "the same yesterday and today and for ever" (Heb. 13:8).

NOTE ON THE EXPRESSION "IN THE BEGINNING" (1:10)

The scholastic authors were fond of treating the term "beginning" (*principium*) as a title of Christ. It is, indeed, plainly such in Revelation 21:6 and 22:13 (cf. Rev. 1:8, 17). But they would also take a verse like Genesis 1:1, "In the beginning God created the heavens and the earth," and impose on it the interpretation that God created all things in or through Christ, who is the beginning. The notion is found in Augustine (*De Trinitate* I.xii.24). In the middle ages a similar understanding of the expression "in the beginning" in verse 10 (=Ps. 102:25) was current. Peter Lombard, for example, in the twelfth century, offers as a mystical interpretation (which involves taking the quotations from Ps. 102 as an address to the Father instead of to the Son): "Thou, O Lord Father, by whom the Son was anointed, didst found the earth in the beginning, that is, through thy Son who is the beginning from the beginning, in accordance with his own words in the Gospel, 'I who am speaking to you am the beginning'" (*Tu, O Domine Pater, a quo unctus est Filius, in principio, id est per Filium tuum qui est*

---

39. Cullmann, *The Christology of the New Testament*, pp. 234, 235. See also p. 98: "... it is just those New Testament writings which most strongly emphasize the deity of Christ which also take his humanity most seriously. Thus we find precisely in Hebrews the boldest of all assertions of Christ's deity: it could not be asserted more strongly than in Heb. 1.10, in which the Son is addressed directly as Creator of heaven and earth."

principium de principio, secundum quod ipse ait in Evangelio: Ego principium qui et loquor vobis). The reference is to John 8:25, and the Latin of the Vulgate in that place undoubtedly at first sight lends itself to such an interpretation; but it is apparently both a misunderstanding and a quasi-literalistic rendering of the original Greek of John 8:25, where, in response to the question, "Who are you?", Jesus says: τὴν ἀρχὴν ὅ τι καὶ λαλῶ ὑμῖν—a text which admittedly presents problems to the translator but which cannot mean what the medieval commentators wished it to mean. (It may be assumed that Jerome intended *principium* not as a nominative but as an accusative corresponding to τὴν ἀρχήν, which can be explained only as an adverbial accusative.)

This interpretation of Hebrews 1:10, supported by the appeal to John 8:25 (Vg), was commonly accepted among the scholastic writers, at least as a legitimate alternative to the more natural exegesis; for it is beyond dispute that our author states that these words of Psalm 102 are addressed *to the Son*. An interpretation which is based on their being addressed to the Father is accordingly inadmissible. Instances of other commentators in which it recurs are Thomas Aquinas in the thirteenth century and Jacques Lefèvre d'Etaples at the beginning of the sixteenth century. Pico della Mirandola (1463–1494) may be mentioned as an example of one who explains the "beginning" of Genesis 1:1 in the same personal way as a reference to Christ (in the concluding portion of his *Heptaplus, Opera Omnia*, Basel, 1572).

> 1:13, 14. *But to what angel has he ever said, "Sit at my right hand, till I make thy enemies a stool for thy feet"? Are they not all ministering spirits sent forth to serve, for the sake of those who are to obtain salvation?*

The seventh and culminating quotation in the catena designed to demonstrate from the scriptures of the Hebrew canon the superiority of the Son to the angels is adduced from the opening words of Psalm 110. The recognition of the messianic significance of this psalm in the apostolic church is amply attested by the frequency with which its authority is invoked in the pages of the New Testament. Citations, either direct or implied, are to be found in the following places: Mark 12:35ff. (= Mt. 22:43ff.; Lk. 20:41ff.), Mark 14:62 (= Mt. 26:64; Lk. 22:69), [Mark 16:19], Acts 2:34f., Romans 8:34, 1 Corinthians 15:25, Ephesians 1:20, Colossians 3:1, and 1 Peter 3:22. And not least in the Epistle to the Hebrews Psalm 110 plays an important part, providing scriptural authentication of the uniqueness and supremacy of Christ, not only as Son and Lord but also as High Priest and Redeemer. In addition to the quotation before us, the psalm is cited or echoed some dozen times (1:3; 5:6, 10; 6:20; 7:3, 11, 17, 21; 8:1; 10:12, 13; 12:2). Indeed, the central doctrinal section, chapters 7–10, is an extended development of the nature of the Son's high priesthood portended by this psalm.

It is evident, then, that Psalm 110:1 was seen by the apostolic authors and teachers as an Old Testament pillar supporting the doctrine of the exalted session and rule of Christ. That this psalm's messianic tenor was accepted by the Jews in the time of Christ is indicated by the encounter narrated in Mark 12:35ff., where Jesus cites this verse in a discussion in the temple concerning the identity of the Messiah, as well as by evidence from other sources. Later rabbinical denials of the psalm's messianic character are to be explained as a reaction to the apostolic teaching that its predictions were fulfilled in the person and work of Jesus.

We have already seen, in the commentary on verse 3 above, that Christ's elevation to the *right hand* of God is his exaltation to the position of supreme lordship and authority. The qualifying clause which the Psalmist adds in the quotation now before us, namely, *till I make thy enemies a stool for thy feet,* should not be taken to mean that the kingship of Christ is something of no more than temporary duration, as though setting a limitation, a *terminus ad quem,* beyond which his reign will not continue; for, as the quotation from Psalm 45 in verse 8 above affirms, his throne is forever and ever. What this clause does assert is that, though he is already exalted, there are still hostile forces to be brought into subjugation (cf. Heb. 2:8, where this theme is taken up and briefly discussed: "we do not yet see everything in subjection to him"); and, further, that the triumph of his dominion will prove to be complete and lasting.

There is a sense, however, in which the Son, having received a mandate, so to speak, from the Father to redeem the elect people and to subdue and eradicate every enemy, reports to the Father that his mission is accomplished and hands over the reins of government. Thus in a passage whose meaning it is impossible for us with our present limited powers of comprehension to grasp adequately Paul writes: "Then [following the advent of Christ at the close of the age] comes the end, when he delivers the kingdom to God the Father after destroying every rule and every authority and power. For he must reign until he has put all his enemies under his feet. . . . When all things are subjected to him, then the Son himself will also be subjected to him who put all things under him, that God may be everything to every one" (1 Cor. 15:24–28). The Son's mediatorial work in redemption and judgment will have been completed, his messianic task fulfilled, the final victory achieved. "The last enemy to be destroyed," says Paul, "is death" (1 Cor. 15:26). The kingdom of life will then be established for all eternity, and the new heaven and new earth will display the fulfilment of Christ's purposes in creation. The redeemed will partake of the perfection of his glorified humanity, and it is in this respect that the Son, and they in him, will continue in subjection to, that is to say in perfect harmony with, the will of the Father. But he who is the Lamb and our King David will reign everlastingly in the midst of the throne (cf. Rev. 7:17; 22:16); and at the sound of the last trumpet the proclamation will go forth: "The kingdom of the world has become the kingdom of our Lord and of his Christ, and he shall reign for ever and ever!" (Rev. 11:15). And then God, the trinitarian God, Father, Son, and Holy Spirit, will be all in all (1 Cor. 15:28).

The radical contrast between the enthroned Son as described in Psalm 110:1 and the subordinate status of the angels—*all* angels—is unmistakably plain from these texts that have been cited. Angels, our author now summarily explains, are *ministering spirits sent forth to serve*, a definition which is reminiscent of Psalm 103:20f.: "Bless the Lord, O you his angels, you mighty ones who do his word, hearkening to the voice of his word! Bless the Lord, all his hosts, his ministers that do his will." Unlike men, whose constitution is a bodily one, they are *spirits*, a fact which is connected with the invisibility and the swiftness of their service. They are, as their name indicates, *sent forth*,[40] that is by God, and it is as God's messengers that they are active in his service. And our author adds the interesting instruction that their ministrations are *for the sake of those who are to obtain salvation*. Theirs is, accordingly, a service unmarred by self-seeking and directed toward a glorious end. This association of the angels with the heirs of salvation had been declared centuries earlier in the words of Psalm 91:11: "He will give his angels charge of you to guard you in all your ways." When the city of Dothan was surrounded by the overwhelming numbers of the Syrian army who had come to capture Elisha, the servant of Elisha was reassured by the exhortation of his master, "Fear not, for those who are with us are more than those who are with them," and his eyes were opened to see that "the mountain was full of horses and chariots of fire round about Elisha" (2 Ki. 6:15–17). It was an angel host that joyfully heralded the birth of the Savior (Lk. 2:13); angels ministered to him after the ordeal of his temptation in the wilderness (Mt. 4:11); angels at the empty tomb announced the resurrection of Jesus from the dead (Lk. 24:4ff.); angels strengthened the disciples who had just witnessed the ascension of their Master from the Mount of Olives with the assurance that he would return in the same way as they had seen him go (Acts 1:10f.); and angels will accompany the Son of man when he returns in the glory of his Father (Mk. 8:38; Mt. 16:27; 25:31; Lk. 9:26; 12:8f.). Later on in our epistle the author assures his readers that in coming to "the city of the living God, the heavenly

---

40. Both the Hebrew מַלְאָךְ and the Greek ἄγγελος come from verbal roots meaning "to send." An angel is a messenger entrusted with a mission by God.

Jerusalem," they have come also to "innumerable angels in festal gathering" (12:22).

The service of the angels, then, is honorable and glorious. But the honor and glory of their service is not to be compared with the honor and glory of the Son's rule. They are but instruments of his kingship and their ministry is but an expression of his sovereignty. Such teaching emphatically disallows any expectation (like that of the Dead Sea Sect) that some angel in particular, such as the archangel Michael, or angels in general will exercise rule and authority in a manner that rivals or surpasses the leadership of Christ in the age to come.

2:1. Therefore we must pay the closer attention to what we have heard, lest we drift away from it.

At this point we come to the first of a number of admonitory passages which are interspersed throughout the epistle (cf. 3:12–4:3; 4:14–16; 5:11–6:8; 10:32–39; 12:3–13; 12:14–17; 12:25–29). These passages serve to demonstrate that the teaching of this epistle is not merely theoretical and unrelated to the realities of everyday life, but is intensely practical and therefore full of intense seriousness. This is true of all the doctrine of the New Testament, in which theology is unfailingly wedded to practice. Theology and life go together. Christian doctrine which is presented to the mind and will, and is received by faith, is proved by experience. As Spicq says, "saving truth is not just speculative, it governs the whole of life." The conjunction *Therefore* points to the essentially logical connection between theology and practice. The teaching our author has given in chapter 1 concerning the absolute supremacy of Christ, in his own person and by virtue of his redeeming work, is of vital importance. To derogate from the honor that belongs to the Son alone and to ascribe it to angels or any other creatures is to destroy the gospel and with it one's own standing before God.

It is precisely because Christ is incomparably superior to all others, whether angels or prophets or (as the chapters that follow will show) national leaders or priests, that *what we have heard,* that is, concerning him who is God's final word to mankind (Heb. 1:2) and whom apostles and evangelists proclaimed as Savior and Lord, is of such crucial importance. The gospel of Jesus Christ stands alone because it is unique (Jn. 14:6; Acts 4:12). Any other "gospel" is no gospel at all and brings a curse, not a blessing (Gal. 1:7–9). To spurn the hearing of the gospel is to disregard not only the preacher but also God who is the source of the saving message. In the speaking of God to us by his Son, the Word become flesh (Jn. 1:14), word and action are perfectly united; and for the believer, who responds with faith and gratitude, this Word is not just a declaration heard with the outward ear, but an energy experienced in the very depth of his being, powerful in the transformation of his existence, and visible in his daily conduct. In view of the infinite grace of God manifested in the sending of his Son into the world to redeem fallen mankind we are indeed under a moral obligation to give the most careful heed to the proclamation of the gospel.

The majority of commentators from Chrysostom onward take the admonitory words *we must pay the closer attention* to mean that the recipients of this letter are being exhorted to be more seriously attentive to the gospel, declared by God's Son, than to the law, which was declared by angels. The next three verses do, it is true, provide a comparison, but from a different line of approach: if, as the history of Israel shows, neglect of the law produced dire consequences, neglect of the gospel must inevitably be disastrous. If the breakers of the law did not go unpunished, certainly dispisers of the gospel cannot expect to do so. Our author is pressing on his readers the extreme seriousness of carelessness and unconcern. Assuming that a comparison is intended, it is perhaps preferable to take this verse as an exhortation to them to apply themselves with much more earnestness than is at present the case to the doctrines of the gospel. Thus the rendering of the Jerusalem Bible: "We ought, then, to turn our minds more attentively than before to what we have been taught." But the probability is that the emphasis intended at this point is superlative rather than comparative, so that the sense is: "We must pay the *closest* attention."[41] Eternal issues are at stake and the gospel by its very nature demands to be treated with the fullest seriousness.

The dangerous consequence of levity or lack of due seriousness where this vital teaching is concerned is that we may *drift away from it*. The metaphor in mind here seems to be that of allowing the current to carry one away from a fixed point through carelessness and unconcern, and, instead of keeping a firm grip on the truth, of failing to maintain a secure anchorage which will keep one from drifting from the gospel.[42]

---

41. Cf. Phillips, "We ought, therefore, to pay the greatest attention." In first-century Greek the superlative form is becoming less common and accordingly the comparative form is often found doing double duty. The adverb περισσοτέρως is a good example of this and probably carries an elative sense not only here but whenever it occurs in the New Testament. The elative sense is favored here by Héring and Moffatt, and Moffatt insists that "there is no idea of demanding a closer attention to the gospel than to the Law."
42. The verb παραρρέω means literally to "flow by" or to "slip away." Plato uses it of something slipping from one's memory (*Laws* 781a), Plutarch of a ring slipping from a finger (*Moralia* 754a), and Aristotle of a crumb going down the wrong way (*De Partibus Animalium* iii.3). Chrysostom suggests that the metaphor is borrowed from Proverbs 3:21,

The imagery may well be related to that of 6:19, where our author speaks of the Christian hope as a "sure and steadfast anchor of the soul." Those to whom this letter is addressed are evidently not far from losing their right to be acknowledged as authentic Christians because of a loss of nerve, a failure of application, or, as Chrysostom puts it, a "wilful negligence" in practicing the faith they profess. Hence the need for the admonitions repeatedly given in this epistle: "we must pay attention ... lest we drift away"; "take care, brethren, lest there be in any of you an evil, unbelieving heart, leading you to fall away from the living God" (3:12); "let us strive to enter that rest, that no one fall by the same sort of disobedience.... let us hold fast our confession" (4:11, 14); "you have become dull of hearing.... you need some one to teach you again the principles of God's word" (5:11, 12); "let us leave the elementary doctrines... and go on to maturity" (6:1); "do not throw away your confidence.... you have need of endurance" (10:35, 36); "let us lay aside every weight... let us run with perseverance the race that is set before us" (12:1); "lift up your drooping hands and strengthen your weak knees" (12:12); "see that you do not refuse him who is speaking" (12:25); "do not be led away by diverse and strange teachings" (13:9). Through sheer apathy they are in grave peril of drifting away from the essentials of the gospel.

2:2, 3a. *For if the message declared by angels was valid and every transgression or disobedience received a just retribution, how shall we escape if we neglect such a great salvation?*

The more precise rendering of the NEB, "the word spoken through angels,"[43] is to be preferred here (the passive is a divine passive, i.e., "spoken" implies spoken *by God*: as in 1:1, God is still the primary speaker). The word spoken by God at Sinai, namely, the law, was communicated *through* angels, who mediated to Moses what God had to say.[44] In both Old and New Testaments there are indications that angels

---

where the LXX uses the same verb: Υἱὲ, μὴ παραρρυῆς, τήρησον δὲ ἐμὴν βουλὴν καὶ ἔννοιαν—certainly a sentiment appropriate to our context in Hebrews. Peter Lombard offers the quaint interpretation, based on the double prefix of the verb in the Vulgate: "*Ne forte pereffluamus*, id est aēternaliter puniamur. Fluimus per poenas mortalis naturae, effluimus peccata addendo, pereffluimus in aeternam damnationem"—an interpretation that is inapplicable to the Greek verb παραρυῶμεν since it is compounded with only one prefix.
43. Ὁ δι' ἀγγέλων λαληθεὶς λόγος.
44. "Λόγος is used, not νόμος," Moffatt comments, "in keeping with the emphasis upon the divine λαλεῖν in the context."

were regarded as having had a part to play in the delivering of the law to Moses. The account in Exodus 19 and 20, where there is no mention of the presence of angels, gives the impression that this was a transaction simply between God and Moses, as indeed it essentially was. Deuteronomy 33:1ff., however, a passage in which Moses is recalling what took place at Sinai, declares that with God were "myriads of holy ones" (v. 2 NEB), which is understood as a reference to the presence of angel hosts. (The Septuagint adds that "angels were with him at his right hand," reflecting either a different Hebrew text or a gloss on the passage.) Psalm 68:17 also speaks of the "thousands upon thousands" that accompanied the Lord at Sinai. In the New Testament Stephen speaks of the law "as delivered by angels" (Acts 7:53; cf. v. 38), and Paul in a similar manner describes the law as "ordained by angels through an intermediary," namely, Moses (Gal. 3:19). Certainly, God spoke to Moses on the mountain, but using angelic mediation, and Moses in turn as he communicated the law served as a mediator between God and the people. This seems to be what is meant by the mention of angels here. Teaching to the same effect is found in the pre-Christian Book of Jubilees (1:27) and in the writings of the first-century Jewish authors Josephus and Philo.[45]

The reference to angels is perhaps somewhat more than incidental. Our author has already adduced scriptural evidence to demonstrate the inferiority of angels to Christ; yet, he now says, the word of the law spoken through their mediation at Sinai was *valid* or binding and unchallengeable,[46] as is evident from the consideration that every infraction of the law *received a just retribution*. The law, of course, was firm and valid precisely because it was spoken by God, not because angels had a role to play in its promulgation; but there is another mediation of great significance in the central teaching of this epistle, that of the Son who is the mediator of the new covenant (8:6; 9:15; 12:24). Here is the immensely greater mediation to men of everlasting redemption sealed by the blood of the incarnate Son himself. The argument, then, is *a fortiori*: if under Moses the law stood firm and its penalties were stringently enforced on those who deliberately or through negligence[47] broke its precepts, it

---

45. Josephus, *Antiquities* XV.v.3; Philo, *De Somniis* i.143.
46. On the connotation of βέβαιος and its cognates βεβαιόω and βεβαίωσις as virtually technical terms implying legal security and validity see A. Deissmann, *Bible Studies* (Edinburgh, 1909), pp. 104ff. and Moulton and Milligan, *sub voc.*
47. Aquinas comments that of the two terms "transgression" (παράβασις) and "disobedience" (παρακοή), the former relates to affirmative and the latter to negative precepts. Spicq and Montefiore propose a distinction between positive and negative sins, that is, between the deliberate breaking of a commandment and disobedience through failure to heed what is commanded. It is difficult to determine, however, whether one or the other of these distinctions is intended here.

cannot but be that the direst consequences await those who are careless and unconcerned[48] about the gospel, which is here described as *such a great salvation*—it is so wonderful that no language is adequate to do it justice.[49] Unlike the law which was, as it were, mediated by word of mouth, the gospel was mediated by the Word-made-flesh. The intensified seriousness of the situation since the coming of Christ is clearly underlined by our Lord's own warning that in the day of judgment it will be more tolerable for Sodom and Gomorrah than for those who spurn the gospel (Mt. 10:14f.; cf. 11:20ff.). "God wishes his gifts to be valued by us at their proper worth," says Calvin. "The more precious they are, the baser is our ingratitude if they do not have their proper value for us. In accordance with the greatness of Christ, so will be the severity of God's vengeance on all despisers of the Gospel."

The law indeed, as Paul insists, is holy and good and also glorious (Rom. 7:12, 14; 2 Cor. 3:7ff.). How could what is God-given be anything less? The problem lies not with the law, which is the divine standard of life (Lev. 18:5; Ezek. 20:11, 13; Neh. 9:29; Lk. 10:28; Gal. 3:12), but with sinful man who is a law-breaker, with the consequence that the law stands over against him as an ordinance of condemnation and death, precisely because it is holy and just. But the glory of the law is completely surpassed by the glory of the gospel because the latter brings life where the former brought death. It is true that sinful man can in the nature of the case never be justified by the works of the law but only by faith through the grace of God in Christ Jesus (Gal. 2:15ff.); yet law and gospel are not in conflict with each other, since, for one thing, the ground of the acceptance of Christ's sacrifice of himself in the sinner's stead was the perfection of his performance of the law and will of the Father, and, for another, through the work of the Holy Spirit, the law which previously was an external instrument of condemnation becomes an internal principle, engraved on the living tablet of the heart, so that the believer now has both the will and the power to fulfil God's law which before he had disobeyed (2 Cor. 3:3ff.). This high doctrine of the law must be borne in mind in the interpretation of this and other passages which speak of the law, for, as Westcott remarks, "throughout the Epistle the law is regarded as a gracious manifestation of the divine will."

---

48. The Greek verb ἀμελεῖν, translated "neglect" here, means precisely to be unconcerned. It is the other extreme from προσέχειν, to pay close attention to or hold firmly to, in verse 1.
49. Teodorico offers the opinion that the comparatively rare term τηλικοῦτος, "such a great," used here rather than τοσοῦτος, "seems to suggest at the same time the two ideas of greatness and of excellence."

2:3b, 4. *It was declared at first by the Lord, and it was attested to us by those who heard him, while God also bore witness by signs and wonders and various miracles and by gifts of the Holy Spirit distributed according to his own will.*

In the knowledge and experience of those to whom this letter is addressed the authenticity of the Christian salvation is attested by the indisputable facts of its dominical origin and its dynamic manifestation in their midst. They are reminded that this salvation *was declared at first by the Lord,* or rather, to render the Greek more accurately, that "it was first spoken by God through the Lord," who is the mediator and the embodiment of this salvation. "The message spoken by God through angels" at Sinai (v. 2) is exactly balanced here by the declaration that the gospel was "spoken by God through the Lord."[50] From this reminder, and in the light of the context, it may be inferred that among the letter's recipients some had been saying in effect: "Our forefathers received the law through angels; we received the Gospel only through men," and were accordingly disposed to suggest that the gospel was inferior to the law — a judgment that could well have been influenced by teaching similar to that of the Dead Sea Sect, in which angels are assigned so elevated a position. This erroneous conclusion is corrected by our author's assertion that, even though it was human evangelists who brought them the saving message, the true mediator of that message is the Son himself, whom he has already shown to be incomparably superior to all angels.

The statement that *it was attested to us by those who heard him* indicates that neither our author nor his readers had received the teaching of salvation directly from the Lord, but, at one remove, from the lips of those who had been instructed by him. This information plainly rules out the admissibility of any "first-hand" apostle or disciple as the writer of our epistle, and at the same time, as Luther, Calvin, and many others have pointed out, it excludes the possibility of Pauline authorship (which was universally accepted during the middle centuries), since, though not himself one of the original apostles, Paul insists that he received the gospel not from men but directly from the Lord (Gal. 1:1, 11ff.). Whether the designation *to us* implies that the author was originally a member of the group or community to whom he is writing, and

---

50. In verse 2 ὁ δι᾽ ἀγγέλων λαληθεὶς λόγος is precisely matched by ἥτις ἀρχὴν λαβοῦσα λαλεῖσθαι διὰ τοῦ κυρίου here. In both places λαληθείς and λαλεῖσθαι are "divine passives," with the implication that it is God who spoke on both occasions. Cf. the same verb in the active voice with God as the subject in 1:1f.: ὁ θεὸς λαλήσας... ἐλάλησεν.... The message of the law was spoken by God through the mediation of angels, δι᾽ ἀγγέλων, at Sinai; the message of the gospel was first spoken by God through the mediation of the Lord, διὰ τοῦ κυρίου. Of the former, moreover, it is said, ἐγένετο βέβαιος, of the latter, ἐβεβαιώθη, which is another mark of the close correspondence in mental and linguistic structure between the two passages.

received the message of the gospel with them, is difficult to determine. The exhortation at the end of the epistle, "Remember *your* [rather than our] leaders" (13:7), seems to tell against it, though it is possible that he had left their company (perhaps to become an evangelist himself) soon after the gospel had been brought to them.[51]

The important thing, however, is that, while the message of salvation was brought to these "Hebrews" by the testimony of men, its pure fountainhead was the Lord himself, who is greater than any angel. Indeed, the description of the law as having been *declared by angels* in the preceding verse is balanced by that of the gospel as having been *declared by the Lord* here. But, once again, a more precise translation is desirable, for the Greek original says "declared *through* angels" and "declared *through* the Lord."[52] The idea conveyed by the preposition in both cases is that of *mediation*, a concept of considerable importance in this epistle. In both instances it is God who speaks (declares),[53] but mediately, through angels in the past and through the Lord now.

But, it may be asked, is not the Son himself God? and is not this indicated by the very title *Lord (Kyrios)*, which both in the Septuagint and in the New Testament is the equivalent of the sacred Hebrew name Yahweh? How then can mediation be intended in the case of the Son? The answer to such questions is that Christ is indeed the *divine* Son, but he is also the *incarnate* Son: he is man as well as God; and the mediation of the Son, who is truly God, depends on his incarnation, which makes him also truly man. An angel is neither God nor man. His service is, as we have seen (1:14), "for the sake of those who are to obtain salvation." But he is not qualified to redeem them. The mediatorial qualification of the Son, however, is infinitely superior to that of the angels, for, as both God and man, he is uniquely qualified to effect reconciliation between God and mankind. As God, the incarnate Son is supreme in power and grace, in contrast to the impotence and resourcelessness of fallen mankind. As man, the incarnate Son is able fully to identify himself with mankind, and in particular in man's place to endure the divine punishment of sin on the cross, thus securing for mankind eternal redemption—a theme developed in this chapter and of major importance throughout the epistle. In Christ mediatorship is raised to an eternal category, truly bridging the gulf between heaven and earth caused by man's sinful rebellion against the sovereignty of his Creator.

The good news of salvation, then, derives from the Lord, whose mediatorship is absolutely other than that of angels, and not from the

51. For further discussion of the question of authorship see Introduction, pp. 19ff.
52. Δι' ἀγγέλων λαληθείς . . . λαλεῖσθαι διὰ τοῦ κυρίου.
53. Λαληθείς and λαλεῖσθαι (see n. 50) are "divine passives."

human agents through whom the "Hebrews" were evangelized. In what our author says here, moreover, we have the structure of the genuine apostolic succession. It is a succession that goes back, not just to the apostles, but through the apostles to the Lord. And it is a succession of evangelism. This is the sum and substance of a passage very relevant to the present theme, where Paul affirms: "There is one mediator between God and men, the man Christ Jesus, who gave himself a ransom for all, the testimony to which was borne at the proper time. For this I was appointed a preacher and an apostle" (1 Tim. 2:5–7). So, too, when Peter preached the word of Cornelius in Caesarea he told him that the "good news of peace by Jesus Christ" began with the Lord himself in Judea, and that he and his fellow apostles who were witnesses of the saving deeds of Christ were commanded to proclaim the message of forgiveness of sins through the name of Jesus (Acts 10:36–43). This succession in which the message of redemption "was declared at first by the Lord" and "then attested by those who heard him" and thereafter transmitted from faith to faith through the succeeding generations to the uttermost parts of the earth is well illustrated in what Irenaeus of Lyons wrote in an autobiographical fragment preserved in the writings of Eusebius of Caesarea. Irenaeus, who flourished during the latter part of the second century, is recalling his boyhood days when he received instruction in the gospel from Polycarp (who suffered martyrdom in 155 or 156), who had been a disciple of John, who in turn was an apostle of Jesus Christ:

> I remember the events of that time more clearly than those of recent years. For what boys learn, growing with their mind, becomes joined with it; so that I am able to describe the very place in which the blessed Polycarp sat as he discoursed, and his goings out and comings in, and the manner of his life, and his physical appearance, and his discourses to the people, and the accounts which he gave of his intercourse with John and with others who had seen the Lord. And as he remembered their words, and what he heard from them concerning the Lord, and concerning his miracles and his teaching, having received them from eyewitnesses of the 'Word of life', Polycarp related all things in harmony with the Scriptures. These things being told me by the mercy of God, I listened to them attentively, noting them down, not on paper, but in my heart. And continually, through God's grace, I recall them faithfully.[54]

The succession of evangelical witness which stretched back through the apostles to the Lord himself was accompanied by corroborating evidences. The latter were in themselves eloquent testimony that the experience of the "Hebrews" as they had responded to the gospel was something more than the work of man. Only God could have performed

---

54. Eusebius, *Hist. Eccl.* V.xx.5ff. (A. C. McGiffert's translation).

the confirming signs they had witnessed. Such wonders were no substitute for the dynamic inward working of the Holy Spirit which amazingly transforms sinners into new men in Christ, but they were, so to speak, God's visible endorsement of the saving message.[55]

It is best to take *signs, wonders,* and *miracles* as belonging together rather than as indicating three different forms of manifestation.[56] The three terms are found in combination again in Acts 2:22, where Peter draws his audience's attention to the "mighty works and wonders and signs" with which Jesus was attested by God, and in 2 Corinthians 12:12, where Paul speaks of the "signs and wonders and mighty works" which indicated that he was a true apostle. "Signs and wonders" (or "wonders and signs") are mentioned together eleven times (Mt. 24:24; Mk. 13:22; Jn. 4:48; Acts 2:43; 4:30; 5:12; 6:8; 7:36; 14:3; 15:12; and Rom. 15:19), while Acts 8:13 speaks of "signs and great miracles" (cf. Ps. 78:43). Each term, however, has its own particular import and contributes a distinctive shade of meaning, so that the use of the terms in combination should not be dismissed as merely tautological. Thus a *sign,* which is the word consistently used in the Fourth Gospel for the miraculous works of Christ, indicates that the event is not an empty ostentation of power, but is *significant* in that, sign-wise, it points beyond itself to the reality of the mighty hand of God in operation. A *wonder* is an event which, because of its superhuman character, excites awe and amaze-

---

55. The truth of the gospel is secure in itself and is not dependent on accompanying signs of the kind mentioned here. This is indicated by the assertion that the message of salvation was "attested," or, better, shown to be firm and sure, by those who had heard the Lord and in turn had passed on the good news to the "Hebrews." The Greek verb is ἐβεβαιώθη, which corresponds to the adjective βέβαιος, "valid," "secure," used in the preceding verse to describe the word of the law. The validity, firmness, and authenticity of the gospel is demonstrated primarily by its dynamic effect in transforming human lives and attitudes. This is the great confirming sign. Other signs are additional and corroborative. See also footnote 58 below.

56. The medieval commentators took "signs" (σήμεια) to mean minor miracles, "wonders" (τέρατα) to mean major miracles, and "miracles" (δυνάμεις) to mean Christian virtues (influenced, no doubt, by the ambiguity of the Vulgate term *virtutes*). Peter Lombard, for example, distinguishes between signs as "lesser acts, such as curing diseases, which physicians can do," wonders as "greater acts which take place contrary to nature," and powers as "acts which are not supernatural" or "spiritual virtues" such as chastity and humility. Herveus comments to the same effect, and also Aquinas, who explains that a sign denotes "what is beyond and above nature, but not contrary to it," a wonder "what is contrary to nature, such as the virgin birth and the raising of the dead," and a power (*virtus*) "what is according to nature with respect to the substance of the deed, but not with respect to the method of doing it, such as the healing of a fever, which physicians can perform, though not instantly"—or "powers signify virtues of the mind, which the Lord gives his preachers, namely, faith, hope, and charity." Distinctions of this kind, however, are indefensible in view of the variations of word order and the virtual interchangeability of the terms in the New Testament, in which, whether separately or in combination, they denote miraculous acts and manifestations.

ment on the part of the beholder. A *miracle* (or literally *power*) emphasizes the dynamic character of the event, with particular regard to its outcome or effect. The mention here of *various miracles* indicates the diversity of these powerful manifestations.

Remarkable evidences of this kind were supplemented by *gifts of the Holy Spirit*, or, more literally, "apportionments of the Holy Spirit"[57]— that is, the experience of the power of the Holy Spirit through the impartation of his gifts. The nature of these charismatic gifts is described in 1 Corinthians 12:4ff. Sovereignly *distributed* by the Holy Spirit, they included, presumably, prophetic utterance, speaking in tongues, and healing powers, and their effect was, as Delitzsch explains, to "raise the human spirit above its usual limitations." It is apparent, then, that, like the believers in Corinth, "the Hebrews" to whom this letter is addressed had been enriched with spiritual gifts (1 Cor. 1:5, 7). As with the Galatians, the supply of the Spirit and the working of miracles went together (Gal. 3:5) and pointed to the fact that in this corroborative manner *God also bore witness*[58] to the greatness of the salvation provided in Jesus Christ.

The qualification *according to his own will* probably relates to God's corroboration of the gospel by signs, wonders, and miracles as well as by charismatic gifts, though some commentators understand it to apply only to the latter gifts. These manifestations are under the control of God, not of man—just as God the Holy Spirit is the dispenser of his gracious gifts and "apportions to each one individually as he wills" (1 Cor. 12:11). God, as Chrysostom observes, "knows what is expedient, and for whom, and apportions his grace accordingly.... You do not know yourself as God knows you. Let us not say, 'What is the purpose of that?' or 'What use is this?' When God dispenses let us not call him to account, for that would be extreme impiety and folly." But Chrysostom is insistent that there is another gift far greater even than the power to raise the dead, to give eyes to the blind, and to do the same things as were done in the time of the apostles: the best gift of all, namely, the "more excellent way" of love (1 Cor. 12:31; 13:1ff.). "Let us then zealously seek this gift," he says; "and, although we may not be able to dispel a fever, we shall be in no way inferior to Paul and Peter and those who have raised innumerable dead. But without this love, though we should perform greater miracles than even the apostles themselves,

---

57. Πνεύματος ἁγίου μερισμοί. As Aquinas points out, *non distribuitur secundum essentiam, sed inquantum dona eius distribuuntur.*

58. The meaning of συνεπιμαρτυροῦντος τοῦ θεοῦ is that together with (συν-) and in addition to (ἐπι-) the message of the gospel, whose truth and power were proved by the response of faith, God bore witness by supernatural signs and spiritual gifts. See also note 55 above.

though we should expose ourselves to innumerable dangers for the sake of the faith, all will be without profit."

2:5. For it was not to angels that God subjected the world to come, of which we are speaking.

The coming age, here called *the world to come*, is the age of the Messiah in which the messianic promises and prophecies of old find their fulfilment. This age, which was obviously future within the perspective of the prophets who foretold its advent, is still future insofar as its ultimate consummation is yet to be manifested. Thus, near the conclusion of the epistle, our author declares that "here we have no lasting city, but we seek the city which is to come" (13:14; cf. Rev. 21:1ff.). But it is also now present, in that the Messiah has indeed come, in the person of the incarnate Son, and by his coming has inaugurated the era of fulfilment. By his life, death, and resurrection he has performed all that was needful for the redemption of fallen man and his world. In him all the promises of God receive their affirmation (2 Cor. 1:20). The miraculous signs and spiritual gifts (referred to in the preceding verse) which accompanied the preaching of the gospel and corroborated its truth are themselves evidence that the messianic age is already here. They are eloquent of the lordship, not of angels, but of Christ (hence the logical conjunction *for*). The promise of an everlasting kingship concerns one who belongs to the line of David and is at this present time being realized (as the verses that follow show) in the exaltation of the divine-human Son who first humbled himself to a position lower than that of the angels in order to procure our redemption.

Accordingly, though the completeness of the new creation is still awaited, even now the Christian experiences "the powers of the age to come" (Heb. 6:5). The new world-order is even now active, and the place of honor and authority belongs to the glorified Son, not, as for example the Dead Sea Sect imagined, to angels or archangels.[59] Our author is about to demonstrate, by the application of Psalm 8 to Christ, that all things, angels included, are placed in subjection to his sovereignty. "The old world, indeed, lost all its *right* to existence and continuance when Christ first came," comments Delitzsch, "but continues nevertheless to exist still as the outward shell of that hidden world of the future which is not yet fully formed within it, but will one day burst from its encasement as a new heaven and a new earth at Christ's second coming

59. See Introduction, pp. 13ff.

(comp. Isa. lxv.17, lxvi.22; 2 Pet. iii.13; Rev. xxi.1). According to its hidden principle and spirit, this world is already present; according to its glorified manifestation and body, it is yet future." The exalted Jesus is already crowned with glory and honor as the head of the new age. It is to him, *not to angels*, that God has subjected all things (vv. 8f. below); for, as Peter explains, Jesus Christ "has gone into heaven and is at the right hand of God, with angels, authorities, and powers subject to him" (1 Pet. 3:22).

2:6–8a. *It has been testified somewhere, "What is man that thou art mindful of him, or the son of man, that thou carest for him? Thou didst make him for a little while lower than the angels, thou hast crowned him with glory and honor, putting everything in subjection under his feet."*

The RSV, *It has been testified somewhere,* fails to reproduce fully the apparent casualness, indeed vagueness, of the formula which introduces this quotation from Psalm 8 (vv. 4 to 6). Literally rendered, it reads: "Somewhere someone has testified, saying." It is characteristic of our author, however, that he is not concerned to provide a precise identification of the sources from which he quotes. It is sufficient for him that he is quoting from Holy Scripture, whose inspiration and authority he accepts without question.[60] God being its primary author, the identity of the human author is relatively unimportant. The fact that the writer of Hebrews apparently regarded it as unnecessary to give a precise identification of the source of the quotation is seen by Chrysostom as an indication that the recipients of the epistle were well acquainted with the Old Testament scriptures—a consideration which tells in favor of their being Jewish rather than Gentile in background. Usually, it is

---

60. "Πού τις is a literary mannerism familiar in Philo," writes Moffatt. ". . . The τις implies no modification of the Alexandrian theory of inspiration; his words are God's words" (cf. v. 8b). To say that the expression πού τις is "familiar" in Philo, with the inference that Philonic influence is discernible here, is, however, an overstatement, since the expression is found only once in all of Philo's writings as part of an introductory formula, namely, in *De Ebrietate* 61. Πού or ὅπου, without τις, occurs just four times. See R. Williamson, *Philo and the Epistle to the Hebrews* (Leiden, 1970), p. 509. Spicq's affirmation that πού τις as part of a formula introducing a quotation is "frequent in Philo" is all the more inexcusable. In any case, the combination πού τις is found in Greek literature from Hesiod onward, and so in itself cannot be regarded as so startlingly unusual. Bengel comments: "Non hic locutus est David de se ipso: quare nomen eius non opus erat poni. Neque subsistendum est in internunciis, sed spectandum verbum DEI, semel *testatum*." Spicq agrees that this manner of introducing the quotation "supposes a very strict conception of the inspiration and authority of Scripture—the human author is of little consequence, it is God who is speaking."

true, he introduces his quotations with assertions that it is God or the Son or the Holy Spirit who is speaking (cf. 1:5, 6, 7, 8; 2:11f.; 3:7; 4:3, 4, 7; 5:5, 6; 8:5, 8; 10:5, 15). Here alone it is the human author, though anonymous as "someone," who is said to be speaking. (In 4:7 God speaks "through David.")

Psalm 8 is an ode on the majesty of God and the insignificance yet at the same time the remarkable dignity of man. It was not regarded by the Jews as one of the specifically messianic psalms, and at first sight it might appear to have little in the way of messianic content. Yet in the New Testament it is repeatedly applied to Christ, that is, treated as messianic. In Matthew 21:16 Jesus himself quotes from this psalm in justification of the messianic acclamation accorded him by the children in the temple; and in 1 Corinthians 15:27 and Ephesians 1:22 Paul teaches that the Psalmist's assertion that God has put all things in subjection under man's feet finds its fulfilment in Christ. Here, in the passage before us, our author does the same. The application to Christ of what this psalm says about man is explained by the fact that the incarnate Son was the perfect, indeed the only perfect, man, and that the intention and achievement of his incarnation was precisely to restore to fallen man the dignity and the wholeness of his existence as he reintegrated in himself the grand design of creation. Psalm 8 relates to the whole of mankind, but it finds its true focus pre-eminently in him who is uniquely the Son of man and in whom alone the hurt of mankind is healed. Only in union with him can man become man as God meant and made him to be.

It has often been pointed out that Psalm 8 is in effect a poetic recapitulation of the account of man's creation found in Genesis 1. The Psalmist contemplates with wonder the glory of man, who, as the crown of God's creation, is entrusted with dominion over all other creatures. Mankind has sinfully betrayed this trust and perverted this power; yet the purposes of God cannot fail, and it is in the man Christ Jesus, as we have said, that these purposes are restored and brought to fulfilment. The author of our epistle accordingly applies these words of the Psalmist, as F. F. Bruce observes, "not to the first Adam but to Christ as the last Adam, the head of the new creation and ruler of the world to come."

Compared with the vastness of the universe which surrounds him, man seems so puny and insignificant: hence the note of amazement in the question addressed to God by the Psalmist, *"What is man that thou art mindful of him, or the son of man, that thou carest for him?"* Our author, who, as Spicq explains, "interprets the texts of the Old Testament, not according to the understanding of their human author, but in the way in which the Christian revelation elucidates them," shows that the answer to this question is already implicit in the words of the psalm itself: the incarnation of the Son of God is the great and ultimate proof of the importance of man. It is not, however, in egocentric self-approval that the worth of man finds expression, but in his status as God's creature and his constitution in the divine image. His true human dignity, destroyed by sin, is restored in Christ. The incarnation not only confirms the value of man in God's eyes but also displays the love of God for his creatures and his power to rehabilitate the world which man in his fallenness has dragged down with himself.

In the interpretation of the psalm which our author is developing, the statement *Thou didst make him for a little while lower than the angels* marks the point of transition from the concept of man-in-general, which was in the Psalmist's mind, to the distinctively Christian concept of man-in-particular, namely, the incarnate Redeemer who in a unique sense is designated the Son of man.[61] The words "for a little while" represent an ambiguous expression[62] which can mean either "by a small degree" or "for a short time." The former sense fits the psalm taken by itself: the status of man is only by a small degree lower than that of the angels.[63] The latter fits the application of this passage to him who is the Son of man, man *par excellence:* for a short time he was made lower than the angels, that is, through his incarnation. This voluntary humiliation was for the redemption of mankind, and the exaltation which followed it guarantees the ultimate exaltation also, in and with him, of redeemed mankind. Enlightened with this knowledge of the destiny of man, it becomes evident that, seen within the perspective of eternity, the position of man below that of the angels can also be described as "for a little while," since in the divine purpose his exaltation above the angels, achieved in Christ, was intended from the beginning. Once again, the superiority of the Son of man to the angels is thrown into relief.

The Hebrew term translated as "angels" in this quotation is *Elohim*, a term which commonly denotes God in the Old Testament. In the Septuagint, however, which our author according to his custom has followed here, the term is rendered "angels," and it is not without significance that the Targum and Jewish commentators also interpret the plural noun *Elohim* in Psalm 8:5 as signifying angels.[64] The same word is again rendered "angels" in the Septuagint when it occurs in Psalms 97:7 and 138:1, and the two occurrences of *Elohim* in Psalm 82 (vv. 1 and 6)

---

61. In the psalm "man" and "the son of man" ("What is man . . . or the son of man . . .") are synonymous terms, the latter being a common semitic form of expression. The title Son of man which Christ used of himself emphasizes the reality of the incarnate Son's humanity. Though our author does not make a connection between the psalm and Christ in this respect, it is an association of sufficient interest to receive our attention.

62. Hebrew מְעַט; Greek βραχύ τι.

63. See pp. 88f. below for a discussion of the implications of this comparison.

64. See also the modern translation of the Psalms issued by the Jewish Publication Society of America and given in *The Psalms* (Soncino Books, London, 1945), ed. by A. Cohen, in which אֱלֹהִים in Psalm 8:6 is translated as "angels."

should similarly be understood of angels or exalted beings. The Septuagint, in fact, gives the right interpretation of these passages in which the translation of *Elohim* as "God" would be misleading.

After the "little while" of abasement the incarnate Son, and in him mankind, is *crowned with glory and honor*. Being one with Christ, his redeemed share in the glory of his reign (2 Tim. 2:12; Rom. 8:17; Rev. 22:5)—and *everything* is placed *in subjection under his feet*—so that in Christ the dominion for which man was originally created is everlastingly established. The motif of humiliation-redemption-glorification-sovereignty is a recurrent theme in this epistle (cf. 1:3f., 13; 2:7ff.; 4:14; 5:9f.; 7:27f.; 8:1; 9:12, 24; 10:12f.; 12:2). The perfection of the Son's sacrifice and the indefectibility of his rule guarantee the fulfilment of the destiny of mankind in him.

2:8b. Now in putting everything in subjection to him, he left nothing outside his control. As it is, we do not yet see everything in subjection to him.

Obvious though the logic may be, our author considers it so important to drive home the truth of the absolute supremacy of the Son that he takes pains to explain to his readers that, if *everything* is subject to the rule of Christ, then there is *nothing*, not even the angelic sphere, which is *outside his control*. There is, indeed, one equally obvious and logical exception to this conclusion, as Paul observes when making a similar application of this passage from Psalm 8 to Christ, namely, that "when it says, 'All things are put in subjection under him', it is plain that he is excepted who put all things under him" (1 Cor. 15:27)—in other words, God, who does the subjecting, is not himself subjected and plainly cannot be included in the totality of things that are subjected to Christ. From this it is clear that the designation "everything" refers to the whole created order of things and not at all to the Creator himself, and also that it is specifically the incarnate Son through and in whom the integrity of mankind is reinstated that God places on the seat of authority.

Some modern commentators, including Delitzsch, Westcott, Moffatt, and F. F. Bruce, understand the statement, *As it is, we do not yet see everything in subjection to him*, to mean that we do not yet see everything in subjection *to man*, rather than to Christ (cf. NEB, "But in fact we do not yet see all things in subjection to man"). Certainly, the fallenness of man has meant that his dominion over all the rest of creation, in accordance with the mandate of Genesis 1:28, has failed of realization; and there is a certain attractiveness about the transition this interpretation gives to the next verse: "We do not yet see everything in subjection to man; but we do see Jesus crowned with glory and honour." But the transition is given more, not less, point when we understand our author to mean that we do not yet see everything in subjection *to Christ*; for while it is obvious that enemy forces are still active and as yet unsubdued in the world, yet the gaze of faith penetrates to the great reality that Jesus is already enthroned on high. Hence the exhortation later in the epistle to look away to Jesus in the midst of the trials and oppositions of our present pilgrimage (12:2). The distinctively christological interpretation of Psalm 8 accords both with the exposition of our author in this passage and also, as we have seen, with that of Paul in 1 Corinthians. Besides, the subjugation of all things under the son-of-man-in-general is achieved only in him who, as the Redeemer of fallen mankind, is the Son-of-man-in-particular. And with him there is no question of failure: the completeness of his dominion is adumbrated by the expression *not yet*. Meanwhile we are not to judge by appearances. All the powers of evil and rebellion and antichristianity so much in evidence in our world do not contradict the fact that judgment already hangs over them because the supremacy of Christ is a present reality. It is this grand theme which our author is now about to develop at greater length.

2:9. *But we see Jesus, who for a little while was made lower than the angels, crowned with glory and honor because of the suffering of death, so that by the grace of God he might taste death for every one.*

As the men and women of faith of the pre-Christian era looked beyond the present appearance of things and fixed their gaze on the heavenly realities (ch. 11), so *we see Jesus*, and in particular, despite every appearance to the contrary, we see him *crowned with glory and honor*. The man of faith knows that Jesus is enthroned because he is sovereign in his own life. The subjugation of the microcosm that is man the believer is itself a guarantee of the ultimate subjugation of the macrocosm that is the totality of things. The very name *Jesus* is the human name of the Son, and the believer's humanity is indissolubly bound to the humanity which the Son assumed for the redemption of the world. Appearances never threatened to contradict the reality more conclusively than when the incarnate Son endured the shameful death of the cross and was laid lifeless in the tomb. But this death, which appeared to be the extinction of all his power, was nonetheless the sovereign expression of his power who declared, "No one takes my life from me, but I lay it down of my own accord; for I have power to lay it down and I have power to take it again" (Jn. 10:18). His death was the predestined manner and moment of our salvation (Acts 4:28). That this is the reality beyond the appearance is confirmed by the resurrection, ascension, and glorification of Jesus, by which, despite all present appearances, the resurrection, ascension, and glorification of those who are one with him by faith is assured. Moreover, the same Jesus who died on earth and is now exalted above all knows and is known by his people (cf. Jn. 10:14) and will return majestically at the end of the age to drive away every false appearance and establish the reality of his dominion for all eternity (Acts 1:11; Rev. 22:12, 16, 20f.).

First the Cross, then the Crown: the exaltation of Jesus was the consequence of his humiliation, not, however, merely the humiliation of his incarnation, but especially the humiliation of the cross; for the incarnation was the means to "the suffering of death" as the end for which he came, and Calvary accordingly is both the explanation and the fulfilment of Bethlehem. Thus Calvary was also the road to glory: it is *because of the suffering of death* that Jesus is now "crowned with glory and honor." For the follower of Jesus, too, the road is one that leads by way of suffering to glory, as 2 Timothy 2:12 reminds us: "if we endure, we shall also reign with him" (cf. 2 Thess. 1:4f.; Acts 14:22, "through many tribulations we must enter the kingdom of God"). Seen within this perspective, the cross is an essential event in the glorification of Jesus (N.B. Jn. 12:23, "The hour has come for the Son of man to be glorified"). Chrysostom, Alcuin, and some later writers in fact speak of the cross here as the glory and honor of Christ; but, strictly speaking, in the present context the cross is seen as preceding and leading to the glorification of the Son. Chrysostom, evidently with John 12:23 in mind, exhorts his hearers: "If Jesus calls what he suffered for your sake 'glory', much more ought you to call 'glory' what you suffer for your Lord." The Christian glories in the first place in the cross of Jesus, the source of his redemption (Gal. 6:14), and then also in the sufferings which he is permitted to endure for Jesus' sake (Acts 5:41; 13:52; Rom. 5:3; 2 Cor. 6:10; 12:9f.; Col. 1:11, 24; 1 Thess. 1:6; Jas. 1:2; 1 Pet. 1:6; 4:13; and Heb. 10:34).

The incarnation of the Son is described here as becoming *for a little while lower than the angels.*[65] The implication that the present status of man is in some sense inferior to that of the angels is plain, but it must be questioned whether any idea of an ontological inferiority of mankind to angels is intended, though this seems to have been the conclusion drawn by many of the patristic and medieval authors. Origen, for example, speaks of angels being "superior to men, so that men, when made

65. Westcott comments on the fact that our author's use of the perfect participle, ἠλαττωμένον, rather than the aorist (ἐλαττωθέντα), indicates that "the human nature which Christ assumed he still retains."

perfect, become like angels."[66] He invokes the support of Matthew 22:30 ("in the resurrection they . . . are like angels in heaven") and its parallel, Luke 20:36 ("they are equal to angels"); but this similarity or equality to angels in the future state is specifically related in the teaching of Christ to the fact that those who are raised to eternal life "neither marry nor are given in marriage," not to the notion of ontological identity. An innate affinity between men and angels was also postulated on the basis of their common possession, alone among God's creatures, of rational natures, and the opinion became widely accepted that the number of the fallen angels was to be compensated for by the number of the redeemed from among men.[67]

All this is idle speculation, however, for although the angelic host and the multitude of the redeemed will together worship God in the eternal realm, as the book of Revelation shows, angels and men are two distinct categories of being within the divine order of creation. As we have seen, if mankind now is "lower than the angels," the destiny of redeemed mankind is to be exalted in Christ higher than the angels. As things are at present, man is an earthly being, while the angels are heavenly creatures; and this consideration indicates the point of comparison intended by our author, it would seem, when he says that "for a little while" the Son "was made lower than the angels": his coming was a "descent" from the heavenly to the earthly sphere. Peter Lombard propounds the interesting view that the description of Christ as becoming lower than the angels refers not to his assumption of our humanity but to his endurance of death, explaining that only God is greater than the human nature, free from all sin, which he assumed, since this perfect manhood is constituted in the image of God.[68] There is truth in this judgment, but the humiliation of the Son consisted in his identification of himself with inferior and fallen man—a humiliation, however, which,

---

66. Origen, *Contra Celsum* iv.29.
67. Cf. Augustine, *Enchiridion* 29: "It pleased God, the Creator and Governor of the universe, that, since the whole body of the angels had not fallen into rebellion, the part of them which had fallen should remain in perdition eternally, and that the other part, which had in the rebellion remained steadfastly loyal, should rejoice in the sure and certain knowledge of their eternal happiness; but that, on the other hand, mankind who constituted the remainder of the intelligent creation, having perished without exception under sin, both original and actual, and the consequent punishments, should be in part restored, and should fill up the gap which the rebellion and fall of the devils had left in the company of the angels. For this is the promise to the saints, that at the resurrection they shall be equal to the angels of God" [Lk. 20:36] (J. F. Shaw's translation).
68. In Peter Lombard man's inferiority to the angels is postulated in terms of his corporeality as well as of his sinfulness. This is a platonic rather than a biblical notion and appears to be incompatible with the assertion that only God is superior to the incarnate Christ, except that Peter Lombard speaks of the *natura humanae mentis* which Christ assumed rather than the *natura humana*. This can only be regarded as a stultifying refinement.

as this present verse asserts, reached its climax and fulfilment in the suffering of the cross.

The order of the clauses in the Greek of this verse is as follows: "We see Jesus (1) who for a little while was made lower than the angels (2) because of the suffering of death (3) crowned with glory and honor (4) so that by the grace of God he might taste death for every one." The semantic interrelationship of these clauses is a matter of dispute among commentators. Does clause (2) go with what precedes or with what follows; in other words, does the suffering of death by Jesus here define the purpose of his humiliation or the cause of his glorification?[69] If the former, then clause (4) has the appearance of being repetitive—though it could be explained as an amplification of clause (2), adding as it does the concepts of "the grace of God" and of the death of Jesus as being "for every one."[70] Taking clause (2) with clause (3), as we have done above, frees the verse from any sense of repetitiveness since the death of Christ is then seen in two different perspectives, first as the prelude to his glorification, and then in its manward aspect as the divine remedy for the human predicament.

It is somewhat surprising to find clause (4) placed where it is, since it speaks of Christ's tasting of death after his being crowned. The more natural order would have been for it to come in the second rather than the last position, so that the verse would then have read: "We see Jesus, who for a little while was made lower than the angels, so that by the grace of God he might taste death for every one, because of the suffering of death crowned with glory and honor." And this is surely the sense intended by the author, involving, as Bengel points out, the literary arrangement of ideas known as chiasmus, in which on the one hand the two outer clauses or concepts and on the other the two inner ones belong together in sense.[71] Spicq, however, argues against this interpre-

---

69. The preposition διά with the accusative (διὰ τὸ πάθημα τοῦ θανάτου) is susceptible of either interpretation.

70. Moffatt, for example, maintains that "ὅπως . . . θανάτου explains and expounds the idea of διὰ τὸ πάθημα (which consists in) τοῦ θανάτου, gathering up the full object and purpose of the experience which has just been predicated of Jesus"; it "resumes and completes the idea of διὰ τὸ πάθημα τοῦ θανάτου."

71. *Chiasmus* from the Greek letter *chi*, χ, which provides a figure for the crossing over of ideas which occur in sequence 1, 2, 3, 4, or, better, A, B, B, A, as follows:

A good example of this is found in Matthew 7:6:
(A) "Do not give dogs what is holy;
(B) and do not throw your pearls before swine,
(B) lest they trample them under foot
(A) and turn to attack you";
where the sense is, "Lest the swine trample them under foot and the dogs turn to attack you" (or "tear you to pieces," NEB). Cf. note 26, p. 49 above.

tation, contending that clause (4) follows logically after the mention of Christ's enthronement. "The resurrection of Christ," he says, "was the condition for the application of the fruits of the passion to all men. If death had held its victim it would have won the victory and the enterprise of salvation would have ended in defeat (cf. 1 Cor. 15:17–18). The crowning of Christ, on the contrary, attests the success of redemption. In other words, the saving efficacy of the death of Jesus was consummated, consecrated, and in a sense ratified by his glorification. The latter is an integral part of redemption and permits Christ in his state of glory to apply the effects of salvation to men (Jn. 12:32)." The truth of these observations is unquestionable, but the purpose clause "so that by the grace of God he might taste death for every one" properly relates to and has its fulfilment in the humiliation of Christ on earth, not his exaltation in heaven; it is a precise definition of the purpose, not of his glorification, but of his incarnation, as the immediately following verse shows. The culminating statement of this great theme of the abasement, suffering, and glorification of the Son, which sounds throughout the epistle, comes in 12:2, where we are pointed to "Jesus, the pioneer and perfecter of our faith, who for the joy that was set before him endured the cross, despising the shame, and is seated at the right hand of the throne of God."

The expression to *taste death* was taken by Chrysostom and many subsequent commentators, including Luther, to denote a brief act of sipping, a participation of death cut short, as it were, by the resurrection of Jesus on the third day;[72] but the significance of the verb "to taste" when used in this common idiomatic sense is to *experience* something, in this case death, to the full. Thus the New Testament speaks of persons in general, other than Christ, "tasting death," that is, being overtaken by and experiencing death (Mk. 9:1; Mt. 16:28; Lk. 9:27; Jn. 8:52). Hence the expression marks the reality both of the humanity and of the dying of Jesus. It is, as Johannes Behm says, "a graphic expression of the hard and painful reality of dying which is experienced by man and which was suffered also by Jesus."[73] In fact, the "suffering of death" and the "tast-

---

72. Cf. Alcuin: "It is fittingly said that he 'tasted death', because he endured it for a short time, so that, once it was vanquished, he might forthwith rise again"; Herveus: "*ut gustaret mortem*, i.e. horariam et non longam"; and Aquinas: "He tastes who does not eat or drink much. Because Christ did not continue in death, but rose again immediately, he tasted it." Calvin remarks, with unwonted indecision: "What Chrysostom expounds as tasting death, as if Christ touched it with the edge of his lips to the point where he emerged from death as victor, I neither refute nor disapprove, although I do not know whether the apostle intended to speak so subtly."
73. J. Behm, *sub voc.* in Kittel, TDNT, I, p. 677. To "taste death" (γεύεσθαι θανάτου) means the same as to "see death" (ἰδεῖν θάνατον) in 11:5 and Luke 2:26 and also in John 8:51 (θεωρεῖν θάνατον). Spicq suggests the possibility of an allusion to "the cup" of Christ's suffering and death mentioned in Luke 22:42.

ing of death," the two expressions which occur in our present verse, mean one and the same thing.

And all that Jesus has done for us is *by the grace of God*. The initiative which procured our redemption is God's, not ours. Were it not for the priority of divine grace we should be without help and without hope. This truth is pressed home by Paul with his threefold insistence that "while we were yet helpless," "while we were yet sinners," and "while we were enemies" God reconciled us to himself by the death of his Son (Rom. 5:6, 8, 10; cf. 2 Cor. 5:18ff.); and by John's reminder that "in this was love, not that we loved God, but that he loved us and sent his Son to be the propitiation for our sins" (1 Jn. 4:10). "This was done," Herveus explains, "*by the grace*, that is the free gift, *of God*, for man did not deserve it; indeed, Christ himself, who tasted death for the salvation of all, is the grace of God, for the Son of God was under no obligation to us that he should die for us."

The manner in which Herveus speaks of Christ as himself the grace of God is reminiscent of a mistaken but interesting reading of the Latin translation of this verse which is found in many of the Latin commentators, and in accordance with which this clause was understood as saying, "so that the grace of God might taste death for every one."[74] Thus Alcuin writes: "He calls him 'grace' because he tasted death for the salvation of all, for there was no obligation for the Son of God to taste death for us, but grace did this" [or "by grace he did this"].[75] There is, however, no possible ambiguity in the original Greek, which can only mean "by the grace of God."

There is, however, an ambiguity in the Greek phrase rendered *for every one*[76] in our version. In the original the pronoun "every one" is singular in number when the plural might have been expected, and may be either masculine or neuter in gender, so that the question arises whether it means "for every person" or "for every thing." If "for every person" is intended, then the phrase is the equivalent of the plural "for all men," as in 2 Corinthians 5:14f. and 1 Timothy 2:6, and "for us all" in

---

74. This is based on the reading of *gratia* in the clause, "ut gratia Dei pro omnibus gustaret mortem" (Vg), as a nominative instead of an ablative. Cf. Peter Lombard: "in order that the grace of God, that is he who is the grace of God himself, because he freely gives, or because he is freely given for us, might taste death"; and Aquinas: ". . . grace, that is Christ himself, who is the Grace of God. This treats *gratia* as a nominative. Christ is called grace because he is the author of grace." Both Peter Lombard and Aquinas recognize the alternative of taking *gratia* as an ablative. The similarity between the comments of Herveus and Alcuin is an example of the indebtedness in general and not infrequently in detail of the medieval commentators to the earlier patristic authors.

75. "Gratia hoc fecit": did Alcuin intend *gratia* as a nominative or as an ablative here?

76. Ὑπὲρ παντός.

Romans 8:32. [77] This is the most natural way to understand it. The possibility, however, of its being a neuter singular cannot be ruled out, in which case the totality or collectivity of that for which Jesus tasted death is emphasized. This may still be interpreted in a personal manner of men, as in John 6:37–40 where Jesus says: "Every one [neuter][78] that the Father gives me will come to me; and him who comes [masculine][79] to me I will not cast out. . . . and this is the will of him who sent me, that I should lose nothing [neuter][80] of all that he has given me, but raise it [neuter][81] up at the last day. For this is the will of my Father, that every one [masculine][82] who sees the Son and believes in him should have eternal life." The neuter singular, then, would stand for the collectivity of the redeemed who in faith have come to Christ. [83]

But it could denote a wider collectivity than this, the totality, namely, of the whole order of creation. Some of the patristic writers understood it in this sense, drawing attention to Paul's teaching in Romans 8:19ff. that the whole creation, now "subjected to futility," longingly awaits the day when it will "be set free from its bondage to decay and obtain the glorious liberty of the children of God." Origen, for instance, regarded Christ as the redeemer not only of mankind but also of all rational beings, and rational beings in his view included the stars

---

77. Cf. the following doctrinally similar passages: 2 Corinthians 5:14, "one died for all," εἷς ὑπὲρ πάντων ἀπέθανεν, where πάντων is masculine, as the next clause shows, "therefore all died," ἄρα οἱ πάντες ἀπέθανον. 1 Timothy 2:6, "who gave himself as a ransom for all," ὁ δοὺς ἑαυτὸν ἀντίλυτρον ὑπὲρ πάντων, where πάντων again is masculine, as is clear from the immediately preceding statement that the man Christ Jesus is the "one mediator between God and men." Romans 8:32, "he gave him up for us all," ὑπὲρ ἡμῶν πάντων παρέδωκεν αὐτόν. Christ is said also to have died or given his life "for us" (Rom. 5:8; 1 Cor. 5:7; 1 Thess. 5:10; Tit. 2:14; 1 Pet. 2:21; 3:18; 4:1; 1 Jn. 3:16; "for me" in Gal. 2:20), "for the ungodly" (Rom. 5:6), "for the unrighteous" (1 Pet. 3:18), "for the sheep" (Jn. 10:11, 15), and "for the church," the totality of the redeemed (Eph. 5:25). These passages provide a solid basis for concluding that ὑπὲρ παντός in Hebrews 2:9 is identical in meaning with ὑπὲρ ἡμῶν πάντων.
78. Πᾶν.
79. Τὸν ἐρχόμενον.
80. Πᾶν . . . μή.
81. Αὐτό.
82. Πᾶς.
83. Regarding the neuter singular πᾶν in John 6:37 C. K. Barrett observes that "the effect of the neuter is to emphasize strongly the collective aspect of the Father's gift of believers," and J. H. Bernard remarks that the "collective use of the neuter singular" occurs in John several times (Jn. 17:2, 24, 1 Jn. 5:4, as well as Jn. 6:37, 39) "and always of the sum of those who have been 'begotten of God' and 'given' by the Father to the Son" (in their commentaries ad loc.). The association of pronouns in John 17:2ff. is particularly interesting: "Thou hast given him power over all flesh (πάσης σαρκός), to give eternal life to all whom thou hast given him (ἵνα πᾶν ὃ δέδωκας αὐτῷ δώσῃ αὐτοῖς ζωὴν αἰώνιον). . . . I have manifested thy name to the men whom thou gavest me out of the world (τοῖς ἀνθρώποις οὓς ἔδωκάς μοι ἐκ τοῦ κόσμου). . . ."

and heavenly bodies as well as men and angels.[84] Theodoret, commenting on our verse, speaks of the cosmic scope of the redemption effected by the sufferings of Jesus; and Ecumenius explains that Christ died not only for men but also for the powers above, "so that he might break down the middle wall of division and unite the things below with the things above."

It is undoubtedly the doctrine of Scripture that man in his fall has degraded the rest of creation with himself and that his redemption involves the restoration of the order of creation to its destined purpose and perfection; but our author's attention is focused on man, and on the perfect Man who by his death brings many sons to glory, delivering them from the fear of death and from lifelong bondage (vv. 10 and 15). "The thought throughout this passage," says Westcott, "is directed to personal objects, and in such a connexion the phrase could hardly mean 'for everything.' "

NOTE ON THE VARIANT READING χωρὶς θεοῦ ("APART FROM GOD") (2:9)

The attestation of the reading χάριτι θεοῦ ("by the grace of God") is exceptionally strong, supported as it is by p[46], by BACD and other uncials, by numerous minuscules, by the Old Latin and other versions, and by the testimony of Origen in the third century (though only twice out of the six times the text occurs in his writings) and of important fathers of the fourth century. By contrast, the evidence for the variant reading χωρὶς θεοῦ ("apart from God") is far from strong, though it was current at a comparatively early date, since Origen, Ambrose, and Jerome attest its presence in manuscripts known to them. Origen, indeed, evidently regarded it as authentic rather than χάριτι θεοῦ, as also did Theodore of Mopsuestia and Ambrose. This consideration in itself completely

---

84. See Origen, *In Joannem* i.34f., 40, and *De Principiis* I.vii, viii; II.i. Origen even takes Paul's assertion that he "became all things to all men" in 1 Corinthians 9:22 and says that much more so the Savior "became all things to all (τοῖς πᾶσι πάντα) in order that he might win all things (πάντα), or make them perfect," and that "clearly he became a man for men and an angel for angels (σαφῶς γέγονεν ἀνθρώποις ἄνθρωπος καὶ ἀγγέλοις ἄγγελος)," citing the appearance of Christ as an angel to Moses at the burning bush (*In Joan.* i.34). But such angelophanies, if they were appearances of Christ, were always *for men*, never for angels, and also, as our author explicitly states in verse 15 of this chapter, it was not the nature of angels but human nature ("the seed of Abraham") that Christ assumed, thus excluding angels and confirming the declaration of the preceding verse that he "partook of the same nature" as ours.

invalidates the later opinion of Oecumenius and Theophylact that the reading χωρὶς θεοῦ was an alteration introduced by the Nestorians in the fifth century to suit their own particular teaching.

In his work De Fide, in which he cites Hebrews 2:9 on a number of occasions, Ambrose follows and treats as doctrinally significant the reading sine Deo. Thus in II.iv he exclaims: "How well the apostle stated, 'so that apart from God he might taste death for all'—lest we should think that it was his divinity and not his flesh that endured that suffering"; and in V.iv he writes as follows: "One and the same person was the Son both of God the Father and of David; for the mystery of the incarnation of God is the mystery of the salvation of the whole of creation, in accordance with what is written, 'so that without God he might taste death for all,' that is, that every creature should be redeemed at the price of the Lord's blood, without any suffering of his divinity."

In his commentary on this passage Theodore of Mopsuestia dismisses the attempt to change χωρὶς θεοῦ to χάριτι θεοῦ as "most ridiculous" (γελοιότατον), explaining it as prompted by an undiscriminating desire to replace scriptural teaching with something that seems easy to understand, and arguing that the expression χωρὶς θεοῦ in no way damages the doctrine of the deity of Christ (Migne, PG, LXVI, 956f.). Certainly, it is a reading that was likely to find favor with any who taught a separation of the natures, and in fact Theodore's writings were later suspected of having "Nestorian" tendencies. His, and Ambrose's, view of the impassibility of the divine nature, however, was thoroughly orthodox. It is a position which has the emphatic support, for example, of Athanasius, who holds that the purpose of the Son's taking a body was that he might surrender it to death in the place of all (see De Incarnatione 8, 9, 10, 20, 22). So also the Tome of Leo affirms that Christ's person was "capable of death in one nature and incapable of death in the other"; Aquinas, commenting on verse 14 below, says that the Son "assumed a nature in which he could suffer and die, which he could not do in the divine nature"; and Calvin declares, in the same place, that "he put on our nature in order to submit himself to the state of death: for God could not undergo death."

It must be objected against the interpretation of Theodore and Ambrose and many other subsequent writers that "apart from God" is a very awkward, not to say questionable, way of expressing the notion "apart from his divinity." As Spicq observes, we should have expected χωρὶς τῆς θεότητος. Yet this reading has not been without its advocates in more recent times. Bengel, for instance, judging, rightly, that χωρὶς θεοῦ, being the more difficult reading, was likely to have been altered to χάριτι θεοῦ, rather than χάριτι θεοῦ to χωρὶς θεοῦ, and drawing attention to the support for the latter in earlier centuries, argues for the authenticity of "apart from God." He understands it in a different way from Theodore and Ambrose, however, taking our author to mean that Jesus tasted death for all, with the exception of God, that is to say, God was not included in those for whom Jesus died; and he cites 1 Corinthians 15:27 as a parallel type of exceptive qualification. It does seem (though Bengel shows no awareness of this early evidence) that Origen and Theodoret may have interpreted the phrase in this way. Thus Origen, in his commentary on John's Gospel, Tome 28, says that "it belonged to Jesus alone to take to himself the burden of the sin of all on the cross (where he suffered) for all 'apart from God'—ὑπὲρ τῶν ὅλων 'χωρὶς θεοῦ' " (Migne, PG, XIV, 721); and Theodoret, when commenting on the passage before us, in which he accepts χωρὶς θεοῦ as authentic, remarks: "If (the angels) rejoice over one sinner, much more when they see so many myriads accounted worthy of salvation are they filled with gladness. It was, then, for men that he endured the redemptive suffering; for the divine nature alone had no need of the healing which then took place—μονὴ γὰρ ἡ θεία φύσις τῆς ἐντεῦθεν γενομένης θεραπείας ἀνενδεής."

That our author intended the sense (favored also in the last century by Bengel's compatriots G. H. A. Ewald and J. H. A. Ebrard) that Jesus tasted death for everyone "with the exception of God" is improbable, however; for it was with reference to mankind (or possibly creation as a whole) that the Son humbled himself and endured the cross, and it is scarcely conceivable that anyone would have imagined that "for every one" without such an explanation might have included God. In any case, as Delitzsch has remarked, for χωρὶς θεοῦ to have this force it should be placed after, not before, ὑπὲρ παντός: even its position in the sentence tells against this sense.

More recently, B. Weiss, A. Harnack (*Studien zur Geschichte des NT*, I, pp. 235f., Berlin, 1931), and G. Zuntz (*The Text of the Epistles: A Disquisition upon the Corpus Paulinum*, p. 34, London, 1953) have contended for the originality of χωρὶς θεοῦ, but in the sense that when Jesus tasted death for everyone he did so "separated from God"—in other words, his was a God-forsaken death, in line with the cry of dereliction from the cross, "My God, my God, why hast thou forsaken me?" (Mk. 15:34). But, as R. V. G. Tasker observes, "the writer would have expressed his thought more naturally by κεχωρισμένος ἀπὸ θεοῦ" ("The Text of the 'Corpus Paulinum,'" NTS, I, iii, p. 184, London, 1955). The advocacy of the authenticity of χωρὶς θεοῦ has, however, been taken up again by J. K. Elliott ("When Jesus was Apart from God: an Examination of Hebrews 2[9]," *The Expository Times*, LXXXIII, 11, pp. 339–341, Edinburgh, 1972). The form χωρὶς θεοῦ, in which χωρίς is followed by an anarthrous noun, "would conform," Elliott points out, "entirely with New Testament usage in general and with Hebrews usage in particular"; whereas the form χάριτι θεοῦ, in which neither χάρις nor the dependent genitive has the article, "does not conform ... with either the New Testament in general or Hebrews in particular." But, in view of the limited range of the evidence (which is not invariable), it is precarious to conclude on this basis that χωρὶς θεοῦ must be the original reading. Elliott does, in fact, regard as "far more significant" the consideration that χωρὶς θεοῦ, in the sense that Christ in his death was separated from God, "agrees fully with the theological stance of Hebrews." Pointing to the significance of Psalm 22 in relation to Christ's passion, he suggests that the author of Hebrews, who explicitly quotes from this psalm in 2:12, was likely to have had the first part of that psalm (notably the opening cry of dereliction) in mind when writing verse 9. And he supposes, further, that the reading χάριτι θεοῦ became standard in the majority of Greek MSS because the reading χωρὶς θεοῦ had come to be associated with Nestorianism. But it is no more difficult to develop a theological justification for χάριτι θεοῦ than it is for χωρὶς θεοῦ, and the poverty of the evidence coupled with the awkwardness of the expression remains a sufficient reason for disallowing the latter reading.

Moffatt conjectures the possibility that the noun *gratia* in the Vulgate rendering—*ut gratia Dei pro omnibus gustaret mortem*—might be (as we have seen some of the Latin fathers treat it) a nominative rather than an ablative, reflecting the nominative χάρις instead of the dative χάριτι in the Greek original, in which "the Grace of God" (χάρις θεοῦ, *gratia Dei*) was intended as a title or designation of Christ. It would then be easily comprehensible that a copyist might misread χάρις as, or "correct" it to, χωρίς. But he prefers the theory of an early corruption of the text (such as had previously been proposed by Wordsworth and Westcott), which views χωρὶς θεοῦ as a gloss either on ὑπὲρ παντός, "for every one," or on οὐδὲν ἀφῆκεν αὐτῷ ἀνυπότακτον, "he left nothing outside his control," in the preceding verse. In the latter case it would represent an assimilation to the explanation, δῆλον ὅτι ἐκτὸς τοῦ ὑποτάξαντος αὐτῷ τὰ πάντα, "it is plain that he is excepted who put all things under him," of 1 Corinthians 15:27, which subsequently "slipped lower down into the text." Tasker (*loc. cit.*) favors the opinion of Tischendorf that χωρὶς θεοῦ is an alteration of χάριτι θεοῦ "made in the light of I Cor. xv.27 to exclude God from the inclusiveness implied in ὑπὲρ παντός." Spicq, rightly in our judgment, insists that the reading χωρὶς θεοῦ must be "resolutely rejected," taking into account both the weight of the textual evidence and also the demands of the context; and he adds that χάριτι θεοῦ "emphasizes the divine initiative of universal salvation" (I, p. 419). To quote Tasker again, with reference to Zuntz's intemperate judgment, "it will certainly seem strange to many Christian readers to learn that the statement that Jesus suffered 'through the grace of God' yields 'a preposterous sense.'" Montefiore, who prefers χωρὶς θεοῦ "on both grounds of intrinsic probability and on the principle of *difficilior lectio potior* (the more difficult reading is to be preferred)," dismisses χάριτι θεοῦ only with slightly more moderation as "a bald phrase, not particularly suited to the context and uncharacteristic of our author." On the contrary, it would be difficult to think of an expression more suited to the context, which is concerned with the goodness of God manifested in the redemption of the world by the death of Christ; and so far is the expression from being uncharacteristic of our author that he uses it again in 12:15 where he urges his readers to see to it that they do not forfeit the grace of God (NEB)—a danger which, as is apparent throughout, provides the chief motive for the writing of this epistle: there is no remedy for them if they outrage the Spirit of grace (10:29), and so they are encouraged to draw near to the throne of grace (4:16), remembering that it is by grace that the heart is strengthened (13:9).

2:10. *For it was fitting that he, for whom and by whom all things exist, in bringing many sons to glory, should make the pioneer of their salvation perfect through suffering.*

The conjunction *For* indicates that our author is now explaining more fully what he has just said concerning the purpose of the incarnation of the Son, namely, that "by the grace of God he might taste death for every one." To the unregenerate mind, for the divine Redeemer to be humbled by incarnation, and much more so by the shame of dying on a cross, seemed totally inappropriate: a crucified Messiah was "a stumbling block to Jews and folly to Gentiles" (1 Cor. 1:23). The purpose of this and the following verses is to show how *fitting* this method of salvation is and, by implication, how totally inappropriate any other notion must be. The fittingness of the divine action in Christ is suggested, to begin with, by the manner in which God is designated here as *he for whom and by whom all things exist.* As Aquinas well observes, this designation describes God as both the efficient cause ("by whom") and the final cause ("for whom") of all things:[85] all creation flows from God and all creation flows to God. To the same effect Paul writes that "from him and through him and to him are all things" (Rom. 11:36). The whole created order is the expression of the will of God, the Creator of all (Rev. 4:11; cf. Neh. 9:6). This being so, the incarnation and the death of Christ, far from being inappropriate, took place in accordance with the design of the divine will: though he suffered and died "by the hands of lawless men," nonetheless it was "according to the definite plan and foreknowledge of God" that he was delivered up (Acts 2:23; cf. 3:18; 4:28; 13:27; Lk. 22:22).

The incarnation and death of Christ were fitting as the effective means to the achievement of the Creator's grand design, namely, the restoration of all things. If all things are not only *by* but also *for* God, it is inconceivable, and it would be in the highest degree unfitting, that he should allow everything to lapse away from himself into a state of lostness and ruin instead of sovereignly taking action to bring about the rehabilitation of all things. The divine purposes are indefectible and the mediation of Christ is the means of their fulfilment. The following passage from Augustine is concerned with the fittingness of the redeeming work of God in Christ:

> Those then who say, What, had God no other way by which he might free men from the misery of this mortality, that he should will the only-begotten Son, God co-eternal with himself, to become man, by putting on a human soul and flesh, and being made mortal to endure death?—these, I say, it is not enough so to refute, as to assert that that mode by which God deigns to free us through the Mediator of God and men, the man Christ Jesus, is good and suitable to the dignity of God; but we must show also, not indeed that no other mode was possible to God, to whose power all things are equally subject, but that there neither was nor need have been any other mode more appropriate for curing our misery. For what was so necessary for the building up of our hope, and for the freeing the minds of mortals cast down by the condition of mortality itself, from despair of immortality, than that it should be demonstrated to us at how great a price God rated us,

---

85. "Ipse enim est *per quem omnia,* sicut per causam efficientem, *et propter quem omnia,* sicut per causam finalem." Westcott, Spicq, and Teodorico are among those who have borrowed this comment, whether directly or indirectly, from Aquinas.

and how greatly he loved us? But what is more manifest and evident in this so great proof hereof, than that the Son of God, unchangeably good, remaining what he was in himself, and receiving from us and for us what he was not, apart from any loss of his own nature, and deigning to enter into the fellowship of ours, should first, without any evil desert of his own, bear our evils; and so with un-owed munificence should bestow his own gifts upon us, who now believe how much God loves us, and who now hope that of which we used to despair, without any good deserts of our own, nay, with our evil deserts too going before.[86]

And Athanasius writes that the great work of redemption "supremely befitted the goodness of God," basing his doctrine on the passage now before us:

The Word of the all-good Father was not unconcerned about the race of men which had been brought into being through him, and which was on the road to destruction, but by the offering of his own body he abolished the death that was their due.

Our author means, he says, that

the rescue of men from the corruption that had come upon them belonged to none other than to the divine Word who also had made them in the beginning.

"What was God to do," he asks,

when men had become brutalized and demonic deception overshadowed everything, hiding the knowledge of the true God? . . . What profit could there be to God who had made them, or what glory, if the men he has created do not worship him but regard others as their makers? For then it would turn out that God had created them for others and not for himself. . . . What, then, was God to do? What was more needful than the renewal of that which was created according to his image, so that thereby men might once more come to know him? But how could this have been effected save by the coming of him who himself is the very Image of God, our Saviour Jesus Christ? Men could not have achieved this, for they have been made only according to the Image; nor could angels, for they are not the images of God. And so the Word of God came in his own person, so that, as himself the Image of the Father, he might create man anew according to the Image.[87]

The humiliation and death of Christ are fitting because this was the effective means of *bringing many sons to glory*. The redeemed are described as *sons*, not in their own right, but by virtue of their union with him who is the only Son and with whom alone God is well pleased (Mk. 1:11; Mt. 17:5). They are sons by adoption, enabled by the Holy Spirit to call God "Father" and sharing in the glorious heritage which is Christ's

---

86. Augustine, *De Trinitate* XIII.x (A. W. Haddan's translation).
87. Athanasius, *De Incarnatione* 10, 13.

(Rom. 8:15–17; Gal. 4:5–7). As Alcuin says, "He is the Son, and we are sons: he true-born, we adopted." Furthermore, as the fall of man, the crown of creation, involved the whole created order in fallenness, so also the restoration of man in Christ involves the restoration of the whole created order and the achievement of the will and purpose of the Creator. Thus Paul pictures the creation as waiting "with eager longing for the revealing of the sons of God," when, at the appearing of Christ, it "will be set free from its bondage to decay and obtain the glorious liberty of the children of God" (Rom. 8:20f.). The bringing of many sons to glory, then, is also the joyful liberation and reintegration of the cosmos.

It is fitting that our Redeemer should have been *made perfect through suffering:* first, because his completely victorious suffering of temptation of every kind (Heb. 4:15) was essential to his achievement of that perfection which qualified him to offer himself on the cross as the spotless Lamb of God in the place of sinners (1 Pet. 1:18f.; 3:18); second, because his suffering and death at Calvary annulled the power of Satan and set free the "many sons" who were destined for glory (vv. 14f. below); and, third, because his own experience of human suffering in the body he assumed has enabled him as a compassionate high priest to aid and strengthen at all times those who are afflicted with trials and temptations (vv. 17f. below; see also the commentary below on 4:15f. and 5:8).

The many sons who are brought to glory have Christ to thank as *the pioneer of their salvation.* As pioneer, he has gone before them, opening up the way that leads to salvation, and also leading them in that way.[88] For him, that way led through suffering to glory and honor (as the preceding verse declares). For them, the way is not different: the route to glory is by way of suffering. As he endured the cross for the joy that was set before him (12:2), so his followers must be willing to accept his leadership through the vale of affliction, reckoning with the Apostle "that the sufferings of this present time are not worth comparing with the glory that is to be revealed to us" (Rom. 8:18). There is, of course, this important distinction, that his suffering for us is unique in that it is the source of our everlasting redemption, whereas our suffering for him is the evidence of our response of devotion to him who is our only Leader. To quote Alcuin again: "He saves, we are saved," and this is the whole reason for that gratitude which impels us to follow him even through suffering. A serious problem with the recipients of this epistle

---

88. The noun ἀρχηγός is difficult to translate satisfactorily. It signifies one who is both the source or initiator and the leader (ἀρχή plus ἄγω), one who first takes action and then brings those on whose behalf he has acted to the intended goal. The same designation is applied to Jesus in 12:2 below and also in Acts 3:15 and 5:31, where, as ἀρχηγὸς τῆς ζωῆς, he is both the source and the means of life.

was that, though they had at first gladly endured suffering, now their zeal was flagging and they were in need of endurance (10:32ff.; 12:12f.). They are urged to look to him who is both the pioneer and the perfecter of their faith (12:2) and who has by his suffering and exaltation opened up the way for them to that glorious realm where he even now is enthroned (10:19ff.). Indeed, the spiritual union of these "many sons" with their Redeemer means that, even though the climactic experience of their redemption is not yet, their own glorification is as good as realized; so Paul is able to say that God has already "raised us up with him and made us sit with him in heavenly places" (Eph. 2:6); for if it is *God* who is bringing these sons to glory, then the completion of this "bringing" is so certain that they can be regarded even now as having been brought to this wonderful consummation. (For further discussion see the note which follows.)

NOTE ON THE SIGNIFICANCE OF THE PARTICIPLE
ἀγαγόντα **(2:10)**

Is it the Father or the Son who is here said to bring many sons to glory? In the Greek, which reads, ἔπρεπεν γὰρ αὐτῷ, δι᾽ ὃν τὰ πάντα καὶ δι᾽ οὗ τὰ πάντα, πολλοὺς υἱοὺς εἰς δόξαν ἀγαγόντα τὸν ἀρχηγὸν ... τελειῶσαι, the participle ἀγαγόντα, which is in the accusative masculine singular, would best agree, so far as appearances go, with the contiguous noun τὸν ἀρχηγόν, which matches it in case, gender, and number. If this association is correct, it would mean that it is the Son, as the pioneer of their salvation, who leads many sons to glory. This interpretation is unobjectionable on theological grounds, and there is indeed a terminological appropriateness, as Bengel points out, in taking ἀγαγόντα τὸν ἀρχηγόν as belonging together, since "ἀρχηγός is compounded of ἀρχή and ἄγω, and ἀρχή is related in the text to τελειῶσαι which follows (cf. ch. 12:2) while ἄγω is related to ἀγαγόντα which precedes." Thus it is as the supreme leader of salvation that Christ leads many sons to glory. There is a strong appeal in this understanding of the verse. Understanding the Son as subject here, Athanasius cites this passage against the Arians. "If all things that were made by the will of God were made by him [Jn. 1:3], how can he himself be one of the things that were made?" he asks. "And since the Apostle says 'for whom and by whom all things exist', how can these men say that we were not made for him, but he for us? If that were so, he ought to have said, 'for whom the Word was made.' "[89] In

---

89. Athanasius, *Encyclical Letter to the Bishops of Egypt and Libya* 15.

a manner that is christologically questionable, Theodore of Mopsuestia makes the eternal Word the subject of the participle ἀγαγόντα and the humanity assumed in the incarnation the object (τὸν ἀρχηγὸν), giving the sense: "It was fitting that the Word, for whom and by whom all things exist, in bringing many sons to glory, should make the Man he assumed (the pioneer of their salvation) perfect through suffering." This interpretation would seem, however, not only to divide the unity of the incarnate Son but also to impair the integrity of his humanity.

The alternative, which is favored by the great majority of scholars, is to take the participle ἀγαγόντα as descriptive of the work of God the Father, and this is perhaps the more natural way of reading the Greek. The most apparent difficulty in construing the sentence in this manner is the lack of a suitable antecedent for ἀγαγόντα. A dative, ἀγαγόντι, might have been expected, agreeing with αὐτῷ in the main clause ἔπρεπεν αὐτῷ, for an agreement with the accusative in the relative clause (δι' ὃν . . .) is improbable (and if there were a connection with the relative clause a genitive, agreeing with the nearer δι' οὗ, would be likely). The solution to this difficulty, however, is to explain ἀγαγόντα as agreeing with the unexpressed subject of the infinitive τελειῶσαι. Comparable constructions occur in Acts 11:12, 15:22, and 25:27.

There is a further difficulty in connection with the tense of ἀγαγόντα. The aorist would properly imply an act that is completed, giving the sense "when he brought" rather than "in bringing" many sons to glory. The opinion that it is the saints of the Old Testament period who are intended here as having already been brought to glory is inadmissible since it is incompatible both with the immediate context and also with the teaching of 11:40 below, that "apart from us they should not be made perfect." Héring explains it as an inchoative or ingressive aorist. Nigel Turner (J. H. Moulton, *A Grammar of NT Greek*, III, Edinburgh, 1963, p. 80) understands it as denoting "coincident action (*by bringing in*)," and similarly Spicq as defining the "intrinsic consequence" of the verb τελειῶσαι. Teodorico sees in the aorist participle an indication of the divine will or intention ("having decided to bring"), much in the same way as it is interpreted by Erasmus, who expounds the sense of the verse as follows: "For it was fitting that he, that is the Father, who wished to bring (*adducere vellet*) not just one Son Jesus but with him many sons to glory, should make him who was the source and leader (*princeps ac dux*) of the salvation of others legitimate and perfect through various afflictions."

The participle ἀγαγόντα is most effectively explained as a proleptic aorist which envisages the work of Christ and its consequences for mankind as a unity. As the glorification of the "many sons," though yet to be experienced, is inseparably bound up with the glorification of him who is uniquely the Son, which has already been realized, the bringing of the many sons to glory is more than assured, it is to all intents and purposes a reality now because of their union with him who is crowned with glory and honor. "The perfecting of Christ," writes Westcott, "included the triumph of those who are sons in Him." The glory that is now his is the glory also of those who are one with him through faith: there is nothing more to be *done*; they await only their entry into its fulness.

2:11. For he who sanctifies and those who are sanctified have all one origin. That is why he is not ashamed to call them brethren.

There is no question that *those who are sanctified* are the company of the redeemed, but to whom precisely does the designation *he who sanctifies* refer? Certainly, the work of "sanctifying" spoken of here is performed by God on man's behalf; the context, however, demands a more narrow definition of the "sanctifier." It may be said at once that it is not the Third Person of the Trinity, the Holy Spirit, who is intended here, for, although it is the special function of him who is the Spirit of Holiness to lead believers into the progressive experience of sanctification or personal holiness, our context is not concerned with the question of sanctification as distinct from justification. The "sanctifying" spoken of here (and elsewhere in the epistle) is descriptive not of one aspect of the Christian life but of the total experience, from regeneration to glorification, of the setting apart of a people ("those who are sanctified") for the praise and service of God; and while this too cannot be known apart from the operation of God the Holy Spirit, it is not the Third Person of the Trinity with whom our author is concerned in this passage. Nor is it the First Person, God the Father, whom he has in mind as the one who sanctifies, though it is true that it is not otherwise inappropriate to describe the Father in this way, since, for example, Christ himself prayed the Father to sanctify the apostles in the truth (Jn. 17:17), and, in the Old Testament, Yahweh assured the people of Israel that it was he who sanctified them (Ex. 31:13; Lev. 20:8; 22:32; Ezek. 37:28). Plainly it is the Second Person, namely, the Son, who is intended, and even more particularly the incarnate Son, who is the subject of this whole passage. So also in the present verse "he who sanctifies" is one and the same with "he who is not ashamed to call them [the sanctified] brethren."

Moreover, the attribution to the Son of this work of "sanctifying" accords well with what is taught elsewhere in this epistle. It is by the Father's will that "we have been sanctified through the offering of the body of Jesus Christ once for all" (10:10); by his single offering of himself Christ "has perfected for all time those who are sanctified" (10:14); his blood is the blood of the covenant by which the believer is sanctified (10:29); and Jesus "suffered outside the gate in order to sanctify the people through his own blood" (13:12; similarly 9:13f.). Such teaching makes it very clear that the "sanctification" of which our author speaks is intimately connected with and flows from Christ's priestly offering of himself on the cross. His consecration of himself is the source of our consecration (cf. Jn. 17:19). Redeemed by the blood of the incarnate Son, the people of God are purified from defilement and constituted holy before their Creator. This explains the rendering of the NEB: "a consecrating priest and those whom he consecrates." The Christian's consecration to God is achieved solely by the reconciling act of Christ at Calvary.[90]

Our author affirms that *all*, that is, the totality comprising the incarnate Son who sanctifies and those whom he sanctifies, *have one origin*, or literally, as in the KJV, "are . . . of one." In the Greek, the pronoun *one*[91] may be either masculine or neuter in gender, and so the question arises as to how it is to be interpreted. If masculine, it must be a person who is intended, and those who take it in this way have variously identified the pronoun with God, Abraham, or Adam. To understand it of God is to place the emphasis on a common *spiritual* origin shared by both sanctifier and sanctified (all are of or from God), and this is how many commentators interpret it, including Chrysostom, Peter Lombard,[92] Aquinas, Delitzsch,[93] Westcott, Moffatt,[94] Windisch, Spicq,[95] F. F. Bruce, and Montefiore. This interpretation is open to objection, however, because it tends to confuse what are really two different categories. God is of course the originator of the whole redemptive work of consecration; but the sanctification (= making perfect, v. 10) of Christ through suffering involved his own suffering on our behalf, whereas the suffering by which we are "sanctified" is not our own, but Christ's; and the Sonship of Christ is his by right of eternal generation, as the Son of God, and of glorification, as the Son of man, whereas our sonship is not by right but by creation in the first place and in particular now by grace, through adoption and incorporation into him who is the eternal Son. The difference between Creator and creature is essential and absolute. Bengel's further objection that if the meaning is "all are of God" this would include the angels, which would be in conflict with what is said in verse 16 below, is not strictly to the point, since in our epistle angels are never associated with the number of "those who are sanctified."

---

90. "The full meaning of ἁγιάζειν," writes Moffatt, "is not developed till 9[13f], where we see that to be 'sanctified' is to be brought into the presence of God through the self-sacrifice of Christ."
91. The phrase is ἐξ ἑνός.
92. Peter Lombard: "We are from one (*ex uno*) . . . for he is from the Father according to deity as his own Son, that is, begotten of his essence, but we are adopted sons."
93. Delitzsch: "The 'one' (of ver. 11) from whom all are derived is God, not as the God of creation (1 Cor. viii.6), but as the God of redemption. . . . God is the One who originally ordained the saving work of sanctification. The Sanctifier, who is Himself first sanctified, and those who are sanctified through Him, are all in this sense FROM God." Chrysostom, however, invokes the support of 1 Corinthians 8:6 for this position.
94. Moffatt: "Jesus and Christians have the same spiritual origin"; Christians "too in their own way are 'sons' of God."
95. Spicq sees a correspondence between ἐξ ἑνός here and χάριτι θεοῦ in verse 9.

The purpose of our author in insisting on the genuineness of the incarnate Son's humanity is better served by those who wish to identify the pronoun *one* with either Abraham or Adam. Bengel, indeed, rightly perceiving that the community of origin of which this verse speaks is that of "the brotherhood and common participation in flesh and blood," approves a twofold reference here: to Adam, in the more general sense that the humanity of Christ is that humanity which is common to all men;[96] and to Abraham, in the more particular sense that the human brotherhood of Christ is shared specifically by those who belong to the Abrahamic line of faith. As, however, Adam is nowhere mentioned throughout the epistle, it is improbable that he is intended here. Abraham, on the other hand, though he is not a figure of central significance, does come into the picture on a number of occasions (6:13; 7:1–9; 11:8–19), and the reference to him in verse 16 below, which is part of the immediate context, might seem to be specially relevant, since there it is said that Christ assumed the nature, not of angels, but of the descendants of Abraham.[97] But if Abraham had been in mind in the present verse it would have been expected that he should be mentioned by name here instead of at a later point in the argument. Nevertheless, to interpret our author to mean here that Christ and his "brethren" have a common descent from Adam or Abraham (cf. Lk. 3:23ff. where the human lineage of Jesus is traced back to Adam, and Mt. 1:1ff. where it is traced back to Abraham) shows a proper appreciation of the thrust of his argument, which is well conveyed by Phillips' rendering to the effect that both sanctifier and sanctified "share a common humanity." Well does Héring remark that "it would be impossible to bar the road to all docetism more forcibly."

It seems preferable, however, to treat the pronoun *one* as neuter and to interpret it as relating primarily to the community of human nature which binds the incarnate Son to us. The context, as we have said, is essentially one of the theology of incarnation. Thus the quotation from

---

96. "If he for whom are all things and through whom are all things had not been man," says Lefèvre d'Etaples, "he would not have been able to suffer. But it is certain that those who are sanctified, that is, who obtain salvation and cleansing from sins through the suffering of Christ, are men from the one man Adam, and, on the authority of Scripture, that Christ who sanctifies and cleanses is a man from the same man." Thus "in the gospel he fears, is weary, and his soul is sad unto death, because he is true man, partaking of flesh and blood as do other men." The identification of the "one" with Adam is favored also by Héring ("The Son, in fact, by his incarnation, has become a descendant of Adam like all men") and Teodorico.
97. This interpretation, which we believe to be correct, is subject to dispute, as the commentary on verse 16 explains below.

Psalm 8 (vv. 6ff.) is specifically applied to the incarnate Savior in his experience of humiliation and exaltation; his incarnation was a necessary prerequisite for his endurance of suffering, as Man for men (vv. 9f.); and in verse 14 it is declared that he partook of our nature of flesh and blood for the express purpose of undergoing death. As Calvin observes, "if we are sinful and unclean, the remedy is not far to seek, because it is offered to us in our flesh." Owen proposes an analogy from the sacrificial logic of the old covenant: "For as in an offering made unto the Lord of the first-fruits, of meat or of meal, a parcel of the same nature with the whole was taken and offered, whereby the whole was sanctified, Lev. ii; so the Lord Jesus Christ being taken as the first-fruits of the nature of the children, and offered unto God, the whole lump, or the whole nature of man in the children—that is, all the elect—is separated unto God, and effectually sanctified in their season." This neuter sense is implicit in the rendering of the NEB, "are all of one stock" (and similarly the JB, "are of the same stock"). Of course, even those who advocate a "spiritual" interpretation have no wish to deny that the incarnation is integral to the writer's argument here. Spicq, for example, remarks that "verse 10 declares that the Saviour could not be perfect apart from sufferings, while verse 11 adds that it is impossible for him to be Saviour apart from incarnation."

From what has been said it follows (*that is why*) that *he is not ashamed to call them*, that is, those with whom and for whom he has become a fellow man, *brethren*. Those whom Christ has redeemed are brothers not merely among themselves but also and particularly of Christ—and this is true in more than a mystical sense, for the historic event of the incarnation has shown that the Son, by becoming man, "is not ashamed" to place himself on the level of their humanity. His taking of flesh and blood is an act of total identification for the purpose of our everlasting redemption. Though he had every cause to be ashamed of us and to abandon us to the judgment we justly deserve, he compassionately abased himself in order that we with him might be raised to glory (Phil. 2:5ff.; 2 Cor. 8:9). It should be emphasized that, as the New Testament consistently shows, and not least this epistle, our brotherhood with Christ rests not solely on the fact of his incarnation, but much more precisely on the redemption which that incarnation enabled him to accomplish at the cross. Our brotherhood is first with him and then and therefore with each other, for it is the brotherhood of the redeemed. Hence the risen Lord refers to his disciples as "my brethren" (Mt. 28:10; Jn. 20:17). With him, and through him, who is "the first-born among many brethren" (Rom. 8:29), we are now able to address God as "our Father." It is indeed a matter for amazement and rejoicing that the beloved and only Son should not have been ashamed to call us brethren!

2:12, 13. *Saying, "I will proclaim thy name to my brethren, in the midst of the congregation I will praise thee." And again, "I will put my trust in him." And again, "Here am I, and the children God has given me."*

At first sight these three quotations from the Old Testament may appear to afford tenuous and scarcely adequate support for the argument our author is intent on sustaining. Such a conclusion, however, reflects rather the widespread unfamiliarity with the Scriptures which prevails in our day and the inadequacy of the contemporary Christian's equipment in the use and application of the sacred text. A noteworthy aspect of the New Testament is the manner in which it shows that Christ and his apostles, when they cited passages from the Old Testament, did not flourish them in isolation as proof-texts uprooted from their environment (something Satan is adept at doing—cf. Mt. 4:6!) but had careful regard to the context from which they were taken. The full significance of a statement can be appreciated only against the background of its total context. Familiarity not only with the particular texts but also with their setting is requisite. Knowledge of this kind could reasonably be assumed on the part of those to whom this epistle was addressed— Hebrew Christians who, as reverent and assiduous students of the Old Testament scriptures, would readily recognize the appropriateness of the context from which these quotations are derived. We have here, as F. F. Bruce points out with reference to the first of these quotations, "a good example of C. H. Dodd's thesis that the principal Old Testament quotations are not isolated proof-texts, but carry their contexts with them by implication" (though Dodd was, of course, far from being the originator of this thesis).

The first of the three quotations comes from a psalm which was of special messianic significance in the apostolic church, namely, Psalm 22. The prophetic relevance of this psalm to the sufferings and death of Christ was clearly perceived by the writers of the Gospels. Indeed, its opening words, "My God, my God, why hast thou forsaken me?", were uttered as Christ's cry of dereliction from the cross (Mk. 15:34; Mt. 27:46). Its seventh and eighth verses apply closely to the mockery hurled at the Savior by his tormentors (Mt. 27:39–43). The fourteenth and fifteenth verses graphically describe the anguish of crucifixion. The sixteenth and seventeenth verses ("a company of evildoers encircle me; they have pierced my hands and feet—I can count all my bones") were also seen as fulfilled in the events of the crucifixion and in the fact that, contrary to custom, Christ's legs were not broken by the soldiers (Jn. 19:31–36). And verse 18, which speaks of the distribution of the victim's garments by the casting of lots, likewise answers precisely to what happened at Calvary (Jn. 19:23f.; Mt. 27:35).

Psalm 22, therefore, was applied with particular appropriateness to the incarnate Son and the afflictions he endured; and verse 22, quoted by our author here, begins the final section of the psalm which is marked by a spirit of joy and victory and is fittingly related to the rejoicing of the exalted Redeemer. The context of the quotation accordingly harmonizes admirably with the theme of the passage before us. The words of the Psalmist now become the words of him who, as the pioneer of our salvation, has passed through suffering to glory: "*I will proclaim thy name to my brethren, in the midst of the congregation I will praise thee.*" The Messiah's *brethren*, as we have previously explained, are those, his fellow men by incarnation and his fellow heirs by reconciliation and adoption, whom he has redeemed by his sacrifice of himself on the cross. The proclamation of God's name is the proclamation of the divine grace and mercy which is the message of the gospel with its promise of a glorious destiny for those who respond to the heavenly call, and its assurance that, as Athanasius says with reference to this passage, the Lord's body is "the root for our resurrection and our salvation."[98] The proclamation of the Good News and the praise of God which accompanies it take place, moreover, *in the midst of the congregation,* or more literally (as in the KJV) "in the midst of the church,"[99] which in the perspective of the New Testament is God's new temple being built up of those "living stones" who are brethren with and in Christ (1 Pet. 2:5; Eph. 2:19–22).

The second and third quotations are from Isaiah 8:13ff., which is another messianic passage. The declaration of verse 14 that the Lord of hosts would become "a sanctuary, and a stone of offence, and a rock of stumbling," was applied directly to Christ by the apostles (see Rom. 9:33; 1 Pet. 2:8; and cf. Lk. 2:34). The cross of Christ is, for every man, either the place of grace or the place of judgment; as Paul says: "we preach Christ crucified, a stumbling block to Jews and folly to Gentiles, but to those who are called, both Jews and Greeks, Christ the power of God and the wisdom of God" (1 Cor. 1:23f.). Thus, once again, the context befits our author's present theme of incarnation and redemption, and the second of the three quotations, "*I will put my trust in him*" (Isa. 8:17), describes the attitude of confidence in God which was characteristic of the incarnate Son. "Trust," comments Aquinas, "is the expectation of help; and trust was found in Christ in that in accordance with human nature he looked for help from the Father in his suffering." This text, then, serves to emphasize effectively that the humanity assumed by the Son made him truly one with us in weakness and temptation (see vv. 17f. below and 4:15), and that in the experience of human weakness

---

98. Athanasius, *De Sententia Dionysii* 10.
99. 'Εκκλησία here is the LXX rendering of the Hebrew קָהָל.

and temptation he displayed that perfect dependence on God which is essential to the realization of the full potential of manhood. In this we see the genuineness of his brotherhood with us.

In the book of Isaiah the third quotation, *"Here am I, and the children God has given me"* (from Isa. 8:18), follows the preceding one without a break. No doubt our author separates it from the second by the formula *and again* because he regards it as pressing home a separate point. The background in Isaiah (in addition to what we have already said) was one of national apostasy. Hence the prophet's stern denunciations to the people of impending judgment, and yet, as the preceding quotation indicated, his confidence in God's sovereign goodness and mercy. This double attitude was symbolized in the names he had given to his two sons: Mahershalalhashbaz, which has the ominous meaning, "the spoil speeds, the prey hastes" (Isa. 8:1ff.), and Shearjashub, meaning, and at the same time expressing his confidence that, "a remnant shall return" (Isa. 7:3). To these prophetic names may be added the significance of Isaiah's own name: "Yahweh is salvation." Our quotation is shortly after followed, moreover (in Isa. 9:6f.), by the famous messianic prophecy of the birth of a Son who was to be the everlasting Prince of Peace and King of Righteousness. Within this setting, then, Isaiah declares: "Behold, I and the children whom the Lord has given me are signs and portents in Israel from the Lord of hosts." Applied to the Christian situation, these words speak of a world under the cloud of God's judgment, but of a world also for whom God has provided a Redeemer; and of a Redeemer to whom God has given *children*, the children, that is, of God,[100] who as Christ's brethren constitute the elect people of God. These are *given* to the Son by the Father; hence the certainty with which Christ affirmed: "All that the Father gives to me will come to me" (Jn. 6:37; cf. Jn. 6:39; 10:29; 17:2, 6, 9, 24; 18:9).

The messianic application of these three texts, then, lends support to our author's doctrine that the incarnate Son is one in humanity with those whom he redeems and whom he calls brothers, the first describing

---

100. Moffatt is surely right when he explains that "the παιδία are God's children, the fellow υἱοί of Christ." F. F. Bruce seems to press the analogy with Isaiah too far when he speaks of Christians as the "children" or "sons" *of Christ*, an idea without parallel elsewhere in the New Testament. Many commentators (for example, Aquinas, Calvin, Spicq) interpret the term *children* here to mean simply "disciples," but this weakens the point of the quotations which is to the effect that the children (begotten by God) given to the Son are his brethren by virtue of incarnation (common humanity) and redemption (restored humanity). It is true that we find Christ as the Master affectionately addressing his followers as "children" or "little children" (Jn. 13:33; 21:5), but this is not a parallel usage of the term; the apostle John uses the same form of address when writing to fellow Christians (1 Jn. 2:1, 12, 28; 3:7, 18; 4:4; 5:21). In any case, the purpose of these quotations is to confirm the truth that those whom Christ redeems are rightly called his *brethren*.

the effectual communication by the triumphant Savior of the redemption he has achieved to his brethren, the second emphasizing the fellow-dependence on God of him who is the sharer of our humanity, and the third declaring the sovereignty of God who by his act of grace in Christ makes us his children (cf. Jn. 1:12) and gives us as brethren to his Son.

2:14. *Since therefore the children share in flesh and blood, he himself likewise partook of the same nature, that through death he might destroy him who has the power of death, that is, the devil.*

This verse is both a recapitulation and a development of what has gone before. The conjunction *therefore* makes it clear that there is a logical link with the preceding argument. The noun *children* is resumed from the text just quoted from Isaiah. The necessity and purpose of the incarnation are now defined with more preciseness than hitherto. Its intention has already been declared: "so that by the grace of God Christ might taste death for every one" (v. 9); and its effect: "bringing many sons to glory" (v. 10), those "sons" being the brethren whom he has sanctified (v. 11). Verses 12 and 13 adduce scriptural support for the reality of the human brotherhood which unites Redeemer and redeemed. The genuineness of Christ's humanity is now affirmed in the most unequivocal terms: *flesh and blood,* [101] a common synonym for human nature, in which *the children share,* in that they are all human beings, is *the same nature* of which *he himself likewise partook.* The doctrine of the incarnation is here so explicitly stated (indeed, purposely overstated, so to speak, since *likewise,* which means in identical fashion, [102] and *the same,* which repeats the emphasis, together give a forceful double insistence) that no possible place is left for the unreal phantom Christ of the docetic heresy by which the church of the first century was threatened. More-

101. The order in the Greek is actually "blood and flesh" (αἷμα καὶ σάρξ), as it is also in Ephesians 6:12. Elsewhere the New Testament has "flesh and blood," reflecting the Hebrew בָּשָׂר וָדָם, which has become an idiomatic expression in English—hence the order in most versions, though the JB retains the Greek order. Some commentators have looked for exegetical significance in the less familiar order used by our author here; Spicq, for example, suggests that the intention behind it was "perhaps to give prominence to the blood which Christ must shed as sanctifier," and Delitzsch similarly and much more positively. It is most unlikely, however, that such a refinement was intended. In view of the occurrence of "blood and flesh" in Ephesians 6:12, where it would be difficult to attach any special meaning to the sequence, it is wiser to conclude that for the Greek ear the order of the words was interchangeable.
102. The adverb παραπλησίως, translated "likewise" in our version, implies, as Spicq says, "a total similarity... it could be translated 'without any difference': Christ was integrally man." Cf. the JB, "equally."

over, that the incarnation was the divine Son's free act on our behalf is indicated by the tenses of the two verbs "share" and "partook." The first, a perfect in the Greek,[103] describes the constant human situation: all men and women, of every generation, have this in common that their nature is "flesh and blood"; whereas the second, an aorist in the Greek,[104] points to the historical event, unique in itself, of the incarnation when the Son of God assumed this same human nature and thus himself became truly man and accordingly truly one with mankind.

This assertion of the common humanity by which Christ is linked to us and we to him is followed by a statement of the primary purpose of the incarnation, namely, *that through death he might destroy him who has the power of death, that is, the devil.* Nowhere does Scripture view the incarnation as a means to some kind of sentimental identification or association of God with men, as though it were a divine tribute to the surpassing dignity of man (a conceit entertained by the mind of Renaissance man), or as though it were by itself a mystical means of raising human nature to a higher, or the highest, level of evolutionary existence (as some more recent "catholic" theologians have supposed). The purpose of the incarnation was specifically that the Messiah might die. Not, of course, that it would have sufficed for him to have assumed any kind of creaturely nature in which he could experience death. Only the assumption of *human* nature could qualify him to fulfil his function of Redeemer, for his human nature fitted him to suffer and die as Man for men, that is, vicariously to bear man's punishment and die man's death on the cross. "He partook of flesh and blood," says Alcuin, "so that he might be enabled to taste death for the children's salvation."

As incarnate, then, Christ was able to die; and it was his incarnation that set the stage for the performance of that great cosmic drama which is at the center of human history and the means of man's deliverance from his fearsome enemy. At the cross, the place of death, the decisive encounter between God and Satan occurred. The Son came into the world precisely for this purpose, that *through death,* his death, he might render ineffective[105] our enemy *the devil* who wields *the power of death.* This has the appearance of a strange and paradoxical statement;[106] for death is the great and inexorable destroyer, and he who has death in his control holds the power of destruction. How can the suffering of death

---

103. Κεκοινώνηκεν.
104. Μετέσχεν.
105. The verb used here, καταργεῖν, which is translated "destroy" in our version, means properly to render inoperative, to nullify. The sense is that the work of Christ undoes the work of Satan, with the implication, certainly, that the devil's defeat will end in his destruction. Cf. the NEB, "break the power," the JB, "take away all the power," Héring, "réduire à l'impuissance," Teodorico, "ridurre all'impotenza."
106. Cf. Bengel: "Paradoxon. Jesus mortem passus, vicit: diabolus mortem vibrans, succubuit."

result in the overthrow of that tyrant who is the prince of death? How can the death of the incarnate Son be anything other than his destruction and the devil's victory?

In considering these questions it should be recognized that the power of death is held by the devil only in a secondary and not in an ultimate sense. Death is indeed the dark reality of his tyranny. But God is still supreme in his sovereignty: unfailingly, it is for him and by him that all things exist, as we have already been reminded (v. 10). Death is not a sphere that has broken loose from God's command. On the contrary, Scripture, as Aquinas observes, clearly teaches that death, like all else, is under God's control (cf. Gen. 2:17; Dt. 32:39; 1 Ki. 2:6; Mt. 10:28; Lk. 12:5; 1 Cor. 15:25f.; Rev. 1:18); and the clinching proof of this is the conquest of death and Satan by the incarnate Son. Besides, the devil is a creature—and, significantly within the present context, an angelic creature—finite and futile in his rebellion, and subject to judgment and destruction. There is no question or possibility of an insoluble dilemma involving a cosmic dualism of God and Satan, as though they were eternally opposed to each other as two equal and ultimate realities. The power of death wielded by the devil is not an absolute power; indeed, death is the sentence of God pronounced against man who sinfully has transferred his allegiance from his Creator to the creature (Gen. 3:1ff.; Ezek. 18:4; Rom. 3:23) and who in doing so has turned his back on God's realm of life in favor of Satan's realm of death. It is in this sense that the devil is said to hold the power of death. But the power which he presently wields is also the power by which he is destroyed (1 Jn. 3:8; Rev. 20:10). Death is the awful reality of divine judgment, not satanic victory. Creation and destruction—and salvation from destruction—belong properly and absolutely to God alone.

When we read that it was *through death* that the devil was overcome, we should carefully consider *whose* death it was that achieved this triumph and *what kind of* death it was that he died; otherwise we shall never have a due appreciation of the logic and the necessity of that death by which we were redeemed. The spectacle of the cross is not that of any man enduring the pains of death, but of the incarnate Son of God in his pure innocence suffering a death which is not his due. It is the death, moreover, of one who, though guiltless, has been tried by legal process and condemned to die the death of a common criminal and in the place of the common criminal (Barabbas), so that it is plain to all that in this death the Innocent One is suffering for the guilty, the Holy One for the unholy. Any other kind of death, peaceful or violent, would have obscured this central truth of the cross. Death, therefore, and more specifically the death of Christ and death of this kind, was necessary for the overthrow of him who had persuaded mankind to abandon life for death. "This of all others seemed the most unlikely way and means," comments Owen, "but indeed was not only the *best*, but the *only way* whereby it might be accomplished." The necessity of Christ's death on the cross is bound up with the demands of the moral structure of God's world. The seriousness of sin and its consequences cannot be ignored. Only by the meeting of its penalties can sin be removed. At the same time, the purposes of God cannot be frustrated, and his love is not contrary to his law. In Christ, the Son of man and only law-keeper, dying in the place of man the guilty law-breaker, the justice and the love of God prevail together; in him God graciously meets the demands of his own moral law which fallen man is totally unable to meet. All, as Paul insists, the whole of our restoration and reconciliation from beginning to end, is of God (2 Cor. 5:18). "Our most merciful God," writes Calvin, "when he willed that we be redeemed, made himself our Redeemer in the person of his only begotten Son." And again: "This is our acquittal: the guilt that held us liable for punishment has been transferred to the head of the Son of God. We must, above all, remember this substitution, lest we tremble and remain anxious throughout life."[107]

Thus the death of Christ for us was the defeat of the devil; but it is not the end of the story, for it was followed by his resurrection, ascension, and crowning with glory and honor (vv. 7–9). This is the great vindication of Christ's saving work, the assurance of its perfection and its acceptance by God, as well as its eternal efficacy for man. It must be plain to all that if Good Friday had not been followed by Easter, that is, if Christ were still dead and buried, then he would be no savior, for Satan, not he, would have been the victor and the power of death would have remained in full force. But the victory is Christ's and, as the next verse declares, he is indeed our all-powerful deliverer. "By the sacrifice of his body he did two things," says Athanasius with reference to this verse: "he put an end to the law of death which barred our way, and he made a new beginning of life for us by giving us the hope of resurrection."[108] And, as he says elsewhere, Christ's victory "vouchsafed a blessing instead of a curse, joy instead of grief, a feast instead of mourning, in this holy joy of Easter."[109]

2:15. *And deliver all those who through fear of death were subject to lifelong bondage.*

The defeat of the tyrant naturally means the setting free of those whom he holds in *bondage*. Rescue is the whole point of the operation.

---

107. Calvin, *Institutes* II.xii.2, II.xvi.5.
108. Athanasius, *De Incarnatione* 10, cf. 20.
109. Athanasius, *Letters* ii.7.

"It is by the bonds of our sins that he held us," comments Peter Lombard; "for they are the chains of his captives. Then Christ came, bound the strong man with the bonds of his passion, entered into his house, that is into the hearts of those where he dwells, and rescued us." The lives enslaved by Satan, instead of being filled with the joy of living, here and hereafter, are dominated and doomed by the *fear of death*. And this enslavement is *lifelong:* it blights the whole of existence.[110] This throws into grim relief the appalling contradiction at the center of the being of unregenerate man, and the futility of his existence—his very living is overcast by the fear of death. The death that man fears, moreover, is not just the physical death that he faces; it is the "second death," the fact that after death there is judgment (Rev. 2:11; 20:6; 21:8; Heb. 9:27). But now, on the cross, Christ has endured that judgment and liberated us from the fear of death and its bondage. By his death he has removed the sting of death, which is sin, and has turned our defeat into victory (1 Cor. 15:56f.). True, the new-man-in-Christ still faces the "first death"; but he does so with the assurance that the resurrection of Jesus, with whom he is one, guarantees his own resurrection to the fulness of eternal life (1 Cor. 6:14; 15:20ff.; 2 Cor. 4:14), that God will indeed bring many sons to glory (v. 10).

Our author is not indulging in theological speculation when he speaks of deliverance from the fear of death. He is expressing the *experience* (which confirms the doctrine) common to all who through faith in Christ have committed themselves to God; for this experience of liberation is not something to be hoped and worked for, but a present reality, won for us by Christ, to be known and to rejoice in here and now. "He who fears death or is not willing to die," says Luther, "is not sufficiently Christian. As yet such people lack faith in the resurrection, and love this life more than the life to come." Calvin writes similarly: "Although we must still meet death, let us nevertheless be calm and serene in living and dying, when we have Christ going before us. If anyone cannot set his mind at rest by disregarding death, that man should know that he has not yet gone far enough in the faith of Christ." Nothing in this whole universe, not even death, has the power to separate the Christian believer from the love of God, the living God, which is in Christ Jesus (Rom. 8:38f.). Truly, for the man of faith death has been swallowed up in victory (1 Cor. 15:54)! This truth should have a profound effect on the Christian's attitude not only to his own death but also to the death of friends and loved ones who "fall asleep in the Lord" (see 1 Thess. 4:13ff.). In this connection Chrysostom deplored, in a memorable homily on this passage, the ostentatious public lamentations that were made

110. "Διὰ παντὸς τοῦ ζῆν, not simply in old age" (Moffatt).

at Christian funerals in his day. "When I behold the wailings in public places," he says, "the groanings over those who have departed this life, the howlings and all the other unseemly behaviour, I am ashamed before the heathen and Jews and heretics who see it, and indeed before all who for this reason laugh us to scorn." He complains that such conduct has the effect of nullifying his teaching on the resurrection and encourages the heathen to continue in unbelief. What can be more unseemly, he asks, than for a person who professes to be crucified to the world to tear his hair and shriek hysterically in the presence of death? "Those who are really worthy of being lamented," he admonishes, "are the ones who are still in fear and trembling at the prospect of death and have no faith at all in the resurrection." And then he drives home his point with these arresting words: "May God grant that you all depart this life unwailed!"

2:16. *For surely it is not with angels that he is concerned but with the descendants of Abraham.*

The Greek verb translated *he is concerned* in our version[111] means literally "to lay firm hold of" or "to appropriate." In the Gospels (Mt. 14:31; Lk. 9:47; 14:4; 23:26) and Acts (9:27; 16:19; 17:19; 18:17; 21:30, 33) it is used in the sense, sometimes friendly, sometimes hostile, of taking hold of a person. Three times (Mk. 8:23; Acts 23:19; 8:9 below, quoting from the Septuagint version of Jer. 31:32) it is used of taking hold of someone's hand, either literally or figuratively. In 1 Timothy 6:12, 19 it is found in the sense of taking hold of eternal life; and in Luke 20:20, 26 of taking hold of Christ's words, that is, seizing on his statements in a hostile manner. It is evident that the meaning of the verb is largely determined by the requirements of the context in which it occurs. How, then, are we to understand the assertion here that Christ "takes hold" not of angels but of the seed of Abraham? The fathers of the early church, both Greek and Latin, interpreted it as descriptive of the Son's assumption (taking to himself) of humanity in the incarnation.[112] Ambrose, for example, says that " 'he took upon him the seed of Abraham' plainly asserts the begetting of a body."[113] This sense was approved also by the scholastic authors. Thus Aquinas comments that "nowhere do we read that he assumed angelic nature, but only 'the seed of Abraham',

---

111. Ἐπιλαμβάνεται.
112. Cf. the Old Latin *adsumpsit* or *suscepit*.
113. Ambrose, *De Fide* iii.11.

that is, human nature." In the sixteenth century we find Erasmus explaining that "Christ did not redeem the fallen angels, nor did he assume their nature."[114] The Reformers were of the same opinion.[115] "This one passage," writes Calvin, "is quite enough to confound Marcion, Manichaeus, and other crazed persons of that sort who deny that Christ was truly man begotten of human seed"; and he adds that "it gives no support to Nestorius, who invented a double Christ as if the Son of God had not been truly man, but had only lived in human flesh."

In the seventeenth century, however, there is evidence of a departure to some degree from the classical interpretation in favor of one which assigns the verb the weaker and more general sense of "to come to the aid of." This is the sense adopted, as was to be expected, by antitrinitarian and Socinian authors;[116] but it is found also in some Roman Catholic commentators, including Cornelius à Lapide and Estius, and, among the Protestant scholars, in Grotius. Owen, who firmly maintains the correctness of the classical interpretation ("the apostle teacheth us . . . that the Lord Christ took unto him, and took on him, our

---

114. Erasmus adds: "*Apprehendit*, . . . id est, *assumit & induit*."
115. Luther, however, follows an interpretation suggested by Chrysostom in accordance with which the verb *apprehendere* depicts the manner in which "Christ pursued after human nature and overtook it when it was fleeing far from him," and cites the parables of the lost sheep and the lost coin which "were sought and found quite obviously not by their own efforts but by the mercy of the seeker." But, though Luther makes no mention of the incarnation here, it is plain that Chrysostom does not exclude it from Christ's action in seeking, finding, and "taking hold" of us. The association of ideas is clearly spelled out in Alcuin, who writes: "Why does he say *apprehendit*? Because, when we were moving away from him and fleeing far from him, he followed and took hold (*apprehendit*) of us, and welded the nature of our frailty into one nature with himself, a wonderful conjunction, since the eternal and immortal was united with the mortal and temporal. . . . He, so great and so wonderful and so glorious, cared so much for our salvation that he became our brother in everything. For this reason he left the angels and the powers of heaven, so that he might take hold of (*apprehenderet*) the lost sheep and, placing it on his shoulder, bring it back to the heavenly kingdom." This interpretation recurs in much the same form in the medieval commentators Herveus and Peter Lombard.
116. The interpretation was not an invention of the seventeenth century. In the previous century, for example, Beza denounces "the cursed impudence of Castellio who twists ἐπιλαμβάνεται to mean 'he assists' (*opitulatur*) by an interpretation that is not only false but also inept." Doubtless antitrinitarians were swayed by culpable prejudice in their approach to this verse, but, leaving out of account their particular presuppositions, the semantic flexibility of the verb ἐπιλαμβάνεσθαι means that the sense "to assist" is both tenable and defensible, and is in fact favored by many modern scholars. The suggestion that σπέρματος Ἀβραάμ ἐπιλαμβάνεται here echoes or is virtually a quotation of σπέρμα Ἀβραάμ . . . οὗ ἀντελαβόμην in the LXX of Isaiah 41:8f. may have some substance so far as vocabulary or phraseology is concerned (though the difference in the verb's prefix should be noticed), but an analogy of sense can hardly be postulated, since in the Isaiah passage the verb is more literal than figurative and does not bear the connotation "to help" or "assist": God, through the prophet, is addressing Israel, "the seed of Abraham, . . . whom I took from the ends of the earth." The reference is to God's taking or ingathering of his people who have been scattered throughout the world as exiles.

human nature, of the seed of Abraham"), points out with reference to the presuppositions of the Socinians that "if the words express that the Lord Christ assumed human nature, which necessarily infers his pre-existence in another nature, their persuasion about the person of Christ is utterly overthrown"—though it would be a mistake to conclude that this explains the basis of Owen's acceptance of the classical interpretation (for which he adduces arguments of a more solid character) rather than the basis of the Socinian approval of the weaker sense of the verb here. What I have called the classical interpretation continued to enjoy general acceptance until more recent times, when it has been widely discarded. Due weight must be given to the consideration that scholars of the caliber of Alford, Westcott, Moffatt, Windisch, and F. F. Bruce (not to mention others) have given their judgment in favor of interpreting the verb in the sense of "assist" or "come to the aid of." This judgment is reflected in many of the modern English versions, as the following examples indicate:

"For verily not to angels doth he give help" (ASV).

"For assuredly it is not to angels that He reaches a helping hand" (Weymouth).

"For of course it is not angels that he succours" (Moffatt).

"For of course it was not angels . . . that he came to help" (Goodspeed).

"After all, he does not make himself the angels' champion" (Knox).

"For it is clear that it is not the angels that he helps" (NTTE).

On the other hand, the plainly incarnational interpretation of the KJV: "For verily he took not on him the nature of angels," seems to be the sense intended in the NEB: "It is not angels, mark you, that he takes to himself," and in the JB: "For it was not the angels that he took to himself," and is quite explicit in Phillips: "It is plain that for this purpose he did not become an angel."

Moffatt even goes so far as to admonish us that "it is a warning against the habit of taking the Greek fathers as absolute authorities" in interpreting the Greek text, "that they never suspected the real sense" of the verb used here. This, of course, is a tendentious comment which begs the question, for we may be certain that they were thoroughly familiar with the verb's various semantic possibilities and gave them due consideration. Granted that the patristic authors were, like other human beings, fallible interpreters of the text of the New Testament, their agreement in the understanding of the verb in this verse is surely a matter of no little consequence for the modern exegete. In any case, what would be the point of saying, "It is not angels but men whom he helps"? Could anyone ever have imagined that Christ came to earth for the purpose of assisting *angels*? Moreover, our author will shortly come on to speak of Christ as the one who *helps* us in the hour of need (v. 18), using, however, and perhaps significantly, a different verb[117] from the one in the verse we are now considering. The rendering "he helps" introduces a comparatively weak note into what is a strong incarnational context, so that it is not surprising that many who favor this interpretation treat the verse as a somewhat paltry parenthesis. We concur with Spicq, rather, in judging the classical understanding of this passage to be the right one. "Christ," he comments, "lays hold of and appropriates, that is to say, assumes, human nature and makes it his own. The present tense underlines the permanence of this union on earth and in heaven."[118]

But why the mention of angels here? The question is asked on the assumption that the author of an epistle which is outstanding even in the New Testament for the concentration and weight of its teaching had some good reason for introducing angels again at this point. An adequate answer is provided on the basis of the hypothesis that this epistle was written for the purpose of exposing the falsity of certain teachings similar to those which the Qumran sect is known to have held.[119] Among these teachings, as we have seen, was the expectation that an angelic personage would be dominant in the mediation of deliverance and the establishment of the awaited messianic kingdom. Our author has already taken pains to demonstrate to his readers the superiority of Christ to any angel (1:4–2:9). He now says in effect: "It follows from what I have told you [for surely] that the nature assumed by the messianic leader must be that of mankind, not of angels; for, while he is in himself superior to angels, he humbled himself to a position lower than the angels by his act of incarnation which united him to our humanity and made it possible for him by suffering and death to overthrow the devil and to deliver us from bondage, and by his resurrection and exaltation to bring us to glory. You must cease, therefore, to focus your hope in any sense on the appearance of some angelic deliverer."

The humanity which the Son took to himself is described here by the expression *the descendants of Abraham* (literally, the *seed* of Abraham). The physical descent of Jesus from Abraham is traced at the beginning of the First Gospel (Mt. 1:1ff.; also Lk. 3:23ff.), and this itself is a testimony to the genuineness of his humanity. The mention of Abrahamic ancestry here, however, denotes something more than that Christ was a Jew by birth. In "taking to himself" the "seed of Abraham" he shows not only that he belongs to but also that he is the fulfilment of the line of the

---

117. Βοηθεῖν. It is worthy of note, as Spicq points out, that the verb ἐπιλαμβάνεσθαι never has this metaphorical sense in the forty odd places where it occurs in the LXX.

118. Spicq, however, is mistaken when he cites Delling as a supporter of the classical interpretation, for Delling explains ἐπιλαμβάνεσθαι in Hebrews 2:16 as meaning "to draw someone to oneself to help" (Kittel, TDNT, IV, p. 9).

119. See Introduction, pp. 13ff.

covenant. The covenant established by God with Abraham is brought to a head and finds its consummation in Christ. This truth is stressed by the Apostle Paul in his letter to the Galatian Christians, with particular reference to the use of the noun "seed" in the singular "Now the promises were made to Abraham and to his seed. It does not say, 'And to seeds', referring to many; but, referring to one, 'And to your seed', which is Christ" (Gal. 3:16). Of course, the "seed" of Abraham, in its covenantal significance, includes others as well as Christ, but only in the sense that they through faith are united to him who is the one "seed." This important doctrine is expounded by Paul in the same passage, where his argument concludes with the following assurance: "In Christ Jesus you are all sons of God, through faith. . . . for you are all one in Christ Jesus. And if you are Christ's, then you are Abraham's seed, heirs according to promise" (Gal. 3:26–29).

Thus in saying that Christ took to himself the seed of Abraham our author places the incarnation within the perspective of the covenant, of which the incarnate Son is the focal point. He is the covenantal seed of Abraham, and his people are one with him by spiritual incorporation into that same seed, without respect to race or culture. In him, they are the "many sons" who are being brought to glory (v. 10), whom he is not ashamed to call "brethren" (v. 11), "the children" God has given him (v. 13), delivered by him from bondage and death (v. 15)—those, namely, who, having received him and believed in his name, he has given the power to become children of God (Jn. 1:12).

2:17. *Therefore he had to be made like his brethren in every respect, so that he might become a merciful and faithful high priest in the service of God, to make expiation for the sins of the people.*

It follows (*Therefore*) that *he had,* of necessity, *to be made like his brethren,* that is, to identify himself completely with mankind, whom he came to rescue, by a true incarnation, involving the assumption not only of flesh and blood but also of all human feelings and sensibilities (*in every respect*).[120] The designation "his brethren" is resumed from verse 11 above, where, as we saw, it signified Christ's fellow humanity with us

120. Κατὰ πάντα, "in every respect," "emphasizes," as Teodorico says, "the completeness of this *assimilation,* removing all doubt regarding the sense of ὁμοιωθῆναι, which might otherwise suggest a likeness that is only external or apparent. The Son became like his brethren not only by community of nature, as has already been stated in verse 10, but also by all the consequences which flow from the nature he assumed and by all the manifestations of human life." What our author says here serves as a comment on Paul's assertion in Philippians 2:7 that Christ was born (literally "became") "in the likeness of men" (ἐν ὁμοιώματι ἀνθρώπων γενόμενος). This likeness is nothing less than complete identification: assimilation, not simulation.

by reason of the authenticity of his incarnation, and also our fellow sonship with him by reason of the redemption he came to achieve. It was precisely this *likeness* to his brethren that qualified him (hence our author's insistence on its necessity) to act as their *high priest*—a title and function, now mentioned for the first time, central to the Christology of this epistle, and, though not applied to Christ elsewhere in the New Testament, thoroughly consonant with the apostolic doctrine of the atoning sacrifice he offered at Calvary. The Son could not have represented men before God, offering, as their high priest, the sacrifice of himself on their behalf and in their place, had he not first become their fellow man. Representation requires identification. Accordingly, our author adds this further explanation, that the Son assumed human nature *so that he might become* what otherwise he could not be, *a high priest*. By the incarnation he becomes man, but his becoming man is also the prerequisite for his becoming a high priest.

His high priesthood, however, is not simply achieved, as it were *ex opere operato*, by his act of incarnation. To achieve the predetermined purpose of his high priesthood, namely, *to make expiation for the sins of the people*, it is essential that he should also *become merciful and faithful*, that is to say, that as the incarnate Son, our fellow man, he should, by his voluntary and victorious endurance of testing and suffering, give proof of his mercy and faithfulness. This is but another way of expressing what has been said in verse 10 about the pioneer of our salvation being made perfect through suffering. While it has frequently and rightly been pointed out that he was merciful with reference to human need and faithful with reference to divine requirement, it may also be said that mercy defines the motivation of his high-priestly office and faithfulness its execution. It was sheer grace that brought him to this world. His pity and compassion for us were not remote sentiments; they were expressed in action, and in our humanity. And the mercy he has for us was dispensed in particular on the cross, where his supreme high-priestly sacrifice was offered for our sakes. Moreover, this mercy of his was made effective by his faithfulness. Having put his hand to the plow, he did not turn back (Lk. 9:62). He fulfilled all that he had promised. Temptation and torment did not turn him aside from his gracious purpose (Mt. 4:1ff.; 16:21ff.). Faithful to the very end, he drained the bitter cup of suffering to its last dregs for our redemption (Mk. 14:36). In bearing our sins, he even bore our forsakenness and our alienation (Mk. 15:34). Our hell he made his, that his heaven might be ours. Never was there such mercy, never such faithfulness, as this!

Christ's faithfulness *in the service of God*, or, more literally, "in the things that pertain to God"[121] (cf. RV), that is to say, in his mediating

---

121. Τὰ πρὸς τὸν θεόν, "with reference to (an accusative of respect) the things that pertain to God."

capacity as the people's high-priestly representative before God, coupled with his mercy displayed in total and compassionate identification, was (as Spicq, following Farrar, remarks) in striking contrast to the remoteness, arrogance, and formalism of the sacerdotal officialdom of his day; and he continues unfailingly to be a high priest who receives even the least and weakest of mankind with gentleness and understanding. How could it be otherwise when the object of his coming was "to make propitiation for the sins of the people." The Greek verb used here[122] means to render propitious or well disposed, to conciliate, and when used intransitively, as in this verse, to make propitiation for (RV, ASV). Misconceptions of the doctrine of propitiation have been chiefly responsible for the modern and mistaken attempt to give the verb the sense of expiate (NEB) or make expiation for (RSV).[123] Expiation is certainly an important aspect of the work of Christ and its effects, but it is the doctrine of propitiation with which our author confronts us at this point. To present propitiation as meaning that the suffering of the Son has transformed the Father from a wrathful God into a well-disposed God is a perilous caricature of biblical truth. For one thing, it introduces an intolerable dichotomy between the Father and the Son, as though the Son by acting independently could somehow induce a change in the Father's attitude, whereas his coming and his saving work were, as we will be reminded later on (10:7–10), entirely in harmony with the will of the Father. There is but *one* God, and we cannot divide him into two "parts," one for us and the other against us. For another thing, the wrath of God, which is the expression of his absolute holiness and righteousness, is his *constant* attitude to sin. It is still manifested against sin. The ultimate day toward which the world is moving is the day of judgment, which is such because it is the day of God's wrath (Ps. 110:5; Prov. 11:4; Zeph. 1:15; Rom. 2:5; Rev. 6:17)—indeed, it is strikingly significant that in this connection Revelation 6:16 even speaks of "the wrath of the Lamb"!

Throughout our epistle there are warnings concerning the reality of the righteous judgment of God. He who is unconcerned about the great salvation God has provided cannot expect to escape just retribution (2:3). An evil, unbelieving heart which leads to falling away from the

---

122. Ἱλάσκεσθαι. For a discussion of the meaning of this verb and its cognates see Leon Morris, *The Apostolic Preaching of the Cross* (Grand Rapids, 1955), chs. IV and V, pp. 125–185; and Roger R. Nicole, "C. H. Dodd and the Doctrine of Propitiation," *Westminster Theological Journal*, XVII, 2 (Philadelphia, May 1955), pp. 117–157.

123. Evidently, the temptation to render ἱλάσκεσθαι as "to expiate" is increased because it makes it possible to treat τὰς ἁμαρτίας τοῦ λαοῦ, "the sins of the people," as the direct object. If this is the direct object, then the sense "to propitiate" is inappropriate, since it is persons, not sins, that one propitiates. But the proper sense of ἱλάσκεσθαι is readily preserved by treating it as intransitive and τὰς ἁμαρτίας as an accusative of respect: the purpose of Christ's high priesthood was "to make propitiation with reference to the sins of the people."

living God is something to be dreaded (3:12). To fail through disobedience to enter God's rest is to suffer eternal loss (4:1, 11). Eternal judgment and the curse of God await despisers of the gospel (6:2, 4–8). Deliberate sin against the light leaves only "a fearful prospect of judgment, and a fury of fire which will consume the adversaries"; for "it is a fearful thing to fall into the hands of the living God" (10:26–31). To refuse him who warns from heaven is to have no part in that kingdom which cannot be shaken; "for our God is a consuming fire" (12:25–29).

But God's love is as constant as his wrath, his grace as firm as his righteousness. He does not have to set aside his wrath in order to begin to be merciful. His hatred of sin and his love for his creatures belong together. Accordingly, even while we were sinners and hostile to him, God displayed his love by sending his Son for the precise purpose that he might be the propitiation[124] for our sins (1 Jn. 4:10; Rom. 5:6, 8, 10). It was by propitiation that love acted; and all along it was God who was acting. To procure our restoration, God himself has met the demands of his own holiness. He has, so to speak, propitiated himself in our place, thereby achieving the reconciliation to himself of mankind, who otherwise were hopelessly alienated and under condemnation because of sin. Hence Paul's assurance to the Corinthian Christians that, where our redemption is concerned, all things, from beginning to end, are of God, "who through Christ reconciled us to himself," since he, God, "was in Christ reconciling the world to himself" and for our sake making him who knew no sin to be sin, "so that in him we might become the righteousness of God" (2 Cor. 5:18–21). This is what our author means here when he speaks of the necessity of the incarnation as the means to the propitiation for sins. In the cross, once again, we see that love and justice meet and are satisfied.

It should be noticed that the language and imagery used by our author in this verse are those of the Day of Atonement, that sacred annual occasion on which the high priest of old entered into the holy of holies with the atoning blood and sprinkled it on the mercy seat, viewed as the place of propitiation[125] since there the blood was ceremonially displayed in the presence of Yahweh. Thus atonement was made, first for the high priest's own sins, and then for the sins of the people. Christ is our high priest, merciful and faithful, who by the sacrifice, not of

---

124. The Greek noun ἱλασμός in 1 John 4:10 (and 2:2) means "propitiation," not "expiation" (RSV). Ἱλασμός and ἱλάσκεσθαι used here by our author are of course cognate terms.
125. In Greek, ἱλαστήριον, as in 9:5 below. The only other occurrence of this term, another cognate of ἱλάσκεσθαι, in the New Testament is in Romans 3:25, where it is used of Christ, probably without intending any reference to the mercy seat, but with exactly the same sense, it would seem, as in 1 John 2:2 and 4:10, where Jesus Christ is described as the propitiation (ἱλασμός) for our sins. For a fuller discussion of the term see Leon Morris and Roger R. Nicole, loc. cit. (n. 122 above).

beasts, but of himself has made propitiation for the sins of the people—not for his own sins, for he, the spotless Lamb of God, was without sins (4:15); hence the mention here of the sins only of the people. This great theme returns and is elaborated later in the epistle (see 7:26ff.; 9:7ff.; 10:1ff.).

2:18. *For because he himself has suffered and been tempted, he is able to help those who are tempted.*

A significant proof of the genuineness of the humanity of him who became our merciful and faithful high priest, and of his true likeness to us, is apparent in that *he himself has suffered and been tempted.* [126] To be tempted is to be put to the test. To give in to temptation is to fall into sin and to fail the test. Christ alone has passed the test by overcoming every single temptation through which he went (Heb. 4:15; 5:7ff.). Fellowship in human suffering and testing begets fellow feeling, that true compassion which is the hallmark of his high-priestly identification with our mortal nature. [127] Some have objected that only by the experience of sin could Christ have evinced full fellow feeling with fallen mankind; but for the incarnate Son to have succumbed to temptation, while it would certainly have meant his becoming a fellow sinner, would also have meant his failure and defeat, with the consequence that he would have been disqualified for the fulfilment of his high-priestly office (cf. Heb. 5:8–10) and unable to come to our aid and lead us in the way of victory. It is a fallacy also to imagine that the fact that he did not fall into sin means that he knows less about temptation than those who have given in to it; for his conquest of temptation, while ensuring his sinlessness, in fact

126. The sense of the Greek ἐν ᾧ γὰρ πέπονθεν αὐτὸς πειρασθείς is effectively conveyed by Phillips' rendering: "For by virtue of his own suffering under temptation." The use of the perfect tense πέπονθεν serves to emphasize that, though the temptation Christ suffered in the flesh is a thing of the past, yet its effect is permanent, the effect, namely, of compassion and understanding as he aids us in the hour of our temptation. Some patristic and scholastic commentators take the expression ἐν ᾧ to mean "in which," explaining it with reference to the human nature he assumed. Thus, for example, Alcuin, "in the humanity in which he suffered," and the Vulgate *in eo in quo passus est ipse* lends itself to this interpretation; cf. Peter Lombard: "that is, in the inferior substance, namely, in the flesh in which he suffered under Pilate." But there is no near antecedent with which to link the relative in order to give it this sense (the nearest would be σπέρματος in v. 16). Thus it is undoubtedly preferable to treat the phrase as adverbial, introducing an explanatory clause and corresponding to the English phrase "in that" (KJV), or "inasmuch as" (cf. RSV "because," NEB "since"). 'Εν ᾧ has the same significance in, for example, Romans 8:3.
127. This fellow feeling is true generally of human relationships—cf. Dido's words in Virgil's *Aeneid* I.630: "Non ignara mali miseris succurrere disco"—but preeminently of Christ in relation to his people.

increased rather than diminished his fellow feeling, since he knows the full force of temptation in a manner that we who have not withstood it to the end cannot know it. What good would another who has failed be to us? It is precisely because we have been defeated that we need the assistance of him who is the victor. "Sympathy with the sinner in his trial," writes Westcott, "does not depend on the experience of sin but on the experience of the strength of the temptation to sin which only the sinless can know in its full intensity. He who falls yields before the last strain."

The help, moreover, which Christ offers to him who is struggling in the midst of temptation is offered not merely as man to man, but as Redeemer to sinner. This help is indeed bound up with the fellow feeling for us and with us of him who has himself endured temptation through to victory, but it is also founded on the atonement he procured for us on the cross and the triumphant power of his resurrection (thus the apostle Paul desired to know not only the fellowship of Christ's sufferings but also, and first, the power of his resurrection: Phil. 3:10). The help that he brings is twofold: in the first place, forgiveness of sins, the annulment of past defeats, and, in the second place, the power (*his* power) to fight and overcome temptation. His own conquest of temptation means for the Christian that the dominion of sin over him has been broken (Rom. 6:14). These two realities, forgiveness and power, are present in the passage before us: he who is our merciful and faithful high priest has both made propitiation for our sins and, himself the victor, *is able to help those who are tempted*. The same association of forgiveness and help is found in the Psalmist's cry as he passed through a time of severe testing: "Help us, O God of our salvation, for the glory of thy name; deliver us, and forgive (show thyself propitious to) our sins, for thy name's sake" (Ps. 79:9).[128] "He saw the human race laid low," comments Alcuin, "bound with the chains of sin, subject to the tyranny of death, and he had mercy on us.... Moreover, in that flesh which he took he suffered many cruel things. Therefore he knows the reality of the tribulation which we suffer. He was tempted, but he was not overthrown."

---

128. The parallel is especially plain in the Greek of the LXX: βοήθησον ἡμῖν, ὁ θεὸς ὁ σωτὴρ ἡμῶν... καὶ ἱλάσθητι ταῖς ἁμαρτίαις ἡμῶν, where the presence of the same two verbs ἱλάσκεσθαι and βοηθεῖν suggests that this verse may well have been in the mind of our author as he wrote Hebrews 2:17, 18. Cf. the comparable passive imperative, ἱλάσθητι, in Luke 18:13 which, in the judgment of Blass-Debrunner (§314), is an example of a "permissive" passive with the sense, "let yourself be disposed to grace."

III. CHRIST SUPERIOR TO MOSES (3:1–4:13)

3:1. *Therefore, holy brethren, who share in a heavenly call, consider Jesus, the apostle and high priest of your confession.*

Although we now move on to a new section of the epistle, the primary theme of which is the superiority of the Son to Moses, the transition is not abrupt but logical, as the conjunction *Therefore* by which it is introduced indicates. The term *brethren* which the author uses to address the recipients of his letter shows that, though they are in need of correction and admonition, he has not ceased to regard them as his fellow Christians and companions in the faith. Its basis as a designation for fellow Christians is the brotherhood which is theirs in and with him who is their incarnate Redeemer, as already expounded in 2:10ff. The term, it is true, is a familiar appellation in all kinds of human associations, and it was common in contemporary Jewish circles, including groups such as the Qumran sect; but Christian brotherhood has deep theological roots and is free from the casualness and superficiality which so frequently demean social relationships. To the designation "brethren" the writer joins the adjective *holy*, thus linking it with another frequent synonym for Christians in the New Testament (particularly in the Pauline writings) which, when it stands by itself, means "holy ones" or "saints."[1] The description of the brethren as "holy" does not imply that they are holy in themselves, but rather "sanctified" or "consecrated" as those who have been chosen and set apart by God (cf. "those who are sanctified" in 2:11 and commentary there). They are brothers because they *share* in the heavenly call, holy because they are *called* to separate themselves to the pure service of God.

The *heavenly call* in which as "holy brethren" they share indicates that the vocation of the Christian has reference to the perfection of heaven, not to the imperfection of earth understood as the environment

1. It would of course be possible to punctuate by placing a comma between ἀδελφοί and ἅγιοι, thus giving a triple vocative: "brothers, saints, partakers of a heavenly call, . . ."

of man's fallenness.[2] The origin of the call is God, "our Father in heaven" (Mt. 6:9; 7:11); and the church of God, the *ecclesia*,[3] is precisely the company or brotherhood of those whom God has called out for himself from this fallen world.[4] The call, moreover, is heavenly in the end to which it leads as well as in the origin from which it springs. It is "the upward call" (Phil. 3:14)[5] summoning the Christian to a heavenly homeland (Heb. 11:16)[6] and to the heavenly Jerusalem (Heb. 12:22).[7] Further, as our author solemnly warns in 12:25ff., to turn a deaf ear to him who speaks from heaven can mean only perdition.

Here the readers are admonished to *consider*, to give thoughtful attention to,[8] *the apostle and high priest of our confession*. The high priesthood of the Son is, of course, a theme of central importance in this epistle; but the designation of Christ by the title "apostle" is without parallel in the New Testament.[9] Something has already been said about the function of Christ as *high priest* in the commentary above on 2:17, and the subject will later on be developed in considerable detail, especially in chapters 5 and 7–10. Suffice it to say at this point that as our high priest Christ is, in the words of Herveus, "intercessor and the one who prepares the way for us to the land of the living, because he intervenes for us and enables us to pass over the waves of this world and over every calamity to the heavenly fatherland."

Unique though the designation of Christ as *apostle* is, its appropriateness is apparent throughout the New Testament and particularly

---

2. Cf. the contrast in 2 Corinthians 5:1 between "our house on earth" (ἡ ἐπίγειος ἡμῶν οἰκία) and the house that is eternal in the heavens (οἰκία αἰώνιος ἐν τοῖς οὐρανοῖς), and in John 3:12 between earthly things (τὰ ἐπίγεια) and heavenly things (τὰ ἐπουράνια).
3. Ἡ ἐκκλησία. In the Christian setting the term, which in the pagan world was used of the assembly of the populace and in the LXX of the congregation of Israel (קָהָל), became revitalized as it was used to connote the community of those whom God has called out (ἐκ-καλέω).
4. "Thus," writes K. L. Schmidt, "although ἐκκλησία is from the very first a secular and worldly expression, it expresses the supreme claim of the Christian community in face of the world. . . . The so-called Christ cult neither was nor desired to be one cult among others. It stood out against all cults in the sense that it stood out against the whole world, even the whole of the so-called religious world. This is all guaranteed by the choice of the self-designation ἐκκλησία, which, as we must constantly emphasize, implies the addition τοῦ θεοῦ (ἐν Χριστῷ)" (Kittel, TDNT, III, pp. 515f.).
5. Ἡ ἄνω κλῆσις.
6. Πατρὶς ἐπουράνιος.
7. Ἰερουσαλὴμ ἐπουράνιος. Cf. also 6:4, 8:5, and 9:23 where ἐπουράνιος is used in a comparable manner.
8. Κατανοήσατε, an intensive compound meaning to apply one's mind (νοῦς) diligently to something.
9. It is only in the Epistle to the Hebrews that Christ is called "high priest" (some dozen times compared with "apostle," which is used here alone), but it is a designation which accords perfectly with the whole biblical doctrine of his sacrificial and atoning death.

in the Johannine literature; for the word "apostle" means "one who is sent,"[10] and Jesus repeatedly describes himself as having been sent by the Father into the world (see Jn. 3:17, 34; 5:36ff.; 6:29, 57; 7:29; 8:42; 10:36; 11:42; 17:3; also 1 Jn. 4:10).[11] In the basic sense of the word, he is indeed the first apostle, the great apostle, and the source of all apostleship. This is plain from the terms with which he commissioned those who are familiarly known as the apostles: "As the Father has sent me, even so I send you" (Jn. 20:21; similarly 17:18). His apostleship is prior to and the ground of theirs.

The question has been raised as to whether this assignation of the title "apostle" to Christ does not correspond to and betoken a continuation of the Jewish concept of the *shaliach*, [12] a Hebrew term synonymous with the Greek *apostolos* but with the special connotation of an envoy who wields plenipotentiary authority. As, for example, Rengstorf[13] and Spicq explain, the rabbinical scholars regarded the priest as God's *shaliach* or envoy, and they, and also Philo, assign the office of high priest to Moses, who was undeniably God's envoy. Insofar, then, as Moses was both apostle and priest he might be considered as providing a typology which found its fulfilment in Christ, who (on the assumption that "apostle" here is the equivalent of the *shaliach* of the Mishna and Talmud) in his capacity as apostle represents God as his plenipotentiary among men, and (as Moses was the people's intercessor before God) in his capacity as high priest represents men in the presence of God. The connection of the former here with the rabbinical figure of the *shaliach* is, however, by no means proved; its likelihood is lessened by the consideration that *shaliach/apostolos* is not part of the terminology of the Old Testament;[14] and in any case the same conclusion is readily reached without calling in the support of the rabbinical usage, as, for example, is

10. Ἀπόστολος: the noun is cognate with the verb ἀποστέλλω, "to send forth."
11. In each case the verb is ἀποστέλλω. It should be remarked that in 1 John 4:10, which declares that God "loved us and sent (ἀπέστειλεν) his Son to be the propitiation for our sins (ἱλασμὸν περὶ τῶν ἁμαρτιῶν ἡμῶν)," the language implies both apostleship and priesthood.
12. שָׁלִיחַ.
13. K. H. Rengstorf, Kittel, TDNT, I, pp. 414ff. With reference to Hebrews 3:1, Rengstorf writes: "Omission of an article before ἀρχιερεύς shows that the phrase constitutes a unity. It gathers up what has been said about Jesus from the standpoint of the decision of the readers (ὁμολογία), namely, that He is the Son (υἱός) in whom God has finally spoken (1:1ff.), and that He is the High-priest who has finally expiated the sins of His people (2:5ff.). In this case ἀπόστολος goes far beyond προφήτης, which is not used of Jesus; and in terms of the absolute ὁ υἱός (1:2) it is best explained by the later Jewish שָׁלִיחַ, i.e., that in the Son there speaks and acts God Himself."
14. In the LXX the only occurrence of ἀπόστολος is in 1 Kings 14:6 in a passage of doubtful authenticity, and then as the rendering not of the noun שָׁלִיחַ but of the passive participle שָׁלוּחַ.

shown by the assertion of Jesus in Luke 9:28: "whoever receives me
receives him who sent me."[15]

Moreover, it is improbable that our author had Moses in mind as the
prototype of the Messiah in his dual office of apostle and priest, for it is
only in a very limited sense that the function of Moses could be described as priestly. The point of comparison between Moses and Jesus in
the verses that follow is that of faithfulness: Moses was faithful as a
steward and Christ as a son (in which also resides the point of contrast).
The present section (3:1–4:13), which concerns Moses, relates primarily
to apostleship rather than priesthood; and it is only at 4:14, where Moses
leaves the stage (not to take it again, apart from incidental mention in
9:19 and 10:28, until 11:23), that the discussion of the high-priestly office
of Christ is resumed and expounded as the central theme of the epistle,
now, however, with reference to Aaron and the levitical priesthood.
Taking this into consideration, it is preferable to understand the designation of Christ as *apostle* and *high priest* to indicate, as Westcott says,
that in him the functions of Moses and Aaron are combined, "both in an
infinitely loftier form." Yet, while the typology of the Aaronic system
found its fulfilment in the sacerdotal work of Christ, there were also
crucial dissimilarities which marked him out as belonging to a different
and indeed unique order of priesthood, so that it would be still more
accurate to say that in him the functions of Moses and Melchizedek are
combined (see especially ch. 7 below). In a discussion of this kind it is
important to remember that the apostolic and high-priestly functions are
indeed unified in Christ: he came (as apostle) in order (as high priest) to
give his life a ransom for many (Mk. 10:45).

An unusual interpretation of the Son's apostleship is given by
Lefèvre d'Etaples, who explains it as referring not to his coming into this
world but of his "going from earth to heaven" to "undertake a legation
to the Father on our behalf." He cites Christ's statement in John 14:12f.:
"I am going to the Father, and whatever you ask the Father in my name,
I will do it." "Behold," says Lefèvre, "our legate and high priest to God
the Father!" But the focus of the passage introduced by the present verse
is on Christ's earthly ministry, rather than on the ministry he now exercises in heaven; hence the past tense of the verbs: "he was faithful to
him who appointed him" (v. 2); "Jesus has been counted worthy" (v. 3);
"Christ was faithful" (v. 6), by which his work completed on earth is
designated.

The question as to whether the phrase "the apostle and high priest

---

15. Spicq's assertion that the term "Siloam," from the same root as *shaliach*, which is
interpreted as meaning "sent" in John 9:7 (Σιλωάμ, ὃ ἑρμηνεύεται Ἀπεσταλμένος), is
intended by the evangelist as applying allegorically to Christ, "the 'envoy' *par excellence*,"
is far-fetched and unwarranted by the context where no such application is even hinted at.

of our confession" means the apostle and high priest of the creed or body of faith we hold or the apostle and high priest to whom we bear witness before the world is academic rather than real; for him whom we confess credally we also confess publicly. Thus, though the term "confession" has a certain ambiguity, the two possible interpretations belong together.

3:2. *He was faithful to him who appointed him, just as Moses also was faithful in God's house.*

Christ has already been described as a *faithful* high priest (2:17). Here the adjective is applied to him again, now with reference more particularly to his performance of the duties that had been entrusted to him as the Father's apostle to us. The imagery is that of a steward appointed to a position of responsibility in a household; thus Christ's faithfulness is defined as being *to him who appointed him,* namely, God. His whole concern was to complete the work he had been sent to do. This motive, which was at the heart both of his coming and of his acting on our behalf, is clearly brought out by the application to Christ later in our epistle (10:7, 9) of the words of Psalm 40:8, "Lo, I have come to do thy will, O God." The knowledge that Christ was utterly faithful to God carries with it the assurance that he is entirely worthy of our trust and confidence.

The verb translated "appointed" in our version (RSV, and also in KJV, NEB, JB)[16] commonly means to "make" or "create." It is used, for example, of God's work of creation in Genesis 1:1 (LXX). Not surprisingly, the Arians seized on this verse, translating it "he was faithful to him who *made* him," and interpreted it to mean that Christ was not the eternal Son but one of God's creatures. Many of the patristic and medieval commentators accepted the sense "made," but explained it as applicable only to the humanity of Christ and not as in any degree compromising the truth of his eternal deity.[17] In his controversy with the

---

16. Ποιεῖν.
17. Alcuin, for example, says that our author "is speaking of the humanity of him who was made of the seed of David according to the flesh, not of his divinity which is not made." The rendering of τῷ ποιήσαντι αὐτόν by *Creatori suo* in the Old Latin version would certainly seem to require some such interpretation. The Vulgate *qui fecit illum* is similarly explained, for example, by Peter Lombard ("of the seed of David according to the flesh"), Herveus ("he was faithful to him who made him, that is, to the Father who according to his humanity created him"), and Aquinas ("not according to his divine nature, because in this respect he was not made or created, but begotten, but according to his human nature"). The support of Romans 1:3, *qui factus est ex semine David secundum carnem,* is consistently invoked for this interpretation, though in the Greek of that verse the verb is γίνομαι, not ποιέω.

Arians we find Athanasius pointing out, with reference to Hebrews 3:2, that "when the Son had taken that which he had to offer on our behalf, namely, his body of the virgin Mary, then it is written of him that he had been created, formed, and made."[18] Again, in another of his writings, he asks: "Who can read this whole passage [Heb. 2:14–3:2] without condemning the Arians and admiring the blessed Apostle, who has expressed himself well? for when was Christ 'made'... except when like us he partook of flesh and blood?" And he explains, further, that our author, when he said that "he was faithful to him who made him," was writing "concerning the Word's human stewardship and not concerning the Word's essence."[19] It is simpler, however, and more appropriate, to understand the verb in the sense of to "appoint," a sense which, indeed, it bears in Mark 3:14 of Christ's appointing of the twelve,[20] and in Acts 2:36 of God's appointing Jesus both Lord and Christ.[21] To take "him who 'made' him" as an absolute statement standing by itself does violence to the context, for the predicate, though not mentioned here, is supplied by what has been said in the preceding verse. Chrysostom puts the right question when he asks, "What did he make him?" and gives the right response when he answers from the context, "apostle and high priest"; that is to say, he was "made" in the sense of "appointed."[22] This is a much more effective line of rejoinder to the Arian misinterpretation of this text, and it is surprising that, instead of pressing it, the fathers seem generally to have incommoded themselves by attempting to combat the Arian interpretation while adopting the Arian translation.

Our author propounds an analogy (just as) between Christ and Moses, who also was faithful in God's house. The allusion is to Numbers 12:7, where God says: "My servant Moses... is faithful in all my house." Here God's "house" means the sphere of Moses' stewardship, the household, in this case comprising the whole "family" of Israel. The apostle Paul draws attention to the commonplace that "it is required in stewards that a man be found faithful" (1 Cor. 4:2 KJV). Moses met this requirement and was commended by God for doing so; but in Christ it was fulfilled in a preeminent manner. This is plain throughout the New Testament, but in the words of Christ recorded in the Fourth Gospel it becomes particularly explicit: "My teaching is not mine, but his who sent

---

18. Athanasius, *De Sententia Dionysii* 11.
19. Athanasius, *Orationes contra Arianos* ii.9.
20. Ἐποίησεν δώδεκα.
21. Καὶ κύριον αὐτὸν καὶ Χριστὸν ἐποίησεν ὁ θεός.
22. This, after all, was also a familiar sense of both *facio* and *creo* in Latin and of corresponding terms in other languages; in English, for example, we speak of a man being made an ambassador or created president.

me. . . . I have not spoken on my own authority; the Father who sent me has himself given me commandment what to say and what to speak. . . . The words that I say to you I do not speak on my own authority; but the Father who dwells in me does his works. . . . [addressing his Father] I have glorified thee on earth by completing the work which thou gavest me to do. . . . I have made known to them thy name" (Jn. 7:16; 12:49; 14:10; 17:4 [NEB], 26). This is the voice of the faithful envoy and steward.

It is strange that Westcott (who is followed by Spicq) should associate the main lesson of this verse with what is acknowledged to be a doubtful reading, namely, the adjective "whole" which in some manuscripts is included before the noun "house," thus: "just as Moses also was faithful in God's whole house," or, as in verse 5 below, "in all God's house."[23] "The point of comparison," according to Westcott, "lies in the fact that Moses and Christ were both engaged, not as other divine messengers with a part, but with the whole of the divine economy. The prophets dealt severally with this or that aspect of Truth, the kings with another region of life, the priests with another. But Moses and Christ dealt with 'the whole house of God.'" The doubtfulness of the reading "whole," which, as the textual evidence shows, was omitted in some important early manuscripts (see n. 23), indicates, however, that this could hardly have been regarded as the main point of exegesis in the early centuries; and, in any case, whichever reading is preferred, the emphasis rests naturally on the adjective "faithful," so that the focus of analogy falls on the faithfulness which characterized the stewardship of Moses on the one hand and of Christ on the other.

3:3. Yet Jesus has been counted worthy of as much more glory than Moses as the builder of the house has more honor than the house.

Though Moses and Jesus are similar in that each was faithful in the execution of his stewardship, it should not be concluded that they are

---

23. Our version reflects the reading ἐν τῷ οἴκῳ αὐτοῦ, which is attested by p[46], p[13], B, the Sahidic, Bohairic, and Fayyumic Coptic versions, and by Ambrose and Cyril among the patristic authors. This attestation, though not quantitatively great, is both early and impressive. The variant reading ἐν ὅλῳ τῷ οἴκῳ αὐτοῦ has a more numerous attestation, including ℵ, A, C, D, the Old Latin, Vulgate, Syriac, Armenian, and Ethiopic versions, and Chrysostom and a few other fathers. This external evidence is somewhat evenly balanced, but the probability is that ὅλῳ was added here in verse 2 under the influence of its presence in verse 5, which reflects the LXX reading. Despite the weight he throws on the term in his exegesis, even Westcott places ὅλῳ between square brackets in the Greek text of his commentary (as do Westcott and Hort and Nestle), thus indicating its doubtful character. The adjective is omitted by RSV, Phillips, and NEB among the modern versions.

therefore on an equality with each other. There is contrast as well as similarity, and our author's purpose is to demonstrate that Jesus is in fact infinitely superior to Moses. The contrast is tellingly illustrated by the reminder that *the builder of the house has more honor than the house.* The concept of Christ as the builder of the house is probably based on the messianic prophecy of Zechariah 6:12f., which declares: "Behold, the man whose name is the Branch: for he shall grow up in his place, and he shall build the temple of the Lord. It is he who shall build the temple of the Lord, and shall bear royal honor, and shall sit and rule upon his throne." It also rests on God's promise to David that he would raise up for him a son who would build a house for God and whose throne would be established forever (1 Chr. 17:11f.). As Mediator, Redeemer, and Lord, Jesus Christ is the builder of the house, the *ecclesia,* of God's people, who as "living stones" are "built into a spiritual house" (1 Pet. 2:5) and "a holy temple" (Eph. 2:21). Moses, a truly great figure, was nonetheless a member of the household and indeed a servant in it (v. 5).

Moreover, the house of Israel in which Moses served as a steward was, like the law he mediated, "but a shadow of the good things to come" and not the final reality (10:1). The Israel of old which he led from the bondage of Egypt and through the wilderness to the land of promise was a type of the true Israel of God redeemed and led to eternal rest by Christ (cf. Heb. 4:1, 8, 11, 14; 1 Cor. 10:6 Gk.; Gal. 3:29; 6:16). The latter is the authentic household of God, built up with the living stones of those who by faith are cemented to Christ and to each other; whereas the former was marred by apostasy and unbelief. Yet there is a real and vital continuity between the two, for in Old Testament times there was a true Israel within Israel, a core of the people of faith, among whom, of course, Moses was outstanding. Hence Paul's assertion that "not all who are descended from Israel belong to Israel, and not all are children of Abraham because they are his descendants" (Rom. 9:6f.). The authentic Israel constitutes "a remnant chosen by grace" on God's part and sustained by faith on man's part (Rom. 11:5, 20; 2:28; and ch. 11 below); and its scope from the very beginning was not narrowly national but universal (Gal. 3:8f.). Thus there is a genuine continuity between the Old Israel and the New Israel, or, rather, there is one true Israel of the people of God throughout all the ages of human history, for, as Herveus observes, "the house of God, which is the Church, comprises the saints of both Old and New Testaments."

The glory that belongs to Moses and the law is, as Paul shows in 2 Corinthians 3:7ff., completely surpassed by the transcendental glory of Jesus and the gospel. So, too, here our author insists that *Jesus is worthy,* as the builder of the house, *of much more glory* than Moses who is but a part of that house. Unlike Moses, the incarnate Son is not merely human but also divine; he was both before Moses and after him; he is the pioneer of Moses' salvation (Heb. 2:10) as well as his creator. It is true that the Son became a servant in the house he had built when he assumed our humanity, so that both he and Moses served in the same household; but he did not cease to be the eternal Son. He who was both Moses' God and his Savior transcended him in his person, in his work, and in his glory.

It had evidently become necessary to remind the recipients of this letter of the unique and unrivalled glory of Christ because, perhaps influenced by teaching similar to that of the Dead Sea Sect,[24] they were actually in danger of putting their trust in Moses, whose return as a messianic figure at the end of the age was anticipated, rather than in him who was their true Deliverer (2:15). Lefèvre d'Etaples dramatically describes the situation:

> See how they ought rather to give heed to Christ and to trust in Christ than in Moses, since it is more important to give heed to God and to trust in God than in a creature. O to whatever sect or denomination you who bear the name of Christ belong, fix your attention on Christ and trust in him and in no other, fix your heart on no one else. He is high priest, he is mediator; otherwise you are trusting more in a creature than in God. Besides, if we desire access to the Father, who is king of all, who would rather trust in a servant as mediator than in the king's son? . . . If Moses could have sufficed you for righteousness and salvation, one so great [as Jesus] would never have been sent to you. . . . He surpasses Moses in glory and in merit: for he is the Son, but Moses is a servant; he is the sanctifier, but Moses is one who has been sanctified; he is free from all sin, even as he has been made perfect in all goodness, but Moses was not without sin.

3:4. *(For every house is built by some one, but the builder of all things is God.)*

Our version is probably correct in treating this verse as parenthetical, momentarily interrupting the line of argument which is resumed in the next verse. The first statement is simply explanatory, the declaration of a general truth which is axiomatic and beyond dispute, namely, that *every house*, whether material or spiritual, *is built by some one*; and the second statement, *but the builder of all things is God*, is corrective of any possible conclusion from the first that there are many competitive builders. While there may be many builders, they are such only in a secondary sense, for they build with the substance, material or spiritual, which God, the sole primary builder, has provided. In Calvin's judgment, the "all things" of which God is said to be the builder here have a

24. See Introduction, pp. 13ff.

reference which is limited to the structure of the church; but it is preferable to understand our author to be affirming the universal truth of the
unique supremacy of God as the architect and constructor of the totality
of things, both the whole created order of the physical world and the
world of his new creation, the household of the church. This does not
reflect in any way adversely on the reality of the deity of Christ; rather
the contrary, for the implication is that he who in the preceding verse
was designated the builder of the house is indeed God. [25] He who, as the
Son of God, is the builder both of the old and of the new creation
(between which, again, there is an indissoluble continuity, the latter
being the consummation of the former) identified himself, as the Son of
man, with his building, becoming the headstone of the corner, chosen
and precious (1 Pet. 2:4ff.). Thus God is the sovereign lord over all
things, from creation to glorification.

3:5, 6a. *Now Moses was faithful in all God's house as a servant, to testify to the
things that were to be spoken later, but Christ was faithful over God's house as a
son.*

The contrast between Moses and Christ, both *faithful*, is now resumed and developed. There are two main points of comparison,
namely, that Moses *as a servant* was faithful *in* God's house, whereas
Christ *as a son* was faithful *over* God's house. As in verse 2, the allusion,
on the part of Moses, is to Numbers 12:7. There Moses is described by
God as his *servant*, a term which, though implying an inferior status,
nonetheless indicated an office which was honorable and dignified. [26] To
be designated "the servant of the Lord" was a high tribute accorded not
only to Moses (Ex. 14:31; Num. 11:11; 12:7; Dt. 3:24; Josh. 1:2; Wisd.
10:16) but also to Abraham, Isaac, and Jacob (Dt. 9:27) and to Job (Job
2:3). But the highest point of its dignity is reached in the messianic

25. Interestingly, an "ambivalence" similar to that which we have here—verse 3 speaking
of Jesus as the builder and verse 4 of God as the builder—occurs in 1 Chronicles 17, where
in verse 10 David is given the promise that "the Lord (Yahweh) will build you a house"
and in verse 12 that the son whose kingdom would be established forever "shall build a
house for me." That promise is fulfilled in Jesus Christ who, as the eternal Son, the Second
Person of the Trinity, is Yahweh who builds the "house," and who, as the incarnate Son
belonging to the line of David, effects the building of that "house" by his atoning sacrifice
of himself at Calvary.
26. The LXX, perhaps recognizing this, renders the Hebrew noun עֶבֶד in Numbers 12:7 as
θεράπων (cf. Vg *famulus*), not δοῦλος. This rendering, θεράπων, is retained here (it occurs
nowhere else in the New Testament). The term δοῦλος, however, is a designation of honor
in the New Testament when it is used of or by those who are Christ's bondservants (Rom.
1:1, etc.).

servant-passages of Isaiah (e.g. 42:1ff.; 52:13ff.), which have their fulfilment in the person and work of the incarnate Son (Mt. 12:18–21; Acts
4:27; 8:32ff.; 1 Pet. 3:21ff., etc.).[27] Christ, too, was a servant in the
household of God, and he alone of all God's servants served with a
faithfulness which was without fault or shortcoming.

Christ, however, in whom we see the summation of all servant-
hood, was something more than the Servant of the Lord *par excellence*
who, like Moses, served *in* the household of God; for he was at the same
time *a son*, indeed *the* son and heir (1:2), and as such he was faithful *over*
that same household (cf. 10:21 below where he is described as "a great
priest over the house of God"). His faithfulness is that of a servant, his
authority that of a son. In other words, he displays himself in a double
capacity, as servant and as sovereign: servant in his mediatorial office
which involved him to the full in the service of the household, and
sovereign by reason both of his eternal Sonship and of the enthronement
that followed his humiliation, and as such the ruler over the household.
He is the promised Son on whose shoulders the government rests (Isa.
9:6). Zechariah's prophecy of the Branch (cited above, p. 132) affirms not
only that he will build the temple of the Lord but also that he "shall bear
royal honor and shall sit and rule upon his throne." In the apostolic
proclamation it is he, the risen and glorified Lord, who has been appointed "supreme head to the church" (Eph. 1:22 NEB; cf. Eph. 5:23;
Col. 1:18). His Sonship is the ground of his authority. The distinction,
then, between Moses as servant in God's household and Christ as Son
over it is one of absolute significance.

A further relationship between Moses and Christ is implied in the
description of the function of the former as being *to testify to the things
which were to be spoken later*—that is, to be spoken by God.[28] That is to say,
an important element of Moses' stewardship was that of witness, not to
himself as though he were the end and fulfilment of God's purposes,
but to realities which were still future and would come to expression in
the incomparably greater person of Christ. As Moffatt explains, "the
position of Moses was one which pointed beyond itself to a future and
higher revelation." Moses, indeed, was a prophet, and, in accordance
with the promise of Deuteronomy 18:15ff., as such he was the prototype
of the Prophet like him whom God would raise up. As he had spoken
the words of God to the people of Israel and had led them from the

27. In these servant-passages the Hebrew עֶבֶד is rendered παῖς by the LXX and in the New
Testament.
28. In the phrase εἰς μαρτύριον τῶν λαληθησομένων, which defines the purpose of Moses'
service as being to testify to the things which would be spoken in the future,
λαληθησομένων is undoubtedly a "divine" passive: the one by whom these things would
be spoken is not specified, because it is plainly God who is intended as the speaker.

bondage of Egypt to the land of promise, so the Coming One would proclaim the words given him by the Father (Jn. 12:49f.) and deliver the Israel of God (Gal. 6:16) from a more terrible tyrant than Pharaoh (Heb. 2:14) and bring them to an inheritance better than that of Palestine (Heb. 11:13–16; 13:14).

The opinion of a considerable number of commentators (including Peter Lombard, Bengel, Spicq, and Héring) that by "the things which were to be spoken" our author means not the gospel which was to be declared in Christ but the things which Moses himself would speak to the people of his day[29] has the effect of weakening the thrust of the passage. The reference, as Luther perceives, is not to "a manifestation of things already at hand" but to "a testimony of things not yet seen." Moses, says Owen, gave testimony to the things of the gospel, "and this was the true and proper end of the whole ministry of Moses." The words proclaimed by Moses were words from God; but they were temporary and preliminary words which, as so much of our epistle teaches, portended the advent of a final and more glorious dispensation. The Mosaic system was as a shadow cast by good things which were on their way but not yet realized (10:1). As the shape of a shadow is related to the form of the substance of which it is the shadow, so the structure of the Mosaic system, not merely in its tabernacle, priesthood, and ceremonial (chs. 5 and 7–10), but even in its history (3:7–4:13, 11:23ff., and 12:18ff.), had a typological affinity with the eternal reality of the gospel; though at the same time, like a shadow, it lacked perfection and permanence. Above all, the testimony of Moses "to the things which were to be spoken later" looked ahead from the provisional and fragmentary utterances of those times to the utterance of God's final Word, spoken in the person of the Son, who himself is The Word (Jn. 1:1), the authentic and eternal reality in whom all the utterances of God find their ultimate meaning and fulness (Heb. 1:1f.; 2 Cor. 1:20). Christ is the true focal point of the Mosaic perspective. Hence the admonition of Christ to his interrogators, "If you believed Moses, you would believe me, for he wrote of me" (Jn. 5:46); and the affirmation of Peter that not only Moses

---

29. Bengel, for example, explains "the things which were to be spoken" as the things which Moses would speak (*quae loquuturus esset Moses*), with a reference to 9:19, and adds "especially regarding Christ" (*de Christo maxime*). He does, however, allow for an extension of the sense to the things which Christ would speak. Héring understands τῶν λαληθησομένων as an explanatory genitive: "the words which Moses would himself proclaim constituted his witness or his message"; and maintains that a dative would have been expected (τοῖς λαληθησομένοις) for the interpretation we have favored. But τῶν λαληθησομένων can equally well be accepted as an explanatory genitive in the latter case, thus: "the words which God would proclaim constituted Moses' witness." As mentioned in note 28, in λαληθησομένων we have a clear example of a *passivum divinum*.

but all the prophets bear witness to Christ (Acts 10:43; cf. Lk. 24:27, 44; Jn. 5:39).

It is interesting and perhaps significant that in the Damascus Rule (Zadokite Document) of the Qumran Sect we find the assertion that God built for his people "a sure house in Israel" (iii.19). The concept is obviously akin to that which we have here in Hebrews 3:3–5 and may be traced back likewise to Zechariah 6:12f. and 1 Chronicles 17:10–12, passages to which attention has already been drawn. It has been suggested[30] that also in the background of our author's awareness was the Targum on 1 Chronicles 17:14, which reads: "I will maintain him faithful in my people, in my house of holiness, and in my kingdom for ever"—the reference being of course to the promised son of David's line whose throne would be established forever. This Targum is suggestive of a link with what is said of Moses in Numbers 12:7. For the Qumran Sect the "house" built by God is interpreted as the community of elect and undefiled persons who have withdrawn themselves from the ungodliness by which the nation and its leaders have become corrupted. If those to whom this epistle was addressed were in danger of coming under the influence of doctrines similar to those propounded by the Dead Sea Sect, this gives all the more force to what our author writes here; for he is then saying in effect: "False notions about membership in the 'house' of which God is the builder are placing you in peril of slackening your attachment to Jesus as your Saviour and Lord. God's 'house' is the house Jesus has built and over which he rules as the Son. To deny him or depart from him (N.B. verses 12ff. below, and 4:1ff., 6:4ff., 10:26ff.) is to exclude oneself from the 'house' of God and will be as disastrous for you as it was for those who because of unbelief perished in the wilderness of old." Accordingly, in what immediately follows, they are solemnly admonished that only they who hold fast to the Christian gospel have a place in this house.

3:6b. And we are his house if we hold fast our confidence and pride in our hope.

Now our author provides a terse but enlightening definition of the "house" of which he has been speaking: it is *we*—persons, the twice born (Peter Lombard), believers (Herveus)—who *are his house*. Paul means precisely the same thing when he speaks of "the household of faith" (Gal. 6:10) and assures the Gentile believers of Ephesus that they

30. By Sverre Aalen, " 'Reign' and 'House' in the Kingdom of God in the Gospels," NTS, 8 (1962), pp. 215ff.; see in particular pp. 234–237.

are "no longer strangers and sojourners, but... fellow citizens with the saints and members of the household of God" (Eph. 2:19; cf. 1 Pet. 4:17). In the commentary on the preceding verses there has been some discussion of the Old Testament background of this concept; as for the New Testament, the opinion of Teodorico may well be correct that the basis or seed-thought for what develops into an important doctrine is the statement of Jesus in Matthew 16:18, "On this rock I will build my church."[31] The structure that is being built is defined by Peter, as previously mentioned, as a "spiritual house"[32] whose construction is of "living stones," that is, persons who through faith are joined and aligned with Christ who is the head cornerstone. The imagery, further, is that of a temple, since at the same time Christians are constituted "a holy priesthood, to offer spiritual sacrifices acceptable to God through Jesus Christ" (1 Pet. 2:5ff.). Similarly, Christians are instructed by Paul that they are "built upon the foundation of the apostles and prophets, Christ Jesus himself being the cornerstone, in whom the whole structure[33] is joined together and grows into a holy temple in the Lord," a temple which is in fact the "dwelling place of God"[34] (Eph. 2:20ff.).

As so frequently in this epistle, however, the status of the Christian is coupled with an admonitory proviso: we are God's house *if*, on condition that, *we hold fast our confidence and pride in our hope.* This is entirely in line with the teaching of Christ, who declared: "If you continue in my word, you are truly my disciples" (Jn. 8:31). F. F. Bruce remarks on the "repeated insistence" of our epistle "on the fact that continuance in the Christian life is the test of reality"; and he adds that "the doctrine of the final perseverance of the saints has as its corollary the sanguinary teaching that the saints are the people who persevere to the end." Admonitions such as our author gives here serve to emphasize the seriousness of the Christian's calling and are thoroughly in line with God's covenant relationship with his people in former times (cf., for example, Dt. 30). God is not beholden to any person or nation: obedience to the terms of the covenant brings blessing; unfaithfulness and apostasy lead to judgment. The verses that follow are designed to instruct the readers of this epistle that the sorry history of Israel under Moses provides a solemn warning to members of the Christian community of the dire consequences of insincerity.

It must not be imagined that our author is speaking only theoreti-

31. The verb οἰκοδομέω used here implies etymologically, though not necessarily semantically, the constructing of a house (οἶκος).
32. Οἶκος πνευματικός.
33. Πᾶσα οἰκοδομή.
34. Κατοικητήριον τοῦ θεοῦ. It will be noticed that the element οἶκος, either by itself (as also of course in Gal. 6:10 and Eph. 2:19; cf. 1 Tim. 3:15) or in combination, persists in these passages.

cally rather than addressing himself to the realities of the situation. His perception of the perilous state of this particular community was what impelled him to undertake the writing of this epistle. His readers, he discerns, are in danger of wavering under the influence of strange ideas and hostile pressures. Like Christians in every age, they are face to face with perplexities and temptations. They are exhorted accordingly not to weaken and retire from the struggle, and reminded that only if they *hold fast* are they God's "house." Nor does an admonition of this kind conflict with the dominical and apostolic teaching that the Christian's eternal security is dependent not on himself but on Christ and his merits alone (cf. Jn. 5:24; 6:37; 10:27–29; Acts 2:47; Rom. 11:6f.; 1 Cor. 1:26ff.; 2 Cor. 5:18ff.; Eph. 2:8–10). But it does mean that a man whose profession of faith is contradicted by the quality of his life should examine himself to see whether he is a Christian at all (2 Cor. 13:5). Security in Christ does not absolve one from personal responsibility: quite the contrary, for the regenerate man is under total obligation to God. Seriousness in believing should manifest itself in seriousness concerning doctrine and conduct. And this is applicable to communities as well as individuals; hence the incitements to the seven churches of the Apocalypse to overcome, to be faithful unto death, and to hold fast until Christ comes (Rev. 2:7, 11, 17, 25f.; 3:5, 11f., 21).

What is said here points to a dwindling of *confidence*, involving inevitably a weakening of evangelical witness,[35] on the part of those to whom this letter is addressed. The *pride* with which they had formerly testified to their Christian *hope*[36] was draining away. We who are Christ's have a hope, as Héring says, "of which we can boast, that is to say, of which we should not be ashamed." The implication is that those to whom this letter is addressed were being tempted to set aside their hope in the return of Christ and the establishment of his everlasting kingdom and to place their confidence in other beings and personages such as those expected in the eschatology of Qumran.[37] They showed signs of ceasing to belong to the number of those who look for the dawning of the Day of the Lord and love his appearing (2 Tim. 4:7f.). Their Thessalonian brethren had been disturbed by affirmations, first, that those Christians who had died were at a disadvantage with respect to the parousia, and, secondly, that the Day of the Lord had already come, and

---

35. The noun παρρησία, translated "confidence" here, means outspokenness and hence boldness, openness, and confidence. Like the verb παρρησιάζομαι, in the New Testament it is most frequently associated with the notion of boldness or confidence in witness and preaching (as reference to a Greek concordance will show). Confidence in belief and confidence in witness go together.

36. The Greek reads τὸ καύχημα τῆς ἐλπίδος. The genitive ἐλπίδος may be described as a genitive of content or definition: the Christian hope is the theme of our boasting or glorying.

37. See Introduction, pp. 13ff.

Paul had found it necessary to correct these misconceptions (1 Thess. 4:13ff.; 2 Thess. 2:1ff.). In the case of our present letter, its recipients would seem to have been heeding suggestions that the expectation of the return of Jesus Christ was a vain hope (cf. 2 Pet. 3:3ff.). But it is a mark of true Christianity that constantly and tenaciously "we rejoice in our hope of sharing the glory of God" (Rom. 5:2).[38] These words of Paul provide an excellent comment on the text before us. The situation which our author is addressing is perceptively summed up for us by Herveus:

> Let us hold fast our confidence, lest suddenly, by reason of some infidelity, we should doubt the possibility of being saved through Christ, and seek help in carnal observances for salvation; but, setting these aside, let us trust without any doubting that Christ alone is sufficient for everything. For it has been shown that Christ is far more noble than Moses, so that we should cling to Christ alone, in whom we have all things, and to the glory of hope, that is, the hope that is glorious because it relates to the joy of heaven, and firm, that is, which endures to the end of life,[39] when what is now hoped for will be received.

3:7–11. *Therefore, as the Holy Spirit says, "Today, when you hear his voice, do not harden your hearts as in the rebellion, on the day of testing in the wilderness, where your fathers put me to the test and saw my works for forty years. Therefore I was provoked with that generation, and said, 'They always go astray in their hearts; they have not known my ways.' As I swore in my wrath, 'They shall never enter my rest.'"*

The author's appeal to his readers to be serious and confident in maintaining the faith and hope that are theirs in Christ is now fortified

---

38. "The idea of τὸ καύχημα τῆς ἐλπίδος," writes Moffatt, "is exactly that of Rom. 5:2 (καυχώμεθα ἐπ᾽ ἐλπίδι τῆς δόξης τοῦ θεοῦ), and of a saying like Ps. 5:12 (καὶ εὐ-φρανθήτωσαν ἐπὶ σοὶ πάντες οἱ ἐλπίζοντες ἐπὶ σέ)."

39. The words "firm... to the end" reflect a longer reading, μέχρι τέλους βεβαίαν κατάσχωμεν, which is supported by a considerable weight of attestation, including the uncials אACD, the Byzantine MSS and Lectionary readings, the Old Latin, Vulgate, Syriac, Coptic (Bohairic), and Armenian versions, a number of patristic authors, and numerous minuscules. Its presence in the Textus Receptus is reflected in the KJV, "if we hold fast the confidence and rejoicing of the hope *firm unto the end.*" The evidence for the omission of μέχρι τέλους βεβαίαν is very much less in terms of quantity, but it includes p⁴⁶, p¹³, and B, as well as Lucifer and Ambrose in the fourth century and, among the versions, the Coptic (Sahidic) and an Ethiopic MS. This is sufficient in quality to cause one at least to hesitate; but when we find the longer expression in the same context in verse 14 below it becomes less doubtful that the shorter reading here in verse 6 is the correct one, the likelihood being that in copying the text familiarity with μέχρι τέλους βεβαίαν κατάσχωμεν in verse 14 led to the inadvertent assimilation of verse 6 to this reading. Most modern editors approve the shorter text, though Souter is an exception, and Nestle and also Westcott and Hort indicate their doubt regarding the longer reading by placing the words μέχρι τέλους βεβαίαν between brackets.

by an extended quotation from Psalm 95, which in turn forms the basis of a solemn admonitory passage intended to warn them against repeating the folly of the Israelites of old, whose disobedience was met by the judgment of God. Plainly, the wilderness setting of this quotation would have had particular appropriateness for a group or community whose expectations were to a greater or lesser degree colored by teachings similar to those of the Dead Sea Sect, for the adherents of the latter had withdrawn themselves to the wilderness with the express intention of reconstructing the exodus situation of their forefathers under Moses, there by discipline and faithfulness to prepare themselves for the establishment of the kingdom of righteousness.[40]

This formula *as the Holy Spirit says* which introduces the quotation has the effect of demanding the serious attention of the readers and emphasizing the extreme seriousness of the warning conveyed in the quotation: it is none other than the Holy Spirit who is admonishing them through this passage of Scripture. While it is doubtless true that the author is not primarily concerned here with the doctrine of biblical inspiration, yet these few words disclose in a manner which is quite unforced the attitude with which he regards Scripture. (It is matched in 10:15 where he introduces another quotation with the words: "And the Holy Spirit also bears witness to us... ," and also, in effect, in 9:8 where, with reference to the regulations prescribed for the construction of the tabernacle in the wilderness, he says: "By this the Holy Spirit indicates. . . .") For him, as for the other apostolic authors, the message of Scripture is the voice of the Holy Spirit. It is plain, too, that, for this very reason, he regards Scripture not as a dead letter of a bygone period but as fully existential in its significance, so that what was spoken or written in the wilderness situation centuries before continues to have a dynamic applicability to the people of God in his own day. This vitality of Scripture in terms of its divine origin and its contemporaneousness is corroborated by a passage like 2 Timothy 3:16 which teaches that not only is all Scripture God-breathed but also and continuously "profitable for teaching, for reproof, for correction, and for training in righteousness"—which is precisely the use to which our author puts the quotation before us. Aquinas comments accordingly:

> The authority of the words arises from this, that they are not the products of human invention, but of the Holy Spirit. . . . He adduces the words of the Old Testament for the New, lest it should be thought that their reference is only to the Old Testament and to a former time, instead of also to the New. And they are words of the Holy Spirit because, as declared in 2 Peter 1:21, "no prophecy ever came by the impulse of men, but men moved by the

40. See Introduction, pp. 13ff.

Holy Spirit spoke from God". For David himself says, in 2 Kings 23:2, of himself: "The Spirit of the Lord spoke through me". This therefore demonstrates the genuineness of the authority, because it derives from the Holy Spirit.

The abiding relevance of this particular psalm (95) is attested not only by its retention in the liturgical worship of the Jewish synagogue but also by its inclusion over the centuries, in the Western Church, as the invitatory psalm (commonly referred to, from its opening word in the Latin version, as the *Venite*) in the worship of Matins or Morning Prayer.

The perverseness of ingratitude and faithlessness is nowhere more strikingly illustrated than in the history of the Israelites in the wilderness. The goodness of God, who had raised up a great leader for them and had brought them safely out of the misery and bondage of Egypt, never failed them. Yet over and over again they rebelled against him and behaved as though he were their enemy instead of their deliverer. In the quotation from Psalm 95 reference is made to one disgraceful instance of their hard-hearted perversity, namely, *the rebellion* which took place *on the day of testing*. The allusion is to the occasion, described in Exodus 17:1ff., when the people grumbled against God and were close to insurrection at Rephidim because they were without water. Their need was supplied by the water which gushed forth after Moses had struck the rock with his rod; but he called the place "Massah," which means "testing," and "Meribah," which means "embitterment" or the rebelliousness that results from it, "because they put the Lord to the test by saying, 'Is the Lord among us or not?' "[41] Some commentators (for example, Delitzsch, Westcott) see here a reference not only to this one incident but also to the similar event described in Numbers 20:1ff.; but, even allowing for the closeness of similarity, the Psalmist's terminology points to the earlier rather than the later occasion, which, however, recalled "the waters of Meribah, where the people of Israel contended with the Lord" (Num. 20:13). A comparable but more general complaint is made in another psalm, where we read: "How often they rebelled against him in the wilderness and grieved him in the desert! They tested him again and again, and provoked the Holy One of Israel. They did not keep in mind his power" (Ps. 78:40ff.). The single shameful incident recollected in the passage cited by our author was characteristic, indeed symptomatic, of their whole attitude of deep-rooted rebellion and unbelief.

Instead of moving forward with a calm confidence in the power and goodness of God, they *put him to the test*. Blind to the fact that it was

---

41. The Greek terms in our text, namely, παραπικρασμός and πειρασμός, correspond to the LXX renderings of the Hebrew words מְרִיבָה, "contention," and מַסָּה, "testing."

they, not God, who were being tested, they set themselves up as judges over God and refused to put their trust in him unless he performed what they demanded—and this in spite of the fact that throughout the *forty years* in the wilderness they *saw his works*. [42] To put God to the test in this way is thus plainly an evidence of unbelief and ingratitude. And it means, further, that, although for forty years they had seen his works, yet they had *not known his ways*. They had seen without knowing, that is, without perceiving what was obvious before their eyes. This was not a matter of incapacity but of unwillingness. They did not want to know, and so they refused to acknowledge, the plain truth about God: in their ungodliness they *suppressed* the truth (Rom. 1:18). They squandered their day of opportunity, the "today" of God's grace (see vv. 13ff. below). In their obduracy they failed culpably to learn the great lesson of God's unfailing faithfulness, with the result that he was *provoked* by the repeated manifestations of their mutinous temper ("They *always* go astray in their hearts") to punish them by causing them to forfeit the blessing of entry into the *rest* that lay ahead for the people of God—that is, in the immediate perspective, rest from their wanderings in the wilderness achieved through entry into and possession of the land of promise. Thus God says, in Numbers 14:22f.: "None of the men who have seen my glory and my signs which I wrought in Egypt and in the wilderness, and yet have put me to the proof these ten times and have not hearkened to my voice, shall see the land which I swore to give to their fathers."

This land, however, was a visible and tangible token which, like a sacrament, pointed beyond itself to a far more wonderful reality, the reality, namely, of the eternal rest of God himself. *This* rest, as our author will show, still awaits the people of God from every age (cf. 4:1–11). Accordingly, we find Chrysostom and Alcuin explaining that three "rests" are spoken of in this section of our epistle: "the first is the rest of the Sabbath on which the Lord rested from his works; the second is in Palestine, on entering which the Israelites were to rest from much toil and misery; and the third, which is the true rest, is the kingdom of heaven, and those who come to this truly rest from their labours and hardships." The same threefold distinction is noticed by later authors,

---

42. The "forty years" would make good sense if taken either in association with what precedes, as is the case in our quotation ("your fathers put me to the test and saw my works for forty years"), or with what follows ("for forty years I was provoked..."). The insertion of the conjunction διό after τεσσεράκοντα ἔτη limits us here to the former connection, but the conjunction is not present in the text of the LXX (or the Hebrew) as it has come down to us. It should be noticed, however, that the latter connection occurs in verse 17 below ("with whom was he provoked forty years?"). This serves to indicate the ambivalence of association, at least in the mind of our author, of the phrase "forty years." Whichever way it is taken, the over-all sense of the passage is not altered.

though a different classification of "three sabbaths" is propounded by Lefèvre d'Etaples, according to whom "the first was that of the Hebrews, the second is that of Christians in this world, and the third is celebrated by the saints in heaven." He adds that "into the first sabbath both those who were admitted and those who were barred from God's [eternal] rest entered, into the second both good and evil Christians enter, and into the third only the faithful and elect will enter." But the difference scarcely amounts to discrepancy. In effect Lefèvre has added a fourth category, the rest which Christians even now experience in Christ in the midst of a variety of afflictions (cf. Mt. 11:28f.), at the same time postulating, quite legitimately, the identity of God's rest (Gen. 2:2f.) with the eternal rest which all the redeemed will enjoy.

Is there some special thrust in the mention of the "forty years" in the quotation from Psalm 95? Spicq suggests that the substitution of *this* generation for "that" generation (as it is in the Septuagint version of the psalm) was intended to sound a note of urgency for the generation contemporary with our author; and F. F. Bruce draws attention to evidence in the Qumran literature "of a belief that God's dealings with Israel, which began with a probationary period of forty years, would be rounded off at the end-time by a probationary period of like duration." He points out that, assuming this epistle to have been written shortly before A.D. 70, it was now almost forty years since Jesus had accomplished his "exodus" at Jerusalem (see Luke 9:31, Greek), "hence the urgency of the present appeal to the readers to take heed 'so long as it is called "today"' (verse 13)." If indeed the recipients of this letter were in some measure disposed to view with favor doctrines distinctive of or similar to those held by the Dead Sea Sect, then the mention of this period of forty years, so significant in the past and now again significant in the reckoning of this community who had returned to the wilderness existence, and the solemn lessons drawn from the history of the Israelites could well have come to them with particular force.[43]

3:12. *Take care, brethren, lest there be in any of you an evil, unbelieving heart, leading you to fall away from the living God.*

The lessons implicit in the preceding quotation from Psalm 95 are now driven home with great plainness. There is a strong logical connection with the words in verse 7 by which the quotation was introduced:

43. See Introduction, pp. 13ff.

"Therefore, as the Holy Spirit says, . . . Take care, brethren, . . ." In other words, the Holy Spirit has said these things not to provide a static record of past occurrences, but to speak an admonitory word, dynamic and existential, to us in our day. In a comparable manner Paul advises the Corinthians that the experiences of the people of Israel in the wilderness are "warnings for us, not to desire evil as they did." "We must not indulge in immorality as some of them did," he continues; ". . . nor grumble, as some of them did. . . . Now these things happened to them as a warning, but they were written down for our instruction, upon whom the end of the ages has come" (1 Cor. 10:6–11).

It is noticeable that our author addresses his readers tenderly as *brethren*, that is, fellow Christians (cf. v. 1 and 2:11ff.), thus indicating that, while he finds it necessary to rebuke them sternly, he does not despair of there being true faith, and faithfulness, among them. He still regards them as a Christian community; but a little leaven (*in any of you*) leavens the whole lump (1 Cor. 5:6) and many can be corrupted by few. The immediate danger is that there should arise *an evil, unbelieving heart*[44] in their midst. The "unbelieving heart" mentioned here is not a heart that has not yet come to belief, but a heart that departs from belief, "a heart not firm in faith" (Aquinas), the evil nature of which is displayed in an act of wilful apostasy.[45] It is not a question of a quasi-passive *falling away* (as our version might seem to suggest), but of a deliberate, rebellious secession from the living God (cf. NEB, "wicked, faithless heart of a deserter"; JB, "a wicked mind, so unbelieving as to turn away from the living God")—precisely, in fact, the sin of the Israelites in the wilderness who, heedless of all their blessings, despised the divine covenant they had sworn to uphold. This is the exact antithesis of the spirit of those who draw near to God "with a true heart in full assurance of faith" (10:22). As Spicq remarks, it is far more serious to commit apostasy after professing belief than never to have come to faith. The same predicament is defined by another apostolic author when speaking of those who have "forsaken the right way" and "gone astray": "For if, after they have escaped the defilements of the world through the knowledge of our Lord and Savior Jesus Christ, they are again entangled in them and over-

44. Literally, "an evil heart of unbelief" (KJV), καρδία πονηρὰ ἀπιστίας—a heart that is evil because it is unbelieving. "The writer does not say, take heed lest there be in any of you a grasping hand, a shifty eye, a sensuous ear," comments Luther. "For before everything else one must see to it that the heart is good, pure, and holy."
45. Ἐν τῷ ἀποστῆναι, "in the commission of apostasy." The construction βλέπετε . . . μήποτε ἔσται may be semitic, as many commentators hold, but it is also effectively graphic, the future indicative depicting the reality of the danger that is ahead of them if they cease to be watchful (βλέπετε, present imperative, "be constantly on the watch"). Exactly the same construction occurs in Colossians 2:8.

powered, the last state has become worse for them than the first. For it would have been better for them never to have known the way of righteousness than after knowing it to turn back from the holy commandment delivered to them" (2 Pet. 2:15, 20f.; cf. Mt. 12:43–45; and especially 6:4ff. and 10:26ff. below).

The apostasy which threatens is like that of the Israelites, too, in that it is a departure *from the living God*, for, of all the nations, it was the Israelites who had knowledge and experience of the living God (cf. Dt. 5:26; Josh. 3:10; 1 Sam. 17:26; Ps. 84:2). Nothing exhibited more clearly the blind folly of the heathen peoples by whom they were surrounded than their custom of offering worship to images which were man-made and lifeless. The absoluteness of the contrast is graphically portrayed by the Psalmist, who writes: "Our God is in the heavens; he does whatever he pleases. Their idols are silver and gold, the work of men's hands. They have mouths, but do not speak; eyes, but do not see. They have ears, but do not hear; noses, but do not smell. They have hands, but do not feel; feet, but do not walk; and they do not make a sound in their throat. Those who make them are like them; so are all who trust in them" (Ps. 115:3–8). Isaiah speaks with scorn of those who carefully fashion and adorn an idol and then fall down and worship it: "They lift it upon their shoulders, they carry it, they set it in its place, and it stands there; it cannot move from its place. If one cries to it, it does not answer or save him from his trouble" (Isa. 46:6f.). Such fabrications are powerless because they are lifeless. "Their idols," declares Jeremiah, "are like scarecrows in a cucumber field, and they cannot speak; they have to be carried, for they cannot walk. Be not afraid of them, for they cannot do evil, neither is it in them to do good. . . . But the Lord is the true God; he is the living God and the everlasting King" (Jer. 10:5–10).

To forsake the living God is always to fall into idolatry. Not that the recipients of this letter were in danger of transferring their worship to images of wood and stone: the constructions of human philosophy and speculation are no less idols, man-made and powerless to save. The essence of all idolatry, whether primitive or sophisticated, is the abandonment of the truth about God for a lie and the worship and service of the creature rather than the Creator (Rom. 1:25). These "Hebrews" were being tempted to relinquish the light of the gospel for the darkness of religious speculation (cf. 6:4ff.), to trust in the appearance of human and angelic figures rather than in the appearance of Jesus Christ, and to submit to earthly structures and earthly authorities—in short, to turn their backs on him who alone is the living God. And, as Peter Lombard observes, "to depart from him is to forfeit life, because in him alone is life."

146

3:13. But exhort one another every day, as long as it is called "today," that none of you may be hardened by the deceitfulness of sin.

An important means for withstanding the enticement to apostasy is that of mutual exhortation or admonition.[46] Christians have a corporate as well as an individual responsibility. Personal concern that is merely introspective and introverted is both selfish and unhealthy. In practice as well as in theory, the truth should not be overlooked that "we, though many, are one body in Christ, and individually members one of another" (Rom. 12:5). Mutual concern and encouragement are of constant value in the church, not least in repelling the menace of false teaching; hence the writer's desire that his readers should *exhort one another* not just occasionally, or in one particular situation, but *every day.* How different might have been the story of the Israelites in the wilderness if only they had daily fostered among themselves a constant faith in God instead of mutually inciting a spirit of rebellion and unbelief! Apostasy is a perennial danger for the church, and we, like those to whom this letter was addressed, should in our day heed the warning provided by the account of the mutual unconcern of the Israelites and the disastrous consequences it brought upon them. Moreover, as Héring remarks, the present verse "reminds us that exhortation and moral encouragement are not a function reserved to the leaders of the church, but a duty of each Christian."

This unremitting encouragement of one another in loyalty and perseverance should continue *as long as it is called "today,"* that is, as long as the present day of God's grace endures. The allusion, of course, is to the quotation from Psalm 95 in verse 7 above. Under Moses, that "day" lasted for forty years in the wilderness, and so long as it lasted the opportunity persisted for the people to heed God's voice and obey his will. As with them, however, the day of divine forbearance will not last forever: it will be succeeded by another "day," the Day of the Lord,

---

46. The opinion that the reflexive pronoun ἑαυτούς, "yourselves," is deliberately used here (παρακαλεῖτε ἑαυτούς) instead of the pronoun ἀλλήλους, "each other," with the purpose of emphasizing the close unity of the Christian body (Westcott, Spicq), attempts too much in the way of interpretation. For one thing, the privileges and responsibilities of Christian corporateness would be no less plain if ἀλλήλους were substituted for ἑαυτούς, and, for another, in the Greek of the New Testament these two pronouns are used interchangeably, as the following passages show: γίνεσθε εἰς ἀλλήλους χρηστοί, εὔσπλαγχνοι, χαριζόμενοι ἑαυτοῖς (Eph. 4:32), ἀνεχόμενοι ἀλλήλων καὶ χαριζόμενοι ἑαυτοῖς (Col. 3:13), and εἰς ἑαυτοὺς ἀγάπην ἐκτενῆ ἔχοντες... φιλόξενοι εἰς ἀλλήλους... ἕκαστος καθὼς ἔλαβεν χάρισμα, εἰς ἑαυτοὺς αὐτὸ διακονοῦντες (1 Pet. 4:8–10; see also Lk. 23:12). In none of these passages can ἑαυτούς or ἑαυτοῖς be said to be naturally susceptible of a reflexive meaning. Bengel's comment combines both the reflexive and the reciprocal: "ἑαυτούς... quisque se ipsum et alterum."

which is the day of judgment for those who have spurned the day of
grace (cf. 2 Pet. 3:8–10). No tragedy is greater than for the members of a
professedly Christian body to fail, through hardness of heart, to recognize the day of grace and opportunity; and of this tragedy the Israelites
in the wilderness and also repeatedly in the subsequent course of their
history are a cautionary example. Our author is anxious that his readers
should not imitate this example.

The purpose of the mutual encouragement which he advocates is
that none of you may be hardened by the deceitfulness of sin. If there should be
a concern of the individual for the community ("exhort one another"),
there should also be a concern of the community for the individual ("lest
any one of you...") in line with the teaching of Paul that "if one
member suffers all suffer together" (1 Cor. 12:26). It would seem that at
this point the apostasy feared by the author was potential rather than
actual, and that the immediate danger, rather than being general, attached to one or two individual members of the group he is addressing.[47] But, in the long term, as, again, the analogy of the body shows,
the infection of one member threatens the infection of the whole. It is
still "today," however: God's day of mercy has not yet closed. The
imitation of the evil example of their forefathers in the wilderness together with its dire consequences can still be averted, and their earthly
pilgrimage can still be crowned with the blessing of entry into God's
own rest.

Sin, nonetheless, is a constantly present reality which makes its
inroads by means of *deceitfulness*. Personified here as it seems to be again
in 12:4 below, sin first deceives and then hardens, leaving its victims in
an irretrievably hopeless position (as 6:4ff. and 10:26ff. explain with
unequivocal frankness). The background of this concept is undoubtedly
the account of the fall (Gen. 3): Satan, with serpent-like guile, insinuates
himself into the consciousness of the woman, whom he completely deceives,[48] and she in turn tempts the man to disobey the word of God,
with the result that the blessing of paradise is exchanged for a curse and
this, the original apostasy, produces a harvest of incalculable bitterness.
"It is rightly called the deceitfulness of sin," Luther declares, "because it
deceives under the appearance of good."

---

47. The clause reads literally, "lest any one of you should be hardened," ἵνα μὴ σκληρυνθῇ
τις ἐξ ὑμῶν. The aorist subjunctive σκληρυνθῇ would seem to imply that hardening had
not yet taken place; whereas, had the present subjunctive been used, it would have
indicated that hardening was already present.
48. Cf. 1 Timothy 2:14, "the woman was completely deceived (ἐξαπατηθεῖσα) and became
a transgressor," where ἐξαπατηθεῖσα is an intensive compound, as the immediately preceding uncompounded ἠπατήθη confirms; and notice the cognate noun ἀπάτη, "deceitfulness," here in Hebrews 3:13.

This phrase "the deceitfulness of sin" [he continues] ought to be understood in a much wider sense, so that the term includes even one's own righteousness and wisdom. For more than anything else one's own righteousness and wisdom deceive one and work against faith in Christ, since we love the flesh and the sensations of the flesh and also riches and possessions, but we love nothing more ardently than our own feelings, judgment, purpose, and will, especially when they seem to be good. For the same reason Christ said, when he healed the paralytic at the Pool of Bethesda, that it was impossible for such people to be able to believe: "How can you believe who receive glory from one another?" (John 5:44). Why are they not able to believe? Because the "deceitfulness of sin", that is, the love of their own righteousness, blinds them and hardens their heart. Yet at the same time they think it a good thing to glory in their own righteousness and be pleased with it, though that indeed is the very worst of all vices, the extreme antithesis of faith. Faith rejoices and glories in the righteousness of God alone, that is, in Christ himself.

3:14, 15. *For we share in Christ, if only we hold our first confidence firm to the end, while it is said, "Today, when you hear his voice, do not harden your hearts as in the rebellion."*

The significance of the clause translated in our version *for we share in Christ*, a more literal rendering of which would be "for we have become partakers of Christ,"[49] is a matter of some dispute (cf. KJV). There is, indeed, a certain ambiguity associated with the Greek noun used here since it may mean either "partakers with" someone in a particular activity or relationship, in which case it denotes "companions" or "partners," as in 1:9 and Luke 5:7 (the only occurrence of the noun outside the Epistle to the Hebrews in the New Testament), or "partakers of," as in 3:1 ("partakers of a heavenly call"), 6:4 ("partakers of the Holy Spirit"), and 12:8 ("partakers of discipline").[50]

The former interpretation is favored here, for example, by Spicq, who points out that the Israelites were companions of Moses in the wilderness and sees an analogous notion in 1:9 above (quoting from Ps. 45) where it is implied that Christians are companions of the royal Son, and also in 2:11 where they are described as his brothers. This is the

---

49. Μέτοχοι γὰρ τοῦ Χριστοῦ γεγόναμεν, the perfect tense of the verb signifying that the readers (and the writer) have become and consequently now are partakers of Christ.

50. The cognate verb μετέχειν, which in the New Testament occurs only in Hebrews and 1 Corinthians, means "to partake of"; see 1 Corinthians 9:10 (to partake of the harvest), 10:17, 21, 30 (to partake of the one bread, of the table of the Lord, of food), Hebrews 2:14 (to partake of the same nature), 5:13 (to partake of milk), and 7:13 (to be part of another tribe). The sense of the verb in 1 Corinthians 9:12 is "to share in."

sense adopted in the NEB, which renders the clause "For we have become Christ's partners," and favored by Montefiore. Moffatt understands the clause as meaning "we have a personal interest in Christ," Delitzsch as signifying that "we are fellow heirs with Christ," corresponding closely with what Paul says in Romans 8:17 (similarly Peter Lombard and JB, "co-heirs with Christ"), and F. F. Bruce in much the same way as indicating "participation with Him in His heavenly kingdom."

Unexceptionable, however, though such opinions may be theologically, participation not in one or other respect but in an inclusive and radical sense seems to be intended here. We agree with Westcott's judgment that the rendering "partakers with Christ" (that is, his fellows or companions) gives a sense that is "far less natural here" and which "as far as it is applicable . . . is included in the more comprehensive idea." Thus Chrysostom and Alcuin explain the participation as that of oneness with Christ, as the body is united to the Head (cf. Rom. 12:5; 1 Cor. 12:27; Eph. 4:15f.). And Owen elucidates the clause as follows: "How, then, are we partakers of him, partakers of Christ? It is by our having an interest in his nature, by the communication of his Spirit, as he had in ours by the assumption of our flesh. It is, then, our union with Christ that is intended, whereby we are made 'members of his body, of his flesh, and of his bones', Eph. 5:30. A participation in the benefits of the mediation of Christ is included in these words, but not firstly intended, only as a consequent of our intimate union with him."

Aquinas postulates a double participation in Christ: "one incomplete, which is through faith and the sacraments, but the other complete, which is through the presence and the beholding of the reality." Of these, the former is too general, however; it could be more precisely and satisfactorily stated as participation through faith and the sacrament of baptism. In other words, the assertion that "we have become partakers of Christ" may be seen as a reference to the faith/baptism event, the decisive moment of conversion through faith in Christ being publicly dramatized by the act of baptism with its symbolism of cleansing from sin in the blood of Jesus (Eph. 5:26; Tit. 3:5; 1 Jn. 1:7) and the death and burial of the old life and resurrection to newness of life in and with Christ (Rom. 6:3ff.)—an event which at the same time looks forward to that ultimately decisive moment of the return of Christ when our incorporation into him will at last be consummated. Hence the importance of a right comprehension of the significance of baptism and its crucial implications for those who have received it. William Tyndale shows how firmly he has grasped this truth when he writes:

> No man that hath the profession of his baptism written in his heart can stumble in the Scripture and fall into heresies, or become a maker of division and sects and a defender of wild and vain opinions.

And the reason for this is that those who have the profession of their baptism written in their hearts

> have utterly forsaken themselves, with all their high learning and wisdom, and are become the servants of Christ only, who hath bought them with his blood; and have promised in their hearts unfeignedly to follow him, and to take him only for the author of their religion and his doctrine only for their wisdom and learning, and to maintain it in word and deed, and to keep it pure, and to build no strange doctrine thereupon.[51]

Here, then, we may hear our author saying in effect: "We have the profession of our baptism written in our hearts, provided we hold our first confidence firm to the end."

Otherwise, the mere reception of baptism as an external rite guarantees nothing; and once again the history of the Israelites in the wilderness provides a salutary warning: "Our fathers," Paul writes, ". . . all were baptized into Moses in the cloud and in the sea. . . . Nevertheless with most of them God was not pleased; for they were overthrown in the wilderness" (1 Cor. 10:1–5). Those to whom our author is writing have all been baptized into Christ; nevertheless, if they follow the evil example of their forebears, they too will meet with God's displeasure and be overthrown—perhaps also in the wilderness if, as is possible, they were being enticed to belittle their baptism into Christ by voices suggesting that baptism of a kind characteristic of the ritual of the Dead Sea Sect was a necessity.[52] Be that as it may, the plain warning before them is that, should they harden their hearts *as in the rebellion*, they are answerable to the same God "who saved a people out of the land of Egypt" and "afterward destroyed those who did not believe" (Jude 5).

Accordingly, our author links authentic participation in Christ with the condition, *if only we hold our first confidence firm to the end*. This conditional clause corresponds closely with the conditional clause at the end of verse 6: "if we hold fast our confidence and pride in our hope."[53]

---

51. William Tyndale, *Exposition of the First Epistle of Saint John* (1531), in *Expositions etc.* (Cambridge, 1849), p. 140. Cf. the comment of Alcuin (on Heb. 4:1): " . . . lest we should desert the promise which we gave to God in baptism and return to the works of unbelief which we abjured in the presence of many witnesses."

52. See Introduction, pp. 13ff.

53. The similarity of the terminology in verse 6 (ἐὰν τὴν παρρησίαν . . . κατάσχωμεν) and in verse 14 (ἐάνπερ τὴν ἀρχὴν τῆς ὑποστάσεως . . . κατάσχωμεν) is enhanced by the fact that the nouns παρρησία and ὑπόστασις are synonymous in this context. In 11:1 below and 2 Corinthians 9:4 and 11:17 ὑπόστασις has this same connotation of confidence or assurance. Spicq's suggestion that the term ὑπόστασις may have been chosen here in order to contrast arrestingly with ἀπόστασις in verse 12 is unconvincing. The tenuousness of the proposed connection is apparent from the fact that the noun ἀπόστασις does not occur in verse 12, but only the aorist infinitive of the verb, ἀποστῆναι, so that it would have to be a matter of subtle innuendo and not at all a plain contrast. Spicq. it seems, owes a debt here to Moffatt's (more guarded) comment: "What a man bases himself on, as he confronts the future, is his ὑπόστασις, which here in sound and even (by contrast) in thought answers to ἀποστῆναι."

The precise sense of the Greek phrase translated in our version as "our first confidence," but more literally "the beginning of (our) confidence," is difficult to determine, for "beginning" could also be rendered as "principle" and "confidence" as "substance" or "foundation." Today the phrase is almost universally understood to mean "the confidence with which we began," that is, when we first became Christians (cf. NEB, "our original confidence"; Phillips, "the trust with which we began"), and this is almost certainly the correct interpretation. But the fact should not be overlooked that the commentators of the early and medieval centuries took the phrase to mean "the principle of the substance or foundation" of the Christian life, this principle being most commonly identified with faith, frequently with reference to 11:1 where our author declares that "faith is the assurance (or substance) of things hoped for."[54] He would then be saying here that "we are partakers of Christ if only we hold the principle of our existence as Christians (namely, faith) firm to the end." This interpretation deserves respectful consideration if only because of its long history; but it seems to rest largely on a metaphysical usage of the term "substance" (*hypostasis*) current in the fourth and subsequent centuries. Hence Luther charmingly advises that "in this place the shoes of philosophy ought to be removed from the feet of the faithful."

Our author himself provides the best explanation of what he means here by the exhortation he gives in 6:11f. below, where he writes: "We desire each one of you to show the same earnestness [as you showed at first, 6:10] in realizing the full assurance of hope until the end, so that you may not be sluggish, but imitators of those who through faith and patience inherit the promises."

> 3:16–19. *Who were they that heard and yet were rebellious? Was it not all those who left Egypt under the leadership of Moses? And with whom was he provoked forty years? Was it not with those who sinned, whose bodies fell in the wilderness? And to whom did he swear that they should never enter his rest, but to those who were disobedient? So we see that they were unable to enter because of unbelief.*

Today many scholars prefer to take verse 15, which is a repetition of the first part of the passage quoted above from Psalm 95, as associated in sense with these verses that follow rather than with what precedes (see, for example, NEB, JB, Teodorico, F. F. Bruce, Spicq, Delitzsch). Thus the NEB starts a new paragraph with verse 15, as follows: "When Scripture

---

54. Ἐστιν δὲ πίστις ἐλπιζομένων ὑπόστασις.

says, 'Today if you hear his voice, do not grow stubborn as in those days of rebellion', who, I ask, were those who heard and rebelled?" This arrangement has much to commend it; however, we have followed the punctuation of our version (RSV), which unites verses 14 and 15 and also gives good sense. That the questions in the verses now before us (16–19) relate to the whole of the passage quoted above in verses 7–11 and not just to the part which is reintroduced in verse 15 does not pose a difficulty, for verse 15 is in effect a return to the passage previously cited, like the re-entry of a theme in music—but not the passage in full, since the repetition of the opening sentence is sufficient to effect the recall of the whole passage.

It should also be mentioned that for centuries verse 16 was interpreted as a positive statement rather than as interrogative in form. This curiosity may be attributed to the pervasive influence of the Latin Vulgate,[55] and it was retained by the editors of the KJV, as follows: "For some, when they had heard, did provoke: howbeit not all that came out of Egypt by Moses." The structure, however, both of the argument and of the Greek text demands a series of questions in verses 16–18; otherwise our author's thrust and incisiveness are impaired.[56] He is not concerned here, as earlier commentators imagined, to draw attention to the fact that there were some (Joshua, Caleb) who did not rebel and provoke God to anger.

Who were they that heard and yet were rebellious? The startling character of the answer to this, the first of the three leading questions proposed in these verses, rests in the fact that the persons involved were none other than *those who left Egypt under the leadership of Moses—all* of them, that is to say, the entire generation that had been set free from bitter bondage and victoriously led forth with Moses at their head from the land of the tyrant. This does not imply that all without exception were guilty of unfaithfulness and apostasy, for the mention of Moses, who was certainly no rebel, is sufficient to remind us that there was a loyal remnant of those whose trust in God remained constant. The point is that this generation, which had firsthand experience of the goodness of God in bringing them from slavery to freedom, comprised the very last group of persons one would have expected to rebel against their Savior God. Still

---

55. "Quidam enim audientes exacerbaverunt: sed non universi qui profecti sunt ex Aegypto per Moysen."

56. If verse 16 is taken in isolation, the interpretation of Vg and KJV is defensible; but this involves treating τινες in that verse as an indefinite pronoun (τινές) instead of as an interrogative (τίνες), even though the corresponding pronouns in verses 17 and 18 (τίσιν ... τίσιν) cannot make sense unless they are interpreted as interrogative. Verse 16 limps badly as a positive statement, but treated as interrogative in form its force and its congruity are restored.

more unthinkable is the prospect of hard-hearted rebellion by Christians against the Lord who at the price of his own life-blood has ransomed them from the dark power of Satan and led them into the glorious liberty of the children of God. Yet this was precisely the danger threatening the community to whom this letter was addressed.

The same Israelites who had been rescued from Egypt were the ones with whom God was *provoked forty years*, and the reason for this provocation was that they *sinned* by abandoning their trust in God, with the consequence that their *bodies fell in the wilderness*. God judged and punished these rebels, who had set out with such protestations of loyalty and obedience, by not permitting them to arrive at the land of promise which was their destination. Only Joshua and Caleb, whose confidence in God had not wavered, and those who at the start of the exodus were immature in years were allowed to enter Canaan (see Num. 14:26ff.). And so a journey which might have taken a few months lasted for forty years—forty years of wandering and not arriving. This period involving the number forty represents, as on other occasions in Scripture (cf. Gen. 7:4, 17; Dt. 2:7; 8:2; Josh. 14:10; Neh. 9:21; Amos 2:10; Jonah 3:4; Mt. 4:2; Acts 1:3; 7:30, 36), a period of divine longsuffering, on the one hand, and, on the other, of testing which culminates in judgment for the unrepentant. It is a period, moreover, as we have seen (p. 144), which could have had particular significance for readers in some measure influenced by teachings akin to those of the Dead Sea Sect.

Again, it was *to those who were disobedient* that God swore *that they should not enter into his rest*, and the failure of this generation to enter was *because of unbelief*. The juxtaposition of unbelief and disobedience indicates the close connection between the two. As Westcott says, "unbelief passed into action." And this is always the case. It is what happened when man first fell from God; it was repeated in the wilderness; and the same disastrous sequence was now threatening the community to whom this letter was sent. The rest from which Adam and Eve were excluded was that of fellowship with God in Eden; the rest forfeited by the rebellious Israelites was that of the promised land; and the rest denied to apostates from the Christian faith is that of the eternal Sabbath of the new heaven and the new earth (Rev. 2:6; 22:1ff.). Furthermore, it was their own unbelief which rendered the people *unable* to enjoy God's rest. They disqualified themselves. Their incapacitation was self-induced. How could it be otherwise when the whole basis of the promised rest is that of trust and security in God? Unbelief engenders unrest. The unbeliever excludes himself from rest (cf. Rev. 22:15); and if this was true of the "rest" of Canaan, how much more is it true of the "rest" of eternity! In the moral structure of the renewed creation there cannot possibly be a place for unbelief or for the unrest which flows from it.

True rest is the enjoyment by the creature of perfect harmony with his Creator, and it can therefore only be *rest in God*. As such, it is totally incompatible with unbelief and disobedience toward God. Hence the *inability*[57] of the rebellious Israelites to enter into God's rest.

> 4:1. *Therefore, while the promise of entering his rest remains, let us fear lest any of you be judged to have failed to reach it.*

In the passage which this verse introduces, our author's purpose is to apply (*Therefore*) to his readers still more insistently the solemn lesson which the history of their forefathers in the wilderness teaches, and in doing so he makes it plain that the scope of the promise of entering into God's rest extends far beyond the historical event of the entry of the Israelites into Canaan under Joshua's leadership. The possession of the land of Canaan was indeed a fulfilment of the promise, but only in a proximate, this-worldly sense. The perspective of faith discerns its ultimate fulfilment in the entry into a heavenly country (11:16) and a heavenly Jerusalem (12:22), in an eternal consummation effected through the redemptive mediation of the incarnate Son. And this perspective is integral to our epistle. It is the key to the understanding of the priestly order of Melchizedek which is realized in the person and work of Christ, our High Priest forever (chs. 5–7), to the understanding of the earthly tabernacle in the wilderness as a type or foreshadowing of the heavenly reality (chs. 8–10), and to the understanding of the outlook of Abraham and other men of faith in the Old Testament period, who in their lifetime did not see the fulfilment of the divinely given promises but fixed their expectation on a heavenly consummation hereafter (chs. 11–13). So, too, here, the Christian readers are advised that *the promise of entering his rest remains*: it still holds good, the door of entry is still open, for the fulfilment is not yet. In the language of Psalm 95, it is still "today" as far as God's promise is concerned; and this indicates both opportunity and responsibility: opportunity in that we live in God's day of grace, and responsibility on our part not to despise or turn away from this privilege.

Hence the admonition *let us fear lest . . .* , for there is no attitude more dangerous for the church than that of unconcern and complacency. Paul's warning, written with reference to the same background of the judgments that overtook the uncaring Israelites in the wilderness,

---

57. Οὐκ ἠδυνήθησαν, on which Westcott comments: "Their exclusion from Canaan was not only a fact (οὐκ εἰσῆλθον), but a moral necessity."

namely, "Therefore let any one who thinks that he stands take heed lest
he fall" (1 Cor. 10:12), is a warning of perennial force; and it is immediately followed by the important assurance that God will not allow
his people to be tested beyond their strength. The first-person plural, *let
us fear*, conveys the genuine sense of solidarity which the writer feels
with those he is addressing, though the danger, as he discerns it, is that
one or more of them (*any of you*) may through a failure of faith deprive
themselves forever of the joy of experiencing the fulfilment of God's
promise of rest. The Christian, too, is a pilgrim journeying toward the
promised goal (cf. Heb. 11:13–16), and there is nothing he should dread
more than to *be judged to have failed to reach it*. The consideration of this
solemn possibility, so startlingly illustrated by the fate of the generation
which perished in the wilderness, should teach him to place his trust not
in the smallest degree in himself but solely and completely in him who
"is able for all time to save those who draw near to God through him"
(Heb. 7:25).[58]

> 4:2. *For good news came to us just as to them; but the message which they heard did
> not benefit them, because it did not meet with faith in the hearers.*

Quite literally, the opening clause of this verse reads, "for we also
have been evangelized just as they were," the perfect tense of the verb[59]
implying, as Spicq observes, the completeness of the evangelization that
had taken place, and thus leaving no room for any excuse to the effect
that the evangelization had been inadequate or deficient. There is a real
equivalence between the *promise* of the Old Testament and the *evangel* of
the New Testament, for their essential content is the same: the former
looks ahead to fulfilment in Christ, the latter proclaims the accomplishment in Christ of what was promised. Thus Paul, using a compound of
the same verb,[60] describes the giving of the covenant promise to Abraham as the preaching of the gospel beforehand to Abraham—his pre-
evangelization (Gal. 3:8).

---

58. Moffatt mentions, disapprovingly, the interpretation of μήποτε... δοκῇ τις ἐξ ὑμῶν
ὑστερηκέναι as meaning, "lest anyone imagine he has come too late for it." This rendering,
however, has been adopted by the translators of the Jerusalem Bible; but it is a sense which
is not well suited to the situation our author is addressing. The danger is that his readers
should fall short of, fail to attain, the rest that has been promised, not come too late for it.
The verb has the same sense in 12:15 below: "See to it that no one fail to obtain (μή τις
ὑστερῶν) the grace of God." Héring offers a rather different line of interpretation: "lest
anyone imagine he has been deprived (ὑστερηκέναι) of entry into the rest because the
promise has failed of fulfilment (καταλειπομένης ἐπαγγελίας)," citing 2 Peter 3:4 where
delay in the fulfilment of a promise is the basis of an argument for its falsity. But, again,
this rendering is unsuited to the context.
59. Ἐσμεν εὐηγγελισμένοι.
60. Προευηγγελίσατο.

But in the case of the Israelites in the wilderness *the message* (evangel) *which they heard did not benefit them,* and the reason for this deplorable eventuality was that it *did not meet with faith in the hearers.* Here we find three things in close association: (1) the message, (2) hearing,[61] and (3) faith. They are present in the same dynamic combination in Romans 10:14: "how are they to believe [faith] in him of whom they have never heard? and how are they to hear [hearing] without a preacher [to proclaim the message]?" It follows that the message by itself, as an isolated concept, is of no avail; to be good news it must be proclaimed so that there is a hearing of it; but, again, merely to hear it is in itself insufficient, for to hearing the response of faith must be added. The generation in the wilderness discovered to their cost that the same evangelical message which they heard and faithlessly rejected became the source of their condemnation. What possible excuse can there be for us if we follow their example? What difference can we plead (*good news came to us just as to them*) except that, if anything, we are all the more culpable, for they had the promise, whereas we have the fulfilment? To us he whom the evangelical message proclaims says: "He who rejects me and does not receive my sayings has a judge; the word that I have spoken will be his judge on the last day" (Jn. 12:48).[62]

---

61. In the Greek, these first two are combined in the phrase "the word of hearing," ὁ λόγος τῆς ἀκοῆς, that is, the word or message which is associated with hearing, ἀκοῆς being a descriptive genitive, and the implication being that the message is intended for people to hear and so must be proclaimed.

62. Our version, *because it did not meet with faith in the hearers,* reflects the reading μὴ συγκεκερασμένος, the nominative masculine singular participle agreeing with the antecedent noun ὁ λόγος, so that the pronoun *it* corresponds to *the message.* This gives good sense and the two adjacent datives, τῇ πίστει τοῖς ἀκούσασιν, can be explained as a dative (τῇ πίστει) governed by the σύν with which the participle (συγκεκερασμένος) is compounded and a dative of reference (τοῖς ἀκούσασιν)—"since it was not mixed with faith in the case of those who heard it." The textual evidence, however, is strongly in favor of the reading συγκεκερασμένους, the accusative masculine plural of the same participial form, which then must agree with the antecedent pronoun ἐκείνους, giving the meaning, "since they were not mingled with. . . ." The two datives that follow are then more awkward to interpret. One possible rendering would be: "since they were not united by faith with those who heard," understanding "heard" in the sense of "obeyed" of which the verb ἀκούω is susceptible (cf. Jn. 8:47). But this is unacceptable because the verb ἀκούω would then convey a sense different from the noun ἀκοή in a verse where the two clearly should coincide in significance (and different also from that of ἀκούσαντες in Heb. 3:16). Another possibility is: "since they were not united with those who heard with faith"; but if this were intended the most natural order of the words would have been μὴ συγκεκερασμένους τοῖς τῇ πίστει ἀκούσασιν (or τοῖς ἀκούσασιν τῇ πίστει). There are variant readings also for the latter participle. One such is the genitive plural τῶν ἀκουσάντων in place of the dative plural, which would give the sense, "since it (the message) was not (or perhaps they were not) united with the faith of the hearers." Another retains the dative plural, but in the passive instead of the active voice, namely, τοῖς ἀκουσθεῖσιν, which must be treated as a neuter, giving the meaning, "since they were not united by faith with the things that were heard." This reading is found in Theodore of Mopsuestia; and it is also reflected in the Vulgate, but in association with the singular μὴ συγκεκερασμένος, the sense then being, "since it (the message) was not united with faith arising from the things they heard"—*non*

4:3–5. *For we who have believed enter that rest, as he has said, "As I swore in my wrath, 'They shall never enter my rest,'" although his works were finished from the foundation of the world. For he has somewhere spoken of the seventh day in this way, "And God rested on the seventh day from all his works." And again in this place he said, "They shall never enter my rest."*

We who have believed enter that rest, in contrast to the wilderness generation whose unbelief excluded them from the promised blessing, the designation "we who have believed" being generally descriptive of the Christian church, the Israel of God (Gal. 6:16), which may properly be defined as the community of *believers*. The prerequisite for admission to membership in this community is simply belief in Christ as Redeemer and Lord, sealed and publicly professed in baptism (cf. Jn. 3:16, 36; 5:24; Acts 8:13; 16:30ff.; Rom. 10:9f.). Thus the aorist tense of the Greek participle here[63] may be interpreted as pointing back to the moment of open profession of belief in baptism: "we who professed to believe and were baptized"; and this being so, it is we, the people of faith now on our earthly pilgrimage following our leader Christ, who are on the way that leads to the promised rest.[64] The prerogative of entry belongs to believers. "The Christian pilgrimage," says Montefiore, "is not an aimless wandering, like that of the Israelites in the desert. It is a deliberate, straight course on a well-mapped route. Every step brings the company of Christians nearer their destination." At the same time, our author is intent on demonstrating the possibility, with the hope that in doing so he will prevent its becoming a reality, that within the community of faith there may be hypocrites or defectors whose position is one of unbelief rather than faith. Any such, of course, do not truly belong to the church, except in a formal and external sense, and the *rest* that is promised does not pertain to them.

The last part of the quotation from Psalm 95 (vv. 7–11 above) is repeated here for the purpose of calling attention again to the fact that *God* has a rest (*my rest*). Although the oath is in the future tense (*They shall never enter into my rest*), the futurity relates not to God's rest as such but to the enjoyment of it by his creatures. We are reminded accordingly that *his works were finished from the foundation of the world*—a reference, as

---

admixtus fidei ex iis quae audierunt. Westcott and Hort conclude "after much hesitation" that "this very difficult passage" probably contains a primitive corruption (see their Note in *The New Testament in the Original Greek,* II, London, 1896, pp. 129f. of the Appendix). Zuntz similarly suggests that the diverse readings represent "a variety of ancient conjectures vainly striving to heal a primitive corruption" (*The Text of the Epistles,* p. 16), and he may well be right. As F. F. Bruce says, however, the sense is plain enough: "the good news had to be appropriated or assimilated by faith if it was to bring any benefit to the hearers."
63. Πιστεύσαντες.
64. Note the present tense, εἰσερχόμεθα: we have not yet entered God's rest in its fulness, but we are "already in process of entering" (Montefiore).

verse 4 explains, to the completion of the works of creation, after which *God rested on the seventh day* (Gen. 2:2). It is noteworthy, as Bengel observes, that Moses mentions an end of each of the first six days, but not of the seventh day—or, as Herveus puts it, that all the previous days had an evening, whereas the seventh day does not have an evening. God's rest, then, is already, and has been since the creation of the world, a reality, and it is future only in relation to the consummation promised to his people, who have yet to enter into it.

The seemingly vague *somewhere* which introduces this Genesis quotation has already been encountered in 2:6 above (see the commentary there). As Aquinas explained long since, it is used here to signify a text that is well known. In the nature of the case, it could hardly betoken uncertainty as to the text's location on our author's part, and there is no necessity for him to give his readers, well versed as they were in the Scriptures, a specific identification of the passage's source. Aquinas is a less reliable guide, however, when he assumes the role of numerologist and advises us that six is the first perfect number, since it is compounded variously of the parts one, two, and three. Thus one times six equals six, three times two equals six, two times three equals six, and one plus two plus three equals six; from which the conclusion is drawn that the perfection or completion of things is designated by the number six, and "after perfection (or completion) rest is promised." Of course, this kind of numerical juggling, which had a special appeal for the medieval mind, really proves nothing, and is ill suited to sane biblical exegesis, smacking as it does of esoteric sophistry. (The numbers four and five are conveniently left out of the reckoning, though it is also a fact that six is compounded of four plus two and of five plus one—not, however, that it was beyond the ingenuity of the scholastic mind to assign a special significance to these combinations as well.) In saying this, however, there is no wish to detract from the solid and impressive character of Aquinas' expository labors, for this is no more than a minor and incidental error of judgment. In this respect he was a man of his age.

4:6–8. *Since therefore it remains for some to enter it, and those who formerly received the good news failed to enter because of disobedience, again he sets a certain day, "Today," saying through David so long afterward, in the words already quoted, "Today, when you hear his voice, do not harden your hearts." For if Joshua had given them rest, God would not speak later of another day.*

The argument proceeds with reference to two stages in the sequence of the history of Israel: (1) the fact that *those who formerly,* in the

time of Moses, *received the good news*[65] of the rest that God had prepared
for his people *failed to enter because of disobedience* does not mean that
God's purpose of bringing his people to this rest has been frustrated and
therefore abandoned, but, on the contrary, that *it remains for some* (persons other than those excluded) *to enter it;* and (2) the fact that *long
afterward,* centuries after Moses' day, God *through David* demarcates[66] *a
certain day* as *"Today"* indicates, further, that the promised rest was still
remaining, unentered, when Psalm 95 was composed. Should anyone
object that a new generation entered into the rest of the land of Canaan
under the leadership of Joshua, the reply is given that if this had been
the rest intended, then *God would not speak later* (in Ps. 95) *of another day.*
This method of argument takes on added force when it is remembered
that when Psalm 95 was written the Israelites were settled in the land of
Canaan, so that the conclusion that a rest other than and beyond that of
Canaan was intended becomes all the more obvious—and it is confirmed
in the course of the subsequent history of the people when they are
expelled and alienated from that territory. What our author is saying is
that God's promise of rest did not and does not have a merely earthly
fulfilment, but is rather eschatological in purport, and therefore still
awaits the people of God in all its fulness. And this accords perfectly
with the insistence later in this epistle (11:13–16, 35; 12:18ff.) that the
expectation of God's people has never been tied to material or earthly
objects, "for here we have no lasting city, but we seek the city which is
to come" (13:14). Hence the propriety of the manner in which our author
here, many centuries again after the Psalmist's day, continues to treat
the promised rest, in its consummating fulness, as future and as a constant hope and incentive for the Christian pilgrim.

> 4:9, 10. *So then, there remains a sabbath rest for the people of God; for whoever
> enters God's rest also ceases from his labors as God did from his.*

The conclusion drawn from the argument which precedes is that
there remains a rest, now described as a *sabbath rest, for* those who
genuinely are *the people of God.* The expression "sabbath rest"[67] links the

---

65. Οἱ πρότερον εὐαγγελισθέντες resumes the terminology of verse 2, ἐσμεν εὐηγγελισμένοι καθάπερ κἀκεῖνοι, and corresponds conceptually to προευηγγελίσατο in Galatians
3:8, where Paul speaks of God having declared the evangel beforehand to Abraham.
66. Ὁρίζει, he appoints or designates in accordance with his sovereign purpose.
67. Σαββατισμός, a Greek noun formed from the Hebrew root שׁבת. It has been suggested
(by Moffatt, Spicq, and others) that the term was coined by the author of our epistle, as it is
not found prior to its occurrence here. It is more probable, however, that the noun was
current in Hellenistic Greek, and particularly in Jewish or Jewish-Christian circles such as

concept of the promised rest still more closely with the account of creation in which the seventh or sabbath day was the day on which God
rested from his labors. An interesting interpretation which appears early
in the second century in the Epistle of Barnabas (XV.4f.) and recurs
spasmodically during the succeeding centuries, finding favor also with
some of the rabbinical scholars, attempts to explain the sabbath rest in a
chiliastic manner. The principle of this interpretation, among Christian
authors, is taken from the affirmation of 2 Peter 3:8 that "with the Lord
one day is as a thousand years, and a thousand years as one day" (cf. Ps.
90:4). Accordingly, the period between the creation and the parousia or
return of Christ is envisaged as a succession of six days of a thousand
years each, culminating in the seventh day or sabbath of Christ's millen-
nial reign. This in turn is to be followed by the ultimate sabbath, the
eighth day which eternally prolongs and consummates the blessings of
the seventh-day rest, a day which dawns but has no evening.

The New Testament, however, affords no valid sanction for a mil-
lennial perspective of this kind. The "sabbath rest" mentioned here is
"not of this creation" (cf. Heb. 9:11), but is the rest of the new heaven
and the new earth which are transposed into the eternity of God and
partake of his unending rest; it is reserved for those whom our author
designates, in covenant terminology, "the people of God" (cf. Jer. 31:33
quoted in 8:10 below), that is to say, those "who believe" and by divine
grace are constituted "a chosen race, a royal priesthood, a holy nation,
God's own people" (1 Pet. 2:7, 9), "the Israel of God" (Gal. 6:16; cf.
3:25ff.; Rom. 9:6f.), the "remnant chosen by grace" (Rom. 11:5). Moreover, to enter *God's rest* means, as the term itself indicates, to cease from
one's labors, just as on the seventh day *God did from his*. Thus in Revelation 14:13 the dead who die in the Lord are pronounced blessed inasmuch as they rest from their labors. There, in the presence of God, says
Peter Lombard, "we shall be at rest and we shall see, we shall see and
we shall love, we shall love and we shall praise. Behold what will be in
the end without end; for what other end is ours than to come to the
kingdom of which there is no end."

It would of course be mistaken to infer that the everlasting rest of
God's people implies an eternity of inactivity. The labors from which
God rests are the works of creation; but he continues to be active in
providence, in judgment, and in grace. And the labors from which the
people of God rest in the heavenly sabbath are the toilings, trials, and

---

the one to whom this epistle was addressed. The likelihood of this is enhanced by the fact
that the cognate verb σαββατίζειν, from which σαββατισμός is formed, occurs in the LXX
on a number of occasions. The further fact that the noun σαββατισμός is also used by the
pagan author Plutarch (d. A.D. 120) points to the same conclusion (*Moralia* 166a).

tribulations of their present pilgrimage; otherwise the sabbath rest will be for them an eternity of joyful service and unclouded worship performed to the glory of him who is their Creator and their Redeemer. The nature of this sabbath rest is nowhere more sublimely described than in Revelation 7:9ff., where the innumerable multitude of the redeemed is composed of those who have come out of great tribulation and who now stand before the throne of God, praising him and serving him ceaselessly in his temple, free at last and forever from hunger, thirst, tears, and every other form of distress. Well may Augustine pray:

> Lord God, grant us peace . . . the peace of rest, the peace of the sabbath, the peace without an evening. All this most beautiful array of things, all so very good, will pass away when all their courses are finished—for in them there is both morning and evening. But the seventh day is without an ending, and it has no setting, for thou hast sanctified it with an everlasting duration. After all thy works of creation, which were very good, thou didst rest on the seventh day, although thou hadst created them all in unbroken rest—and this so that the voice of thy Book might speak to us with the prior assurance that after our works . . . we may find our rest in thee in the sabbath of life eternal.[68]

4:11. *Let us therefore strive to enter that rest, that no one fall by the same sort of disobedience.*

The verb translated *strive* here[69] means to make haste, to be in earnest, to concentrate one's energies on the achievement of a goal. Thus this exhortation incites the recipients of the letter to display a spirit of zeal which is the exact opposite of the spirit of unconcern that proved so disastrous for their forefathers in the wilderness and to which they themselves are in danger of capitulating (cf. 10:35f., 39; 12:12 below). *That rest* of which the author has been speaking is not something to be trifled with; it calls for full seriousness and intensity of application on the part of those who wish *to enter* into its enjoyment. The issue is eternal in its consequences, for the sole alternative to entry is exclusion. Hence the need to be serious and, like the apostle Paul, to stretch out for what lies ahead and press toward the goal of God's heavenly rest (Phil. 3:13f.). Charles Simeon used to say, when he looked on the portrait of Henry Martyn who as a young man burned himself out for the gospel in distant lands: "There, see that blessed man! What an expression of countenance! No one looks at me as he does; he never takes his eyes off me,

---

68. Augustine, *Confessions* xiii.35f.
69. Σπουδάζειν.

and seems always to be saying, 'Be serious—be in earnest—don't trifle—don't trifle!'"[70]

Once again, as in the opening verse of the chapter ("let us fear"), the author associates himself with his readers by the use of the first-person plural, *let us . . . strive*, thus expressing his oneness with them in Christ and in effect issuing a warning not only to them but to himself as well. His prayer is that *no one* (here too repeating the structure of verse 1, "lest any one of you") should *fall by the same sort of disobedience*, suggesting again that it was a few rather than all who seemed to be in danger of imitating the evil example of the wilderness generation, but with the awareness at the same time that a little leaven is sufficient to leaven the whole lump. *Disobedience*[71] led to the downfall of the Israelites of old, and this is true of all in every generation who disregard God's will and despise his covenant. Christ's teaching of his apostles in the upper room was to precisely the same effect when he warned them that as a branch cannot bear fruit unless it abides in the vine, so the life that does not abide in him is unblessed and unfruitful, for separated from him it is capable of nothing, but, like a worthless branch, withers and is thrown into the fire and burned (Jn. 15:1ff.). And the instrument with which a disobedient human branch is pruned away from him who is the True Vine is, as the next verse shows, the sharp sword of God's word.

4:12. *For the word of God is living and active, sharper than any two-edged sword, piercing to the division of soul and spirit, of joints and marrow, and discerning the thoughts and intentions of the heart.*

The logical connection, indicated by the conjunction *For*, between this verse and what precedes lies in the consideration that disobedience, mentioned at the conclusion of the previous verse, involves the notion of disobedience to a *word* that has been spoken to express the will of the speaker (in this case God). The word of God in particular can never be disobeyed with impunity precisely because it is the word *of God*, whose speaking cannot be idle and without effect. Although the title "Word" is applied elsewhere to the Son (Jn. 1:1ff.) and this identification is made here by many of the patristic[72] and medieval commentators, it is an

---

70. H. C. G. Moule, *Charles Simeon* (1892; repr. 1965, London), p. 108.

71. Ἀπειθεία. The reading ἀπιστίας is found in p[46] and several other witnesses in place of ἀπειθείας. This may be explained as due in part to the general similarity in appearance of the two words and in part to the close conceptual relationship that there is between unbelief and disobedience (cf. Heb. 3:18f. and the commentary on p. 154 above).

72. See, for example, the quotation from Athanasius in note 79 below (p. 167).

inappropriate line of interpretation within the present context. Our author, for instance, likens the word of God here to a sharp sword, but, as
Bengel observes, Christ the incarnate Word is never said to be a sword
but to wield a sword (citing Josh. 5:13; cf. also Rev. 1:16, 2:12, 19:15,
where a sharp, two-edged sword, symbolizing as here his penetrating
word, is said to issue from his mouth). Furthermore, as Montefiore
points out, the "word" (*logos*) "here has nothing to do with Hellenistic
concepts of the rational element in creation." It is the expression, communicated to man, of the will and purpose of God, the terms of his
covenant of grace, the warnings of judgment against unfaithfulness.

The divine word is, first of all, *living and active*. It is no dead letter,
no utterance lost as soon as spoken in an unresponding void. As the
word of the living God it cannot fail itself to be living. And as God is the
God who acts with power, his word cannot fail to be active and powerful.
Its effectiveness derives from its source, which is God himself, and from
its purpose, which is the will of God; and neither God nor his will is ever
subject to frustration and defeat. God's word, says Lefèvre d'Etaples, "is
not a transient and evanescent word which when uttered is immediately
diffused through the air and perishes, but it is a permanent word, not
carried off, not dispersed, not diffused, but sustaining and binding together all things." The essential character of the word of God in its
inexhaustible vitality and dynamic efficacy is clearly defined in Isaiah
55:11, where God says through his prophet: "so shall my word be that
goes forth from my mouth; it shall not return to me empty, but it shall
accomplish that which I purpose, and prosper in the thing for which I
sent it." The vigor and the potency of his word are seen in its operation
as his creating word (Gen. 1:3ff.; Heb. 11:3), his sustaining word (Heb.
1:3), and his regenerating word (2 Cor. 4:6; 1 Pet. 1:23).

God's word is described, further, as *sharper than any two-edged
sword*. This means that as the instrument of God's mighty acts it is more
powerful and penetrating than the keenest instrument devised by man.
Paul similarly calls the word of God the sword of the Spirit (Eph. 6:17),
again placing it in a category distinct from and far above any merely
human weapon. As God's sword it is double edged: it never fails to cut;
there is no blunt side to it. Otherwise the two edges have been variously
interpreted, for example, by Tertullian[73] and Augustine[74] as the two
Testaments, and by Herveus and others as denoting the twofold function of God's word in speaking of temporal as well as of eternal things.

---

73. Tertullian, *Adversus Judaeos* 9, where he writes of the sword which is "the divine word
of God, doubly sharpened with the two Testaments of the ancient law and the new law."
74. Augustine, *De Civitate Dei* xx.21: "Scripture says that the word of God is a doubly
sharp sword, on account of the two edges, the two Testaments."

Such explanations, however, are far from satisfactory. If special significance is to be assigned to the details of symbolical language—and it is a procedure which is open to some question—it would be preferable to suggest that the word of God, like a sword with two sharp edges, always cuts with one side or the other, that is to say, either in a saving or in a judging manner. Thus, on the one hand, Christ proclaims, "The words that I have spoken to you are spirit and life" (Jn. 6:63), and, on the other hand, he says of him who rejects him, "The word that I have spoken will be his judge on the last day" (Jn. 12:48). The same sword cuts both with an edge of life and with an edge of death (cf. 2 Cor. 2:15f.). With this sword Peter cut his hearers to the heart savingly on the Day of Pentecost (Acts 2:37) and shortly after pierced the consciences of another audience to their condemnation (Acts 5:33; cf. 7:54).

The *piercing* character of the word of God is such that it penetrates to the innermost depth of man's being, causing *the division of soul and spirit, of joints and marrow*. It is hardly necessary to inquire whether this means a separation of soul from spirit and of joints from marrow—in other words, a separation within both the immaterial and the physical nature of man—or of soul and spirit from joints and marrow—in other words, a separation between the immaterial and the physical aspects of his nature. Yet Alcuin and numerous other authors offer the explanation that the soul (*psyche*) is that principle of animal life which unites man to the beasts, while the spirit (*pneuma*) is the rational or intellectual faculty which lifts man above the beasts and unites him to the angels. Alcuin passes over the significance of the joints and marrow in silence, but Herveus, inconsistently making a transition from a literal to a figurative method of interpretation, suggests that the joints can be understood of the conjunctions of the thoughts and the marrow of their intentions (thus in effect postulating an equivalence with the clause that immediately follows). While, doubtless, the distinctions he proposes are not pointless (see, for example, the threefold division of spirit, soul, and body in 1 Thess. 5:23), our author is not concerned to provide here a psychological or anatomical analysis of the human constitution, but rather to describe in graphic terms the penetration of God's word to the innermost depth of man's personality. Even Luther, with his ethical interpretation, reads too much into the text when he explains that "the word of the Lord pierces even to the dividing of both joints and marrow, because it separates the limbs and marrow from evil affections, thus purifying not only the heart but also the body." The point is, rather, that no separation could be more intimate than that between soul and spirit or between joints and marrow; that, as Calvin says, "there is nothing so hard or firm in a man, nothing so deeply hidden that the efficacy of the word does not penetrate through to it."

The mention of soul and spirit and of joints and marrow, then, serves to convey effectively the notion of the extreme power of penetration of the word of God, to the very core of man's being. These elements of his constitution, further, both visible and invisible, indicate that the whole of man's nature, both bodily and spiritual, is involved in the encounter with that piercing word; for man functions as a single unified entity, in such a way that the pneumatic and the psychic cannot be dissociated from the somatic. The complex intangible personality of man is essentially an incarnate personality: were it not so, the incarnation of the Son of God for the purpose of man's redemption and the expectation of a bodily resurrection would be void of meaning.

As the word of God penetrates to the innermost recesses of man's being it does so as his "critic" or judge, *discerning*, that is, passing judgment on,[75] *the thoughts and intentions of the heart.* Nothing could be more inaccessible and intangible, humanly speaking, than the notions and motives concealed in the furthest depths of man's mind. No scalpel can dissect them, no electronic detector can discover them. Only God's word can pierce through to this intangible realm, and it does so in a manner that is both dynamic and critical. *The heart* here, of course, is not the anatomical organ, but designates, as constantly in Scripture, the central seat of human personality, the deep fount of man's life in all its aspects, spiritual, intellectual, moral, and emotional. It is here, in this radical center of human selfhood, that the word of God does its work. That is why the effects it produces are radical and critical for the being of man in its entirety. And that is why this sword of the Spirit, which the Christian is given to wield, is the most powerful weapon in the whole universe. "O thou elect blade and sharpest sword," exclaims an ancient author, "who art able powerfully to penetrate the hard shell of the human heart, transfix my heart with the shaft of thy love.... Pierce, O Lord, pierce, I beseech thee, this most obdurate mind of mine with the holy and powerful rapier of thy grace."[76]

4:13. *And before him no creature is hidden, but all are open and laid bare to the eyes of him with whom we have to do.*

This verse drives home in the plainest possible language the truth inherent in what precedes. The fact that the word of God penetrates, like a sharp sword, to the innermost center of man's selfhood means that

75. Κριτικός.
76. *Liber Meditationum* xxvii, in *Augustini Opera*, IX (Lyon, 1664), p. 299.

every single detail and aspect of the human person is fully and inexorably open to the gaze of God. There is *no creature*, [77] that is, not one single thing in the whole of creation, which is *hidden*, or, literally, unexposed, [78] *before him*. There is a natural transition from "the word of God" in the previous verse to "God" himself here, for the word of God is not only the activity of God but also his revelation of himself, whether it be in judgment or in salvation. As God is its source so also he is its fulfilment, and there is therefore the closest association between God and the word by which he effectively acts and reveals himself. "The author passes insensibly," says Spicq, "from the notion of the word of God to God himself, and finally identifies them, since the word was truly in the place of the omniscient and omnipresent God, and received its power and its qualities only from him." Clearly, as God is by his word the creator and sustainer of the whole order of creation, *all*, that is, all things, [79] which includes all men, *are open and laid bare* to him. There is not and cannot be any part of reality which is unknown or incomprehensible to him who is the source of all being and the fount of all knowledge. Every creaturely covering and pretext is stripped away. [80] There is no recess, no dark depth, that is not wide open [81] before him (cf. 1 Cor. 4:5).

This profound and solemn truth is one that man in his fallenness does not like to face: it is damaging to his self-esteem; it destroys his

---

77. Κτίσις, "creature," is used here in the same comprehensive sense as in Romans 8:39.
78. Ἀφανής.
79. Πάντα, neuter plural. "We see," says Athanasius in a comment on Hebrews 4:12f., "that he applies the name 'creature' to all things that have been brought into being; but he recognizes the Son as the Word of God who is distinct from created things. Indeed, by saying that 'all things are open and laid bare to the eyes of him with whom we have to do', he indicates that he is other than *all*" (*Contra Arianos* ii.72). In this way Athanasius uses the passage for the refutation of Arian error.
80. The Greek word translated "open" here is the adjective γυμνός, which means "naked."
81. The Greek word translated "laid bare" here is the perfect participle passive τετραχηλισμένα, found only here in biblical Greek. Its derivation from τράχηλος, "throat," is evident, and the context shows that in its current meaning it was synonymous with γυμνός (naked, open) and οὐκ... ἀφανής (not hidden, i.e., manifest). Thus the contemporary sense of the term is apparent, and that is the important thing for the semantic work of exegesis. How the verb τραχηλίζειν acquired this meaning is, however, far from clear. It has been variously explained as having originally meant to seize someone by the throat (Philo), to hang by the neck (Chrysostom), to lay a victim out supine and powerless (Theodoret), and to bend the neck back or to force the head back so as to expose the throat preparatory to administering the *coup de grâce* (Ecumenius). Hesychius explains the participle τετραχηλισμένα as meaning πεφανερωμένα, i.e., the equivalent of "laid bare" as in our English version. Aquinas, working with the Vulgate, proposes a distinction between *nuda* and *aperta*, taking the former to mean "bare" in a superficial sense and the latter "open" in depth (*quia nihil est ita occultum in re, quod Dei cognitionem effugiat*); but a refinement of this kind is difficult to justify. The opinion of Delitzsch is that "τραχηλίζειν, which undoubtedly means to seize by the throat and throw back the head, receives here its secondary meaning from the context, without needing any archeological illustrations."

proud pretensions to wisdom and competence; and it discloses the futile superficiality of all the elaborate defenses which he seeks to erect against God (cf. 2 Cor. 10:4f.). But God sees all things, as man never can, in the ultimate light of their undisguised reality; his gaze penetrates beneath the surface and beyond every specious façade to the radical heart of our being (cf. 1 Sam. 16:7). Indeed, a man's knowledge even of his own self is faulty and inadequate; and wisdom begins in his recognition of this fact and in the prayer that God therefore will search him and know him and reveal to him the true depths of his depravity and also the wonders of divine grace (cf. Ps. 139). The man who acknowledges that he is now and that he will be hereafter "naked and exposed to the eyes of the One with whom we have to reckon" (NEB),[82] and that the discernment of God is always without error and his judgment righteous and equitable (Isa. 11:3f.), is a man who is standing on the threshold of divine grace; for it is against the background of human guilt and powerlessness that the grace of God which, in Christ, brings forgiveness and victory is most particularly displayed; and it is to this theme that our author now turns.

82. In the expression πρὸς ὃν ἡμῖν ὁ λόγος the word λόγος is best understood in the sense of "account" or "reckoning," which is the sense it bears again in 13:17 below (cf. Rom. 14:12, "each of us shall give account [λόγον δώσει] of himself to God"; also 1 Pet. 4:5; Mt. 12:36; 18:23; 25:19; Lk. 16:2). Commentators have drawn attention to what appears to be an effective play on words: the λόγος, word, of God cuts through to the very depth of our being; ... with this God we have a λόγος, reckoning, to give; and the standard or reference-point of this reckoning will be precisely the word of God.

IV. CHRIST SUPERIOR TO AARON (4:14–10:18)

4:14. Since then we have a great high priest who has passed through the heavens, Jesus, the Son of God, let us hold fast our confession.

"After terrifying us, the Apostle now comforts us," comments Luther; "after pouring wine into our wound, he now pours in oil." The Christian, conscious though he rightly is of his utter inability to stand uncondemned before the judgment throne of God, should nonetheless be filled with confidence, not in himself but in Christ; for he has *a great high priest* to stand in his place and answer for him. The concept of Jesus as our high priest is resumed from 2:17–3:1, a passage which is in close correspondence with verses 14–16 here. It is not themselves but this high priest that Christians should unceasingly consider (3:1; cf. 12:2), and for three good reasons: first, because he has made propitiation for their sins (2:17; cf. 1:3); second, because he who by his own experience knows what it is to pass through the ordeal of temptation is standing by to help them win the victory in the hour of their testing (2:18); and, third, because he "has passed through the heavens" and is preparing and securing for them that eternal rest which has been promised to the people of God (3:18–4:11; cf. Jn. 14:2f.). The knowledge of these truths should be a source of unfailing encouragement to the Christian pilgrim as he perseveres to the end; and his confidence is strengthened by the further assurance that in Jesus we have a *great* high priest—that is to say, no ordinary high priest, but the high priest *par excellence*, unique in his power and supremacy.[1]

The greatness of this high priest who surpasses all others is indi-

---

1. The force of the adjective "great" (μέγας) here is indicated by the consideration that in Hebrew the title "high priest" is literally "great priest," כֹּהֵן גָּדוֹל—cf. ἱερεὺς μέγας in 10:21 (also ποιμὴν μέγας in 13:20). Thus "great high priest" signifies, as Luther explains, "the greatest of all priests," being equivalent, for the Hebrew mind, to saying, "great great-priest." So also Montefiore observes that the expression suggests "that Jesus is greater than the levitical high priests"; cf. Bengel: *"archisacerdos magnus,* major *archisacerdote levitico."*

cated by the assertion that he *has passed through the heavens:*[2] that is to say, in contrast to the high priest of the levitical order who once a year passed from the sight of the people as he took the blood of atonement into the earthly sanctuary, Jesus, our great high priest, at his ascension passed from the sight of the watching apostles as he entered once for all into the heavenly sanctuary, there to appear on our behalf (Acts 1:9; cf. Heb. 8:1ff., 9:11ff. and 24ff., where this theme is developed more fully). Our author is speaking of something far more than a spatial journey, like that of some cosmonaut: his language is that of transcendence. Not only did Jesus *ascend,* but in doing so he completely *transcended* all the limits of time and space. His transcendence guarantees his uniqueness, his greatness.

Alcuin sees a contrast at this point between Moses and Jesus. "Moses, the leader of the people to whom a transitory rest was promised," he writes, "did not enter into the rest which he frequently promised the people." This was also true, of course, of Aaron, their high priest. "But our priest," Alcuin continues, "is the sponsor of a better promise, and, opening the way for those who believe in him, he first entered into the rest promised to the people who belong to him"—a rest which is not transitory but eternal.

The competence of him who is our great high priest as redeemer and mediator is assured by the fact that he is both *Jesus,* the son of Mary, and also *the Son of God:* the incarnate Son, being both truly man and truly God, is alone qualified to bridge the gulf between sinful man and his holy Creator. "The two titles are placed side by side," Westcott says, "in order to suggest the two natures of the Lord which include the assurance of sympathy and power." As divine, he is one with God; as incarnate, he is one with man; and as God-man, he is competent to accomplish the great work of reconciliation whereby harmony between God and man is re-established. The Son of God came to our aid in the incarnation in order that as our fellow man he might take our place on the cross and then by his resurrection, ascension, and glorification open the way for us into the presence of God himself.

It is perhaps necessary to emphasize that it is *Jesus* who has passed through the heavens as our transcendent Lord—the same Jesus who was born in Bethlehem and died at Calvary. The identity between the one who walked in Palestine and the one who is now crowned with glory and honor is essential for the ultimate glorification of our re-

---

2. It is unnecessary to detect here, as, for example, Spicq does, an allusion to the rabbinical doctrine of a series of seven heavens. The plural usage, οὐϱανοί, is best explained as an assimilation to the Hebrew word for "heaven," שָׁמַיִם, which is plural in form, and in the New Testament it occurs interchangeably with the singular form of the noun, οὐϱανός.

deemed humanity. There is no place in the New Testament for any docetic concept of the risen Christ. Resurrection means bodily resurrection or it means nothing at all. Provided, then, with this exalted high priest who is at one and the same time Jesus and the Son of God, no exhortation could be more logical than our author's here that we should *hold fast our confession*. And, contrariwise, nothing could be more senseless than for us to abandon our confession because of the enticement of teachings foreign to the gospel or because of the pain of the contest (cf. 12:1ff.; 13:9). Yet this was precisely what the recipients of this letter were in danger of doing, as we have already seen. Hence the need for the earnest repetition of this exhortation throughout the epistle: "we are his house if we hold fast our confidence and pride in our hope . . . we share in Christ if only we hold our first confidence firm to the end . . . let us hold fast the confession of our hope without wavering . . . do not throw away your confidence . . . let us run with perseverance the race that is set before us . . . lift your drooping hands and strengthen your weak knees" (3:6, 14; 10:23, 35; 12:12). The "confession" we are to hold fast is the same as that mentioned in 3:1 above: it is the belief that is both inwardly entertained by the heart and outwardly professed before men. Peter Lombard describes it as "the faith of the heart together with the confession of the mouth, so that faith is present also in the mouth" (that is, in witness). Paul speaks to the same effect in Romans 10:9f., where belief in the heart and confession with the lips are closely conjoined with each other, and in 2 Corinthians 4:13, where he writes, with reference to Psalm 116:10: "Since we have the same spirit of faith as he who wrote, 'I believed, and so I spoke', we too believe, and so we speak."

4:15. For we have not a high priest who is unable to sympathize with our weaknesses, but one who in every respect has been tempted as we are, yet without sinning.

Transcendentally exalted though he is, it would be quite wrong to imagine that our great *high priest* is remote from the realities of our human experience. His involvement with us is guaranteed, as the preceding verse implies, by the fact that the glorified Lord is still Jesus, the incarnate Son: his identification with us has not ceased because he has passed into the heavenly sanctuary. There is no question of any incapacity on his part to *sympathize with our weaknesses*, for it was precisely our weaknesses that he embraced and made his own when he took our nature upon himself. The purpose of his coming was, in fulfilment of the prophecy of the messianic servant, to make our weaknesses his own (Mt. 8:17; Isa. 53:4). Thus his humanity was not a pretense or a mas-

querade; and the reality of the temptations he endured follows from the
reality of the human nature he assumed.

Temptation itself is neutral: to be tempted indicates neither virtue
nor sinfulness; for the proper connotation of temptation is testing, or
proving, and virtue is in the resistance and overcoming of temptation,
whereas sin is in yielding and capitulation. Our high priest's experience
of temptation corresponded *in every respect* to ours. From first to last he
was being put to the test, whether by enticements to self-concern, popular acclaim, and ambition for power when assailed by Satan in the
wilderness (Mt. 4:1ff.), or by the temptation in the garden to draw back
rather than go through the dreadful ordeal that lay before him (Mt.
26:38ff.), or by the taunt hurled at him even as he hung in agony on the
cross: "If you are the Son of God, come down from the cross" (Mt.
27:40ff.). Were the recipients of this letter being tempted to lapse into
apostasy (6:4ff.; 10:29ff.)? Their high priest knew this temptation too, for
relentlessly, in the wilderness and at Gethsemane and Calvary and even
through the lips of Simon Peter, who had acknowledged him to be "the
Messiah, the Son of the living God," Satan tempted him to abandon his
mission by turning aside from the shame and scandal of the cross (Mt.
16:16, 21–23). To have succumbed to these inducements would have
been the sabotage of our salvation and a failure of trust and obedience
on his part—in other words, an act of apostasy. His whole life on earth
was one of testing and proving: thus he spoke of the members of the
intimate circle of the apostles, when Calvary was approaching, as those
who had continued with him in his temptations (Lk. 22:28). And not
only has he led the way to victory through temptation, but in doing so
he has also gained the profoundest fellow feeling for our weaknesses, at
the same time demonstrating that our human frailty is the opportunity
for the power of God and for the triumph of his grace (2 Cor. 12:9f.).

That our high priest did not merely survive the severe testing
through which he passed but was in fact completely victorious over
every single temptation is made plain by the addition of the phrase *yet
without sinning.*[3] The implications of this qualification are highly signifi-

3. Philo could also speak of the sinlessness of the high-priestly Logos, but how totally
different is his incorporeal and ethereal Logos from the Word who became flesh and dwelt
among us of the Christian gospel (Jn. 1:1, 14)! What could the former possibly know of
human temptation? "Philo, too, suggests that the *Logos* as high priest should be sinless (*De
Spec. Leg.* i.230)," observes Montefiore; "but then Philo's *Logos* had no experience of the
frailties inherent in adult existence." To have this fellow feeling he must be fellow man,
and as such tempted in the same way as we are tempted. Peter Lombard's comment is to
the point: "A man who has had no experience of affliction, and who has not endured
everything in his own senses, cannot possibly know the affliction of the afflicted. But
Christ knows it, not just because as God he knows all things, but because as man he has
endured the same things as we endure."

cant. For one thing, had Jesus fallen into sin by giving way to temptation he would himself have been in need of atonement, and thus at no higher level than the high priests of old for whom a sacrifice was first necessary in expiation of their own sins (Heb. 7:27), and no more competent than they were to procure eternal redemption for others. For another thing, for him, who by the offering up of himself was to be the sacrifice as well as the sacrificer, to have been stained by sin, would have incapacitated him to serve as God's Lamb without blemish or spot and rendered his offering unacceptable (cf. Jn. 1:29; 1 Pet. 1:19; Eph. 5:2). The sinlessness of Jesus, achieved by his complete conquest of temptation, was an essential prerequisite for the accomplishment of our redemption by his sacrifice of himself on the cross. As Héring remarks, "the sinlessness of Jesus does not consist in an absence of human weakness, but in an ever renewed victory over temptations." Moreover, his sinlessness meant that the temptations came to him with a sharpness far greater than is known to us whose minds and wills have become dull through frequent failures. This sinlessness, it should be stressed, is not something passive, a mere state of being, but the achievement of Christ's active conquest of temptation. Indeed, it is entirely synonymous with the complete *obedience* learned by him through all he endured, by which his *perfection* was won and established, and which fitted him to become the source of our eternal salvation (Heb. 2:10; 5:8f.; 7:26; 1 Pet. 3:18; 1 Jn. 2:1; 3:3, 5).

4:16. Let us then with confidence draw near to the throne of grace, that we may receive mercy and find grace to help in time of need.

In the levitical system that had prevailed up till the time of Christ's advent only the high priest was permitted to approach into the sanctuary of God's presence, and then only once a year, on the Day of Atonement, when he passed from sight into the holy of holies. The people, however, were excluded from the divine presence because of their sinfulness and prohibited from drawing near. But the atonement effected by Christ's sacrifice of himself on the cross opened the way that had hitherto been closed. This was dramatically symbolized by the rending of the temple curtain from top to bottom at the time of the crucifixion, indicating that through an act of divine grace access into the holiest place was now available to all the people of God (Mk. 15:38; Mt. 27:51; Heb. 10:20). The reality corresponding to this symbolic event is pressed home by our author here. Sinners are no longer commanded to keep their distance in fear and trembling, but, on the contrary, are now invited to *draw near*, and to do so *with confidence*. The passage of their great high priest through the heavens (v. 14) has opened the way for them into the presence of God himself. Christ's perfect sacrifice on their behalf has been accepted; their sins have been cancelled; united to him by faith they now have free access with him into the presence-chamber of God. And while it is still *the throne* of God's majestic sovereignty that they approach, yet it is now, on the basis of the reconciliation achieved by God in Christ, the throne *of grace*. Hence the unhesitating boldness with which we may draw near.[4]

The problem with those to whom our author is writing is that instead of drawing near they are in danger of drawing back (cf. 10:35). In the face of opposition they are showing signs of a loss of confidence and even of turning away from the faith into apostasy. The genuineness of the faith they have professed must be demonstrated by a confident approach to God at all times in Christ: to draw back is the act of the apostate. The hardness of the struggle should be an inducement to the Christian to draw near to the throne of God's grace, rather than to draw back and abandon the conflict; for just as in the tabernacle of old to enter the holy of holies was to stand before the mercy-seat, so the throne of God's grace is also his mercy-seat, with the result that in drawing near he is certain to *receive mercy* and to *find grace* which manifests itself in providing *help in time of need*, that is, help which is opportune and appropriate to the particular need of the moment.[5]

Referring to the striking contrast between the former situation, under the old covenant, when the high priest alone had access to the presence of God, and the present situation, under the new covenant, in which all who participate in Christ are invited to approach the divine presence with boldness, Spicq points out that "this is nothing less than a revolution in the fundamental conception of religion and one of the most important revelations of the epistle"; for "only Christianity can give sinful creatures the boldness to present themselves before God."

> 5:1. *For every high priest chosen from among men is appointed to act on behalf of men in relation to God, to offer gifts and sacrifices for sins.*

The logical connection with what precedes (to which the conjunction *For* points) is that fellow humanity, such as Christ took to himself in

---

4. "Our approach . . . is τῷ θρόνῳ τῆς χάριτος, for grace is now enthroned" (Moffatt).
5. It is grace which is active in sending "timely help" (NEB), χάριν . . . εἰς εὔκαιρον βοήθειαν. The mercy-seat (ἱλαστήριον) in the holy of holies is mentioned in 9:5 below; for further observations see the commentary there.

the incarnation, involving fellow feeling with our susceptibility to human weakness and temptation, is a necessary qualification for one who is to function as our high priest—though for the moment our author is speaking more generally of the qualities and duties required of *every high priest*, as a pattern to which Christ also must conform. An essential characteristic of high priesthood is that the holder of this office is *chosen from among men:* only one who is himself man is fitted to serve as the representative of his fellow men before God. No angel, for example, would be capable of assuming such an office. It is in particular as man that a high priest is qualified *to act on behalf of men.* In this connection Luther offers the appropriate admonition that "it is not enough for a Christian to believe that Christ was instituted high priest to act on behalf of men, unless he also believes that he himself is one of these men for whom Christ was appointed high priest." We see this principle in operation under the old covenant in the requirement that Moses was to take Aaron and the whole priestly company "from among the children of Israel," whom they were to represent (Ex. 28:1; Num. 8:6). The high priest's action on behalf of men, moreover, was *in relation to God.* His function, in other words, was that of a mediator, not between man and man, but as man's representative before God. This was the significance of the high priest's entry into the holy of holies, the sanctuary filled with the glory of God's presence, on the Day of Atonement: an act which portended the entry of him who is our great High Priest into the true sanctuary above after he had made peace by the blood of his cross, thus becoming the surety and mediator of a better covenant between God and man (cf. Heb. 7:22; 8:6ff.; 1 Tim. 2:5f.).

Another point of significance is suggested by the statement that every high priest *is appointed,* the passive voice implying that he does not appoint himself, and therefore that it is an office compatible with humility and service, not pride and ambition. This theme is developed in verses 4ff. below. Thomas Aquinas, fitting his remarks to the conditions of his day, comments that a high priest "is not appointed for the sake of glory, nor for the sake of amassing riches, nor for the sake of enriching his relatives"; and he adds that "if anyone inquires how he is going to profit his attitude is not pastoral but mercenary."

A primary function of a high priest, as he represents his fellow men before God, is the offering of *gifts and sacrifices.* The expression "gifts and sacrifices" is best understood here as a general description of the offerings over which the high priest officiated. There is no necessity to explain the two terms as signifying the unbloody and the bloody sacrifices respectively, as Peter Lombard, Delitzsch, Westcott, Teodorico, and numerous other commentators have wished to do; for in 8:4 below the single term "gifts" is used in a comprehensive sense of all the priestly offerings (cf. Mt. 5:23), and is evidently synonymous with the "gifts and sacrifices" mentioned in the preceding verse, which repeats what is said in the verse now before us (cf. also Heb. 9:9).[6] The two words, in fact, have a wide range of connotation in the Old Testament, and they present two different aspects of the same thing: the offering which was sacrificed, whether animal or vegetable, bloody or unbloody, was first brought as a gift, so that it was both a gift and a sacrifice.

Particularly important is the purpose of these gifts and sacrifices: they were offered, our author states, *for sins*. In saying this there is little doubt that he has especially in mind all that was done by the high priest on the Day of Atonement, specifically related as it was to the expiation of the sins of all the people (Lev. 16). The high priest was something far more than a cultic or liturgical specialist. His office was concerned, above all, with the radical problem of human sinfulness and the need of the people for reconciliation with God. This was the intent of all his sacerdotal actions, which reached their highest expression on that one day in the year when the sins of the people were confessed over the head of the scapegoat and the blood of sacrifice was sprinkled on the mercy seat within the holy of holies for the purpose of making an atonement, "because of the uncleanness of the people of Israel, and because of their transgressions, all their sins" (Lev. 16:16).

5:2, 3. *He can deal gently with the ignorant and wayward, since he himself is beset with weakness. Because of this he is bound to offer sacrifice for his own sins as well as for those of the people.*

There is a correspondence between what is said in 4:15 above with specific reference to Jesus as our "great high priest," that he is able "to sympathize with our weaknesses," and what is said here about the high-priestly office in general, that its incumbent *can deal gently*[7] with those for whose sakes he ministers, *since he himself is beset with weakness*. Sympathy, or compassion, and gentleness in dealing with others go

---

6. Moffatt (who is followed by F. F. Bruce) observes that "the phrase recurs in *Ep. Aristeas* 234 (οὐ δώροις οὐδὲ θυσίαις) and is a generic term for sacrifices or offerings, without any distinction."

7. The verb μετριοπαθεῖν was used in the Aristotelian philosophical tradition in the sense of to moderate one's feelings or passions and so to avoid excesses either of enthusiasm or of impassivity, the latter of which (ἀπάθεια) was cultivated by the adherents of Stoicism. Here, however, the sense is to moderate one's attitude toward others, that is, to treat with magnanimity instead of severity. Our version (RSV), to "deal gently with," and NEB, to "bear patiently with," bring out the sense well. Μετριοπαθεῖν occurs only here in biblical Greek.

together; and this compassionate gentleness springs from a community of weakness. As we have seen, the weakness Christ experienced in his human nature, which is the basis of his fellow feeling with us in our weakness, displayed itself in the temptations with which he had constantly to do battle and in the pain and suffering he endured, culminating in the experience of the ultimate weakness of death (2:9, 10, 14, 17, 18; 4:15). Our author, however, is now speaking of that weakness which is the consequence not so much of human nature as of human depravity. The weakness which results from the fallenness of man explains the need for the levitical high priest *to offer sacrifice for his own sins as well as for those of the people*,[8] and this is a weakness in which Christ did not share, for, as we have already seen (4:15), he was without sin, and consequently was under no necessity to offer sacrifice for himself (see 7:26f. below).

That Christ did not share in our sinfulness does not in any degree invalidate this fellow feeling for us and with us in our weakness. The common ground with us was that of his fellow humanity which was subject to temptation or testing. The difference between him and us is that he unfailingly overcame temptation, whereas we have been overcome by temptation. For him to have been our fellow in defeat would have been of no worth to us. The levitical high priests were sinners and therefore in need of atonement no less than the people on whose behalf they ministered. Hence the imperfection of that system with its constantly repeated sacrifices which could never take away sins and cleanse the conscience (cf. Heb. 10:1–11). What we, and they, needed was not a fellow loser but a winner; not one who shares our defeat but one who is able to lead us to victory; not a sinner but a savior. For Jesus to have been our companion in evil would have vitiated his high priesthood and rendered him no more capable of being our redeemer than were the high priests of old. By reason of its very inadequacy, the old order awaited the appearance of the perfect and final high priest who would offer up

---

8. The present tense of the verb ὀφείλει should be noticed: the high priest "is bound or obliged" to offer sacrifice for his own as well as the people's sins. This may be no more than the statement of a general truth; but the accumulation of occurrences of the present tense in connection with the function of the high priest and the levitical worship throughout the epistle would seem to imply rather definitely that the levitical system was still in operation when this epistle was written. If so, the temple would still have been standing, and this in turn would indicate a date for this epistle prior to A.D. 70. Cf. the string of present tenses in verses 1–4 here: λαμβανόμενος... καθίσταται... προσφέρῃ... μετριοπαθεῖν δυνάμενος... περίκειται... ὀφείλει... προσφέρειν... λαμβάνει... κακούμενος. (See Introduction, pp. 30ff.)

The expression προσφέρειν περὶ ἁμαρτιῶν is virtually a technical expression meaning "to offer a sin offering," since the phrase περὶ ἁμαρτιῶν, or more frequently the singular περὶ ἁμαρτίας, stands for the sin offering in the LXX. See, for example, Leviticus 16:25, and cf. note 60 below (p. 397) on περὶ ἁμαρτίας in 10:6.

the perfect and final sacrifice—perfect because, not now the inadequate offering of some dumb and uncomprehending beast, it is the fully equivalent offering of his own unblemished and victorious self, as our fellow man, and final because it avails for all sin and for all eternity. (See also the commentary above on 2:18 and 4:15.)

Those with whom the high priest is competent to deal gently are described here as the *ignorant and wayward*, that is to say, those who have sinned whether through offending in ignorance of the divine law or through wandering away from the path of the will of God which has been set before them. The perversity of the human heart is such that, even if it should be possible for a person to be free from sins of waywardness, yet no man can claim to be free from sins of ignorance or inadvertency. (See Lev. 4 for the sacrifices prescribed in the levitical system for those who sinned unwittingly.) Atonement is necessary for sins that are both known and unknown, if man is to be fully delivered from the power of evil. It was, then, for the ignorant as well as the wayward that the offerings and sacrifices of the Old Testament were instituted. Belonging to a category quite distinct from them were those persons who sinned presumptuously or "with a high hand" and who, because they thereby wilfully excluded themselves from the grace and blessing of God, were ordered to be cut off from among his people (Num. 15:27ff.; cf. Ps. 19:13). For such there is no offering prescribed, or prescribable: they are beyond recall. The high priest's atoning sacrifice was offered, accordingly, for all the sins of the people except the sin of rebellion or apostasy, which was a defiant renunciation of the divinely given covenant. And this was the irremediable sin which those to whom this epistle is addressed were in danger of committing: hence they are warned that to return to unbelief is to fall away from the living God, that there is no possibility of restoration for those who have committed apostasy, and that there remains no sacrifice for sins if they sin deliberately after receiving the knowledge of the truth (3:12; 6:4–6; 10:26).

5:4–6. *And one does not take the honor upon himself, but he is called by God, just as Aaron was. So also Christ did not exalt himself to be made a high priest, but was appointed by him who said to him, "Thou art my Son, today I have begotten thee"; as he says also in another place, "Thou art a priest for ever, after the order of Melchizedek."*

The implication of verse 1, namely, that a high priest, since he is "chosen" and "appointed," does not select himself or seize this office as it were by violence, is now expounded, first of all by the negative assertion that he *does not take the honor upon himself,* and then by the positive assertion that *he is called by God.* The appointment, properly understood, is dependent on the calling of God: it is not a human institution but a divine vocation. This principle is illustrated by reference to Aaron (*just as Aaron was*), the first of the long line of levitical high priests, who was installed by Moses in accordance with instructions received from God (Ex. 28:1ff.). The divine appointment of Aaron was confirmed, moreover, at the time of the revolt of Korah, Dathan, and Abiram who accused him of having exalted himself to a position of prominence and whom Moses rebuked with these words: "It is against the Lord that you and all your company have gathered together; what is Aaron that you murmur against him?" (Num. 16:11). Subsequently, the sprouting of Aaron's rod alone among the rods of the leaders convinced the rebellious Israelites that he was indeed the man whom God had chosen and not one who had arrogated the high priesthood to himself (Num. 17:1ff.; cf. Heb. 9:4).

Spicq suggests that our author may have had in mind the leading sacerdotal families of Jerusalem in his day, who were not descendants of Aaron, but had sought for themselves the high-priestly office and been elevated to it by Herod the Great. Such men, though approved by the state, were not approved by God. Their appointment accordingly was invalid and debasing in its effect on true religion, for their spirit was one of ambition and arrogance instead of humility and self-effacement. Herveus relates what is said here in verse 4 to the abuses of his day, as follows: "Those who are eager to seize ecclesiastical honours to which they have not been divinely called are struck down by this statement; for he who puts himself forward and seeks his own glory does not achieve honour if he becomes a bishop or prelate in the church, but usurps a right that does not belong to him and makes plunder of the grace of God; and therefore he receives not blessing but cursing." Luther also offers some pointed comments: "The office of a bishop is nothing if it be not a work—and, moreover, a 'good work,'" he says, with 1 Timothy 3:1 in mind, "not a life of idle luxury. The others who climb to the top, and let us be honest about it, in the desire for a life of idleness and pleasure and high office—nay rather who lust after these things—these are they who 'take the honour upon themselves.'"

So also, that is, in conformity with this pattern of humility and vocation, *Christ did not exalt himself to be made a high priest,* or, as the NEB renders it, "he did not confer upon himself the glory[9] of becoming high

9. This is a closer translation of οὐχ ἑαυτὸν ἐδόξασεν.

priest," but, in accordance with his calling, *was appointed* by the Father. This is the reality of the situation to which Christ himself bore consistent testimony. Thus, for example, he declared: "If I glorify myself, my glory is nothing; it is my Father who glorifies me" (Jn. 8:54). The sayings of Christ recorded in the Fourth Gospel make it emphatically plain that the glory which the Son sought with intense singleness of purpose was the glory of the Father who had sent him (Jn. 7:18; 8:42; 9:4; 10:18, 25, 38; 11:42; 12:28, 44f., 49f.; 14:7, 9, 13, 24, 31; 15:8, 23; 16:27f.; 17:1, 4ff.). Indeed, if one thing is stressed throughout the New Testament it is that, in assuming the office of savior and high priest, so far was the Son from exalting and glorifying himself that he accepted it knowing full well that it meant for him the experience of the darkest depths of humiliation, rejection, agony, and death. His office-bearing was the furthest possible remove from self-glorification. To put it colloquially, there was nothing in it for him—only the certainty of unutterable anguish and alienation and immolation suffered vicariously for our redemption.

Yet the cross of Christ is also the glory of Christ. This moment of his solitude and self-sacrifice is also the moment when he is glorified, not indeed self-glorified, but glorified because in him God is glorified and the divine purpose for the redemption of the world is now accomplished (cf. Jn. 12:23; 13:31; Heb. 10:9f.). And the awful glory of his humiliation is followed by the resplendent glory of his exaltation—not, again, self-exaltation—when, raised to the right hand of the Majesty on high, the glory of his triumphant redeemership is, so to speak, added to the glory, which he now resumes, of his eternal sonship (cf. Heb. 1:3; 2:9; 12:2; Acts 3:13; Phil. 2:5–11; Jn. 17:4f., 24).

The assertion that *Christ*, the Messiah, God's servant anointed for this high-priestly office, was assigned his appointment *by him who said to him* ... corresponds to the general statement of the preceding verse that every high priest is *called by God*. This calling of Christ is seen by our author as having been prophetically proclaimed in two passages from the Psalms, the first of which (Ps. 2:7) has already been cited as finding its full significance in him who is now enthroned on high (1:5; see commentary there), while the second (Ps. 110:4) is virtually to become the theme-text of the central part of our epistle (see 5:10; 6:20; 7:1ff., 11, 15, 17, 21). The collocation of these two messianic affirmations, namely, "*Thou art my Son, today I have begotten thee*," and "*Thou art a priest for ever, after the order of Melchizedek*," shows how closely within the perspective of the history of redemption the Sonship and the Priesthood of Christ belong together, corresponding to the combination of deity and humanity in the theanthropic person of the Mediator (though Sonship is also closely associated with the resurrection and exaltation of the incarnate Savior—see pp. 53ff. above). This union of Sonship and Priesthood was, indeed, implied in the opening paragraph of the epistle, where (1:2f.) it is precisely the Son who is spoken of as having, priestlike, "made purification for sins."

As the Son's proper dignity is to reign in glory (Ps. 110:1, cited at 1:13 above), so also, as incarnate Mediator, it is his function to officiate as high priest (Ps. 110:4). The royal and the sacerdotal offices are united in him. The author of our epistle is, in effect, emphasizing the truth that there is but *one Messiah*, unique both in his sonship and in his priesthood. By contrast, the adherents of the Dead Sea Sect looked for the coming of *two* messianic figures, a lay, royal (Davidic) personage and a priestly (Aaronic) personage. If indeed our author has the Qumran teaching in mind,[10] his instruction here and in the chapters that follow demonstrates, on the basis chiefly of Psalm 110:4, that they were wrong in two important respects: first, because there is only one messianic personage, both King and Priest, and, second, because his priestly category is that of Melchizedek, not Aaron. Of course, under the Qumran scheme a descendant of David, who belonged to the tribe of Judah, and a descendant of Aaron, who belonged to the tribe of Levi, could hardly be expected to coincide in one person. It is especially significant, then, that in the one person and category of Melchizedek, who was both king of Salem and priest of God Most High (Gen. 14:18; Ps. 110:1, 4; Heb. 7:1), there is a union of the royal and priestly functions. The significance of the priestly *order of Melchizedek* is developed at length in chapter 7. For the present, it is sufficient to mention, in the words of Westcott, that Melchizedek "represented a non-Jewish, a universal priesthood," and that "in relation to the priesthood he occupies the position which Abraham occupies in relation to the Covenant." But the immediate purpose of the two quotations given here from the Psalms is to corroborate the doctrine that Christ's high-priestly office was not from himself but from God.

5:7. In the days of his flesh, Jesus offered up prayers and supplications, with loud cries and tears, to him who was able to save him from death, and he was heard for his godly fear.

When our author speaks of Christ's *flesh* here, he means the human nature which he took to himself in the incarnation. As we have seen (2:14ff.; 4:15), the true humanity of him who is our high priest assures us of his fellow humanity and therefore of his fellow feeling, or compas-

---

10. See Introduction, pp. 13ff.

sion, with us and his sympathetic understanding of our human weakness. *The days of his flesh* designate the period during which "the Word became flesh and dwelt among us" (Jn. 1:14; cf. Gal. 2:20; Phil. 1:22, 24; 1 Pet. 4:1f.); and throughout this time on earth it was the custom of the incarnate Son to maintain fellowship with and to express his dependence on the Father by means of prayer and supplication (see Mk. 1:35; 6:46; Lk. 5:16; 6:12; Jn. 17:1ff., etc.). Alcuin, indeed, asserts that "all things that Christ did in the flesh were prayers and supplications for the sins of the human race." The *prayers and supplications* mentioned here, however, belong to a particular occasion rather than to the general practice of Christ, since they were *offered up* by him *with loud cries and tears,* that is, in a situation of extreme anguish. Furthermore, they were addressed *to him who was able to save him from death,* which implies a situation in which he was facing the prospect of death.

The occasion intended is beyond doubt that of Christ's agony in the Garden of Gethsemane, where, face to face with the awful reality of the cross, he sensed the overwhelming horror of the ordeal that lay before him and besought the Father that, if possible, this cup might be removed from him (Mk. 14:32ff.). Gethsemane saw the concentration of the compassionate anguish of the incarnate Son in the fulness of its intensity. Hitherto he had never failed to be moved to compassion in the presence of human need and affliction (Mk. 1:41; 8:2; Mt. 9:36; 14:14; 15:32; 20:34); his weeping at the tomb of Lazarus gave proof of the depth of the sympathy with which the sorrows of this world affected him (Jn. 11:33ff.); and the blind folly of the unconcern of the populace to whom he had come as deliverer drew from him cries and tears (Mt. 23:37f.; Lk. 13:34f.; 19:41ff.). But now in the Garden the moment has come, in his self-identification with mankind, to plumb human depravity and fallenness to its very depths as he prepares, in all his innocence and purity, to submit himself in the place of sinners to the fierceness of God's wrath against the sins of men. This meant an experience incomparable in the horror of its torment, from which his whole being shrank instinctively but which was inescapable if the purpose of his coming was to be achieved.

It is essential to understand the reason for this extremity of anguish. Something infinitely more than the fear of physical suffering and death is involved—though it is true that to suffer and die unjustly and in ignominy is an experience from which human flesh naturally recoils and a bitter affront to the dignity of the person. But to attribute Christ's distress in the Garden of Gethsemane, as, among others, Spicq and Teodorico do, to the fear of a painful execution is hopelessly inadequate. In the annals of human endurance there are many who, whatever their inward feelings, have faced a cruel end with calmness and courage: to interpret Christ's "loud cries and tears" as indicating a collapse of his resolution as the hour of crisis arrives not only portrays him as less admirable in this respect but also is inconsistent with the character of him to whom with one voice the Evangelists bear testimony; for the Gospels show us one who is at all times steadfast and intrepid, and not least as he repeatedly informs his disciples that a violent death awaits him in Jerusalem (Mt. 16:21ff.; 17:22f.; 20:17ff.; Mk. 8:31ff.; Lk. 9:22; Jn. 10:11, 17f.; 11:7f., 16; 16:32f.). Christ's way, from first to last, was the way of the cross (Mk. 8:34; 10:45; Lk. 9:23). He was the Lamb of God appointed for slaughter (Jn. 1:29, 36). He came to die: this was the supreme purpose of the incarnation (Heb. 2:9, 14). The cross, therefore, was the fulfilment of his mission, and he moved onward to it with an inflexible determination.

The agony of Christ at Gethsemane was occasioned by something other and deeper than the fear of physical death; for what he faced was not simply a painful death but also judgment—the judgment of a holy God against sin, *our* sin, which is the experience of the "second death" (Rev. 20:14; cf. 9:27 below), the disintegrating experience of separation from God. Hence the terrible cry of dereliction from the cross: "My God, my God, why hast thou forsaken me?" (Mk. 15:34). In a real but deeply mysterious manner, which no words of man can explain, the incarnate Son as he hung on the cross endured the desolating anguish of being torn away from his Father. He took our sins, the sins of the whole world (1 Jn. 2:2), upon himself at Calvary in order that there he might bear our judgment, the Righteous for the unrighteous (1 Pet. 2:24; 3:18). It was then, on that cross, that "God made him who knew no sin to be sin for our sake, so that in him we might become the righteousness of God" (2 Cor. 5:21). For this reason the second death has no power over those who by faith are one with him who as our Sin-Bearer endured the second death in our place; and for them the first death, which is the death of the body, holds no terror because the bodily resurrection of Jesus is the guarantee that they too will rise to everlasting life (1 Cor. 15:20; 2 Cor. 4:14). The dread with which he approached the cross is explained, as Calvin says, by the fact that in the death that awaited him "he saw the curse of God and the necessity to wrestle with the total sum of human guilt and with the very powers of darkness themselves." The "loud cries and tears" which accompanied Christ's supplication are to be understood, then, in relation to the indescribable darkness of the horror that he, our High Priest, was to pass through as, on the cross, he bore not only the defilement and guilt of the world's sin but also its judgment. At Gethsemane and at Calvary we see him enduring our hell so that we might be set free to enter into his heaven.

The description of the Father, to whom the petitions of the incarnate

Son were offered, as *him who was able to save him from death*, can, as Aquinas observes, be understood in two ways: either as meaning "him who was able to save him from the experience of dying" or "him who was able to save him by raising him from the dead." The former deliverance would, indeed, have been welcome to Christ, who naturally shrank from draining the bitter cup that was now set before him; but he who had come to do the Father's will, which involved the offering up of his body for us (10:9f. below), turned away from the temptation to avoid the cross and held fast to the purpose of his coming, as he affirmed: "My Father, if this cannot pass unless I drink it, thy will be done" (Mt. 26:42). He was, however, "saved from death" inasmuch as on the third day he rose triumphantly from the grave; and it is in this sense that *he was heard*, that is to say, his prayer was granted. Thus Herveus comments, " 'He was heard', because in the resurrection he received what he sought." The same principle of total dependence on God and devotion to his will should be characteristic of the life of every Christian, not least when he finds himself confronted with the prospect of death, as the apostle Paul learned through the affliction which prostrated him in Asia. "I felt," he writes, "that I had received the sentence of death; but that was to make me rely not on myself but on God who raises the dead" (2 Cor. 1:8f.).

The entreaty of the incarnate Son was heard, moreover, *for his godly fear*. The Greek noun translated "godly fear" here[11] means religious carefulness or concern for the honor of God, or, as Delitzsch puts it, "watchfulness over ourselves, so as to avoid whatever might displease him." The sense is well conveyed by the marginal comment of the Jerusalem Bible: "It was because the prayer of Christ in Gethsemane was a prayer of total submission to the will of his Father that it was heard and answered." The term does not denote subjective fear, or terror, whether of a physical or psychological nature, though this is the interpretation which some have wished to place on it, including Calvin, Grotius, Owen, Bengel, Zahn, Héring, and Montefiore. As it would not make sense to say, "he was heard for his fear (sc. of death)," a different translation is proposed, namely, "he was heard (in such a way that he was delivered) from fear."[12] Thus Héring asks, "In what did his being heard consist?" and answers, "In this, that he was set free from fear."

11. Εὐλάβεια. Cf. the cognate participle εὐλαβηθείς in 11:7.
12. This interpretation of εἰσακουσθεὶς ἀπὸ τῆς εὐλαβείας is forced and unnatural. The appeal to Hebrews 10:22, ῥεραντισμένοι... ἀπὸ συνηδήσεως πονηρᾶς, "sprinkled from an evil conscience," is not convincing, for while ceremonial sprinkling is closely bound up with the concept of *deliverance from* guilt (hence the rendering of our version, "sprinkled clean from"), it can hardly be maintained that hearing and deliverance are so closely connected with each other that "he... being heard was set free from fear" (the English diglot translation) is the proper sense of εἰσακουσθεὶς ἀπὸ τῆς εὐλαβείας.

Owen asserts that "fear internal and subjective is intended" and that "God relieved him against his fear, removing it and taking it away, by strengthening and comforting of him." Phillips renders it: "His prayers were heard; he was freed from his shrinking from death." But the more natural sense of the Greek is that he was heard because of[13] his godly reverence; and this accords better with the context, for his petitions were offered "to him who was able to save him from death," not from fear, and, as we have already remarked, the proof of his having been heard is his resurrection from the dead, with the consequence that he has become "the source of eternal salvation to all who obey him" (v. 9). Due consideration should be given, further, to the fact that our author uses the same Greek noun in 12:28 below (this is its only other occurrence in the New Testament), where the sentiment which is encouraged can only be reverence toward God, not a feeling of subjective fear. Indeed, there is a close parallel between that passage and this, for the admonition to "offer God acceptable worship" there corresponds to the offering up of prayers and supplications which are heard (accepted) here, and in both places there is the association with the disposition of godly reverence or solicitude.

Another view which has been advanced is that Jesus besought deliverance, not from death on the cross, but from dying in the Garden of Gethsemane.[14] Attention is drawn to the utterance of Christ in the garden, "My soul is very sorrowful, even to death" (Mk. 14:34; Mt. 26:38), and to Luke's narration that an angel appeared and strengthened him (Lk. 22:43). On this interpretation, it would be plain that the prayers and supplications of Christ were heard, because he did not die at Gethsemane. Hewitt, who favors this explanation, remarks that "no greater calamity could possibly have fallen on mankind" than for Christ to have succumbed there; and this comment calls forth the following rejoinder from F. F. Bruce: "But why? Once he had said, 'Not my will, but thine, be done', the offering up of his life at any subsequent moment must have constituted 'a ransom for many', as he had said it would (Mark 10:45)." In this respect, however, Hewitt is right, for had Christ died privately in a garden (or in his bed), or even publicly by the hand of an assassin, the true significance of his death would not have been apparent. He might have been mourned as a good man or venerated as a hero. But something more than, so to speak, mere dying was required. A judicial process leading to his condemnation, while plainly innocent, as a common criminal and his public execution as such were a necessity,

---

13. The preposition ἀπό in the expression ἀπὸ τῆς εὐλαβείας is to be understood in the sense of "arising from," "as the result of."

14. For some discussion of this view see *The Expository Times*, VI (1894–95), pp. 433f.

so that it might be seen that his death was the sacrifice of the innocent for the guilty. The cross, being both the symbol and the reality of the greatest possible shame, assures us, further, that the reconciling grace of God which flows from it reaches to the most wretched and depraved of sinners. Hence the rightness of the judgment that, had Christ died in the Garden of Gethsemane, "he could not have made atonement on the cross, and so his whole life's work would have been frustrated."[15] But the opinion that the cup which he prayed might be removed from him was that of his private and premature death in the garden is unacceptable, because it is clear throughout the Gospels that the cup he had come to drain was that of his substitutionary blood-shedding on the cross (cf. Mt. 20:22; 26:39, 42; Mk. 14:36; Lk. 22:42; Jn. 18:11). From the beginning there was but one cup, the cup of the cross, and but one way, the way of the cross, with the consequence that only he who takes up his cross and follows Christ is worthy of him (Mt. 10:38; 16:24; Mk. 8:34; Lk. 9:23; 14:27).

Another theory, remarkable only for its inappropriateness, has been suggested by Héring, who says that "the Synoptic Gospels enable us to see how Jesus could have been released from experiencing the cross" because "he could have requested the Father to take his soul to himself at that moment in Gethsemane." He adds that "it would have been a relatively pleasant death, somewhat like that of the Buddha Gautama in the gardens of Kusinara"; and he too claims the support of the utterance, "My soul is very sorrowful, even unto death," which he wishes to interpret expansively as meaning, "I am sorrowful to the point of desiring death," understood as indicating "a peaceful death at Gethsemane." Such an end would have spared Jesus the bitter experience of condemnation and crucifixion; but to stretch the text in this way is hardly conducive to sober exegesis.

5:8–10. *Although he was a Son, he learned obedience through what he suffered; and being made perfect he became the source of eternal salvation to all who obey him, being designated by God a high priest after the order of Melchizedek.*

The "godly fear" mentioned in the preceding verse manifested itself in the *obedience* of Christ, and that obedience was *learned*, that is, it was achieved as a personal reality, *through what he suffered*, for his perseverance in the performance of the Father's will, which was the purpose of his coming, meant his walking the road of suffering that led to the cross.

15. *The Expository Times, loc. cit.* See also the commentary on 2:14 above.

At Gethsemane, to which the preceding verse alludes, he wrestles with and accepts the impending and climactic suffering of Calvary, and in doing so he completes the perfection of his obedience to the will of the Father.

The astonishing thing is that he "learned obedience in the school of suffering" (NEB), *although he was a Son,* or better, as Phillips renders it, "Son though he was," understood as implying "Son of God though he was";[16] for as the holy and eternal Son of God he was under no necessity to learn obedience. It is a commonplace, as our author well knows (12:5ff.), that obedience is learned painfully by our fallen humanity, so prone to disobedience. But in this respect we are very different from him who is our High Priest, for he, as we have already seen (4:15; cf. 7:26f.), was entirely free from sin, the essence of which is disobedience, and therefore in no need of learning obedience by the discipline of painful correction. Yet, as the incarnate Son who fully shares our humanity, it was essential to his work as mediator and redeemer that he should accumulate the perfection of obedience, through his undeviating conquest of temptation, preparatory to the culminating act of his obedience on the cross, where he offered himself to the Father as a sacrifice for sinful and disobedient mankind (2:14ff.). In its furthest reference, Christ's obedience was "obedience unto death, even death on a cross" (Phil. 2:8; cf. 12:2 below). As the incarnate Son, then, it was absolutely necessary for him to learn obedience, since his obedience was essential for the offsetting of our disobedience. Accordingly, the apostle Paul teaches that "as by one man's disobedience many were made sinners, so by one man's obedience many will be made righteous" (Rom. 5:19). The coming of Christ, therefore, itself an act of obedience, meant his choosing the way of suffering; not, however, like the sinful sons of men, the suffering of painful correction, but the suffering involved in the conquest of sin, and above all the suffering of the cross where he, the obedient Son, offered himself on behalf of us who are disobedient sons (cf. 1 Pet. 3:18).

It is with reference to this suffering that Jesus was *made perfect;* indeed, what is said here is a reaffirmation of the teaching already given in 2:10 that Christ was made "perfect through suffering." This perfection was progressively achieved as he moved on toward the cross which marked the consummation of his suffering and obedience. His perfec-

---

16. The Greek reads, καίπερ ὢν υἱός. The inclusion of the indefinite article in the RSV and KJV detracts from the force of this concession; and the rendering of υἱός as "son" with a small "s," as in the NEB, gives it a merely general sense which is out of place here. "Here the remarkable thing," says Moffatt, "is that Jesus had to suffer, not because but although he was υἱός, which shows that Jesus is Son in a unique sense; as applied to Jesus υἱός means something special."

tion consisted in the retention of his integrity, in the face of every kind of assault on his integrity, and thereby the establishment of his integrity. Had he failed at any point, his integrity would have been impaired and his perfection lost, with the consequence that he would have been disqualified to act as mediator and redeemer. What was essential was that, starting, like Adam, with a pure human nature, he should succeed where Adam had failed. His sufferings both tested and, victoriously endured, attested his perfection, free from failure and defeat. This he himself dramatically declared by his triumphant utterance from the cross: "It is finished!" (Jn. 19:30), which in the light of what is said here in Hebrews may be understood as signifying, "I have retained my integrity to perfection," as well as, "My work of redemption is perfectly accomplished."[17]

The perfection, then, of the Savior's unstained manhood capacitated him to endure the ultimate suffering of the cross for us, who because of our sin are stained and defeated and in need of salvation. It is thus, the perfection of his life leading up to the perfection of his death, that *he became the source of eternal salvation*. In this affirmation, too, the thought of Hebrews 2:10 is recapitulated, for the description of Christ here as "the source of eternal salvation" corresponds to his designation there as "the pioneer of our salvation." He, and no one else, is the cause[18] of man's redemption: it is from him that it flows to us. His bearing of our imperfection, the punishment of which he endured and exhausted, made available his perfection for the rehabilitation of mankind—with the qualification, however, that the eternal salvation of which he is the source is a reality in the experience only of those *who obey him*. As Westcott observes, "continuous active obedience is the sign of real faith";[19] and this applies quite pointedly to the recipients of this letter whose obedience shows signs of wavering. Here again, then, they are being reminded, as previously they have more forcefully been reminded (cf. 2:3; 3:12ff.; 4:11), that this great salvation belongs only to those who persevere in obedience to Christ.

The "designation" of Christ as *high priest* both precedes and follows the incarnation. It precedes it in that the coming of the Son into the world was in accordance with the predetermined purpose of God for the redemption of the world—thus those who are God's redeemed people were chosen in Christ before the foundation of the world (Eph. 1:4); and

---

17. The cry from the cross, τετέλεσται, corresponds to τελειωθείς here, both verbs being formed from the same root. Moffatt suggests that there may be "a side-allusion to the death-association of these terms."
18. Greek: αἴτιος.
19. This interpretation is indicated by the present tense of the participle in the phrase πᾶσιν τοῖς ὑπακούουσιν.

it follows the incarnation in that what was before intended and anticipated is now completed, so that through his life, death, and exaltation
Christ is revealed as our great High Priest. Moreover, he is this in a
unique sense; hence the definition, in fulfilment of Psalm 110:4, *after the
order of Melchizedek,* which places him in a category quite distinct from
that of the levitical order of the old covenant. The discussion of the
important implications of this distinction is postponed, however, while
the author addresses to his readers another of the solemn admonitory
passages which are a characteristic feature of the epistle (5:11–6:19). The
fact is that their spiritual immaturity is an embarrassment to him and he
feels the necessity of attempting to arouse them from their lethargy by
warning them again in unequivocal terms of the serious dangers which
attend their present attitude. The affirmation of Psalm 110:4, already
introduced in verse 6 above, is taken up again at the end of chapter 6,
where it is followed by a prolonged exposition of the significance for the
Christian believer of the designation of Christ as our priest forever after
the order of Melchizedek.

5:11, 12a. *About this we have much to say which is hard to explain, since you have
become dull of hearing. For though by this time you ought to be teachers, you need
some one to teach you again the first principles of God's word.*

The theme which the author has just mentioned, namely, the
priesthood of Christ which belongs to, and indeed constitutes, the order
of Melchizedek, is of such importance that, understandably, he has
much to say concerning it.[20] But, unfortunately, what he wishes to communicate on this theme is *hard to explain*—not, however, because it belongs to the realm of esoteric mystery which only the enlightened few
are capable of entering (Windisch), or because the author feels himself
inadequate as an instructor, but because those to whom he is writing are
dull of hearing. This, in turn, does not suggest that the latter are in
themselves intellectually or spiritually inferior; for it is not a question of
what they are by nature but of what they have *become*[21] by default, the
implication being that this was not the case with them originally. They
have become slack, and their slackness has affected their attentiveness
and their capacity to receive and retain solid instruction. Indeed, if they

20. Montefiore prefers to take the relative pronoun in the expression περὶ οὗ as masculine,
"about whom," i.e., about Melchizedek, rather than neuter, "about which," i.e., about
this matter.
21. The perfect tense of the verb γεγόνατε conveys this sense very clearly.

do not stir themselves from their culpable inertia they may expect to find themselves, like the Hebrews of Ezekiel's day, "a rebellious house, who have eyes to see, but see not, who have ears to hear, but hear not" (Ezek. 12:2; cf. Jer. 6:10; Zech. 7:11f.). For this reason our author is conscious of the difficulty of the task which faces him as he seeks to instruct his readers in the doctrine of Christ's high priesthood.

He complains that *by this time,* that is, taking into account the considerable period of time that has elapsed since their conversion (which we may assume to be several years), they *ought to be teachers.* This should not be taken to mean that they ought all to be in official teaching positions in the church,[22] but rather that they ought by now to be sufficiently advanced in their comprehension of Christian doctrine to be able to instruct and edify those who are still young in the faith. Deplorably, however, they are so far from having maintained normal progress that they have slipped back to a stage where they are themselves in need of a teacher to instruct them *again* in *the first principles of God's word.* Their spiritual comprehension corresponds, to their shame, to that of children in the kindergarten who, unable to read or write, have to start at the very beginning by learning the ABCs.[23]

5:12b–14. *You need milk, not solid food; for every one who lives on milk is unskilled in the word of righteousness, for he is a child. But solid food is for the mature, for those who have their faculties trained by practice to distinguish good from evil.*

One who is so unadvanced that he needs to be introduced once more to the ABCs of the faith is no better than *a child*[24] in spiritual

---

22. Cf. Bengel's comment on the noun διδάσκαλοι, "teachers": "vocabulum non muneris, sed facultatis."

23. The Greek here is striking: the expression τὰ στοιχεῖα τῆς ἀρχῆς τῶν λογίων τοῦ θεοῦ means literally "the rudiments (or ABCs) of the beginning of the oracles of God" and carries the reproachful implication that those who are being addressed need to start again not even at chapter one, but, as it were, with the elements of the alphabet that precede chapter one. The phrase τὰ λόγια τοῦ θεοῦ should not be taken to mean the Old Testament scriptures here (as, for example, Westcott understands it, and as is the meaning in Acts 7:38 and Rom. 3:2), but is a description rather of the message and teaching of Christianity, which is equivalent, as the immediate context shows, to ὁ τῆς ἀρχῆς τοῦ Χριστοῦ λόγος, "the rudiments of Christianity" (NEB; literally, "the word—or instruction—of the beginning of Christ"), in Hebrews 6:1. Chrysostom takes "the first principles" to mean instruction concerning the human nature of Christ and the medieval commentators explain the phrase as a reference to the articles of the creed.

24. The noun translated "child" in our version (RSV) is νήπιος, to which the Latin *infans* corresponds exactly (literally, one unable to speak: νη+επος, *in+fari*). The rendering "infant" of the NEB is preferable; cf. "babe," KJV, "baby," JB. In 1 Corinthians 3:1 the RSV renders the plural as "babes."

understanding: *milk* is the only diet suited to his immature condition, *not* the *solid food* of sound Christian doctrine. To go on living on milk, mere baby-food, is indicative of arrested development, and the recipients of this letter have evidently failed to advance beyond, or have relapsed into, a state of spiritual infancy. Instead of being strong and well developed, they are weaklings in the faith. A comparable situation in Corinth had caused Paul to write to the Christians there in similar terms: "I, brethren, could not address you as spiritual men, but as men of flesh, as babes in Christ. I fed you with milk, not solid food; for you were not ready for it; and even yet you are not ready" (1 Cor. 3:1f.).[25] The tragic pattern was not unique even in the apostolic age, and it has repeated itself all too frequently in the subsequent centuries of the church's history.

Our author explains that the underdeveloped individual who can tolerate only a diet of milk *is unskilled in the word of righteousness.* The considerable diversity of opinion regarding the precise meaning of the expression "the word of righteousness"[26] is attributable to the wide range of senses of which the term "word" (*logos*) is susceptible in the New Testament as well as elsewhere. Some, including Delitzsch and Weiss, take the author to mean here that those whom he is addressing are incapable of correct speech, or, in other words, of the utterance of right and sound doctrine, basing their opinion on the fact that etymologically the Greek noun translated "child" in our version signifies one who is unable to speak.[27] But etymology and semantics are not at all necessarily one and the same thing, and it is most improbable that any such connection was intended by, or even occurred to, the writer of Hebrews. Others, including Chrysostom and Moffatt, understand the phrase to have an ethical connotation, signifying moral truth or right conduct and corresponding to the ability to distinguish between good and evil of which verse 14 speaks. The context seems better served, however, if, with Westcott, Windisch, Spicq, and Teodorico, we interpret the expression in a more specifically theological sense, so that "the word of righteousness" indicates the teaching about righteousness which is fundamental to the Christian faith, namely, the insistence on Christ as our righteousness (1 Cor. 1:30; cf. 2 Cor. 5:21) as opposed to self-righteousness or works-righteousness (cf. Phil. 3:9; Tit. 3:5; Gal. 2:16; Rom. 3:21ff.; Lk. 18:9ff.). As Spicq says, "the first Christian instruction

---

25. There is no necessity to conclude that the striking similarity between these two passages points to the dependence of one author on the other, for this is a common enough manner of speaking. The same metaphor is found, for example, in Philo and in Stoic writings of the period.
26. A literal rendering of λόγος δικαιοσύνης.
27. Νήπιος. See note 24 above.

involves initiation into justification by faith." It is on this foundation that the whole structure of the Christian faith is erected, and it is precisely this foundation which the Hebrew readers are in danger of despising and abandoning (see 6:4ff.; 10:29). The author is now seeking, as it were, to wean them from the debility of the milk-stage, into which they have sunk back, and bring them on to the solid diet of the doctrine of the high priesthood of Christ, who, as their Melchizedek, is the King of Righteousness (7:1f.).

Solid food, however, is for *the mature,* that is, for those who have progressed beyond the helplessness of infancy to a position of adult competence and responsibility. Within the biblical perspective, perfection belongs properly only to God, and absolute maturity, which coincides with perfection, has been achieved at the human level, as we have seen (2:10; 4:15; 5:8f.), only by the incarnate Son, Jesus Christ. Perfection is, indeed, the goal toward which the Christian should always be advancing, as our author is about to emphasize (6:1; cf. 12:1f.; Mt. 5:48), but which he will not attain until the appearance of the glorified Redeemer at the end of the age, when, seeing him as he is, the believer will at last be fully conformed to the likeness of his Lord (1 Jn. 3:2). Meanwhile the Christian's maturity is relative—relative in terms of the degree to which he has advanced from his spiritual infancy on the journey to the perfection of Christ-likeness (cf. 2 Cor. 3:18). Hence Paul's declaration: "I have not yet reached perfection, but I press on, hoping to take hold of that for which Christ once took hold of me" (Phil. 3:12 NEB). The criterion, or canon, of maturity is always the fulness of the perfection of Christ (Eph. 4:13). Those who are not being nourished and strengthened by the solid food of sound doctrine are no better than spiritual infants in danger of never reaching Christian manhood: their great need is to *grow up* into Christ (Eph. 4:15).[28]

Our author explains that the "mature" persons of whom he is speaking are *those who have their faculties trained by practice to distinguish good from evil,* in other words, Christian athletes who as the result of single-minded self-discipline and application to the contest on which they have entered are persons of spiritual sensitivity and discernment. And it is not just a hardy few but all believers who should show this

28. Westcott comments as follows regarding the sense of τέλειος ("mature") here: "A man is said to be τέλειος who has reached the full maturity of his powers, the full possession of his rights, his τέλος, his 'end'.... As compared with the child, the full-grown man is τέλειος physically, intellectually, socially (comp. 1 Cor. xiii.10f.; Gal. iv.3); as compared with the fresh uninstructed convert, the disciplined and experienced Christian is τέλειος (1 Cor. xiv.20; ii.6; Eph. iv.13; Phil. iii.15; Col. i.28; iv.12; James i.4).... He is absolutely τέλειος in whom each human faculty and gift has found a harmonious development and use, who has fulfilled the destiny of man by attaining the likeness of God (Gen. i.26)."

athletic zeal; hence the exhortation addressed to all, in 12:1 below, to run the race unencumbered and with perseverance. Like the serious athlete who trains himself so that he is in the peak of condition for the contest, the mature Christian is equipped to face responsibly the demands and endure to the end the rigors of the conflict by the habitual exercise of his powers.[29] No longer a child in the faith, his maturity is displayed in his discernment, by the use of which he is able to distinguish between what is good and what is evil. "How may our senses be exercised?" Alcuin asks; and he replies: "By the use and frequent study of Holy Scripture; just as the psalmist says that the man who meditates on the law of the Lord day and night is blessed" (Ps. 1:2).

Good and evil should not be understood merely in an ethical sense here as signifying good conduct and evil conduct, but more particularly, as the context requires, in a comprehensive theological sense, namely, of good and evil, or true and false, doctrine, which would include moral teaching. The power of discernment is something very necessary in those who are "mature" enough to be "teachers," and something to be expected of those who, like the recipients of this letter, have been members of the Christian church for a number of years.

6:1, 2. *Therefore let us leave the elementary doctrines of Christ and go on to maturity, not laying again a foundation of repentance from dead works and of faith toward God, with instruction about ablutions, the laying on of hands, the resurrection of the dead, and eternal judgment.*

The conjunction *Therefore* indicates that there is a close link in thought and logic with the preceding passage: the author has rebuked his readers for their arrested growth as Christians, of which their spiritual immaturity and dullness of comprehension and discernment are symptomatic; now he exhorts them to do something about it, to shake themselves out of their torpor and to grow up into intelligent and

---

29. The noun translated "faculties," τὰ αἰσθητήρια, means the faculties or senses of perception, here used metaphorically of spiritual sensitivity. These faculties are developed through use and training, the perfect participle passive γεγυμνασμένα which qualifies τὰ αἰσθητήρια being borrowed from the vocabulary of the athletic contests; and the noun ἕξις, "practice," from the same root as the verb ἔχω, corresponds to the Latin *habitus* (*habeo*): habitual training builds up fitness for the contest. Affinities that have been pointed out between the language of this passage and that of Greek philosophy and the pagan mysteries are affinities of vocabulary only, not of substance. In the latter, for example, τέλειος describes the initiate, whereas in the Christian perspective the initiate is no more than νήπιος, one who becomes τέλειος only in the ultimate (eschatological) completion of his redeemed manhood in the perfection of Christ-likeness.

energetic adulthood, lest the curse of God, instead of his blessing, should rest on them. *The elementary doctrines of Christ* correspond to "the first principles of God's word," and the incitement to *go on to maturity* follows on what has been said of those who are "mature," in verses 12 and 14 respectively of the previous chapter. Our author now openly confronts those whom he is addressing with the challenge which was implicit in the reproaches of 5:11–14; but he does so in no spirit of pharisaical self-righteousness, for, good instructor that he is, he identifies himself with them and invites them to join with him in united progress as (appealing to them in the first-person plural) he says in effect, "Let *us* move forward together." This sense of community in progress is intensified in the Greek text by the fact that the expression translated in our version as "let us go on" means literally "let us be carried forward,"[30] suggesting that it is not a matter of the learners being carried by their instructor, but of both being carried forward together by God.[31] Paul speaks to the same effect in Romans 8:14 when he declares that "all who are led by the Spirit of God are sons of God"; and Peter, using the same verb as our author uses here,[32] asserts that the prophets of old were "moved by the Holy Spirit" (2 Pet. 1:21). The energy, hidden and inward, of the Holy Spirit is the true dynamic of spiritual growth: where evidence of Christian development and progress to maturity is lacking it must be doubted whether there has been a genuine experience of the Holy Spirit's activity. Hence the extremely solemn character of the warning which is about to be offered (vv. 4–8). At the same time, however, our author is convinced that the gospel seed has fallen into good ground and will produce a harvest to the glory of God, though not necessarily in the case of every one of those to whom he is writing. Where there is a true experience of the work of God, it is a work which, precisely because it is of God, cannot fail or come to nothing. As Owen somewhat quaintly expresses it, "then if the holy gales of the Spirit of God do breathe on us, are we in a blessed tendency towards perfection."

To *leave* the elementary doctrines does not mean to despise or abandon them any more than a pupil who has learned the ABCs can then dispense with the alphabet. The letters of the alphabet are indispensable in the formulation and communication of the most advanced learning; for progress to maturity is always cumulative. So, also, the first principles of Christian truth are basic to every stage of development and are

---

30. Φερώμεθα ἐπί.

31. In other words, φερώμεθα should be interpreted as a divine passive, implying the agency of God. "He says 'let us be carried', and this refers to being impelled by the Holy Spirit" (Thomas Aquinas).

32. The Greek reads: ὑπὸ πνεύματος ἁγίου φερόμενοι.

no less essential at the end than they are at the beginning. The point is that the beginning is not a stopping-place; it is the door to progress and the springboard to achievement.

The "elementary doctrines of Christ," or, literally, "the word (or instruction) of the beginning of Christ,"[33] from which the readers are being exhorted to advance, may best be understood as referring to the first simple presentation of the gospel message. What this involves is well illustrated by the content of Peter's address to a Hebrew audience on the Day of Pentecost (Acts 2:22ff.). The central thrust of his proclamation is the presentation of Jesus as Messiah and Lord, in whom the Scriptures find their fulfilment, whose death was in accordance with the redemptive purpose of God, and who is now risen and exalted over all. This message evokes the response of repentance, faith, and baptism. For the three thousand persons who professed conversion on that occasion it was the starting-point of the Christian life. But ahead of them stretched the road to spiritual maturity. Hence the important additional information that from then on"they devoted themselves to the apostles' teaching and fellowship, to the breaking of bread and the prayers" (Acts 2.42), and hence, also, the more advanced instruction in Christian truth conveyed by the epistles of the New Testament which, as the repositories of the apostles' teaching, constitute a veritable school of theology. By their neglect of this further instruction those to whom this

33. Ὁ τῆς ἀρχῆς τοῦ Χριστοῦ λόγος. Writing on "Exegesis of Hebrews vi.1f." in NTS, 13 (July 1967), pp. 378ff., J. C. Adams contends that τοῦ Χριστοῦ should be interpreted as a subjective rather than as an objective genitive, so that the expression means "the original teaching of Christ" as something distinct from the salvation he accomplished. The readers, he explains, "have accepted the message of Jesus, but not his person and work." They represent a point of view in primitive Christianity "which placed great emphasis on the teaching of Jesus"; and this teaching "can without difficulty be seen as consistent with the Jewish religion." Adams claims that in none of the six rudiments of the faith mentioned here (repentance, faith, washings, laying on of hands, resurrection, judgment) "is there any reference to anything specifically Christian," and that "they are in fact all part of the faith of a Jew." The readers, then, are being exhorted to leave behind them the original teaching of Christ, which on this interpretation is one and the same with the basics of the Jewish faith. But it is quite contrary to the attitude of the writers of the New Testament to regard the teaching of Christ, or any part of it, as no better than common Jewish beliefs and therefore dispensable. The very thought would have been shocking to the apostolic mind. And the assertion that there is nothing specifically Christian in any of the elements listed here is surely to beg the question; for if our author is speaking of Christian repentance, faith, etc., then the list is indeed specifically Christian. It would no doubt be attractive, and ease some of the exegetical problems of the passage, if the readers are being encouraged to abandon beliefs that are distinctively Jewish rather than Christian; but it is impossible to believe that "the elementary doctrines of Christ" (whether the genitive τοῦ Χριστοῦ is taken as objective or subjective) can be anything but specifically Christian doctrines, as the tenor of the immediate context certainly seems to require. This, moreover, is the understanding of the passage from the earliest times onward—a consideration of some moment!

letter is addressed are in danger of stopping at the starting-post and even of stultifying their claim to be contestants in the Christian race.

A *foundation* is something that is either there or not there; it is not something that, once laid, can be laid again. Consequently, there can be no question of *laying again* the foundation on which the Christian life is built. The foundation is described here as consisting of "the elementary doctrines of Christ," which are listed under six heads, namely, repentance, faith, cleansing, laying on of hands, resurrection, and judgment. Briefly stated in this manner, they are characteristic of the evangelistic preaching and practice of the apostles as recounted in the book of Acts, which may be called the book of the missionary church whose first task is that of laying the foundation of the gospel.

The six component fundamentals of the faith resolve themselves naturally into three related pairs: (1) repentance and faith, (2) cleansing and laying on of hands, and (3) resurrection and judgment. An alternative, or perhaps additional, arrangement which fits the text may be schematically represented as follows:

Foundation: (1) repentance
            (2) faith
            (3) teaching concerning (a) cleansing
                                    (b) laying on of hands
                                    (c) resurrection
                                    (d) judgment.

Both arrangements are effectively brought into combination with each other in the Jerusalem Bible, which translates: "the turning away from dead actions and towards faith in God; the teaching[34] about baptisms and the laying-on of hands; the teaching about the resurrection of the dead and eternal judgment." We shall now consider each of these "elementary doctrines" in turn.

Repentance from dead works. This was the main theme of the preach-

---

34. Our version (RSV) and the translation of the NEB are based on the adoption of the reading of the accusative διδαχήν instead of the genitive διδαχῆς, and it is then natural to understand the four genitives that follow, namely, βαπτισμῶν, ἐπιθέσεως, ἀναστάσεως, and κρίματος, as descriptive of the instruction to which διδαχήν refers. The accusative case is to be explained as being in apposition to θεμέλιον. The reading διδαχήν seems to us preferable both because the witnesses attesting it, though few, are weighty and early (p⁴⁶ B it^{d(e)} syr^p) and because with the long string of genitives on either side it is more likely that διδαχήν was altered to διδαχῆς than the other way around. However, even if the genitive form is preferred, the four nouns in the genitive mentioned above are still best taken as descriptive of διδαχῆς, for this seems to be the implication of the conjunctive particles, τε . . . τε . . . καί, which belong to the last three components (βαπτισμῶν διδαχῆς, ἐπιθέσεώς τε χειρῶν, ἀναστάσεώς τε νεκρῶν, καὶ κρίματος αἰωνίου). In that case, διδαχῆς is in series with the preceding genitives μετανοίας and πίστεως and with them is descriptive of θεμέλιον.

ing of John the Baptist, who, stressing that the judgment of God was at hand, admonished the sanctimonious Pharisees and Sadducees to "bear fruit that befits repentance" and the tax collectors to exact no more than was legal and the soldiers to abstain from bullying and intimidation (Mt. 3:7ff.; Lk. 3:7ff.). The call to repentance was clearly sounded also by Christ, who warned his hearers that if they did not repent they would all perish (Lk. 13:3ff.); and it was a constant ingredient in the evangelistic exhortation of the apostles (cf. Acts 2:38; 3:19; 20:21; 26:20). Repentance is the changing of one's mind and attitude, the reversal of one's position, displayed in the renunciation of self-adequacy and in turning to God in sorrow for sinfully robbing him of the glory which is due to him alone. This is the first step on the road which leads the sinner back home to the Father. It is the moment when he "comes to himself" (Lk. 15:17), and in doing so turns away from the course he has pursued to this point. Thus our author speaks of *repentance from*, and specifies that from which the repentant man turns as "dead works."

The expression *dead works*, which recurs in 9:14, is not used in any other New Testament writing, but it presents briefly and suggestively, like a sort of theological shorthand, the teaching of Scripture regarding the state of unregenerate man and his activities. The effect of sin is deadly (Rom. 6:23; 7:11), with the consequence that before repentance and faith man is described as being dead in his sins (Eph. 2:1, 5; Col. 2:13). Accordingly, his every sin is a dead work, as Calvin says, "either because it works death or because it arises from the spiritual death of the soul." Within the purview of the New Testament the dead works of unregenerate men may be classified, though only in a general manner, under two heads, Gentile and Jewish, depending on the background of those who are in view. The dead works of the Gentile milieu are associated with licentiousness and idolatry (cf. Gal. 5:19ff.; Eph. 4:17ff.; Col. 1:21). They are works of which the man who comes to repentance is ashamed, as he now recognizes their barren and unprofitable nature and the end of death and perdition to which they lead (Rom. 6:20f.; Phil. 3:18f.). For the religious Jew, however, it is the merely external and self-righteous compliance with the requirements of the law which gives rise to his dead works (cf. Mt. 5:21ff.; 23:1ff.). His sin is, if anything, worse than that of the idolater, for, though outwardly righteous in men's eyes, inwardly he is full of hypocrisy and iniquity (Mt. 23:28; cf. Rom. 2:28f.). The law, so far from justifying him, condemns him, because, together with every other man, he is a law-breaker who has in fact neglected the very essence of the law which is love (cf. Mt. 5:43ff.; Mk. 12:28ff.; Rom. 13:10; Gal. 5:14; Jas. 2:8), and as such he is subject to judgment and death (cf. Rom. 2:23f.; 3:20, 23; Gal. 2:16ff.; 2 Tim. 1:9; Tit. 3:5). Alienation from God, who is the source of all life, whether through the idol-worship and immorality of heathendom or through the self-centered religiosity and works-righteousness of Judaism, can result only in death; hence the necessity of repentance from dead works and, beyond repentance, of the atonement made available to us by the blood of Christ which purifies the conscience from dead works to serve the living God (Heb. 9:14).

Faith toward God. This describes the "positive" act of trust and self-commitment which follows and balances the "negative" act of repentance and renunciation. The two acts are inseparably complementary and, like the two faces of a coin, together form a unity. If repentance is a turning away from the former life of dead works, faith is a turning toward God for newness of life in Christ. Accordingly, we find Jesus commencing his ministry in Galilee with the declaration: "The time is fulfilled, and the kingdom of God is at hand; repent and believe the gospel" (Mk. 1:15); and the sum of Paul's proclamation, wherever he went, to both Jew and Gentile, was "that they should repent and turn to God and perform deeds worthy of their repentance" (Acts 26:20; cf. 20:21). Indeed, faith in itself always presupposes repentance. Thus not to have faith in Christ means to die in one's sins (Jn. 8:24), since absence of faith also argues an absence of repentance. Similarly, the Philippian jailer, on asking what he must do to be saved, is exhorted to have faith in the Lord Jesus (Acts 16:30f.), for the reality of repentance is implicit in his question concerning salvation. Faith, because of its connotation of the denial of all self-adequacy and complete trust in God, is the hallmark of the people of God (cf. Gal. 3:6f., 9, 26). Christians therefore are also known as "believers," that is, people who have faith (cf. 1 Tim. 4:3, 12; 5:16, etc.).

If it is asked why "faith toward God" rather than "faith in Christ" is included here among the fundamental doctrines, the answer is that the purpose of Christ's coming was to bring mankind back to that attitude of spontaneous trustfulness toward God, departure from which led to our condition of fallenness and alienation. It is through the mediation of the Son that we return to the Father (Jn. 14:6) and thus recover the meaning and integrity of our existence. Faith in Christ is faith toward God; and this involves the reversal of the ungodliness of sinful man which expresses itself, as Paul observes, in the suppression of the truth about God, the denial of his eternal and sovereign power, and the refusal to honor him as God or to give thanks to him for his goodness (Rom. 1:18–21). In Christ the restoration is effected of the Creator/creature relationship which is absolutely basic not only to man's existence but also to his self-understanding and self-realization. Calvin's equation of "faith" here with the summary of the faith found in the articles of the creed is surprisingly inept.

Instructions about ablutions. The significance of this "elementary doctrine" is much less easy to determine. In a list of Christian fundamentals one would expect to find baptism included; for the practice of baptism in the triune name of Father, Son, and Holy Spirit belonged integrally to the commission entrusted by the departing Lord to his apostles (Mt. 28:19), and repentance, faith, and baptism together form the pattern of Christian conversion and initiation from the Day of Pentecost onward (cf. Acts 2:38, 41; 8:12f., 36; 9:18; 10:47f.; 16:14f., 30–33; 18:8; 22:16). But it is not obvious that baptism is intended because, for one thing, the Greek noun that occurs here[35] is not used elsewhere in the New Testament for the sacrament of baptism,[36] and, for another, on every occasion where baptism is mentioned it is the singular, not the plural, noun that is employed (this consideration, however, does not rule out the possibility that the plural here may be an exception to the rule). The same noun, it may be added, is found again in 9:10 below and in verses 4 and 8 of Mark 7, each time in the plural and designating Jewish ceremonial washings or ablutions.

Those who understand the term as a reference to baptism have offered a diversity of explanations for the use of the plural form here. Some (for example, Theodoret, Owen, and Moulton and Milligan, following Chase) have suggested that as many persons were baptized so there were many baptisms—on the Day of Pentecost, for instance, there were, presumably, three thousand baptisms. But it is an unsatisfactory solution of the problem, because in this catalogue of fundamental matters a direct and exclusive reference to Christian baptism would rightly be expected to be in the singular, just as the items which follow are in the singular; otherwise, on the basis of this interpretation, simple consistency would have required a plural sequence of (many) baptisms, (many) layings on of hands, (many) resurrections, and, possibly, (many) judgments. But the fact is that we have here one plural in the midst of a sequence of singulars, and the attempt must be made to explain the significance of this exception. The explanation that it means the baptisms of many persons is far from convincing. Héring speaks of the temptation to correct the plural to the singular, but it is a temptation he manages to resist.

Others (for example, Teodorico) have taken the plural to signify the

---

35. Βαπτισμός, which is found here in the plural in the expression βαπτισμῶν διδαχῆς. The noun regularly used of Christian baptism is βάπτισμα.

36. Colossians 2:12 would be an exception, if the reading ἐν τῷ βαπτισμῷ is preferred to ἐν τῷ βαπτίσματι. Both readings can claim strong support, and the editors of the United Bible Societies' edition of the Greek New Testament have adopted the former. Other modern editors, however, have favored the latter—for example, NEB (Tasker), Souter, Nestle, Westcott, and Hort.

practice of triple affusion or immersion in the baptismal rite, in accordance with which affusion or immersion took place at the mention of each name of the Persons of the Trinity. This, however, would hardly have been described as three baptisms, but rather as three parts of the one act of baptism; and in any case, though this practice developed early on,[37] there is no evidence that it was known or approved in the apostolic church.

Another conjecture rests on the mention in the *Apostolic Tradition* of Hippolytus, early in the third century, of a preparatory washing which took place on the Thursday before the Sunday when baptism was administered. F. F. Bruce, who favors the hypothesis that this letter was addressed to a group of Hebrew Christians in Rome, inclines to the view that the plural noun may be explained as indicating baptism proper plus this preliminary rite of cleansing, suggesting that though "this pre-baptismal bath has no warrant in the New Testament," yet "it may well have been a legacy from Roman Judaism"—on the ground that the writing of Hippolytus, himself a Roman presbyter, reflects the situation in Rome of his day. But it is difficult to see how any solidity can be granted to an explanation of this kind which involves a supposition built on a supposition, namely, that the Jewish-Christian community in Rome included a non-conformist baptist group and that some elements of their ablutionary ritual were adopted by the Roman church; and in any case it is always a precarious device to read back into the New Testament observances which are found in the post-apostolic centuries. This is especially so with the ceremonial of initiation described by Hippolytus, which is elaborate to a degree far beyond anything suggested in the New Testament.

Also unsatisfactory are the attempts that have been made to explain the plural noun in terms of later distinctions regarding permissible modes or equivalents of baptism. Thus Augustine, Peter Lombard, and Herveus are among those who distinguish between baptism of water, which is normal, baptism of penitential tears, or of desire, where, as in the case of the penitent thief, water-baptism is not available, and baptism of blood, that is to say, of martyrdom. Others, including Aquinas, postulate a threefold distinction between baptism of water, of fire, that is, of the Holy Spirit, and of blood (*fluminis, flaminis, et sanguinis*). Athanasius, Theophylact, Lefèvre, and others take it as a reference to the wrongful practice of the repetition of baptism, but this again was something that developed later in the church. Alcuin interprets the

---

37. Evidence that the practice was accepted in the second century is found in the *Didache* vii.1ff., and in Tertullian, *De Corona* 3 and *Adversus Praxean* 26. Cf. also *Didache* ii.7, where triple affusion is allowed as an alternative to triple immersion.

plural simply, and rather weakly, as an allusion to the variety of causes for receiving baptism.

Yet another interpretation identifies the "ablutions" mentioned here with the various ceremonial washings prescribed under the old covenant (see, for example, Ex. 30:18ff.; Lev. 6:27; 13:54; 14:8; 16:4, 24, 26, 28; 22:6; Num. 19:7ff.; 31:32ff.). The "instruction about ablutions," then, would be to the effect that such ritual cleansings are now abrogated because of the perfect cleansing procured by the shedding of Christ's blood and symbolized in baptism (cf. 9:9–14 below). This interpretation, favored by Weiss and others, seems to be reflected in the renderings of the RSV ("ablutions") and the NEB ("cleansing rites"), and it is certainly consistent with the significance of the same term in 9:10 below and Mark 7:4, 8. If, indeed, the community to whom this letter is addressed felt an attraction to teachings similar to those propounded by the Dead Sea Sect,[38] this explanation would be so much the more appropriate; for the leaders at Qumran were evidently much concerned that their members should be carefully instructed regarding the ceremonial washings which they practiced. Thus the *Manual of Discipline* emphasizes that a man who is not genuinely repentant and obedient to God "cannot be cleared by mere ceremonies of atonement, nor cleansed by any waters of ablution, nor sanctified by immersion in lakes or rivers, nor purified by any bath"; he remains unclean "so long as he rejects the government of God and refuses the discipline of communion with him"; the outward ceremony, to be effective, must correspond to an inward disposition of submissiveness: "Only thus can it [his flesh] really be sprinkled with waters of ablution. Only thus can it really be sanctified by waters of purification." This denunciation of any *ex opere operato* doctrine of ritual washing is reinforced by the admonition that "no one is to go into water in order to attain the purity of holy men," since "men cannot be purified except they repent their evil" and "God regards as impure all that transgress his word." The eschatological triumph of truth is awaited when, "like waters of purification [God] will sprinkle upon [man] the spirit of truth, to cleanse him of all the abominations of falsehood and of all pollution. . . ."[39] Old Testament prophecies like Isaiah 44:3 and Ezekiel 36:25ff. (cf. also Num. 19:19) lie behind these teachings. The serious concern for authenticity in the practice of religion, including the observance of lustral prescriptions, manifested in these writings is noteworthy; but the Christian message to the Dead Sea Sect in the first

---

38. See Introduction, pp. 13ff.
39. *The Manual of Discipline* iii.4f.; iv.21; iii.9. The translation is that of T. H. Gaster, *The Scriptures of the Dead Sea Sect* (London, 1957). For a precise instruction regarding ritual ablutions see *The Zadokite Document* x.10–13.

century, and to all in every age who seek for cleansing and purification, is that the reality adumbrated in the ancient ceremonies and promised through the prophets has found its fulfilment in Jesus Christ, who by his blood-shedding his made full and final purification for sins (Heb. 1:3; 9:14, 22ff.; 13:20f.; 1 Jn. 1:7).

Complementary, in our judgment, rather than alternative, to this interpretation is the view of Lünemann, Delitzsch, and many others that the use of the plural term by our author here refers to the varieties of baptism familiar in the early setting of the Jewish-Christian church, namely, the Jewish baptism of proselytes, the baptism of John, and the baptism of Jesus, all baptisms in or with water. To these might be added the promised experience of baptism with the Holy Spirit (cf. Mt. 3:11; Mk. 1:8; Lk. 3:16; Jn. 1:33; Acts 1:5; 11:16). Plainly, the baptism of John was superseded by that of Jesus, and there is one striking occasion in the New Testament where a dozen disciples in Ephesus had to be apprised of this fact (Acts 19:1–7). It could appropriately be said that this was an instance of Paul giving "instruction about baptisms." Shortly prior to this incident, the Alexandrian Apollos, when he came to the same city, required and received similar instruction from Priscilla and Aquila before he travelled on to Greece (Acts 18:24ff.). Héring suggests that these events accord well with the hypothesis that Apollos was the author of our epistle. Likewise Montefiore comments that if the epistle emanated from Ephesus and was written by one who had needed to be taught that there was a baptism beyond that of John, and who had then submitted to baptism in the name of the Lord Jesus and to the laying on of hands, as described in Acts 19:5f., the author "would have had to have instruction on the two water rites and also on the laying on of hands." This, again, would seem to fit Apollos well, though Montefiore does not mention him by name here.[40]

We conclude, then, that our author is referring here to instruction regarding washings and baptisms, but, quite naturally, with particular respect to Christian baptism, by which all others are surpassed and replaced. Indeed, whichever way one approaches the question, it seems impossible, and rightly so, to remove Christian baptism from the center of the picture.

The laying on of hands. This is another designation which, like the preceding one, has invited a diversity of interpretations because of the lack of an explanatory context. It is plain that in the early apostolic

---

40. On the question of authorship see Introduction, pp. 19ff. Montefiore is a strong supporter of the claims of Apollos, in the Introduction to his commentary, pp. 9ff. It is of some interest that Josephus uses the term βαπτισμός of John's baptism (*Antiquities* XVIII.v.2). Héring wonders whether foot-washing (see Jn. 13:4–15) might be among the "ablutions" intended by our author.

church baptism and the laying on of hands were closely connected with each other. Generally, it would seem, baptism preceded laying on of hands (cf. Acts 8:16f.; 19:5f.), and this would accord well with the order we have here; but at least on one occasion this order was reversed (Acts 9:17f.). The conferring of the Holy Spirit was associated with the laying on of hands in these particular instances; but the reception of the Holy Spirit could take place before baptism and without laying on of hands (Acts 10:44, 47f.). Indeed, the laying on of hands does not seem to have been an invariable practice: there is no mention of it, for example, in the accounts of the conversions of the three thousand on the Day of Pentecost or of Lydia or of the Philippian jailer (Acts 2:41; 16:15, 33).

Elsewhere in the New Testament laying on of hands is used in the act of blessing (cf. Mt. 19:13–15) and in the healing of the sick (cf. Mk. 6:5; 16:18; Lk. 4:40, etc.; Acts 28:8). Together with prayer, it seems to have been customary in the ordination or commissioning of persons for various kinds of service (cf. Acts 6:6; 13:3; 1 Tim. 5:22; 2 Tim. 1:6). The Roman Catholic commentators understand the laying on of hands to indicate the rite of confirmation.[41] Thomas Aquinas, for example, observes that "in confirmation the Spirit is given for strengthening in order that a man may boldly confess the name of Christ before men." The moderation of this viewpoint, which is not dissimilar from that of Calvin and the Anglican Book of Common Prayer, contrasts with the general Catholic propensity to exalt confirmation at the expense of baptism. Calvin, indeed, acknowledges that "the origin of this rite came from the apostles," but complains that "afterwards it was turned into a superstition" involving the mutilation of baptism. The apostles, he says, "intended by this sign to confirm the profession of faith which adolescents make when they pass from their childhood." "Today," he adds, "we must retain the institution in its purity, but we must correct the superstition." This is sound counsel; but the whole question of the theology and history of confirmation is a vexed one,[42] and in this case also too many scholars still succumb to the temptation to read back into the New Testament the involved teaching and ceremonial of a later period.

Surprise has been expressed by some that our author has not included "the breaking of bread" in this list of subjects on which basic

41. Spicq comments that "the neophyte would be instructed in the difference between the χάρις conferred by baptism and the χαρίσματα transmitted by the laying on of hands." Where, however, is such a distinction to be found in the New Testament, which in any case surely teaches that grace precedes baptism, or, in other words, that grace is the ground rather than the effect of baptism?

42. For a valuable and detailed discussion of the baptism-confirmation issue see G. W. H. Lampe, *The Seal of the Spirit* (London, 1951); see also my *Confirmation in the Church Today* (Grand Rapids, 1973).

instruction was given, either before or after "the laying on of hands." They feel that this apparent omission impairs the completeness of the list, and that the mention of the one gospel sacrament (baptism), to which allusion is made by the use of the term "ablutions" or "washings," would be expected to be followed by the mention of the other gospel sacrament (the eucharist). Jeremias, for example, suggests that "the conspicuous absence of the eucharist from the list of subjects taught to beginners is probably to be explained by the consideration that the doctrine of the eucharist was among the subjects reserved for the 'mature.'"[43] This, however, is improbable, for there is no indication in the New Testament that the breaking of bread was reserved for those who had reached a prescribed degree of maturity; on the contrary, it was a practice observed by all baptized Christians from the very beginning (Acts 2:42). The simplest explanation is that the subjects listed here in verse 2 were expounded in pre-baptismal instruction, whereas the breaking of bread, which, in contrast to baptism, is not an initiatory rite but a sacrament of Christian growth for the initiated, had its place in post-baptismal instruction. It is a matter of some interest, though the case is not entirely parallel, that the Nicene Creed has a clause on baptism but none on the eucharist, especially as the need for a pre-baptismal standard of instruction seems to have provided the original impulse for the formulation of credal statements (though in the earlier Apostles' Creed there is an article neither on baptism nor on the eucharist). Both Apostles' and Nicene Creeds contain clauses on resurrection and judgment, subjects which now await our attention.

The resurrection of the dead and eternal judgment. These, the two final components in the doctrinal foundation, belong to the eschatological perspective of the apostolic church. The whole sweep of the Christian spectrum is taken in at a glance, as it were, by passing immediately from baptism and imposition of hands, that is, the ceremonies of initiation, to the great events of the consummation of all things, resurrection and judgment. And this reminds us of the truth that, in the realism of the faith, the end is already present in the beginning, and the beginning is the window through which the end is viewed. Thus baptism, which is the first event, is the symbol of the judgment of the unregenerate life and of resurrection to newness of life in Christ, which, in its fulness, is the ultimate event; and the laying on of hands is the symbol of the eternal blessing which replaces the curse of man's fallenness borne by

43. J. Jeremias, *The Eucharistic Words of Jesus* (New York, 1955), p. 84. Elsewhere he states rightly, in our judgment, that the themes listed here "belonged to the instruction preparatory to primitive Christian baptism"; *Infant Baptism in the First Four Centuries* (London, 1960), p. 30.

Christ on the cross. What our author is, in effect, leading up to is this: that baptism, though, in a dramatic manner, it is the germ or seed of resurrection to eternal life, will produce a harvest of judgment for him who receives it and then despises it, and that the blessing implicit in the laying on of hands will turn to cursing for him who spurns the gracious working of the Holy Spirit. Apostasy, in short, is the repudiation of one's baptism and the sin against the Holy Spirit. This is the thrust of the solemn warning of verses 4ff. below.

Indissolubly bound as it is to the fact of the rising from the tomb of Jesus Christ, who is himself the resurrection and the life (Jn. 11:25), the resurrection of believers at the last day is a cornerstone of the Christian faith, as Paul explains in 1 Corinthians 15. Coupled with this is the resurrection of unbelievers, including apostates, not, however, to life, but to judgment (cf. Dan. 12:2; Mt. 25:46; Jn. 5:24, 28f.; 2 Pet. 2:9; 3:7; Jude 14f.; Rev. 20:11ff.). This judgment, eternal in its effects, means the complete elimination of evil and its consequences from God's creation and the establishment of the new heaven and the new earth in which righteousness dwells (2 Pet. 3:13)—the glorious fulfilment, in other words, of all God's purposes in creation and the absolute vindication of his gracious and sovereign lordship.

6:3. *And this we will do if God permits.*

There is a division of opinion among the commentators as to whether the demonstrative pronoun *this* here refers to the more advanced teaching which the writer proposes to give his readers (cf. 5:11), in which case the plural pronoun *we* designates the author alone (as in 5:11) and he is saying in effect, "and I intend, God willing, to give you this instruction," or whether it refers to the need to advance to maturity (v. 1), in which case the plural pronoun *we* designates both author and readers and he is saying in effect, "and, God willing, we shall go on to maturity together." Obviously, his instruction and their maturity are closely interrelated, hence indeed the writing of this epistle. Moffatt's attempt to relate this verse to the fundamentals just enumerated, with the sense, "I will go over such elementary truths with you, God willing," not in this letter, but when, as the author plans to do, he pays them a visit in person (13:23), is unconvincing, because the connection is too remote, and less suited to the context than the alternatives we have mentioned. It is true that Paul adds a similar proviso, "if the Lord permits," when writing to the Corinthians of his hope of spending some time with them (1 Cor. 16:7), but this consideration can hardly be allowed to influence our interpretation here, for there, unlike here, the meaning is quite explicit. Moreover, the present verse is related to what follows as well as to what precedes it—and there is no hint in this context of an intended visit. The pronoun *this* links it with what has already been said, and the conjunction *For* at the beginning of the next verse shows that there is a link also with what comes next.

We may be sure that the qualification, "if God permits," is something far more than a pious cliché. The point is that the Christian's life is in the Lord's hands and all his planning is subject to the overruling will of God. The principle is explained in a characteristically practical manner by James in his epistle (Jas. 4:13–15). We have already seen that the Greek text of verse 1 above, translated in our version as "let us . . . go on to maturity," means literally "let us be carried forward (*sc.* by God) to maturity," and that, accordingly, it is God who enables us to make progress toward the maturity of those who are well instructed in the deep truths of the faith, but always, as our author repeatedly emphasizes, in conjunction with our own earnest effort and application. We may take the affirmation, "this we will do," then, as an expression of confidence on the part of the author in the reality of his readers' experience of grace and therefore in their capacity for instruction and spiritual progress. At the same time, however, as the ensuing verses plainly show, they, or at least some among them, are in serious danger of falling right away if they do not stir themselves and give proof that they are what they profess to be.

6:4–6. *For it is impossible to restore again to repentance those who have once been enlightened, who have tasted the heavenly gift, and have become partakers of the Holy Spirit, and have tasted the goodness of the word of God and the powers of the age to come, if they then commit apostasy, since they crucify the Son of God on their own account and hold him up to contempt.*

The author now returns to the grave theme of apostasy which he has already broached in 3:12ff. above and which he will take up again in 10:26ff. and 12:25ff. It is apparent, therefore, that his concern is not simply lest his readers should remain at a standstill on the threshold of the Christian life, immature and unfruitful in the faith they profess (5:11ff.), but, something far worse, lest there should be a relapse into unbelief in their midst. The danger of apostasy, it must be emphasized, is real, not imaginary; otherwise this epistle with its high-sounding admonitions must be dismissed as trifling, worthless, and ridiculous. Certainly, in our author's judgment, the situation is one of extreme gravity.

He is addressing readers whose loss of confidence and whose flagging will to persevere in the Christian race (10:35f.; 12:3, 12) point alarmingly to the possibility of their dropping out of the contest altogether, and in doing so of placing themselves beyond all hope of restoration.

Six things are predicated of the spiritual experience of those whom *it is impossible to restore again* if they rebel against the faith they claim to hold.

1. They have professed *repentance*. This should be understood in the light of what is more fully stated in verse 1, namely, "repentance from dead works and faith toward God." Genuine repentance is a once-for-all turning of the back on the old way of life; it is "repentance that leads to salvation and brings no regret" (2 Cor. 7:10), a decisive, unrepeatable moment in the transition from death to life symbolized publicly by the act of baptism; and as such it belongs to the foundation on which the new life in Christ is erected. Consequently, it is unthinkable that by a second crisis of repentance this foundation stone can be laid over again (v. 1). This does not mean that there is no place for repentance on the part of the man who has truly turned to Christ. On the contrary, the sins and shortcomings of which he is daily guilty call for daily repentance and forgiveness (1 Jn. 1:8–2:2); but even so, thanks to the grace of God which enabled him to make the decisive initial move of turning and trust, he has left behind him his former ungodly life and is on the road that leads to holiness and glory.

2. They belong to *those who have once been enlightened* (the expression recurs in 10:32 below). The same verb[44] is used in John 1:9 of the activity of the eternal Word who came into the world to enlighten men. Through faith in him believers have been enlightened in the very depths of their being (Eph. 1:18; cf. 2 Tim. 1:10). Satan, on the other hand, blinds the minds of unbelievers "to keep them from seeing the light of the gospel of the glory of Christ"; but for those who have been transformed by the grace of the gospel this satanic darkness has been dispelled by the shining in their hearts of "the light of the knowledge of the glory of God in the face of Christ" (2 Cor. 4:4, 6).[45] This accords closely with what is said in chapter 10 below, where "to be enlightened" (v. 32) evidently corresponds to the experience of "receiving the knowledge of the truth" (v. 26). The grace of enlightenment carries with it logically plain responsibilities. Thus Paul admonishes the Ephesian Christians: "Once you were darkness, but now you are light in the Lord; walk as children of light. . . . Take no part in the unfruitful works of darkness" (Eph. 5:8,

---

44. Φωτίζειν.
45. In both of these verses the Greek word translated "light" is the cognate noun φωτισ-μός.

11)—these "unfruitful works of darkness" being the equivalent of the "dead works" (v. 1 above) from which in baptism the Christian professes to have separated himself.

From at least the second century onward the expression "to be enlightened" was interpreted as a reference to baptism. Justin Martyr (d. 165), for instance, states that the term "enlightenment" was used in his day as a synonym for Christian baptism, and he himself calls the person baptized "the enlightened one";[46] and the Peshitta Syriac version actually renders the present passage as "who have gone down into baptism." The baptismal ceremony, in which the candidate's repentance from dead works and resurrection to newness of life in Christ are dramatically portrayed, had become, within two centuries after the apostolic age, the climax of a prolonged period of preparatory instruction and the moment when the convert to Christianity professed as it were before the world his turning from the darkness of sin to the light of Christ. In the controversy over re-baptism in the fourth century this text was adduced as specifically forbidding the repetition of baptism. And its association with baptism persisted, and, it could be said, became entrenched, so that in the thirteenth century we find Thomas Aquinas explaining that "enlightened"[47] means enlightened through baptism, and that "baptism is appropriately called enlightenment[48] since baptism is the principle of spiritual regeneration in which the understanding is illuminated by faith." Again, early in the sixteenth century Lefèvre d'Etaples asks: "What is 'who have once been enlightened'?" and replies: "Undoubtedly who have once been baptized; for baptism is termed the sacrament of *photismata*, that is, of enlightenments,[49] by most of our scholars." Long before Aquinas and Lefèvre, Chrysostom made a nice distinction when he observed that "the heretics have baptism, but not enlightenment."[50] To what extent baptism and its significance may have been in our author's mind as he wrote this passage is a question to which we shall return.

3. They *have tasted the heavenly gift.* The explanation of "the heavenly gift" as a description of the eucharist, which is literally "tasted," has proved attractive to some, especially if the "enlightenment" of the preceding clause has been taken as a reference to baptism. On this understanding, the two gospel sacraments are then placed

46. Ὁ φωτισθείς: *First Apology* 61, 65.
47. *Illuminati.*
48. *Illuminatio.*
49. *Photismatum hoc est illuminationum sacramentum.*
50. Chrysostom, Homily on John 1:1: βάπτισμα . . . ἔχουσιν, οὐ φώτισμα. They have the external ceremony without the corresponding internal reality; thus he adds: βαπτίζονται μὲν σώματι, ψυχῇ δὲ οὐ φωτίζονται.

neatly side by side. It is an interpretation which has recently been taken up approvingly by Teodorico, who relates the "heavenly gift" to the teaching of Christ in John 6:31ff. where he speaks of himself as the bread of life given by the Father from heaven. F. F. Bruce, too, while conceding that this "heavenly gift" need not be restricted to the eucharist, suggests that "it may indicate the whole sum of spiritual blessings which are sacramentally sealed and signified in the eucharist." But it is unlikely that "tasting" is intended here in a physical sense, that is, of consuming the eucharistic elements, especially as its usage in the clause after the next ("tasted the goodness of the word of God"), within this same sentence, is quite clearly metaphorical.[51] This eucharistic interpretation, moreover, does not appear to have been current in the early centuries. Chrysostom, for example, understands the "heavenly gift" to mean the forgiveness of sins, and in this he is followed by numerous other commentators (Alcuin, Peter Lombard, Herveus, Lefèvre d'Etaples, etc.). Many others expound it in a somewhat more general sense of the gospel and the benefits it confers. According to Aquinas, it is God-given grace; and Spicq, similarly, remarks that the Greek word translated "gift" here[52] is "a technical term almost equivalent to grace." To "taste the heavenly gift," then, may perhaps best be understood as signifying to experience the blessing which God freely and graciously bestows in Christ.

In our discussion of 2:9 above, where Christ is said to have tasted death, we noticed that some commentators have wished to give the verb "tasted" a diminutive connotation, as though our author were saying that Christ only briefly sipped death; so also here a few (but, interestingly, not the same) commentators, including Owen, Westcott, and Montefiore, take "tasting" to indicate no more than a temporary or superficial participation. The metaphorical usage of the verb "to taste," however, does not seem to warrant an interpretation along these lines, accurate though the reading of the situation may otherwise be. The two occurrences of the verb in this passage are parallel to the assertion of 1 Peter 2:3, "you [Christians] have tasted the kindness of the Lord." Behind such statements is discernible the influence of the invitation of Psalm 34:8, "O taste and see [that is, prove] that the Lord is good," where no diminished or inadequate experience is implied.

4. They *have become partakers of the Holy Spirit*. There is a certain but perhaps deceptive attractiveness about the suggestion that the se-

---

51. Of the 14 times, apart from the instance now before us, that the verb γεύομαι occurs in the New Testament seven are literal and seven are metaphorical, five of the latter (including 2:9 above) in the sense of tasting, i.e., experiencing, death.
52. Δωρεά.

quence here of "enlightenment," "tasting the heavenly gift," and "participation of the Holy Spirit" is in correspondence with the "instruction about ablutions" (interpreted as a reference to Christian baptism) and the "laying on of hands" mentioned above in verse 2 (through there are only two items there as compared with three here). Thus, for example, Teodorico and F. F. Bruce offer the opinion that by the three things mentioned here baptism, eucharist, and the laying on of hands are intended—eucharist having been passed over in silence earlier. Delitzsch arrives at a more precise correspondence by his supposition that "enlightenment" is the equivalent of catechetical instruction and the "heavenly gift" the grace imparted in baptism (the two together thus answering to the "instruction about ablutions" of v. 2), while the "partaking of the Holy Spirit" is the same as the imposition of hands. But conjectures of this kind must be treated with caution, if only because in the Acts of the Apostles there is no fixed pattern for the impartation of the Holy Spirit, which takes place sometimes with and sometimes without imposition of hands, sometimes before and sometimes after baptism. The sequence, moreover, of baptism, laying on of hands, and eucharist which later gained acceptance in the church is different from the sequence which, as we have seen, some have thought they could discern here.

Leaving such questions aside, we may conclude that those who are addressed in this letter became "partakers of the Holy Spirit" by the reception of the gifts or impartations of the Holy Spirit mentioned earlier in 2:4, and that these gifts in turn are identical with the charismatic apportionments enumerated by Paul in 1 Corinthians 12:4ff., which, as both places affirm, are sovereignly distributed in accordance with the divine will. These spiritual gifts, as 2:3 above testifies, confirmed the truth and power of the gospel when it was proclaimed to those to whom this letter was written.

5. They have *tasted the goodness of the word of God*. As we have seen, the metaphorical use of the verb "to taste" implies to experience something in a manner that is real and personal. We prefer here to translate the Greek, as in the KJV, as "tasted the good word of God"[53] and, with Spicq and Teodorico, to treat the expression "the good word" as a synonym for the good news which is the gospel (cf. JB, "the good message").[54] "This word is called good," comments Aquinas, "because

---

53. Καλὸν γευσαμένους θεοῦ ῥῆμα.

54. The expression καλὸν ῥῆμα corresponds to the Hebrew הַדָּבָר הַטּוֹב (cf. Josh. 21:43; 23:15, etc., LXX). The attempt of Westcott, Montefiore, and some others to sustain a distinction between ῥῆμα as some special utterance and λόγος as the whole message of the gospel is misplaced, since the evidence shows that the two terms are used interchangeably (as, e.g., in Acts 10:36f. quoted below), and, further, that the Hebrew דָּבָר, conformably with this, is

it is the word of eternal life." And Alcuin explains "the good word" as meaning "the evangelical doctrine." Within the sphere of influence of this good word the recipients of this letter had entered into the experience of the blessings that belong to the gospel.

6. They have tasted also *the powers of the age to come.* These powers may confidently be identified with the signs, wonders, and miracles mentioned earlier in 2:4 as accompaniments of the preaching of the gospel.[55] They are the dynamic evidence of the activity of the Holy Spirit within the community of believers, manifested particularly perhaps in miraculous healings and deliverances. As such, moreover, they testify to the fact that "the age to come" is already upon them, since its powers are operative in their midst. Looked at from the perspective of the Old Testament, this "coming age," so long expected, has truly dawned with the advent of Christ and the achievement of his work of reconciliation, followed by the outpouring of the Holy Spirit on all flesh. Hence the keynote of the public ministry of Jesus is the proclamation: "The time is fulfilled, and the kingdom of God is at hand" (Mk. 1:14f.). Christ's coming ushers in "the last days" (cf. Heb. 1:2; Acts 2:16f.; 1 Jn. 2:18; Jude 18). But, at the same time, it is apparent that in the biblical purview the coming of the final age is in two stages; and this conception is closely bound up with the doctrine of the two comings of Christ. At his first coming, Christ by his incarnation, death, and resurrection accomplished all that was necessary for the redemption of the world and the reconciliation of man to God. The new creation is even now taking place in the lives and communities of Christian believers. The principles of the new age are at this moment active through the operation of the Holy Spirit. But the consummation is not yet. The fulness is yet to come. And it will come when Christ appears the second time in the glory of his eternal majesty and his exalted manhood. Meanwhile the Christian, who is being transformed from glory to glory as he is increasingly molded into the likeness of him who is the true Image of God (2 Cor. 3:18), enjoys a genuine experience of the powers of the age to come. The conquest of sin in his own life is the assurance that the triumphant Christ will finally drive out all imperfection, not only from his people but also from the

---

translated sometimes by the one, sometimes by the other. Particularly relevant is Peter's assertion, with reference to Isaiah 40:8, which indicates that ῥῆμα by no means implies something other or less than the gospel (εὐαγγέλιον): "That word (ῥῆμα) is the gospel which was preached (εὐαγγελισθέν) to you." The same apostle addresses Cornelius in the following terms: "You know the word (ὁ λόγος) which he sent to Israel . . . , the word (τὸ ῥῆμα) which was proclaimed throughout all Judea" (Acts 10:36f.). So, too, Paul speaks of "the word (τὸ ῥῆμα) of faith which we preach" (Rom. 10:8).

55. It should be noted that δυνάμεις, translated "miracles" in 2:4, is translated "powers" here.

whole of his creation. The believer's *taste* of the powers of the age to come, real and dynamic though it is, is but a *foretaste* of the glorious banquet which awaits him (cf. 1 Cor. 13:9–12; Acts 3:19–21; Phil. 3:20f.; 2 Pet. 3:13; 1 Jn. 3:2; Rom. 8:18, 23; 2 Cor. 1:22; Eph. 1:13f.; 1 Pet. 1:4f.; Rev. 7:13ff.; 19:9; 21:1ff.).

These six blessings have necessarily been discussed separately and in turn, but it is important to realize that they are but different aspects and manifestations of the one great blessing which the reception of the gospel brings. They are components of a unitary experience of evangelical grace in the life of the believer. Certainly, it seems scarcely credible that one who has in some definite sense experienced all this should then fall away from this state of blessedness. Yet this is the dreadful possibility that is envisaged in this passage. The situation is hardly eased by suggesting, as some (including Spicq) have done, that the author is expressing himself in a merely hypothetical manner: "*If* anyone should become apostate, it would be impossible to restore him," with the implication that a defection of this kind would actually never take place.[56] The author, we are reminded, goes on to express his confidence with regard to those he is addressing in verse 9, where he says: "Though we speak thus, yet in your case, beloved, we feel sure of better things that belong to salvation" (cf. also 10:39). This is then taken as an indication that his warning about the impossibility of restoration for the apostate does not answer to reality and is little better than the invention of a bogey for the purpose of frightening them into being better Christians. But the end does not justify the means, and to resort to subterfuge and deception, and that too within so solemn a context, would be subchristian and incompatible with the whole tenor of the epistle. What, in any case, would be the point of warning them of the danger of apostasy and then assuring them that, after all, they are in no danger of falling into apostasy? Any such procedure would be self-defeating. The confidence expressed in 6:9 and 10:39 arises from the certitude that a true work of God has taken place in their midst; but this does not exclude the possibility that some of their number are rebellious at heart and, unless there is a radical change, will find that they have reached the point of irremediable apostasy.

Attempts have been made (by Ambrose,[57] Aquinas, Wordsworth, Spicq, and others) to soften the import of the language by proposing that "impossible" here means impossible *for man*, but not for God, and

---

56. There is, as a matter of fact, no "if" in the Greek text, though the rendering of the participle παραπεσόντας in a conditional sense is quite justifiable. The NEB rendering is better suited to the context: "for when men have once been enlightened, etc. . . . and after all this have fallen away, it is impossible to bring them again to repentance."
57. Ambrose, *De Poenitentia* ii.2.

invoking the support of a text like Mark 10:27 ("With men it is impossible, but not with God; for all things are possible with God"). But the notion of "impossibility" is used absolutely here, without any such qualification. Still less substantial is the supposition of Erasmus and Bengel that "impossible" means no more than "difficult," for this is to do violence to language.[58] Such a sense is, as Calvin observes, "wholly foreign to the meaning of the word." Nor is the explanation of Wordsworth, Delitzsch, and others convincing that what is intended here is that it is impossible for the renegades envisaged to be restored *as long as* they persevere in the betrayal of the faith they formerly professed. F. F. Bruce rightly remarks that "to say that they cannot be brought to repentance so long as they persist in their renunciation of Christ would be a truism hardly worth putting into words," and that "the participle 'crucifying'[59] is much more appropriately taken as causal than temporal in force: it indicates *why* it is impossible for such people to repent and make a new beginning." This is how our version (RSV) understands it: there is no possibility of their restoration "since they crucify the Son of God on their own account. . . ." (The NEB rendering is to the same effect.)

An interpretation that has had much currency through the centuries of the church's history is that which explains the expression to "restore again"[60] as signifying to baptize again. Not long after the apostolic age the theory was developed that the washing of baptism was equivalent to the cleansing of the blood of Christ, but that this cleansing covered only those sins committed prior to baptism; for sins committed after baptism Christ's blood no longer availed and there was no place for repetition of repentance and forgiveness. Such teaching is found in the *Shepherd of Hermas*[61] and is restated more fully in Clement of Alexandria,[62] and subsequently receives considerable elaboration in the self-expiatory demands of the penitential system in this life and in the flames of purgatory hereafter. The teaching that the one permissible substitute for baptism was the blood of martyrdom, which, it was held, like the blood of Christ effected the purging of all sin, led to the practice, on the one hand, of postponing baptism until the hour of death and, on the other, of deliberately seeking martyrdom, since by either method it was hoped that one would be free of the peril of a spiritual relapse in this world and unencumbered by sin as one entered the future world. Motivated

---

58. The reading *difficile* in the Latin version of the sixth-century Codex D (Claromontanus) which they cite affords no real confirmation since this is clearly an earlier attempt to soften the sense of "impossible" and not a solution of the problem.
59. Ἀνασταυροῦντας.
60. Πάλιν ἀνακαινίζειν.
61. Commandment iv.3.
62. Clement of Alexandria, *Stromateis* ii.13.

though teaching of this kind may have been by concern for the purity of the church, it is nonetheless seriously unevangelical, for the New Testament plainly instructs us that grace and forgiveness and the cleansing of Christ's blood are freely available to the Christian believer who falls into sin and turns in repentance to God (cf. Heb. 4:15f.; 10:19–23; 1 Jn. 1:7–9; 2:1f.). Moreover, the reference in the passage before us is not to sin as it manifests itself in the lives of Christians, but to a particular disposition involving a repudiation of grace so grave that it has the effect of permanently severing those who display it from the body of Christ.

Early in the third century, Tertullian, governed by the rigorist presuppositions of the Montanism which he embraced in his later years, regarded repentance and forgiveness for sins such as adultery to be appropriate only to the heathen, that is, at the moment of baptism. For the Christian, or baptized person, however, repentance and forgiveness for a sin of this degree of seriousness he considered unthinkable: "For who will fear to squander what he has the power of afterwards recovering?" he asks. "Who will be careful to preserve to perpetuity what he will be able to lose *not* to perpetuity? Security in sin is likewise an appetite for it. Therefore the apostate will recover his former 'garment', the robe of the Holy Spirit, and the renewal of the 'ring', the sign and seal of baptism, and Christ will again be 'slaughtered' "—the imagery is that of the parable of the prodigal son (Lk. 15:22f.), but with overtones from the passage before us. And there would seem to be another echo of our passage when, after citing 1 Corinthians 6:9–11, where Paul affirms that immoral, dishonest, and dissolute persons will not inherit the kingdom of God, and then adds: "And such were some of you; but you were washed, you were sanctified, you were justified in the name of the Lord Jesus Christ and in the Spirit of our God," Tertullian explains that "in as far as Paul puts on the paid side of the account such sins *before* baptism, in so far *after* baptism he determines them irremissible."[63] In the next century both Ambrose[64] and Jerome[65] state that sects such as the Montanists, who denied the possibility of repentance in the case of church members who had fallen into serious sin, and the Novatians, who denied that those who had lapsed under persecution could be restored to fellowship, claimed that their rigorist position was justified on the basis of the apostolic teaching of a passage like Hebrews 6:4–6. Indeed, the favor with which groups like this that had been denounced as heretical regarded the Epistle to the Hebrews is said by Filaster (d. ca. 397) to have been a cause of the difficulty this writing encountered in

---

63. Tertullian, *De Pudicitia* 9, 16.
64. Ambrose, *De Poenitentia* ii.2.
65. Jerome, *Adversus Jovinianum* ii.3.

gaining admission to the New Testament canon.[66] In the midst of the Novatian controversy Cyprian had exclaimed:[67] "I wonder that some are so obstinate as to think that repentance is not to be granted to the lapsed or to suppose that pardon is to be denied to the penitent," referring to Novatians and Montanists respectively.

The situation to which the author is addressing himself, however, involves considerably more than the question of the irremissibility of a particular sin. It is not so much an act as an attitude of which he is speaking—an attitude, to be sure, which will disclose itself in disgraceful acts inconsistent with a profession of Christian faith. Yet even an act of adultery coupled with virtual murder, as in the case of David, does not necessarily betray an attitude of apostasy. That David's true attitude, despite the enormity of his sin, was not that of apostasy is plain from the content of Psalm 51. A *life* that once professed obedience to Christ but now openly blasphemes his name and denies his gospel is the mark of the apostate. 1 John 5:16f. speaks of the commission by a Christian brother of a sin which, wrong and dishonoring to Christ though it is, is not "unto death," but at the same time affirms that there is such a thing as "sin unto death" into which a "brother," that is, a member of the Christian community, may fall. The one guilty of the latter is evidently beyond praying for, but the precise nature of "sin unto death" is not explained. A clue to what is intended is available, however, in the warning of Christ against "eternal sin" (Mk. 3:29). This warning was called forth by the calumnious assertion of the scribes that Christ himself was demon-possessed and cast out demons by the prince of demons—in other words, that the power at work in him was satanic and not divine. This was, in fact, the sin of blasphemy against the Holy Spirit, since from first to last the dynamic of Christ's life was the dynamic of the Holy Spirit (cf. Mk. 1:10f.; Lk. 1:35; 4:18–21), his deeds were manifestly good, not evil, and evil cannot be the source of good (Mk. 3:22ff.; Mt. 12:22ff.; Lk. 11:14ff.; 12:10). By closing their eyes to the plain evidence that the kingdom of God had come upon them and wickedly describing as satanic the signs that the Holy Spirit was powerfully and beneficially acting in and through Jesus, these professors of godliness betrayed an attitude of hardened hostility to the truth. Members of the covenant people though they were, they refused to glorify God for the evidence that his promises were so clearly being fulfilled in their presence. They showed themselves to be hard-hearted enemies of the light that had

---

66. Filaster, *De Haeresibus* 41. Calvin charges that "the western fathers preferred to deny the genuineness of the epistle because the Novatian sect were their enemies, and they were not strong enough in doctrine to be equal to refuting their arguments."
67. Cyprian, Epistle to Antonianus 22.

come into the world (Jn. 1:19-21). Such blasphemy against the Holy Spirit is sin for which there is no forgiveness (Mk. 3:29). "The apostle is not talking here about theft or perjury or murder or drunkenness or adultery," comments Calvin. "He is referring to a complete falling away from the gospel, in which the sinner has offended God not in some one respect only but has utterly renounced his grace."

This sin, then, or sinful disposition, is sin against the light. It is sin committed, not in ignorance, but in the face of knowledge and even experience of the truth—not the sin of those who are "ignorant and wayward" (Heb. 5:2) but of those who "sin deliberately after receiving the knowledge of the truth" (Heb. 10:26). It is the sin which brought the direst judgment upon the Israelites of old, and also the sin by which in the first days of the gospel their descendants proved themselves unworthy of eternal life (Acts 13:46). To enter into the light and then to reject that light in favor of the darkness of unbelief incurs the judgment of being broken off from the tree of life (cf. Rom. 11:17ff.). Within this perspective we can understand Paul's otherwise enigmatic statement in 1 Timothy 1:13 that, though he had blasphemed and persecuted and insulted Christ, yet he received mercy because he had acted "ignorantly in unbelief": in other words, his unbelief was capable of receiving God's pardon (on his acceptance of the gospel) because his opposition had been exercised in the darkness of ignorance (sinful and therefore culpable in itself), whereas the man who rebels as an apostate after professing faith in Christ and entering into the sphere of evangelical blessing is not acting "ignorantly in unbelief," but by a deliberate and calculated renunciation of the good he has known he places himself beyond forgiveness and renewal.

In our epistle the calamitous history of the Israelites of old is repeatedly set before the readers as a warning against the imitation of their evil example (2:1f.; 3:12ff.; 4:1f., 11; 10:28ff.; 12:25ff.), while at the same time they are urged to emulate the example of unwearying perseverance of the faithful core of the community (ch. 11). The principle affirmed in Romans 9:6 applies equally in the sphere of the Christian church, to the effect that not all are of the church who are in the church; or, as another apostle says of some who professed to be Christian but were in fact anti-Christian: "They went out from us, but they were not of us; for if they had been of us, they would have continued with us; but they went out, so that it might be clear that not all in our company truly belong to it" (1 Jn. 2:19; the last clause is the NEB rendering). This same principle finds fuller expression in Christ's parable of the sower (Mk. 4:1-20). Four types of reception of the good seed of the gospel are depicted, but only one is genuine. In one type Satan immediately snatches away the word that has been sown. In another, the word is received with joy, and with rapid and even spectacular results, but without being deeply rooted, so that the response is apparent rather than real, and, "when tribulation or persecution arises on account of the word, immediately they fall away." A third class of hearers seemingly gives evidence of more permanent and solid results, "but the cares of the world, and the delight in riches, and the desire for other things, enter in and choke the word, and it proves unfruitful." Only those who receive the seed of the word into "good soil" really "hear the word and accept it and bear fruit." It is not enough to have the name of the Lord on one's lips in worship and invocation. Even to prophesy and to cast out demons and to do mighty works in the Lord's name does not necessarily guarantee trueness of heart (Mt. 7:21–23; 25:11f.). Jesus knew very well that it is all too possible to honor God with the lips while the heart is far from him (Mk. 7:1–8). Many of the same voices that cried "Hosanna" (a petition for salvation, Ps. 118:25) and hailed Jesus as king on Palm Sunday insistently demanded his crucifixion on Good Friday. Genuine confession with the lips springs only from belief that is deeply rooted in the heart (Rom. 10:9f.).

To turn to individual cases, Paul had the sad experience of being deserted by his erstwhile fellow worker Demas, who was lured away by "love of this present world" (2 Tim. 4:10; cf. Philem. 24; Col. 4:14; Mk. 4:18f.). Simon Magus, who professed belief and was baptized, was shortly afterwards rebuked by Peter as being "in the gall of bitterness and in the bond of iniquity" (Acts 8:9ff.)—though in this instance, it is true, he was urged to repent and pray for forgiveness; tradition strongly affirms, however, that Simon became a megalomaniacal heresiarch. But no defection is more startling than that of Judas Iscariot, one of the Twelve, no less, who for the duration of our Lord's ministry was blessed with the special privilege of being constantly in his presence, enjoying the warmth of his friendship, receiving his sublime instruction, and witnessing his wonderful works, and yet who sold his heart to Satan and betrayed the Master he had followed so long and so closely (Lk. 22:3; Jn. 13:2). Furthermore, the apostate condition of his heart, though known to Jesus, was not even suspected by the rest of the Twelve, to whom it was unthinkable that any of their number could prove to be a traitor (Mk. 14:18f.; Lk. 22:21–23).

The sin of apostasy, then, is a grim (and far more than a merely hypothetical) possibility for persons who through identification with the people of God have been brought within the sphere of the divine blessing. They may be baptized, as Simon Magus was, occupied in Christian labors, as Demas was, endowed with charismatic gifts, preachers even, healers of the sick and casters out of demons, and privileged to belong to an inner circle of disciples, as Judas was (Mk. 6:12f.; Mt. 10:5ff.), and yet

their heart may be far from the One they profess to serve. Such considerations from elsewhere in the New Testament throw light on the passage that is before us. The Hebrew Christians who are being addressed
had to all appearances been incorporated into the church of Christ: they
had professed repentance, been enlightened, tasted the heavenly gift,
partaken of the Holy Spirit, and experienced the goodness of the word
of God and the powers of the age to come; but, despite all this, they, or
at least some among them, had failed to such a degree to show spiritual
progress that it was doubtful whether they had grasped even the first
principles of the faith (5:11–6:2). The author fears that they are in imminent danger of slipping away into reprobation. As 10:26f. shows, wilful
or deliberate repudiation of the truth they have known would place
them beyond the scope of that grace whose benign influences have been
shed upon them. Such persons, of their own choice, withdraw themselves from the sphere of redemption and take their stand with those
who *crucify the Son of God* and *hold him up to contempt.* [68] They now show
themselves in their true colors. They join the ranks of the mob that yells
"Crucify him, crucify him!" and that wickedly derides and insults the
suffering Savior; and they do this *on their own account,* that is, in their
own persons and of their own volition: they are not content that others
should have scorned him apart from them.

The patristic authors, we may affirm, were wrong-headed in their
wish to explain that this passage, despite its categorical declaration to
the contrary, should not be understood as excluding all possibility of
repentance to such persons. Regrettably, their judgment at this point
was affected by the problems presented by the rigorist sects of their
times. But their insistence on the impossibility of the repetition of baptism is another matter and is deserving of closer consideration. A somewhat typical assertion is that of Chrysostom: "What, then, is repentance
excluded? God forbid! but the renewing again by baptism." Jerome relates the whole passage to Christian baptism and its significance:
"Surely we cannot deny that they have been enlightened and have
tasted the heavenly gift and have been made partakers of the Holy Spirit
and have tasted the good word of God." [69] Ambrose contends that "it is
evident that the writer was speaking of baptism from the very words in
which it is stated that it is impossible to renew unto repentance those
who have fallen, inasmuch as we are renewed by means of the laver of

---

68. The tenses of the Greek participles are significant: the aorist participle παραπεσόντας
indicates a decisive moment of commitment to apostasy, the point of no return; the
present participles ἀνασταυροῦντας and παραδειγματίζοντας indicate the continuing state
of those who have once lapsed into apostasy: they keep on crucifying the Son of God and
holding him up to contempt.
69. Jerome, *Adversus Jovinianum* ii.3.

baptism"; and in support of this interpretation he cites the teaching of Romans 6:4 where Paul says that "by baptism we were buried with Christ into death, so that as Christ was raised from the dead by the glory of the Father we too should walk in newness of life." He further understands the admonition of Ephesians 4:22–24 as a reference to the significance of baptism: "Put off your old nature . . . and be renewed in the spirit of your minds, and put on the new nature, created after the likeness of God in true righteousness and holiness." Ambrose goes on to expound the association between baptism and the crucifixion of Christ: "This, too, is plain, that in him who is baptized the Son of God is crucified, for our flesh could not do away sin unless it were crucified in Jesus Christ"; for, as Paul teaches again, "all we who were baptized into Christ Jesus were baptized into his death," and "we know that our old self was crucified with him" (Rom. 6:3, 6). Thus baptism signifies that "Christ is crucified in us, so that our sins may be purged through him, that he, who alone can forgive sins, may nail to his cross the handwriting which was against us" (Col. 2:14). From this teaching the conclusion is drawn that as Christ was once crucified and died for sins once so there is but one baptism, which cannot be repeated without violating the principle of Christ's once-for-all sacrifice.[70] Chrysostom's comments are to precisely the same effect.

Now it may very well be that the danger confronting those whom our author is addressing involved, in effect, the repudiation of their baptism. The New Testament undoubtedly affirms a very high doctrine of baptism, and in favor of interpreting the passage in the light of the baptismal event is the series of participles in the aorist tense,[71] which would appropriately point back to the moment of initiation through a rite which dramatically and publicly symbolizes the candidate's turning from the darkness of unbelief to the light of the gospel. The cardinal significance of baptism is explained by Paul to Titus, in a passage which has clear affinities with the one before us. "God saved us," he declares, "not because of deeds done by us in righteousness, but in virtue of his own mercy, by the washing of regeneration and renewal of the Holy Spirit, which he poured out upon us richly through Jesus Christ our Savior, so that we might be justified by his grace and become heirs in hope of eternal life" (Tit. 3:5–7). Reduced to a single phrase, baptism is "the washing of regeneration." The external element of this washing is water, but the water is a sacramental symbol which graphically points to an internal reality, "renewal in the Holy Spirit," who effectively applies to the believing heart cleansing from sin by the blood of Jesus Christ (cf.

---

70. Ambrose, *De Poenitentia* ii.2.
71. Φωτισθέντας . . . γευσαμένους . . . γενηθέντας . . . γευσαμένους.

1 Jn. 1:7; 5:6; 1 Pet. 3:21). That is to say, as Augustine taught long ago, the element of water must be linked to the word of the gospel, otherwise there is no sacrament.[72] Accordingly, Paul tells the Ephesian Christians that Christ's cleansing of his church is "by washing of water in the sphere of the word" (Eph. 5:26); and Paul himself, at his conversion, was exhorted by Ananias: "Be baptized, and wash away your sins, calling on his name" (Acts 22:16; similarly 2:38). The internal and essential reality of Christian baptism is the Holy Spirit. Thus the baptism of Christ, in contrast to the baptism of John (and for that matter the proselyte baptism of the Jews), is described as baptism with the Holy Spirit (Mk. 1:8, par.; Jn. 1:33); and thus Christ admonished Nicodemus: "Truly, truly, I say to you, unless one is born of water and the Spirit, he cannot enter the kingdom of God" (Jn. 3:5).

Furthermore, the regeneration which Christian baptism portrays is symbolized by the sequence of descent into and under the water and ascent from the water, signifying self-identification with the death, burial, and resurrection of Christ. "In baptism," Paul reminds the Colossians, "you were buried with him, in baptism you were raised to life with him, through your faith in the active power of God who raised him from the dead" (Col. 2:12 NEB). The far-reaching implications of this baptismal union with Christ in death, burial, and resurrection are expounded at length in Romans 6:1ff. The plain logic of baptism, then, is that one has died to the old life of sin and been raised to newness of life in Christ. And as the death of Christ for sinners is, as our epistle repeatedly emphasizes, once for all, never to be repeated, so also this determines the once-for-all character of Christian baptism. This emphasis comes through in the present passage in the declaration that "it is impossible to restore again to repentance those who have *once*, and therefore unrepeatably, been enlightened . . . tasted the heavenly gift . . . become partakers of the Holy Spirit . . . tasted the goodness of the word of God and the powers of the age to come"—the term "once" qualifies not just the first verb but the whole sequence of verbs, showing that it is a unitary experience, a single, decisive event that is spoken of here.

A repetition of baptism suggests the possibility of a repetition of the crucifixion of Christ; and to revert from the evangelical faith professed and dramatized in baptism to a state of mutinous unbelief is to put Christ and his cross to open mockery. The following comments by Lefèvre d'Etaples are very much to the point in this connection:

> It is not said simply that it is impossible for persons to be restored to repentance, but that it is impossible for those who crucify again the Son of God in themselves and make him a figure of shame to be restored to

72. Augustine, Tract. LXXX.3, on the Gospel of John.

repentance, which is precisely what those do who, having fallen away after receiving the baptismal enlightenment, imagine that they can be restored as penitents by means of a repetition of baptism. For through baptism we die, are buried, and rise again with Christ; and this is something that can happen only once. For the Lord died once, was buried once, and rose again once. Is not to crucify Christ a second time in a second baptism to set him up as a figure of extreme shame: as though his having been crucified, dead, and buried once were insufficient for the redemption of the world?

Like so many others in the preceding centuries, Lefèvre d'Etaples goes on to affirm, inconsistently with this passage, that while the way is not open for the repetition of baptism it is always open for the return of the penitent. Of course, the very possibility of lapsing from all that one's baptism signifies discountenances any doctrine of automatic regeneration, *ex opere operato*, through baptism, as though the external rite itself guaranteed the internal reality. Indeed, the whole issue of this passage may be said to revolve around the question whether the internal reality, to which the external rite is designed to testify, is truly present or not.

Our conclusions concerning the first six verses of chapter 6 may be summed up as follows: that verses 1 and 2 relate to the response of repentance and faith to the preaching of the gospel followed by the basic instruction which precedes baptism; and that verses 4 through 6 describe the irremediable state of those who, having publicly confessed allegiance to Christ in baptism, subsequently turn their backs on the gospel and thereby renounce their baptism and all that is implied by it. Repudiating their profession that Christ was crucified for them and they with him, they show that their true place is with those rejecters who display their hatred by crucifying him. Such apostates are not genuine branches of him who is the true vine; they do not abide in him and so they are cut off and cast away (Jn. 15:1ff.).

Finally, when the redeeming blood of Christ is applied by the Holy Spirit to the very heart of a man's being, it is a work of God that cannot fail. This means that those who are genuinely Christ's do not fall away into apostasy. Where there is a work of God, whether in creation or in re-creation, whether in judgment or in grace, that work, simply because it is *God's* work, cannot fail to achieve its purpose in accordance with the divine will. Thus Paul is assured that God who began a good work in the Philippian believers will bring it to completion at the day of Jesus Christ (Phil. 1:6); and he encourages Timothy, at a time when he is faced with the defection of Hymenaeus and Philetus, with the reminder that God's foundation is firm and secure, bearing this seal: "The Lord knows those who are his" (2 Tim. 2:19). The mystery of divine election is the guarantee that Christ will not have died in vain and that the purpose of his coming into the world will be fulfilled without any hint of frustration.

This was the certain confidence of the incarnate Lord himself, who declared: "All that the Father gives me will come to me; and him who comes to me I will not cast out" (Jn. 6:37), and who assured his disciples that those to whom he gave eternal life would never perish and that no one would be able to snatch them from his hand (Jn. 10:28). How, indeed, can the life he gives be described as eternal if for one reason or another it may fail or be cut off?

It is plain that our author does not contemplate the possibility that the work of God in the lives of those to whom he is writing may fail or be frustrated, for he expresses confidence concerning them, and that confidence is based on the assurance that God's word and God's work, which have been powerful in their midst, cannot falter (cf. 6:9ff., 17ff.; 10:39 below; note also his request for their prayers in 13:18—a strong mark of his confidence regarding the genuineness of their relationship to God). What he has reason to fear is that some among them who have professed Christian faith, enjoyed Christian fellowship, and engaged in Christian witness may prove to be hypocrites and enemies of Christ and, by turning away from the light they have known, show that they do not belong to God's people at all.

> 6:7, 8. *For land which has drunk the rain that often falls upon it, and brings forth vegetation useful to those for whose sake it is cultivated, receives a blessing from God. But if it bears thorns and thistles, it is worthless and near to being cursed; its end is to be burned.*

The point of the admonition which has just been given is pressed home by the use of a simple parable. The soil enjoys the benefit of *rain* frequently showered upon it for its enrichment and fertility, so that it in turn may by its fruitfulness be of benefit to others. In fulfilling this function it is blessed of God. Spiritual productiveness is a manifestation of the operation of divine grace; for it is God who sends the rain of his mercy upon the soil of human lives, and who also as the husbandman tends his vineyard (Jn. 15:1)[73] and gives the increase (1 Cor. 3:6f.). But if instead of the benefaction of seasonable fruits the soil produces *thorns and thistles*, then a curse is upon it and its worthless harvest awaits the judgment of destruction by fire. So, too, the man who has been brought within the sphere of the blessings of the gospel so graciously showered on mankind by Almighty God and has publicly professed faith in Christ

---

73. Compare the description of the Father as ὁ γεωργός in John 15:1 and γεωργεῖται, "it is cultivated," here.

crucified and associated himself with the company of the redeemed, and whose life then produces the baneful crop of "thorns and thistles,"[74] that is, of hostility to the Son of God and conduct incompatible with his profession, invites not the blessing but the curse of God upon himself, and his end is the fire of judgment (cf. 12:29 below; Phil. 3:19; Mt. 3:10, 12; 5:22; 13:30, 42, 49f.; 18:8f.; 25:41; Jn. 15:6; 2 Pet. 3:7, etc.). Origen remarks, in reference to these verses, that "every one's will, if untrained and fierce and barbarous, is either hardened by the miracles and wonders of God, growing more savage and thorny than ever, or it becomes more pliant and yields itself up with the whole mind to obedience, if it is cleared from vice and subjected to training."[75]

The affinities of this parable with the account of creation and the fall would not have been missed by the Hebrew readers of this letter. God's creation mandate for the earth was: "Let the earth put forth vegetation, plants yielding seed, and fruit trees bearing fruit in which is their seed, each according to his kind, upon the earth" (Gen. 1:11); and this beneficent productivity of the soil followed the sending of rain upon the earth (Gen. 2:5, 9). But with the entry of sin into the world and the fall of man into apostasy from God, a curse is pronounced which extends beyond Satan and man to the whole created order, including the ground and its productivity: "Cursed is the ground because of you ... thorns and thistles it shall bring forth to you..." (Gen. 3:17f.). The readers would doubtless also have recollected the not dissimilar parable of the vineyard in Isaiah 5:1ff. which, after being carefully planted and tended, yielded wild instead of sweet grapes, with the consequence that judgment is pronounced over it: "I will make it a waste; it shall not be pruned or hoed, and briers and thorns shall grow up; I will also command the clouds that they rain no rain upon it." The explanation is added that "the vineyard of the Lord of hosts is the house of Israel, and the men of Judah are his pleasant planting"; that is to say, the very ones who had enjoyed the blessings of God's gracious covenant were the ones who had fallen away into apostasy and invited God's judgment upon themselves.

Chrysostom finds it comforting that the sterile ground is not said to be actually cursed but only *near to being cursed,* for he takes this to imply that there is still opportunity for repentance and reform. This, however, seems to be a misunderstanding of the author's meaning, and it is an

---

74. Thomas Aquinas, in company with other medieval commentators, quaintly interprets "thorns" as indicating lesser sins and "thistles" greater sins. Chrysostom, no less quaintly, observes that "with good reason did he call sin a 'thistle'"—or more strictly, a three-spiked burr, τρίβολος—"for on whatever side you grasp it, it wounds and pierces, and is unpleasant even to look at."
75. Origen, *De Principiis* III.i.10 (from the Latin version).

interpretation which is ill fitted to the context. "The nearness of the curse," as Spicq well observes, "does not imply that the threatened judgment can be avoided by a sudden and unexpected fertility of the earth. This would be out of harmony with the condemnation without appeal pronounced against apostates, of whom the sterile earth is a figure." Spicq refers to 8:13 below, where exactly the same idiom appears in connection with the old covenant which is described as being "near to vanishing away,"[76] remarking that "the disappearance of that which is obsolete cannot be considered as susceptible of being avoided." To the same effect, in Mark 1:15 and Matthew 3:2 and 4:17, where it is declared that the kingdom of God is at hand, or near,[77] it is regarded as having already arrived (cf. Mt. 12:28).[78] "It is a nearness of contact," to quote Spicq again.[79] This understanding is confirmed, further, by the assertion that the *end* of the barrenness of which our author speaks is *to be burned.*

6:9, 10. *Though we speak thus, yet in your case, beloved, we feel sure of better things that belong to salvation. For God is not so unjust as to overlook your work and the love which you showed for his sake in serving the saints, as you still do.*

Despite the preceding admonition concerning the serious danger of apostasy, our author is confident that those to whom he is writing are firmly founded in the faith. This does not mean that the warning is after all unnecessary or unrealistic. As we have seen (5:11f.), they are in general so far from making spiritual progress that to all intents and purposes they need to be instructed again in the first principles of the Christian faith. A stagnant situation is always an unhealthy one, and indeed potentially fatal, and there is a real peril that their community as a whole or some of their number in particular may decline into apostasy and reprobation. The light of a church, once vital and flourishing, can be extinguished and all too frequently has been extinguished, as history shows only too plainly. This, too, is the force of the warnings contained in the letters to the seven churches of the Apocalypse (Rev. 2 and 3).

At the same time, however, there is confidence that a genuine work of grace has taken place in their midst. Though the danger signals are

76. Compare κατάρας ἐγγύς here and ἐγγὺς ἀφανισμοῦ in 8:13.
77. Ἤγγικεν.
78. Ἔφθασεν ἐπί.
79. Cf. Moffatt's comment: "There is no thought of mildness in the term ἐγγύς, it being used, as in 8:13, of imminent doom, which is only a matter of time. Meanwhile there is the ἐκδοχή (10:27)."

plain to see, and even though, it may be, some are already showing themselves to be turncoats, the gospel has not been preached to no purpose. As with the church in Ephesus, whose members, while threatened with the removal of their lampstand, are commended for their works, their toil, their patient endurance, and their opposition to those who are false apostles and Nicolaitans (Rev. 2:2–6), so also here our author speaks approvingly of the work and love of his readers in ministering to their fellow Christians. Paul displays a similar confidence with regard to his apostolic labors. Despite the many serious problems and aberrations which disturbed the churches he addressed, he could never doubt that God would give an eternal increase to the faithful sowing and watering of the good seed of the gospel. Thus he tells the Christians in Rome of his assurance respecting them (Rom. 15:14); to the Corinthians, whom he has had to rebuke in the sternest terms, he declares: "I have great confidence in you, I have great pride in you" (2 Cor. 7:4); he is certain that God's work begun among the Philippians will not fail to be brought to its destined completion (Phil. 1:6); the Galatians, who have been hindered in the race and are in danger of losing their liberty in Christ, will, he is persuaded, respond to his correction (Gal. 5:1, 7–10). The great principle which gives rise to this confidence is the absolute sovereignty of the God of grace and the indefectibility of his work in the lives of men. From first to last regeneration is of God (2 Cor. 5:18ff.), hence it is secure. Whatever is of man is fallible and insecure. But those who have experienced the power of God's redeeming grace in Christ know that this has been effected in fulfilment of "the purpose of him who accomplishes all things according to the counsel of his will," that in Christ they are "sealed with the promised Holy Spirit," and that therefore the glorious inheritance which is theirs is guaranteed for all eternity (Eph. 1:11–14).

It is considerations of this kind which cause our author to tell his readers that he is assured, where they are concerned, of *better things*, better, that is, than the relapse into infidelity against which he has been warning them, things, in other words, that *belong to salvation* rather than apostasy. The affectionate manner in which he addresses them here as *beloved* confirms his confidence in them as well as his love for them. And this confidence is bolstered by the recollection of their *work* and their *love* on behalf of their brethren in the faith, involving, as 10:32ff. below indicates, the endurance of severe affliction, exposure to public obloquy, loss of possessions, and ministry to those who for their faith had been thrown into prison. This confidence is confirmed, further, by the knowledge that *serving the saints* is for them not just a thing of the past but something they are still doing. The love shown to their fellow Christians, moreover, is *for his sake*, or, more literally, it is love shown "to his name."[80] This implies that their coming to the assistance of their brethren is evidence of their willingness to identify themselves with the stigma attaching to the name of Jesus, and thus of the genuineness of their love for him.

There is no necessity to conclude that "saints" is a term used here specifically to designate the Christians of the mother church in Jerusalem and that to "serve" or minister to them means the sending of financial aid, with the further inference that the community to whom this letter is addressed must have been located in some country other than Palestine;[81] for it is a clear fact that in the New Testament Christians in general are referred to as "saints," including those to whom this letter was sent (13:24)—whether they live in Rome, Corinth, Ephesus, Colossae, Thessalonica, or Jerusalem. In any case, the implication of 10:32ff. below is that the sphere of love and ministry to which our author is referring is that of his readers' own, rather than of some other, community. If, then, by "saints" Christians in Jerusalem are intended, this would provide an argument, rather, for locating the recipients of this epistle in or near that city and against locating them in some country, like Italy, outside of Palestine.

The assurance that *God is not so unjust as to overlook* the *work* and *love* of these Hebrew Christians has been cited by Roman Catholic apologists as supporting the doctrine of the meritorious character of good works. Good works, it is maintained, are deserving of a reward and establish, as it were, a claim upon God. Thus, for example, Thomas Aquinas in commenting on this passage affirms the distinction between the merit of good works performed before justification (*meritum congrui*) and the merit of good works performed after justification (*meritum condigni*). This distinction, however, entrenched though it is in Roman Catholicism, is alien to the emphatic biblical teaching of the incapacitation of man through sin with its corollary of the justification of man by virtue only of the free and all-sufficient grace of God in Christ Jesus, so that the redeemed sinner can but testify with Paul, "By the grace of God I am what I am" (1 Cor. 15:10). As Calvin explains, the author "is clearly not discussing here the cause of our salvation, and therefore no conclusion should be drawn from this passage about the merits of works." And more recently Montefiore has written: "There is no doctrine here of the merit of good works. Nor is there any suggestion of a recompense for services rendered, but rather for the love which must issue in good works if it is real love."

---

80. Εἰς τὸ ὄνομα αὐτοῦ.
81. Thus F. F. Bruce comments: "When the writer refers to his readers' long-standing and continued ministering 'to the saints' (Ch. 6:10), we may reflect that throughout the apostolic age the Jerusalem church is more prominent as a recipient than as a giver of such ministry" (p. xxxii).

Certainly, the Christian is exhorted to produce good works, as a good tree bears good fruit and is known by that fruit; and the production of good fruit in his life is something for which he is held responsible. But as the principle or root of faith is implanted within the heart by God's grace, so also the growth and the harvest of good works that spring from that root are to be attributed to the power and the goodness of God enabling him to do what he is commanded to do. This is the teaching given by Paul to the Ephesians when he says: "God, rich in mercy, for the great love he bore us, brought us to life with Christ even when we were dead in our sins.... For it is by his grace you are saved, through trusting him; it is not your own doing. It is God's gift, not a reward for work done. There is nothing for anyone to boast of. For we are God's handiwork, created in Christ Jesus to devote ourselves to the good deeds for which God has designed us" (Eph. 2:4–10 NEB). Similarly he writes to the Philippians: "Work out your own salvation with fear and trembling; for God is at work in you, both to will and to work for his good pleasure" (Phil. 2:12f.). And again, when he informs the Corinthians that he worked harder than any of the other asrpostles, he adds: "though it was not I, but the grace of God which was with me" (1 Cor. 15:10). Here, then, our author interprets the work and the love shown by his readers to others in Christ's name as a sign that God was truly at work within them. Such loving labor is pleasing to God, for as an evidence of God's working within, it is at the same time a manifestation of the graciousness of God himself. Being "in the Lord," it is "not in vain" (1 Cor. 15:58); God adds his blessing to it (Jas. 1:25). God, who is just, never overlooks the works of love and service that spring from a good heart of faith. Thus, in like manner, even when reproving the church in Ephesus for departing from its first love and its first works and exhorting it to repent, the Lord says: "I know your works, your toil and your patient endurance, and how you cannot bear evil men.... I know you are enduring patiently and bearing up for my name's sake, and you have not grown weary" (Rev. 2:2–5). The commendation increases the solemnity of the rebuke and the warning.

6:11, 12. *And we desire each one of you to show the same earnestness in realizing the full assurance of hope until the end, so that you may not be sluggish, but imitators of those who through faith and patience inherit the promises.*

The author's deep concern for the spiritual progress of his readers is further conveyed in the Greek verb translated here *we desire*,[82] the strong

---

82. Ἐπιθυμοῦμεν.

sense of which is more effectively communicated by translating it "we long" (NEB) or "it is our earnest wish" (Phillips); for it is, as Moffatt says, "a term charged with intense yearning." His affectionate longing, moreover, extends to *each one* of them: as a true pastor of Christ's flock, the well-being of every individual is a concern close to his heart. He addresses them, as Chrysostom observes, not with the authority of a teacher but with the affection of a father. It is natural for parents to desire earnestly that their children should advance in strength of mind and body; so also the Christian pastor longs that those committed to his charge should go on to maturity (v. 1). Arrested growth, whether physical or spiritual, is a tragedy. The Christian life must be marked by progress and perseverance *until the end* (cf. Mt. 10:22; Mk. 13:13; Rev. 2:26). Its direction is ever onward and upward (cf. 12:1f. below), and *hope* is one of its distinguishing characteristics—hope that is securely founded on the promise and the power of God, and which itself is the dynamic impulse that drives us on toward the goal.

As in these two verses, so throughout the epistle the close association between faith and hope is apparent. "True faith," as Calvin remarks, "always goes hand in hand with hope." The invitation to faith is not an invitation to inactivity but to the perseverance of pilgrimage, for Christ is not only the source but also the goal of our salvation, the end as well as the beginning. Faith indeed rests upon the alpha, but it also displays itself as hope directed toward the omega (cf. Rev. 22:13). While it is true, therefore, as Paul assures the members of the church in Rome, that "we are justified by faith" and our standing is "in grace," yet this does not imply that we may stand still or withdraw from the conflict, for, as Paul adds, "we rejoice in our hope of sharing the glory of God," and, this being so, "we rejoice in our sufferings, knowing that suffering produces endurance, and endurance produces character, and character produces hope, and hope does not disappoint us, because God's love has been poured into our hearts through the Holy Spirit which has been given to us" (Rom. 5:1–5). In the case of the recipients of this letter, similarly, *earnestness*, the *same* as they have already showed, is demonstrated by endurance in suffering and perseverance in loving service, and is itself the clear evidence of *the full assurance of hope*. It is not surprising, then, that our author is alarmed at the indications that his readers are becoming *sluggish* and at the possibility that the dwindling of their enthusiasm could cause them even to contemplate dropping out of the race (cf. 10:35f.; 12:1, 12); for sluggishness, which is only one degree removed from stagnation, is a symptom of the clouding over of the perspective of hope.

No more stirring example of this perspective of hope could be found than that afforded by the patriarchs and heroes of the faith of the past, who received the promises and believed them but did not see their fulfilment. Yet *through faith* in God's word *and patience*, which bore witness to the vital nature of their hope, they showed that they belonged to the company of those who *inherit* and make their own *the promises*. Despite severe trials and afflictions, they believed and endured in the assurance that their hope in the blessings announced to them would not be disappointed. The specific example of Abraham is mentioned in the verses that follow, but then this grand theme is set aside while our author instructs his readers in the doctrine of the priesthood of Christ as contrasted with that of the Mosaic system, to be resumed, however, and developed in chapter 11, which is justly renowned for the nobility of its thought and expression.

6:13–15. *For when God made a promise to Abraham, since he had no one greater by whom to swear, he swore by himself, saying, "Surely I will bless you and multiply you." And thus Abraham, having patiently endured, obtained the promise.*

Of those whose example of faith and patience is to be imitated Abraham in particular is singled out here; for he was pre-eminent among all the heroic figures of the old dispensation for his unwavering faith in the promises of God and his patience in awaiting their fulfilment. It was his faith that engendered his firm hope that, though delayed, the fulfilment of the promises would not fail, and this hope stimulated his patient perseverance through prolonged and perplexing testings. To quote Paul's memorable words, "in hope he believed against hope"—that is to say, despite all appearances to the contrary, his confidence in God's word remained unshaken. "No distrust made him waver concerning the promise of God, but he grew strong in his faith as he gave glory to God, fully convinced that God was able to do what he had promised" (Rom. 4:18, 20f.).

God, moreover, confirmed his promise to Abraham by an oath. Undoubtedly, it seems strange to find God represented as resorting to an oath, since an oath is ordinarily sworn with reference to God as the source and sum of all that is true and trustworthy. Furthermore, it is, strictly speaking, between men that the necessity for the taking of oaths arises, because of the uncertainty and unreliability, due to sin, of human words and promises. That God should bind himself by an oath is a reflection not on the divine credibility but on the perversion of the human situation. God's oath, indeed, though in itself redundant since his word is absolute truth (Jn. 17:17), is a condescension to human frailty. For God to have sworn by someone or something other than himself would have implied, either that the person or thing by which he swore was greater than himself, and therefore that he must be less than God, and his word, like man's, less than absolutely certain, or, since there is nothing greater than God, that the thing by which he swore, being other than God and therefore finite and impermanent, would accordingly invest his oath with finitude and impermanence (and incidentally controvert the nature of an oath, which, as v. 16 will remind us, is to swear by someone greater than oneself and especially by the ultimate and eternal reality of God's being).[83] God, however, reinforced Abraham's faith in the promise by means of an oath, and, *since he had no one greater by whom to swear, he swore by himself.* God's word, as we have remarked, inasmuch as it is *God's* word, cannot fail and stands in no need of strengthening; but for Abraham's sake, and in view of the low level of credibility belonging to the promises of fallen mankind, God made his promise doubly secure, as it were, by an appeal to the infallible integrity of his own self.

The passage quoted here is Genesis 22:16f., and it is of particular interest that the occasion was the offering up by Abraham of Isaac, the son of the promise, in obedience to the command of God. The patriarch's trust in the integrity of God and his promise could not have been put to a more severe test, for the fulfilment of the covenant which God had made with him depended on the life and the line of Isaac, and the instruction to slay his son had the appearance of the failure of the divine word (cf. Gen. 12:2f.; 13:15f.; 15:5f., 18; 17:7, 9, 15, 19, 21; 18:18f.; 21:12). Abraham's confidence in that word and its fulfilment was so firm, however, that he obeyed without question the command to offer up his son Isaac, convinced, as our author points out in 11:19 below, that God would, if need be, raise him from the dead and thus vindicate the trustworthiness of the promise. It should be noticed, too, that God's reaffirmation of the promise with an oath took place *after* this trial of Abraham's faith. In the light of this consideration it is plain that Abraham's faith in the infallibility of the promise associated so intimately with Isaac was unwavering even before God added an oath for its confirmation. Indeed, seen within this context, the divine oath is a response to Abraham's great faith, not to his doubt. It is the token of God's approval and pleasure that his servant has come through this most

---

83. In Strack-Billerbeck the explanation of Rabbi Eleazer ben Pedat (third century) of Exodus 32:13 is quoted as follows: "Moses said to God: Lord of the world, if thou hadst sworn by heaven or by earth, I would have been able to say: As heaven and earth shall pass away, so also thine oath shall pass away. But now that thou hast sworn by thy great Name (by thyself), as thy great Name lives and abides eternally, so also shall thine oath continue secure in all eternity" (*Berakhot* 32a).

grievous testing without giving way to doubts and questionings. Accordingly, the promise which the oath introduces is expressed with special emphasis: *"Surely* (assuredly)[84] I will bless you and multiply you."

And thus, our author continues, *Abraham, having patiently endured, obtained the promise.* The testing of his trustful obedience by the command to offer up Isaac was the climax of many years of patient endurance for Abraham. Undeterred by delays and trials he clung tenaciously to the promise, and in doing so he made it his own special possession: he *obtained* it (cf. 11:33 below); by testing and perseverance he laid hold of it, proving this finally by the triumph of his faith as he received Isaac back virtually from the dead and thus in a real sense *obtained* his only son and with him the promise, which God now reaffirmed and strengthened with an oath. And so it is a great thing not only to receive the promise but also to *obtain* it (or *attain* it, NEB). This the majority of the people of Israel, the nation descended from Abraham through Isaac, failed to do because of the hardness of their hearts;[85] and this the Hebrew Christians to whom this letter is addressed are also in danger of failing to do, unless they imitate the faith and persistence of Abraham. Lefèvre d'Etaples comments finely on this passage, as follows:

> They are sluggish who, impatient of labors and the long delays of the promised blessings, cease from doing good or prefer to follow present pleasures and are opposed to those who persevere.... But those who are patient are not broken by any delay, are not diverted by any blandishments, are not cast down by any adversities, from the hope of those blessings, and they bear all things and do all things for the sake of him who solely by his goodness promises such good things to those who have faith and hope in him. And lest those who trust and hope should ever relax their faith and patience and become less confident, he swore by himself, so that they might have absolute certainty regarding the promise and as they persevere further might no more doubt those blessings than if they were a present possession.

---

84. The emphatic Hebrew idiom of the infinitive absolute followed by the finite form of the same verb is imitated to some degree in the Greek text by preceding the finite verb with the participle of the same verb: εὐλογῶν εὐλογήσω... πληθύνων πληθυνῶ. This in turn is rendered literally in the KJV: "blessing I will bless... multiplying I will multiply." The emphasis is best conveyed, however, by the use of an intensifying adverb, as in our version (RSV); cf. "I vow that I will bless you abundantly..." (NEB), "Assuredly I will bless you..." (Weymouth).

85. See Romans 11:7, where the same verb ἐπιτυγχάνειν is used as here. Paul declares that, despite having received the promises (cf. 9:4), Israel failed to obtain, οὐκ ἐπέτυχεν, because the people were hardened, but that the company of the elect did obtain, ἐπέτυχεν; so also here, Abraham not only received the promise (cf. Heb. 11:17) but also obtained it, ἐπέτυχεν.

6:16–18. *Men indeed swear by a greater than themselves, and in all their disputes an oath is final for confirmation. So when God desired to show more convincingly to the heirs of the promise the unchangeable character of his purpose, he interposed with an oath, so that through two unchangeable things, in which it is impossible that God should prove false, we who have fled for refuge might have strong encouragement to seize the hope set before us.*

So great is the general unreliability of human utterance that the use of an oath has become common practice when a statement or promise is made which is intended to be absolutely firm and binding. In this fallen world men, whose words have lost the authority that should belong to them, are accustomed to *swear by a greater than themselves*, in particular by God, seeking by this means to invest their utterance with that ultimate and inviolable authority which belongs to and derives from God himself. When *disputes* arise, that is, when the reliability of one person's word is questioned by another, an oath is accepted as *final for confirmation*,[86] and such an oath serves as a guarantee of good faith. To swear by God, "who never lies" (Tit. 1:2), or, in other words, to call God to witness that one is speaking the truth and acting honorably, is the highest affirmation of trustworthiness that any man can make. When God speaks, however, there is no one greater to whom he can appeal, as we have been reminded in verse 13, and so in reaffirming his promise to Abraham it was by himself that he swore. The oath was added not because God's word was in need of any kind of support, for in the nature of the case his word is indefectibly firm and reliable (which is the whole reason for swearing by God's name), but because, the human situation being what it is, God in his goodness *desired to show more convincingly*,[87] to underline, as it were, with a double assurance, *the*

---

86. For the evidence that the expression εἰς βεβαίωσιν, translated "for confirmation" here, belongs to the technical terminology of Egyptian civil law, see G. A. Deissmann, *Bible Studies* (Edinburgh, 1909, 2nd edn.), pp. 104–109. "The context of the passage," he asserts, "is permeated by juristic expressions—as is the Epistle to the Hebrews as a whole. That this Egyptian legal formula, persistent through hundreds of years, occurs here also, deserves our notice. We do not need to give it the same sharply defined sense it had in Attic jurisprudence (*guarantee in regard to a sale*): it must be interpreted more generally; at all events it is still a technical expression for a legal *guarantee*" (p. 107). It would seem that Deissmann regards this expression as belonging to the supposed Alexandrian background of the author of our epistle. On the question of authorship see Introduction, pp. 19ff.

87. Though comparative in form, περισσότερον, translated "more convincingly" here, is probably not comparative in sense. Cf. the occurrence of the other adverbial form περισσοτέρως in 2:1 and 13:19 and the notes in those places. In meaning it is emphatic and elative, "especially." Here, then, περισσότερον βουλόμενος ὁ θεὸς ἐπιδεῖξαι could be translated "when God wished to make especially plain."

unchangeable character of his purpose;[88] and to this end *he interposed with an oath.*[89] This he did for the sake not only of Abraham but also of all *the heirs of the promise*, whose line starts with Abraham and continues on through Isaac and the men and women of faith of the old dispensation (as expounded in ch. 11 below), and right on to the present moment, with Christ as the focal point of fulfilment; for the line is the line of faith, and specifically faith in Christ, in whom the promise has its realization (Jn. 8:56; Gal. 3:7–9, 16f.; 2 Cor. 1:20). All who by faith are united to Christ are heirs of the Abrahamic promise. Accordingly, Paul tells the Galatian believers: "If you are Christ's, then you are Abraham's off-spring, heirs according to promise" (Gal. 3:29).

God, then, guaranteed his trustworthiness *through two unchangeable things,*[90] namely, his word of promise and his oath in confirmation of that word, *in which it is impossible that God should prove false.* God's absolute truthfulness was thus doubly established, in order that we might have *strong encouragement to seize,* that is, to lay firm hold of and appropriate as our own, *the hope set before us,* or, more fully expressed, the glorious goal on which our hope is fixed. With this powerful incentive there is no excuse for sluggishness (vv. 10 and 11), for the encouragement of God's word and oath is constantly there for those who have turned their backs on the passing allurements of this world and *have fled for refuge.* Where is this refuge to which they have fled? When our author says here "we have fled for refuge" and, in 13:14 below, "here we have no lasting city, but we seek the city which is to come," the implication (suggested by Spicq and some others) is possible that those to whom he is writing have been driven from their homes by persecution and have become exiles or displaced persons; but it is far from being certain, and, if this was their situation, he would more likely have addressed them as "you," since, obviously, he is addressing them from a distance and to that extent his situation is not the same as theirs. But he says "we,"

88. Like βεβαίωσις (n. 86 above), ἀμετάθετος belongs to the legal terminology of the time and signifies a ruling or contract which is incapable of being set aside or annulled. Τò ἀμετάθετον, rendered "the unchangeable character" here, indicates the irrevocability of God's purpose as expressed in the promise and confirmed by the oath.
89. The verb μεσιτεύειν, which occurs nowhere else in biblical Greek, means properly to "intervene" or "mediate." The translation of ἐμεσίτευσεν as "interposed" corresponds to the Vulgate "interposuit," but the KJV rendering "confirmed it by an oath" (similarly NEB, "guaranteed it by an oath") is probably the correct sense here (so Teodorico, Bonsirven, Windisch, and others). It is a sense that is attested in the papyri and in Philo.
90. Δύο πραγμάτων ἀμεταθέτων: the irrevocability of God's purpose (n. 88 above) is established by two irrevocable realities, his promise and his oath. The same adjective is used in both places.

which is comprehensive, and it is of much greater importance to recognize that his language here and elsewhere applies to all believers of every age and clime, whatever their immediate circumstances may be: we are all strangers and pilgrims in this world on our way to the heavenly city. For every Christian, whether exiled or in his homeland, imprisoned or free, to "flee for refuge" is to turn to Christ and in him to find salvation and security (cf. Acts 9:35; 11:21). Our hope in him, as the next verse declares, is "a sure and steadfast anchor of the soul."

"The hope set before us" is the assurance that at last we shall be with Christ and be like Christ (Jn. 14:3; 1 Jn. 3:2), that ours will be the ultimate joy of witnessing and sharing in his eternal glory (Jn. 17:24), the experience, in short, of that imperishable inheritance which is ours in Christ (1 Cor. 2:9; 1 Pet. 1:3ff.). This is indeed a hope worth seizing; and, while it is appropriated by faith, it is far removed from all the uncertainties and disappointments that attend merely human hopes, for it is founded on the infallible and irrevocable verities of God's promise and God's oath.

Of parallel interest and significance is the consideration that the announcement of Christ's eternal priesthood after the order of Melchizedek, as affirmed in Psalm 110:4 and quoted in 7:20f. below, was also established with an oath. The addition of an oath in both instances serves to emphasize strongly the abiding importance in the divine scheme of salvation of the priestly order of Melchizedek as well as of the Abrahamic covenant. Both the promise and the priesthood achieve their unique and permanent fulfilment in Christ. In each case the introduction of an oath has the effect of concentrating the attention on matters of such eternal consequence, and confirming the integrity of God's redeeming purpose.

Many commentators point out that the legitimacy of employing an oath to mark the binding character of one's word may be derived from this passage. Aquinas, for example, says: "In this you have an example that an oath is not of itself unlawful, since Scripture attributes nothing to God which of itself is sinful."

> 6:19, 20. *We have this as a sure and steadfast anchor of the soul, a hope that enters into the inner shrine behind the curtain, where Jesus has gone as a forerunner on our behalf, having become a high priest for ever after the order of Melchizedek.*

Unlike the insecure sentiment which passes for hope in this transient world, the hope of the Christian, centered as it is in Christ, is so firm that it is possible for our author to describe it as *a sure and steadfast anchor for the soul.* The term "soul" (*psychē*) here denotes not an immaterial aspect of man's existence but "human life regarded as the life of an individual being with consciousness and will (Mt. 10:28; 16:26; Lk. 9:56; 12:19f.; Jn. 12:27; 2 Cor. 1:23; 12:15; Phil. 1:27; 1 Thess. 2:8)."[91] The *personal* security of the man whose hope rests on Christ is intended. The metaphor of an anchor in itself effectively portrays the concept of fixity, for the function of an anchor is to provide security in the face of changing tides and rising storms. Human anchors cannot hold man's life secure in the stresses and troubles that assail it; but the anchor of Christian hope is unfailingly sure and steadfast. There is an immense contrast between the former restless and meaningless existence which those who have "fled for refuge" (v. 18) have left behind them and the stability which, through fixing their confidence in Christ, they now enjoy. Even though this imagery is not used elsewhere in Scripture, it is not surprising that in the early days of the church, in the midst of physical insecurity and persecution, the anchor was adopted as the symbol of Christian hope and certainty and as a reminder that hereafter there will be calm after the tempest (cf. Heb. 4:9f.).[92] The anchor of hope, as Aquinas observes, "fixes the soul firmly in God in this world, which is like a kind of sea."

There is this difference, however, that, whereas sailors cast their anchors down into the depths to grip the ocean bed, the Christian's anchor ascends to the supreme heights of heaven: it is *a hope that enters into the inner shrine behind the curtain;* for, to quote Aquinas again, "there is no stability in this present life in which the soul may find security and rest." Calvin writes similarly that "our hope rises and flies aloft because it finds nothing to stand on in this world; it cannot rely on created things, but finds rest in God alone." Herveus, moreover, perceives a pleasing analogy in connection with the hiddenness of the anchor and its hold. "In the case of sailors," he says, "the sands in which the anchor is fixed and holds are hidden and invisible, and yet the sailors are secure, although they cannot see how the arms of the anchor are held. So also we, placed as we are amid the waves of this world, do not see the heavenly realities, and yet we are so joined to them through hope that we cannot be moved by any onset of fear."

The "inner shrine behind the curtain" into which the anchor of Christian hope enters is a reference to the holy of holies, that sacred inner chamber in the wilderness tabernacle and subsequently in the

---

91. H. Mehl-Koehnlein in *Vocabulary of the Bible,* ed. by J.-J. von Allmen (London, 1958), p. 251—American title *Companion to the Bible* (New York).
92. Spicq remarks that in the catacomb of Priscilla alone some 66 representations of the anchor have been found.

Jerusalem temple which was separated from the outer chamber known as the holy place by a curtain. This inner shrine was the place of the glory of God's presence, from which all but the high priest on one day of the year were excluded; but now, thanks to the perfect atonement accomplished by Christ, access into the heavenly sanctuary of God's eternal presence, of which the earthly shrine was a shadow and a symbol (cf. Heb. 8:5; 9:11f., 23f.), has been made open to all who by faith have laid hold of the hope that is set before us in him. The entry of the ascended Christ into the heavenly sanctuary means also the penetration of our hope into the presence-chamber of God himself, for Christ is our hope (1 Tim. 1:1): he and our hope are identical, so that on the Christian pilgrimage it is precisely Christ in us who is the hope of glory (Col. 1:27).

The Christian hope, then, is bound up with the realization that in entering the reality of the heavenly sanctuary *Jesus has gone as a forerunner on our behalf.* Although he has gone before, he has not deserted us; for a forerunner is one who goes on ahead in order to open up the way for those who follow after. In this respect the high priesthood of Christ is quite different from that of the old order, because the Aaronic high priest was no forerunner: in no sense did he open up the way for the people to follow him into the holy of holies, since, as has been mentioned, he alone was permitted to enter this most sacred place, and then only once a year, while the people were strictly forbidden to draw near. By contrast, however, Jesus, as our forerunner, has opened up the way for God's people, who formerly were excluded, so that now in him they have access into the very presence of God, and are encouraged to draw near with full confidence (see 4:16 and 10:19ff.). The ground of this confidence is the great truth that Jesus has, by way of Bethlehem and Calvary, *become a high priest for ever after the order of Melchizedek;*[93] and this is the theme—central to the doctrine of this epistle, previously introduced but then interrupted at 5:10—of the unique and all-sufficient high priesthood of our Lord and Savior Jesus Christ, which our author now takes up in the chapters that follow.

Notice that it is *Jesus* who is our forerunner into the heavenly sanctuary. The New Testament knows nothing of the distinction, fashionable in our day, between "the historic Jesus" and "the risen Christ," with its implication that the cross marked the end of the former and that Easter and the ascension relate only to the latter. It is a distinction which leaves us with a docetic Christ. The apostles, however, consistently proclaim, and without embarrassment, that it was *Jesus* who was raised from the dead (Acts 2:32), who ascended into heaven (Acts 1:9), who has

---

93. As Spicq remarks concerning the expression ἀρχιερεὺς γενόμενος, "the aorist participle evokes the incarnation and the sacrifice of the cross."

been exalted and glorified (Phil. 2:9), and who is coming again (Acts 1:11); and this teaching is amply confirmed in our epistle, in which it is *Jesus* who after the humiliation of incarnation and death has been crowned with glory and honor (2:9), who as our great high priest has passed through the heavens (4:14), to whom as our victorious and exalted Savior we, the runners of the Christian race, are urged to look (12:1f.; cf. 3:1), to whom as the living mediator of the new covenant we have come (13:24), who as the risen shepherd of the sheep continues to tend his flock (13:20f.), and who, in short, is the same yesterday and today and forever (13:8). If it were not one and the same Jesus, then all that is said and written about resurrection, ascension, glorification, and return is no more than empty words. Here, then, it is *Jesus* who has gone before us into the glory of the divine presence as our pioneer, our fellow, and our merciful and faithful high priest (2:10–17).[94]

EXCURSUS I: THE SIGNIFICANCE OF MELCHIZEDEK

The aura of mystery which surrounds the person of Melchizedek is not entirely or even primarily due to the fanciful roles that have been assigned to him in the course of the centuries, but springs, rather, from the enigmatic manner of his encounter with Abraham, as briefly described in the narrative of Genesis 14, and the laconic mention of him, centuries later, in the 110th Psalm. These are the only two references to Melchizedek in the whole of the Old Testament; yet they are sufficient to indicate that he is a figure of unusual significance. Who is this personage to whom Abraham, the great founder and progenitor of the nation of Israel, paid homage and whose name is associated with an eternal order of priesthood? It is hardly surprising that he became the subject of speculation, much of it extravagant, in both Jewish and Christian circles. The canonical Christian answer to the conundrum of the significance of Melchizedek is developed with logical precision by the author of the Epistle to the Hebrews who shows his importance within the typological perspective of the scheme of redemption. The fact that none of the other New Testament authors gives attention to Melchizedek does not imply that he was regarded as irrelevant by them, any more than that the institution of the Lord's Supper is explained only once in the Epistles implies that this sacrament was little esteemed in the apostolic church. Just as the writing of the First Epistle to the

---

94. "Christ," comments Spicq, "is identical as πρόδρομος with the ἀρχηγός of 2:10, and the accent is manifestly placed on his humanity, 'Ιησοῦς, for it is as man that he will be followed by his brethren."

Corinthians provided the proper occasion for a careful discussion of the importance of the eucharist and the resurrection, so also the writing of Hebrews provided the proper occasion for a careful discussion of the importance of Melchizedek. In each case, the authors were addressing situations which called for the discussion, respectively, of these particular themes. It is natural to infer that any theme which is developed in the pages of the New Testament, even if only in one place, was considered important for the church as a whole and accordingly widely expounded. This is certainly the view of the patristic writers.

Our author's answer to the question of Melchizedek's significance will be discussed later in the exegesis of chapter 7. Here it is proposed to survey historically the various attempts that have been made to understand and interpret the meaning of this intriguing figure. That our author is resurrecting an otherwise dead theme is most improbable, if only because it is the custom of the New Testament writers to address themselves to matters that are currently under discussion. This judgment is confirmed by evidence which clearly indicates that speculation regarding the eschatological significance of Melchizedek was very much in the air at the time the New Testament was being written. Quite the most striking piece of evidence is that of the scroll fragments discovered in Cave 11 at Qumran, in which Melchizedek is presented as the eschatological deliverer cast in the role of champion of the faithful Jewish remnant who have not defiled themselves by serving Belial. His advent marks the great Day of Atonement and Year of Jubilee and his dignity as chief of the heavenly hosts is so exalted that his supremacy matches that ascribed to the archangel Michael elsewhere in the Dead Sea Scrolls—so much so that an identity between the two may be assumed.[1] This being so, we can see that the teaching given here concerning the true significance of Melchizedek is not unconnected with that which has already been given concerning the proper function of angels.

This is witness enough to the existence of a definite and apparently well-developed contemporary background of speculation concerning the significance of Melchizedek as a powerful eschatological figure; and it may be assumed that such teaching was by no means limited to the monastic group at Qumran, but

---

1. The 11QMelch document has been assigned a date in the first half of the first century. For the reconstruction and discussion of the text see A. S. van der Woude, "Melchisedek als himmlische Erlösergestalt in den neugefundenen eschatologischen Midraschim aus Qumran Höhle XI," *Oudtestamentische Studiën*, 14 (1965), pp. 354–373; M. de Jonge and A. S. van der Woude, "11Q Melchizedek and the New Testament," NTS, 12 (1966), pp. 301–326; J. A. Fitzmyer, S. J., "Further Light on Melchizedek from Qumran Cave 11," JBL, 86 (1967), pp. 25–41. On the history of interpretation and speculation connected with Melchizedek see F. J. Jérôme, *Das geschichtliche Melchisedech-Bild und seine Bedeutung im Hebräerbrief* (Strasbourg, 1917); G. Wuttke, *Melchisedech der Priesterkönig von Salem: Eine Studie zur Geschichte der Exegese* (Giessen, 1927); J. Carmignac, "Le document de Qumrân sur Melkisédeq," *Revue de Qumrân*, 27 (1970), pp. 343–378; and J. Coppens, *Les Affinités Qumrâniennes de l'Epître aux Hébreux* (Louvain, 1962). "The function of Melchizedek," de Jonge and van der Woude point out, "as heavenly deliverer who protects the faithful people of God and as chief of the heavenly hosts runs parallel with that of the archangel Michael in the Dead Sea Scrolls, and in late Jewish and early Christian literature. Michael and Melchizedek are, however, not identified explicitly in the Qumran texts at our disposal. This identification is only found in certain medieval Jewish texts" (*ut supra*, p. 305).

was an expectation shared in common with other circles in the Judaism of the first century, not least by those of Essene persuasion. Hence, the necessity, if the assumption is correct that the recipients of this epistle were being attracted by doctrines similar to those of the Dead Sea Sect,[2] for our author to lead them to a correct understanding of Melchizedek and his importance. Certainly, the combination of regal and priestly functions in a single person is historically discernible in the Maccabean leader Simon who was confirmed as "leader and high priest in perpetuity until a true prophet should appear"; for not only was he in full charge of the temple but he was also supreme military commander and civil potentate, distinguished as such by "the purple robe and the gold clasp" (1 Macc. 14:41ff.; cf. the similar prerogatives of his predecessor Jonathan, 9:30f.; 10:20f.), and the combination of religious and civil authority was in general characteristic of his successors in the Hasmonaean line. This, however, is a matter of history, and a particular state of emergency, not eschatology. But a strand of expectation similar to that disclosed in the Cave 11 fragments, though without any mention of Melchizedek by name, may perhaps be preserved in the Levi section of the *Testaments of the Twelve Patriarchs*. There it is foretold that God will raise up a new priest who "will execute a judgment of truth upon the earth in the fulness of days," bringing peace among men and joy in heaven, and causing sin and lawlessness to cease (*Testament of Levi* 18). But the probability is that the anticipated advent of this kingly priest, or priest-king, rests on the messianic "Branch" prophecies of Zechariah, in which, with predictive symbolism, the high priest Joshua (who typifies him who was to bear the same name, Jesus our Joshua) has a crown placed on his head and receives the promise that "the man whose name is the Branch . . . shall build the temple of the Lord, and shall bear royal honor, and shall sit and rule upon his throne" (Zech. 6:11ff.; cf. 3:6ff.). There is no suggestion in the *Testaments*, however, that this eschatological priesthood will be anything other than levitical, and it is important to remember that the Dead Sea Sect was quite definitely awaiting the restoration of the genuine levitical priesthood. It is apparent, therefore, that in this major respect contemporary Jewish expectation was incompatible with the teaching of the Epistle to the Hebrews, which proclaims the abolition of the temporary and imperfect levitical order and the establishment in its place of the unique and eternal order of Melchizedek.

Of course, the rabbinical commentators could not ignore Melchizedek since he appears in the Torah, and, as we shall see later, they did indeed discuss his significance and identity. But as the rabbinical evidence, far back though its roots may go, belongs in the main to a later period and gives indications of being influenced by the necessity to react to the position assigned to Melchizedek in Christian doctrine, it will be considered later. Suffice it to say for the present that of the two best-known contemporary Jewish authors Josephus speaks of Melchizedek only as a figure of past history, doing little more than recount the Genesis narrative of his encounter with Abraham,[3] while Philo finds in Mel-

---

2. See Introduction, pp. 13ff.
3. Josephus, *Bell. Jud.* vi.438; *Ant.* i.180f.

chizedek a subject for abstract allegorical and metaphysical interpretation,[4] so much so that "speculative philosophical thinking strains the concrete historical person to the very limit of the possible."[5] Neither Josephus nor Philo betrays any interest in Melchizedek as an eschatological figure.

Turning to the Christian authors of the post-apostolic centuries, it is in Justin Martyr (d. ca. 165) that we first come across the use of Melchizedek for polemical purposes in the Jewish-Christian debate, as one whose priesthood, fulfilled by the advent of Christ, is universal in scope, though with a predilection for the Gentiles. The argument turns on the supposition that Melchizedek was uncircumcised and accordingly was "a priest of those who were in uncircumcision," and particular significance is attached to the consideration that the circumcised Abraham paid him tithes and was blessed by him. From this the conclusion is drawn that Christ, in whom the priestly order of Melchizedek is fulfilled and comprehended, was intended to be the Priest of those in uncircumcision, that is to say, non-Jews; though it is added that those of the circumcision who approach him in faith and seeking his blessing will be received and blessed by him.[6] This notion that the reception and blessing of Abraham by Melchizedek symbolizes the reception and blessing of the circumcision by the uncircumcision has no place in the interpretation offered by the author of the Epistle to the Hebrews. It is a notion, however, which seems to have become widely accepted, for it recurs in Tertullian (d. ca. 220)[7] and in Epiphanius (d. 403), who asserts that Abraham's offering of homage to an uncircumcised priest was intended to keep the circumcision from boasting in itself and presaged not only the impermanence of the levitical order but also the ultimate transference of the priesthood to that order which had preceded Levi and Aaron.[8] According to the Genesis account, however, Abraham was not yet circumcised when he met Melchizedek, since circumcision was not introduced until a number of years later (Gen. 17:22ff.). This must be regarded as somewhat of an embarrassment for the theory that the encounter between Abraham and Melchizedek was an encounter between circumcision and uncircumcision!

Another opinion which is noticeably unmentioned in our epistle, but which quite certainly became firmly established as a stock interpretation, at least until the time of the Reformation, held that Melchizedek's provision of bread and wine on the occasion of his encounter with Abraham foreshadowed or anticipated the institution of the sacrament of the eucharist by Christ. It is found, for example, in Clement of Alexandria (d. ca. 215),[9] Cyprian (d. 258),[10] for whom this constituted the main significance of Melchizedek, Epiphanius (d. 403),[11]

---

4. Philo, *Legum Allegoriae* iii.79ff.; *De Migratione Abrahami* 235f.; *De Congressu Quaerendae Eruditionis Gratia* 99.
5. O. Michel, "Μελχισεδέκ," Kittel, TDNT, IV, p. 569.
6. Justin Martyr, *Dialogue with Trypho* 33.
7. Tertullian, *Adversus Marcionem* v.9; *Adversus Judaeos* 2f.
8. Epiphanius, *Adversus Haereses* II.i.35ff.
9. Clement of Alexandria, *Stromateis* iv.25.
10. Cyprian, Epistle 63, to Caecilius.
11. Epiphanius, *loc. cit.*

Chrysostom (d. 407),[12] Jerome (d. 420),[13] Augustine (d. 430),[14] who sees in this event the first appearance of the Christian sacrament, and Theodoret (d. ca. 458), and it is commonplace in the works of the medieval commentators. At the Council of Trent it received a nod of approval,[15] and it is not surprising that "catholic" scholars have continued to propound it right up to the present time.

The Reformers, however, rejected this analogy, not only because it is passed over in silence by the author of the Epistle to the Hebrews (Luther and Calvin, for instance, make no reference to it in their commentaries on this epistle), but also because they could find no support for it in the Genesis narrative, particularly the interpretation that the bringing forth of bread and wine by Melchizedek was in order that he might offer it as a sacrifice to God, with the supposed consequence that his action was intended as a type of the Roman Catholic sacrifice of the mass. The Genesis account, they objected, does not say that Melchizedek sacrificed the bread and wine, or offered it to God, and the attempt to associate it with the Roman mass could not be justified. "What does this have to do with Christ, who did not sacrifice bread and wine but distributed it to his disciples?" asks Luther. ". . . Christ says: 'Do this in remembrance of me'; that is, 'Take, eat and drink this bread and cup, and proclaim my death'. He does not say: 'Sacrifice the bread and the wine.'"[16] The attempt, Calvin remarks, is in effect subversive of the doctrine of the mass held by Roman Catholics: "For in order to bring Melchizedek into agreement with themselves, it will be necessary for them to concede that *bread* and *wine* are offered in the mass. Where, then, is transubstantiation?"[17] In any case, as Owen points out, the supposed sacrifice of bread and wine would be destructive of our author's purpose, which is to demonstrate the superiority of the priesthood of Melchizedek over that of Levi, since the offering of bread and wine was something enjoined in the levitical system (see Lev. 7:13; 23:13, 18) and would not, therefore, have been a distinguishing mark in the case of Melchizedek.

It is all the more interesting, then, to find so strongly Reformed a scholar as Jonathan Edwards in the eighteenth century postulating a connection between the bread and wine of Melchizedek and the bread and wine of the eucharist, though of course without any intention of granting validity to the argument employed by Roman Catholics to justify the doctrine of the mass. "Another remarkable confirmation Abraham received of the covenant of grace," he writes, "was when he returned from the slaughter of the kings; when Melchizedek, the king of Salem, the priest of the most high God, that great type of Christ, met him, and blessed him, and brought forth bread and wine. The bread and wine signified the same blessings of the covenant of grace that the bread and wine does in the sacrament of the Lord's supper. As Abraham had a seal of the covenant in circumcision that was equivalent to baptism, so now he had a seal of

12. Chrysostom, Homily on Psalm 110.
13. Jerome, Epistle 73, to Evangelus.
14. Augustine, *De Civitate Dei* xvi.23.
15. Session 22, On the Sacrifice of the Mass, ch. 1.
16. Luther, *Lectures on Genesis* (14:18).
17. Calvin, *Commentary on Genesis* (14:18).

it equivalent to the Lord's supper."[18] The worth of this interpretation must, however, remain very doubtful. While there is undoubtedly, and understandably, a strong attraction in an analogy along these lines, it is difficult to believe that our author would have passed by so good an opportunity of teaching a typological lesson had it been acknowledged or approved in the apostolic church. The Genesis account, indeed, gives no indication that the provision of bread and wine by Melchizedek was in any way a sacramental act. It was, rather, a generous act of hospitality intended for the refreshment of Abraham, who was fatigued after the military expedition on which he had been engaged.

Some idea of the speculation concerning the identity of Melchizedek in the early Christian centuries may be gained from a letter which Jerome wrote to a presbyter named Evangelus.[19] The latter had sent Jerome an anonymous work in which it was maintained that Melchizedek who blessed so great a personage as Abraham must have been divine rather than human, and was in fact a manifestation of the Holy Spirit in the guise of a man. Jerome informs his correspondent that, while Origen (in his commentary on Genesis, now lost) and his pupil Didymus held that Melchizedek was an angelic being, the other, and more reliable, church authors he had consulted—Irenaeus, Hippolytus, Eusebius of Caesarea, Eusebius of Emesa, Apollinaris, and Eustathius—were united in their judgment that Melchizedek was a human being, an inhabitant of Canaan, and king of Jerusalem. He adds that this was the view also of learned Jewish interpreters. In his work *On the Faith* Ambrose appears to insist that this is the settled understanding of the church, which, he says, does not regard Melchizedek as an angel, "as Jewish triflers suppose, but a holy man and a priest of God . . . a type of Christ—but only a type to which Christ corresponds as the reality: for a type is the shadow of the reality."[20] It is somewhat surprising, therefore, to find Ambrose positively identifying Melchizedek elsewhere in his writings with God[21] and with the Son of God.[22] This confusion on the part of Ambrose may well indicate that speculative and extravagant theories regarding Melchizedek were still current in the church late in the fourth century.

The judgment of Jerome and the others mentioned may, however, be taken as generally accepted and approved by the orthodox theologians. It is endorsed by Cyril of Alexandria (d. 444), who emphatically affirms that Melchizedek was no more than a man, a type of the perfection of Christ, and not a manifestation of the Holy Spirit or of an angel or some other heavenly power exercising the priestly function.[23] Epiphanius also concurs, pointing out that the fact that nothing is known of the parentage of Melchizedek does not mean that he was more than human, for we are equally ignorant of the parentage of Elijah and Daniel and others in the Old Testament whose humanity is acknowledged by all. He

---

18. Jonathan Edwards, *A History of the Work of Redemption,* in *Works,* I (London, 1840), p. 544.
19. Jerome, Epistle 73, to Evangelus.
20. Ambrose, *De Fide ad Gratianum* iii.11.
21. Ambrose, *Hexaemeron* i.3.
22. Ambrose, *De Abrahamo* i.3.
23. Cyril of Alexandria, *Glaphyra in Genesim* ii.

cites John 3:13: "No one has ascended into heaven but he who descended from heaven."[24]

The identification of Melchizedek with the Holy Spirit was particularly associated with certain gnostic heretics. Hippolytus records that the second-century banker Theodotus taught that Melchizedek was "the greatest power," that is, divine, and in fact greater than Christ.[25] A similar belief was characteristic of the sect known as the Melchizedekians, who, according to Epiphanius, broke away from the Theodotians. It was the view also of Origen's pupil Hierax, who attempted to justify the identification of Melchizedek with the Holy Spirit by linking the designation of Psalm 110:4, "a priest for ever after the order of Melchizedek," with the intercessory activity of the Holy Spirit on behalf of the saints mentioned in Romans 8:26f., which he interpreted as a specifically priestly work. Epiphanius offers the rejoinder that nowhere is it said that the Holy Spirit assumed flesh or appeared in a theophany.[26]

A later sect supposed that the appearance of Melchizedek was a theophany not of the Third but of the Second Person of the Trinity, or, in other words, a manifestation of the Logos before the incarnation. But Epiphanius put his finger on the weak spot in this hypothesis: "If Melchizedek resembles the Son of God," he says, "he cannot at the same time be the same as the Son of God; for how can a servant be the same as his master?"[27] It is a view, however, which has continued to have its advocates. John Brown, for example, writing in the middle years of last century, asserts that it had supporters in his day. He counters the opinion, in a manner similar to Epiphanius, by observing that "it appears very plain that Melchizedek and the Son of God are two different persons"; for "Melchizedek is said to have been 'made like unto the Son of God', and the Son of God is said to have been 'made a high priest after the order of Melchizedek'"; so that "it is scarcely possible to conceive two persons more clearly distinguished." He explains, further, that, as the author of our epistle insists, "to the exercise of the priesthood on the part of the Son of God the possession of human nature was absolutely necessary." Moreover, "to argue from the superiority of the priesthood of Melchizedek to Aaron and his sons to the superiority of the priesthood of Christ, supposing Melchizedek and Christ the same person, is obviously a paralogism."[28] In our own day the interpretation of Melchizedek

---

24. Epiphanius, *loc. cit.*; see also Theodoret, *Dialogues.*
25. Hippolytus, *Refutatio Omnium Haeresium* vii.24.
26. Epiphanius, *loc. cit.* An early source-work on the various heresies was probably the *Syntagma* of Hippolytus, now lost, but largely reproduced in the "Collection of Thirty-Two Heresies" appended to Tertullian's *De Praescriptione Haereticorum*, but from a later hand (Pseudo-Tertullian), and in Epiphanius and Filaster. See B. Altaner, *Patrology*, pp. 172, 185f.
27. Epiphanius, *loc. cit.*
28. F. F. Bruce cites J. B. McCaul, who wrote a commentary on the Epistle to the Hebrews which was published in 1871: "Cunaeus... believes, as Ewald does, and I do," says McCaul, "that Melchizedek was the Second Person of the Ever Blessed Trinity, the Divine *angel of the Lord*, who continually appeared to the Fathers under the Old Testament dispensation.... If Melchizedek was 'without beginning of days or end of life', but 'abideth a priest continually', how can it be believed of him that he was a mere mortal?... Melchizedek, as the Divine *Logos*, existed from eternity."

as identical with the pre-incarnate Christ has been accepted by A. T. Hanson, who maintains that "according to the author of the Epistle to the Hebrews Christ appeared to Abraham in the person of Melchizedek, thereby vindicating the superiority of the coming messianic priesthood to the coming Levitical priesthood."[29] His view is of course open to the same objections.

The Pelagians, it may be noticed in passing, seized on Melchizedek as an example of a man who, in accordance with their presuppositions, lived a sinless and perfect life. Augustine, for instance, quotes from a work of Pelagius in which Melchizedek is included, together with Abel, Enoch, Abraham, Isaac, Jacob, Joshua, Samuel, Elijah, Daniel, and others, in a list of those who not only, negatively, lived without sin, but also, positively, led holy lives.[30]

The theory that Melchizedek and Noah's eldest son Shem were one and the same person was introduced by rabbinical scholars before the end of the first century with the purpose, it would seem, of counteracting the superior importance assigned by Christians to Melchizedek as a type of Christ on the basis of the doctrine of the Epistle to the Hebrews. This intention notwithstanding, it soon gained a considerable degree of acceptance in Christian circles. Epiphanius, it is true, mentions it as an opinion of the Samaritans, and attempts to prove that Shem could not have been alive when Abraham met Melchizedek.[31] But Jerome, while recognizing it as a common Jewish opinion, sees no chronological problem and in fact is attracted by the theory. According to Genesis 11, Abraham was a direct descendant of Shem, and Jerome considers it appropriate that in meeting his ancestor he should have paid him tithes and been blessed by him.[32] This judgment is repeated in the commentators of the following centuries. Luther in his day describes it as "the general opinion" which is founded on "the general conviction of the Hebrews." "Even though not much depends on whether their conviction is right or wrong," he says, "I gladly agree with their opinion." The identification of Melchizedek with Shem pleases him, he adds, "because there was no greater patriarch at that time, especially in spiritual matters."[33] Calvin, however, rejected the theory, observing that "the Lord would not have designated a man, worthy of eternal memory [Shem], by a name so new and obscure [Melchizedek] that he must remain unknown."[34] Moreover, as Spicq remarks, "the identification is implausible because the 'genealogy' of Shem is perfectly well known," whereas one of the main points in our author's argument is the absence of any genealogy in the case of Melchizedek. One may add that it would also invalidate the conception of Levi, as yet unborn but in the loins of Abraham, paying tithes to Melchizedek as though to a priesthood of a different order, because, if Melchizedek is Shem, then Levi was no less in Melchizedek's loins than he was in Abraham's, and the distinction which is proposed falls to the ground.

29. A. T. Hanson, "Christ in the Old Testament according to Hebrews," *Studia Evangelica*, Vol. II, Part I (1964), pp. 398ff.
30. Augustine, *De Natura et Gratia* 36.
31. Epiphanius, *loc. cit.*
32. Jerome, *loc. cit.*
33. Luther, *Lectures on Genesis* (14:18).
34. Calvin, *Commentary on Genesis* (14:18).

At first, as has been mentioned, the Jews had venerated Melchizedek as a heavenly being to whom an important role was assigned in the eschatological kingdom; but with the development of the controversy with the Christians, who saw the realization of his order of priesthood in the person and work of Christ and by the same token the abolition of the levitical order, they found it convenient to interpret his significance in a manner less threatening to the superiority of Abraham and the Aaronic priesthood. For Abraham to behave with deference in the presence of his ancestor was entirely natural and commendable, they argued, for such conduct befits the address of the younger man to the older, without at all implying that the former is inferior to the latter. The tenuous thread on which the rabbinical identification of Melchizedek with Shem hung seems to have been a line which connected Noah's description of Yahweh as the God of Shem (Gen. 9:26) with the designation of Melchizedek as the priest of God Most High (Gen. 14:18). The situation was hardly eased, however, for, as we have seen, many Christians regarded the supposed identity of Shem and Melchizedek with approval without diminishing their belief in Melchizedek's typological significance and his superiority to Abraham and Levi.

Consequently, the rabbinical authors took refuge in a strangely hostile attitude to Melchizedek which taxed to the limit their ingenuity in explaining away the far from unfavorable references to him in the biblical record. To all intents and purposes the identification with Shem is forgotten. His priesthood, it is now contended, must have beeen essentially levitical and was communicated by him to Abraham and so on down to Levi. The silence about his parentage is accounted for by the calumny that he was the child of a prostitute—though this (such are the contradictions in which the Jewish apologists entangled themselves) would in fact have disqualified him for priestly service. The tithe which Abraham paid him was not from his own property but from the spoils of battle, so that it was not a mark of homage from the lesser to the greater. Indeed, a slight grammatical ambiguity in the Hebrew text emboldened some to contend that the tithe was actually paid the other way around, by Melchizedek to Abraham! It was even contended that the priesthood was taken away from Melchizedek and given instead to Abraham on the ground that Melchizedek was guilty of the impiety of blessing Abraham before he blessed God, as follows: "Blessed be Abraham by God Most High... and blessed be God Most High" (Gen. 14:19f.). The attempt was made, too, to interpret Psalm 110 as applying to Abraham, despite the fact that previously it had been universally recognized as one of the messianic psalms.[35]

We shall now turn to the Christian understanding of the significance of Melchizedek as it is expounded by our author in this central section of his epistle, and in doing so we shall find that the implications of the two references to Melchizedek in the Old Testament, brief though they are, carry profound importance for the Jew as well as the Christian.

---

35. See M. Simon, "Melchisédech dans la polémique entre juifs et chrétiens et dans la légende," *Revue d'Histoire et de Philosophie Religieuses*, 17 (Paris, 1937), pp. 58ff. The same negative attitude to Melchizedek is apparent in the commentary of the modern Jewish scholar Chief Rabbi J. H. Hertz on *The Pentateuch and Haftorahs* (American edition, Vol. I, 1941), who asserts that "Melchizedek was evidently a convert of Abraham's" (p. 53)!

7:1, 2. *For this Melchizedek, king of Salem, priest of the Most High God, met Abraham returning from the slaughter of the kings and blessed him; and to him Abraham apportioned a tenth part of everything. He is first, by translation of his name, king of righteousness, and then he is also king of Salem, that is, king of peace.*

The designation of Melchizedek as *king of Salem* and *priest of the Most High God* is taken directly from Genesis 14:18. Though our author offers no information on the subject, Salem seems to have been identified as Jerusalem at the time when he was writing. This at any rate is the explanation preserved in the tradition of the Targums and given by Josephus,[1] and it seems to have been generally accepted in the early church, as, for example, Jerome attests.[2] Jerome expresses his disagreement with this identification, however, maintaining that the place referred to is located near Scythopolis and was still called Salem in his own day, and that the ruins of Melchizedek's palace were still visible there. He adds that it is the city to which Jacob is said to have come, in the region of Shechem (Gen. 33:18f.), and that it is the same as the Salim, some eight miles south of Scythopolis, near which John the Baptist conducted his ministry (Jn. 3:23). But, on the other hand, Salem and Zion (Jerusalem) are clearly synonymous in Psalm 76:2. If the question is still unresolved, it is evidently not regarded as a matter of importance by our author and it need not detain us further here.

That "the Most High God," whose priest Melchizedek was, was not the title of some heathen deity, but the same sovereign God whom Abraham worshipped, is evident from the manner in which, in the Genesis narrative, Abraham speaks to the king of Sodom of "the Lord God Most High, maker of heaven and earth," or "the Most High God Yahweh, maker of heaven and earth." This description corresponds with the "God Most High, maker of heaven and earth," whom Melchizedek invokes (Gen. 14:18–22), and points to the conclusion that Melchizedek, like Abraham, was a worshipper of Yahweh, the one true God. The qualification "most high," then, should not be understood in a polytheistic sense, as though indicating the highest among many deities, but as designating the one and only God who is supreme in his sovereignty over the whole of existence. Accordingly, we see these two

---

1. Josephus, *Bell. Jud.* vi.438; *Ant.* i.180f.
2. Jerome says that "all" the Christians of his day (*nostri omnes*) identified Salem with Jerusalem. The hybrid etymology then current, which explained Jerusalem as compounded of Greek and Hebrew elements (ἱερός, "holy," plus שלם, "peace"), he rightly dismisses as "manifestly an absurdity." A more consistent, Semitic, etymology indicates, however, that the meaning of the name Jerusalem is "foundation of Salem" or "city of Salem," which would tell in favor of the identification of Salem with Jerusalem. This opinion reappears in the medieval commentators.

ancient personages united in the profoundest possible manner at the religious heart of their being.

There is, beyond doubt, something momentous as well as mysterious about the occasion in the remote past when *this Melchizedek*, appearing unannounced on the scene, *met Abraham returning from the slaughter of the kings and blessed him*. The reference is to "the battle of the four kings against five" described in Genesis 14:1ff. The four kings, led by Chedorlaomer of Elam, had routed the five kings, including the king of Sodom, and carried off Lot, Abraham's nephew, who had settled in Sodom (Gen. 13:12). Abraham, on receiving news of this, gathered and armed a band, set off in pursuit, and, attacking by night at a place near Damascus, defeated the four kings and rescued Lot and the others who had been taken captive. It was on his return from this excursion that the historic encounter with Melchizedek took place, when Melchizedek brought forth bread and wine for Abraham's refreshment and pronounced a blessing upon him, and Abraham presented tithes of all the spoils to Melchizedek. The obvious inference, which is explained in verses 4ff. below, is that in confrontation with Melchizedek, from whom he received the priestly benediction and to whom he paid homage, Abraham was face to face with one who was his superior.

Aquinas allegorizes the details of the narrative, explaining that the four kings indicate "the four principal vices, opposites of the four cardinal virtues, which hold in captivity the faculty of reason, nephew to the virtues, once the five bodily senses have been overcome." He also expounds in scholastic fashion the perfection of the number ten—a line of thought suggested by the mention of the tithe or tenth part—and goes on to the precarious conclusion that "it was in order that he might signify that the fulness of all perfection is from God that Abraham gave tithes." Speculative interpretations of this kind, however, which disregard the plain meaning of the text, and are the product of fanciful ingenuity, do not serve the interests of sound exegesis.

Our author, it is important to notice, invests Melchizedek not with allegorical but with typological significance. He is content here to draw attention to the messianic significance of the Hebrew names Melchizedek and Salem, the former of which means "king of righteousness" and the latter "peace." Accordingly, as *king of righteousness* and *king of peace* Melchizedek is presented as the type of the messianic priest-king, the marks of whose kingdom are righteousness and peace. In Christ we see the appearance of the expected everlasting king promised to David's line under whom righteousness flourishes and peace abounds (Ps. 72:7; cf. Ps. 97:2; 98:3, 9); he is "the Prince of Peace," of the increase of whose government and peace there shall be no end (Isa. 9:6f.); he is the long-awaited king who will speak peace to the nations (Zech. 9:9f.), and "the righteous Branch," whose name is "The Lord our Righteousness" and who administers justice in his glorious reign (Jer. 23:5f.; 33:15f.). As king he is just, and as priest he justifies all who trust in his atoning sacrifice (Rom. 3:26; 5:8f.).

7:3. He is without father or mother or genealogy, and has neither beginning of days nor end of life, but resembling the Son of God he continues a priest for ever.

The explanation of the typological significance of Melchizedek now turns, unhesitatingly, to what is *not* said about him in the Genesis narrative. It is a form of argument from silence which has parallels in Philo and also in later rabbinical literature, where, generally, it is of a fanciful nature. The silence is eloquent insofar as Melchizedek is a type of Christ. It does not imply that that he was a superhuman being or a manifestation of God. This silence is, as Bengel observes, full of mystery, especially in the setting of the Old Testament, and it is not surprising that our author should regard the omission of any mention of parentage or posterity as remarkable. For one thing, in the early chapters of Genesis, in which genealogy is so prominent a feature (cf. 5:1ff., the book of the generations of Adam; 10:1ff., the generations of the sons of Noah; 11:10ff., the generations of Shem; 11:27ff., the generations of Terah, Abraham's father), Melchizedek is the only personage among the worshippers of the one true God whose ancestry and descendants receive no mention. For another thing, as our author is now about to describe the character of the priesthood of Melchizedek, and to compare it with that of the levitical order of priests, for whom the line of descent was a matter of essential importance, it is especially noticeable that Melchizedek is introduced in isolation from all family bonds.

The description *without father or mother or genealogy,* accordingly, should not be taken literalistically to mean that Melchizedek had no parents or family, nor does the statement that he had *neither beginning of days nor end of life* intend us to understand him as an eternally existent being who experienced neither birth nor death. The point is that these assertions apply positively to Christ, not to Melchizedek. The significance of the biblical silence is that it marks Melchizedek out as a type who in these respects *resembles the Son of God,* who alone exists everlastingly, from eternity to eternity. Surrounded by this silence, Melchizedek is the figure, but Christ is the reality. The incarnate Son, it is true, insofar as he was one with us in our humanity, had a human mother and a human genealogy (cf. Mt. 1:1ff.; Lk. 1:26ff.; 3:23ff.; Rom. 1:3), and a human birth as well as a human death (of which our author has much to say). But as the Son of God he is eternally the same and his years will never end (Heb. 1:12; 13:8).

The silence of Genesis 14 with regard not only to the origin and termination of Melchizedek's life but also to any priestly succession is typological, too, in that it gives the impression of a continuous and uninterrupted priesthood, which again finds its fulfilment in the messianic antitype, who, in accordance with the declaration of Psalm 110:4, *continues a priest for ever.* His priesthood, as our author will shortly explain, is characterized by "the power of an indestructible life" (v. 16); it does not pass from him to others "because he continues for ever" (v. 24). The silence of Scripture is, in fact, as Herveus observes, the silence of the Holy Spirit, who "wished in accordance with a higher counsel to be silent about these things so that he might in every respect exhibit a figure of the Lord."[3]

It is strange to find patristic and medieval authors appealing to the verse before us as though it supported their notion of a celibate New Testament priesthood. Thus, for example, we find Jerome affirming that the qualification "without genealogy" means that Melchizedek was unmarried, and so childless and without posterity, in a place where he is advocating celibacy of the clergy,[4] even though he does not conclude from this same verse that Melchizedek was without parents and experienced neither birth nor death. Such is the inconsistency of special pleading! Herveus is another who contends that the priests of the New Testament must, like Melchizedek, be without genealogy or, in other words, without wives, since by having wives "they would profess that they were priests of Jewish, not Christian, institution." Apart from the fact that it is most unlikely that "without genealogy" could mean "childless," let alone, by further inference, "unmarried," it is astonishing to find Christian scholars turning a blind eye to the absolutely plain and indeed emphatic teaching of this epistle, and not least this present chapter from which they select the expression "without genealogy," that the Christian priesthood is uniquely fulfilled in the sole person of Christ and, without succession or transference to others, belongs to him alone. True enough, Peter speaks of Christian priests, but only in terms of a

---

3. Cf. Calvin: "It must not be thought to be an omission either by accident or by lack of thought that he is given no family connection, and that there is no word of his death. The truth is that the Spirit has done this purposely so as to elevate him for us above the common herd of men."

4. Jerome, *Adversus Jovinianum* i.23. In a manner characteristic of his Christology, Theodore of Mopsuestia imports into this verse a distinction between the deity and the humanity of Christ, explaining that "without mother" is said of the Word's eternal generation from the Father, while "without father" betokens the humanity he assumed of the Virgin Mary. This, however, is to stretch the passage beyond its natural sense and to impose a division which is not there.

priesthood that is common to *all* Christians, who together in Christ constitute a spiritual priesthood (1 Pet. 2:5, 9). Logical consistency, then, would require these authors to prescribe celibacy for all Christians. They do not do so because, while no doubt intending to be scriptural, in this instance they are seeking a biblical peg on which to hang a particular preconception.

As we have seen,[5] the identification of Melchizedek with an angelic being who was expected to fulfil a prominent role in the eschatological age was regarded by the patristic writers as a characteristically Jewish notion, and there is evidence to suggest that the Dead Sea Sect entertained a view similar to this. The question arises whether it may at least be part of our author's intention to demonstrate the falsity of all such speculation since all that is portended by Melchizedek in the Old Testament has been and is being fulfilled in Christ. In the early part of the epistle he has already established the superiority of the Son to angels (1:4–2:16); is he now resuming the controversy with specific reference to contemporary speculation concerning Melchizedek? The suggestion has been made that the statements here and in verse 8 would "make more sense if the author of Hebrews understood Melchizedek to be an (arch)angel," because "if this were the case it would make it possible to take at face value the description of Melchizedek in Hebrews 7:3, 8 and to understand the thrust of the passage to be the subordination of Melchizedek, the angel, to the pre-existent heavenly Son of God even though his priesthood was of a higher order than that of Levi."[6]

This suggestion, however, is ill suited to the context, in which Melchizedek is presented in an entirely favorable light in comparison with Levi and as a type of Christ. There is no hint here of a polemic against a speculative image of Melchizedek. This does not mean that our author was unaware of current speculations of this kind; far from it, for he has already addressed himself to them, and if there is a polemic against false notions of Melchizedek as an eschatological angelic power it is to be found not here but in the early section of the epistle. The purpose now is not negative, but positive and constructive, namely, to develop the true understanding of the significance of Melchizedek in relation both to Levi and to Christ. The controversial issue is no longer angels but the levitical priesthood and its ministrations which the advent of Christ has rendered obsolete.

---

5. See Excursus I, pp. 237ff. above.
6. A. J. Bandstra, "*Heilsgeschichte* and Melchizedek in Hebrews," *Calvin Theological Journal*, 3 (1968), pp. 36ff.

7:4-7. *See how great he is! Abraham the patriarch gave him a tithe of the spoils. And those descendants of Levi who receive the priestly office have a commandment in the law to take tithes from the people, that is, from their brethren, though these also are descended from Abraham. But this man who has not their genealogy received tithes from Abraham and blessed him who had the promise. It is beyond dispute that the inferior is blessed by the superior.*

The argument now developed is quite plain and easy to grasp. The purpose is to demonstrate *how great* Melchizedek is in comparison with Abraham—a superiority that is especially startling in view of the fact that Abraham is himself *the patriarch*,[7] that is, the ancestral founder of the Hebrew people, the one to whom the covenant *promises* concerning his posterity had been given by God, and therefore the possessor of a position of primacy in the long history of the Jews. The great boast of the Jews was that they were the descendants of Abraham, the friend of God and the recipient of the promise (cf. Jn. 8:33, 39; Mt. 3:9; Phil. 3:4f.). But here is someone in their own Scriptures who is manifestly Abraham's superior. The author draws his readers' attention[8] to the remarkable consideration that Abraham, eminent patriarch though he was, *gave* Melchizedek *a tithe of the spoils* and was *blessed* by him. No proof is needed for what, as an accepted principle of human relationships, is *beyond dispute*, namely, *that the inferior is blessed by the superior*, and, equally, that the person who receives tithes is superior to the person who pays them. Herveus, in a manner consistent with the implications of the passage, presses the logic one stage further: "If Melchizedek, who was a sign and shadow, is preferred to Abraham and to all the levitical priests, how much more Christ, who is the truth and the substance! . . . If a type of Christ is greater than he who has the promises, how much more so is Christ himself!"

The custom of tithing was enjoined under the Mosaic legislation on all the people of Israel, with the exception of the Levites. The tithes, whether of crops or of livestock, were assigned to the Levites (Num. 18:21ff.), who because of their special religious function in the community were debarred from participation in any territorial inheritance (Dt. 10:8f.; 12:12). The Levites, accordingly, were the recipients of *tithes from*

---

7. The definite article in the expression ὁ πατριάρχης conveys the sense of "the great patriarch" or "our great patriarch." In the Greek text the position of this description at the end of the sentence lends further enhancement to this emphasis.
8. The verb θεωρεῖτε, which could be read as either indicative or imperative, has more thrust if it is taken as the latter. Its sense is somewhat stronger than the rendering "see" of our version and is better conveyed by the KJV and the NEB, "consider."

the people, who were at the same time *their brethren* because, like them, they had *descended from Abraham.* Among *the descendants of Levi* the sacerdotal office proper belonged to Aaron and his male posterity, who constituted the Aaronic succession of priests. To the rest of the Levites the role of assistants in the maintenance of the tabernacle (or later the temple) and its ministrations was entrusted. Of the tithe which they received from the people they in turn passed on a tithe, "the tithe of the tithe," to the Aaronic priests for their sustenance (cf. Num. 3:5ff.; 18:1ff., 25ff.; Neh. 10:37ff.).

Our author's assertion that *those descendants of Levi who receive the priestly office have a commandment in the law to take tithes from the people* raises the question how this is to be reconciled with the Mosaic prescription in accordance with which, as has been mentioned, the priests themselves actually received only a tithe of the tithe paid by the people to the Levites. It may be that he is speaking somewhat loosely, without having this specific distinction in mind, to the effect that it was to the priestly tribe of Levi that the people paid tithes; or it may be, as Aquinas suggests, that it was the Aaronic priests alone who received but did not pay tithes, since even the Levites, who received the people's tithe, paid in turn a tithe to the priests; or, in line with this, "the people" here may possibly mean all who were not priests, that is, the Levites together with the non-Levites, since it was from this totality that the priests ultimately received their tithe. Another explanation is that our author's statement would apply to the situation obtaining in his own day, when, according to the evidence of the rabbinical literature,[9] the practice had developed and become established of, so to speak, by-passing the Levites and paying the people's tithes directly to the priests. This would solve the question, but as a solution it must itself be regarded as questionable, not only because our author's custom is to relate his argument to the situation defined in the Old Testament, but also because the immediate context indicates that he has in mind the reception of tithes by "Levi" (v. 9)—the more general term to which "Aaron" would answer as the more specific. If there is some impreciseness here in the manner in which he expresses himself it is of no real consequence, since it in no way invalidates the thrust of his argument.

---

9. See J. Jeremias, *Jerusalem zur Zeit Jesu,* Part II (Leipzig, 1929), pp. 2ff.; E. Schürer, *History of the Jewish People in the Time of Jesus Christ,* II, i (Edinburgh, 1885), p. 248. "The central administration on the part of the priests extended to the *tithe* as well," says Schürer, "which in point of fact was delivered, not to the Levites, but to the priests, in whose hands the further disposal of it was then left." Josephus describes how this situation was abused by unscrupulous priests (*Ant.* XX.viii.8; ix.9; cf. *Vita* 12).

7:8–10. *Here tithes are received by mortal men; there, by one of whom it is testitifed that he lives. One might even say that Levi himself, who receives tithes, paid tithes through Abraham, for he was still in the loins of his ancestor when Melchizedek met him.*

Here, that is, in the case of the descendants of Levi (v. 5), it is *mortal men,* or, more literally, dying men,[10] by whom *tithes are received;* whereas *there,* that is, in the case of Melchizedek, they are received, from Abraham, *by one of whom it is testified that he lives.* The expression "it is testified" means "it is testified in the scriptural record"; hence the NEB rendering, "one whom Scripture affirms to be alive." The point is the same as that already made, rather more fully, in verse 3. Genesis 14 says nothing about the death of Melchizedek; he is presented only as a *living* personage, and in this respect he serves as a figure or type of Christ whose priesthood is permanent because he continues forever (v. 24 below). Thus Aquinas comments: "*It is testified,* in Scripture, *that he lives,* that is, no mention is made of his death, not because he did not die, but because he symbolizes a priesthood that abides eternally." The inference of Psalm 110:4 that he who is a priest after the order of Melchizedek is a priest *for ever* (Heb. 6:20 and v. 21 below) is drawn from what is tacitly and typologically implied in the very structure of the Genesis narrative.

But significance is found, further, in the consideration that, in accordance with the strong (though by no means exclusively) Jewish concept of family solidarity, it is permissible to argue that Abraham's payment of tithes was at the same time Levi's payment of tithes to Melchizedek, since Levi *was still in the loins of his ancestor when Melchizedek met him.* Paul's reasoning is of the same kind when he teaches, on the basis of the solidarity of the human race in Adam, that when Adam sinned all sinned (Rom. 5:12) and that the death of Adam was the death of all (1 Cor. 15:22). It is a parallel that is remarked by Peter Lombard and Herveus, the latter of whom says that "just as when Adam sinned those who were in his loins sinned, so when Abraham paid tithes those who were in his loins were tithed." Both seminally and by representation Levi was present in the person of his great-grandfather on this occasion. It may be affirmed, therefore, that Levi *who receives tithes*—this is something characteristic of the levitical status—actually *paid tithes through Abraham.* In this historic encounter, then, what was established was not simply a precedent but a whole relationship, the significance of which is permanent:[11] namely, that the order of Melchizedek, fulfilled in Christ,

10. Ἀποθνήσκοντες (rather than θνητοί) ἄνθρωποι.
11. The permanent import of what took place on the occasion of Abraham's (and, in accordance with the argument, Levi's) meeting with Melchizedek is brought out in the

253

is superior to the order of Levi, which with the advent of Christ is surpassed and superseded.

If it is objected that by precisely the same line of argumentation it could be maintained that Christ, whose lineage is traced back to Abraham (Mt. 1:1f.; Lk. 3:34), paid tithes through Abraham to Melchizedek, this must be granted. At the same time, however, certain important qualifications must be introduced. The parallel relates only to Christ as Son of man, not as Son of God; for as the incarnate Son he identified himself with mankind (Heb. 2:11, 14) and with mankind's need for the institution of that high-priestly office of which Melchizedek was a figure. It is true that as the incarnate Son he performs the priestly work of offering up his humanity vicariously on the cross for our redemption; but in doing this he is still the Son of God acting on our behalf, and it is as the eternal Son that he continues a priest forever after the order of Melchizedek. That is why Melchizedek is said to resemble the Son of God (v. 3). He who is our high priest is none other than he through whom the world was created and by whose word of power the universe is carried forward to its destined consummation (1:2f.).

Our author, indeed, is not unaware of Christ's human descent from Abraham (2:16), but, as he will soon point out (v. 14 below), in this connection his association is not with the tribe of Levi but with the nonpriestly tribe of Judah, so that he is disqualified for the office of the levitical priesthood. His priesthood, accordingly, is of another order, and it achieves that which the levitical priesthood could never achieve (9:9; 10:4). Yet the very imperfection of the levitical system points to the necessity for the provision of an atonement that will be fully and eternally effective, as the rest of this chapter explains (vv. 11ff.). The former priesthood was but an insubstantial shadow (8:5; 10:1); the priesthood of Christ is the reality that abides forever.

In Christ, therefore, Abraham and Melchizedek meet again, and they not only meet, but, as figures of the temporal and eternal orders, in him they are united into one eternal reality. Thus, as both Son of man and Son of God, Christ bridges the gulf which separates man and his

---

Greek by the sequence of finite verbs in the perfect tense: Melchizedek "has received tithes" (δεδεκάτωκεν) from Abraham and "has blessed" (εὐλόγηκεν) him (v. 6); and Levi, who receives tithes, "has paid tithes" (δεδεκάτωκαι) through Abraham (v. 9). These perfects, says Spicq, have "the force of the present" and "perhaps indicate that the consequences of these events are permanent." As J. H. Moulton affirms, the use of the perfect in this manner is "a marked feature" of our author's style, and he explains them and the perfects that occur in 7:13 (μετέσχηκεν), 9:18 (ἐγκεκαίνισται), 11:17 (προσενήνοχεν), and 11:28 (πεποίηκεν) in the same way (A Grammar of New Testament Greek, I, pp. 142, 143f.). Moffatt, to the contrary, and too summarily, dismisses them as aoristic perfects.

guilt on the one side and God and his righteousness on the other; by his atoning priestly sacrifice of himself on the cross he fulfils the requirements for a reconciliation that is complete and everlasting; and in his exaltation the glory of the Son of God becomes also the glory of the Son of man and of all those sons of men who through faith are forever made one with him.

7:11, 12. *Now if perfection had been attainable through the Levitical priesthood (for under it the people received the law), what further need would there have been for another priest to arise after the order of Melchizedek, rather than one named after the order of Aaron? For when there is a change in the priesthood, there is necessarily a change in the law as well.*

The argument is now advanced by a consideration which arises from the history of revelation. The appearance of Melchizedek on the stage of patriarchal history is fleeting and dramatic. He is identified as king of Salem and priest of the Most High God, but nothing is said in Genesis 14 about an *order* of Melchizedek. Only in Psalm 110, in the midstream, as it were, of the history of the Israelites, is there an isolated, and for this reason cryptic, mention of one who is "a priest for ever after the order of Melchizedek." The psalm, which expresses the expectation of the establishment of a messianic priesthood and kingdom, was written some hundreds of years after the inauguration of the levitical order. This in itself is eloquent of the imperfection and impermanence of the levitical order, since it is obvious that, *if perfection had been attainable through the Levitical priesthood*, it would have been superfluous and indeed meaningless to speak of *another priest* belonging to a different order, *rather than one named after the order of Aaron*. Thus the plain implication of this flash of revelation is that the old and inferior order is to be superseded by a new and superior order, which, compared with the inadequate and temporary nature of the former, will be distinguished by full and abiding efficacy.

The Dead Sea Sect looked for the appearance of two messianic or anointed figures, one priestly, "the messiah of Aaron," and the other lay and kingly, "the messiah of Israel," when, following the conclusion of the present era, the golden age was to be ushered in by a new prophet (in fulfilment of the prophecy of Dt. 18:15, 18). The expected high priest would be of the Aaronic family and thus of the levitical order, and under him the ancient sacerdotal system would be restored in its pure and original form. In the council of state, moreover, his dignity would be that of "head of the entire community of Israel"; associated with him would be "the heads of the Aaronic priestly families"; and subordinate to him, the kingly lay messiah of the line of David, and then in turn "the chiefs of the armed forces," "the heads of the families of the community," and "the sages" or scholars.[12] If, as has been suggested,[13] those to whom our epistle is addressed were Hebrew Christians who had in some way been influenced by teaching similar to that of the Dead Sea Sect, the relevance of our author's demonstration of the superiority of the order of Melchizedek, fulfilled in the unique person of Jesus Christ, who is at the same time both messianic priest and messianic king, becomes all the more apparent.

The parenthetical statement, *for under it* (that is, the levitical priesthood) *the people received the law,* is a reminder of the close interdependence between the priestly and the legal systems; for the levitical priesthood and its ministrations were instituted by Moses simultaneously with his communication of the law of God to the people of Israel. The Greek phrase translated in our version as "under it" would be more accurately rendered "on the basis of it" (thus NEB, "it is on this basis that the people were given the law") or "in association with it." The law and the priesthood belonged together for the simple reason that, since the law, representing the divinely ordered standard of conduct and character, was universally broken (cf. Rom. 3:9–23), there was a continuous necessity for the ministry of mediation and reconciliation which the levitical priesthood provided, even though imperfectly. Hence the Mosaic legislation coincided with and was inseparable from the provision of a priestly system.

From this interrelationship between law and priesthood it follows that *when there is a change in the priesthood there is necessarily a change in the law as well.* A new order of priesthood presupposes a new disposition of law. The introduction of a new and different order of priesthood necessitates the setting aside of the law insofar as its prescriptions for the regulation of the old priesthood and its ministry are concerned, and the provision of a new law by which the new system is governed. This is boldly described by Paul as the "law" of faith, the principle of which is that the Christian man is "justified by faith apart from the works of the law" (Rom. 3:27f.). The problem of the old system was twofold. First, all, priests and people alike, were breakers of the law, and the fact that the priests of the levitical order were themselves sinners incapacitated them for offering up an adequate and perfect sacrifice; indeed, they had first to offer sacrifice for their own sins before presenting an offering for

12. *Manual of Discipline for the Future Congregation of Israel.*
13. See Introduction, pp. 13ff.

the sins of the people (see v. 27 below; 5:3). Second, no unwilling and uncomprehending animal, such as was offered under the old system, was competent to serve as a true substitute for the human sinner. For these reasons the Aaronic priests were occupied, in conformity with the requirements of the Mosaic law, with an endless repetition of sacrifices—a repetition which was necessary because of, and which threw into strong relief, the imperfection of the system. The system itself was an eloquent witness to the need for a new and better order of priesthood which would operate on the basis of a new and effective principle of justification.

The "change in the priesthood" is seen in this, that he who as a priest forever constitutes the order of Melchizedek is, unlike the Aaronic priests, a keeper of the law, and thus not himself in need of redemption, and also in this, that his sacrifice was the sacrifice, not of a brute beast, but of himself, the incarnate Son. On the cross he offered himself as Man for man, the Righteous One for the unrighteous (1 Pet. 3:18), the sinner's unique and fully adequate substitute. Hence the once-for-allness, the unrepeatability, of the sacrifice of Christ, and the perfection of his priesthood, which our author emphasizes with such insistence (vv. 23ff. below; 9:11ff., 24ff.; 10:1ff., 11ff., etc.). Within the sphere of the new "law" of faith the Christian believer is no longer under law but under grace (Rom. 6:14). As a law-breaker, the very law which he has broken has become to him an instrument not of justification but of condemnation; but through faith in him who is the only law-keeper, and who in his own body has paid the penalty of the sinner's law-breaking, he stands fully justified before God (Rom. 5:1f., 6ff.).

The "change in the law" is seen in this, that, with the establishment of the order of Melchizedek, the numerous precepts of the law respecting the function of the levitical priesthood have been abrogated and have fallen into desuetude, and, as we have seen, have been replaced by the new principle or "law" of faith. It was this change in the law, at the very heart of the gospel, which was so violently resented by those Jews who were wedded to their own legalistic principle of works-righteousness. Those who put Stephen, the first Christian martyr, to death did so on the ground that he had declared that the advent of Jesus of Nazareth meant a change in the customs which Moses, their great law-giver, had delivered to them (Acts 6:14). The hostility which Paul, who himself had been a fanatical legalist and opponent of the gospel of grace (Acts 8:3; 9:1f.; Phil. 3:5f.), encountered from the Jews was engendered chiefly by the charge that his teaching was contrary to the law and the temple (Acts 21:28). Like the apostle Paul, however, our author is intent on showing that the gospel is not subversive of the law, but the provision of that perfection which the law could never achieve. Though the regulations concerning the levitical priesthood have passed with the passing of that priesthood, yet the essence of the law, which is love and obedience, not only continues in force but is made possible of fulfilment by the gospel; for in accordance with the promises of the new covenant the law ceases, for the Christian, to be an external instrument of condemnation and becomes an internal principle of the will of God which, through the gracious enabling of the Holy Spirit, re-born humanity delights to perform. Thus the change in the priesthood involves both a change in the law, in the sense that all the regulations governing the old order are now superseded and set aside forever, and also a change in the relationship of man to the law in its essence as summarized in the decalogue, in that under the new covenant which comes into operation together with the new priesthood the law is now written in the heart, so that through divine grace man is able joyfully to glorify God by performing his will which previously he had opposed (see on 8:6 below; also Jer. 31:33; Ezek. 11:9; 2 Cor. 3:3ff.).

In the order of Melchizedek both law and priesthood are still intimately bound up with each other, but now in a relationship of perfection and fulfilment. The precepts regulating the old imperfect order of priesthood have been set aside together with that priesthood because the long-promised new covenant is now a glorious reality. By the grace of God manifested in the person and work of Christ, our Melchizedek, the human situation has undergone a radical transformation.

7:13, 14. *For the one of whom these things are spoken belonged to another tribe, from which no one has ever served at the altar. For it is evident that our Lord was descended from Judah, and in connection with that tribe Moses said nothing about priests.*

That Psalm 110 is a messianic psalm was commonly acknowledged by the Jews (cf. Mk. 12:35–37); and the very fact that the great priestly figure mentioned in the psalm belongs to an order other than that of Levi, specified as the order of Melchizedek, in itself signified that the one whose coming was expected would not be a member of the tribe of Levi. Moreover, the kingly character of this personage, as defined in the opening section of the psalm, presupposes his connection with the tribe of Judah, and more particularly with the line of David, in accordance with the promises concerning the advent of a Davidic king whose kingdom would be everlasting (2 Sam. 7:12ff.; Isa. 9:6f., etc.). Our author's contention throughout, of course (not to mention the citing of the psalm for the same purpose by other New Testament writers), is that Psalm 110 has received its fulfilment in the incarnation, death, and exaltation of Jesus Christ. But under the old covenant the tribe of Levi was the sole priestly tribe, whereas *the one of whom these things are spoken,* in Psalm 110, *belonged*[14] *to another tribe, from which,* because of the Mosaic regulations, *no one has ever served at the altar,* that is, fulfilled a priestly calling and function as defined in the Mosaic system. Now *it is evident,* as a perfectly well-known fact,[15] when we consider the lineage of *our Lord,* that he *was descended from Judah, and in connection with that tribe Moses said nothing about priests.* The verb translated "was descended" here[16] actually has the contrary meaning of "has arisen,"[17] though it may be granted that in a statement concerning lineage they share a certain synonymity. To turn away from the more precise translation, however, is to weaken the messianic thrust of the sentence, for, as many commentators have justly pointed out, the concept of one who is to "arise" has a messianic significance in Scripture. Malachi 4:2, for example, promises the rising of him who is the sun of righteousness; Numbers 24:17 foretells the appearance of a star out of Jacob; 2 Peter 1:19 speaks of the rising of the morning star in our hearts (cf. Isa. 61:1; Lk. 1:78; Rev. 2:28); and the prophets also predict the raising up for David of one described as a righteous Branch (Isa. 11:1; Jer. 23:5f.; 33:15; Zech. 3:8; 6:12; cf. Rev. 22:16). Consequently, the assertion that our Lord has *arisen* from Judah carries a distinctly messianic connotation.

Alcuin observes (and it is an observation which is found in some of the other commentators) that the priesthood was transferred "from tribe to tribe, from the priestly to the kingly tribe, so that the same tribe might be both kingly and priestly." The genealogies given by Matthew (1:1ff.) and by Luke (3:23ff.) provide proof that Jesus belonged to the tribe of Judah and therefore could make no claim of levitical lineage. Consistently with this information, we find Jesus repeatedly

14. The Greek verb μετέσχηκεν, "partook of," is the same verb as was used in 2:14 (μέτεσχεν) of Christ's partaking of human nature. "The choice of this word," says Westcott, "points to the voluntary assumption of humanity by our Lord." Spicq comments as follows: "The verb μετέχω, which emphasizes the humanity of Christ (2:14), is a happy choice to suggest that the new priest did not wish to participate in the privileges of the levitical line. He had nothing in common with this tribe; it was completely foreign to him (ἑτέρας, cf. v. 11). The perfect expresses a condition of fact, both historic and official; beyond doubt it is intended to accentuate the absolute incompatibility, resulting from his birth, between Christ and the priesthood in terms of the conditions of the validity prescribed by the old legislation."
15. Πρόδηλον is an intensified adjective which means (with the addition of the unexpressed verb) "it is perfectly obvious"; cf. JB, "everyone knows," Phillips, "it is a matter of history." Κατάδηλον in the next verse is a similar and synonymous intensified form.
16. Ἀνατέταλκεν. Compare the synonymous verbs ἀνίστασθαι in verse 11 and ἀνίσταται in verse 15.
17. Cf. KJV, "sprang," NEB, "is sprung."

addressed in the Gospels as the "Son of David" (cf. Mt. 15:22; 21:9; Mk. 10:47f.; Jn. 12:42) and designated by Paul a descendant of David according to the flesh (Rom. 1:3; similarly 2 Tim. 2:8). In view, then, of the plain teaching of our epistle concerning the human line of Jesus and its clear confirmation in the rest of the New Testament, and also the implications of Psalm 110 together with the inherent inadequacy of the levitical system itself, it is surprising to encounter attempts in the post-apostolic centuries to bring together the lines of Levi and Judah as though in this combination the fulfilment of the priestly and kingly messianic prophecies was to be found.

This association of Judah with Levi instead of with Melchizedek is undoubtedly the result of an improper endeavor to accommodate Christianity to Judaism in such a way that the levitical system would not be threatened, especially as the form of worship to be restored in the eschatological kingdom. But it is a compromise which is destructive of the Christian position because it is essentially unevangelical, for the very reasons expounded with such care and insistence in this epistle. The Dead Sea Sect, as we have seen,[18] expected the advent of two messianic figures, one priestly, of the order of Levi, and the other kingly, of the line of David; and if, as has been supposed,[19] our epistle was written, at least in part, with the purpose of counteracting teachings identical with or similar to those of this community which had proved attractive to the recipients, then the emphasis on Christ's priesthood as being of the order of Melchizedek, and thus as outmoding and superseding the levitical order, may well have been intended to offset the erroneous expectation of the reinstitution of the levitical system of worship and sacrifice.

There is ample evidence in the apostolic writings of the threat which judaizing influences and sects presented to the Christian church. There is evidence, too, that the particular type of judaizing influence against which our author is intent on warning his readers succeeded, in the post-apostolic period, in bringing about just such a conflation of incompatible Christian and Jewish notions as he had feared. In the work entitled *The Testaments of the Twelve Patriarchs* we have what appears to be the manifesto of a second-century judaizing sect whose members attached particular importance to the role of Levi and Judah in the eschatological kingdom.[20] The picture is not free from confusion and inconsistency, however. In some places it would seem that a single mes-

---

18. See pp. 255f. above.
19. See Introduction, pp. 13ff.
20. For the text of *The Testaments of the Twelve Patriarchs* see R. H. Charles's edition of the Greek version and his English translation, both published in 1908, at Oxford and London respectively; also his *The Apocrypha and Pseudepigrapha of the Old Testament in English*, II (Oxford, 1913), pp. 282ff.; cf. also M. de Jonge, *The Testaments of the Twelve Patriarchs: a Study of their Text, Composition, and Origin* (Assen, 1953); E. Schürer, *A History of the Jewish*

sianic personage is expected in whom the priestly and kingly functions will be combined; in others, that there are to be two eschatological leaders, one priestly and one kingly. The explanation for this may be either that the author failed to express himself with clarity and precision, or that he failed to achieve any kind of consistent assimilation of the one-figure expectation of Christianity to the two-figure expectation of Judaism. In the *Testament of Levi*, for example, the appearance of a king from Judah, who will establish a new priesthood after the fashion of the Gentiles, is anticipated (§8). This is the new priest, who will execute judgment and truth upon the earth in the fulness of days (§18). The *Testament of Dan* foretells that one shall arise "from the tribe of Judah and of Levi" who will be "the salvation of the Lord" and will make war against Belial (§5); the *Testament of Gad* declares that Judah and Levi are to be honored because from them the Lord will raise up a Savior to Israel (§8); and similarly the *Testament of Joseph* enjoins that they are to be honored because from them shall arise the Lamb of God who will by his grace save all the Gentiles and Israel (§19). Exhortations to the same effect are found in the *Testaments of Reuben* (§6) and *of Simeon* (§7). In the *Testament of Judah*, on the other hand, it is affirmed that the Lord has given the kingdom to Judah and the priesthood to Levi, but that the kingdom is set below the priesthood, so that in the eschatological hierarchy Levi will have the first place and Judah the second (§§21, 25; cf. also *Issachar*, §5). This seems to reflect a two-figure expectation of the type that is present in the teaching of the Dead Sea Sect.

It is impossible to overlook the importance repeatedly assigned to Levi and Judah in the *Testaments of the Twelve Patriarchs*, and at the same time it is noticeable that there is not a single mention of Melchizedek, who, one might judge, has purposely been omitted as a figure no longer congenial to the Jews because of the significance attached to him in Christian exegesis. Consistent with this silence is the absence of any reference to Psalm 110. The canonicity of the Epistle to the Hebrews was widely acknowledged in the early post-apostolic period, though later

---

People in the Time of Jesus Christ, Div. II, Vol. III (Edinburgh, 1886), pp. 114ff.; G. R. Beasley-Murray, "The Two Messiahs in the Testaments of the Twelve Patriarchs," JTS, XLVIII (1947), pp. 1ff. De Jonge opposes the widely held interpolation theory, according to which a Christian author inserted distinctively Christian interpolations into an originally Jewish work and at the same time made such adjustments and modifications as he considered desirable. He holds it, rather, to be the work of a Christian, imprecise in his theology, who made use of Jewish material in which he was interested. De Jonge, however, is unable to offer a solution to the question of the circumstances and location of the work's composition. We would wish at least to postulate an affinity with and perhaps a line of descent from the amalgam of Christianity and Judaism which the author of the Epistle to the Hebrews is concerned to discountenance. Jean Daniélou, indeed, maintains that this work, *The Testaments of the Twelve Patriarchs*, "offers so many similarities with the Qumran scrolls that it may be viewed as an Essenian document" (*The Dead Sea Scrolls and Primitive Christianity*, 1958, p. 115).

there was hesitation over its authenticity in the Latin Church. The extent to which the speculation which associated Christ with Levi rather than with Melchizedek came to be accepted in the church is difficult to determine. It would seem very probable that it was a factor of consequence in the development of the sacerdotal concept of the Christian ministry which spread so rapidly in the church, even though, as Bishop Lightfoot reaffirmed in a famous essay, the apostolic church "has no sacerdotal system" and in the New Testament definitions of the forms of ministry "there is an entire silence about priestly functions."[21]

Teaching similar to, and perhaps influenced by, that found in the *Testaments of the Twelve Patriarchs* occurs in the latter part of the second century in the writings of Irenaeus, who asserts that Christ "was begotten as king and priest from Levi and Judah according to the flesh."[22] It is not that Irenaeus was unfamiliar with the Epistle to the Hebrews, for there are indications to the contrary in his extant works, and Eusebius informs us that Hebrews was mentioned and quoted by him in works which are now lost.[23] (Eusebius himself speaks equivocally of Aaron and Melchizedek with reference to his own ministry.)[24] Origen, in the third century, seeks to retain the levitical order together with that of Melchizedek, arguing that what is said about Melchizedek in our epistle and in Psalm 110 applies only to Christ, while the Aaronic priesthood is continued in the ministry of the Christian church. "We say accordingly," he writes, "that men can be high priests according to the order of Aaron, but according to the order of Melchizedek only the Christ of God."[25] That the priesthood of Melchizedek is fulfilled in Christ alone is true enough, but our epistle teaches with the clearest possible emphasis that the introduction of the order of Melchizedek means the disappearance of the order of Levi; consequently any suggestion that the latter is still in force in the ministry of men is inadmissible and shows a surprising disregard of the instruction so plainly given by our author. No more legitimate is the attempt to justify an association of Jesus with the tribe of Levi on the ground that Mary, the mother of Jesus, was a kinswoman of Elizabeth, the mother of John the Baptist, who was "of the daughters of Aaron" (Lk. 1:5, 36). Jesus, as we have seen, was acknowledged to be a son of David of the tribe of Judah, and in any case it does not follow that because Mary had a kinswoman of the tribe of Levi she too must have been a Levite.[26]

---

21. J. B. Lightfoot, *St. Paul's Epistle to the Philippians*, pp. 179, 184.
22. Irenaeus, *Fragm.* 17, in W. W. Harvey, *Sancti Irenaei Libros quinque adversus Haereses, etc.*, Tom. II (Cambridge, 1857), p. 487.
23. Eusebius, *Hist. Eccl.* V.xxvi.
24. *Hist. Eccl.* X.iv.23.
25. Origen, *Commentary on the Gospel of John* i.3.
26. A. Plummer, *A Critical and Exegetical Commentary on the Gospel according to S. Luke* (Edinburgh, 1910), writes: "Levites might marry with other tribes; and therefore Elisabeth,

What is remarkable is that, notwithstanding the plain doctrine of the Epistle to the Hebrews, by the middle of the third century the Christian ministry has come to be widely understood in terms of the levitical priesthood of the old covenant. This is strikingly evident in the writings of Cyprian, who, to quote Bishop Lightfoot again, "treats all the passages of the Old Testament which refer to the privileges, the sanctions, the duties, and the responsibilities of the Aaronic priesthood, as applying to the officers of the Christian Church."[27]

7:15–17. *This becomes even more evident when another priest arises in the likeness of Melchizedek, who has become a priest, not according to a legal requirement concerning bodily descent but by the power of an indestructible life. For it is witnessed of him, "Thou art a priest for ever, after the order of Melchizedek."*

The argument runs as follows: the imperfection of the levitical system is implied by the very fact that, while that system is still functioning vigorously and without challenge, the Psalmist mentions another order of priesthood whose priest is a priest forever, for there would have been no point in saying this if the system then in operation were effective and irreplaceable (v. 11); but *this has become even more evident* now that *another priest*, who is not a Levite (vv. 12–14) and therefore of a quite different order, has actually appeared on the scene of history.[28] In the nature of things, the fulfilment is clearer than the prediction. His manifestation, moreover, is full of significance precisely because it is *in the likeness of Melchizedek*. In Christ, what was promised and foreshadowed has come to pass. The nature of this "likeness" has already been indicated in the first three verses of this chapter: there it is said of Melchizedek that "resembling the Son of God he continues a priest for ever"; here, that the incarnate Son is "in the likeness of Melchizedek."[29] The correspon-

---

who was descended from Aaron, might easily be related to one who was descended from David. This verse is not evidence that Mary was not of the house of David" (p. 25, on Lk. 1:36). F. Godet, *A Commentary on the Gospel of St. Luke* (Edinburgh, 1875), says with reference to the same verse: "Mary's being related to Elizabeth in no way proves, as Schleiermacher [and, one may add, some of the early church authors] thought, that Mary did not belong to the tribe of Judah. There was no law to oblige an Israelitish maiden to marry into her own tribe. Mary's father, even if he was of the tribe of Judah, might therefore have espoused a woman of the tribe of Levi" (I, p. 94).

27. Lightfoot, *op. cit.*, pp. 256f.

28. On the significance of the verb "arises," ἀνίσταται, see the commentary above on verse 14 (p. 259) and also note 16. The structure of the sentence here in verses 15 and 16 is hypothetical—εἰ . . . ἀνίσταται, "if another priest arises"—and this adds effect to the argument, but the reference, as the over-all context shows, is to the *fact* that the priest adumbrated in Psalm 110 has now come in the person of Jesus Christ.

29. The cognate expressions ἀφωμοιωμένος in verse 3 and κατὰ τὴν ὁμοιότητα here in verse 15 should be noticed.

dence is pressed from both sides. The likeness is explained both negatively and positively: negatively with respect to the the Aaronic priesthood, since Christ, not being of the tribe of Levi, *has become a priest* in a manner *not according to,* indeed altogether in contradistinction to, the *legal requirement concerning bodily descent,* that is, the requirement of levitical lineage, which was binding in the sphere of the Aaronic order; and positively in view of the consideration that the scope of his priesthood is determined *by the power of an indestructible life.* This important qualification is inherent in the assertion of Psalm 110 that the priest after the order of Melchizedek is to be a priest *for ever.* Where there is a priest forever there is obviously no necessity for a law regarding priestly succession, for the very idea of succession is ruled out in the case of him whose priesthood is forever (see vv. 23ff. below).

There is, however, no more than a *likeness* between Christ and Melchizedek, a likeness which is suggested by the mysterious silence of the Genesis narrative concerning the birth and death and the parentage and posterity of Melchizedek. Within this setting, the figure of Melchizedek is a semblance or shadow, a signpost pointing to someone greater than himself. He is like a primeval John the Baptist who testifies in effect: "After me comes one who ranks before me, for he was before me" (Jn. 1:30). The *reality* foreshadowed by Melchizedek is Christ, the One who is *for ever,* first, because he is the eternal Son, and, second, because by his incarnation and sacrifice of himself he *has become* mankind's high priest, who by the power of his resurrection from the dead and the glory of his exaltation to the right hand of the Majesty on high has redeemed and raised up with himself our fallen nature. He who died once for us now lives, never again to die (Rom. 1:4; 6:9; 1 Cor. 15:20). The crown has followed the cross, and it is this *power of an indestructible life* which guarantees that he is indeed our priest *for ever.*

7:18, 19. *On the one hand, a former commandment is set aside because of its weakness and uselessness (for the law made nothing perfect); on the other, a better hope is introduced, through which we draw near to God.*

The *former commandment* refers in particular to the legislation whereby the levitical priesthood and its succession were regulated (vv. 11ff. above). This legislation has been *set aside,* or cancelled,[30] *because of*

---

30. Ἀθέτησις ... γίνεται, "cancellation has taken place." The noun ἀθέτησις, which occurs in the New Testament only in our epistle, here and in 9:26, is shown by the papyri to have been familiar in legal usage, often in conjunction with ἀκύρωσις, in the sense of annulment or cancellation (cf. A. Deissmann, *Bible Studies,* 1909², pp. 228f.). It is an appropriate term, accordingly, to describe the annulment of a legal enactment.

its weakness and uselessness in the sense that it was incompetent to effect the justification of sinners before God. The law is a principle of life only to the man who fulfils the righteousness it prescribes (Rom. 10:5); but to the law-breaker it becomes an instrument of death (Rom. 7:10–12; 2 Cor. 3:7ff.), and the human predicament is precisely that of the law-breaker. Hence the addition of the explanatory comment that *the law made nothing perfect.* It must be understood, then, that the law is ineffective only in relation to sinful man, and that the deficiency is located in sinful man rather than in the law; for in itself, as Paul insists, the law is holy and spiritual (Rom. 7:12, 14): it is, after all, *God's* law.

Our author's primary concern, however, is with that part of the law ("a former commandment") which prescribed and controlled the sacrificial system, but which, though fitted to make man deeply conscious of his sinfulness and alienation and of his need for forgiveness, was not competent to keep him from sinning or to achieve a state of permanent reconciliation between him and God. Herveus observes that "although some were made perfect under the law, it was not from it that they had perfection, but from grace." The cause of their perfection was no different from the cause of ours, namely, the perfect offering of him who is a priest forever after the order of Melchizedek (cf. Heb. 11:40). The constant repetition of the sacrifices of the levitical order lays bare their ineffectiveness (10:1ff.); the blood of brute beasts could never achieve the cleansing of the conscience from sin and the restoration of the sinner to fellowship with his Maker (9:9; 10:4). There was need all along for a different order of priesthood which by the offering of a single all-sufficient sacrifice would make perfect for all time those for whom it was offered (10:14), and in doing so would make available to mankind *a better hope.*

Our author is in effect pleading with his readers not to revert to the imperfection of the old and outmoded system. With the advent of him who is our great High Priest the better hope has been *introduced:* what possible advantage could there be in exchanging the better for the worse? Why lose hold of the fulness of Christ in favor of the incompleteness of the system he has annulled? They have indeed already been urged to seize firm hold of the hope set before them, for this hope in Christ enters into the heavenly sanctuary itself (6:18f.). Similarly here, he assures them that it is through this better hope that *we draw near to God.* They are in real danger of ignoring or neglecting the wonderful privilege that is theirs in Christ of confident access to the throne of divine grace. Hence the urgent and repeated exhortation to exercise this privilege with boldness (4:15f.; 10:19ff.). The thrust of our author's argument in the present passage may effectively be summarized in the words Paul wrote to the Christians in Rome, when he said that "by sending his Son in the likeness of sinful flesh and for sin" God "has done what the law, weakened by the flesh, could not do" (Rom. 8:3). The hope of the Christian, focused as it is on the Son of God, is not something shifting and uncertain, but secure and substantial; for the word and the work of God in Christ on which it rests can never fail or be set aside.

These considerations fully justify the description of the hope which is made real within the sphere of the new covenant as "a better hope"; but at the same time the description itself implies that hope was not lacking during the period of the old covenant. By comparison, however, the hope of the old is far inferior to that of the new. The contrast is between the promise and the fulfilment, the shadow and the substance, the weak and the powerful, the transient and the permanent, the imperfect and the perfect. As chapter 11 below will show, the saints of the Old Testament were men and women of hope as well as, indeed because they were, men and women of faith, for, by definition there, "faith is the assurance of things hoped for" (11:1). But their hope concentrated itself in the expectation of the coming of him who, as the mediator of the new covenant and their "priest for ever," would at last take away the sin of the world; whereas we are privileged actually to live in the new age in which he who is our Melchizedek has superseded Levi and his order. Like them, we too are pilgrims, and in company with them we shall participate in the glorious and eternal consummation of Christ's kingdom; but through him who has now come we enjoy that access into the presence of God himself which was not open to them when they were pilgrims on this earth. "The person who still holds to or wishes to restore the shadows of the law," says Calvin, "not only obscures the glory of Christ but also deprives us of a tremendous blessing, in that he puts a distance between us and God, to approach whom freedom has been granted us by the gospel."

7:20–22. *And it was not without an oath. Those who formerly became priests took their office without an oath, but this one was addressed with an oath, "The Lord has sworn and will not change his mind, 'Thou art a priest for ever.'" This makes Jesus the surety of a better covenant.*

Psalm 110 provides yet another link in the chain of the argument which demonstrates the superiority of the order of Melchizedek to that of Levi: *Jesus*, the *"priest for ever"* in whose person the priesthood of Melchizedek finds its fulfilment, is *the surety of a better covenant* in view of the fact that his priesthood, in contrast to that of the levitical succession, was established by God *with an oath*. We have already been reminded earlier in the epistle (6:13ff.) that when God made his great covenant promise to Abraham he confirmed it with an oath, thus establishing for all time "the unchangeable character of his purpose" (6:17). What is true of the covenant with Abraham is true also of the institution of the order of Melchizedek, for here too the fact that *the Lord has sworn* is at the same time the assurance that he *will not change his mind*—not, of course, that God is otherwise fickle and unreliable, but that within the sphere of human undependability he graciously makes his promise, which in itself is absolutely firm, doubly secure in the mind of man by the addition of an oath.

Moreover, not all God's ordinances are intended to continue in perpetuity. This is especially apparent, in the context of the present discussion, in the case of the old covenant and the priesthood so closely associated with it. Our author has already argued (v. 11) that the very mention of another order of priesthood in Psalm 110 points to the temporary and inadequate nature of the levitical order, and he now finds that the order of Melchizedek was established *not without an oath*, whereas there is no question of a divine oath in connection with the institution of the priesthood of Aaron.[31] It is a matter of exceptional significance that the covenant with Abraham and the declaration concerning the priestly order of Melchizedek were both confirmed by God with an oath, for under these two heads all the gracious promises and prophecies which precede the coming of Christ are gathered, and with the coming of Christ both the evangelical covenant and the evangelical priesthood burst into fulfilment.

As, under Moses, the old and inferior covenant and the old and inferior priesthood belonged together, so now, in Christ, the new and better covenant and the new and better priesthood are closely bound up with each other. Of the latter, by virtue of the oath from above and on the basis of the perfection of his priestly offering, Jesus, the incarnate Redeemer of our humanity, is *the surety:*[32] he is the guarantor, he who is

---

31. The periphrastic construction in verse 21, οἱ μέν ... εἰσὶν ἱερεῖς γεγονότες, which is repeated in verse 23 (where ἱερεῖς follows γεγονότες) and may be translated "those have become priests," is wrongly given an aoristic sense in the English versions, for the periphrastic perfect comprehends the whole levitical system from its inauguration up to the present, that is, the time when this epistle was being written, and the implication is that at the time of writing there still were such priests in office. See Introduction, pp. 30ff.

32. The Greek term ἔγγυος, "surety," which is found only here in the New Testament, was common in legal and promissory documents of the period (see Moulton and Milligan, *sub voc.*) and means a guarantor (so NEB) or one who stands security. What is said here is in contrast to the mention, with reference to the Mosaic legislation concerning the levitical priesthood, of annulment or setting aside, ἀθέτησις, in verse 18. Jesus himself is our security that there will be no annulment of this new and better covenant. For literary occurrences of ἔγγυος see Liddell and Scott and Kittel, TDNT. Moffatt, Spicq, and Teodorico suggest that our author's usage of ἔγγυος here may be a case of paronomasia, induced by the assonance and proximity of ἐγγίζομεν in verse 19. This, however, is unlikely.

for ever, that the better covenant, of which he is the substance, will not fail or be set aside. That is why it is described, in 13:20, as "the eternal covenant."

> 7:23–25. *The former priests were many in number, because they were prevented by death from continuing in office; but he holds his priesthood permanently, because he continues for ever. Consequently he is able for all time to save those who draw near to God through him, since he always lives to make intercession for them.*

Of particular significance in the development of our author's argument is the consideration that the priests of Aaronic descent *were many in number*.[33] The multiplicity of such priests in a long succession over the centuries was necessitated by the fact that, as sharers in our common mortality, *they were prevented by death from continuing in office:* the inevitability of death, by which sooner or later every individual priesthood was terminated, meant also the inevitability of the passage of the priesthood from one man to another and from one generation to another. Hence the necessity for legislation to regulate the line of priestly descent (vv. 11ff. above). By contrast, Christ has no place in this legal line of succession because he is not a member of the priestly tribe of Levi: his priesthood, therefore, must be of a different order (vv. 15ff. above). But an even more important reason why Christ is not subject to any regulation relating to parentage and succession is that his priesthood is characterized by "the power of an indestructible life" (v. 16). As a priest who, in accordance with the affirmation of Psalm 110, *continues for ever* and who therefore *holds his priesthood permanently,* there is neither need nor place for any kind of priestly succession in his case. Because he does not pass away his own priesthood does not pass away, nor is it passed on to others; there can be no question of his passing on to others an office which is uniquely and uninterruptedly his.[34] "There is," as Calvin ob-

---

33. The RSV rendering of οἱ μὲν πλείονές εἰσιν γεγονότες ἱερεῖς διὰ τὸ θανάτῳ κωλύεσθαι παραμένειν as "the former priests were many in number, because they were prevented by death from continuing in office" is not strictly accurate, since the force of the Greek is to suggest that there were levitical priests still in office when these words were written. See note 31 above, on verse 21, where our author uses the same formulation. The sense is effectively brought out in the NEB: "Those other priests are appointed in numerous succession, because they are prevented by death from continuing in office." In other words, our author is speaking of a present situation, and so one that is not yet past, even though from the viewpoint of Christian theology the advent of Christ means the abrogation of the order of Levi. The present force of the Greek has clear implications for the dating of our epistle. See Introduction, pp. 30ff.
34. The adjective ἀπαράβατος, rendered adverbially in our version as "permanently," is susceptible of a variety of interpretations: "unchangeable" (KJV), "perpetual" (NEB), "in-

serves, "no death that prevents Christ from performing his office. Therefore he is the only and the perpetual priest." "He is the one and only priest," writes Peter Lombard, viewing the matter from the reverse angle, "and this could not be unless he were immortal; just as under the law the priests were many because they were mortal." It is true that Christ did die, and that this death was the essential priestly offering for man's sins; but his death was not the termination of his priesthood, or the moment of its transition from him to someone else, for he rose from the grave, the victor over death, and now continues as our sole and ever living high priest. With Paul we confidently affirm: "We know that Christ being raised from the dead will never die again; death no longer has dominion over him" (Rom. 6:9). This gives the answer to the question put by Christ's own hearers, who failed to see how the long-expected and ever continuing Deliverer could also be lifted up in death. "We have heard from the law that the Christ remains for ever," they said. "How can you say that the Son of man must be lifted up?" (Jn. 12:34; cf. Jn. 8:35). To the seer on Patmos the glorified Savior says: "Fear not, I am the first and the last, and the living one; I died, and behold I am alive for evermore" (Rev. 1:17f.).

Most important of all, the truth that he who is our Mediator and High Priest "continues for ever" carries with it the inescapable consequence (*consequently*) that *he is able for all time* and in all completeness[35] *to save those who,* putting their whole trust in his priestly offering of himself on their behalf, *draw near to God through him* (cf. v. 19 above; 4:16; 10:22). How could we hope to draw near to the eternal God through a priest who is dead or subject to death (as is the case with every other priest, and indeed with every creature)? How can we who draw near to God through Christ fail to be eternally secure in view of the fact not only that *he always lives* but also that as our ever living priest he never ceases *to make intercession* for us in the heavenly sanctuary? With him as our inter-

---

defectible" (F. F. Bruce), "inviolable" (Westcott), "interminable" (Delitzsch) represent one line of exegesis, while "that cannot pass to another" (Erasmus), "that doth not pass from one to another" (Owen), "intransmissible" (Héring, Teodorico), "inalienable" (Spicq, Montefiore), "non-transferable" (Moffatt), "that needs no successor" (Phillips) represent another. Such evidence as the papyri afford seems to favor the former, but this is more than counterbalanced by the preference of the Greek fathers for the latter understanding. In our view, the appropriateness of the term is enhanced by its ambivalence: the priesthood of Christ does not pass to another precisely because it is a perpetual priesthood.

35. The expression εἰς τὸ παντελές is at the same time a resumption and an amplification of the εἰς τὸν αἰῶνα of Psalm 110:4. Like the term ἀπαράβατος (see preceding note), it is enriched by its ambivalence, combining the notions of perpetuity on the one hand—thus "for all time" (RSV), "*in perpetuum*" (Vg)—and of completeness on the other—thus "absolutely" (NEB), "fully and completely" (Phillips), "totally" (Héring), "*ad plenum sive perfecte*" (Erasmus). As Owen says, "we may take the words in such a comprehensive sense as to include the meaning of both these interpretations."

cessor, supporting us by his strength and surrounding us with his love, there is no force that can daunt or overpower us (cf. Phil. 4:13; Rom. 8:37).[36]

The rabbinical scholars assigned an intercessory function to the angels,[37] and it is quite possible that the recipients of this epistle were being enticed to look to angels as their intercessors instead of to Christ. Whether this was so or not, our author makes it perfectly plain that as Christ is the sole mediator of the new covenant so also he is our sole intercessor, for intercession is itself an activity of mediation (cf. 1 Tim. 2:5; Rom. 8:34; 1 Jn. 2:1f.). To rely upon angels or saints or any other finite beings for their intercessions is not only futile; it also betrays a failure of confidence in the adequacy of Christ as our intercessor, and it is to honor the creature rather than him who is our Creator and Redeemer (cf. Rom. 1:25). Nor should it be imagined that the interceding of the Son on our behalf implies that he is pleading with an ill-disposed Father to change his attitude toward us, for such a concept is seriously at variance with the teaching of our epistle and indeed of the whole of the New Testament; it does violence to the trinitarian harmony of the Godhead. Father, Son, and Holy Spirit are one in deity, in will, and in love. The Son himself is the expression of the Father's attitude toward us, and, enthroned as he is at the right hand of the Majesty on high, his intercession is always, and can only be, at one with the good pleasure of the Father. Paul places the divine attitude in its true perspective in these memorable words: "He did not spare his own Son, but gave him up for us all; and with this gift how can he fail to lavish upon us all that he has to give?" (Rom. 8:32 NEB). Seen in this light, there is no room for distortion and misunderstanding of the purpose of Christ's heavenly intercession. "His once-completed self-offering," says F. F. Bruce, "is utterly acceptable and efficacious; His contact with the Father is immediate and unbroken; His priestly ministry on His people's behalf is never-ending, and therefore the salvation which he secures to them is absolute."[38]

---

36. For a fuller discussion of the meaning of the intercession of Christ in the heavenly sanctuary see Excursus III on "The Blood of Jesus and His Heavenly Priesthood," pp. 329ff. below, especially pp. 351ff.

37. See Strack-Billerbeck.

38. "The modern description of Christ pleading in heaven his passion, 'offering His blood', on behalf of men has no foundation in the Epistle," Westcott insists. "His glorified humanity is the eternal pledge of the absolute efficacy of his accomplished work. He pleads, as the older writers truly expressed the thought, by His Presence on the Father's Throne" (p. 230).

7:26. For it was fitting that we should have such a high priest, holy, blameless, unstained, separated from sinners, exalted above the heavens.

The rendering of our version, *it was fitting that we should have such a high priest*, does not do full justice to the force of the original, which may better be translated, "such a high priest exactly befitted us,"[39] that is to say, answered exactly to the requirements of the predicament in which we, as fallen creatures, were placed. *Such a high priest* refers to the description developed in the argument which precedes and leads up to this point (as also the conjunction *For* shows), while the brief definition which follows is no more than a summation of the teaching that has been given. The notion of "fittingness" (*it was fitting*) has little in common with the predilection for neat correspondences and counterbalances that we find in the mentality of medieval scholasticism.[40] Our author is speaking not of the fitting together of some divine parlor puzzle but of the serious necessities of the human situation. He has already drawn his readers' attention to the consideration that it was fitting for God to make him who is the pioneer of our salvation perfect through suffering (2:10); and now here he spells out the qualities of this high priest who is perfectly fitted to our needs, who is appropriate in that he has in his own person met the strict proprieties, in terms both of law and grace, of our situation, and who accordingly mediates between God and man with complete effectiveness. His unique qualifications are summarized in what follows in this and the next two verses. As a portrait of perfection it is compounded of the worthiness of his works no less than of the purity of his person.

To begin with, our High Priest is described as *holy, blameless,* and *unstained*, which, Teodorico suggests, may be taken in turn as expressive of the sanctity of Christ in relation to God ("holy," so also Bengel), in relation to his fellow men ("blameless"), and in relation to himself ("unstained"). The designation *holy* has a specifically messianic connotation

---

39. In the Greek, τοιοῦτος γὰρ ἡμῖν καὶ ἔπρεπεν ἀρχιερεύς, the καί, which is strong by its position, effectively intensifies the statement; cf. NEB: "Such a high priest does indeed fit our condition," where "indeed" represents the καί.
40. Anselm provides a good example of the medieval notion of fittingness as he attempts to prove how fitting the virgin birth of Christ was. "God," he explains, "can make a human being in four ways: either from a man and a woman, which is the normal way; or from neither man nor woman, as he created Adam; or from man without woman, as he made Eve; or from woman without man, which was something he had not yet done. Accordingly, to demonstrate that this last method also lay in his power, and was held over for this very purpose, nothing is more fitting than that he should take that man about whose origin we are inquiring from a woman without a man" (*Cur Deus Homo?* ii.8). This notion of fittingness as a test of divine competence and ingenuity is foreign to the mind of the scriptural authors.

in the thought of the apostles. This is evident in the evangelistic use made by both Peter and Paul of Psalm 16:10—"Thou wilt not let thy Holy One see corruption"—which would appear to have been an accepted element in the apostolic proclamation of the resurrection of Jesus as the fulfilment of prophecy (Acts 2:27; 13:35).[41] It is true that in both the Old and the New Testaments God's people are described as holy,[42] but theirs is a holiness not their own; it is a holiness which results from their being chosen and set apart by God and from the operation of divine grace within their lives; above all their holiness is holiness in Christ. For there is only one among men who is holy in the absolute sense of the term, namely, Jesus Christ, the Word-become-flesh, the sanctifier of those who are being sanctified (Heb. 2:11), who through eternal ages will be praised as the One who alone is holy (Rev. 15:4; cf. Rev. 16:5). The perfection of his holiness offsets the deficiency, indeed the absence, of ours. As he uniquely is God's Holy One, it is essential, if we are to be able to stand before God, that we should find acceptance in him with whom alone God is well pleased (cf. Mk. 1:11; Eph. 1:6). The awareness of this necessity indicates how *fitting* it is for us that our High Priest should himself be absolutely holy.

Christ is qualified to save us also in that he is *blameless:* in person and character he is entirely free from all that is evil and harmful, both in action and in motivation.[43] By contrast, because of the root of sin within us, in ourselves and in our dealings with others we are inescapably evil and harmful and our lives are soiled by false motives and unworthy deeds. How remarkable, then, to find him arraigned and condemned before a criminal court as an evil-doer, despite his judge's repeated declaration of his blameless innocence (Lk. 23:4, 14f., 22)! What is the meaning of this, except that there was no hope that we, guilty sinners as we are, could receive acquittal before the divine tribunal, were it not that he, the only righteous One, took our guilt upon himself and in our place endured the judgment that rightly belongs to us? Truly, it is by his wounds that we have been healed (1 Pet. 2:22–24; 3:18)! In this, too, we see how *fitting* it was for us that our Sin-Bearer should himself be altogether blameless.

The *unstained* character of Christ's person is a further attestation of

---

41. The adjective ὅσιος used by the author of Hebrews here is the same as that used in the LXX of Psalm 16:10, τὸν ὅσιόν σου.

42. In Scripture God's people are frequently called οἱ ἅγιοι, "holy ones," "saints." The use of ὅσιος is much less frequent.

43. The adjective ἄκακος, which occurs only here and in Romans 16:18 in the New Testament, describes the absence of all that is bad and wrong.

his competence to mediate between man and God. Far from being some-thing merely superficial or ceremonial, this freedom from all defilement belonged to the integrity of his being; and in this respect, too, there is a significant contrast between our Priest of the order of Melchizedek and the priests of old. They, it is true, were required to be undefiled and without blemish, but the standards demanded of them were of a formal and external nature, involving, for example, the avoidance of contact with dead bodies and the absence in their own persons of physical deformity or mutilation (cf. Lev. 21:1ff., 16ff.). Inwardly, however, they were stained with sin; hence the need (mentioned in the next verse) for them to offer sacrifice for their own sins before doing so for the sins of the people. But Jesus our High Priest is unstained *throughout*. Through his complete obedience and his victorious conquest of every temptation he has become perfect forever (v. 28 below; also 2:10; 4:15; 5:8), and as such he is "the source of eternal salvation to all who obey him" (5:9), for by virtue of his unstained character he was qualified to offer up the sacrifice of himself on our behalf, as of "a lamb without blemish or spot" (1 Pet. 1:19), and therefore wholly acceptable to the Father. Had he been stained with any defilement he would have been incapacitated to achieve this great redemption on our behalf and the purpose of his coming would have been frustrated. How *fitting*, therefore, that he should have been completely without stain or blemish!

The high-priestly qualification next added, namely, that he who is our Melchizedek should be *separated from sinners*, brings into a single focus the central implication of the three preceding definitions of his person as holy, blameless, and unstained. There is, in fact, a long-standing dispute over the precise connotation of the expression "sepa-rated from sinners": does it mean a separation by reason of the sinless-ness of his human life while he was on earth or a separation by reason of his removal from this fallen earthly scene to the pure glory of heaven? Herveus actually gives three possible interpretations. The expression means, he says, either that he was "set apart from the company of sinners, so that he was touched by no taint of sin from their company," or that he was "immune from all sin and separate from the company of other priests, among whom none is without sin" (this idea of separation from the levitical priests, who were all sinners, is propounded by Alcuin and recurs in some other medieval commentators), or that "his associa-tion is not now with mortal men, who, so long as they are in this life, cannot be free from sin."

This last interpretation requires the expression to be taken with what follows rather than with what precedes, so that Christ is under-stood as being "separated from sinners" because he has been "exalted above the heavens." Luther ("Christ is seated in heaven where there are no sinners"), Bengel,[44] Delitzsch, Moffatt,[45] Héring, Spicq, and Montefiore are among those who favor this sense. Delitzsch, for example, explains that Christ is now "so separated from evil men as to be henceforth unassailable by them" and that this is "in virtue of his exaltation"; and Spicq comments that "while he kept company with sinners during his mortal life (Mt. 9:10; 11:19), to the extent of being judged as one of them and finally of being delivered into their power (Mk. 14:41), since his ascension he has been preserved from contact with them."

The concept of Christ as now being remote from sinners in this quasi-physical sense is, however, inappropriate to the immediate context and indeed to the thought of the epistle as a whole, which emphasizes *nearness* rather than remoteness—the nearness of Christ to mankind through his incarnation (2:10ff.) and the nearness of the sinner, through Christ, to the throne of God's grace (4:14ff.; 10:19ff.). The separateness of Christ from sinners of which our author speaks here points rather to his separation from that which constitutes them sinners, namely, their sin. In terms of the humanity which he assumed for their sakes he is not separate from them, even in his exalted and glorified state, for it is precisely a *fellow*-humanity, the purpose of which is to "bring many sons to glory" (2:10). A key to the meaning of the expression is indeed available to us in what has already been said in 4:14f. above, for here we have what is virtually a repetition of the assertion there, that "we have a great high priest who has passed through the heavens, Jesus, the Son of God" (corresponding to "exalted above the heavens" that follows here), ". . . who in every respect has been tempted as we are, yet without sinning" (corresponding to "separated from sinners" here).[46]

The point, then, is that Christ, who is "holy, blameless, unstained," is *ipso facto* "separated from sinners." Self-evidently, the category of sinners is a category to which he does not belong. "He is described as separated from us," writes Calvin, "not because he rejects us from his society, but because he is uniquely distinguished from us in that he is free from all defilement." And Owen explains the significance of the

---

44. "Separatus est, relicto mundo" is Bengel's terse comment.
45. "The next two phrases go together," says Moffatt. "Κεχωρισμένος ἀπὸ τῶν ἁμαρτωλῶν is intelligible in the light of 9:28; Jesus has ἅπαξ sacrificed himself for the sins of men, and in that sense his connexion with ἁμαρτωλοί is done. He is no levitical high priest who is in daily contact with them, and therefore obliged to sacrifice repeatedly. Hence the writer at once adds (v. 27) a word to explain and expand this pregnant thought; the sphere in which Jesus now lives (ὑψηλότερος κτλ.) is not one in which, as on earth, he had to suffer the contagion or the hostility of ἁμαρτωλοί (12:2) and to die for human sins."
46. The terminology here, κεχωρισμένος ἀπὸ τῶν ἁμαρτωλῶν, is reminiscent of χωρὶς ἁμαρτίας in 4:15.

phrase as follows: "He was every way, in the perfect holiness of his nature and his life, distinguished from all sinners. . . . And so it became us that he should be. He that was to be a middle person between God and sinners, was to be separate from those sinners in that thing on the account whereof he undertook to stand in their stead." How could he have offered an all-sufficient sacrifice for the sins of others if he himself had not been entirely free from sin? It was only as he himself had been tested and proved perfect that he could become the source of eternal salvation to others (5:9).

We are told, finally, that he who is our Melchizedek has been *exalted above the heavens*. The language, as in 4:14 above, is that of transcendental reality. It embraces the triumph of Christ's resurrection, ascension, and glorification, and it portrays the supreme perfection of our ever living High Priest in the sanctuary above. The height of the glory to which he has been exalted far surpasses all possibilities of mundane experience and human description. As Westcott says, our author is here speaking of Christ's "elevation above the limitations of sense." Paul is speaking of the same great reality when he affirms that "he who descended is he also who ascended far above all the heavens, that he might fill all things" (Eph. 4:10). The truth of the transcendental glory of our ever living High Priest guarantees to us the existential reality of his person and work, for it assures us that he is not just a figure of the past, but also of the present and the future, indeed of eternity (Heb. 13:8). The power of his all-sufficient atoning work is available without diminishment to us today as it was to the believers of the first century, and it is so because he who died for us is alive from the dead and enthroned on high. Were he merely a figure of past history, overtaken and held by death, he could be no mediating high priest for us today. But Christ, alive and supremely exalted as he is, is truly our contemporary and our ever present Lord. In this respect, too, we see how *fitting* it is, how entirely appropriate to the satisfaction of the requirements for our restoration to God, that we should have "such a high priest."

7:27. He has no need, like those high priests, to offer sacrifices daily, first for his own sins and then for those of the people; for he did this once for all when he offered up himself.

From the postulation of the perfect innocence of Christ, as defined in the preceding verse, it follows that, unlike the levitical high priests, he was under no necessity to offer a sacrifice *first for his own sins* before doing so for the sins of others. This is a further significant point of contrast between him and *those high priests* of the Aaronic line, for (as already mentioned in 5:3 above) because they were without exception sinful mortals, themselves in need of reconciliation no less than *the people* in whose stead they ministered, they were required to sacrifice a sin offering on their own behalf before doing so on behalf of others (see Lev. 16:6, 11, 15). This procedure, moreover, had to be followed with interminable repetition (*daily*). Such considerations in themselves testify emphatically to the imperfect character of the Aaronic priesthood and its ministrations and to the need for another priesthood which would be free from frustrating inadequacies and therefore finally and eternally effective.

The use of the qualification *daily* here has presented a particular problem to commentators, because there is no indication in the Old Testament that the high priest was obliged every day to offer sacrifices for himself and for others. This was certainly true of *one day* in every year, namely, the Day of Atonement—a fact of which our author is well aware (see 9:7, 25). The suggestion of some, then, that the writer is simply confused or at fault through unfamiliarity with the detailed arrangements of the levitical system is hardly convincing. Others have supposed the qualification "daily" to mean on each Day of Atonement; but it would be a strange kind of mentality that says "daily" when "yearly" is intended, and, again, it would be incompatible with the fact that the author actually says "yearly" in 9:7, 25 below. Still others have wished to identify the offerings referred to here with the daily (morning and evening) cereal offerings enjoined in Leviticus 6:14ff.; these, however, could not be strictly classified as sin offerings, and in any case they were the concern of the priests in general rather than of the high priest in particular. The solution proposed by Delitzsch, that "the meaning of this sentence must be, that Christ has no need to do that *daily* which the high priest does *annually*, and which, if needing to be repeated at all, must be repeated continually every day, in order to effect a complete atonement for continually emergent cases of sin," is no more satisfactory. It is an argument that defeats its own purpose, for clearly any concept, even though hypothetical, of the repetition of Christ's sacrifice, whether it be yearly, daily, or a thousand times a day, is incompatible with the logic of its once-for-all adequacy, on which the author of our epistle insists with such emphasis, and relegates it to the level of the imperfection of the levitical system and its constantly repeated sacrifices; indeed, to contemplate a situation in which Christ would have to do daily what the levitical high priest did only yearly would seem in effect to relegate it to a lower level. In brief, no hypothesis can possibly justify the attachment of the condition "if needing to be repeated at all" to the sacrifice of Christ, and it is inconceivable that our author could have intended any such thing.

Much more plausible is the supposition that the writer of Hebrews is addressing himself to the situation which prevailed in his own day. His contemporary, the Jewish scholar Philo of Alexandria, speaks of the high priest as offering prayers and sacrifices day by day;[47] and indeed more than two centuries earlier, in the intertestamental period, we find Jesus the son of Sirach asserting that the Aaronic sacrifices "were to be burnt entirely, twice each day for ever" (Ecclus. 45:14 JB). But it must be questioned whether the reference of these passages is to anything more than to the daily cereal offerings described in Leviticus 2:1ff. and 6:14ff., in connection with which there was no requirement for the high priest to offer "first for his own sins and then for those of the people." Spicq, however, regards it as "likely that at that time the original distinction between the various sacrifices had been obliterated and that they were all regarded as, directly or indirectly, expiatory of sin"; and he cites the Jerusalem Talmud to the effect that it was open to the high priest to officiate at the daily sacrifices according to his pleasure throughout the year.

Owen draws attention to the regulations concerning the sin offering as given in Leviticus 4, where the high priest (here described as "the anointed priest") is required, whenever he sins, to sacrifice a young and unblemished bull for a sin offering (vv. 3ff.). This is followed by instructions regarding sin offerings for the whole congregation of Israel and for different individuals (vv. 13ff.). It would no doubt have been justifiable to describe these sin offerings in a general manner as "daily" sacrifices. Yet the hard fact remains that the specification "first for his own sins and then for those of the people" applies in a particular manner to the sacrificial sequence of the annual Day of Atonement, as prescribed in Leviticus 16.

Taking these various considerations into account, it is perhaps best to suppose that our author is speaking both generally and particularly in this verse, in such a way that when he says "daily" he has in mind the complex daily sacrificial routine performed by high priest as well as priests, whereas when he says "first for his own sins and then for those of the people" his thought is moving from the general to the particular, and is in fact beginning to focus on that great festival which was the annual consummation of the whole sacrificial system. Certainly, from now on, the center of interest becomes the significance of the entry of our Melchizedek into the heavenly holy of holies once for all, in fulfilment of the typology of the entry of the Aaronic high priest into the earthly holy of holies once a year, and his opening of the way for us into the divine presence, in contrast to the levitical dispensation under which the people were totally excluded from the innermost sanctuary.

47. Philo, *De Specialibus Legibus* iii.131.

When Christ our High Priest offered sacrifice *he did this once for all.* This all-important affirmation not only attests the eternal completeness and efficacy of this "one sacrifice for sins for ever" (10:12 KJV) but also confirms the negation and abolition of every other sacrificial system. The advent of what is final and eternal leaves no further place for what is temporary and inadequate. Henceforward the expression "once for all," or (within this context) the equally emphatic term "once," becomes a keynote in the great theme which our author is now developing.[48] The contrast between the levitical order and the order of Melchizedek could not be more marked: the former comprising a numerous succession of mortal and sinful priests offering over and over again a multitude of sacrifices, a system by its very nature stamped with imperfection and impermanence; the latter comprising but *one* priest, one because of the spotless sanctity of his ever continuing life, who offered up but *one* sacrifice, one because of its all-sufficient fulness, susceptible therefore of neither addition nor repetition, the sacrifice, moreover, not of some uncomprehending beast, but of *himself,* the beloved Son of God, who by reason of his incarnation was able to offer up himself in our stead. "As four things are to be taken into account in every sacrifice," writes Herveus, "namely, what is offered, to whom it is offered, by whom it is offered, and for whom it is offered, he who is our one true Mediator, reconciling us to God by a sacrifice of peace, remained one with him to whom he offered, became one with those for whom he offered, and as the person who offered was one and the same with what was offered[49].... So great is this sacrifice that, although it is one and once offered, it suffices to eternity."

7:28. *Indeed, the law appoints men in their weakness as high priests, but the word of the oath, which came later than the law, appoints a Son who has been made perfect for ever.*

The close interrelationship between *the law* and the levitical priesthood has already been noticed in verses 11 and 12 above, and the *weakness* of the *high priests* appointed under the old system has been shown in two main respects: first, in that they were mortal, and consequently "were prevented by death from continuing in office" (v. 23), and, sec-

48. Ἐφάπαξ, "once for all," occurs here and in 9:12 and 10:10, and ἅπαξ, "once," in 9:7, 26, and 28 within the context of which we are speaking.
49. In the medieval commentators there are many borrowings from the earlier patristic authors. The fourfold relationship of Christ's sacrifice propounded by Herveus here, and also by Peter Lombard in his comments on 8:5, in the twelfth century, is found in the eighth century in Alcuin (commenting on 8:3 below), and there can be little doubt that it goes back to the fourth century or even earlier.

ond, in that they were sinful, and consequently were under necessity to offer sacrifice for their own sins before doing so for the sins of the people (v. 27). Because of their weakness these former high priests were incapable of making an atonement infinite in its worth and eternal in its effect. It is true, indeed, that our author has also associated weakness with the high-priestly office of Christ, and, further, that the weakness known by Christ was precisely *human* weakness, the result of his assumption of our humanity by the act of incarnation—weakness shown in the reality of the frailty, fatigue, and temptation he endured (2:14ff.; Mt. 4:2; Mk. 4:38; Jn. 4:6, etc.), in the reality of the suffering he passed through (Heb. 5:7f.), and in the reality of the bitter death he experienced (7:27; 12:2)—with the consequence that he is indeed able "to sympathize with our weaknesses" (4:15). But the point now is that he was totally dissimilar from the levitical high priests not only because his high priesthood was neither stained with sin nor terminated by death, but also because he triumphed completely over the weakness, *our* weakness, with which he was beset: in temptation he knew no defeat, in suffering he endured to the end, and in death he was sovereign, proving by the glory of his resurrection that he had power both to lay down his life and to take it again (Jn. 10:18). Thus he victoriously learned obedience and was made perfect through his sufferings (Heb. 2:10; 5:8f.). We see, then, what is meant here by the description of Christ as *a Son*[50] *who has been made perfect for ever,* in this vital respect so different from the *men in their weakness* whom *the law appoints as high priests.*[51]

The word of the oath is of course a reference to the declaration of Psalm 110:4 ("The Lord has sworn and will not change his mind, 'Thou art a priest for ever'"), the significance of which has already been explained in verses 20ff. above. This oath clearly stands in contrast to the law, since, as our author observes (cf. v. 11 above), it *came later than the law* (Ps. 110 belonging to a period subsequent to the law-giving at Sinai), the point being that if the law, and with it the levitical priesthood, had been sealed with perfection, what possible need could there have been for a later oath concerning the appointment of another priest belonging to a different order? The very time sequence points to the incompetence of the priesthood instituted under Moses to provide what it portended.

50. It is difficult to bring out in translation the pregnant implication of the anarthrous use of the noun υἱός, "Son," here and elsewhere in the epistle (1:2; 3:6; 5:8). See the note on ἐν υἱῷ, 1:2 above. Teodorico remarks that the use of υἱός in these places without the article serves to emphasize "the inimitable relationship which unites our new High Priest to God."

51. The use of the present tense in this statement, ὁ νόμος ἀνθρώπους καθίστησιν ἀρχιερεῖς, "the law appoints men as high priests," further strengthens the impression that at the time when this epistle was being written the levitical priesthood was still functioning, with the implication that the Jerusalem temple was still standing. See Introduction, pp. 30ff.

The contrast between the assertion that "the law appoints men" and the assertion that "the word of the oath appoints a Son" should also be noticed: the plural "men" recalls the multiplicity of the high priests in their succession under the old order (v. 23), but the singular "Son" recalls the uniqueness of Christ, our great High Priest of the order of Melchizedek, who "continues for ever" (vv. 16, 24, 25) and who accordingly is without fellow or successor. The term Son is, indeed, of central significance in our epistle. Thus God who formerly spoke by the prophets has now, and finally, spoken in the person of his Son through whom the world was created (1:1f.); the ministering angels are not to be compared with him to whom God has said, "Thou art my Son" and who, as the appointed heir of all things, shares in the glory of the Father's sovereignty (1:5, 8, 13); faithful Moses ministered in God's household as a servant, but Christ was faithful over God's household as a Son (3:5f.); yet, although his status was that of Son, he obediently suffered and overcame, with the result that he has become the source of eternal salvation to all who trust in him (5:8–10); and so also here, it is not sinful and mortal men who are appointed by the word of the oath but One who in his own right is the eternal Son and who by his self-offering has procured everlasting reconciliation for us.

Thus this verse condenses and recapitulates within the briefest possible compass the main theme of the epistle up to this point. Teodorico describes the three verses 26–28 as "a hymn to the High Priest[52] . . . as though an outburst of the joy of humanity which has at last found the high priest qualified to understand its weaknesses and to come to its aid: so far above us and so near to us; himself in need of no cleansing and able to cleanse and expiate all our guilt; so different from the levitical priests and so much more effective in the function of his sacerdotal mediation."

> 8:1, 2. *Now the point in what we are saying is this: we have such a high priest, one who is seated at the right hand of the throne of the Majesty in heaven, a minister in the sanctuary and the true tent which is set up not by man but by the Lord.*

The theme continues to be that of the unique high priesthood of Christ. As the argument proceeds, however, it will become increasingly apparent that there are not only aspects of discontinuity but also typological affinities between the old system of the sanctuary set up under Moses and the eternal order of Melchizedek established in Christ; for the old order, imperfect and temporary though it was, did more than cry out for the provision of an order that would be effective and abiding:

52. Cf. Moffatt's engaging *obiter dictum:* "It is generally misleading to parse a rhapsody. . . ."

it was also designed to teach that the way of atonement was the way of sacrifice and substitution and to arouse the hope that in due course God himself would send the perfect victim for the removal of all sin (cf. Jn. 1:29). The affirmation of the two verses now before us constitutes *the point* (the "main point," NEB), the *leitmotif*, of this central section of the epistle.

In his development of the Melchizedek theme our author is not indulging in idealistic speculation. He is speaking of fact, not theory; for it is precisely *such a high priest* that *we have:* he is real and he is ours! And he is ours because, unlike the levitical high priests, who were earthbound and sooner or later were removed from the scene by death, his high priesthood is prolonged for eternity *in heaven,* where (resuming the language and the perspective of Ps. 110:1—cf. Heb. 1:3, 13; also 10:12; 12:2) he *is seated at the right hand of the throne of the Majesty* on high, whence also he exercises a ministry that is universal and without limitation. "Unlike all earthly priesthoods," comments Spicq, "that of the Son of God is performed in heavenly glory with a dignity that is kingly and a power that is divine." The expression "the Majesty in heaven" is, like the similar expression in Hebrews 1:3, a periphrasis for God himself. The exalted and glorified Son shares the Father's "throne," the "right hand" of which is the position of privilege and authority. When, at length, every hostile force has been subdued (as promised in Ps. 110:1 = Heb. 1:13 and Ps. 8:6 = Heb. 2:8), then, his work of cosmic mediation completed, he will deliver the kingdom to the Father, and thus God will be all in all (1 Cor. 15:24—28).

Elevated to this position of eminence, our ever living High Priest is the *minister*[53] in that *sanctuary*[54] which is *the true tent.*[55] It is described as

---

53. The noun λειτουργός, which our author uses here, specifically designates the priestly minister in Isaiah 61:6 and Jeremiah 33:21 (LXX). The verb λειτουργεῖν, "to minister," and the noun λειτουργία, "ministry," are commonly employed to describe the service of tabernacle and temple in the Old Testament. Erasmus, for example, observes that λειτουργός "non simpliciter sonat *ministrum,* sed plerunque *ministrum sacrorum.*"

54. The phrase τῶν ἁγίων λειτουργός is susceptible of a variety of interpretations. A number of patristic authors treated the genitive τῶν ἁγίων as masculine and accordingly interpreted the phrase to mean "a minister of the saints," which in itself is appropriate enough. Alcuin explains that "the souls of the saints are this tabernacle in which he ministers with eternal joy." If, however, the genitive is understood as being neuter, then two other possibilities arise: either "a minister of holy things," which is how Luther took it—and it is worth remarking that Philo uses the same expression, in the order λειτουργὸς τῶν ἁγίων, of the levitical priest in this sense (*Legum Allegoriae* iii.135; cf. *De Fuga* 93); or "a minister of the sanctuary," which is the accepted interpretation today, the sanctuary intended being the heavenly holy of holies. The justification for this conclusion is our author's repeated designation of the wilderness holy of holies as τὰ ἅγια (9:8, 12, 24, 25; 10:19; 13:11; in 9:2 it is used of the holy place; cf. also τὸ ἅγιον in 9:1 and ἅγια ἁγίων in 9:3). It can hardly be doubted that this usage, within the immediate context, in which Jesus is conceived as having entered as our High Priest into the heavenly holy of holies, determines the authentic understanding of the expression here.

55. Our version's rendering of τῶν ἁγίων λειτουργὸς καὶ τῆς σκηνῆς τῆς ἀληθινῆς as "a

"the true tent" because, in contrast to the perishable tent or tabernacle which accompanied the Israelites in their wilderness wanderings, the heavenly reality into which the ascended Lord has entered is the genuine sanctuary, the imperishable holy of holies. The sense of the expression is clearly given in 9:24 below, where our author declares that "Christ has entered, not into a sanctuary made with hands, a copy of the true one, but into heaven itself, now to appear in the presence of God on our behalf." The wilderness sanctuary was but a shadow; the sanctuary of which Christ is the minister is the reality (v. 5 below; cf. also Heb. 10:1; 1 Cor. 10:1ff.). The latter is "the true tent" because, in contrast to the former, it *is set up not by man* (cf. Ex. 33:7) *but by the Lord.*

This mode of thought is no mere reproduction of the idealism of Plato and his followers, according to which all earthly entities correspond and are fashioned according to their specific heavenly prototypes, or ideas, as particulars to their universals. Yet the fact that Platonism exercised a determining contemporary influence on Alexandrian philosophy—including that of Philo, who also speaks of an earthly and a heavenly sanctuary—should not be left out of account; for it is undeniable that in this epistle our author gives much attention to the correspondence of the earthly to the heavenly, as of the copy to the reality.[56] He does so, however, in such a way as to demonstrate this correspondence in its true perspective, which is particularly the soteriological perspective of the relationship between the temporal and the eternal under the providential grace of God. But in doing this he is intent on the application of his teaching in a practical manner to the specific situation which has evoked this letter—something very different from indulgence in abstract philosophizing. It seems clear that the readers whose condition he is addressing are in danger of stultifying their Christian profession by a preoccupation with the transitory, and now superseded, worship and priesthood of the levitical system. This diagnosis would apply, obviously, with considerable appropriateness to persons fascinated to a greater or lesser degree by tenets similar to those of the Dead Sea Sect, whose adherents were intent on restoring the pattern of life, with its

---

minister in the sanctuary and the true tent" (similarly KJV, Phillips, JB) is somewhat maladroit. The "sanctuary" and the "true tent" should be understood as referring to the same thing and the καὶ accordingly is epexegetic and should be translated as "even," thus: "a minister of the sanctuary, even (or which is) the true tent" (cf. NEB). For discussion of the expression "the true tent" see Excursus II on pp. 283ff. below.

56. Cf. the interesting passage in the apocryphal writing *The Wisdom of Solomon,* a product of pre-Philonic Alexandrian Judaism: "Thou didst tell me to build a temple (ναόν) on thy sacred mountain and an altar in the city which is thy dwelling-place, a copy of the sacred tabernacle (μίμημα σκηνῆς ἁγίας) prepared by thee from the beginning" (9:8). The reference here, of course, is not to a heavenly sanctuary but to the earthly temple which Solomon erected.

structures and observances, which characterized the wilderness experience of the Israelites under Moses.

There is indeed a sanctuary, but it is not on this earth (he is saying to them), and a priesthood, but it is fulfilled in Christ, our glorious High Priest of the order of Melchizedek. They are not to fix their expectations on mundane shadows but on the heavenly reality. Jesus our forerunner has opened for us the way, hitherto barred, into the sanctuary of God's presence and favor. The eternal rest which the Israelites in the wilderness failed to achieve belongs to us who trust in him (4:1ff.). For he who is now enthroned above is still ours. His ascension was indeed a return to the glory from which he first descended (cf. Jn. 7:33; 8:14; 13:3; 17:5); but it was a return with a difference. He left as the Son of God. He returned both as Son of God and also, by reason of the incarnation, as Son of man. He left as Lord. He returned both as Lord and also as Minister on our behalf in the presence of the Father. He left as King. He returned both as King and also as High Priest and Intercessor for those whom he is not ashamed to call his brethren (Heb. 2:11). He left as Sovereign. He returned also as Savior. He who sustains the whole of creation is now also the pioneer and the guarantor of our redemption (Heb. 1:1–3; 2:10; 12:2).

EXCURSUS II: THE MEANING OF "THE TRUE TENT" IN HEBREWS 8:2 and "THE GREATER AND MORE PERFECT TENT" IN HEBREWS 9:11

A number of commentators have interpreted these two expressions as signifying the body or humanity of Christ. Owen, for example, expounds "the true tent" of 8:2 as meaning "the human nature of the Lord Christ himself," explaining that "he is the only way and means of our approach unto God in holy worship, as the tabernacle was of old," that "the human nature of Christ is the only true tabernacle wherein God would dwell personally and substantially," and that "we are to look for the gracious presence of God in Christ only." Bengel is among those who are of a similar mind. The rather long and involved sentence which comprises 9:11, 12 may be paraphrased as follows:

> After coming (to earth) as high priest of the good things fulfilled by his coming, Christ achieved our eternal redemption and then entered once and for all into the sanctuary, through the greater and more perfect tent not made with hands, that is not of this creation, and (he did so) not through the blood of goats and bullocks but through his own blood.

283

Chrysostom and some later patristic authors, including Theodoret, Primasius, and Ecumenius, understood this "greater and more perfect tent" to denote the body which the Son assumed in the incarnation, and this understanding has had distinguished advocates ever since.

The justification for this interpretation is sought in the symbolical usage of the term "tent" (σκηνή) elsewhere in the New Testament. Christ himself spoke of his body as "this temple" (ναός) which he would raise up in three days (Jn. 2:19–22; cf. Mk. 14:58; 15:29)—the allusion being primarily to his resurrection from the dead, but also, more cryptically, to the impending cessation of the temple worship which was historically the successor of the tent worship in the wilderness and functionally synonymous with it. John describes the incarnation of the Word as the "pitching of his tent" (ἐσκήνωσεν) in our midst (Jn. 1:14). Paul calls our present mortal body "our earthly tent dwelling" (ἡ ἐπίγειος ἡμῶν οἰκία τοῦ σκήνους) and also quite simply "the tent" (τὸ σκῆνος; 2 Cor. 5:1, 4). Peter uses the same metaphor when he refers to his approaching death as "the laying aside of his tent" (ἡ ἀπόθεσις τοῦ σκηνώματός μου; 2 Pet. 1:13, 14). And, in a manner reminiscent of John 2:19ff., Paul writes of the body of the Christian as the temple or sanctuary of the Holy Spirit (ναός; 1 Cor. 6:19; 2 Cor. 6:16).

On the basis of this symbolism, then, "the true tent" of 8:2 and "the greater and more perfect tent" of 9:11 are interpreted as a manner of speaking of the human body by means of which Christ accomplished our eternal redemption, for it was this body that enabled him to function as our high priest and in particular to offer himself in our place on the cross. This "tent" can be described as "true" or "greater and more perfect" in comparison with the tabernacle of old because of the eternal perfection of the atonement which has been procured through its instrumentality. But the fuller definition of 9:11, namely, that it is "not made with hands, that is, not of this creation," raises some problems; for while the qualification "not made with hands" suggests a contrast with the former tent which, though erected in accordance with the divine pattern, was a human construction from earthly materials, the explanation of this phrase as meaning "not of this creation" would appear to call in question the genuineness of that humanity supposedly designated as "the greater and more perfect tent," and therefore to render doubtful the reality of the Son's identification of himself with mankind. Theophylact, indeed, in the eleventh century, states that this text was adduced by heretics as proof that Christ's body was of a docetic or ethereal character. Heretical conclusions of this kind were customarily countered, however, by the explanation that the miracle of the virgin birth afforded adequate justification for defining Christ's humanity as being "not of this creation." Thomas Aquinas, to give an example, suggests that "the greater and more perfect tent" of 9:11 may be interpreted to mean either "the tabernacle of heavenly glory" or "the body of Christ in which he fought against the devil." In support of the latter interpretation he cites Psalm 19:4, "He placed his tabernacle on earth" (Vulgate)— a text of questionable relevance; and he explains that it is *greater* because "in him dwells all the fulness of the Godhead bodily" (Col. 2:9), *more perfect* because "we have seen his glory, glory as of the only begotten of the Father, full of grace and truth" (Jn. 1:14), and *not made with hands* because it is "not the product of male seed."

Turning to the Protestant commentators, Owen does not specifically mention the virgin birth, but his explanation of "not of this creation" is to the same effect. "Although the substance of his human nature was of the same kind with ours," he writes, "yet the production of it in the world was such an act of divine power as excels all other divine operations whatever . . . in its constitution and production it was an effect of the divine power above the whole order of this creation." Calvin expounds the phrase more vaguely: while admitting that the body of Christ "was certainly created of the seed of Abraham and subject to sufferings and death," he maintains that at this point the author "is not concerned with the material body or its quality but with the spiritual power which comes to us from it." His exegesis of the "tent" concept in terms of Christ's body is, however, very plainly stated:

> The word "sanctuary" is properly and fittingly applied to the body of Christ because it is the temple in which the whole majesty of God dwelt. He is said to have made through his body a way to ascend into heaven because he consecrated himself to God in that body: in it he was sanctified to be true righteousness and in it he prepared himself to make his sacrifice. . . . He has entered heaven through his own body because he now sits on the right hand of the Father. He intercedes for us in heaven because he has put on our flesh and consecrated it as a temple to God the Father and has sanctified himself in it to make atonement for our sins and gain for us eternal righteousness.

Owen seems to be no less confident that this is the correct interpretation, as the following excerpts show:

> This tabernacle, whereby he came a high priest, was his own human nature. . . . Herein dwelt "the fulness of the Godhead bodily", Col. ii.9—that is, substantially; represented by all the pledges of God's presence in the tabernacle of old. This was that tabernacle wherein the Son of God administered his sacerdotal office in this world, and wherein he continueth yet so to do in his intercession. . . . The human nature of Christ, wherein he discharged the duties of his sacerdotal office in making atonement for sin, is the greatest, the most perfect and excellent ordinance of God, far excelling those that were most excellent under the old testament.

There is, undoubtedly, much that is attractive in this line of interpretation. But, well suited though it may be to teaching which is found elsewhere in the New Testament, there are reasons for regarding it as exegetically inappropriate within the present context of the Epistle to the Hebrews. For one thing, in the passages cited in support of this interpretation the association between the tent or the temple and the body is clearly indicated; but there is no such indication in our epistle. For another, when Christ speaks of raising in three days a temple not made with hands ("he spoke of the temple of his body," as the evangelist explains, Jn. 2:21), it is clear that he intended the glorified body with which he rose from the dead (Jn. 2:22); and likewise when Paul teaches that, even though his present earthly tent dwelling should be dismantled in death, the Christian has "a building from God, a house not made with hands, eternal in the heavens," he too is referring to that ultimate transformation in which the believer is invested with a glorified body similar to that of the risen Jesus. Guided by this understanding, exegetical consistency would surely demand that "the true tent" and "the greater and more perfect tent" should be explained as referring (if indeed this is what our author means) not to the body assumed by Christ at Bethlehem but rather to the glorious body of his resurrection—not, of course, that there are two bodies, but two different states of the same body: the one humble, the other exalted; the one earth-bound, the other transcendental (as Paul teaches in 1 Cor. 15:42ff.).

Another interpretation, which starts virtually from the same premise but follows a somewhat different course, is that which makes use of the Pauline identification of the church as the body of Christ (Eph. 1:22f.). Cornelius à Lapide, indeed, takes our author to be speaking of the church quite simply, without any allusion to the concept of the body of Christ. Thus he writes on Hebrews 9:11:

> I conclude that this tabernacle is the Church of Christ gathered here on earth, pilgrim and militant, which Christ himself founded, of which he said in ch. 8:2 that it is a tabernacle set up by the Lord and not by man; for this is identical with the description here, "a tabernacle not made with hands, not of this creation," in other words, not the product of human skill and fashioning, as was the first tabernacle fashioned by Bezaleel. For the tabernacle fittingly represents the Church... in which Christ in dying on the cross offered himself to the Father, as a victim for the sins of men; and just as the high priest used to go from and through the holy place into the holy of holies, so Christ (and we with Christ) passed from his Church militant here on earth to the Church heavenly and triumphant.

The step of linking the concepts of "body" and "church" is deliberately taken by Westcott, whose search for "some spiritual antitype to the local sanctuary" is controlled by the prerequisites which demand that it must both "represent the Presence of God" and "offer a way of approach to God"—requirements which he believes are met in the redeemed and perfected humanity which is the community of the church.

> Through this glorified Church [he writes] answering to the complete humanity which Christ assumed, God is made known, and in and through this each believer comes nigh to God. In this Body, as a spiritual Temple, Christ ministers. As members of this Body believers severally enjoy the Divine Presence. ... It enables us to connect redeemed humanity with the glorified human Nature of the Lord, and to consider how it is that humanity, the summing-up of Creation, may become in Him the highest manifestation of God to finite being, and in its fulness that through which each part is brought near to God.

But this interpretation, too, has its problems. It is reached by using one metaphor (the tent for the body) as the basis for another metaphor (the body for the church), with the consequence that the exegesis has a distinctly mystical quality. It reflects, moreover, a characteristic tendency of Westcott's thought in accordance with which Christ is regarded, evolutionistically, as *Consummator Mundi*, the one in whom the whole unfolding process achieves its culmination—hardly the perspective of the writer of Hebrews! And in any case it is difficult to see what sense there could be in saying, as according to Westcott's understanding we must suppose the author of our epistle to be saying, that "through the greater and more perfect tent, that is his body understood as signifying the Church, Christ entered once for all into the sanctuary"; for, however rightly Christ may be said to work or minister through the church, there is no way in which one can speak of his having entered into the heavenly sanctuary through the church: the church is not the means of his entry into the heavenly sanctuary, but, to the contrary, he is the means of the church's entry, and it is precisely on the ground that we have a great High Priest in the sanctuary above that those who constitute the church are invited confidently to draw near to the throne of grace through the new and living way which he has opened for us (4:14–16; 10:19–22).

The comparable opinion that the sanctuary into which Christ enters is the souls or hearts of God's people is open to criticism of the same order. This explanation is found as early as the fourth century in Gregory of Nazianzus.[1] In our own day it has received the approval of F. F. Bruce, who writes as follows (on 9:11):

> What then is the nature of the spiritual temple in which God dwells? When Stephen maintained that "the Most High dwelleth not in houses made with hands", he confirmed his statement by quoting Isa. 66:1f. But in that same prophetic context God declares that in preference to any material temple He chooses "him that is poor and of a contrite spirit, and that trembleth at my word". And this means that He prefers to make His dwelling with people of that character, as is shown by the similar words of Isa. 57:15: "For thus saith the high and lofty One that inhabiteth eternity, whose name is Holy: I dwell in the high and holy place, with him also that is of a contrite and humble spirit". Our author stands right in this prophetic tradition when he affirms that the people of God are the house of God: "whose house are we, if we hold fast our boldness and the glorying of our hope" (Ch. 3:6).

This, however, unexceptionable though it may otherwise be theologically, is still a questionable exegesis of the passage in question. The affirmation of 3:6 is not the same as that of 9:11; and, though the people of God are described as a "house" (or "household"), they are not anywhere called a "tent." "The thought of our author must be distinguished here from that of the Fourth Evangelist and from that of Paul," writes Montefiore (on 8:5). "For Paul the congregation of Christians formed the Temple of God (1 Cor. iii.16; 2 Cor. vi.16; Eph. ii.21). According to the Fourth Evangelist, Jesus when he prophesied that in three days he would raise up the temple, was speaking 'of the temple of his body' (John ii.21). But for our author, heaven is to be identified with the heavenly sanctuary, and Jesus entered it at his ascension."

As a matter of curiosity, it may be mentioned that the sixteenth-century Roman Catholic scholar Catharinus attempted to explain "the greater and more perfect tent" as a reference to the Virgin Mary, through whom Christ appeared as our high priest in this world. If this raises even more acutely the question of

---

1. Gregory of Nazianzus, *Ad Julianum* (alluding to 8:2).

the understanding of the definition "not of this creation," no doubt the Roman Catholic apologist would propose that the answer is to be found in the dogmas of the immaculate conception and the assumption into heaven of the Virgin Mary—but this in turn would raise other and more serious questions.

Another view, which maintains a close analogy between what is said here about Christ and the action of the high priest in the wilderness tabernacle, supposes that as the high priest of old passed through the holy place into the holy of holies so our High Priest is envisaged as passing "through the greater and more perfect tent" (corresponding to the holy place) before "he entered once for all into the sanctuary" (corresponding to the holy of holies). On this interpretation, Christ at his ascension passed through the outer chamber of the heavens, that is, beyond this earth where the altar of the cross was situated, and entered into the inner chamber of God's own presence. Thus over a century ago John Brown expounded 9:11 as follows:

> Our Lord offered his sacrifice on the earth, as the Jewish high priests did without the tabernacle; and having offered his sacrifice on the earth, He passed through the visible heavens, as they passed through the outer tabernacle, into the heaven of heavens, of which the most holy place was an emblem. He entered into the holy place [by which the writer evidently means the holy of holies] through the visible heavens, which are represented in the Old Testament Scriptures as the tabernacle of Jehovah—His outer court, throughout which are scattered displays of grandeur and beauty worthy of the antechamber of the great King, the Lord of hosts—a tabernacle certainly greater, more magnificent, more perfect, more highly finished, than the Mosaic tabernacle, with all its curious embroidery and costly ornaments—a tabernacle formed immediately by the hand of God, who "in the beginning stretched out the heavens as a curtain."

Among our contemporaries both Héring and Spicq propound a similar interpretation. According to the former: "The tabernacle is presented here as the way, the sanctuary as the destination. . . . He passes through the holy place, identified as heaven, in order to enter into the holy of holies." And according to the latter: "Jesus, after his resurrection and by means of his ascension, passed through the heavens to arrive at the presence of God." Spicq refers to 4:14, "we have a great high priest who has passed through the heavens," and to 7:26, where it is asserted that he is "exalted above the heavens" (cf. Eph. 4:10). Another advocate of this interpretation is Helmut Koester, who offers the following explanation of the expression "the sanctuary and the true tent" (8:2):

> This is not a hendiadys, but expresses that Christ's office includes both the service in the sanctuary of heaven itself (τὰ ἅγια) *and* the entering by passing through the heavenly regions (ἡ σκηνή) = the ascension! It also becomes clear here that the author of Hebrews is more interested in the opening of the way into the heavenly sanctuary than in the performance of a service within the sanctuary of heaven.[2]

---

2. Helmut Koester, "Outside the Camp: Hebrews 13:9–14," *Harvard Theological Review*, 55 (1962), pp. 309f.

The judgment of the last sentence is surprising; leaving that aside, however, the term σκηνή is used in our epistle of the holy place through which the levitical high priest passed to enter the holy of holies (ἡ πρώτη σκηνή, 9:2, 6, 8, and perhaps 21), yet it is also used of the holy of holies (9:3) and of the tabernacle *in toto* (8:5; 13:10). The description of ἡ σκηνή in 8:2 as ἀληθινή, "the *true* tent," well defines the sanctuary of which Christ is now the minister, but is scarcely appropriate as a description of the heavenly regions through which the ascending Lord passed. Besides, if the latter interpretation were correct, one would have expected the way to be mentioned before the destination. And, further, that a hendiadys is indeed intended by "the sanctuary and the true tent" is confirmed by the singular number of the pronoun ἥν in the relative clause which follows— ἥν ἔπηξεν ὁ κύριος: our author could hardly have meant that the Lord set up only a heavenly holy place, especially as the focus of his attention is on the high-priestly entry of Jesus into the heavenly holy of holies. In fact, throughout these chapters our author's perspective does not include the concept of a holy place above, as distinct from the holy of holies, precisely because, now that the curtain between the two has been abolished and the way opened up by him for all into the heavenly holy of holies which is the sanctuary of God's presence, the distinction no longer exists.

The ineptitude of this interpretation appears, too, from the fact that the qualification of 9:11, "not made with hands, that is, not of this creation," applies just as little to the visible heavens as it does to our earth, since both belong equally to "this creation" and both are praised throughout Scripture as the works of the divine Creator (Gen. 1:1; Ps. 19:1, etc.). This consideration alone is enough to disqualify the distinction made by those who propose this type of interpretation. The analogy between the old and the new must not be pressed too far, for there is a radical change in the situation as the result of the sacrifice which the incarnate Son offered on the cross. The rending of his flesh at Calvary was accompanied by the rending of the curtain which separated the holy place from the holy of holies (Heb. 10:20; Mt. 27:51). This symbolized, as we have already observed and as 9:8 plainly indicates, the abolition of the outer chamber and the removal of the barrier which hitherto had excluded the people from entry into the chamber of God's presence. Now the way is clear for all God's people, who together in Christ constitute a holy priesthood (1 Pet. 2:5), to approach with boldness the throne of divine grace. This is the new and living way of which our author speaks in 10:19f.

It is our understanding, then, that the author of the Epistle to the Hebrews means here not two things but one; that is to say, that the sanctuary into which Christ has entered is the same as that tent which is described as "true" and "greater and more perfect." The correctness of this judgment is confirmed by the assertion of 9:24 that "Christ has entered, not into a sanctuary made with hands, a copy of the true one, but into heaven itself, now to appear in the presence of God on our behalf," in which we find the sanctuary into which Christ has entered defined by precisely the same terms that are used to define the *tent* in 8:2 and 9:11, namely, *true* and *not made with hands*. This linguistic correspondence shows in a striking manner that the "sanctuary" and the "tent" are the same thing. In 8:2 our author declares that Christ our High Priest is now "in heaven," where he ministers "in the sanctuary which is the true tent," and in 9:11f. that he entered into the heavenly holy of holies through his entry into "the greater and more perfect tent." If there is a suggestion of a distinction in the latter passage, it is no more than this, that, in conformity with the imagery of the wilderness tabernacle, Christ is envisaged as entering the true tent (of heaven) which contains the true sanctuary (of God's presence). But as the curtain which divided the tent into two chambers has now been abolished, it is easy to see how in the true order of things tent and sanctuary can be treated as synonymous terms.

The contrasts and correspondences to which we have drawn attention may be presented schematically as follows:

The Mosaic tabernacle	The heavenly reality
"on earth" (8:4f.)	"in heaven" (8:1)
"an earthly sanctuary" (9:1)	
"set up by man" (8:2)	"set up by the Lord" (8:2)
"made with hands"	"not made with hands,
"of this creation" (9:11)	that is, not of this creation" (9:11)
"a sanctuary made with hands" (9:24)	"not a sanctuary made with hands" (9:24)
"a copy and shadow" (8:5)	"the true tent" (8:2)
"a copy" (9:24)	"the true sanctuary" (9:24)
	"the greater and more perfect tent" (9:11)
	"heaven itself" (9:24)

8:3, 4. *For every high priest is appointed to offer gifts and sacrifices; hence it is necessary for this priest also to have something to offer. Now if he were on earth, he would not be a priest at all, since there are priests who offer gifts according to the law.*

The opening statement of verse 3 is a resumption of what has been said already in 5:1: whenever a *high priest is appointed* the primary purpose is that he should *offer gifts and sacrifices.* This being so, it follows (*hence*) that *this priest,* namely, Christ, must necessarily also *have something to offer;* otherwise he would improperly be described as a priest. Alcuin explains that the necessity spoken of here applies to "the days of his flesh," since "while he was in the eternal nature of his divinity he did not have anything to offer, but he took from us what he was able to offer, that is, human flesh." "What," he asks, "is so suitable for sacrifice as mortal flesh for mortal men?" And, as Aquinas points out, what distinguishes Christ's offering, as compared with the sacrifices of old, is that "it was pure, since his flesh had no stain of sin (Ex. 12:5) . . . it was appropriate, since it is appropriate that man should make satisfaction for man ... and it was suitable for sacrifice, since his flesh was mortal (Rom. 8:3)."

That Christ's offering is limited to a single sacrifice is indicated by the singular pronoun *something:* there is no suggestion that he offers a plurality of "gifts and sacrifices," for to do so would be incompatible with the unique and total sufficiency of the one sacrifice he offered on the cross. Nor may it be concluded that in some sense he re-offers or re-presents this one sacrifice in the heavenly sanctuary, for this too would conflict with our author's insistence not only that his sacrifice of himself was done once for all, in contrast to the repetitious offerings of the levitical system, but also that it took place here on earth, on the altar of the cross, "outside the camp" (7:27; 9:25, 27; 10:10, 12, 14; 13:12).[1] "Jesus' present ministry in heaven is intercession, not offering," says Montefiore; "and so it was in the past that he had to have had something to offer."

The observation of verse 4, that if Christ *were on earth,* with reference, that is, to his eternal priesthood, *he would not be a priest at all,* is based on the fact that *there are priests who offer gifts,* and that they do so *according to the law.* Our author has already explained why there is no place for another priestly order on earth in 7:11ff. The earthly order is the order of Levi, as required by the Mosaic law. Christ did not belong to the tribe of Levi, but to the tribe of Judah, "and in connection with that tribe Moses said nothing about priests" (7:14). It follows, therefore, that his priesthood belongs to a sphere that is not earthly. This consideration in no way stultifies the priestly character of the Son's incarnation to the end that he might offer his humanity in sacrifice here on earth; for the cross in turn was a means to a further end, namely, the restoration of our humanity and its exaltation with himself to the glory which is now his. He who has gone to heaven is the One who first came from heaven; the true sanctuary in which he now appears in the presence of God on our behalf is heaven itself (9:24); and the abiding sphere of his priesthood is heavenly and eternal, not earthly and temporal. Thus from the very beginning the gaze of the believer has been fixed, not on the earthly shadow, but on the heavenly reality; for this life is the time of pilgrimage, not rest, and this present world, prior to the renewal of all things, is

---

1. The distinction between the present infinitive προσφέρειν, used of the action of high priests in general, and the aorist subjunctive προσενέγκῃ, used of the action of Christ in particular, should be noticed. Thus, for example, F. F. Bruce comments: "The fact that προσενέγκῃ is aorist (subjunctive) is consistent with our author's repeated emphasis on the singularity of the sacrifice which Christ offered." So also Spicq: "Observe the aorist προσενέγκῃ: a sacrifice offered once-for-all, instead of the present προσφέρῃ (9:25)." For further discussion see Excursus III, "The Blood of Jesus and His Heavenly Priesthood," pp. 329ff., especially pp. 345ff.

the realm of all that is transitory, and is thus no fit sphere for him who is our High Priest forever (4:1; 11:10, 13–16; 12:2).

The statement, in the present tense, that "there are priests who offer gifts according to the law,"[2] is another of the indications in this epistle that the levitical priesthood was still in existence when it was written, and thus that the Jerusalem temple was still standing, with the consequence that the date of its composition must have been prior to A.D. 70.[3]

> 8:5. *They serve a copy and shadow of the heavenly sanctuary; for when Moses was about to erect the tent, he was instructed by God, saying, "See that you make everything according to the pattern which was shown you on the mountain."*

The ministry of the levitical priests, our author explains, is associated with[4] *a copy and shadow of the heavenly sanctuary,*[5] not with the true and eternal reality. But to call it "a copy and shadow" does at least mean that the tent in the wilderness had a definite correspondence with the heavenly reality, though only to a limited degree. It was a *copy*, much as a drawing or plan of a building corresponds in scale and representation to the building but is not the building itself, since a two-dimensional diagram, however appropriate it may be for instruction and guidance, can never be the same thing as the three-dimensional structure it delineates; or as a model is not comparable in reality and splendor to the reality it portrays in miniature. It was also a *shadow* inasmuch as a shadow presupposes a body or substance which casts a shadow, though the shadow itself is incorporeal and insubstantial.[6] There is,

2. The construction is a genitive absolute in which there is a combination of two present participles, the second of which is substantival: ὄντων τῶν προσφερόντων κατὰ νόμον τὰ δῶρα, "there are those who offer gifts according to the law."
3. Cf. also the present tenses in verse 3: πᾶς γὰρ ἀρχιερεὺς εἰς τὸ προσφέρειν... καθίσταται (similar expressions are used in 5:1 and 7:28 above). See Introduction, pp. 31ff.
4. Once again a present tense is used of the operation of the levitical priests: λατρεύουσιν, "they serve," indicating that the temple ministry had not yet ceased. See preceding verse and Introduction, pp. 30ff.
5. Our version (RSV) evidently links λατρεύουσιν τῶν ἐπουρανίων with τῶν ἁγίων λειτουργός in verse 2, and thus interprets τὰ ἐπουράνια to signify τὰ ἄγια τὰ ἐπουράνια, "the heavenly sanctuary." NEB understands the phrase similarly: "they minister in a sanctuary which is only a copy and shadow of the heavenly." Vg and KJV, however, take τὰ ἐπουράνια here to mean simply "heavenly things."
6. Cf. Col. 2:17, where σκιά is contrasted to σῶμα. Bengel, Moffatt, and Teodorico are among the commentators who prefer to treat ὑπόδειγμα καὶ σκία, "a copy and shadow," as a hendiadys, denoting "a shadowy outline."

however, a real correspondence between a shadow and the substance of which it is the shadow.

The important thing is to possess the substance, not the shadow, the reality, not the copy. Yet the very language our author uses serves to suggest that if, as has already been demonstrated, there are fundamental differences between the order of Levi and the order of Melchizedek, there are nonetheless significant affinities. There is, in other words, a principle of continuity as well as a principle of discontinuity. The new not only replaces but also fulfils the old. The type both points forward to and receives its meaning from the antitype. But, as the context indicates, the complete perspective involves still more than this, for the antitype is also the archetype. The reality comes not only after but also before the copy and the shadow. Jesus Christ is the first as well as the last (cf. 13:8). Every earthly entity is preceded by the mind and the purpose of God.

Thus the earthly tabernacle which Moses erected was constructed *according to the pattern*[7] revealed to him on Mount Sinai. Both its origin (the mind of God) and the truth it prefigured (the true tent, v. 2) were heavenly, not earthly. It was the shadow cast by the reality. And as Moses was *instructed by God*[8] the wilderness sanctuary was not the result of merely human planning and construction. It was designed to display, in a typical manner, deep truths concerning the need of man and the grace of God. There was, as Calvin says, a real spiritual meaning in everything; but at the same time, he adds, "there is no cause for us to be excessively curious and to seek some sublime mystery in every nail and in other similar details, as Hesychius and a good many ancient writers laboured to do." As we learn that we are to worship God only in the manner which he has ordained, so also we must acknowledge that "there are no true religious symbols except those which conform to Christ."

What was this pattern in accordance with which the Mosaic tabernacle was constructed? F. F. Bruce is one of those who maintain, on the basis of the precise meaning of Exodus 25:40, that it was something visible, and therefore that Moses received more than simply verbal instruction. This would suggest that Moses was shown either a model or some other kind of representation. Delitzsch holds that Moses was actually given a sight or vision of the heavenly archetypal reality itself, "not a mere plan of the earthly tabernacle, but a real manifestation of the heavenly world, of which that tabernacle was to be a type"; though he

---

7. The Greek noun is τύπος (*type*): the pattern was that of the wilderness structure, which was the "copy and shadow" of the heavenly reality.
8. The agent is not expressed in the Greek, but the verb κεχρημάτισται is rightly interpreted as a divine passive: Moses was instructed *by God*.

qualifies this assertion by adding, somewhat inconsistently it would seem, that "we must suppose the manifestation to have been made, by a divine operation, in such a form as to have fitted it to serve as a model for the earthly building." Jewish thought more or less contemporary with the period of our epistle postulated, it is true, a definite association of the form of the wilderness structure with the heavenly reality. The *Apocalypse of Baruch*, for example, affirms that when God showed Moses "the likeness of the tabernacle and all its vessels" on Mount Sinai he also showed him the heavenly Jerusalem, as he had previously given the same revelation to Adam before he sinned and to Abraham "by night among the portions of the victims."[9]

Philo, of course, explains what took place in a characteristically platonizing manner. Moses, he writes, "saw with the soul's eye the immaterial forms of the material objects about to be made"; but then "these forms had to be reproduced in copies perceptible to the senses," which in turn constituted the blueprint for the material tabernacle. He was the recipient "not of shadows but of the actual archetypes." Moses, then, is described as "the artificer of the archetypes," but Bezaleel as "the artificer of the copies of these."[10] Though, however, Philo postulates a distinction between the earthly and the heavenly, the shadow and the reality, it does not follow, as some have imagined, that his philosophy is the fount from which the author of Hebrews derived his thought. T. H. Robinson, for instance, declares that "we cannot mistake the fact that we have here Platonism as expounded by Philo and other Jewish-Alexandrian philosophers," and Moffatt asserts of our author that "the philosophical element in his view of the world and God is fundamentally Platonic"—though he is willing to admit that he elaborates his thought "in an altogether new form, which went far beyond Philo."[11]

There is, however, almost literally a world of difference between the thought of Philo and the perspective of the Epistle to the Hebrews. For the former, the complex Mosaic system is a philosopher's model of the metaphysical universe, and the "reality" which engages his attention is that of the archetypal "ideas" of Plato. But for the author of Hebrews metaphysical speculation holds no attraction; his overmastering concern is with the soteriological significance of the divinely appointed tabernacle and its ceremonial for fallen mankind, and the achievement in Christ of that eternal reconciliation which the levitical system could never achieve.[12] If there is any affinity with Platonic idealism, it is, as F. F.

9. II Baruch 4:2–7.
10. Philo, *Vita Mosis* ii.72ff.; *De Plantatione* 27; *Legum Allegoriae* iii.102.
11. Moffatt, pp. xxxi and 106.
12. Coincidences in terminology between Philo and Hebrews cannot be interpreted to imply coincidences in meaning and doctrine. Philo's use of τύπος, for example, is quite

Bruce remarks, "our author's language, and not his essential thought, that exhibits such affinity." To the same effect is the judgment of Ronald Williamson, who insists that, "although something like the language of Philonic Platonism may be found in 8:5, there is no trace in that verse, or indeed anywhere else in the Epistle, of the fundamental attitudes or convictions which constitute Platonism either in its original or in its Philonic form."[13]

It is idle to inquire concerning the manner in which Moses was shown the pattern of the tabernacle at Sinai. That he saw some kind of model or representation is just as unlikely as that he was granted an ecstatic viewing of the heavenly sanctuary itself. An earthly type can be no more than an aid in the apprehension of eternal truth; but the heavenly reality cannot be reduced to scale, because it transcends all that we know and experience, and the transcendental can never be contained within the finite and fallen categories of our world. The instructions Moses received on the mountain were followed in the construction of the tabernacle, but we may be sure that we who live after the advent of Christ have a clearer comprehension of its typological significance than he had, man of faith though he was (11:23ff.; cf. 1 Pet. 1:10–12). Yet there are mysteries here which exceed our powers of understanding, privileged though we are with the fuller light of the New Testament, and which will be revealed only when at last we know even as we are known (1 Cor. 13:12). Nevertheless, the evangelical teaching our author gives is plain and adequate, namely, that our unique High Priest Jesus Christ, following the offering up of the perfect sacrifice of himself on our behalf, has entered into the true sanctuary, which is heavenly, not earthly, and that in doing so he has also opened up the way into the very presence of God himself for us who before were excluded because of our sin. The divine purpose is reflected in our author's concern, which is to set clearly before us the great realities of the eternal redemption that God has provided for us in his Son.

8:6, 7. *But as it is, Christ has obtained a ministry which is as much more excellent than the old as the covenant he mediates is better, since it is enacted on better promises. For if that first covenant had been faultless, there would have been no occasion for a second.*

The introductory phrase, *but as it is,* [14] has the effect of emphasizing the fundamental contrast between the ministry of Christ and that of the

---

different from what we have here in the Epistle to the Hebrews. See R. P. C. Hanson, *Allegory and Event* (London, 1959), p. 91.

13. Ronald Williamson, *Philo and the Epistle to the Hebrews*, p. 557.

14. The force of νυνὶ δέ is logical rather than temporal, though of course the temporal

old order. As in verse 2 above Christ is designated a "minister" with specific reference to his high-priestly presence in the heavenly sanctuary, so here the *ministry* which belongs to him is that of his unique high priesthood.[15] He is said to have *obtained* this ministry in the sense that he has *attained*[16] it—that is to say, his earthly ministry completed, Christ has won his way to, or taken over by right of achievement, the ministry in the true sanctuary above. And his ministry is *much more excellent* than *the old*, not only because the heavenly is exalted in comparison with the earthly and the eternal reality superior to the temporary copy, but also because *the covenant* mediated by Christ *is better* in that *it is enacted on better promises*. Here again, in a manner characteristic of the epistle, the essential superiority of the new order to the old is affirmed. In 7:22 Christ has already been described as "the surety of a better covenant," an affirmation based on the divine oath establishing the everlasting nature of his priesthood (7:21; Ps. 110:4) and on the eternal efficacy of the eternal sacrifice he offered; and now it is said that he *mediates* a better covenant (similarly in 9:15 and 12:24 he is called "the mediator of a new covenant")—in contrast, no doubt (as in 12:24), to Moses, whom Paul designates the "mediator" of the law (Gal. 3:19), the covenant heart of which was the demand, "Do this, and you will live" (Lk. 10:28; Lev. 18:5; Ezek. 20:11, 13, 21; Rom. 10:5; Gal. 3:12). To the same effect, we read in the Fourth Gospel that "the law was given through Moses," in contradistinction to the declaration that "grace and truth," which constitute the essence of the new covenant, "came through Jesus Christ" (Jn. 1:17). In the apocryphal Jewish work *The Assumption of Moses*, belonging to the early part of the first century, Moses describes himself as "the mediator of God's covenant" (I.14); and Philo is another contemporary of the apostles who speaks of Moses as "mediator," but with reference to his role as intercessor for the people when they had provoked God's anger by their worship of the golden calf.[17]

The mediation of Christ is superior to that of Moses because the covenant he brings into operation is "enacted on better promises." The Greek verb rendered "enacted" here suggests that the "better covenant"

---

factor is inevitably involved in the argument. The expression occurs again in 9:26 and 11:16 (νὺν δέ); cf. 1 Corinthians 15:20.

15. Λειτουργία here corresponds to λειτουργός in verse 2. See note 53, p. 281.

16. The verb τέτυχεν requires a strong sense here rather than the weak sense of the NEB, "the ministry which has fallen to Jesus," which betokens merely what happens to fall to one's lot. The strong sense, which is amply attested both in the classical authors and in the contemporary papyri, involves the notion of achievement, success, and victory.

17. Philo, *Vita Mosis* ii.166.

has a legal relationship (cf. NEB, "it is legally secured").[18] This, as we have seen, was very evident in the case of the old covenant, which was inextricably bound up with the giving of the law through the mediation of Moses, so much so that a change in the priesthood necessarily meant a change in the law (7:11f.). This change, as has been pointed out above on 7:11f., involved both the abolition of all the legal regulations concerning the levitical priesthood and its ministry and also the keeping of the moral law by the incarnate Son, so that he might in our place endure the penalty of our law-breaking and make his perfect righteousness available to us. His high-priestly work of atonement has activated the "better promises" of the new covenant—promises fulfilled in the cleansing of our consciences from the deadly contagion of sin, in the planting of the love of God and his will in our hearts, and in the restoration of that intimate fellowship with our Creator which the curse we brought on ourselves had destroyed (cf. vv. 8ff. below; 9:14; 10:4, 16f., 19ff.). "Now that the truth is present, what need is there for the figurative and the vestigial?" asks Lefèvre d'Etaples. "Once we have received superior things, indeed the ultimate and the best things, why should imperfect and incomplete things detain us any longer? The sacrifice of the eternal High Priest immeasurably surpasses every other sacrifice. . . . Therefore what is inferior has ceased."

If that first covenant had been faultless, it is obvious that *there would have been no occasion for a second.* The logic is identical with that applied in 7:11 with reference to the levitical order of priesthood, which was integrally bound up with the old covenant, and the mention of Melchizedek, the high priest of the new covenant. If the former had been perfect, there would have been no point in speaking of any other order. Precisely because the first covenant was not "faultless" there was need for a second which would be faultless. The "fault" of the old covenant lay, not in its essence, which, as we have said, presented God's standard of righteousness and was propounded as an instrument of life to those

---

18. Significantly, the same verb, νομοθετεῖν, is used here of the new covenant as is used in 7:11 of the inauguration of the old covenant (the only occurrences of this verb in the New Testament; cf. the nouns νομοθεσία, Rom. 9:4, used of "the giving of the law" through Moses, and νομοθέτης, Jas. 4:12, used of God as the supreme "Lawgiver"). The two basic meanings of νομοθετεῖν are (i) to give or frame laws and (ii) to ordain by law. The relative pronoun ἥτις, which is the subject of the verb νενομοθέτηται, may have either διαθήκη, "covenant" (as in the versions and commentators), or λειτουργία, "ministry," as its antecedent. In favor of the latter is the connection between law and priesthood in the old covenant already made in 7:11, which means that to connect law and ministry (= priesthood) here when speaking of the new covenant would follow naturally and logically. On the other hand, the consideration must be weighed that elsewhere covenant and promises rather than priesthood and promises go together.

who should keep it, but in its inability to justify and renew those who failed to keep it, namely, the totality of fallen mankind. The new covenant went literally to the heart of the matter, promising man, as it did, a new and obedient heart and the grace truly to love both God and his fellow man (Ezek. 11:19f.).

8:8a. *For he finds fault with them when he says.*

In this clause, which introduces an extended quotation from the prophecy of Jeremiah setting forth the distinctive terms of the new covenant, the subject of the verb *says* is not named in the Greek. It could be translated "he says," in which case the pronoun could be understood of God or of Jeremiah, or "it says," meaning that Scripture says. It is unlikely that Jeremiah is intended, since he is not mentioned by name, though it is true that he was speaking as the mouthpiece of God when he uttered this prophecy, as the words "says the Lord" in the opening sentence of the quotation indicate. It is our author's custom, however, to introduce citations from Scripture without specifying who is speaking, but in such a way as to leave no doubt that God is the intended subject (see 1:5, where our version actually supplies "God" as the subject, 6, 7, 8, where "he says" is supplied, and 13; 2:12; 4:3, 4, 7; 5:5, 6; 10:30; 11:18, a divine passive; also 3:7 and 10:15, where the Holy Spirit is designated as the speaker; and 10:5 and 15, where the words quoted are assigned to Christ as the speaker; there are also some quotations which are introduced in an impersonal or indefinite manner, e.g., 2:5; 3:15; 7:17; 12:6; one which has Moses as the speaker, 9:20; and one which is without any kind of introductory formula, 10:37).

The expression *he finds fault* forms a link with what has just been said in the preceding verse about the first covenant not being faultless. The basis on which, so to speak, God "faults" the old covenant is suggested by the definition of the new covenant in the passage from Jeremiah that follows, namely, that the former could not supply the new heart of regeneration which the latter guarantees. The rendering "he finds fault *with them*," which seems to be universally approved today, is ill suited to the declaration cited from Jeremiah, which is one of promise to the people rather than of finding fault with them; and it is preferable (adopting a strongly attested variant reading in the Greek text) to translate this introductory clause: "for he finds fault (*sc.* with the first covenant) when he says *to them*":[19] the promise of a new covenant clearly

19. The Greek reads μεμφόμενος γὰρ αὐτοὺς λέγει, with αὐτοῖς as a variant for αὐτούς. As the verb μέμφεσθαι can govern either an accusative or a dative, with either reading the

implies "fault-finding" with the old covenant. Understanding the pronoun "them" in this way as referring to those to whom the prophecy was originally addressed, rather than as referring to those with whom God finds fault, preserves the sequence of thought from the preceding verse which is plainly indicated by the logical conjunction *For*. Thus our author is saying: "If that first covenant had been faultless, there would have been no occasion for a second; for he finds fault (with that first covenant) when he says to them: 'The days will come ... when I will establish a new covenant ...' not like the covenant that I made with their fathers.'"

8:8b–12. *"The days will come, says the Lord, when I will establish a new covenant with the house of Israel and with the house of Judah; not like the covenant that I made with their fathers on the day when I took them by the hand to lead them out of the land of Egypt; for they did not continue in my covenant, and so I paid no heed to them, says the Lord. This is the covenant that I will make with the house of Israel after those days, says the Lord. I will put my laws into their minds, and write them on their hearts, and I will be their God, and they shall be my people. And they shall not teach every one his fellow or every one his brother, saying, 'Know the Lord,' for all shall know me, from the least of them to the greatest. For I will be merciful toward their iniquities, and I will remember their sins no more."*

The chief characteristics of the new covenant that appear from this quotation may be summarized as follows:

(1) The prophecy when uttered by Jeremiah referred to a future age of grace and blessedness; hence the divinely given promise: *The days will come ... when I will establish a new covenant.* Jeremiah's own day, in fact, was a day of disruption and disaster, and this in itself was recognized as

---

Greek could mean "for he finds fault with them when he says." If, however, the dative αὐτοῖς is preferred, then μεμφόμενος γὰρ αὐτοῖς λέγει could also mean "for he finds fault when he says to them," taking αὐτοῖς with λέγει instead of with μεμφόμενος. The documentary evidence weighs in favor of αὐτοῖς as the authentic reading; for while αὐτούς has the support of Sinaiticus (the first hand), Alexandrinus, and Claromontanus (the first hand) uncial MSS of the fourth, fifth, and sixth centuries respectively, the Armenian version, and the fifth-century patristic authors Euthalius and Theodoret (each variant is found once in Chrysostom in the fourth century), αὐτοῖς boasts the impressive combination of the Chester Beatty Papyrus 46 (ca. 200), Sinaiticus (corrected), and Vaticanus (fourth century), and is found in the third-century writer Origen and in the majority of the Byzantine MSS and the majority of the lectionaries. The rendering of the Latin versions, *vituperans enim eos dicit*, could be based on either reading, though if it is αὐτοῖς, it is clearly associated with μεμφόμενος, not λέγει. If the commonly accepted rendering is retained, then it must be supposed that our author is pointing out that it was with the covenant-breaking people rather than with the old covenant itself that God found fault ("for they did not continue in my covenant," v. 9); but this weakens the logical connection with the preceding verse.

a condign judgment on the people because of their wilful disobedience and contempt for the covenant which they had engaged themselves to observe; for to spurn the blessing which the covenant promises is to invite the cursing which it threatens (see, for example, Jer. 11). Jeremiah's prophecy, therefore, was like a shaft of light penetrating the darkness of desperate apostasy and focusing on a glorious future time when God would be truly loved and obeyed.

(2) The inauguration of the new covenant would be due entirely to the gracious initiative of God: *I will establish a new covenant*, he says. God is its author and its operator, bringing it into being and making it effectual in the lives of his people. This new covenant, *not like the covenant* made with the people through Moses, would be of grace, not of works; radical, not external; everlasting, not temporary; meeting man's deepest need and transforming his whole being, because from beginning to end it would be the work, not of man, but of God himself.

(3) The new covenant would bring together those who had been divided by bitterness and hostility: it was to be established *with the house of Israel and with the house of Judah*. The promise of the reunion of Israel and Judah was symbolical of the healing of every human breach and the reconciliation of all nations and persons in Christ, the seed of Abraham in whom all the peoples of the earth are blessed and united (Gal. 3:8f., 16, 27–29) because he "has broken down the dividing wall of hostility" (Eph. 2:14). What God accomplishes through Christ is nothing less than the reconciliation of the world to himself (2 Cor. 5:19ff.).

(4) The new covenant would be quite distinct from the old covenant: it is *not like the covenant that [God] made with their fathers on the day when [he] took them by the hand to lead them out of the land of Egypt*. The law can never be a principle of justification for sinners, but only a principle of condemnation precisely because they have failed to keep its precepts. Hence Paul's universal declaration that "no human being will be justified in his sight by works of the law" (Rom. 3:20). This explains the failure of those under the old order to *continue in [God's] covenant*, with the consequence that God *paid no heed to them* ("abandoned them," NEB). The new order, however, is distinguished by God's promise that he *will put [his] laws into their minds and write them on their hearts*, and that he *will be their God, and they will be [his] people*. In other words, the law which formerly was external and accusing now becomes internal, an element of the redeemed nature, and a delight to fulfil; and the new covenant is the sphere, not of abandonment, but of unceasing fellowship with God, who, by virtue of the perfect atoning sacrifice of Christ our Law-Keeper, is *merciful toward their iniquities* and *will remember their sins no more*. In the new creation, then, the people of God rejoice in the constant benediction of his presence and delight to do his will, and this means that all will know him, *from the least of them to the greatest*.

At the same time there are definite points of contact between old and new covenants. The God who *establishes* the new is the same God who *made* the old.[20] Since God is the author of both, each is good and glorious, though the goodness and glory of the latter far surpass the goodness and glory of the former (cf. v. 6; Rom. 7:12–16; 2 Cor. 3:7–9). And it is the same law that is associated with both old and new covenants. Though the Christian believer is not justified by the works of the law, but by the law-keeping and self-offering of Another on his behalf, yet the law of God is the standard of holiness required of him; only now he is enabled to love and obey the commandments of God which before he hated and disobeyed. The promise, "I will put my laws into their minds,[21] and write them on their hearts,"[22] is fulfilled in his experience. Thus there is no suggestion of antinomianism here or anywhere else in the New Testament, which is the book of the new covenant, nor is there any antithesis between law and love. Love, indeed, love of God and love of man, is the summary of the law (Lk. 10:26f.; Rom. 13:8–10), and our love for Christ is demonstrated precisely in the keeping of his commandments (Jn 14:15). Loving obedience, accordingly, should be one of the distinctive marks of genuine Christianity. As the law is a signpost to the will of God, so the concern of the Christian should always be to honor God by walking joyfully in the way of his will.

A further point of contact is found in that the promise, "I will be their God, and they shall be my people," is the same as the promise that God gave to the Israelites, with the condition that its fulfilment was dependent on their observance of the Mosaic covenant (Ex. 6:7; 29:45f.; Lev. 26:12; Dt. 26:18f.; 29:12f.). By their repeated acts of apostasy, however, the people cut themselves off from the enjoyment of the blessings of this promise; and it is only now, following the redeeming work of the Son and the universal outpouring of the Holy Spirit by the ascended Lord, that God, in Christ, dwells in the innermost being of his people, who together constitute the temple of the living God (1 Pet. 2:5; 1 Cor. 3:16f.). But it is only eschatologically, with the introduction of the new heaven and the new earth, populated with the multitude of the redeemed, that this covenant promise attains its ultimate fulfilment. Then at last, and everlastingly, God "will dwell with them, and they shall be his people, and God himself will be with them" (Rev. 21:3). In this

---

20. The Greek verbs translated in our version "I will establish" and "I made" are συντελέσω and ἐποίησα respectively, but neither in the Hebrew original nor in the Greek of the LXX are two different verbs used. The LXX verb διατίθεσθαι is in fact cognate with the noun διαθήκη, "covenant."

21. NEB, "in their understanding"—a better rendering of εἰς τὴν διάνοιαν αὐτῶν.

22. In the expression ἐπὶ καρδίας αὐτῶν the noun καρδίας is almost certainly genitive singular ("heart") rather than accusative plural ("hearts"). The singular corresponds with the singular of the Hebrew original and also with the singular διάνοιαν in the preceding clause.

intimate and uninterrupted relationship there will be no need to urge others to "know the Lord," because all, "from the least of them to the greatest," will know him. The reason for their being there is, indeed, that they know God; for to know God is itself life eternal (Jn. 17:3). As the essence of sin is unwillingness to know God and to glorify him as God (Rom. 1:18ff.), so without forgiveness and removal of sin there can be no knowledge of God and of the blessing of his presence. Hence the promise of mercy with which this quotation ends; and this forgiving and reconciling mercy has been procured for us by the high-priestly mediation of our Savior Christ.

> 8:13. *In speaking of a new covenant he treats the first as obsolete. And what is becoming obsolete and growing old is ready to vanish away.*

In the prophecy of Jeremiah which has just been cited the mere designation of another covenant as *new* carries with it the implication that *he* (either Jeremiah or, more probably, God speaking through Jeremiah) *treats the first* covenant, mediated through Moses, *as obsolete.* Within the prophetic perspective, which focuses on the better promises of the new covenant (v. 6), the old is clearly seen as outmoded and destined to be discarded. The shadow of its impending abolition already lies upon it. The utterance of the prophecy is sufficient proof that the first covenant can be regarded only as *becoming obsolete and growing old,* and therefore as *ready to vanish away* when in due course the new and eternal covenant of grace is established.

This seems to be the right way to understand this verse. It is possible, however, that the latter part of the verse represents the viewpoint of the author of our epistle, in which case we would have here another indication that when he was writing the ministry and ritual associated with the former covenant and its priesthood were still being observed in Jerusalem. He senses, in the light of Christ's prediction of the destruction of the temple (Mk. 13:2; cf. Acts 6:14; 7:48), that this old order "will shortly disappear" (NEB). This is the opinion, for example, of Delitzsch, who comments that "the temple service, though to continue it may be a few years longer in outward splendour, is only a bed of state on which a lifeless corpse is lying." If this should be the correct understanding, then we have here another pointer to the conclusion that our epistle must have been written prior to the sack of Jerusalem in A.D. 70.[23]

---

23. See Introduction, pp. 30ff.

NOTE ON THE DEAD SEA SECT AND THE NEW COVENANT

The instruction concerning the senescence and displacement of the old covenant in consequence of the institution of the new covenant would have come with special force to persons who had shown themselves susceptible to the influence of teachings similar to those of the Dead Sea Sect; for the Qumran Community, in anticipation of the arrival of the messianic age, had bound itself in allegiance to a "new covenant"—a covenant, however, which was not really new, but in fact a renewal or reaffirmation of the old covenant of the Mosaic dispensation. The outlook of this Sect may be taken as more or less common to the Essene movement in general. Thus at Qumran "the formal congregation of the community" was to consist of "twelve laymen and three priests schooled to perfection in all that has been revealed of the entire law." The priests would "have knowledge of the covenant of justice" and "be qualified to offer what will be indeed 'a pleasant savour' to the Lord"; while the laymen would "constitute a household of integrity and truth qualified to maintain the covenant as an everlasting pact" (*Manual of Discipline* viii.1ff.). Believing that "God still remembered the covenant which he had made with their forebears," and that he had "raised from the priesthood men of discernment and from the laity men of wisdom," the members of the Dead Sea Sect identified themselves as "those of Israel who repented and departed from the land of Judah to sojourn in 'the land of Damascus'" (the expression is taken from Amos 5:7 and applied to their place of voluntary exile by the Dead Sea), where (now allegorizing the language of Num. 21:18) they "dug the well" of the law. Within this framework they regarded themselves as "the men who entered the covenant in 'the land of Damascus.'" Any who "entered the covenant" but subsequently "broke through the bounds of the law" would "be 'cut off from the midst of the camp' at the time when God's glory is made manifest to Israel" (*Zadokite Document* vi.1ff., viii.21).

From these passages it is evident that the expectation of the Qumran Community was fixed on an ideal restoration of the Mosaic covenant rather than the introduction of a genuinely new covenant, and thus was at variance with the apostolic understanding of the fulfilment of the ancient prophecies. Their doctrine of justification, in stark contrast to the doctrine of justification by faith in the unique saving work of Christ which is at the heart of the evangelical interpretation of the new covenant, was a doctrine of justification by the works of the law—the very position which the ex-Pharisee Paul had found it necessary to abandon (Rom. 3:20, 27f.; 5:1; Gal. 3:2, 10f.; Phil. 3:8f.). This is very plain in the following passage from the *Zadokite Document* (B.xx.27ff.):

> Howbeit, all that hold fast to these enactments, going and coming in accordance with the Law; that hearken to the voice of the Teacher; that make confession before God, saying: Just and truthful are thy judgments against us, for we have done wickedly, both we and our fathers, in that we have gone contrary to the statutes of the covenant; all who raise not their hands against his holy statutes or his righteous judgments or his truthful ordinances; ... all who give ear to him who imparts the true interpretation of

the Law and who do not controvert the right ordinances when they hear them—all of these shall rejoice and their hearts shall be strong, and they shall prevail over all that dwell in the world. And God will accept their atonement, and because they took refuge in his holy name they shall indeed see salvation at his hand.

Covenanters these Jewish reformers might be, but in the old and sterile sense, not in the new and dynamic sense of the Christian gospel. Indeed, their position, for all its sincerity and dedication, was unevangelical and belonged to an order that was "obsolete" and "ready to vanish away"—or rather that was already superseded now that Christ had come and, by offering the perfect sacrifice for the sins of the world, inaugurated the age of the new covenant. It was, therefore, not a position with which any Christian ought to be entangled.

9:1. *Now even the first covenant had regulations for worship and an earthly sanctuary.*

In the Greek, the word "covenant" is not present, so that a literal rendering of the original would read: "Now even the first had regulations for worship, etc." But the translators have rightly, in the interests of clarity, supplied the term "covenant," since in the immediately preceding verse (8:13) the same expression, *the first,* is used with reference to the former covenant. (The logical sequence of thought and the terminological correspondence tend to be interrupted by the chapter division, which of course had no place in the original.) In the past there have been those who have maintained that the reference here is not to the first covenant but to "the first tent," that is, the Mosaic tabernacle in the wilderness. They were influenced, no doubt, by the occurrence of this expression in the verse which follows;[24] but this interpretation is invalidated by the consideration that "the first tent" of verse 2 does not designate the former tabernacle in its entirety (as correspondence with v. 1 would require) but only the first or outer chamber of the tabernacle, namely, the holy place, as the description of its contents clearly shows. The point of the verse now before us is that *the first covenant* had its own *regulations for worship* and that these were related to what took place in the *earthly sanctuary* of the wilderness tabernacle. Our author is about to describe the ceremonial associated with the former covenant and this

24. Our version (RSV) renders σκηνὴ ... ἡ πρώτη in verse 2 as "a tent... the outer one," in other words the first chamber to which one who was entering the tabernacle would come. The addition of σκηνή to ἡ πρώτη in verse 1 has very inferior attestation and is doubtless the result of a scribal gloss. It is found in numerous minuscule manuscripts, the Coptic version, and Theodoret and Cosmas. According to Delitzsch it was imported into the Textus Receptus from the Complutensian Bible of 1520.

requires some explanation of the plan of the tabernacle and the rites which were conducted within its precincts. What follows is, in fact, an explanation of these "regulations for worship,"[25] with particular reference to the parallels and contrasts between them and the high-priestly ministry of Christ.

The expression "an earthly sanctuary" denotes a sanctuary of this earth as distinct from the heavenly sanctuary in which our great High Priest now ministers. This sense of the adjective translated "earthly" here[26] is dictated by the context. Thus our High Priest is enthroned in heaven (8:1); he is not on earth (8:4); the earthly sanctuary is but a copy and shadow of the heavenly (8:5; 9:23); Christ has entered, "not into a sanctuary made with hands"—"that is, not of this creation" (9:11)—". . . but into heaven itself" (9:24). Some of the patristic authors, however, understood the adjective to connote "open to the world," "available to all." Chrysostom, for example, explains that the sanctuary is called "cosmic" because all were permitted access to it and in the temple the places were clearly designated where priests, Jews, proselytes, and non-Jews might assemble. True, however, though this may be of the temple, it does not apply to the tabernacle, which could hardly be described as an international institution, and it is of the tabernacle in the wilderness that our author is speaking here.

Another patristic view is that of Ecumenius, who draws attention to the threefold division of the tabernacle into courtyard, holy place, and holy of holies and identifies the "cosmic sanctuary" with the first of these, in which the brazen altar stood and to which all the people without distinction were permitted access with their offerings.[27] Photius offers a similar interpretation.[28] But this explanation is no more acceptable;

---

25. Δικαιώματα λατρείας. Some, including Luther, have wished to take λατρείας as an accusative plural rather than as a genitive singular, giving the sense: "the first covenant had regulations, services, and an earthly sanctuary." In verse 6 below, which speaks of the priests performing their "ritual duties" (λατρείας), it is in fact an accusative plural. But it is more natural to treat the same form here in verse 1 as a genitive singular which defines the term δικαιώματα.

26. Κοσμικός, that is, belonging to the κόσμος or created order of things (NEB renders it "material"). Thus Héring explains it as signifying "that which is in the world." This is also a good classical sense. Its only other occurrence in the New Testament is in Titus 2:12, where it has an ethical, but related, connotation: τὰς κοσμικὰς ἐπιθυμίας, "worldly passions." There is no semantic evidence to justify the suggestion that κοσμικός here might have the same sense as κόσμιος, "well ordered," which occurs in 1 Timothy 2:9; 3:2. The proposal of B. F. C. Atkinson (mentioned by F. F. Bruce, p. 181) that τὸ ἅγιον κοσμικόν should be understood to mean "the holy ritual" (that is, treating κοσμικόν as the noun and ἅγιον as the adjective) would have some attraction if it could be shown that κοσμικός was ever used substantivally and in this sense.

27. Ecumenius; see K. Staab, Pauluskommentare aus der Griechischen Kirche (Münster, 1933), p. 465.

28. Photius; see Staab ut supra, p. 648.

first, because here in verse 1 our author is speaking of the tabernacle in general or as a whole and it is only in the next verse that he begins to speak specifically of its component parts; second, because when he does speak specifically he describes only the outer and inner chambers of the tent-structure and does not even mention the courtyard; and, third, because (and this objection applies equally to Chrysostom's opinion) the Greek adjective connotes what belongs to the world, the created order, rather than the idea of openness to all comers.

It is interesting to find Jewish scholars contemporary with our author using the same adjective, or equivalent terminology, to express their view of the tabernacle and the temple in their structure and ceremonial as cosmic or universal in significance. Thus Josephus maintains that every one of the objects associated with the tabernacle "was intended to recall and represent the universe,"[29] that the measurement of the tabernacle was "an imitation of universal nature,"[30] its ceremonial cosmic in meaning,[31] and the magnificent combination of its material an "image of the universe";[32] and Philo expounds all the numbers, proportions, and colors of the tabernacle as an allegory of the harmony of the universe,[33] and correspondingly envisages "the whole universe"[34] as in the highest and truest sense God's temple.[35] This line of interpretation was adopted later on by a number of patristic writers. Theodore of Mopsuestia, for instance, speaks of the "cosmic sanctuary" as a "symbol of the universe,"[36] and Theodoret says that "the tabernacle was called 'cosmic' because it provided a figure of the whole world."[37]

This, however, is not our author's way. He is interested neither in minute and detailed significances nor in the tabernacle as an allegorical model of the universe. Certainly, he sees a typological or symbolical relationship between the wilderness tabernacle and the sanctuary above, with reference in particular (vv. 11ff. below) to what took place on the Day of Atonement when the high priest, after offering sacrifice for the people, passed into the inner shrine of God's presence; but there is a complete absence of "cosmic" speculation. Indeed, so far from expounding the perfection of the earthly sanctuary, he constantly insists on its imperfection and its transitoriness as he steadily points his readers to the

29. Josephus, *Ant.* iii.180.
30. Josephus, *Ant.* iii.123.
31. Josephus, *Bell. Jud.* iv.324—τῆς κοσθικῆς θρησκείας.
32. Josephus, *Bell. Jud.* v.212.
33. Philo, *Vita Mos.* ii.77ff.
34. Philo, *De Spec. Leg.* i.66—τὸν σύμπαντα . . . κόσμον.
35. Philo, *ibid.*
36. Theodore of Mopsuestia, Migne, PG, LXVI, 964—σύμβολον τοῦ κόσμου.
37. Theodoret, τύπον ἐπέχουσαν τοῦ κόσμου παντός.

glorious and abiding reality of the heavenly sanctuary into which Christ has now entered on our behalf. By its very nature the earthly sanctuary belongs to this present world, and as such it is one of those things which pass away (cf. Mt. 24:35; 1 Jn. 2:17). The unshakable realm is the realm of the new creation (Heb. 12:26ff.).

The past tenses which occur in this section—"the first covenant *had* regulations . . . a tent *was* prepared" (vv. 1, 2)—raise the question as to whether they indicate that the levitical ceremonial of tabernacle and temple was now entirely a thing of the past, as some modern scholars have concluded, among whom may be mentioned Weiss, Windisch, and Jeremias. We have already seen in a number of places, however, that our author uses the present tense of the levitical worship, as though it were still in operation;[38] and, indeed, very shortly he will use the present tense again of these functions of the old order (see vv. 6f.). Accordingly, we must judge that the temple was still standing and that its services were still being performed. The past tenses used here are appropriate in view of the fact that our author is speaking of the original tabernacle set up under Moses in the wilderness—as is confirmed by his choice of the term "tent" and also by the consideration that the ark of the covenant and its contents, as described in verse 4, disappeared without trace following the destruction of the temple of Solomon.

9:2. For a tent was prepared, the outer one, in which were the lampstand and the table and the bread of the Presence; it is called the Holy Place.

The sanctuary or tabernacle proper (v. 1) was divided by a curtain into two chambers known as the holy place and the holy of holies. *The Holy Place*[39] was the first or *outer*[40] tent, which was entered from the courtyard, and in this chamber, twenty by ten cubits in area and ten cubits in height, the following objects were placed:

(1) *The lampstand,* made of beaten gold, which stood at the south side. It had seven branches (or, better, six, three on either side of the central stem, with the top of the stem forming the seventh lamp) and its seven lamps were kept alight day and night.

---

38. See Introduction, pp. 30ff.

39. At first sight ἅγια looks like a nominative feminine singular describing and agreeing with σκηνὴ . . . ἡ πρώτη, and this would indeed be a legitimate way of construing it; but it is preferable to read it as a nominative neuter plural corresponding with the LXX term τὰ ἅγια for the "holy place." Montefiore, however, is one who prefers to interpret ἅγια as qualifying σκηνή ("this Tent is called Holy").

40. Literally, "the first tent," σκηνὴ . . . ἡ πρώτη, that is, the first from the viewpoint of one entering the tabernacle.

(2) *The table and the bread of the Presence*[41]—a hendiadys, as has often been pointed out, meaning "the table together with the loaves displayed on it," table and loaves being regarded, quite naturally, as a unit. The loaves, twelve in number, were arranged in two rows of six and were replaced by freshly baked loaves each sabbath day. The table of show-bread, to follow Tyndale's familiar translation, stood at the north side of the holy place.

(3) *The altar of incense*, made of pure gold, which stood centrally before the curtain separating the holy place from the holy of holies. It is a surprise that the altar of incense is in fact omitted in the description of the furnishings of the holy place given here and is included (in v. 4 below) in the furnishings that belong to the holy of holies. The question which this arrangement raises will be discussed in the section of the commentary that follows. Suffice it to say, for the moment, that it is most improbable that we are confronted with the result of an early dislocation in the text. It is true that in the Codex Vaticanus (fourth century) and in the Coptic (Sahidic) and Ethiopic versions the golden altar of incense is added to the objects designated in verse 2 as belonging to the holy place and omitted from verse 4; but this must be taken as reflecting an attempt to correct, by transposing the phrase from verse 4 to verse 2, any impression that the location of the altar of incense was in the holy of holies rather than the holy place.

9:3–5. *Behind the second curtain stood a tent called the Holy of Holies, having the golden altar of incense and the ark of the covenant covered on all sides with gold, which contained a golden urn holding the manna, and Aaron's rod that budded, and the tables of the covenant; above it were cherubim of glory overshadowing the mercy seat. Of these things we cannot now speak in detail.*

The second curtain was the barrier separating the holy place from the holy of holies. No other, or first, curtain has been mentioned by our author, but he has two in mind, the first being the curtain to which one

---

41. Literally, "the display of the loaves," ἡ πρόθεσις τῶν ἄρτων. In Mark 2:26 (Mt. 12:4; Lk. 6:4) the expression "the loaves of display," τοὺς ἄρτους τῆς προθέσεως, is used. Though the basic sense of both expressions is the same, the latter corresponds more closely with the Hebrew original לֶחֶם פָּנִים, "bread of the face," that is, bread displayed before the face of God or in the presence of God. The rendering "bread of the Presence" (not strictly a translation of the Greek) in our version (RSV) and NEB is somewhat misleading. The formula favored by our author here corresponds with that found in the LXX of 2 Chronicles 13:11, προθέσεις ἄρτων, for מַעֲרֶכֶת לֶחֶם. Cf. 1 Chronicles 9:32 and 23:39, where the formula corresponds with that found in the Synoptic Gospels, namely, τῶν ἄρτων (or τοὺς ἄρτους) τῆς προθέσεως, for לֶחֶם הַמַּעֲרֶכֶת.

entering the tabernacle would come as he passed from the courtyard into the holy place. To move on further into the innermost sanctuary of the holy of holies he would have to pass through the second curtain. Like the curtain which formed the outer walls of the tabernacle (prescriptions for which are given in Ex. 26:1ff.), this second or inner curtain which screened the holy of holies from the holy place was made of fine twined linen, woven with blue, purple, and scarlet and adorned with the figures of cherubim, and supported by pillars of acacia wood overlaid with gold. The designation of the inner sanctuary as *the Holy of Holies* follows closely the Hebrew idiom,[42] the force of which is that of an emphatic or elative superlative: of all the divisions of the tabernacle this place was the most holy. The same idiom is used of things which were to be treated as "most holy," such as the furnishings and vessels of the tabernacle (Ex. 30:29) and the various offerings associated with the priestly ministry (Lev. 2:3, 10; 6:17, 25, 29; 7:1, 6, etc.).

It is the holy of holies, and not, as we would have expected, the holy place, which is described as *having the golden altar of incense.* How is this apparent discrepancy to be explained? Luther, who oscillates between the opinions that it is, on the one hand, a golden altar and, on the other, a golden censer, that is intended, actually attempts to argue that there must have been an extra altar in the holy of holies which was used by the high priest on the Day of Atonement ("a third altar," that is, in addition to the altar of incense in the holy place and the brazen altar of sacrifice in the courtyard); but he fails to convince even himself. Some commentators have wished to solve the problem by supposing that our author is simply guilty of an error or misconception. Moffatt may be allowed to speak for those who have decided that he was a non-Palestinian without firsthand knowledge of the temple and its contents, and therefore that the present inaccuracy is the result of "the vague language of the pentateuch about the position of the altar of incense."[43] There is undoubtedly a degree of imprecision regarding its location.

---

42. See Exodus 26:33, etc., קֹדֶשׁ הַקֳּדָשִׁים, where the LXX rendering is τὸ ἅγιον τῶν ἁγίων. The plural form ἅγια ἁγίων, employed by our author, is also found in the LXX—for example, 1 Kings 8:6; 2 Chronicles 4:22; 5:7. Josephus uses the completely singular form (τοῦ) ἁγίου (τὸ) ἅγιον (*Ant.* iii.125; *Bell. Jud.* v.219). The simple plural τὰ ἅγια, which our author also uses (vv. 8, 12, 24, 25 in this chapter and 10:19; cf. 8:2) probably corresponds with the simple singular τὸ ἅγιον, found in Leviticus 16:2, 3, 16, 17, 20, 23, 27. Such an expression, which in itself is more general and less emphatic, is shown by the context to relate specifically to the holy of holies. See note 54 on 8:2 above (p. 281).

43. Moffatt supposes, further, that the author of Hebrews was dependent on the Septuagint for his knowledge of these things. He remarks that the preposition ἀπέναντι in Exodus 30:6 "may mean 'opposite' or 'close in front of' the curtain—but on which side of it?" But ἀπέναντι is an adequate rendering of the Hebrew לִפְנֵי, which seems to be no less inexplicit.

Thus Exodus 30:6 says it was to be placed "before the veil that is by the ark of the testimony" (cf. 40:26), and Exodus 40:5 requires it to be situated "before the ark of the testimony," without even mentioning the curtain. In the description of Solomon's temple, indeed, the altar of incense is spoken of as "belonging to the inner sanctuary" (1 Ki. 6:20, 22). The ceremonial prescriptions for the Day of Atonement, however, would seem plainly to indicate that it was in the holy place that the altar of incense was located (Lev. 16:18). Yet it must be admitted that the vagueness of the Old Testament specifications would afford some excuse for misunderstanding on the part of one who was uninstructed in the precise arrangement of temple and tabernacle.

But our epistle offers little justification for the conclusion that its author was ill informed in a matter which must have been common knowledge among persons of Jewish origin. The proper position of so important an article as the altar of incense was hardly a subject of doubt or dispute. It was universally known in Jewish circles, and for anyone in the position of an instructor (like our author) to have believed it to be located in the holy of holies would have been laughable. Delitzsch well remarks that, "even supposing him to have been an Alexandrine Jew, he must have been a monster of ignorance and forgetfulness to be capable of such a mistake." Certainly, it was not a misconception shared by his contemporary Philo of Alexandria, who specifically states that the lampstand, the table of showbread, and the altar of incense were located in the vestibule or antechamber, that is, the holy place, as distinct from the inner sanctuary of the holy of holies.[44] Josephus, another Jewish contemporary, is no less explicit.[45] It is impossible to doubt that the disposition of the various furnishings of the Jewish shrine was perfectly familiar to the average Jew in the first century of our era. The place of the altar of incense in the outer sanctuary during this period is confirmed by Luke's account of the experience of the father of John the Baptist, Zechariah, a priest of the division of Abijah, when in accordance with the duty assigned to him he went into the sanctuary to burn incense (Lk. 1:5ff.). This he could have done only at the altar of incense in the holy place, since an ordinary priest was not permitted to enter the holy of holies.[46] The assumption, then, that our author, with his deep interest

44. Philo, *Vita Mos.* ii.94f., 101–104; *Quis Rev. Div. Her.* 226.
45. Josephus, *Bell. Jud.* v.216ff.; *Ant.* iii.139–147, 198.
46. There is an early Christian tradition that Zechariah was high priest and that the occasion described by Luke was the Day of Atonement, with the consequence that Zechariah must then have passed through the holy place into the holy of holies. The identification of Zechariah as high priest is found as early as the second century in the apocryphal *Protevangelium of James* and recurs in Ambrose (in his commentary on Luke) in the fourth century and in later writers. One of the reasons adduced by Luther to "justify the assumption that there was a third altar in the holy of holies is that in the opinion of

in the ritual of the Jewish sanctuary, was ignorant of so elementary a matter as the position of the altar of incense in the holy place must be judged unreasonable.

A quite different solution, which also can boast a long history, is offered by those who maintain that what our author is speaking of here is not the altar of incense but a censer (thurible) or incense-shovel. This understanding of the Greek noun[47] numbers among its advocates Theophylact, Anselm, Aquinas, Luther,[48] Grotius, Bengel, and Alford, and is adopted in the KJV ("the golden censer") and its history may be traced back at least as far as the Vulgate Latin version of Jerome in the fourth century.[49] It is a sense, further, which is in line with such evidence as we have of the meaning of the term in classical Greek and in the Septuagint.[50] On this interpretation, then, the article intended is not the altar of incense which stood in the holy place, but the censer or some similar vessel which the high priest is said to have used on the Day of Atonement when he entered the holy of holies, and which, it is supposed, was kept in the inner sanctuary. An auxiliary utensil of this nature would, however, have been of minor significance and unlikely to receive special mention. In any case, it would have been made of brass, not gold, and in fact there is no mention in the Old Testament of any such thing as a *golden* censer. Moreover, that the term used here was currently employed to denote specifically the altar of incense is confirmed by the consideration that precisely the same term designates this

---

many Zechariah, the father of John the Baptist, is thought to have been the high priest, because it is written that the angel Gabriel appeared to him standing on the right of the altar of incense." The high priest, however, would never have been designated "a certain priest" (ἱερεύς τις), nor could it be said of the high priest on the Day of Atonement that it "fell to him by lot" to offer incense in the sanctuary (Lk. 1:5, 8f.). There is no room for doubt that Zechariah was one of the common run of priests and that he was on duty at this time because the priestly division to which he belonged was responsible for one of its recurring spells of temple ministry. The coveted privilege of burning incense in the holy place (permitted only once in a lifetime) was assigned by the casting of lots.

47. Θυμιατήριον.

48. This is Luther's conclusion, despite his preceding arguments for the existence of a third altar located in the holy of holies. "What shall we say," he writes, "to the Apostle who simply says without qualification that there was a golden censer in the holy of holies? It may be said that there was such a censer in the holy of holies since the priest carried one there during the feast of the Atonement. And such is my view until I learn differently."

49. The Vulgate translation of θυμιατήριον is *turibulum*. The Old Latin rendering, however, is *altare*.

50. It is found, for example, in Herodotus (IV.162, where the form is θυμιητήριον) and Thucydides (VI.46) and in the LXX of 2 Chronicles 26:19 and Ezekiel 8:11, and also in IV Maccabees 7:11. The Hebrew word מַחְתָּה, LXX πυρεῖον, in Leviticus 16:12, translated "censer" in KJV, RSV, JB, "firepan" in NEB, denotes the vessel, doubtless of brass, not gold, filled with live coals taken from the altar of burnt offering in the courtyard which the high priest carried into the holy of holies, where he mingled incense with the coals, thereby generating an aromatic cloud that enveloped the mercy seat.

particular object in the writings of Philo and Josephus, both acknowledged experts in Jewish customs.[51]

As a solution, moreover, it actually creates a difficulty much more serious than the one it is intended to solve; for if the Greek word is interpreted as meaning a censer or some other minor utensil it follows that our author has failed to mention so important an object as the altar of incense in his description of the main furnishings of the tabernacle. It is difficult to believe that he could have been guilty of so improbable a lapse. And it may be judged no less improbable that our author imagined the altar of incense to be located in the holy of holies, because, if that had been the case, it would then have been accessible to one man, the high priest, on one day only of the whole year, the Day of Atonement, when alone it was permissible for him to enter the inner sanctuary; whereas it was a well-known fact that incense was burnt on this altar every day of the year, both morning and evening, so that it was called "a perpetual incense" (Ex. 30:7f.). Interestingly enough, the Jewish writing known as *The Apocalypse of Baruch* (vi.7), which belongs to the same period as the Epistle to the Hebrews, describes the holy of holies as containing not only the mercy seat and the tables of the law but also the altar of incense together with the vestments of the high priest, the forty-eight precious stones with which these were adorned, and all the sacred vessels of the tabernacle; and there is no question of error or misapprehension on the part of the authors of this writing.

It would seem sensible to conclude that our author, so far from being guilty of ignorance or eccentricity, was, as Spicq judges, following a liturgical tradition which recognized a special doctrinal association between the altar of incense and the holy of holies. As Keil and Delitzsch point out, "its place was to be in front of the curtain, which concealed the ark of the covenant (xxvi.31), 'before the capporeth' (xl.5), so that, although it really stood in the holy place between the candlestick on the south side and the table on the north (xxvi.35, xl.22, 24), it was placed in the closest relation to the *kapporeth*, and for this reason is not only connected with the most holy place in 1 Kings vi.22, but is reckoned in Heb. ix.4 as part of the furniture of the most holy place."[52] Similar considerations lead Lange to the decision that we should "rather find a theological

---

51. The term θυμιατήριον is used, too, in the second-century versions of Exodus 30:1 of Theodotion and Symmachus. The LXX reading is θυσιαστήριον θυμιάματος. Of the earlier Alexandrian patristic authors Clement and Origen also designate the altar of incense by the noun θυμιατήριον.

52. C. F. Keil and F. Delitzsch, *Biblical Commentary on the Old Testament*, Vol. II, Exodus (Edinburgh, 1878), p. 208.

idea than an archaeological error" in the passage before us.[53] Certainly, the distinctive Christian understanding which our author is intent on imparting, and which evidently involves the association of the altar of incense with the holy of holies, the former symbolizing the prayers of God's people and the latter the heavenly sanctuary, is confirmed in Revelation 3:8f., where it is said that, in the celestial reality, incense is offered "with the prayers of all the saints upon the golden altar before the throne."

The alignment of the brazen altar of sacrifice, the golden altar of incense, and the mercy seat, though each was located in a different division of the tabernacle or its precincts, namely, in the courtyard, the holy place, and the holy of holies respectively, was undoubtedly an arrangement of the greatest significance. The straight line which connected these three with each other indicated clearly the line of propitiation and atonement appointed by God. Accordingly, on the Day of Atonement the high priest entered into the holy of holies bearing with him the blood of the spotless victim vicariously slain on the altar of sacrifice and also the incense from the altar of incense which, when sprinkled on the live coals, generated a sweet-smelling cloud symbolical, as we have mentioned, of the prayers of the people as the atoning blood was applied to the mercy seat. Indeed, the closeness of the association was further demonstrated by the fact that the blood of the sin offering was also applied by the high priest to the altar of sacrifice and the altar of incense (Lev. 16:17ff.; Ex. 30:10). Bearing in mind that the principal focus of our author's exposition is the Day of Atonement and

---

53. J. P. Lange, *A Commentary on the Holy Scriptures*, Vol. II, Exodus (New York, 1870), pp. 125f.

Some commentators find it significant that our author does not say *in which* here, as he did when speaking of the contents of the holy place in verse 2, but now uses the participle *having* (ἔχουσα). They maintain that this variation is intentional and exegetically important, on the ground that the expression "in which" can only denote what is actually located *in* a place, whereas the participle "having" is designed, they contend, to convey a different shade of meaning. Grotius, for example, asserts that "we are said to have what we are using" (*habere enim dicimur quod in nostro usu est*); and Owen comments as follows: "And of this altar he says not that it was in the *second tabernacle*, but that *it had it*. And in that expression he respects not its *situation*, but its *use*." Similarly, Westcott affirms that the substitution of "having" for "in which" "itself points clearly to something different from mere position." This line of interpretation may be possible, but its validity here must be judged doubtful, if only because when the participle ἔχουσα is repeated in this same passage it plainly means "holding" or "containing," and it is difficult to see how this is not the equivalent of ἐν ᾗ, "in which." In fact ἐν ᾗ and ἔχουσα alternate with each other: the outer tent in which (ἐν ᾗ) were the lampstand and the table ... the holy of holies having (ἔχουσα) the altar and the ark, which contained (ἐν ᾗ) a golden urn holding (ἔχουσα) the manna and Aaron's rod and the tables of the covenant. Do we really have something more here than a stylistic variation?

the fulfilment of all that its ceremonial portended in the perfect high-priestly work of Christ, the appropriateness of his association of the altar of incense with the holy of holies becomes evident.

The ark of the covenant, which the Israelites were taught to treat as peculiarly sacred, was the most important object located in the holy of holies. It was a box or chest made of acacia wood, 2½ cubits long, 1½ cubits wide, and 1½ cubits high, *covered on all sides,* that is, both inside and outside, *with gold,* and with rings of gold at each corner through which the staves of acacia wood overlaid with gold, for raising and transporting it from one place to another, were inserted (Ex. 25:10–15).

The tables of the covenant, that is, the two tablets of the decalogue given to Moses on Mount Sinai, were placed in the ark; hence its designation as "the ark of the covenant" (Ex. 25:16), for the law was the standard to which, as the people of the covenant, the Israelites were required to conform: breakers of the law were *ipso facto* breakers of the covenant. As the tablets of the law were also designated simply "the testimony," testifying as they did to the holiness demanded by God of his people and against those who disobeyed their prescriptions, the ark was also known as "the ark of the testimony."

With the destruction of Solomon's temple in 587 B.C. the ark disappeared from the scene, and in the second or post-exilic temple, which remained standing until the sack of Jerusalem in A.D. 70, the holy of holies was completely empty, the former position of the ark being demarcated by a slab of stone known as "the stone of foundation." The emptiness of the holy of holies in this later temple is not only implied by Josephus[54] but also remarked on by the Roman historian Tacitus.[55] The actual fate of the ark is unknown, though different strands of Jewish legend variously related that it, together with other contents of the holy of holies, was carried away by an angel,[56] or hidden, with the altar of incense, by Jeremiah in a cave on the mountain from which Moses viewed the promised land,[57] or, according to the tradition of the Samaritans, buried by Moses on Mount Gerizim, awaiting the advent of the messianic prophet promised in Deuteronomy 18:15ff.[58] The Christian seer, however, contemplates the revelation, not of an earthly ark (cf. v. 1 above and vv. 11f. and 23f. below), but of "the ark of God's covenant,"

---

54. Josephus, *Bell. Jud.* i.152f. and *Ant.* xiv.71f., describes Pompey's forceful entry into the temple in Jerusalem in 63 B.C. and his finding of the lampstand, the table, various vessels, censers, spices, and a sum of sacred money, all of which would have been located in the holy place. The implication is that the inner sanctuary was empty.

55. Tacitus, *Histories* v.9, states that the fact that the sanctuary was empty was common knowledge in his day.

56. II Baruch vi.7.

57. II Maccabees 2:4–8.

58. Josephus, *Ant.* xviii.85ff.

which is displayed when the temple of God is opened in heaven (Rev. 11:19).

The golden urn holding the manna and Aaron's rod that budded were also, according to our author, *contained* in the ark. Exodus 16:32–34 describes how Aaron fulfilled the instruction of Moses to take a jar and put an omer of manna in it and to "place it before the Lord, to be kept throughout your generations." The Hebrew text, it may be noted, does not say that it was a golden jar or urn; but this is how the Septuagint describes it (reflecting, no doubt, a Hebrew reading in the text used by the translators), and it was also a definition current in contemporary Judaism, as Philo witnesses.[59] There is no reason to doubt that the urn was in fact of gold. But the affirmation of Exodus 16:34 that "Aaron placed it before the testimony" would seem to indicate that it was set in front of rather than in the ark; and the same may be said of the account in Numbers 17:10f. of the placing of Aaron's rod "before the testimony." Delitzsch, however, argues that the position of the pot of manna (and, by the same token, the rod of Aaron) inside the ark is "a natural conclusion" from the words of the Hebrew original. It would at least seem reasonable to suppose that if the urn and the rod were originally placed in front of the ark, yet subsequently, for the sake of convenience (for example, when carrying the ark from one place to another), they were placed inside it.

According to rabbinical tradition, indeed, the ark contained a number of objects, specified as the two silver columns by which the tables of the law were said to have been supported, the fragments of the original Sinai tablets which Moses broke when he came down and found the people worshipping the golden calf (Ex. 32:19), a copy of the Torah, and the names by which God was invoked by the high priest before the ark; not, however, the urn of manna and Aaron's rod which this same tradition located beside or before the ark. The categorical assertion of 1 Kings 8:9 and 2 Chronicles 5:10 that "there was nothing in the ark except the two tables of stone which Moses put there at Horeb" does not clash with what is said here in the Epistle to the Hebrews, since the reference is to the ark when it was brought into Solomon's temple, whereas our author is speaking of the much earlier period of the tabernacle in the wilderness. Delitzsch, in fact, is of the opinion that "the very terms of this statement may almost seem to imply that other things had been there formerly."

Though the wilderness manna and Aaron's rod have perished long since, the Christian who overcomes is promised that he will be given "the hidden manna" to eat (Rev. 2:17), that heavenly nourishment with

59. Philo, *De Congressu* 100.

which God eternally sustains his faithful servants. And through union with Christ he whose life previously was productive only of dead works (Heb. 6:1) is now enabled to bring forth much good fruit to the glory of God (Jn. 15:4, 5, 8; Gal. 5:22f.). The same power that caused Aaron's lifeless rod to bud, blossom, and bear fruit (Num. 17) is even more wonderfully at work in his experience.

The cherubim of glory above the ark of the covenant *overshadowing the mercy seat* are the last furnishings of the holy of holies to be mentioned here. The mercy seat was a panel or slab of pure gold, 2½ cubits long by 1½ cubits wide, which fitted exactly over the top of the ark of the covenant; and the cherubim were two figures, also made of beaten gold, standing at either end of the mercy seat with which they were integrally connected, and facing inward toward each other, their wings stretched out and overarching the mercy seat (Ex. 25:17ff.). They are described as "cherubim of glory," not because they were gloriously or beautifully fashioned, as, for example, Aquinas supposed, but because it was between them that the glory of God's presence appeared above the mercy seat, as promised in Exodus 25:22: "There I will meet with you, and from above the mercy seat, from between the two cherubim that are upon the ark of the testimony, I will speak with you." The glory in the holy of holies is thus the *shekinah* glory of God's presence in the midst of his people (cf. Ex. 40:34ff.; Lev. 16:2; 2 Sam. 6:2; 1 Ki. 8:10f.; 2 Chr. 5:13f.; Ps. 80:1; Isa. 37:16).

The Greek noun *hilastērion*,[60] translated *mercy seat* in our version (and in KJV), is the term ordinarily used in the Septuagint to render the Hebrew *kapporeth*,[61] which means simply "covering." This Hebrew word was descriptive in a literal sense, because, as we have seen, the mercy seat exactly covered the ark of the covenant. But it may well also have had a symbolical significance from the earliest times in that, as Westcott and others have pointed out, it was interposed between the tables of the law contained in the ark, by which the sinner stood condemned, and the glory of God's holy presence. This is certainly the implication of the Greek *hilastērion*, which means a place of propitiation. On the great annual Day of Atonement the culminating moment of propitiation and reconciliation came when the high priest, on entering the holy of holies, sprinkled the blood of atonement on the mercy seat in the awesome presence of God's glory (Lev. 16:14ff.). It may reasonably be assumed that the same association between the atoning blood of sacrifice and the mercy of God was in the mind of the Psalmist when he exclaimed: "Blessed is he whose transgression is forgiven, whose sin is

---

60. Ἱλαστήριον, to which the Latin *propitiatorium* (Vg) corresponds exactly in meaning.
61. כַּפֹּרֶת.

covered.[62] Blessed is the man to whom the Lord imputes no iniquity" (Ps. 32:1f.). For the Christian, the rightness of linking the blood of atonement which was shed at Calvary with the mercy of God is confirmed both in the argument our author is about to develop (see vv. 11ff. below) and in the only other place in the New Testament where the noun *hilastērion* occurs, namely, Romans 3:25, a passage in which Paul applies the term directly to Christ: God, says the Apostle, set Christ Jesus forth "to be a propitiation,[63] through faith, by his blood" (ERV). F. F. Bruce observes appropriately that the mercy seat or place of propitiation is "viewed by our author as the earthly counterpart of the 'throne of grace' to which he has already exhorted his readers to draw near for help in the hour of need (Ch. 4:16)."

It is plain, especially in the Epistle to the Hebrews, that the tabernacle and its ministry fulfilled a symbolical function which has an important bearing on God's purposes of redemption in Christ. But the question arises regarding the extent to which symbolical significance should be sought and found: the temptation to allegorize every little detail is one which many, in most ages of the church, have been unable to resist. In so carefully ordered a system the structure and service of the tabernacle should not be regarded as meaningless, and it is not wrong to seek typological significances. But some limits must be set, otherwise a fertile imagination can lead, and frequently has led, to all sorts of extravagant interpretations. The tendency is discernible, for instance, though to a restricted degree, in Alcuin, who explains that the seven lights of the lampstand are the seven gifts of the Spirit and that the ark is the flesh of our Savior, containing the manna of his divinity and Aaron's rod, the symbol of Christ's priesthood.

The medieval commentators pursued this line of interpretation to the point where every minute particular was regarded as heavily pregnant with esoteric significance and their allegorizing enthusiasm carried them far beyond the limits of sane exposition. Peter Lombard, for example (to select a typical schoolman), expounds the holy place as

---

62. Significantly, the Hebrew verb כפר (*kaphar*), "to cover," has a radical identity with the noun כַּפֹּרֶת (*kapporeth*), "mercy seat."

63. The precise connotation of ἱλαστήριον in Romans 3:25 is a matter of dispute among exegetes, but its connection with the concept of reconciliation is clear, and its usage in the LXX to render the Hebrew *kapporeth* has to be taken into account. As the place of mercy in the holy of holies, which finds the fulfilment of its typology in the entrance of Christ into the heavenly sanctuary through his own blood (v. 12 below), the *hilastērion*, both in the passage before us and in Romans 3:25, may properly be brought into association with the declaration of 1 John 2:2, that "Jesus Christ the righteous is the propitiation for our sins" (where the cognate noun ἱλασμός is used), and with the covenant promise of Jeremiah 31:34 already cited in 8:12, namely, "I will be propitious toward their iniquities" (where the cognate adjective ἵλεως is used).

signifying the church militant here on earth and the holy of holies the church triumphant in glory. The golden lampstand is Christ shining with virtue and wisdom in the midst of the faithful. The three lights on the right side of the stem are the believers of this age of grace, and the three on the left side the faithful who lived before the advent of Christ. Every detail of the lampstand's ornamentation is full of spiritual significance (Ex. 25:31ff.)—the almond-shaped cups, for instance, are the saints who are fitted to receive and to transmit to others the oil of grace. For Peter Lombard, too, the seven lights are the seven gifts of the Spirit which dwelt most fully in Christ and which are distributed to the faithful in accordance with his will. The table is Holy Scripture which supplies the food of life. The loaves are the twelve apostles and their vicars who offer the incense of prayer to God. The thurible is Christ, full of the fire of love, ever interceding for us. The ark is Christ, in whom are all the treasures of wisdom and knowledge (Col. 2:3). One cubit of its length signifies perseverance in doctrine, and the other cubit perseverance in labor, while the extra half-cubit signifies the imperfection of human capacities; and similarly its breadth signifies the perfection of love and its height the perfection of hope, but again the half-cubits our own imperfection. The four rings are the four Evangelists, through whom Christ is carried to the four quarters of the world and to whom the golden carrying-rods, that is, preachers shining with wisdom, are ever attached. The urn of manna in the ark is the soul of Christ filled with wisdom. The rod signifies Christ's priestly authority; the tablets, that he is the giver of the law; the mercy seat, that he is our propitiation; and so on, with much more of the same kind.

All this contrasts noticeably with the reserve of our author, who shows no inclination to develop a detailed allegorical interpretation of this kind. He seems instead deliberately to avoid any sort of over-elaboration, making specific mention of only a few important matters and then adding, *of these things we cannot now speak in detail.* The implication is that there was no necessity for him to give a more detailed description of the structure and furnishings of the tabernacle. Indeed, excessive attention to minor details could only have the effect of obscuring the main thrust of the important teaching he has to communicate concerning the high-priestly work of Christ and the everlasting covenant he has sealed with his own redeeming blood. As Calvin warns, "philosophizing beyond reasonable bounds (as some do) is not only futile but also dangerous."

It may be added that in the early apostolic period the Jewish scholar Philo had carried his particular philosophical type of allegorical interpretation of the Old Testament to extremes so fanciful that they were never subsequently surpassed, and that two centuries later the Christian scholar Origen (another Alexandrian!) took the lead, which he has held ever since, as the champion allegorizer of the Christian church.

9:6, 7. *These preparations having thus been made, the priests go continually into the outer tent, performing their ritual duties; but into the second only the high priest goes, and he but once a year, and not without taking blood which he offers for himself and for the errors of the people.*

Our author has given a brief summary of the structure and contents of the tabernacle (*These preparations*),[64] and he now turns his attention to the priestly ceremonial conducted in the two chambers, and more especially in the inner holy of holies. First he explains that *the priests,* that is, the priests of the levitical order without distinction, *go continually,* day after day, in accordance with the Mosaic requirements, *into the outer tent,* or holy place. The ritual duties performed by them there were three in particular: (1) the tending from evening to morning of the golden lampstand to ensure that its lamps were kept burning without interruption (Ex. 27:20f.); (2) the burning of incense on the altar of incense each morning and evening when the lamps were dressed (Ex. 30:7f.); and (3), in contrast to the two duties already mentioned, which were performed daily, the weekly replacement, on every sabbath day, of the loaves on the table of showbread (Lev. 24:8f.). The book of Leviticus contains detailed prescriptions regarding the functions and responsibilities of the priests, not only in the holy place but also in the sacred precincts. A summary of these duties is given in 1 Chronicles 23:24–32.

In distinction from these daily activities and assignations in the anterior sanctuary, *the second,* or inner, sanctuary of the holy of holies saw no activity at all, except *once a year* when the Day of Atonement came around. This was the tenth day of the seventh month (Lev. 16:29), known as Tishri, in the season of autumn. And the *only* person permitted to enter the holy of holies on this annual occasion was *the high priest.* His entrance, further, was *not without taking blood* with him—that is to say, he had no inherent right of entry on the basis of his own holiness, for he, like the rest of the people, was a sinner in need of atonement. Thus the sanctity of this shrine was safeguarded by the most careful prescriptions which excluded not only the general populace but even the priests themselves and sanctioned the entry of the high priest on but a

---

64. The "preparations" in the clause "these preparations having thus been made," τούτων δὲ οὕτως κατασκευασμένων, relate back to the statement of verse 2 that "a tent was prepared," σκηνὴ γὰρ κατεσκευάσθη.

single day of each year, while, as Westcott observes, "even he entered only in the power of another life." All this served to make dramatically plain to the Israelites that the way into the presence of God was closed to them because of their sinfulness which separated them from their Creator, and that it was only through the blood of a sacrifice offered in their stead that they could hope to find mercy and forgiveness.

At the same time, however, it was plain that the perfect and all-sufficient sacrifice was not offered under the levitical system, for the way into the holy of holies remained barred and the ritual of the Day of Atonement was repeated year after year. Moreover, the high priest who represented them before God was himself incapacitated by his own imperfection from effecting fully and finally that reconciliation which they needed, for, as we have mentioned, he, like them, was a sinner in need of forgiveness, and accordingly he offered the blood of sacrifice *for himself* as well as *for the errors of the people* (a requirement already noticed in 5:3 and 7:27). But the imperfection extended beyond the high priest to the victim which was sacrificed, for it is evident that a brute beast can never be a proper substitute for man whom God created in his own image; and so the multiplicity of animal victims in itself pointed to the need for one adequate victim who would bear away the sins of the world.

The ritual of the Day of Atonement is described in Leviticus 16. First, the high priest offered a bull as a sin offering for himself at the brazen altar of sacrifice in the courtyard of the tabernacle and carried some of its blood into the holy of holies, where, in the enveloping cloud of incense, he sprinkled it on and before the mercy seat; then he killed one of a pair of goats as a sin offering for the people and repeated the same ceremonial with blood from this victim. This done, he came out and laid his hands on the head of the remaining goat, confessing over it "all the iniquities of the people of Israel, and all their transgressions, and all their sins." This goat was then led into the wilderness symbolically bearing away all their sins, never to return. Properly understood, the ritual of the Day of Atonement in its various parts was sacramental in character, inviting the people to look beyond the sign to the reality, yet to be fulfilled, when the perfect high priest would come, able to represent them without hindrance of sin in the presence of God, and would offer the perfect sacrifice for the forgiveness and the removal of their sins forever.

The Greek noun translated *errors* in our version means literally "ignorances,"[65] and should be understood as designating those sins which are committed inadvertently or in ignorance. It thus matches the

65. Ἀγνοήματα.

thought of 5:2 above, where our author has spoken of "the ignorant and wayward,"[66] that is, those who sin unintentionally or through human frailty (Lev. 4:1f.; 5:17ff.), as distinct from those who sin in deliberate and rebellious defiance of God and his law. High-handed sin was a mutinous repudiation of the covenant bond between God and his people, a wilful withdrawal from membership in the people of God, and as such was irremediable. An equivalent situation is envisaged in 10:26 below, where it is asserted that, "if we sin deliberately after receiving the knowledge of the truth, there no longer remains a sacrifice for sins." The term used by our author here is, then, entirely appropriate to describe the nature of those sins for which sacrifice was offered by the high priest on the Day of Atonement. Though resulting from ignorance and infirmity, they were nonetheless sinful and defiling and in need of expiation; and all without exception are sinners in this respect, for, as Chrysostom remarks, no one is guiltless of such sinning.

The present tenses used in these two verses of the functioning of the levitical priesthood[67] conform with the usage elsewhere in the epistle. They are most naturally taken at their face value, rather than as historic presents (Moffatt), indicating that the temple in Jerusalem was still standing at the time of the composition of our epistle.[68] "The sacred writer regards indeed the old covenant as passed away and superseded," comments Delitzsch, "but its ritual worship has still a dying life and present existence."

> 9:8–10. *By this the Holy Spirit indicates that the way into the sanctuary is not yet opened as long as the outer tent is still standing (which is symbolic for the present age). According to this arrangement, gifts and sacrifices are offered which cannot perfect the conscience of the worshiper, but deal only with food and drink and various ablutions, regulations for the body imposed until the time of reformation.*

The Holy Spirit, regarded as the inspirer of the sacred text, is said to *indicate* certain truths in connection with the tabernacle, whose pattern of construction and scheme of worship were revealed to Moses by God (8:5).[69] The fact that none but the high priest was permitted to pass through the curtain into the holy of holies, and then only on one day of the year, carried with it the negative consequence that *the way into the*

---

66. Οἱ ἀγνοοῦντες καὶ πλανώμενοι.
67. ... εἰσίασιν ... ἐπιτελοῦντες ... προσφέρει.
68. See Introduction, pp. 30ff.
69. Aquinas observes that "this contradicts those heretics who say that the Old Testament comes not from the Holy Spirit but from an evil God."

sanctuary,[70] that is, the inner chamber symbolizing the place of God's presence, was *not yet opened* so that there might be freedom of access for all. The phrase "not yet" signifies the hope and expectation that the time would come when the way to the throne of divine grace would indeed be open to all—a hope that was fostered, positively, by the promises and prophecies concerning the coming of him who would be a priest forever after the order of Melchizedek and the inauguration of the new covenant when the closest communion would prevail between God and his people, and, negatively, by the obvious inadequacy of the whole levitical system to provide a radical cure for the ills of mankind. Clearly, however, the fulfilment of these expectations was deferred *as long as the outer tent was still standing,* that is to say, as long as the old system with its imperfections remained in force.[71] That force was cancelled when the purpose of Christ's coming was achieved at Calvary, for there the old levitical priesthood with its multiplicity of sacrifices was superseded by his unique and everlasting priesthood with its single all-sufficient sacrifice. The annulment of the old order was signified by the rending of the curtain which barred the way into the holy of holies: the moment of Christ's death on the cross was the moment when full atonement was made for the sins of the whole world (1 Jn. 2:2) and when access into the sanctuary of God's presence was procured for man.

As in verses 2 and 6 above, where the holy place is plainly intended, the Greek expression rendered *the outer tent* in our version means literally "the first tent."[72] Many modern commentators, as well as our version and JB, argue that our author is unlikely to have changed the meaning of the expression from the holy place to the tabernacle as a whole at this point. If this understanding is correct, the point would seem to be that the outer tent or holy place was regarded as blocking the way into the sanctuary of God's presence for the mass of the people, for whom entry even into the holy place was prohibited. They were

---

70. The Greek, τὴν τῶν ἁγίων ὁδόν, is interpreted in the Peshitta to mean "the way of the saints"; but τῶν ἁγίων must be understood here as a neuter rather than a masculine genitive plural, and more precisely as designating the inner sanctuary of the holy of holies (as in 8:2, in vv. 12, 24, and 25 of this chapter, and in 10:19). See note 54 above, on 8:2, and note 42, on 9:3. Westcott suggests that the designation τὰ ἅγια may have a more general connotation here, so that, while it must include the holy of holies, it may comprehend the holy place as well. "The people," he says, "had no way into the Holy Place which was open to the priests only; the priests had no way into the Holy of Holies which was open to the high priest alone." But in the whole of the present context it is plain that the great need of all was entry into the inner shrine of God's presence where everlasting mercy is to be found.

71. In the Greek ἔτι τῆς πρώτης σκηνῆς ἐχούσης στάσιν the expression ἔχειν στάσιν is more than a periphrasis for to continue in existence. As Teodorico observes, its force is to have legal standing or official sanction. Whatever lacks or loses this is annulled and set aside.

72. Ἡ πρώτη σκηνή.

excluded not only from the holy of holies but also from the ante-chamber or *aditus* of the holy of holies. So long, then, as the holy place continued standing they had no hope of immediate access to God. But the rending of the curtain meant the abolition of the distinction between the holy place and the holy of holies, indeed the abolition of the holy place (of which there is no mention when our author describes the heavenly reality). In Christ, God's people constitute a holy priesthood with full right of access into the divine presence (cf. Heb. 10:19ff.; 1 Pet. 2:5). The term "tent," however, can designate the tabernacle as a whole (as in 8:5, vv. 11 and 21 of this chapter, and 13:10), and this is how the older commentators interpreted it and more recently Héring and F. F. Bruce, as well as the KJV and the NEB ("the earlier tent"); and it seems preferable to understand it here in this more general sense. So long as the former tabernacle, the center of operations of the levitical priest-hood, continued to have standing there was no cleansing of the con-science and no freedom of approach to the mercy seat of God.

The old order of things, says our author, *is symbolic* (literally, "a parable") *for the present age*, [73] by which he means that "the Mosaic ritual was a parable in action" (Spicq) for "the present time of the new dis-pensation, in which the types and shadows of the old are being fulfilled" (Delitzsch). The parabolic significance of the levitical practices, both in their analogies and in their contrasts, has already received some atten-tion in the two preceding chapters, but will now be more fully ex-pounded, with particular reference to the fulfilment in Christ of all that was portended but not effected by the ceremonial of the Day of Atone-ment. The parable enacted in the worship of the tabernacle involved the offering of *gifts and sacrifices* (cf. 5:1) and thus pointed to the need of sinners for forgiveness and reconciliation. These gifts and sacrifices,

---

73. It is unnecessary to seek a precise term, such as τῆς πρώτης σκηνῆς or στάσιν, as the antecedent for ἥτις in the clause ἥτις παραβολὴ εἰς τὸν καιρὸν τὸν ἐνεστηκότα. As F. F. Bruce says, "the antecedent of ἥτις may be the whole situation of vv. 6–8, ἥτις being attracted to the gender and number of παραβολή." This agrees with the opinion of Bengel, Teodorico, Spicq, etc. The use of the perfect participle ἐνεστηκώς or ἐνεστώς to designate a time or event that is "now present" rather than, as some have wished to explain it, "close at hand" or "impending" is confirmed by its usage elsewhere in the New Testament; cf. Romans 8:38 (ἐνεστῶτα, "things present," as contrasted with μέλλοντα, "things to come"), 1 Corinthians 3:22 (where the same contrast recurs), 1 Corinthians 7:26 (τὴν ἐνεστῶσαν ἀνάγκην, "the present time of stress"), Galatians 1:4 (τοῦ αἰῶνος τοῦ ἐνεστῶτος, "the present evil age"), and similarly the use of the indicative in 2 Thessalonians 2:2 (ὡς ὅτι ἐνέστηκεν ἡ ἡμέρα τοῦ κυρίου, "alleging that the Day of the Lord is already here," NEB). Owen takes our author to be referring not to his own time, that is, the present Christian era, but to the age that *then* was, that is, the time that was present to the Israelites of old. This would mean that the practices associated with the tabernacle were a parable to them; but it is more likely that he means that these things have lessons to teach us, and in the first instance his readers, in our present age (cf. 1 Cor. 10:1ff.).

however, *cannot*[74] *perfect the conscience of the worshipper*. Their inadequacy, as has already been explained (7:18f., 27), and as will be further explained (10:1–3), is indicated by their constant repetition and by the inferior character of the sacrificial victims; yet their obvious imperfection, coupled with the promise of a new order, arouses the hope of the provision of a perfect offering for sin.

The conscience is properly man's inner knowledge of himself, especially in the sense of his *answerability* for his motives and actions in view of the fact that he, as a creature made in the image of God, stands before and must give an account of himself to his Creator. As a sinner, who has failed to keep the loving standard of God's law, he has an inner consciousness of his guilt and of his need for cleansing and restoration. The levitical ceremonial was incompetent to provide that perfection of reconciliation, that completeness of justification before God, which the sinner so radically needed. The prescriptions of the Mosaic system were external rather than internal in character, involving as they did regulations regarding *food and drink and various ablutions*, which by reason of their externality are appropriately described as *regulations for the body*. By way of example it is sufficient to mention the careful distinction between clean animals that could be eaten and unclean animals that could not be eaten (Lev. 11:1–47), the prohibition of wine for Aaron and his sons when they were ministering in the sanctuary (Lev. 10:8ff.) and for the Nazirite at all times (Num. 6:2ff.), and the great variety of ablutions, sprinklings, and cleansings for many different purposes (Lev. 11:28, 40; 14:1ff.; 15:1ff.; 16:4, 28; Num. 8:5ff.; 19:7ff., 14ff., etc.). A deeper purification, which would penetrate to the very heart of man's being, was essential if true reconciliation was to be effected.

Not that these ceremonies of old were empty ceremonies—far from it, for, as our author has said, they constitute a parable, pointing through and beyond themselves to the promised reality of perfection that was yet to come. In association with covenant promise and messianic prophecy, which they were designed to illustrate (for imperfect ordinances have no worth in isolation), they stimulated a longing for the perfect sacrifice that God would provide for his people. They performed a sacramental function as signposts directing the worshippers to the all-sufficing provision which in the intention of God was already available to them. But as such they were anticipatory: the unique sacrifice offered by the eternal High Priest of the order of Melchizedek was not yet. Hence the assertion that the regulations were *imposed* (or "in force,"

---

74. Notice, once again, the present tenses of the verbs: "gifts and sacrifices are offered (προσφέρονται) which cannot (μὴ δυνάμεναι) perfect the conscience." The implication is that the temple ritual had not yet been discontinued. See Introduction, pp. 30ff.

NEB)[75] *until the time of reformation,* that is, until the day when everything would be put right[76] and the shadow replaced by the substance. This "time of reformation" has already been defined in the terms of Jeremiah's prophecy of the new covenant and its fulfilment in Christ (Heb. 8:7ff.).

The sacramental nature of the provisions of God for his people in the Old Testament period is apparent in the manner in which these provisions were closely bound up with the covenant promises of everlasting blessing. The horizon of the men and women of faith was not limited to the externalities of a promised land or an earthly sanctuary, which in the nature of the case belonged to this present passing world. With the divine promises affixed to them, these things became "visible words" which fostered a perspective that was firmly focused on the eternal reality. Thus Christ assured the Pharisees: "Your father Abraham rejoiced that he was to see my day, and he saw it and was glad" (Jn. 8:56). And our author declares that the patriarchs desired "a better country, that is, a heavenly one," and that they were not to be disappointed, for God "has prepared for them a city with foundations" (11:10, 16); and, further, that Moses endured adversity "as seeing him who is invisible" (11:29). The external provisions, therefore, coupled with the promises, were welcomed and understood by them in this sacramental manner, as signs pointing away from themselves to an everlasting spiritual reality. Though during their earthly pilgrimage they did not receive what was promised, yet "they saw it and greeted it from afar" (11:13). Their justification, like ours, was in Christ, grounded in the perfection of his atoning work; for, as in the mind and purpose of God Christ is the Lamb slain from the foundation of the world (Rev. 13:8; 1 Pet. 1:19f.), so their justification in Christ is as sure as ours who live in the age of fulfilment. They looked forward in faith to the justifying sacrifice; we look back in faith to the same justifying sacrifice. "Only this difference was between them and us," writes Archbishop Cranmer of the Old Testament believers, "that our redemption by Christ's death and passion was then only promised, and now it is performed and past. And as their sacraments were figures of his death to come, so be ours figures of the same now past and gone. And yet it was all but one Christ

---

75. Ἐπικείμενα, "incumbent upon," would seem to be more or less equivalent to ἐχούσης στάσιν, "having legal standing," in verse 8. In the present context both expressions describe a system that is "in force."

76. In the Greek phrase μέχρι καιροῦ διορθώσεως the noun διόρθωσις, which indicates the setting straight or restoring of what is out of line, is a hapax legomenon in biblical Greek. F. F. Bruce suggests that it might be rendered "the New Order," since the coming of Christ "involved a complete reshaping of the structure of Israel's religion."

to them and us, who gave life, comfort, and strength to them by his death to come, and giveth the same to us by his death passed."[77]

Here, again, we may ask whether our author, in admonishing his readers that the levitical "gifts and sacrifices... cannot perfect the conscience of the worshiper" and that all the other "regulations for the body" were only "until the time of reformation," has not teaching similar to that of the Dead Sea Sect in mind. Though the members of this community had withdrawn into the wilderness, the sphere of their belief was still that of the Mosaic law and the levitical priesthood. They hoped that their observance of the law would atone for guilt as effectively as the sacrifice of burnt offerings and that their company would itself be a holy sanctuary and a reservoir of the pure priesthood.[78] Their withdrawal, indeed, was intended only as an interim measure, until such time as the temple was purified and the authentic priesthood restored. Meanwhile they religiously observed the "regulations for the body" prescribed in the Mosaic legislation. If, as has been conjectured,[79] those to whom this letter was addressed showed signs of being influenced by the outlook of the Qumran Community, they would have had special need of the reminder that the levitical system with all its gifts and sacrifices and its regulations for the body was not only inadequate to cleanse the conscience but also was no longer in force now that the time of reformation had come.

9:11, 12. *But when Christ appeared as a high priest of the good things that have come, then through the greater and more perfect tent (not made with hands, that is, not of this creation) he entered once for all into the Holy Place, taking not the blood of goats and calves but his own blood, thus securing an eternal redemption.*

The imagery in these verses is that of the Day of Atonement, and there is a close logical connection with what has already been said in verse 7 about the ministry of the levitical high priest on that annual occasion. There we had the shadow; here we have the reality. *When Christ appeared*[80] the whole situation was altered. The levitical high

77. Thomas Cranmer, *Works*, I (Cambridge, 1844), p. 60.
78. *The Manual of Discipline* ix.4–6.
79. See Introduction, pp. 13ff.
80. The Greek reads Χριστὸς δὲ παραγενόμενος, and the contemporary evidence indicates that the verb παραγίνεσθαι was commonly in use as a synonym for ἔρχεσθαι, "to come" (see Moulton and Milligan, *sub voc.*). The verb does not necessarily suggest the majestic arrival of a great personage, as some scholars (for example, Westcott, Spicq, Teodorico) have wished to understand it. The commonplace sense undoubtedly accords with the usage of παραγίνεσθαι elsewhere in the New Testament (as reference to a Greek concordance will show), and it is the sense that should be retained here. Another possible meaning of the verb, favored by some here, is "to come to our assistance," but, once again, our judgment should be governed by the contemporary semantic evidence.

priests were incompetent to provide the good things that God had promised; but with the appearance of him who is the High Priest after the order of Melchizedek these are rightly described as *the good things that have come,* for in his high-priestly work the new covenant and its promises find their fulfilment (2 Cor. 1:20). According to a variant reading, however, Christ is the high priest "of the coming good things."[81] If this reading is correct, the reference could be either to the good things which were coming from the point of view of those who lived in the Old Testament period (cf. Heb. 10:1), and which his advent brought to fulfilment, or the good things which are coming from the point of view of those who live in the present Christian era, and which belong to the consummation of his second advent (cf. Heb. 13:14; 1 Cor. 2:9; Rom. 8:18). While both variants can claim solid support, the reading reflected in our version seems more likely to be the correct one.

Be that as it may, the good things that are ours in Christ come to us in two stages: united to him, we are indeed the heirs of all things (Rom. 8:17; 1 Cor. 3:21–23), but it is only hereafter that we enter into the fulness of our heritage (1 Pet. 1:4; 1 Jn. 3:2). Christ's atoning work is the source from which all the blessings of the new covenant flow: hence Paul's rhetorical question, "he who did not spare his own Son but gave him up for us all, will he not also give us all things with him?" (Rom. 8:32); yet these gracious gifts, though already enjoyed in him, are not yet known in their fulness, for the best is kept till the last (cf. Jn. 2:10)—a "last," however, that is also a beginning and a continuation and that has no limit or measure. Our present experience of the transforming power of the indwelling Spirit is but the pledge or earnest of the ineffable completeness of that transformation which awaits the people of God in the glory of eternity (cf. Eph. 1:13f.; 2 Cor. 1:22). Thus the good things both have come and are coming; and the two stages in which we experience them, the foretaste and the fulness, are closely connected, as effect to cause, to the two comings of Christ, the one past and the other still future.

The interpretation of what is designated "the greater and more perfect tent (not made with hands, that is, not of this creation)" has

---

81. Both readings can claim early and extensive support. Ἀρχιερεὺς τῶν γενομένων ἀγαθῶν, which lies behind the rendering of our version, is found in Papyrus 46 (where the equivalent γεναμένων is written) and Codex Vaticanus and also in Origen in the first half of the third century, while ἀρχιερεὺς τῶν μελλόντων ἀγαθῶν is attested by Codex Sinaiticus and Codex Alexandrinus, accepted by Jerome in the Vulgate (*pontifex futurorum bonorum*), and incorporated into the Textus Receptus. It seems likely that the latter reading is attributable to a copyist's error, resulting from an unconscious assimilation to 10:1 which speaks of the law as having a shadow "of the good things to come," τῶν μελλόντων ἀγαθῶν. Delitzsch, however, contends that γενομένων is an error in transcription, "occasioned by παραγενόμενος," and Moffatt is of the same opinion, though he suggests that, alternatively, the alteration may have been caused by "a pious feeling that μελλόντων here (though not in 10¹) was too eschatological."

been discussed above in Excursus II (pp. 283ff.), and a discussion of the significance of the blood of Jesus and the scope of his heavenly high priesthood follows in Excursus III (pp. 329ff.).

Notice should be taken of three unfortunate errors in the rendering of verse 12 given by our version (RSV). (1) It was not into *the Holy Place* that Christ entered but into the holy of holies.[82] (2) It was not *taking* but through or by virtue of[83] his own blood that he entered. (3) He did this, not *thus securing* but having secured[84] an eternal redemption[85] for us. The levitical high priest alone of all the priests was permitted to present himself "before the Lord" in the holy of holies on behalf of the people; so also, but transcendentally, Jesus our High Priest has presented himself on our behalf in the glory of the heavenly sanctuary. The levitical high priest was permitted entry into the holy of holies only once every year (v. 7), on the Day of Atonement—a finite, annual "onceness"; so also, but transcendentally, Jesus our High Priest has entered *once for all* into the true sanctuary above—an infinite "onceness," without any repetition, because of the eternal worth of his atoning sacrifice. The levitical high priest passed into the holy of holies only after, and on the basis of, the shedding of the blood of the sacrificial victim[86] at the altar in the courtyard outside the sacred tent; so also, but transcendentally, Jesus our High Priest first secured our eternal redemption by the sacrifice of himself in the "courtyard" of this world, and then, by virtue of his own blood, passed from sight "into heaven itself, now to appear in the presence of God on our behalf" (v. 24 below).

---

82. The Greek τὰ ἅγια, which may designate the sanctuary as a whole or the holy place or the holy of holies, is repeatedly used for the holy of holies in our epistle. See notes on 8:2 (54, p. 281), 9:1 (39, p. 307), and 9:3 (42, p. 309). In each case the sense is determined by the demands of the context.

83. Διά with the genitive.

84. The aorist participle εὑράμενος plainly means that Christ entered into the heavenly sanctuary *after he had secured* an eternal redemption: the securing of our eternal redemption took place at the cross and was followed by his entry into heaven. The one great prerequisite of his triumphant entry into glory was his sacrificial death and blood-shedding on earth. See Excursus III.

85. The root meaning of the Greek noun λύτρωσις, "redemption," and the verb λυτρόω, "redeem," is that of deliverance (λύω, "loose," "set free"). The religious significance is already established in the Old Testament, where it is God who graciously provides for the deliverance or redemption of his people. Especially significant was their deliverance from the bondage of Egypt, celebrated annually in the observance of the passover, which pointed sacramentally to the deeper need of release from the bondage of sin, which in turn was graphically presented in the ritual of another annual festival, that of the Day of Atonement. The true fulfilment, to which, as our epistle teaches, these ceremonial occasions pointed, is provided in the perfect redemption achieved for us by Christ.

86. It is true that the blood of only one calf and one goat was shed on the Day of Atonement, but the plural "goats and calves" is appropriately used by our author here because as year succeeded year a multiplicity of goats and calves was sacrificed.

EXCURSUS III: THE BLOOD OF JESUS AND HIS HEAVENLY PRIESTHOOD

In the eighteenth century J. A. Bengel (1687–1752) propounded, with a passion and at a length that are alike uncharacteristic of the economy of expression by which his most celebrated work is distinguished, the theory that in the suffering and death of Christ his blood was totally poured out, so that not one drop remained in his body. This total effusion of his blood, says Bengel, was not limited to the suffering on the cross, but extended from the agony in the garden, where his sweat was like great drops of blood, to the scourging in the praetorium, and then to the piercing of hands and feet by the nails that fastened him to the cross, and, after death, the effusion that resulted from the thrusting of the spear into his side. He held, further, that this blood, even after it had been shed, was preserved from all corruption. Justification for this conclusion was sought in the declaration of 1 Peter 1:18f. that "we were redeemed not with corruptible things such as silver and gold, but with the precious blood of Christ." According to Bengel, "the *preciousness* of that blood excludes all *corruption.*" Its supreme value requires its imperishability.[1]

What, then, happened to this precious blood which Jesus shed? Bengel rejects the opinion that at the resurrection it was somehow restored to the vascular system of Christ's body, maintaining rather that at the ascension the blood that had been shed was carried by Christ, in separation from his body, into the heavenly sanctuary. With reference to Hebrews 9:12, he says:

> Christ entered into the sanctuary *through his own blood* (not just *after* the blood had been shed, or *by virtue of* its effusion, or *when* it had again been taken into his body, but THROUGH the blood); therefore he as the high priest carried his own blood, in separation from his body, into the sanctuary, and at the time of his entry or ascension Christ kept his blood apart from his body. His body was bloodless [*exsangue*]; not inanimate [*exanime*], however, but living [*vivum*].

Had the blood been in his body, Bengel contends, there would not have been a correspondence with the typology of the Old Testament, where the high priest entered the sanctuary with the blood of animals, and it is important, he adds, to "preserve the analogy between type and antitype" (a principle he cites from Witsius). Bengel fails, however, to take into account the fact that biblical analogies cannot be pressed into correspondence at every point; and, indeed, the particular analogy on which he wishes to insist here is hardly favorable to his hypothesis, for, while it is true that the high priest of old entered the sanctuary with the blood of sacrifice in separation from himself, his own blood was at the same time freely flowing within his body—that is to say, he himself was not at all in a bloodless state. If analogy is enforced at one point it cannot be enforced at another, and it is clear that on this basis those who maintain that Christ's blood

---

1. Bengel, *Gnomon Novi Testamenti*, at Hebrews 12:24.

was restored to his risen body can equally well claim the support of analogy. It is indisputable that in the Epistle to the Hebrews there are many analogies and correspondences, but no less striking are the contrasts and differences which are brought to light between the levitical priesthood and the priesthood of Christ.

Among those whose support Bengel claims are Chrysostom, who says that Christ's blood "was taken up into heaven," with the result that "we partake of blood that has been carried into the sanctuary, the true sanctuary" (Homily 33 on Heb. 13), and Calvin, who comments as follows on Hebrews 10:19:

> The blood of beasts, since it immediately undergoes putrefaction, could not long retain its vigour; but the blood of Christ, which is corrupted by no putridity, but ever flows with pure colour, is sufficient for us even to the end of the world. No wonder slain animal victims had no power to give life once they were dead; but Christ who rose again from the dead to bestow life on us, pours his life into us. This is the perpetual consecration of the way, because in the presence of the Father the blood of Christ is always in a sense [quodammodo] distilling for the irrigation of heaven and earth.

Again, on 13:11f.:

> In order that he might atone for the sins of the world Christ took his own blood into the heavenly sanctuary.

And on 13:20:

> It seems to me that the apostle means that Christ rose from the dead in such a way that his death was not abolished but retains its power eternally; as though he had said, "God raised up his Son, but in such a way that the blood, which he shed once in death, continues powerful after the resurrection for the ratificiation of the eternal covenant and brings forth its fruit just as if it were for ever flowing."

In the first of these quotations from Calvin the Reformer's manner of expression is unusually forced and even fanciful. What he is intent on saying, it seems, is that the blood-shedding of Christ was no ordinary blood-shedding; its effects were not momentary but eternal, and they were not geographically limited but universal in their scope. It does indeed sound strange to be told that Christ's blood is "always distilling for the irrigation of heaven and earth," but this is no more than a figure of speech (quodammodo), even though not a particularly happy one. Similarly, in the last of the three quotations he is saying that the power of Christ's atoning death, which is identical with the power of his blood, is in no way annulled by the event of the resurrection. Christ is no longer dead, but risen and alive forevermore; yet his sacrifice on the cross avails for the repentant sinner "just as if" (though this is not actually the case) "it were for ever flowing."

But what of the second of the quotations from Calvin and the one from Chrysostom, in which Christ is said to have taken or carried his blood into the heavenly sanctuary? In his extended presentation of his thesis that Christ's blood was carried into heaven in separation from his body Bengel leaves no room for doubt regarding his own position; but where commentators speak in a briefer and more incidental manner (as is the case with Chrysostom and Calvin in the places cited) caution should be observed in attributing the same or similar teaching to them. It is hardly without significance that in their comments on 9:12 and 12:24, where, more than anywhere else, those who hold that Christ carried his blood into heaven would be expected to expound this view, neither Chrysostom nor Calvin says a single word about such an interpretation. When John Owen (1616–1683), to take another example, commenting on 12:24, says that the blood shed by Christ, which, according to our author, "speaks" to God, did so speak "when it was shed" and "continues so to do in that presentation of it in heaven," it might be inferred that he held that the blood shed by Christ on earth was taken by him into heaven and is there continually "presented" to the Father. That this, however, is not at all Owen's doctrine, and thus that in the place mentioned he is writing of the presentation of Christ's blood in heaven only in a manner of speaking, not in a literal sense, is demonstrated by what he has previously written at considerably greater length when commenting on 9:12, where it is said that Christ entered into the heavenly sanctuary *through* his own blood:

> The apostle [he says] is so far from using the particle διά [*through*] improperly for σύν [*with*], so to frame a comparison between things wherein indeed there was no similitude, as they [the Socinians] dream, that he useth it on purpose to exclude the sense which σύν [*with*] would intimate: for he doth not declare with what the high priest entered into the holy place, for he entered with incense as well as with blood; but what it was by virtue whereof he so entered as to be accepted with God. . . . It is a vain speculation, contrary to the analogy of faith, and destructive of the true nature of the oblation of Christ, and inconsistent with the dignity of his person, that he should carry with him into heaven a part of that material blood which was shed for us on the earth. This some have invented, to maintain a comparison in that wherein none is intended. The design of the apostle is only to declare by virtue of what he entered as a priest into the holy place. And this was by virtue of his own blood when it was shed, when he offered himself unto God. This was that which laid the foundation of, and gave him the right unto the administration of his priestly office in heaven.

To return to Bengel: it is his conviction that the blood of Christ now forever separated from his risen and glorified body remains eternally the blood that was shed. He mentions the vision of the heavenly Christ in Revelation 1:14, where his head is described as *white*, from which some have drawn the inference that the whiteness was to be attributed to bloodlessness—an exceptionally jejune piece of special pleading, as is the conclusion derived by some from Luke 24:39 ("See my hands and feet, that it is I myself; handle me and see; for a spirit has not flesh and bones as you see that I have") that the risen Savior had flesh and bones, but no blood. On the same principle of logic it could be argued that he had no skin or hair, since they are not mentioned, but only flesh and bones. The consideration is left out of account that the normal conception of flesh involves the presence of blood as a component part; and in any case it is difficult to imagine how the spectators could reasonably have been invited to "see my blood." Bengel, however, does not "allege" these inferences as evidence, realizing, no doubt, that they are scarcely compatible with solid exegesis.

But he evidently feels himself to be on more secure ground when offering the explanation that in the supper of the Lord, instituted by him as a reminder of his death, the body and the blood of Christ are set before us symbolically in separation from each other. It must be objected, however, that this is putting asunder two things that God has joined together, and it is surely preferable to understand the twofold structure of the eucharist as a theological hendiadys, the presentation of a single truth by means of two particular aspects of its reality. The "body of Christ" here speaks to us of a *victim*, and, what is more, a truly *human* victim, who was thus fully qualified to serve as our substitute, and did so on the cross where "he himself bore our sins in his body" (1 Pet. 2:24); and the "blood of Christ" here speaks to us of the *sacrificial* nature of his death, in which his precious blood was voluntarily shed for the forgiveness of our sins (Mt. 26:28; 1 Jn. 1:7). In line with this understanding, and contrary to Bengel's supposition, the author of our epistle speaks both of our being "sanctified through the offering of *the body* of Jesus once for all" (10:10) and of our being "sanctified by *the blood* of the covenant" (10:29), and thus, so far from teaching a disjunction of the body from the blood of Jesus, testifies to the virtual interchangeability of the terms "body" and "blood" in reference to Christ's redeeming death and its sanctifying effect—a reference which includes the eucharist, in view of the significance of that sacrament.

This conclusion is confirmed, moreover, rather than contradicted by the declaration of John 6:53 (another "proof-text" adduced by Bengel): "Truly, truly, I say to you, unless you eat the flesh of the Son of man and drink his blood, you have no life in you"; for in the discourse to which this statement belongs the correct manner of interpreting these words has already been given in verse 35, where Christ asserts: "He who comes to me shall not hunger, and he who believes in me shall never thirst"—that is to say, to come to Christ is to eat his flesh and to believe in him is to drink his blood: but to come to Christ and to believe in him are two different ways of saying the same thing; hence, again, a hendiadys.

Bengel insists, however, that now in heaven the outpoured blood of Christ, in separation from his body, is present before the eyes of God. By way of answer to those who maintain that the blood must have returned to the body of the risen Jesus to ensure the completeness of his glorified humanity, he affirms that, while the circulation of the blood is a necessity for natural or animal life, it is not so for the life of glorification, in which everything is of God. Presumably, then, the same should be postulated of the eschatological body of the believer which is to be made like Christ's glorified body (Phil. 3:21). And, by the same token, it might be asserted that Christ's (and the believer's) resurrection body has no more need of a digestive system than it has of the circulation of blood. Yet the risen Lord, on the same occasion when he displayed himself as having "flesh and bones," showed that he was able to eat and assimilate food (Lk. 24:41ff.). Not that this explains anything, for the fact is that the resurrection body of Jesus (and of the believer) belongs to a new and higher category of existence and will remain a mystery to be explained only when it is experienced.

The blood of Jesus, transported separately into heaven, is, according to Bengel, repeatedly sprinkled there for the removal of sin. Bengel finds support for this opinion in the writings of the English mystic Thomas Bromley (1629–1691), who is cited to the effect that the blood of the eternal covenant is sprinkled in the heavenly sanctuary, and that our great High Priest continues to perform this act of sprinkling from time to time for the purpose of assuaging the wrath of God which is aroused by sin. In more recent times Henry Alford (1810–1871) has propounded a similar view when commenting on Hebrews 12:24, which speaks of the blood shed by Jesus as "the blood of sprinkling." He writes as follows:

> And if Moses had blood wherewith to sprinkle the people, much more Jesus, of whom Moses was a shadow. And therefore the Writer, enumerating the great differences of our Sion from their Sinai, though he has not recounted their blood of sprinkling, as not being worthy of mention in the face of the terrors of God's law, mentions ours, by which we were redeemed unto God, and assigns it a place in the heavenly city, next to, but separate from, Jesus Himself in his glorified state. If we come to enquire how this can be, we enter on an interesting but high and difficult subject, on which learned and holy men have been much divided. Our Lord's Blood was shed from Him on the Cross. And as his Body did not see corruption, it is obvious to suppose, that His Blood did not corrupt as that of ordinary men, being as it is so important a portion of the body. Hence, and because his resurrection Body seems to have been bloodless—see Luke xxiv.39 ["flesh and bones"!]: John xx.27 [the invitation to Thomas to probe the supposedly bloodless wound-prints], and notes—some have supposed that the Blood of the Lord remains, as it is poured out, incorruptible, in the presence of God. On such a matter I would neither affirm nor deny, but mention, with all reverence, that which seems to suit the requirements of the words before us. By that Blood we live, wherever it is: but as here it is mentioned separately from the Lord Himself, as an item in the glories of the heavenly city, and as "yet speaking", it seems to require some such view to account for the words used.[2]

John Keble (1792–1866) may be cited as one who, apparently, held that the blood of Jesus was reunited with his resurrection body. Thus he speaks of Christ's "glorified body with all its wounds, his blood which he poured out on the cross but on his resurrection took again to himself," and of his ascension into heaven "with that body and blood."[3]

The notion, however, that the blood shed by Christ in his passion and death is incorruptible, and that it is now in the heavenly sanctuary, whether reassimilated into his glorified body or in separation from him, is inappropriate and naive. It involves a strange confusion of the physical and the spiritual. In no place do the scriptural accounts say that every drop of Christ's blood was drained from his body, or that the blood which was shed in one way or another participated in incorruptibility and in the resurrection. Certainly, common experience would lead us to expect that the body taken down from the cross was not entirely bloodless, however great the loss of blood may have been. After all, the blood is distributed throughout every portion of the human body, not only in the large arteries and veins but also in the minute capillary networks. To seek

---

2. Henry Alford, *The Greek Testament*, IV (London, 1861), p. 256.
3. John Keble, *On Eucharistical Adoration* (Oxford, 1857), pp. 66f.

support for the view that the risen Lord was a bloodless being from passages like Luke 24:39 and John 20:27 has the appearance of a desperate device. Though there is a genuine continuity between the body of humiliation and the body of glory, in speaking of the resurrection body of Christ or of the believer's glorified body hereafter we are speaking of a category of existence which transcends anything of which we at present have experience. All we can say is that "what is sown is perishable, what is raised is imperishable," that "it is sown in dishonor, it is raised in glory," that "it is sown in weakness, it is raised in power," that "it is sown a physical body, it is raised a spiritual body," and that "just as we have borne the image of the man of dust, we shall also bear the image of the man of heaven" (1 Cor. 15:42ff.). But our experience of this great transformation is *not yet*. Accordingly, meanwhile we must be content to say: "It does not yet appear what we shall be, but we know that when he appears we shall be like him, for we shall see him as he is" (1 Jn. 3:2).

It is wrong-headed, then, to be curious or concerned about what happened to the blood which Jesus shed. The important thing is that *it was shed*—by virtue of the incarnation, which made it possible for Christ, as Son of man, to shed his blood for men. Being truly *human* blood, it was susceptible to the same consequences as happen to other human blood that is shed. We may at least (and perhaps at most) assert that the body of Christ's resurrection was, by the power of God, the human body in the perfection of its glorification, and as such the prototype as well as the firstfruits of the bodies of our resurrection. The preciousness of the blood of Christ inheres not in the physical blood as such but in the perfection of the unique sacrifice of himself which he offered and of which the precious blood is a synonym.

The untenability of the negative deduction from a verse like Luke 24:39, which mentions only flesh and bones, that Christ's risen body was bloodless, becomes perfectly plain when the same type of exegetical logic is applied to the declaratory statement of 1 Corinthians 15:50 that "flesh and blood cannot inherit the kingdom of God," which would compel one to conclude that the resurrection body is not only bloodless but also fleshless (a conclusion that was in fact drawn by the Socinians). This, however, would involve a contradiction, since the one text assigns and the other denies flesh to the resurrection body. Such is the peril of a crass literalism that does not show proper regard for the manner of speaking and for the context of such biblical statements. In both cases a figure of speech is employed, not a precise literal definition: "flesh and bones" in Luke 24:39 and "flesh and blood" in 1 Corinthians 15:50 are both descriptive of the body as a whole (*synecdoche,* in which a part stands for the whole). In the former passage, the purpose is to emphasize the reality of the resurrection as a *human* and *bodily* resurrection; in the latter, the reference is to the human body in its present mortal and corruptible state as distinct from the glorified and incorruptible character of the resurrection body.[4]

* * * * *

4. As J. Behm observes (Kittel, TDNT, I, p. 172, *sub* "αἷμα"), "σάρξ καὶ αἷμα = בָּשָׂר וָדָם: an established Jewish (though not OT) term for man, whether as individual or species, in his creatureliness and distinction from God." Cf. Matthew 16:17; Galatians 1:16; Ephesians 6:12.

A distinctive opinion regarding the significance of the term "blood" in Scripture has become associated with the name of B. F. Westcott (1825–1901), whose viewpoint is summed up in the statement that "the blood poured out is the energy of present human life made available for others."[5] Applied to Christ, this means that by his blood-shedding he made "the virtue of his life accessible to the race." Westcott refers the reader to his earlier commentary on the Epistles of John[6] in which he endeavored to show that "the Scriptural idea of Blood is essentially an idea of life and not of death." The biblical justification for this view is sought in certain Old Testament passages which identify blood with life: Genesis 9:4 (which prohibits eating "flesh with its life, that is, its blood"); Deuteronomy 12:23 (a similar prohibition: "for the blood is the life; and you shall not eat the life with the flesh"); and especially Leviticus 17:10f. (which to the injunction against eating blood—"for the life of the flesh is in the blood"—adds the instruction relating to the blood of sacrifice: "and I have given it for you upon the altar to make atonement for your souls; for it is the blood that makes atonement, by reason of the life"). From such declarations Westcott argues that "by the outpouring of the Blood the life which was in it was not destroyed, though it was separated from the organism which before it had quickened"; and he postulates a distinction between the death of the victim occasioned by the shedding of its blood and the life of the victim which, supposedly, by the release of its blood is made available in life-giving virtue for the benefit of others—a distinction which he maintains is apparent in the two stages of the ritual performed on the Day of Atonement, first, by the shedding of blood at the altar of sacrifice and, second, by the sprinkling of that same blood in the sanctuary of the tabernacle.

This view had in fact already been developed at greater length by William Milligan in his book *The Resurrection of Our Lord*.[7] Much is made by Milligan of the assertion of Genesis 4:10 that the voice of Abel's blood cried to God from the ground, which is taken up in Hebrews 12:24 where it is declared that the sprinkled blood of Jesus "speaks more graciously than the blood of Abel." "What speaks," Milligan contends, "must either be, or must be thought of as being, alive."[8] This, however, is an inadmissible interpretation to impose on what is so clearly a figure of speech. By the same method it could equally well be argued that the affirmation of Hebrews 11:5, that through faith Abel, though dead, is still speaking, implies that Abel must be alive, despite the assertion that he is dead, because otherwise he could not still be speaking. This would manifestly be nonsensical. The point in 12:24 is that the blood of Abel, that is, his murder by the hand of his brother, cried out to a just God for vengeance, whereas the blood of Christ, willingly shed on the cross, speaks or assures us of pardon and reconciliation.

Further, it is unrealistic to speak of the shedding of a victim's blood as denoting the liberation of life which is thereby made available for the benefit of

---

5. B. F. Westcott, *The Epistle to the Hebrews* (London, 1889), Additional Note on 9:12, "On the use of the term 'Blood' in the Epistle" (pp. 293ff.).
6. B. F. Westcott, *The Epistles of St. John* (London, 1883), Additional Note on 1 John 1:7, "The Idea of Christ's Blood in the New Testament" (pp. 34ff., 2nd edn., 1886).
7. W. Milligan, *The Resurrection of Our Lord* (London, 1881).
8. *Ibid.*, p. 278.

others—and it is *biblically* unrealistic, since throughout Scripture the shedding of blood in death means not the *release* of life but the *loss* of life.[9] Nor will it do to explain, as Milligan does, that such blood is not physically but "ideally" alive, for mystical exegesis of this kind is confusing rather than enlightening. On the basis of this hypothesis, moreover, the conclusion might logically be drawn that, as the life of Christ was released and made available to the world in the act of his blood-shedding on the cross, there is no proper necessity for his resurrection from the dead: the regenerating life is there in the outpoured blood; what need is there for a risen and living Redeemer in addition to this? In the New Testament, however, it is not the life supposedly inherent in the outpoured blood, but the life of the *risen* Lord which, through the operation of the Holy Spirit, is the dynamic principle of the revitalization of the Christian believer. This is what Paul calls "the power of his resurrection" (Phil. 3:10).

An important consideration which should not be left out of account is that Scripture does not speak of the blood as life in isolation from the flesh: it is *the life of the flesh;* that is to say, it is properly described as the life only so long as it belongs to the *living* person. To describe it as life in separation from the living being is an unreasonable straining of the sense assigned to the term. "To shed blood," as Johannes Behm asserts, "is to destroy the bearer of life and therefore life itself." "Blood" therefore "signifies 'outpoured blood', 'violently destroyed life', 'death', or 'murder.'" This is the sense in which it used of the slaying of Jesus in Matthew 27:4, 24 and Acts 5:28, and of the prophets, saints, and witnesses of Jesus in Matthew 23:30, 35; Luke 11:50f.; Revelation 16:6; 17:6; 18:24; and 19:2. "The interest of the New Testament," says Behm, "is not in the material blood of Christ, but in his shed blood as the life violently taken from him. Like the cross, the 'blood of Christ' is simply another and even more graphic phrase for the death of Christ in its soteriological significance."[10] Similarly, F. J. Taylor writes that "the phrase 'the blood of Christ' . . . is a pictorial way of referring to the violent death upon the cross of shame voluntarily endured for men by Christ (Rom. 3:25; 5:9)."[11] That this equation Blood = Death is congenial to the mind of the writer of Hebrews is clearly demonstrated in 12:4, where he says (literally): "In your struggle against sin you have not yet resisted unto blood." No one disputes that "unto blood" here means "unto death" (cf. JB, "to the point of death"). It would be impossible to illustrate more plainly that the term "blood," when used in this manner, is synonymous with "death," and particularly death of a violent nature.

*   *   *   *   *

9. See Leon Morris, "The Biblical Use of the Term 'Blood,'" JTS, New Series, 3 (1952), pp. 216ff. A careful survey of the evidence leads Morris to the conclusion that in the Old Testament the term "blood" signifies life violently taken rather than the continued presence of life available for some new function, in short, death rather than life," even where the reference is to atonement, and that "it seems tolerably certain that in both Old and New Testaments the blood signifies essentially the death."
10. J. Behm, *loc. cit.*, pp. 173, 174.
11. F. J. Taylor, "Blood," *A Theological Word Book of the Bible,* ed. by Alan Richardson (London, 1950).

The view that it is in heaven, rather than on earth, that our High Priest offers the sacrifice of himself was propounded in the seventeenth century by the Socinians on the basis of their own characteristic interpretation of 9:12–14. There is no mention here, they argued, of the offering of Christ's blood or of the cross, and from this they concluded that the self-oblation of Christ of which our author speaks takes place, not on earth, but in the heavenly sanctuary. To this John Owen objects that it was precisely in the offering of his blood that Christ offered himself, and that to suggest that the sacrifice of Christ took place or takes place in heaven "utterly overthrows the whole nature of his sacrifice," and, furthermore, that "our redemption is everywhere constantly in the Scripture assigned unto the blood of Christ and that alone" (see Eph. 1:7; Col. 1:14; 1 Pet. 1:18f.; Rev. 5:9). Nowhere, as Owen points out, is the appearance of Christ in heaven called his sacrifice or offering of himself. The Socinian construction destroys the analogy of the tabernacle ceremonial, in accordance with which the sacrifice at the altar *preceded* the high priest's entry into the holy of holies, and undermines the incarnation's primary purpose, the substitutionary atonement accomplished at Calvary; and it also does violence to the text, which declares that it was *after* he had secured (εὑράμενος, aorist) our eternal redemption, and *through* or by virtue of (διά) his own blood, that he entered into the heavenly sanctuary (Heb. 9:12).

Delitzsch, in company with a number of other German scholars, understands the offering spoken of in 9:25 to mean an offering in the sanctuary above, but only in the sense of Christ's presentation of himself on our behalf in heaven, and without in any way wishing to bypass the cross or minimize the centrality of its significance for our redemption. But this interpretation is based on a misunderstanding of the passage. The offering mentioned in verse 25 is clearly connected with the notion of suffering, and is therefore a reference to the cross on earth and the suffering of Christ there, which cannot be repeated. In 9:24–28 our author speaks, in fact, of three different "appearings" of Christ: in verse 24 he speaks of Christ's present appearing "in the presence of God on our behalf"; in verse 26, of his past appearing "once for all at the end of the age to put away sin by the sacrifice of himself"; and in verse 28, of his future appearing, "not to deal with sin but to save those who are eagerly waiting for him."[12] His sacrifice of himself for sins belongs, as our author repeatedly emphasizes, to his first appearing when he came to earth in order that, as the incarnate Son, through death he might deliver us from the bondage of sin (2:14f.).

Another view, associated in the main with "catholic" scholarship, is that in the heavenly sanctuary a perpetual sacrificial offering by Christ of himself takes place. It is a view which is commonly linked with a particular doctrine of eucharistic sacrifice taking place simultaneously here on earth. Hebrews 8:3 (on which see commentary above) is cited in support of the argument that if Christ is

---

12. A different verb is used for each of the three "appearings." In verse 24 ἐμφανισθῆναι is, appropriately, virtually a technical term for the official presentation of oneself in order to report on a commission accepted and completed. In verse 26 πεφανέρωται is descriptive of the Son's manifestation to men through the incarnation. And in verse 28 ὀφθήσεται seems to stress the visible character of his appearance to men for the second time.

not offering sacrifice he cannot fulfil the priestly function, and that therefore his role in heaven must be that of a constantly sacrificing priest. Because of the emphatic teaching of the New Testament, and not least the Epistle to the Hebrews, regarding the final, once-for-all character of Christ's atoning sacrifice on the cross, it is hardly open to anyone to suggest that in heaven he offers an atoning sacrifice other than that which he offered on the cross; consequently, the explanation is proposed that it is a perpetual offering of this same sacrifice that takes place in the heavenly sanctuary.

The concept, however, is much confused. Not only are the suffering and death of the cross unrepeatable, but they are also unprolongable. Christ lives to suffer and die no more. Therefore what is conceived of as a self-offering in heaven cannot be the same thing as the self-offering on earth. The notion of the presentation of a *fait accompli*, apart from being biblically questionable, would hardly meet the sacerdotal requirements of this theory. Rightly understood, it is the *efficacy* of the one offering made at Calvary, not the offering itself, which is perpetual. But the concept of the offering of an atoning sacrifice in the heavenly sanctuary would seem to a considerable degree to be dictated by an *a priori* notion of the eucharist as, so to speak, an extension of Calvary in our earthly sanctuaries and a means of uniting the worshippers with Christ and his offering. The Roman Catholic sacrifice of the altar, though bloodless, is seen as one, sacramentally, with the sacrifice of the cross. The immolation of the sacred victim takes place not so much again and again (though phenomenally this would seem to be so) as perpetually, and corresponds to and is simultaneous with the sacrifice continuously being offered in heaven. Christ, apparently, has been cast in the part of a eucharistic priest sacrificing in the sanctuary above.

Although the doctrine of eucharistic sacrifice is not recent, the concept of Christ's continuous sacerdotal self-offering in the heavenly sanctuary seems to have been developed only in modern times. Thomas Aquinas, for example, makes a precise distinction between the earthly offering of the sacrifice of Christ and its heavenly consummation, between the event of the sacrifice and the effect of the sacrifice. Of the ceremonial on the Day of Atonement he remarks that "it is noteworthy that the goat and the calf were slain, not in the holy of holies, but outside," and declares that "likewise Christ has entered into the holy of holies, that is, into heaven, furnishing a way of entry for us by the power of his own blood which he shed for us here on earth." Insisting that "the passion and death of Christ are never to be repeated," he also affirms that "the efficacy of his sacrifice remains for ever."[13] Aquinas defends the description of the eucharist as a sacrifice by invoking the Augustinian principle that the images of things are called by the names of the things of which they are the images: "the celebration of this sacrament," he says, "is an image representing Christ's suffering, which is his true sacrifice; accordingly the celebration of this sacrament is called Christ's sacrifice." And on this same basis it is equally true "that Christ was sacrificed even in the figures of the Old Testament"; hence the declaration of the New, that he is "the Lamb slain from the foundation of the world."[14] But the notion of a perpetual sacerdotal self-offering by Christ in heaven is unknown to Aquinas.

13. Thomas Aquinas, *Summa Theologiae* 3a.22.5.
14. *Summa Theologiae* 3a.83.1.

This is evident from the quotation just given, for it would be impossible, with reference to the Old Testament figures, to imagine a self-sacrifice in the heavenly sanctuary when Christ had not only not yet entered the heavenly sanctuary as high priest but also had not yet offered up himself on earth; and it is also evident from the comments of Aquinas on 9:24, where he makes no attempt to advocate any such opinion. "The Apostle," he says, "is alluding to the ritual of the old law, according to which the high priest, when he entered the holy of holies, stood before the mercy seat in order that he might pray for the people; so also Christ entered into heaven, in so far as he is man, in order that he might be the advocate before God for our salvation."

Early in the sixteenth century, it is true, Jacques Lefèvre d'Etaples speaks of a perpetual self-offering of Christ in the heavenly sanctuary, when commenting on 9:24ff.: "After once entering into the holy of holies above, he continues in the presence of God offering himself without intermission for all who are to be saved even to the end of the world." At first sight, this seems like a departure from the doctrine of Aquinas, but in fact in his exposition of 7:26ff. Lefèvre propounds a view entirely in harmony with that of Aquinas. Stressing that it was by *one* offering that Christ made satisfaction for the sins of the whole world, an offering "more powerful than the innumerable victims offered with endless repetition" under the former dispensation, he affirms that "those things which are performed daily in the ministry of his priesthood [that is, in the observance of the eucharist] are not repetitions of his offering but rather the remembrance and recollection [*memoria ac recordatio*] of that one same victim who was offered once only," in conformity with the command, "Do this in remembrance of me." This indicates an agreement between Lefèvre and Aquinas regarding the perpetual virtue and efficacy of Christ's one sacrifice offered not in heaven but on earth, and consequently the self-offering in heaven spoken of in the former quotation must be taken to mean Christ's *presentation* of himself in the presence-chamber of the sanctuary above as our advocate and intercessor.

It is worthy of remark that in the Roman Catholic position officially formulated at the Council of Trent in the mid-sixteenth century no doctrine of a continuous high-priestly offering in the heavenly sanctuary is propounded. The Tridentine fathers, in fact, do no more than mention the heavenly session of Christ, contending that his presence at the right hand of the Father is not repugnant to the belief that he is "truly, really, and substantially" present in the sacrament.[15] The perpetuity of Christ's priesthood is seen as achieved in the sacrament which he instituted and bequeathed to the church as "a visible sacrifice, such as the nature of man requires, whereby that bloody sacrifice, once to be accomplished on the cross, might be represented and its memory remain even to the end of the world."[16] The Catechism of the Council of Trent adds nothing to this teaching. Officially, then, Roman Catholicism envisages the continuing priesthood of the glorified Christ as finding its sacerdotal fulfilment in the daily offering on earth of the sacrifice of the mass, which is regarded as one with that of Calvary.

In the controversy between John Jewel and Thomas Harding shortly after

15. Decree on the Sacrament of the Holy Eucharist, Session XIII.i.
16. Doctrine of the Sacrifice of the Mass, Session XXII.i.

the conclusion of the Council of Trent, Harding professed to maintain the precarious position that "Christ offered and sacrificed his body and blood twice: first, in that holy supper unbloodily, . . . and afterward on the cross, with shedding of his blood"; and he also postulated a third offering which took place in heaven simultaneously with the offering on the cross, thereby teaching the offering of the sacrifice in heaven even before the entry of Christ into the heavenly sanctuary, though thereafter it is explained as continuing forever. "At the very same instant of time," he says, "we must understand that Christ offered himself in heaven invisibly (as concerning man) in the sight of his heavenly Father, and that from that time forward that oblation of Christ in heaven was never intermitted, but continueth always for our atonement with God, and shall without ceasing endure unto the end of the world." The doctrine of the perpetual offering of sacrifice in the heavenly sanctuary had in fact been advocated unsuccessfully by some of the delegates at the Council of Trent and is reflected in these sentiments expressed by Harding. But the day for it to be fully developed was not yet. Meanwhile Harding, when pressed by Jewel, goes on to explain that by the continually enduring oblation of Christ in heaven "we understand the virtue of his oblation on the cross ever enduring, and not the oblation itself with renewing of pain and sufferance continued." As, moreover, he declares that on earth "we do perpetually celebrate this oblation and sacrifice of Christ's very body and blood in the mass, in remembrance of him, commanded so to do until his coming," it would appear that his position is not radically different from that of Aquinas. His language, however, contains the seeds of a quite different line of speculation.[17]

Some years later the notable Roman Catholic scholar Robert Bellarmine (1542–1621) asserted that the concept of Christ's everlasting priesthood demanded that he should always be offering sacrifice. Thus he writes, with reference to 7:27 (9:25f.): "When Paul says that there was no necessity for Christ to offer himself frequently he is obviously speaking of the bloody oblation, which was fully sufficient, indeed of infinite cost and worth. . . . With respect, however, to the eternal priesthood of Christ, it is necessary that he should frequently offer, by himself or by his ministers, not indeed in a bloody manner, but in some other manner."[18] In support of this opinion he cites 8:3, from which, he argues, it necessarily follows that "Christ is not a high priest for ever unless he offers something assiduously" and that "it is not enough that he once offered himself in a bloody manner." How, then, does he continuously offer himself? "Without doubt," Bellarmine answers, "in the most blessed eucharist," the sacrament which he instituted and now celebrates daily by his ministers.[19] Within this same perspective comes Christ's heavenly intercession, for it is explained as taking place in association with the eucharistic sacrifice, "which is continually offered by Christ to God through human ministry."[20] Here, once again, the

17. John Jewel, *Works* (Cambridge, 1847), pp. 717, 718f.
18. Robert Bellarmine, *De Missa* I.vi.
19. Bellarmine, *De Sacramento Eucharistiae* VI.xvi.
20. Bellarmine, *De Missa* I.vi.

notion of a perpetual offering of sacrifice by Christ is conceived in terms of eucharistic offering on earth rather than self-immolation in heaven.

* * * * *

The Socinians, as has already been remarked, taught that Christ's high-priestly function, including his offering of himself, had its commencement not on earth but on his entry into the heavenly sanctuary. Teaching very much to the same effect has become current in our day, though presumably its advocates otherwise have little if any sympathy for the distinctive opinions of Socinianism. At the beginning of this century, for example, Charles Gore wrote that in the sacrificial ritual of the Day of Atonement "the moment of offering and of atonement was not the moment of the slaying of the victim, but that of the entrance of the high priest with the blood of the victims into the most holy place to sprinkle it upon the mercy seat"; and he argued accordingly that "in the Epistle to the Hebrews all that goes before the ascension is the preparation of Christ for His priestly work," that "it is at His entrance into heaven, and not upon the cross, that He accomplishes His atonement for us," and that "his work as high priest, which begins with His entrance into heaven, is perpetual."[21] The Englishman Gore was, apparently, to some degree indebted to the Scottish scholar A. B. Davidson for these views, though it is unlikely that Davidson would have found himself in agreement with the manner in which they were developed, in particular eucharistically, by Gore. In his commentary on the Epistle to the Hebrews Davidson had declared that it was certain "that all the Son's priestly acts in heaven belong to the sphere of his Melchizedek priesthood" and that it was doubtful "if the Epistle anywhere regards the Son's death considered merely in itself as a priestly act." It is the Son's entry into heaven, he says, which "is the culminating point of His atoning sacrifice—is strictly the atoning point itself." At the same time, however, he insists that "the idea that in any sense He repeats the offering of himself, or that He continues it, is wholly absent from the Epistle."[22]

This line of interpretation, which, in combination with the doctrine of eucharistic sacrifice, has become characteristic of much contemporary Anglo-Catholic theology, was elaborated and systematized by F. C. N. Hicks in his book *The Fullness of Sacrifice*. Hicks is severely critical of "the habit of interpreting the Cross as the ultimate Christian altar."[23] Indeed, he maintains that the world which the author of our epistle and the other writers of the New Testament had in mind was one "in which such an error as the equating of sacrifice with death would have been inconceivable." "The rule is," he contends, "that the work of the priest, as priest, does not begin until after the death" of the victim that is offered up. In his view, then, "the Cross is not itself the Sacrifice," though it has

21. Charles Gore, *The Body of Christ* (London, 1901), pp. 252, 253.
22. A. B. Davidson, *The Epistle to the Hebrews* (Edinburgh, 1882), pp. 150, 151, 153; cf. also pp. 196ff.
23. F. C. N. Hicks, *The Fullness of Sacrifice* (London, 1930; 3rd edn. 1946), p. 235.

its place in the sacrificial action and sequence; and it is not until the entry into the heavenly sanctuary that the effective work of sacrifice is performed. Following the lead given by Milligan and Westcott, Hicks postulates the identification of the blood that is shed with the life of the victim (released and made available in the act of blood-shedding) and affirms that "the blood, in fact, needs to be dissociated from the idea of death," indeed deplores "the fatal identification between sacrifice and death."[24]

This disjunction of blood-shedding from the notion of death is fundamental to Hicks' argument, though, as we have seen, it is consonant with the usage neither of the Epistle to the Hebrews nor of the rest of Scripture. It is also strangely at variance with the doctrine of the Book of Common Prayer of the Church of England, of which Hicks was a bishop, for the Prayer Book speaks plainly of "the sacrifice of Christ's death," of the Lord's Supper as "a sacrament of our redemption by Christ's death," and of the Father's merciful gift of his "only Son Jesus Christ to suffer death upon the cross for our redemption," where, "by his one oblation of himself once offered" he made "a full, perfect, and sufficient sacrifice for the sins of the whole world." Certainly, it is by the precious blood of Christ that we have been redeemed, but the blood is "like that of a lamb without blemish or spot" (1 Pet. 1:18f.); that is to say, the focus is in reality on the act of blood-shedding which took place when Christ as the pure and innocent victim died for our sins on the cross. The argument that the New Testament writers (who, Hicks advises us, "know their subject") stress the virtue of the blood rather than of the death of Christ, on the supposition that blood and death mean two different things, cannot reasonably be sustained, as the two examples which follow demonstrate. First, when Paul asserts in Romans 5:9 that "we are justified by his blood," this can hardly imply, as Hicks wishes, a distinction between the death of Christ as backward-looking and the blood of Christ (equated with life) as forward-looking, for, as Paul says immediately after, we who are now reconciled to God were so reconciled by the *death* of Christ; and, as justification and reconciliation belong together as the consequence of the redeeming work of our High Priest, to be justified by Christ's blood and to be reconciled to God by his death both speak, harmoniously, of the one saving event of the cross and its significance. Second, to take an example from our epistle, in 9:16–18—"where a will ($\delta\iota\alpha\theta\eta\varkappa\eta$) is involved, the *death* of the one who made it must be established.... Hence even the first covenant ($\delta\iota\alpha\theta\eta\varkappa\eta$) was not ratified without *blood*"—there is a clear identification between death and blood.

Like Bengel, Hicks postulates a theologically significant distinction between the flesh of Christ and the blood of Christ—a distinction that is produced by emphasizing the copula *and* in places such as John 6:53, "Unless you eat the flesh of the Son of man *and* drink his blood... ," and 1 Corinthians 11:26, "as often as you eat this bread *and* drink the cup...." But, as we have shown above in connection with the former of these passages, eating Christ's flesh and drinking his blood belong together in the one response of the sinner who comes in faith to

24. *Ibid.*, pp. 241, 240, 242f.

Christ. So also in the words of the institution of the eucharist the eating of the bread and the drinking of the wine testify unitedly, as a single act, to the redeeming death of Christ, the benefits of which are appropriated by the believer. Hence the Apostle completes his account by admonishing the Corinthian Christians that every time they eat the sacramental bread and drink the sacramental wine they "proclaim the Lord's *death* until he comes." The wine (blood), equally and in union with the bread (flesh), proclaims the *death* of Christ by which our redemption has been purchased. The redemptive efficacy of the death of Christ is identical with the redemptive efficacy of his blood. Both belong to and take their significance from the single event of the cross. The specific purpose of the incarnation, our author affirms, was that "by the grace of God he might taste *death* for every one" (2:9).

If it is only with his entry into heaven that Christ's priestly activity begins, it undoubtedly follows that there is a necessity for priestly sacrifice to be offered there. Though (as we have already mentioned) the doctrine of the perpetual offering of sacrifice in the sanctuary above was advocated by some in the sixteenth century, without, however, gaining official sanction, it was not till the next century that it was fully formulated. While the roots of the position of Hicks and other like-minded Anglican scholars may be traced back to this earlier current of Roman Catholic thought, the theory they developed was marked by a measure of restraint and moderation not apparent in the prototype. The French Roman Catholic scholar Louis Thomassin (1619–1696), for example, held that the sacrifice of the cross was not only once offered but is also continuously offered, and that it was only after his resurrection that Christ, on entering the heavenly sanctuary, specifically assumed the dignity and office of high priest. He propounded an identity between the cross below and the sacrifice above, arguing that "Christ's own abode and dwelling place is heaven and the sacrifice itself is also heavenly, because, although the victim is slain on earth, it is slain here in order that it may be placed there on its proper altar, and may be offered there for an eternal burnt offering." Accordingly, the One who in glorified manhood stands before the Father in heaven "does not cease to offer a solemn sacrifice and to plead and to offer himself, and without intermission to sacrifice a burnt offering and a perpetual sacrifice."[25]

Language of this kind seems, unfortunately, to be governed by preconceptions which are incompatible with the perspective of the New Testament. Nowhere does our author, or any other canonical writer, teach that the incarnate victim "is slain here in order that it may be placed there on its proper altar" and "offered there for an eternal burnt offering." Christ entered heaven not as victim but as victor. His entry is his exaltation: his humiliation, of which the cross was the deepest expression, is now behind him (Phil. 2:8f.). "We know," says Paul, "that Christ being raised from the dead will never die again; death no longer has dominion over him" (Rom. 6:9). In any case, there was no altar in the holy of holies and consequently never any suggestion that the victim slain outside at the

---

25. Louis Thomassin, *Theological Dogmas* X.x.9; xi.13; xii.3. See Darwell Stone, *A History of the Doctrine of the Holy Eucharist*, II (London, 1909), pp. 382ff.

altar of sacrifice was then carried in and sacrificed as a burnt offering in that inner sanctuary. The earthly sanctuary, which is the shadow of the heavenly reality, is defined in Hebrews 9:1ff. in terms of the tent: the outer courtyard with its altar of sacrifice corresponds to the reality of the cross, placed here on earth, and consequently has no counterpart above. The notion, then, of the repetition or extension of Christ's atoning sacrifice on an altar which is imagined to belong to the heavenly sanctuary is inadmissible. Extravagant language of this sort probably intends less than it says, but even so it is seriously misleading insofar as it shifts the focus of the atoning sacrifice from the earthly to the heavenly scene.

This view of the offering of the atoning sacrifice in heaven, conjoined with the concept of its offering on earth in the eucharist, was embraced, but less extremely expressed, by the adherents of the Tractarian Movement in the nineteenth century. Thus in 1850, the year before he abandoned the Church of England for the Church of Rome, Henry Edward Manning wrote that "Christ truly offers Himself for us perpetually both in heaven and earth," that "His intercession is the perpetual presenting of His own sacrifice, that is, of Himself, bearing the wounds of His Passion," and that, whether in heaven or on earth, "it is but one act still, one priesthood, and one sacrifice," since in heaven Christ offers himself "in visible presence" and on earth "by his ministering priesthood... in the Sacrament of His Body and Blood."[26] And in the middle of the present century A. G. Hebert formulated the view which may be taken as characteristic of contemporary Anglo-Catholic theology in the following terms:

> The idea that the death of the victim was the centre of sacrifice is simply false. The animal was killed not in order that its life might be destroyed (for 'the blood is the life'), but that the life offered in death might become available for the holy purposes of sacrifice... the Sacrifice which was enacted in time on Calvary... now is offered by Him at the heavenly altar.[27]

In certain Anglican circles, then, the opinions that the sacrificial blood speaks not of the death of the victim but of the release of his life for the world, and that the priestly work of Christ commences not on earth but only with his entry into the heavenly sanctuary, have won acceptance.

*   *   *   *   *

A more extreme development of the doctrine that Christ began to fulfil his priestly function only after his entry into heaven has recently come from the pen of a Roman Catholic writer, Walter Edward Brooks. Arguing from the assertion of Hebrews 7:16 that Christ "has become a priest by the power of an indestructible life" (κατὰ δύναμιν ζωῆς ἀκαταλύτου), Brooks maintains that Jesus "is eter-

26. H. E. Manning, *Sermons*, IV (London, 1850), pp. 223ff.
27. A. G. Hebert, "A Root of Difference and of Unity," in *Intercommunion*: A Report of the Theological Commission appointed by the Continuation Committee of the World Conference on Faith and Order together with a selection from the material presented to the Commission (London, 1952), pp. 239, 242.

nal priest from the moment of his resurrection-exaltation because he possesses from that moment a life that does not end." The following quotations indicate the main lines of his position:

> Since Jesus' priestly office is based on a life that cannot end and is exercised in the heavenly tent, it is inconceivable that his sacrifice would have been offered before the resurrection experience. For then he was not a priest, but now he is a priest forever and his sacrifice must correspond to his priesthood.... The death of the victim was essential but preparatory. At-one-ment through expiation was achieved by the manipulation of the blood. This was the saving event and on the Day of Atonement it took place within the holy of holies.... He enters in with his blood and presents himself to the Father. Drawing on the analogy of the Day of Atonement coupled with an accurate conception of Jewish sacrifice and the understanding that Christ's priesthood is not of this earth but only begins with the reception of the life that does not end, we are justified in seeing his sacrifice reach its climax in the holy of holies of the eternal tent.... Now to say this is not to say that the cross is unessential. However, it is to stress the fact that the priestly work of Christ begins only after the death and reaches its *terminus* in the heavenly sphere and that the act of offering there is perpetual. The cross is not the sacrifice. It is rather part of the preparation for the heavenly sacrificial ministry of our high priest and is thereby essential but not all-sufficient. It is not the altar on which the sacrifice of Jesus begins and ends.[28]

A closer examination of the teaching of the Epistle to the Hebrews will show, however, that these conclusions are not justified. In the first place, the KJV rendering of δύναμις ζωῆς ἀκαταλύτου as "the power of an endless life," which Brooks adopts, is not entirely satisfactory. It is more accurately translated by the RSV and the JB as "the power of an indestructible life" or, similarly, by the NEB as "the power of a life that cannot be destroyed." The reference is to a life not merely which, from a certain point onward, has no end, but also which has no beginning. This is clearly brought out earlier in the same chapter where the author, in comparing Christ with Melchizedek, says that he "has neither beginning of days nor end of life" (7:3). His life is indestructible because it is the ever continuing life of the Son of God (7:24f.); and while it is true that the priestly office of Christ is specifically associated with the incarnate Son, who by the incarnation is capacitated to die, and to die as Man for man, yet, as Chalcedon insisted long since, he does not and cannot cease to be the eternal Son of God.

Second, to "make intercession," as our High Priest does in the heavenly sanctuary for "those who draw near to God through him" (7:25), is not the same thing as to offer up a victim in sacrifice. The place of sacrifice was outside the tent at the altar of sacrifice, to which, in the Epistle to the Hebrews and throughout the New Testament, the cross of Calvary corresponds. Moreover, as there was no altar of sacrifice within the earthly tent, it is wrong and inconsistent to

---

28. W. E. Brooks, "The Perpetuity of Christ's Sacrifice in the Epistle to the Hebrews," JBL, 89 (1970), pp. 208, 208f., 211, 212.

postulate the existence of such an altar in the sanctuary above. Nor is this conclusion shaken by the declaration of 8:3 that since every high priest is appointed to offer gifts and sacrifices, "it is necessary for this priest also to have something to offer." For one thing, the text does not say that he must have something which he can *perpetually* offer. For another, the verb "to be" is not included in the Greek text, though it is implied, and it has to be supplied in an English translation. One must decide, therefore, whether ὅθεν ἀναγκαῖον would better be rendered "therefore it *is* necessary" or "therefore it *was* necessary." Westcott accordingly comments: "It has been debated whether ἦν or ἐστίν should be supplied with ἀναγκαῖον. If the reference is to the offering of the cross, as seems to be required by the type and the context, then ἦν must be supplied." The tense of the verb προσενέγκη is also significant. If the author had intended to say that it *is* necessary for Christ to have something *to offer continuously* the present rather than the aorist would have been appropriate to his purpose, προσφέρη rather than προσενέγκη. But the aorist προσενέγκη weighs against the notion of a perpetual offering, and all the more so when it is considered in association with the present infinitive προσφέρειν used in the earlier part of the verse of the constantly repeated offering of the old-style high priests. To quote Westcott again: "This offering is described as made once for all (προσενέγκη contrasted with προσφέρη ix.25; comp. c.vii.27). The one sufficient offering was made by Christ as the condition of entrance into the sanctuary *through his own blood* (c.ix.12). On this his intercession is based. That intercession knows no end or interruption; and therefore no second offering is required, as in the case of the Levitical High-priest, who made a fresh offering every year in order that he might again enter and repeat the intercession which had been made before."[29] The fact is, as Wilfrid Stott has pointed out, that when referring to the work of the Aaronic high priest the author of our epistle "invariably uses the present tense, showing its continuous character" (5:1, 3; 8:3a, 4; 9:7; 10:1, 2, 8), whereas, "in contrast with this, when he speaks of Christ's offering he invariably uses the aorist" (8:3b; 9:14, 28; 10:12).[30]

Third, that the offering of himself on the cross was the focal and consummating moment of the high-priestly work of Christ in its sacrificial aspect is plainly the teaching of 2:14ff., where the purpose of the incarnation is defined as follows: "so that through death he might break the power of . . . the devil, and might liberate those who, through fear of death, had all their lifetime been in servitude" (NEB); or again, as reflected by another facet of the prism of redemption, "so that he might become a merciful and faithful high priest in the service of God, to make propitiation for the sins of the people." His mercy or compassion is explained in terms of his suffering: "because he himself has suffered and been tempted, he is able to help those who are tempted" (cf. 4:15f.); and his faithfulness is explained in terms of his obedience, which of course is inseparable from his suffering (cf. 3:1ff.; 5:8ff.; 10:7ff.). The summit both of his obedience

29. See note 1, p. 291 above.
30. Wilfrid Stott, "The Conception of 'Offering' in the Epistle to the Hebrews," NTS, 9 (1962), p. 65.

and of his suffering was the cross (12:2; Phil. 2:8). The cross, far from being isolated from or merely preparatory to Christ's priestly work, is the very center and heart of that work. It was when, or after, he had made purification for sins (καθαρισμὸν τῶν ἁμαρτιῶν ποιησάμενος, another aorist!) that he sat down at the right hand of the Majesty on high (Heb. 1:3). So, too, 6:20 declares that Jesus has entered the heavenly holy of holies "as a forerunner on our behalf, *having become* (γενόμενος) a high priest for ever after the order of Melchizedek," the aorist participle indicating that it was prior to his entry into heaven that he became our high priest.

This high priesthood belongs to the incarnate Christ in humiliation as well as in glorification, but always the central focus is on Calvary as the culmination of his obedience and suffering and as the place of his perfect and eternally availing sacrifice. Our author's language is marked by precision and consistency throughout the epistle. Thus, to give some further examples, in 9:12 he asserts that Christ entered once for all into the sanctuary above *after* he had secured (εὑράμενος) our eternal redemption. This is the proper connotation of the aorist participle, and it is regrettable that it is not brought out in the RSV ("thus securing...") or the NEB ("and secured..."); though the KJV ("having obtained...") and Phillips and the JB ("having won...") render it accurately. Again, 9:28 assures us that Christ, "having been offered once (ἅπαξ προσενεχθείς, another aorist!) to bear the sins of many" at his first advent, "will appear a second time, not to deal with sin but to save those who are eagerly waiting for him." And yet another aorist participle, in 10:12—"when he had offered for all time a single sacrifice for sins (μίαν ὑπὲρ ἁμαρτιῶν προσενέγκας θυσίαν εἰς τὸ διηνεκές) he sat down at the right hand of God" (cf. 1:3)—conveys the same emphasis on the finality and the pastness of the unique sacrifice of Calvary. Nowhere is there any mention of a sacrifice that is prolonged in some manner or continuously offered in the heavenly sanctuary.

The teaching of our epistle on this important theme has been well explained by F. F. Bruce, who writes as follows (on Heb. 9:12):

> Aaron certainly carried the sacrificial blood into the holy of holies, but our author deliberately avoids saying that Christ carried His own blood into the heavenly sanctuary. Even as a symbolic expression this is open to objection. There have been expositors who, pressing the analogy of the Day of Atonement beyond the limits observed by our author, have argued that the expiatory work of Christ was not completed on the cross—not completed, indeed, until He ascended from earth and "made atonement 'for us' in the heavenly holy of holies by the presentation of His efficacious blood". But while it was necessary under the old covenant for the sacrificial blood first to be shed in the court and then to be brought into the holy of holies, no such division of our Lord's sacrifice into two phases is envisaged under the new covenant. When upon the cross He offered up His life to God as a sacrifice for His people's sin, He accomplished in reality what Aaron and his successors performed in type by the twofold act of slaying the victim and presenting its blood in the holy of holies. The title of the Anglican Article XXXI speaks rightly "of the one oblation of Christ finished upon the cross."

And Oscar Cullmann very properly warns that "the danger of falling back to the level of Old Testament priesthood arises when the high priest must always present the sacrifice anew":

> Christian worship [he continues] in the light of that "one time" which means "once for all time" is possible only when even the slightest temptation to "reproduce" that central event itself is avoided. Instead, the event must be allowed to remain the divine act of the past time where God the Lord of time placed it—at that exact historical moment in the third decade of our chronology. It is the saving consequences of that atoning act, not the act itself, which become a present event in our worship. The Lord present in worship is the exalted *Kyrios* of the Church and the world, raised to the right hand of God. He is the risen Lord who continues his mediating work on the basis of his unique, completed work of atonement.[31]

Finally, our epistle describes the glorified Savior who has entered the tabernacle above in two ways: (1) as seated and (2) as interceding. The session of Christ is first mentioned in the opening section, at 1:3, and it recurs at 8:1, 10:12, and 12:2. To speak of him as being seated symbolizes not only his sovereign enthronement but also the completion of the redemptive work he had come to earth to perform (cf. Mk. 10:45: "The Son of man came . . . to give his life as a ransom for many"); and in particular it is important to notice that such language is incompatible with the notion that Christ is perpetually offering priestly sacrifice in heaven—otherwise there would be no point in the contrast propounded in Hebrews 10:11f. between the priests of the old dispensation daily *standing* as they repeatedly offer the same sacrifices and Christ, our unique High Priest, *seated* in glory, his one all-sufficient sacrifice for sins now a thing of the past. It is not surprising, therefore, that those who advocate the notion of the offering of sacrifice in the heavenly sanctuary customarily link it with Christ's heavenly intercession, as though this intercession were the same thing as his constant pleading by means of the continuous offering of his sacrifice in the tabernacle above. This is a notion, however, which is read into rather than out of the Epistle to the Hebrews. Christ's intercession, mentioned only as such in 7:25, is undoubtedly identical with what 9:24 speaks of as his appearing in the presence of God on our behalf. The complete acceptance of his sacrifice on the cross for the sins of mankind is signified by the fact of his exaltation; and his acceptance means also the acceptance of all those who by faith are one with him. Hence the confidence with which we are invited to draw near, on the basis of his atonement, to the throne of grace (4:16; 10:19ff.).

Wilfrid Stott draws attention to 2 Samuel 7, a passage quoted in Hebrews 1:5 and probably echoed in 3:6, as an example of the combination of session with intercession—in fact "the only passage in the Scriptures where prayer is spoken of with the posture of sitting," the picture being that "of David as king seated before Jehovah and claiming that the Covenant which has been promised shall be fulfilled." Relating this to the imagery of our epistle, he concludes: "Thus it would seem that the picture in the writer's mind is of a royal priest who is

---

31. O. Cullmann, *The Christology of the New Testament* (London, 1959), p. 99.

seated, as David was, before God, not pleading a sacrifice, but 'having accomplished' already the 'cleansing', mediated the New Covenant and now seated in royal state and claiming the fulfilment of the Covenant promises for his seed."[32] Christ's intercessory activity, as Cullmann says, "is always effective because of his once-for-all work" and "is a genuine high priestly act."[33]

The force and clarity with which our author expresses himself are unmistakable. Christ, he insists, "has no need, like those high priests, to offer sacrifices daily . . . ; he did this once for all when he offered up himself" (7:27). Again: By the will of the Father "we have been sanctified through the offering of the body of Jesus Christ once for all. . . . For by a single offering he has perfected for all time those who are sanctified. . . . 'I will remember their sins and their misdeeds no more'. Where there is forgiveness of these, *there is no longer any offering for sin*" (10:10, 14, 17, 18). How is it possible in the face of such affirmations to hold that the Epistle to the Hebrews does not teach in the most emphatic manner the all-sufficient finality of the cross of Christ as the altar of our eternal redemption?

* * * * *

It remains for us to examine rather more fully the nature and significance of our Lord's high-priestly activity in heaven. This will be considered under three headings, namely, representation, benediction, and intercession, all of which, however, are closely interrelated.

(1) *Representation*. "Christ," according to 9:24, "has entered into heaven itself, now to appear in the presence of God on our behalf." There in that sublime sanctuary which is the very presence-chamber of God the risen and glorified Savior presents himself, not to claim benefits for himself, for he is crowned with glory and honor (2:9), but as our Representative and Mediator to receive for us the eternal blessings which his atoning death has procured. Yet these blessings are not, so to speak, external to or apart from himself, for in presenting himself at the throne of grace he presents also those who through divine grace have been made one with him. It is the union of believers with Christ that ensures their acceptance before God. The royal favor with which he is received embraces at the same time those who are one with and in him. As Paul says, God "raised us up with him, and made us sit with him in the heavenly places in Christ Jesus" (Eph. 2:6). The Christian's whole and only status before God is *in Christ*. True and wonderful though this is, however, the sphere of the Christian's existence is still here on earth. He is still beset by temptations; he is hampered by weakness and frustrated by failings; he falls short of "the measure of the stature of the fulness of Christ" (Eph. 4:13); the perfection for which he longs is not yet. He needs a holiness not his own, made available to him by the Lamb of God who has made atonement for his sins and who now interposes himself as his representative in the heavenly sanctuary. And this is the representation which Christ fulfils as he appears in the presence of God for us.

32. W. Stott, *loc. cit.*, p. 67.
33. Cullmann, *op. cit.*, p. 102.

In the earthly sanctuary the levitical high priest entered into the holy of holies taking with him the blood of the victim that had been slain outside at the altar of sacrifice. In himself, this high priest had no more right of entry than did the people for whom he was acting, for he, like them, was a sinful man for whose sins, no less than for those of the people, atonement had to be made. Accordingly, the blood he carried into the holy of holies was not his own but the blood of the victim which had been offered up in his stead. Our great High Priest, however, being entirely without sin, had no need to take the blood of another into the sanctuary; nor did he need to present his own blood, for since the blood was the token of the life that had been offered up in sacrifice, and since he was both offerer and offering, he, the sinless and glorified incarnate Son, presents not his blood but *himself* in the heavenly sanctuary, into which he has the full and inalienable right of entry. This unique victim, unlike the victims of old, is not left outside, but in the power of his risen life he himself, and none other, has passed into the holy presence of God, where "he has gone as a forerunner on our behalf" (Heb. 6:20). It is he himself, in all the perfection of his, and our, exalted manhood, who now represents us there.

(2) Benediction. An important function of the royal high priest is to bestow the divine blessing upon the people of God. Thus we read in Leviticus 9:22f.: "Then Aaron lifted up his hands toward the people and blessed them; and he came down from offering the sin offering and the burnt offering and the peace offerings. And Moses and Aaron went into the tent of meeting; and when they came out they blessed the people, and the glory of the Lord appeared to all the people." And the form of the high-priestly blessing, which is simply the declaration of the blessing which comes from God, is given in Numbers 6:22ff.: "The Lord said to Moses, 'Say to Aaron and his sons, Thus you shall bless the people of Israel: you shall say to them, The Lord bless you and keep you: the Lord make his face to shine upon you, and be gracious to you: the Lord lift up his countenance upon you, and give you peace. So shall they put my name upon the people of Israel, and I will bless them.'" So also Melchizedek, priest of God Most High, blessed Abraham (Heb. 7:1, 7; Gen. 14:19), and in doing so he prefigured the blessing which was to flow from him who is our Melchizedek to all who through faith are the children of Abraham (cf. Gal. 3:29). Indeed, the blessing promised to the world through the seed of Abraham is, as Paul teaches, concentrated and fulfilled in the single person of Christ (Gal. 3:8, 16f.).

The blessing which our heavenly High Priest bestows from the true sanctuary above is made effective through the outpouring of his Holy Spirit upon all flesh. Hence the affirmation of Peter on the Day of Pentecost: "Being therefore exalted at the right hand of God, and having received from the Father the promise of the Holy Spirit, he has poured out this which you see and hear" (Acts 2:33). Through the blessing which the outpouring of the Holy Spirit guarantees to us our Redeemer exercises in our midst his threefold office of prophet, priest, and king. As prophet, he who is the Truth continues to teach us through the apostles whom he himself had taught, and to whom he had specifically promised that the Holy Spirit would teach them all things and bring to their remembrance all that he had said to them (Jn. 14:6, 26). Accordingly, in the apostolic doctrine of the New Testament we have the authentic doctrine of

Christ himself, and through these writings he does not cease to lead us, as our Prophet, into everlasting truth. The New Testament scriptures belong to the benediction of our exalted High Priest.

The central truth with which we are blessed thanks to the enlightening action of the Holy Spirit is the knowledge of the gospel of our Lord and Savior Jesus Christ. But the Spirit of Christ not only brings us face to face with evangelical truth, he also applies the saving work of Christ to our hearts and lives. Through the blessing of the Holy Spirit which Christ has poured out from heaven we are enabled to experience the regenerating power of God. The benefits of the Savior's atoning death are made a vital and transforming reality, so that we who, like the prodigal in the parable, are alienated from God by the rebellion of our sin are blessed by restoration to the family relationship, calling penitently and joyfully on God as our Father, as "the Spirit bears witness with our spirit that we are the children of God" (Rom. 8:14ff.).

So we experience the reconciling priestly work of Christ in our lives; and so also, by the operation of the same Holy Spirit, we surrender ourselves to his service as our king. It is the Holy Spirit who enables us to "sanctify Christ as Lord in our hearts" (1 Pet. 3:15), so that we may know daily the benediction of his sovereign rule in our lives. Our heavenly High Priest "is seated at the right hand of the throne of the Majesty in heaven" (Heb. 8:1); but the same crucified Jesus, whom God raised up and made both Lord and Christ, is at the same time, through the blessing of the outpoured Holy Spirit, enthroned in every believing heart (cf. Acts 2:36ff.). Thus the blessing of the prophetic, priestly, and kingly work of Christ becomes a dynamic reality in the experience of the Christian.

(3) *Intercession.* Because his priesthood is everlasting, Christ "is able for all time to save those who draw near to God through him, since he always lives to make intercession for them" (Heb. 7:24f.). Our Lord's intercession above is his continuing high-priestly work whereby, in conjunction with the work of the Holy Spirit in our midst, he achieves the divine purpose of "bringing many sons to glory" (2:10). It is, as we shall see, a most important and necessary work. "So great and glorious is the work of saving believers unto the utmost," John Owen comments, "that it is necessary that the Lord Christ should lead a mediatory life in heaven, for the perfecting and accomplishing of it. . . . It is generally acknowledged that sinners could not be saved without the death of Christ; but that believers could not be saved without the life of Christ following it, is not so much considered." The most eloquent symbols of the intercessory function of the high priest are found in the prescriptions for the sacerdotal garments which Aaron was to wear. In the shoulder-pieces of the ephod two onyx stones were set on which the names of the sons of Israel were engraved. These stones are designated "stones of remembrance," because Aaron bore "their names before the Lord upon his two shoulders for remembrance." And attached in front to the two shoulder-pieces of the ephod was the breastpiece in which were set twelve precious stones, in four rows of three, also engraved with the names of the twelve sons of Israel; so that Aaron bore "the names of the sons of Israel in the breastpiece of judgment upon his heart" when he went into the sanctuary, "to bring them to continual remembrance before the Lord" (Ex. 28:6ff.; 39:1ff.). Thus the people of God were carried by name into the divine presence, sup-

ported, as it were, in their weakness on the strong shoulders of their high priest, and bound closely to his loving and compassionate heart. Their high priest was their remembrancer.

He who is the Good Shepherd knows his own sheep by name (Jn. 10:3, 13). As High Priest he intercedes for them by name in the heavenly sanctuary, supporting them with his victorious strength and ceaselessly surrounding them with his love. In the hour of testing his help is always at hand (Heb. 2:18). Precisely because "we have not a high priest who is unable to sympathize with our weaknesses, but one who in every respect has been tempted as we are, yet without sinning," we are encouraged to "draw near with confidence to the throne of grace, that we may receive mercy and find grace to help in time of need" (4:15f.). In his hour of trial Stephen, filled with the Holy Spirit, sees the heavens opened and Jesus standing at God's right hand to support him in martyrdom and to welcome him into his glorious presence (Acts 7:55).

Our Lord's intercession on our behalf is always infallible in its effectiveness. This we see even during his earthly ministry, when, for example, he assures Simon Peter as the time of his testing approached: "I have prayed for you that your faith may not fail; and when you have turned again [as the Master's intercession ensures that he will] strengthen your brethren" (Lk. 22:31f.). What confidence it should give us, not only that our High Priest always intercedes for us, but also that the Father always hears the Son (Jn. 11:42)! And it is in the "high priestly prayer" of John 17 in particular that we have a glimpse of our Redeemer engaging in the sacred work of interceding with the Father for those who are his: "I am praying for them; I am not praying for the world but for those whom thou hast given me, for they are thine. . . . Holy Father, keep them in thy name, which thou hast given me, that they may be one even as we are one. . . . I do not pray that thou shouldest take them out of the world, but that thou shouldest keep them from the evil one. . . . Sanctify them in the truth; thy word is truth. . . . I do not pray for these only, but also for those who believe in me through their word, that they all may be one. . . . Father, I desire that they also, whom thou hast given me, may be with me where I am, to behold my glory which thou hast given me in thy love for me before the foundation of the world. . ." (Jn. 17:9, 11, 15, 17, 20, 24).

His intercession is our security. "Who will be the accuser of God's chosen ones?" Paul asks in Romans 8:33f. "Will it be God himself? No, he it is who pronounces acquittal. Who will be the judge to condemn? Will it be Christ—he who died, and, more than that, was raised from the dead—who is at God's right hand? No, he it is who pleads our cause" (NEB mg., that is, "intercedes for us," RSV). Obviously, then, nothing can possibly separate us from the love of God in Christ Jesus our Lord, nothing in the whole of creation—not tribulation, distress, persecution, hunger, nakedness, peril, sword, not even death (Rom. 8:35ff.). When Christians fall into sin, Jesus Christ is still their righteousness, for it is still in him, and not to the smallest degree in themselves, that they are justified before God. There in the heavenly sanctuary he intercedes as their advocate (paraclete). "If any man should sin," says John, writing to Christian believers, "remember that our advocate before the Father is Jesus Christ the righteous, the one who made personal atonement for our sins" (1 Jn. 2:1f. Phillips).

Moreover, our Lord's advocacy in heaven is reinforced, so to speak, by the advocacy of the Holy Spirit within us here on earth, in accordance with his promise that when he was glorified he would pray the Father, who would then send another advocate (paraclete) to be constantly with us, even the Spirit of truth (Jn. 14:16f.; cf. 7:39; 16:7). The sending of the Holy Spirit is a comprehensive blessing for which we are indebted to the intercession of Christ! And the Holy Spirit, who "bears witness with our spirit that we are children of God," inwardly "helps our weakness; for we do not know how to pray as we ought, but the Spirit himself intercedes for us with sighs too deep for words," and he does so, of course, in harmony with the will of God (Rom. 8:16, 26f.). Hence the apostolic injunction to "pray at all times in the Spirit" (Eph. 6:18). The intercession of the Holy Spirit in the temple of our bodies (1 Cor. 6:19) is united with the intercession of the Son in the sanctuary of heaven and brings the joy of heaven into every believing heart.

It follows that, since Christ is the sole Mediator between God and men (1 Tim. 2:5) and our perpetual Intercessor in the presence of God, there is no place for any other intercessor or mediator. To imagine that saints or angels can be influenced to intercede for us is not only a delusion; it is to cast doubt on the perfect adequacy of the intercession of Christ on our behalf and thus to deprive ourselves of the fulness of the security which is available to us only in Christ. Our Lord clearly taught that no man can come to the Father except by him (Jn. 14:6) and that our requests to God are to be made in his name (Jn. 14:13f.; 15:16; 16:23, 24, 26), precisely because there is no other name which avails and prevails with God (cf. Acts 4:12).

In considering the intercessory work of our heavenly High Priest, there is absolutely no place for the notion of any kind of "dualistic" situation, as though a well-disposed Son were attempting to persuade a hostile Father to regard us with favor. God is not divided, and there is always perfect harmony between Father and Son. The oneness in purpose and performance in the relationship between the Father and the Son was plainly and constantly taught by our Lord, as the following quotations show: "Truly, truly, I say to you, the Son can do nothing of his own accord, but only what he sees the Father doing; for whatever he does, that the Son does likewise. . . . I have come down from heaven not to do my own will, but the will of him who sent me. . . . And he who sent me is with me; he has not left me alone, for I always do what is pleasing to him. . . . I and the Father are one. . . . He who believes in me, believes not in me but in him who sent me. And he who sees me sees him who sent me. . . . Believe that I am in the Father and the Father in me" (Jn. 5:19; 6:38; 7:16; 8:29; 10:30; 12:44; 14:11). So also Paul asserts that the whole of our redemption, from beginning to end, is from God, since "God was in Christ reconciling the world to himself" (2 Cor. 5:18f.). And the author of our epistle places the words of Psalm 40, "Lo, I have come to do thy will, O God," on the lips of Christ, explaining that "by that will we have been sanctified through the offering of the body of Jesus Christ once for all" (10:7-10). The grace of God precedes and is the sole cause of our restoration: thus "God shows his love for us in that while we were yet sinners Christ died for us" (Rom. 5:8). Christ himself is the supreme manifestation of the love of God for us his creatures (1 Jn. 4:9f.).

The intercession of the Son, then, is in no sense a pleading with the Father to change his attitude toward us. Nor does the Father have to be reminded of the full redemption that he himself has provided for us in his Son—the very thought is preposterous! The presence in heaven of the Lamb bearing the marks of his passion is itself the perpetual guarantee of our acceptance with God, who gave his Son to be the propitiation for our sins. In ourselves, however, though we have the forgiveness of our sins through the blood of Jesus Christ and though we are united to him in love and trust, we are unworthy because Christ has not yet been fully formed within us (cf. Gal. 4:19) and we still sinfully fall short of the glory of God (cf. Rom. 3:23). This consideration explains our continuing need of the advocacy and intercession of him who alone is accounted worthy before God (cf. Rev. 5:1–10). It is in his worthiness that even now we rejoice in the blessings of the divine favor, for by the grace of God his merit has been reckoned to us as our merit, his heaven has become our heaven, and his eternal glory our eternal glory.

9:13, 14. *For if the sprinkling of defiled persons with the blood of goats and bulls and with the ashes of a heifer sanctifies for the purification of the flesh, how much more shall the blood of Christ, who through the eternal Spirit offered himself without blemish to God, purify your conscience from dead works to serve the living God.*

The theme of the infinite superiority of Christ's high-priestly sacrifice to the sacrifices of the levitical order is now further developed. We have already seen that the system which the coming of Christ rendered obsolete was characterized by the offering of sacrifices incapable of achieving the renovation of the sinner, and therefore constantly repeated, whereas the perfection of Christ's sacrifice means that it was offered once-for-all and is never to be repeated (7:23ff.). This implied what our author now states explicitly, namely, that, in contrast to the old ceremonial, which of itself was superficial and external (though faith in the reality to which as a type it pointed led to the appropriation of the promised covenant blessings awaiting their fulfilment in Christ), the work of the incarnate Son penetrated right to the heart of the matter: it was *inward,* not outward, *radical* instead of superficial, purifying *the conscience,* not just the flesh, and therefore fully and finally effective as a remedy for the sickness of mankind.

Our author alludes to two typical rites of the old order: first, *the sprinkling . . . with the blood of goats and bulls,* [1] which took place on the

---

1. The following instances of the sprinkling of persons with sacrificial blood may be mentioned: the sprinkling of the people with the blood of the covenant by Moses at Sinai (Ex. 24:8) and the sprinkling of Aaron and his sons by Moses with blood from the altar and with anointing oil for their consecration (Ex. 29:21; Lev. 8:30). No sprinkling of persons

annual Day of Atonement, when a bullock was sacrificed as a sin offering for the high priest and a goat as a sin offering for the people (see pp. 319f. above). The plural "goats and bulls" is to be explained by the yearly repetition of these sacrifices; or it may be, as F. F. Bruce suggests, that we have here a more general allusion to sacrifices additional to those offered on the Day of Atonement. Second, *the sprinkling with . . . the ashes of a heifer*, which was prescribed for the ceremonial cleansing of any person who had been in contact with a dead body (Num. 19). The latter rite involved the choice of an unblemished red heifer which had not labored under the yoke and which was slaughtered outside the camp. The priest dipped his finger in the heifer's blood and sprinkled the blood seven times in the direction of the tabernacle. After that, the carcass was completely burned in his presence, and as it was burning the priest threw cedar wood, hyssop or marjoram, and scarlet wool into the flames. The ashes of the heifer were gathered and kept outside the camp, where they were used in the preparation of "the water for impurity,"[2] that is, water to be ritually employed for the sprinkling of persons and objects contaminated through association with a dead body.

Various explanations have been offered regarding the symbolism of this particular ritual. Peter Lombard, for example, asserts (among other things) that the red heifer is the infirm flesh of Christ, since the female beast signifies fleshly infirmity and its red color the blood of his passion; that it was without blemish because the flesh of Christ was free from sin; that it had not been subjected to the yoke because Christ was not subjugated to sin, but in fact liberated those so subjugated; that its blood was sprinkled because Christ shed his blood for the remission of sins; and that the cedar wood, the hyssop, and the scarlet wool represent hope, faith, and charity. Owen writes: "Red is the colour of guilt, Isa. i.18, yet was there no spot or blemish in the heifer: so was the guilt of sin upon Christ, who in himself was absolutely pure and holy. No yoke had been

---

was involved, however, in the ritual of the Day of Atonement, which is the occasion we may assume was in our author's mind when he mentions the blood of goats and bulls. This consideration tells against the manner in which our version (RSV) has rendered the Greek at this point. If the Greek text is taken quite literally, then the sprinkling refers only to the ashes of the heifer and not to the blood of goats and bulls, the participle ῥαντίζουσα agreeing with the feminine singular noun σποδός as its antecedent, not with the neuter singular noun αἷμα. Nonetheless, it could well belong to both σποδός and αἷμα, being attracted, as is common in Greek, into agreement with the number and gender of the nearer of the two antecedents; if this is the case, our author must be understood as speaking of sprinkling with blood in a general sense. It seems preferable, however, to associate the sprinkling here only with the ashes of the heifer, and this is how it is understood in both the KJV ("if the blood of bulls and goats, and the ashes of a heifer sprinkling the unclean, sanctifieth . . .") and the NEB ("if the blood of goats and bulls and the sprinkled ashes of a heifer have power to hallow . . .").

2. In the Hebrew מֵי נִדָּה (*mē niddāh*).

on her: nor was there any constraint on Christ, but he offered himself willingly." In the opinion of Delitzsch, "the fragrance of the cedar wood would act against the odour of death, the hyssop was regarded by all antiquity as an instrument of purification, and the crimson band, coloured with the cochineal dye, may... have symbolized life." B. F. C. Atkinson, to cite a more recent author, holds that the cedar wood represents the cross, the hyssop, as the instrument of sprinkling, the blood-shedding of Christ, and the scarlet thread the cleansing effected by that blood.[3] The legitimacy of pressing every detail to serve a typological purpose must, however, be regarded as questionable. It is a practice which leads to the extremes of fanciful ingenuity and it is certainly not our author's method. Yet it cannot be denied that there is such a thing as typological significance. The question is, Where is the line to be drawn? And the answer to this question, it may be suggested, lies between those interpretations where there is a wide range of disagreement and those interpretations where there is a general consensus of judgment. Thus in the case of the red heifer it is generally agreed that its unblemished condition symbolizes the sinlessness of Christ, the sacrificial ritual of purification the cleansing effected by the blood of Christ, and its offering outside the camp the suffering of Christ outside the gate (see 13:11f.). Our author, however, does not pause even to mention significances of this kind here.

What he is concerned to emphasize at this point is that this ritual *sprinkling of defiled persons*, whether with blood or with the water for impurity, effected no more than *the purification of the flesh*, which is contrasted with the purging of *the conscience* effected through the blood of Christ. The term "flesh," accordingly, must be understood here as signifying that which is merely external, in distinction from the "conscience" which denotes what is essentially internal and radical. It was only in a *superficial* sense that the blood or ashes of the animals sacrificed under the levitical system could be said to achieve cleansing. The ceremonial involved did not penetrate *to the heart* of man's need, which is the cleansing of his conscience whereby he knows himself to be condemned as guilty before God. Such ceremonial was only the shadow, though not without promise, and not the substance; "for it is impossible that the blood of bulls and goats should take away sins" (10:4).

The argument proceeds *a fortiori:* if the blood of these animal sacrifices served for the cleansing of persons defiled in this external sense, *how much more shall the blood of Christ* achieve the radical inward cleansing of the conscience. As Herveus observes, "if the shadow purifies the flesh, how much more does the truth purify the soul!" There is a funda-

3. B. F. C. Atkinson, *The Book of Numbers* (London, 1956), p. 128.

mental difference between the animals sacrificed in the levitical system and the unique sacrifice by Christ of himself in the priestly order of Melchizedek. Animals are not moral creatures; the unblemished condition of those victims offered up was merely external and superficial in character for the purposes of ritual symbolism; and neither by nature nor in any moral sense were they fitted to take the place of man who is answerable for his conduct and morally defiled in his conscience at the deep center of his being. By contrast, Christ, the incarnate Son, is a fellow human being, partaking of our own human nature (2:14), and therefore, as man, fully qualified to stand in for us as our substitute, and, as one *without blemish*,[4] that is, as a man morally perfect with an undefiled conscience before God (4:15; 7:27), competent to offer up the completely efficacious sacrifice of his own unblemished person in satisfaction for our sins and for the purifying of our consciences. It is not merely superficially but in the very depth of his being that our Redeemer is without blemish and thus that his sacrifice of himself deals in *a radical manner* with the alienating and disintegrating effects of human sinfulness.

Herveus means the same thing when, commenting on verse 23 below, he speaks of the rationality of man as compared with the brutish nature of animals and emphasizes the unsuitability of slaying "brute animals as victims for rational men."

> There was need [he writes] for a man who could be offered for men, so that a rational sacrifice might be offered for the rational sinner and might obliterate the guilt of the first parent. But what sacrifice, seeing that a man without sin was not to be found? How could a sacrifice offered for us cleanse us from the contagion of sin if it itself was not free from the contagion of sin? A defiled offering certainly could not cleanse defiled persons. Therefore, in order that there might be a rational victim it was necessary for a man to be offered, so that he might truly cleanse man from sin—a man, and one without sin. But what man would be without sin if he were descended from the commingling of sin? Accordingly, the Son of God entered the virgin's womb on our behalf. There he became man without sin for us, he offered his body as a sacrifice for us, presenting for sinners a victim

---

4. The adjective ἄμωμος (*amōmos*), "without blemish," occurs seven times in the New Testament and its cognate ἀμώμητος twice. The sense varies between "without blemish," as here, and "without blame" (cf. Eph. 1:4; Col. 1:22; 2 Pet. 3:14); but because of the plain ethical implications the two senses are closely connected with each other. The original force of the root μωμ-, however, as in the verb μωμάομαι, is that of blame. It is of particular interest that the translators of the Septuagint used this Greek stem μωμ- (*mōm-*), and especially the noun μῶμος, as an equivalent of the Hebrew מוּם (*mūm*), "blemish." The virtual identity in sound and structure between the two terms is obvious. In the adjective ἄμωμος the initial α is, of course, privative, giving the sense "without blemish." This same adjective is used to translate the Hebrew תָּמִים (*tāmīm*), meaning, positively, "perfect" or "upright," and, negatively, "unspotted," with which also, though to a lesser degree, it is somewhat homophonous.

without sin who was able by reason of human nature to die and by reason of righteousness to cleanse.

The spontaneous character of Christ's sacrifice is disclosed in the assertion that he *offered himself:* it was his doing, and in this free and voluntary act of self-offering he fulfilled the purpose of his coming into the world (Mk. 10:45; 1 Tim. 1:15). Hence his emphatic declaration: "I lay down my life that I may take it again. No one takes it from me, but I lay it down of my own accord. I have power to lay it down, and I have power to take it again" (Jn. 10:17f.). Here, again, there is an absolute difference between Christ's offering of himself and the animals that were sacrificed by the levitical priests. The latter, as irrational beasts, were brought involuntarily and uncomprehendingly to the place of sacrifice; they were brute beasts, lacking all understanding of what was being done. But Jesus, the incarnate Son and our fellow man, was no brute beast devoid of wit and will: "he set his face to go to Jerusalem" (Lk. 9:51); "For this purpose I have come to this hour," he affirmed, ". . . and I, when I am lifted up from the earth, will draw all men to myself," saying this, as the evangelist explains, "to show by what death he was to die" (Jn. 12:27, 32f.). Christ's sacrifice on the cross was his own free action on our behalf.

Moreover, it was *through the eternal Spirit* that he made this unblemished offering of himself to God. The significance of the phrase "through the eternal Spirit" has long been a matter of dispute. Alcuin interpreted it to mean "through the Holy Spirit," and this in fact is the reading found in the Vulgate, which doubtless reflects an early gloss and which inevitably fixed the "Catholic" understanding of the expression for centuries. But it coincides with the interpretation of Bengel and numerous other Protestant commentators; and, indeed, there is nothing inappropriate in the explanation that *Christ,* God's Chosen One anointed with the Holy Spirit for the fulfilment of his mediatorial high-priestly office (cf. Isa. 42:1; 61:1; Mk. 1:10, par.; Lk. 4:18), lived the perfect life and offered the perfect sacrifice in the power of that same Spirit. Thus, for example, F. F. Bruce asserts that "behind our author's thinking lies the portrayal of the Isaianic Servant of the Lord" who "in the power of the Divine Spirit . . . accomplishes every phase of his ministry."

Others, however, understand the phrase as a specific reference, not to the Third Person of the Trinity, but to the essential nature of Christ as the divine and therefore eternal Son of God. Thus Westcott explains that "in virtue of His inseparable and unchangeable Divine Nature Christ was Priest while He was victim also"; and Spicq identifies the "eternal spirit" of this passage with "his very personality or his own power, of transcendental worth, which ensures for him an eternal life and priesthood even by way of death." This interpretation accords well with the teaching already given, that Christ has become a priest "by the power of an indestructible life" (7:16)[5] and that "he holds his priesthood permanently, because he continues for ever" (7:24). This teaching, in turn, flows from the similitude of the priesthood of Melchizedek, who, as portrayed in Genesis 14 and Psalm 110, "has neither beginning of days nor end of life, but resembling the Son of God continues a priest for ever" (Heb. 7:3). No finite, temporal creature could ever offer himself as a propitiation of eternal efficacy for the sins of the whole world (1 Jn. 2:2).[6] It has rightly been observed that "only one endowed with *eternal* spirit could give to His sacrifice the character of an *eternal* redemption."[7]

5. "What the author had called ζωὴ ἀκατάλυτος (7[16]) he now calls πνεῦμα αἰώνιον," says Moffatt. "The sacrificial blood . . . resulted in an eternal λύτρωσις because it operated in an eternal order of spirit, the sacrifice of Jesus purifying the inner personality (τὴν συνείδεισιν) because it was the action of a personality, and of a sinless personality which belonged by nature to the order of spirit or eternity. . . . The implication (which underlies all the epistle) is that even in his earthly life Jesus possessed eternal life. Hence what took place in time upon the cross, the writer means, took place really in the eternal, absolute order. Christ sacrificed himself ἐφάπαξ, and the single sacrifice needed no repetition, since it possessed absolute, eternal value as the action of One who belonged to the eternal order. . . . Αἰωνίου closely describes πνεύματος (hence it has no article). What is in the writer's mind is the truth that what Jesus did by dying can never be exhausted or transcended. . . . It was because Jesus was what he was by nature that his sacrifice had such final value; its atoning significance lay in his vital connexion with the realm of absolute realities; it embodied all that his divine personality meant for men in relation to God."
6. "A mere creature," comments John Brown, "can never yield more obedience than it owes for itself. . . . It was the living God manifested in flesh who was both our High Priest and victim."
7. H. H. Meeter, *The Heavenly High Priesthood of Christ* (Grand Rapids, 1916). p. 138. So also Geerhardus Vos explains that the expression "through eternal spirit" means "through the heavenly aspect of His deity" (*The Teaching of the Epistle to the Hebrews*, Grand Rapids, 1956, p. 114). "The clause διὰ πνεύματος," he writes elsewhere, "is to be explained from the fact that the purification which the readers need is a purification in the sphere of the spirit, a purification of the conscience." He holds, further, that "the personal initiative, the voluntariness form the most important element in the πνεῦμα-character of the offering"; and he concludes that "the passage actually implies the deity of the Saviour and the familiar dogmatic thought of his deity imparting transcendent efficacy to his sacrifice, not so much, however, in virtue of the bare fact of its being deity, but rather because in virtue of its specific character of heavenly spirit it suited exactly the sphere in which the purification was to be accomplished and the finality, absoluteness which were required for it" ("The Priesthood of Christ in the Epistle to the Hebrews," *The Princeton Theological Review*, 5 [1907], pp. 590–592).
   The absence of the article tells, if anything, in favor of this interpretation; but it cannot in itself be regarded as decisive in view of the fact that there are nearly 50 instances in the New Testament of the anarthrous use of the designation πνεῦμα ἅγιον (see Mt. 1:18, 20; 3:11; Mk. 1:8; Lk. 1:15, 35, 41, 67; 2:25 [cf. the following verse, with article]; 3:16; 4:1; Jn. 1:33; 7:39 [where πνεῦμα, clearly signifying the Holy Spirit, is found both with and without the article]; 20:22; Acts 1:2, 5; 2:4 [both without and with the article]; 4:8; 6:3, 5; 7:55; 8:15, 17 [cf. the following verse, with article], 19; 9:17; 10:38; 11:16, 24; 13:9, 52; 19:2 [twice; cf. v. 6, with article]; Rom. 5:5; 9:1; 14:17; 1 Cor. 2:3 [πνεῦμα]; 12:3; 2 Cor. 6:6; 1 Thess. 5:6; 2 Tim. 1:14; Tit. 3:5; 1 Pet. 1:12; Jude 20; and two instances which have already occurred in our epistle, 2:4 and 6:4). It is, then, the theological context in which the expression "through eternal spirit" occurs which governs our questioning of the explanation that it is a reference to the Holy Spirit. The expression could well be translated "through his eternal spirit."

In the context before us we have an unmistakable contrast between the sacrifices under the old system of animals which, as we have remarked above, became the involuntary, uncomprehending, and passive victims on the altar, and the sacrifice of Christ, who actively, of his own will, and in full consciousness of what he was doing, offered himself, and determined to do so in the eternal realm of his perfect freedom and absolute power. Consequently, the difference between the levitical offerings and Christ's self-offering was infinite rather than relative. Beza comments accordingly: "To the blood of beasts our author opposes the blood of him who was not only man, like others, but also God; for by the designation 'eternal spirit' I understand the infinite efficacy of the Deity in the humanity he assumed, which consecrated the whole of his sacrifice."[8]

The conscience, furthermore, is purified by the blood of Christ *from dead works*. This radical purging, accomplished at Calvary, is the ground of the reconciliation provided by God in Christ. From man's side there is the necessity for "repentance from dead works," to which our author has previously referred (6:1); though it must not be imagined that this repentance is in any sense a meritorious "work" of man—if it were, it would contradict the apostolic emphasis on the full and sole sufficiency of the work of Christ on our behalf—but the result of the grace of God operating within his heart and bringing him to repentance (cf. Heb. 12:15–17; Eph. 2:8–10). This truth is admirably stated in the declaration of absolution in the Anglican Book of Common Prayer, where to the assurance that God "pardons and absolves all those who truly repent and unfeignedly believe his holy Gospel" is added the exhortation, "Wherefore let us beseech him to grant us true repentance. . . ."

There are three main senses in which the works of the unregenerate may be described as "dead." First, they are "dead" works because they

8. "The *perfect spirit* which led Christ to give Himself as a sacrifice," writes H. H. Meeter, "or to use the terminology of the author in 10:1–10, the *absolute voluntariness* was indispensable, if a sacrifice were to have atoning value. Absolute voluntariness however to do the will of God cannot exist without perfect knowledge of what that will of God for redemption requires. Hence *absolute intelligence* is likewise necessary. The animal was entirely unconscious of what the whole performance meant. As little could there be thought of any will by the animal to undergo the suffering. But even for a man, granted even that he be a perfect man, but nothing more than man, it would be impossible to fulfil these two absolute requirements for an atonement sacrifice. It lies wholly beyond the possibility of any human being, temporal spirit as he is, fully to know the omniscient will of the eternal God. And having no full knowledge of the contents of that will, it follows of course that an absolute obedience to that will is out of the question. But Christ offered himself through the eternal spirit that characterized Him as the eternal Son of God. Therefore He, and forsooth He only of all that were ever one with our race, had a perfect knowledge of what that will of God demanded for redemption. . . . In the clear conscience of His eternal spirit He could therefore say as no man could: 'Lo, I come to do Thy will, O God', 10:9" (*op. cit.*, pp. 137f.).

proceed from him who, by reason of his sinfulness, is dead toward God. The person who is dead in trespasses and sins is incapable of performing "living" works which are acceptable to God. Only when he has been turned from his self-centeredness and restored to the God-centeredness in and for which he was created—that is to say, only when he has by divine grace been "made alive together with Christ" (Eph. 2:1–5)—can his works cease to be "dead" works. Second, the works of the unregenerate are "dead" because they are essentially sterile and unproductive; they yield no living harvest. How could they, since they are the mark of the person whose existence shows no regard for God who is the source of life? These are works of time, not eternity; works of lust, not love; works of the flesh, not of the Spirit (Rom. 6:21; Gal. 5:19ff.). Third, such works are "dead" not only because they proceed from deadness and are accompanied by deadness but also because they end in death: they lead to judgment and perdition (Rom. 6:21, 23; Phil. 3:19f.; Rev. 21:8). These dead works which spring from deadness and lead to death speak very plainly of the disastrous nature of the human predicament and of the desperate need for the purging and liberation of the conscience from the tyranny of death (Heb. 2:15)—the need, that is, for man's renewal at the very root of his being.

Many commentators have thought that in this passage a connection is intended between the dead works from which the blood of Christ purifies the conscience and the defilement resulting from contact with a dead body (which, however, our author does not mention) from which sprinkling with the heifer's ashes effected fleshly purification. Thus, for example, Alcuin comments: "If anyone touches a dead body he is polluted. And here if anyone touches a dead work he is contaminated in his conscience. Dead works are sins. . . . If he who touched a dead body was not permitted to enter the temple, how much more is it impossible for him who has dead works to enter heaven!" Chrysostom, Aquinas, Owen, and Moffatt are among the many others who have postulated this analogy between "dead bodies" and "dead works," and it is certainly an analogy well worth bringing out. But, while our author would doubtless have approved it, it is open to question whether he had it in mind. It is possible that he left it to be inferred instead of stating it explicitly, though the manner in which he states and compares the blood of animals and the purification of the flesh on the one hand and the blood of Christ and the purification of the conscience on the other is nothing if not explicit.

The purging of the conscience from dead works by the blood of Christ is not an end in itself. It is rather the beginning which opens the way for the realization of the end or purpose of our redemption. And that end is described here as *to serve the living God*. What begins with

God also ends with God. It does not end with man. Moreover, the work of God, ever dynamic as it is, does not lead to a static result—a motionless state, as it were, of purgation. God's work is, and must be, dynamic in its effect, that of dynamic service. In the Christian experience everything is "to the praise of his glorious grace which he freely bestowed on us in the Beloved" (Eph. 1:6), and it is unthinkable that the living God could be served by anything but living works, that is, works that spring from the new life in Christ engendered through the dynamic operation of the Holy Spirit in the human heart. In Paul's words, we are "created in Christ Jesus for good works, which God prepared beforehand, that we should walk in them" (Eph. 2:10). "We are not cleansed by Christ," writes Calvin, "so that we can immerse ourselves continually in fresh dirt, but in order that our purity may serve the glory of God."

There is a striking antithesis here between "dead works" and "the living God." They are two incompatibles. Yet these Hebrew Christians to whom our author is writing are in danger of committing the gross contradiction of professing to serve the living God and at the same time reverting to the dead works which are the mark of the unregenerate. Disobedience and dead works go together, and they are in danger of imitating the very disobedience which caused the downfall of so many of their fellow Israelites before them (4:11). Indeed, they are in danger of becoming guilty of that worst of all dead works, sinning deliberately against the light of the truth which has been made known to them (6:4ff.; 10:26), and thus of incurring the awful consequence of falling into the hands of the living God (10:31) who is a consuming fire (12:29). If, however, their consciences have indeed been purified from dead works, then this will openly display itself in the willingness and gratitude with which they dedicate themselves to the service of the living God.

NOTE ON THE PURPOSE OF THE REFERENCE TO "THE ASHES OF A HEIFER" IN HEBREWS 9:13

The mention of the blood of goats and bulls seems entirely appropriate in a context which is so patently concerned with the ceremonial of the Day of Atonement; but the allusion to the sprinkling with the ashes of a heifer is unexpected and, apparently, unrelated except in a somewhat incidental manner to the main thrust of the argument. The primary emphasis is on the cleansing efficacy of the blood of Christ in comparison with the merely superficial cleansing effected by the blood of goats and bulls. It may be explained, quite rightly, that the ritual associated with the ashes of the red heifer and the "water for impurity" was related, as was Christ's death, to the need for purification on the part of those who were in a condition of defilement, and, further, that Christ's immolation, like that of the heifer, took place "outside the camp" (13:11f.— though here, also, it is plain from the context that our author has in mind the symbolism of the Day of Atonement and our purification by virtue of the blood of Christ). But the impression remains that the mention of this ritual might well have been omitted.

Yet to dismiss out of hand the author's introduction of this particular observance as incongruous or unnecessary would be rash. It would seem wiser to assume that he had some good reason for mentioning it. And it is possible to suggest such a reason, on the supposition that those to whom his letter was addressed showed signs of being influenced by the teaching and practice of the Dead Sea Sect or some similar isolationist group.[9] The burning of the red heifer was one of the Mosaic ordinances which the members of the Qumran Community were in a position to observe, since it was not a rite performed in the precincts of the tabernacle (or temple) but outside the camp (or the city of Jerusalem). Solemnly bound as their Zadokite priests were to abide by the covenant of Moses and its laws, the probability is that, unable because of their self-imposed separation from Jerusalem and its temple to offer up those sacrifices which involved the shedding and sprinkling of blood within the confines of the sanctuary (as on the Day of Atonement), they would meticulously have observed a purificatory ordinance of this kind which was independent of city and temple, especially in view of the plentiful evidence that questions and methods of purification were of great importance to their community.

It may, however, be more than a probability. *The Manual of Discipline* prescribes that every year, "so long as Belial continues to hold sway," a review or examination of the members of the Community is to take place, the object of which is that every man, priest, levite, or layman "may be made aware of his status in the community of God in the sense of the ideal eternal society." Anyone who stubbornly shows a rebellious spirit "cannot be reckoned as among those essentially blameless. He cannot," it is affirmed, "be cleared by mere ceremonies of atonement, nor cleansed by any waters of ablution,[10] nor sanctified by immersion in lakes or rivers, nor purified by any bath. . . . For it is only through the spiritual apprehension of God's truth that man's ways can be properly directed. . . . Only by the submission of his soul to all the ordinances of God can his flesh be made clean. Only thus can it really be sprinkled with waters of ablution.[11] Only thus can it really be sanctified by waters of purification."[12] From this passage it is apparent that included among the rites of purification

9. See Introduction, pp. 13ff.
10. *Mē niddāh*, "water for impurity."
11. *Mē niddāh*, "water for impurity."
12. *The Manual of Discipline*, 1QS ii.19ff. (T. H. Gaster's translation).

practiced by the Dead Sea Sect was sprinkling with the "waters of ablution," that is, waters with which the ashes of the red heifer had been mingled.

We have, then, a situation prevailing at the time when the Epistle to the Hebrews was written which would give particular point to the mention of the rite of sprinkling with the ashes of a heifer if the supposition is correct that the recipients of the letter were being enticed to imagine that the observance of this rite might be advantageous to them, Christians though they now professed themselves to be. Acquiescence would have amounted to a denial of the sole and total sufficiency of the sacrifice of Christ for their purification. Even the emphasis, commendable in itself, of *The Manual of Discipline* on the need for "spiritual apprehension" and "submission of the soul" could be dangerously misleading, hence our author's insistence that the levitical ordinance was superficial in character and could never achieve the cleansing of the defiled conscience. He cannot condone any challenge to the uniqueness and the perfection of the sacrifice offered once-for-all by our High Priest after the order of Melchizedek.[13] "A good, pure, quiet, and joyful conscience," says Luther, "is nothing else than faith in the remission of sins, which nobody can have save in the Word of God, which proclaims to us that the blood of Christ is shed for the remission of sins.... Still more, it is not even enough to believe that it was shed for the remission of sins, unless we believe that it was shed for the remission of our own sins."

> 9:15. *Therefore he is the mediator of a new covenant, so that those who are called may receive the promised eternal inheritance, since a death has occurred which redeems them from the transgressions under the first covenant.*

Christ's blood-shedding has achieved what the old covenant with its priesthood and sacrifices was incapable of achieving, namely, the purification of the conscience from dead works to serve the living God; *therefore,* by reason of this, *he is the mediator of a new covenant*—new not only in that it is different from the old covenant but also in that it supersedes it. The theology of the covenant belongs integrally to the argument of this central section of the epistle: Jesus has already been described both as the surety or guarantor and as the mediator of a better covenant (7:22; 8:6); the prophetic promise of the new covenant and its blessings has been quoted at length from Jeremiah 31:31ff. (8:8ff.); and the very fact of the announcement and provision of a new and better covenant has been explained as indicative of the inadequacy and imperma-

---

13. For further discussion, see John Bowman, "Did the Qumran Sect burn the red heifer?" *Revue de Qumrân,* I (1958), pp. 73ff. F. F. Bruce suggests a connection with Isaiah 52:15 rendered, "so shall he sprinkle many nations" (cf. E. J. Young, *Studies in Isaiah,* 1954, pp. 199ff.; H. L. Ellison, *The Servant of Jehovah,* 1953, pp. 29f.), where, he judges, "the allusion may well be to the sprinkling of the water for the removal of impurity."

nence of the former covenant, whose institutions were earthly and temporal compared with the heavenly and eternal realities of the new (8:7, 13; 9:1ff.).

Our author would certainly not wish to suggest that the necessity for a *new* covenant supposes the failure or impracticability of God's purposes in connection with the old covenant. There is no question of the old having been tried and found unsatisfactory with the consequence that God was obliged to try something new. Even from the beginning of what is called here (and in 8:7, 13 and 9:1) the *first* covenant the need for a new dispensation whose provisions would be marked by perfection and permanence was recognized. Indeed, as the argument of this epistle has already shown, the logic of the situation under the earlier system, with its endless repetition from generation to generation of a multiplicity of sacrifices, cried out for the provision of the one perfect sacrifice which would meet once and forever the requirements of the human predicament.

But there is a further important consideration which shows that the new covenant was not some kind of divine attempt to rectify the mistakes of an earlier experiment, namely, that there was a still earlier covenant which antedated what is described here as the "first" covenant. This was the Abrahamic covenant, established, according to Paul, 430 years prior to the inauguration of the Mosaic covenant but in no sense invalidated by the interposition of the latter (Gal. 3:15–18). The promise made to Abraham that in his seed all the nations of the earth would be blessed was fulfilled precisely in Christ (Gal. 3:16). Accordingly, the Abrahamic covenant is continuous with the new covenant, as its root, and identical with it. Thus the advent of Christ demonstrated that God was acting "to remember his holy covenant, the oath which he swore to our father Abraham" (Lk. 1:72f.). The "new" covenant, therefore, not only superseded the "first" or Mosaic covenant but was also antecedent to it, and so was anything but an emergency measure. In any case, the purposes of God are settled and not subject to the uncertainties and fluctuations of our human situation, and it would be a strange concept of God which portrays him as engaging in a hit-or-miss experiment or resorting to a novel scheme in order to counteract the frustrations of an earlier failure. The new covenant is not new to God but to us, as, in the sequence of history, it supersedes and transcends the former covenant given through the mediation of Moses.

How, then, are we to understand the interlude of the Mosaic covenant? The answer to this question is given in Galatians 3:19ff., where Paul states that the law "was added because of transgressions, till the offspring should come to whom the promise had been made"—that is, until the advent of Christ, in whom, as we have said above, the covenant promise made to Abraham receives its fulfilment. The law did not change the human situation, but it threw it into relief; for the inability of man to keep its demands made unmistakably clear his guilty state before God. Man's great and radical need is justification; but the law can never justify the law-breaker. Despairing of his efforts to achieve righteousness by his works, man's only hope was to turn away from himself and to seek the refuge of faith in the pardoning grace which had been promised. Thus "the law was our custodian until Christ came, that we might be justified by faith" (Gal. 3:24). In itself, however, the law, except for the forms and ceremonies that pertained to the ministry of the levitical priesthood, was not something transient. Since it defines the standard of righteousness, which is at the same time the standard of love (Mk. 12:30f.; Rom. 13:8–10), required of man if he is to find acceptance with God, the law, so far from being just an interlude, continues as an integral element of the new covenant; indeed, in accordance with the promise attached to the new covenant, it is now written on the hearts of God's people (Heb. 8:10). The transition from the Mosaic covenant to the new covenant of which Christ is the mediator is the transition from the principle of works to the principle of grace, from weakness to power.

The basis of Christ's mediatorship of the new covenant is *a death which has occurred*. The association of a covenant and its solemnization with death, particularly in the form of a sacrifice with the shedding of blood, appears to have prevailed from the earliest times. Thus the slaughter of animal victims accompanied the establishment of the covenant with Abraham (Gen. 15:9ff.; cf. Jer. 34:18); the ratification of the covenant between Jacob and Laban involved the offering of sacrifice (Gen. 31:54); the Mosaic covenant was inaugurated with the building of an altar, the offering of sacrifices, and the sprinkling of the people with "the blood of the covenant" upon their acceptance of the terms of the covenant (Ex. 24:3ff.; cf. Zech. 9:11 and vv. 19ff. below); and an altar was built again, for the offering of sacrifice, when the Israelites reaffirmed their allegiance to the covenant on the passing of the leadership from Moses to Joshua and the crossing of the Jordan into the land of promise (Dt. 27:1ff.). The new covenant has this in common with the old, that it too came into operation through the sacrificial death of an innocent victim on behalf of the people.

The blessings which flow from the death by which the new covenant has been established are here summarized under two heads. (1) *Redemption from the transgressions under the first covenant,* that is, deliverance from the guilt and condemnation which the law pronounces against all law-breakers and which the blood of brute beasts could never remove (see vv. 9f., 13f. above, and 10:4). Thus the new provides the antidote to the inadequacy of the former covenant. The new overcomes the incompetence of the old. As Aquinas says, "the new covenant is superior to the old because it is able to do what the old could not." The Hebrew nation, to which the recipients of this letter belonged, was to a special degree guilty of "transgressions under the first covenant," for, as those to whom the law had been entrusted, and boastful of this privilege (cf. Rom. 2:17ff.), they were in a heightened sense law-breakers through their failure to keep the terms of the covenant which they had sworn to observe. But now, at last, the great prophecy of the new age, "I will be merciful toward their iniquities, and I will remember their sins no more" (Jer. 31:34, cited above, Heb. 8:12), finds its fulfilment—but not without cost, for deliverance comes only on the payment of the price of redemption, which is the death and blood-shedding of him who is the incarnate Son of God, our true fellow (Heb. 2:14f.). The efficacy of this redemption, moreover, extends not only to those who have lived since the advent of Christ but also, retroactively, to those who trusted the promises prior to their fulfilment in his coming (as the next paragraph explains). The perfection that is ours in Christ is theirs also (11:39f.).

(2) *Reception of the promised inheritance.* The promise of this inheritance[14] is that of the new covenant cited in 8:8ff. above, which, as we have said, has its roots in the covenant made with Abraham many centuries earlier, to whom God promised, by an everlasting covenant (Gen. 17:7, 19), that he and his posterity, destined to be an innumerable multitude, would possess the land as an everlasting possession (Gen. 12:7; 13:15, 16; 17:2, 5, 8; 22:17). This covenant promise was fulfilled in an external and this-worldly sense, as the Israelites themselves freely acknowledged when they obtained possession of the land under the leadership of Joshua and subsequently became a great and numerous nation. "All came to pass" (Josh. 21:43–45; cf. Dt. 10:22; 24:5; Num. 23:10; 1 Ki. 3:8; Dt. 26:3; Neh. 9:7–9, 23–25; and cf. Ex. 23:31 and Josh. 1:4 with Gen. 15:18). Yet because of the transitory nature of earthly possessions and the mortality of man which makes certain his separation sooner or later from the acquisitions of this life, it was impossible that an "everlasting covenant" promising an "everlasting possession" and an "eternal inheritance" could find the completeness of its fulfilment in the present order of things. The physical land and the posterity that in due course inherited it were in effect sacramental in character: they constituted a sign, visible and passing, which pointed beyond itself to a reality, as yet

---

14. The Greek ὅπως ... τὴν ἐπαγγελίαν λάβωσιν οἱ κεκλημένοι τῆς αἰωνίου κληρονομίας reads literally "so that those who are called may receive the promise of the eternal inheritance." To "receive the promise" here (as also in the expression κομίσασθαι τὴν ἐπαγγελίαν or τὰς ἐπαγγελίας in 10:36 and 11:39; cf. 6:12, 15, 17) means to enjoy or experience the fulfilment of the promises, to receive what was promised. This sense is well conveyed by the rendering of our version: "... receive the promised eternal inheritance."

invisible, which would be permanent. And this is precisely what our author teaches. Although Abraham and the other early patriarchs died without seeing the fulfilment of the covenant promise, they were not therefore excluded from the enjoyment of what had been promised. It would indeed have been somewhat of a mockery if Abraham, the prime recipient of the promise, had been debarred by vicissitude and death from the experience of its benefits. His gaze, however, and that of the other patriarchs and believers of old, was fixed on a fulfilment which is other-worldly. They looked for "a better country, that is, a heavenly one" (11:13–15). Patiently enduring, they seized the hope that was set before them and through the victory of their faith "obtained the promise" (6:15, 18).

The fruition of the promised eternal inheritance, moreover, is granted to *those who are called*—called, that is, by God. This consideration in itself ensures the full effectiveness of the covenant and its promises. All is of God and all is of grace (2 Cor. 5:18). God who has made provision for the blessings of this eternal inheritance also by his calling guarantees that there will be inheritors to enter into the enjoyment of it, for his calling is always and indefectibly *effectual* calling. His word is his deed (cf. Gen. 1:3ff.; Isa. 55:11f.); accordingly, those whom he calls he also leads on through justification to glorification (Rom. 8:30)—in other words, to the eternal inheritance, in which not only believers of this present age but also believers who lived before the coming of Christ, and, greeting the fulfilment of the promise from afar, died in faith (Heb. 11:13), will participate with joy and endless thanksgiving. The promise of an eternal possession and an innumerable posterity receives its ultimate fulfilment in the consummation of all things when the great multitude of the redeemed which no man can number will everlastingly praise and serve God in the perfection of the new heaven and the new earth (Rev. 7:9ff.; 21:1ff.), thus bringing the divine purpose of creation to the fulness of fruition.

9:16, 17. *For where a will is involved, the death of the one who made it must be established. For a will takes effect only at death, since it is not in force as long as the one who made it is alive.*

The mention of the promised inheritance which is received on the basis of the redeeming death of Christ suggests the analogy from everyday life of the principle of inheritance, in accordance with which the provisions of a last will and testament become effective only on the death of the testator. Rather more than analogy is involved, however, since the Greek word *diathēkē* which is used here can mean either "covenant" or "testament," and at this point in the argument there is an easy transition from the sense of "covenant" to the sense of "testament." Within the present context there is in fact a close association of ideas, for, as we have seen (p. 366), the connection of a covenant and death, particularly in the form of the shedding of blood in sacrifice, was commonplace in the history of the Hebrews, not to mention other peoples. But an association of this kind was not a necessity. The covenant between David and Jonathan, for example, involved no death in its initiation, but the exchange of personal possessions (1 Sam. 18:3f.), and the establishment of God's covenant with Noah was related, it seems, only to the rainbow as the symbol of its firmness (Gen. 9:8ff.). In the case of a last will and testament, however, the death of the testator is invariably required before the terms of his disposition can become operative. Hence our author's appeal to the universally acknowledged rule that *where a will is involved, the death of the one who made it must be established, because a will is not in force as long as the one who made it is alive,* but *takes effect only at death.* [15] Where death is the effective basis of a covenant, as, pre-eminently, with the death of Christ and the implementation of the new covenant, it is the death of one offered in sacrifice; but death of any kind, violent or peaceful, suffices for the provisions made by a testator in his will to take effect. The sacrificial death of Christ, therefore, answers the demands both of a covenant and of a testament.

A further point of affinity between a last will and testament and the biblical concept of a divine covenant is that both originate from a single initiator. A will represents the wish of but one person, the testator alone, regarding the distribution of his possessions at his death. The beneficiaries under the terms of the will, though certain conditions may be demanded of them before they enter into the enjoyment of the inheritance, are not the will's authors. So also God is the sole author of the covenant which he appoints for his people, while their obedience to its terms is required if they are to enjoy the benefits it conveys.

---

15. It is interesting that the terminology of 8:10, citing Jeremiah 31:33, ἡ διαθήκη ἥν διαθήσομαι, corresponds to that of verse 16 here, ἡ διαθήκη ... τοῦ διαθεμένου. In 8:10, however, the context demands the sense of "covenant" for διαθήκη, which is the translation there of the Hebrew בְּרִית (*berith*). Another parallel of terminology is found in Luke 22:20 and 29 (accepting the longer reading of v. 20 as authentic), where Christ speaks of the wine as "the new covenant (ἡ καινὴ διαθήκη) in my blood," and then says (v. 29), "I confer (διατίθεμαι) a kingdom on you" (JB). This may well be another example of the semantic covenant/testament ambivalence, so that Christ may be understood as saying in the latter verse: "I will or bequeath a kingdom as your inheritance." It is possible, too (as, for example, Moffatt maintains), that in Galatians 3:15 and 17 there is a play on the double sense of the term διαθήκη. This is plainly the understanding of the RSV and the NEB. The JB translates διαθήκη as "will" in both verses.

Deissmann insists, perhaps somewhat too vigorously, on the unilateral signification of the term *diathēkē* when he maintains that "no one in the Mediterranean world of the first century A.D. would have thought of finding in the word *diathēkē* the idea of 'covenant'" and that "to St. Paul the word meant what it meant in his Greek Old Testament, 'a unilateral enactment', in particular 'a will or testament.'" From this he proceeds to the conclusion that nothing less than what is "ultimately the great question of all religious history: a religion of grace or a religion of works?" is at stake.[16] In speaking of Paul, of course, Deissmann has primarily the Epistles to the Romans and to the Galatians in mind; his judgment, however, is comprehensive and in the nature of the case extends to the usage of the term in the Epistle to the Hebrews. Oversimplified though his pronouncement may be, there is too much truth in what he says for it to be dismissed as merely an oversimplification. The unilateral character of God's covenants with Noah and Abraham is plain, for in both cases God speaks unequivocally of "my covenant" which "I establish" (Gen. 9:8ff.; 17:2, 7, 19). This is true also of the Mosaic covenant in which the law and its specifications are sovereignly decreed by God from above. And this is certainly true of the new covenant, which is formulated in its entirety by God in accordance with his will (see Jer. 31:31) and owes its fulfilment in Christ solely to the initiative of divine grace. In the nature of the case God and man, Creator and creature, the Infinite and the finite, and, still more particularly, the Holy One and the sinner, do not meet and bargain together on equal terms. The encounter between God and man can never be the same as the encounter between man and man. The issue is one of theology, *biblical* theology, rather than of etymology.[17] God's covenant dealings with his creatures, moreover, are dealings of grace, not tyranny, for it is through his covenant that God in his sovereignty mercifully meets with man, takes him into his counsels, and raises him to participation in his glory.

While God himself, the source of all life, is not subject to death and would therefore inappropriately be cast in the role of testator, yet in Christ, who is God Incarnate and whose purpose in becoming man was that "he might taste death for every one" (Heb. 2:9), God capacitates himself, so to speak, for the fulfilment of this role. Christ is God in action on our behalf (2 Cor. 5:19). The inheritance God has promised his people takes effect and comes into force, in the manner of a will, on the death of the incarnate Son. The wonder and the mystery of divine grace

---

16. A. Deissmann, *Light from the Ancient East* (New York, 1908, 2nd edn.), p. 341.
17. In this connection the use of the Greek term διαθήκη (*diathēkē*), which commonly means a legal disposition by one person, rather than συνθήκη (*synthēkē*), which is the usual term for a covenant between two persons, would seem to be particularly appropriate as a rendering of the Hebrew noun בְּרִית (*berith*) when it signifies a "covenant" appointed by God.

is this, that the deathless Son of God should become the mortal Son of man, so that, though still eternally sovereign as God, as man he might die for mankind[18] and, rising from the grave, unite mankind with himself in the enjoyment of his everlasting inheritance. As F. F. Bruce says: "All analogies from ordinary life must be defective when they are applied to Him who rose from the dead and is thus able personally to secure for His people the benefits which he died to procure for them. He is testator and executor in one, surety and mediator alike."

The cross of Christ is the dawning of the endless day of the new covenant, as the old order with all its imperfection and insufficiency is done away for good; it is the instrument of death whereby the promised inheritance becomes a present reality; and it is the means of purification and reconciliation by which sinners are restored to sonship and made fellow heirs with Christ and partakers of his glory (Rom. 8:15–17).

NOTE ON THE TERMINOLOGY OF HEBREWS 9:16 AND 17

The language used by our author is marked by the precision of the technical legal document. "Where a will (διαθήκη) is involved," he says, "the death of the one who made it must be established (φέρεσθαι, that is, brought forward in evidence). For a will takes effect only at death (ἐπὶ νεκροῖς βεβαία), since it is not in force (μήποτε ἰσχύει) as long as the one who made it (ὁ διαθέμενος) is alive." This terminology corresponds with the legal stereotype which long prevailed. An interesting confirmation is available in the text of the last will and testament of Gregory of Nazianzus who died A.D. 389. The will opens with these words:

> I Gregory, bishop of the catholic church in Constantinople, living and mentally alert, sound in knowledge and intellect, have appointed this as my will (διέθεμην τὴν διαθήκην μου ταύτην). I order and desire that it is to be accepted as valid and in force (κυρίαν καὶ βεβαίαν) before any court of law and any authority.

And it concludes in the following manner:

> I Gregory, bishop of the catholic church in Constantinople, have read this will (ἀναγνοὺς τὴν διαθήκην) and approve all that I have written in it with

---

18. Thus Ambrose writes, De Fide iii.11: "He is the Mediator of a better covenant. But where there is testamentary disposition the death of the testator must first come to pass.... Howbeit, the death is not the death of his eternal Godhead, but of his weak human frame."

my own hand, and I order and desire that it should be accepted as binding (καὶ ἰσχύειν αὐτὴν κελεύω καὶ βούλομαι).[19]

With reference to the significance of the noun διαθήκη, Westcott attempts to defend the retention of the sense "covenant" in the verses before us by explaining that in the death of the victim the death of the covenant-maker is symbolically represented—that his death is "introduced upon the scene" or "set in evidence" in the act of sacrificing the life of the victim rather than "alleged" or "established" as a fact. But this fits ill with our author's plain declaration that a διαθήκη "is not in force as long as the one who made it is alive." Special attention should be given to the emphatic affirmation of Moulton and Milligan that in the papyri and inscriptions of the period the word διαθήκη "means *testament, will,* with absolute unanimity, and such frequency that illustration is superfluous." By contrast, the noun συνθήκη "is to the last the word for *compact,* just as διαθήκη is always and only the word for *will.*" However:

> Any thought of some special 'Hebraic' flavour about the use of διαθήκη for *covenant* is excluded by the isolated but absolutely clear passage in Aristophanes (*Birds* 439), where *compact* is the unmistakable meaning. This passage is enough to prove that διαθήκη is properly *dispositio,* an 'arrangement' made by one party with plenary power, which the other party may accept or reject, but cannot alter. A will is simply the most conspicuous example of such an instrument, which ultimately monopolized the word just because it suited its differentia so completely. But it is entirely natural to assume that in the period of the LXX this monopoly was not established, and the translators were free to apply the general meaning as a rendering of בְּרִית. For this course there was an obvious motive. A covenant offered by God to man was no 'compact' between two parties coming together on equal terms. Διαθήκη in its primary sense, as described above, was exactly the needed word.
>
> Passing thus to the NT, we ask whether we are bound to keep to one rendering throughout. Westcott and W. F. Moulton in their commentaries on Heb 9[16f.], and formerly G. Milligan (*Theology of the Epistle to the Hebrews,* pp. 166ff.) held that *covenant* must stand everywhere. Deissmann (*St Paul,* p. 152) insists on *testament* everywhere.... Now, we may fairly put aside the idea that in LXX 'testament' is the invariable meaning: it takes some courage to find it there at all. But on the other hand, a Hellenist like the *auctor ad Hebraeos* or even a Jew like Paul, with Greek language in the very fibre of his thought, could never have used διαθήκη for *covenant* without the slightest consciousness of its ordinary and invariable contemporary meaning. He would use the 'Biblical' words—'Biblical' being in this case synonymous with 'archaic'—but always with the possibility of a play on the later meaning of the word. This is what comes in Heb 9[15ff.] (probably also in Gal 3[15]).... Deissmann, among other difficulties, would have to prove that in iii/B.C. the older general meaning, established by Aristophanes, was extinct. The view to which we have capitulated, after strongly supporting the Westcott doctrine, is less heroic than consistent holding to one English word, but it can claim to account for its inconsistency.

---

19. Gregory of Nazianzus, Migne, PG, XXXVII, 389ff.

Calvin asserts that "this single passage gives proof that the epistle was not written in Hebrew, because in Hebrew ברית means a covenant but not a testament," whereas "in Greek διαθήκη includes both." But Owen allows a wider range to *berith*, which is, he says, "of a large signification and various use." "Frequently," he continues, "it is taken for a 'free grant and disposition' of things by promise, which hath the nature of a testament."

> And in the old covenant there was a free grant and donation of the inheritance of the land of Canaan unto the people; which belongs unto the nature of a testament also. Moreover, both of them, a covenant and a testament, do agree in the general nature of their confirmation, the one by blood, the other by death. Hereon the apostle, in the use of the word διαθήκη, doth diversely argue both unto the nature, necessity, and use of the death of the mediator of the new testament. He was to die in the confirmation of it as it was a testament, he being the testator of it; and he was to offer himself as a sacrifice in his blood, for the establishment of it, as it had the nature of a covenant.[20]

9:18–20. Hence even the first covenant was not ratified without blood. For when every commandment of the law had been declared by Moses to all the people, he took the blood of calves and goats, with water and scarlet wool and hyssop, and sprinkled both the book itself and all the people, saying, "This is the blood of the covenant which God commanded you."

Having explained that the terms of the new covenant, of which Christ is the mediator, became effective by virtue of his death, just as, by way of illustration, a will comes into force at the death of the testator, our author reminds his readers that *even the first covenant* (now returning to the earlier connotation of the term) *was not ratified*, or inaugurated,[21]

---

20. For further discussion of the significance of the term διαθήκη and the interpretation of Hebrews 9:16–17 see the following: Spicq, Excursus IX, "Les Deux Alliances," II, pp. 285ff.; G. Quell and J. Behm, "Διαθήκη," in Kittel, TDNT, II, pp. 106ff.; J. Swetnam, "A Suggested Interpretation of Hebrews 9,15–18," *The Catholic Biblical Quarterly*, 27 (1965), pp. 373ff.; J. Barton Payne, *The Theology of the Older Covenant* (Grand Rapids, 1962), pp. 78ff.; Meredith G. Kline, "Dynastic Covenant," *The Westminster Theological Journal*, XXIII (1960), pp. 1ff.; Geerhardus Vos, "Hebrews, The Epistle of the Diatheke," *Princeton Theological Review*, 13 (1915), pp. 587ff., 14 (1916), pp. 1ff.; J. Behm, *Der Begriff Διαθήκη im Neuen Testament* (1912); F. O. Norton, *A Lexicographical and Historical Study of Διαθήκη* (1908); E. Riggenbach, "Der Begriff der Διαθήκη im Hebräerbrief," *Theologische Studien Theodor Zahn zum 10 Oktober dargebracht* (1908), pp. 289ff.; O. Palmer Robertson, unpublished thesis on "The People of the Wilderness: The Concept of the Church in Hebrews" (1966), pp. 38ff., in the library of Westminster Theological Seminary, Philadelphia.
21. The Greek verb here is ἐγκεκαίνισται. In the LXX ἐγκαινίζειν means "to make new," "to renew" (Isa. 16:11; 1 Sam. 11:14; 2 Chr. 15:8; Ps. 51:10) or "to dedicate" (1 Ki. 8:63; 2 Chr. 7:5; cf. 1 Macc. 4:36, 54; 5:1). The latter sense is favored by the KJV here, the implication being the dedication of something *new* (καινός). Hence the sense of "to introduce something new," "to initiate," "to inaugurate" (NEB), inauguration and dedication being

without blood. While, as we have said above, any type of death suffices for activating the provisions of a will, the designation "blood" here specifies the act of blood-shedding connected with the offering of sacrifice, which is associated more particularly with the establishment of a covenant. Thus at the inauguration of the Mosaic covenant (see Ex. 24:3ff.) burnt offerings and peace offerings of oxen were sacrificed to the Lord by specially appointed young men. Moses then took half the blood from these offerings and threw it against the altar which he had erected at the foot of Mount Sinai. This was followed by his reading of the book of the covenant, in which he had written the divine precepts, to the assembled Israelites, who responded: "All that the Lord has spoken we will do, and we will be obedient." The remainder of the sacrificial blood was then sprinkled over the people by Moses, with these words: "Behold, the blood of the covenant which the Lord has made with you in accordance with all these words."

Now it is evident that our author's summary of the procedure of this inaugural occasion does not coincide at every point with the account given in Exodus 24. No mention is made there of the sacrifice of *calves and goats,* but only of oxen; nothing is said there of any ceremonial involving the use of *water and scarlet wool and hyssop;* and there is no indication that *the book* as well as all the people was sprinkled with blood. How is this divergence to be explained? Moffatt maintains that our author is treating the pentateuchal account "with characteristic freedom," Montefiore that he is doing so "uncharacteristically"! Spicq and Teodorico suggest that he is following an oral tradition rather than the sacred text itself. Owen judges that "he gathers into one head sundry things wherein the sprinkling of blood was of use under the law, as they are occasionally expressed in sundry places"; and Calvin to the same effect, that "he seems to have mixed together the various kinds of expiations which have the same reference," adding that "there is nothing absurd in this since he is dealing in general with the question of cleansing in the Old Testament which was by blood."

The mention of "calves" instead of oxen is hardly a problem since the Hebrew word used in Exodus 24:5 is applicable to bovine animals of any age and is in fact translated in the Septuagint by a diminutive.[22] The addition of "goats," however, presents something of a difficulty, not merely because goats are not involved in the account of Exodus 24, but more particularly because they were associated with sin offerings, which

---

closely related concepts. "Inaugurate" is basically the sense of the same verb (ἐνεκαίνισεν) in 10:20—the only other occurrence of the verb in the New Testament. The rendering of our version (RSV), "to ratify," fails to convey the meaning accurately.

22. Μοσχάρια, cf. μόσχοι here.

apparently were not offered on the occasion in question. Delitzsch, Moffatt, Spicq, and others suggest that the expression "calves and goats" or its equivalent (see "goats and calves," "goats and bulls," vv. 12f. above, and "bulls and goats," 10:4) was a commonplace or portmanteau expression in connection with the blood sacrifices of the Old Testament, comparable to the expression "gifts and sacrifices" (v. 9 above and 5:1 and 8:3). Westcott supposes that the sacrifices offered on this occasion conformed to the patriarchal type of sacrifice rather than to the levitical pattern, which had not yet been introduced, and particularly to the prototype of all inaugural covenant-sacrifices when Abraham slaughtered, among other animals, a three-year-old heifer and a three-year-old she-goat (Gen. 15:9f.). Another suggestion is that the inclusion of goats here betrays an association in our author's mind with the ceremonial of the Day of Atonement, which provides the framework for his argument and on which both bulls and goats were sacrificed (see again vv. 12f. above and 10:4).

There is a further possibility, namely, that the words "and goats" represent a later addition to the text of our epistle. Their omission is supported by "an impressive combination of witnesses."[23] The shorter reading may indeed be the result of a scribal decision to make what is said here conform to what is read in Exodus 24:5. But it is perhaps more likely that the longer reading is an undesigned assimilation to the expressions "goats and calves" and "goats and bulls" in verses 12 and 13 above. The latter is the judgment of Zuntz,[24] F. F. Bruce, and the NEB.

"Water and scarlet wool and hyssop," which also receive no mention in the ritual described in Exodus 24, were particularly associated in Jewish ceremonial with the operation of sprinkling. Thus, for example, the procedure prescribed for the ritual cleansing of a leper involved the use of water and scarlet wool and hyssop together with cedarwood: two clean birds were chosen and one of them killed "in an earthen vessel over running water"; the remaining, live, bird was then taken and with the cedarwood, the scarlet wool, and the hyssop was dipped in the blood of the bird that had been killed; and after this blood had been sprinkled seven times over the person being cleansed of leprosy, the living bird was allowed to fly away to freedom (Lev. 14:1ff.; cf. Num. 19:6, 18). The hyssop, or marjoram, was apparently tied with the scarlet

---

23. Bruce M. Metzger, *A Textual Commentary on the Greek New Testament* (London and New York, 1971), p. 668.
24. G. Zuntz, *The Text of the Epistles* (London, 1953), pp. 54f. "The words in question are spurious," Zuntz asserts: "they were added on the model of ver. 12. The interpolation is given away by the facts that its wording and its positions vary, that it is absent from the Peshitta and the Harklean, and that it is omitted by Chrysostom."

wool to a cedarwood stick, thus forming a sprinkling implement which was dipped in the blood diluted with water. This, presumably, was the common method of sprinkling, and there is no reason why it should not have been used by Moses in the procedure described in Exodus 24. Delitzsch regards this addition to the Mosaic account as "a natural and obvious one."

Again, in Exodus 24:7, we are told that Moses "took the book of the covenant and read it in the hearing of the people," but there is no mention of the book being sprinkled by him. As, however, it was the custom under the old system for "almost everything" to be purified with blood (v. 22 below), it was only to be expected that, on the day of the solemn ratification of the former covenant, Moses would have sprinkled not only the altar he had built and the people but also the book he had written. In any case there is nothing unreasonable in the assumption that in his amplification of the pentateuchal narrative our author is following a strong and approved tradition. Aquinas offers the suggestion that as this was the first consecration under the former covenant all future ceremonies of sanctification were in effect contained in it, and especially that of the Day of Atonement (Lev. 16) and that connected with the red heifer (Num. 16), the former involving the blood of calves and goats, and the latter water, scarlet wool, and hyssop. Thus understood, our author relates everything back to this original.

The blood used by Moses on this occasion was designated by him *the blood of the covenant* because, as we have seen, it belonged to the special ceremony at which the people, after hearing him read the book of the covenant, pledged their obedience to its precepts and were then sprinkled with this blood. The precise words attributed to Moses in Exodus 24:8 are the following: "Behold the blood of the covenant which the Lord has made with you in accordance with all these words." The extent to which our author's quotation varies from this is not significant, except for the probability that the form "This is the blood of the covenant" is an assimilation to the words used by Christ at the institution of the eucharist: "This is my blood of the covenant" (Mk. 14:24; Mt. 26:28; cf. Lk. 22:20; 1 Cor. 11:25), thereby implying a bond between the two occasions. To partake of the eucharistic cup is to declare in faith and with gratitude one's acceptance of the new covenant in Christ's blood (Lk. 22:20). Precisely the same association is implied by the description of Christians in 1 Peter 1:2 as those who are "sanctified by the Spirit for obedience to Jesus Christ and for sprinkling with his blood." With the shedding of the blood of Jesus Christ the shadow of the blood-shedding inaugurated under Moses has given place to the eternal and all-sufficient reality.

9:21, 22. And in the same way he sprinkled with blood both the tent and all the vessels used in worship. Indeed, under the law almost everything is purified with blood, and without the shedding of blood there is no forgiveness of sins.

In the same way as the inauguration of the former covenant at Sinai was accompanied by the sprinkling with sacrificial blood, the tabernacle, upon its completion, and everything that belonged to it—*the tent and all the vessels used in worship*—were sanctified by this means. The difficulty with our author's affirmation here is, once again, the silence of the Pentateuch, which contains no record of the tabernacle and its vessels being sprinkled by Moses with blood. What is clearly stated is that "the tabernacle and all that was in it" was anointed with oil for the purpose of its consecration (Ex. 40:9ff.; Lev. 8:10f.). But blood was also an integral element in this ceremony of consecration, for the blood of a bull which was slain as a sin offering was applied to the horns of the altar of sacrifice and poured out at the base of that altar; and the blood of a ram, sacrificed as a burnt offering, was sprinkled on the altar, and the same was done with the blood of a second ram after it had been applied to certain parts of the person of Aaron the high priest. Moreover, both blood and oil were sprinkled on the persons and the vestments of Aaron and his sons, thereby setting them apart as holy (Ex. 29:10ff.; Lev. 8:30). This, at least, points to an association of blood with oil in the rite of consecration. Further, in the ritual prescribed for the Day of Atonement the blood of the sacrificial victims was sprinkled on the mercy seat in the holy of holies, on the altar of incense in the holy place, and on the brazen altar in the court of the tabernacle (Lev. 16:14ff.).

It is worthy of remark that Josephus writes[25] in a manner wholly in agreement with our author at this point when he describes how, at the time of the inauguration of the tabernacle and its worship, for a period of seven days Moses purified not only the priests and their vestments but also the tent and its vessels[26] both with oil and with the blood of bulls and goats which were slaughtered each day. We may conclude that both Josephus and our author are following the solid tradition of their day, the authenticity of which there is no reason to doubt. Delitzsch explains that the blood was "the negative (as removing impurities), the oil the positive instrument of sanctification (as symbolically imparting grace)." "That the vessels of the sanctuary, and the sanctuary itself, needed such purification," he adds, "was the result partly of their origin, as made by

---

25. Josephus, *Ant.* iii.206.
26. There is a basic identity of language: Josephus, τὴν τε σκηνὴν καὶ τὰ περὶ αὐτὴν σκευή; Hebrews 9:21, τὴν σκηνὴν δὲ καὶ πάντα τὰ σκευὴ τῆς λειτουργίας.

human hands, and partly of their use, as visited or handled by the unclean."

Under the law, that is, within the framework of the Mosaic system, it is, *indeed,* an established principle that *everything is purified with blood*—or *almost* everything, for there are a few exceptions to the rule. This principle is concisely stated in the words (perhaps a familiar saying)[27] *without the shedding of blood[28] there is no forgiveness of sins.* It is, of course, a principle which is at the very heart of the Christian gospel with its insistence that the shedding of the blood of Jesus Christ is the sole source of cleansing and reconciliation for the sinner (cf. 1 Jn. 1:7; 1 Pet. 1:18f.; Rev. 1:5; 7:14; 12:11; and v. 14 above). What was foreshadowed under the law is fulfilled in Christ. Once again (see p. 376), the language used here is strongly reminiscent of the words with which our Lord instituted the eucharist: "This is my blood of the covenant, which is poured out for many for the forgiveness of sins" (Mt. 26:28).

The ablutions with water to which some commentators have pointed as exceptions to the rule, such as those prescribed in Leviticus 15 and Numbers 19, were hygienic as well as ceremonial and in any case do not seem to have been isolated from the practice of blood-shedding (cf. Lev. 15:14f., 29f.; Num. 19:2ff.). The purification by fire of metal articles captured in battle was also hygienic (Num. 31:21ff.), though here too there was the additional requirement that the water of impurity should be used (v. 23; cf. Num. 19:2ff.). A more relevant exception was that permitted in Leviticus 5:11ff., according to which a person who was so poor as to be unable to afford either two turtle doves or two young pigeons, let alone a lamb or a goat (vv. 6f.), might bring a tenth of an ephah of fine flour for a sin offering. This, however, was not a setting aside of the principle that "without shedding of blood there is no forgiveness of sins," but a gracious concession to the condition of an individual in extreme poverty: the principle was there in intention and his humble offering of flour was accepted in place of the animal victim whose blood would ordinarily have been shed for his sins.

---

27. Cf. Phillips: "as the common saying has it—'No shedding of blood, no remission of sin.'" Delitzsch and some others cite the later rabbinical dictum (which may well have been long in existence), אֵין כַּפָּרָה אֶלָּא בַּדָּם, "there is no atonement except in blood."
28. Many scholars, including Montefiore, F. F. Bruce, Spicq, Moffatt, and Delitzsch, express the opinion that the noun αἱματεκχυσία, "blood-shedding," was coined by our author since there is no trace of the term prior to its appearance in this epistle. It is inherently improbable, however, that he or any other New Testament author invented and used new-fangled words. The likelihood is that this and other novel (novel, that is, only so far as the literary evidence goes) terms in the New Testament were in current circulation and therefore readily recognized and understood by the contemporary readers. Significantly, thanks to the accumulating evidence from non-literary sources, the list of *hapax legomena* in the New Testament is a dwindling one.

9:23. *Thus it was necessary for the copies of the heavenly things to be purified with these rites, but the heavenly things themselves with better sacrifices than these.*

The distinction already expounded in 8:2–5 is resumed here. There it was said that earthly (levitical) priests "serve a copy[29] and shadow of the heavenly sanctuary"[30] (8:5), whereas Christ our High Priest is "a minister in the sanctuary and the true tent, which is set up not by man but by the Lord" (8:2). Here, similarly, "the copies[31] of the heavenly things" are contrasted with "the heavenly things themselves."[32] *The copies of the heavenly things* are, as in 8:5, the wilderness tabernacle and its various furnishings and appointments, and *these rites* with which *it was necessary* for them *to be purified* are the various sacrifices involving the shedding of blood alluded to in the preceding verse. This much is plain. But what does the author mean when he says that "the heavenly things themselves" must also be purified? And what are the "better sacrifices than these" by which this purification is achieved?

To take the latter question first, there is general agreement among commentators that the plural *better sacrifices* is not a precise but a generic plural, corresponding or accommodated to the plural "these rites" in the first clause of the verse: the inferior sacrifices of the levitical system called, speaking generally, for better sacrifices. To be specific, however, they were superseded not by many sacrifices but by *one*, namely, the unique and fully adequate self-offering of the incarnate Son on the cross of Calvary (as our author repeatedly insists—see 7:27; 9:12, 14; 10:10, 12, 14, so that he is not open to the charge of imprecision). His is the "one sacrifice for sins for ever" (10:12 KJV). Hence it is described here as *better:* it accomplishes once and for all that complete and eternal redemption which the imperfect sacrifices of the former system never could accomplish.

But, turning now to the former of the two questions asked above, in what sense are we to understand the affirmation that "the heavenly things themselves" needed to be "purified"? It is clear from the verse which follows and from 8:5 above that the expression "the heavenly things" designates the sanctuary above which is "heaven itself," the reality of which the earthly sanctuary was but a shadow. The interpreter is faced with the problem of explaining how the heavenly reality, where the pure presence of God dwells, can be conceived as requiring any kind of purification. The explanation offered by Delitzsch and others, that

29. Ὑπόδειγμα.
30. Τὰ ἐπουράνια.
31. Τὰ ὑποδείγματα.
32. Αὐτὰ τὰ ἐπουράνια.

379

heaven needed cleansing in the sense, first, that it had been darkened as the light of God's love had been replaced by the cloud of his wrath against sin and, second, that it had been rendered unapproachable to man because of man's sin, is unacceptable; for it is a serious misconception to imagine that the wrath of God is opposed to the love of God, or that these are two mutually exclusive motions or emotions in the Deity. God's wrath, no less than his love, is the expression of his holiness and purity, nor does he set aside wrath in order to display love; indeed, the cross is the supreme manifestation of the love and the wrath of God meeting together, for there the love of God absorbed the wrath of God as the incarnate Son enacted the love of God by taking both the sinner's place and his punishment. Moreover, the unapproachability of heaven to sinful man argues the need for the purification, not of heaven, but of the sinner: to redeemed mankind, cleansed from sin and sanctified by the Holy Spirit, heaven, previously closed, now lies open (10:19ff.).

Also unsatisfactory is the opinion of Héring and others that the purification in question was effected by the dismissal of Satan from heaven (cf. Lk. 10:18; Jn. 12:31; Rev. 12:7ff.) and with him the removal of all defilement. Appeal is made to Ephesians 6:12, which speaks of the powers of wickedness in heavenly places, and to 2:14f. above, where Christ is spoken of as overcoming the devil who has the power of death and delivering those he has held captive; but, while the victory of Christ is indeed the death-blow for Satan and the vindication of his own supreme lordship, the judgment and perdition of the devil were sure even apart from what took place at Calvary. It is inconceivable, further, that the glorious presence of God should be in any danger of defilement because of the rebellion of Satan.

Another view, propounded by, among others, Spicq, Lünemann, and Owen, is that the "purification" of "the heavenly things themselves" means the "inauguration" or "consecration" of the heavenly sanctuary by reason of the "better" sacrifice of Christ. Support for this view is sought from our author's assertion above that the Mosaic covenant was inaugurated with blood (v. 18) and that under the law almost everything was purified with blood (v. 22), the conclusion being drawn that in the present context "to purify" and "to inaugurate" are equivalent terms. There is much to attract in this proposal, which has both simplicity and strength. In contrast to verses 19 to 22, however, which certainly refer to the inauguration of the former covenant, verse 23 is quite general in its scope, and this would seem to present a difficulty; but it could well be treated as a parenthetical comment.

Another interpretation, which can claim a long history and includes among its advocates Chrysostom, Peter Lombard, Herveus, Luther, Cornelius à Lapide, Estius, Teodorico, F. F. Bruce, and Montefiore, understands "the heavenly things" mentioned here, or "the heavenly sanctuary" (as the same expression is translated in 8:5 above), to be the people of God who together constitute the church or temple of God, "a spiritual house, a holy priesthood, to offer spiritual sacrifices acceptable to God through Jesus Christ" (1 Pet. 2:5). Bruce explains that "in order to be a spiritual house of this kind they must have experienced regeneration and cleansing by 'sprinkling of the blood of Jesus Christ' (1 Pet. 1:2, 19, 22f.)." This concept, it can be argued, corresponds as antitype to the action of Moses, recounted in verse 19 above, when he sprinkled all the people with the blood of the covenant. True though this is, it is difficult to see how, except in a subsidiary manner, an interpretation along these lines is suited to the exegesis of the verse before us, for it requires an identification between "the heavenly sanctuary," or, as the next verse defines it, "heaven itself" into which the risen Christ has entered, and the community of the redeemed. The new temple is indeed being built with the living stones of Christian believers within whom Christ dwells, but this concept is not the same as that of the transcendental sanctuary into which the risen Lord entered at his ascension. Nor is the situation clarified by the supposition that our author means that "by the removal of the defilement of sin from the hearts and consciences of the worshippers the heavenly sphere in which they approach God to worship him is itself cleansed from this defilement" (F. F. Bruce, and similarly B. Weiss); for to speak thus is to speak really of the cleansing of sinners, not of heaven. The heavenly sphere is in fact inaccessible to uncleansed sinners (cf. Rev. 21:27); therefore to postulate its cleansing from the defilement it would otherwise have contracted if access had been possible to uncleansed sinners is to postulate a situation which is not factual but rests upon an unfulfilled and unfulfillable condition.

There is no need to seek precise and detailed parallels and correspondences between the cleansing ritual with its multiplicity of applications under the old system and the purification which is made available under the new. The former is complex and repetitious, the latter simple and comprehensive in its uniqueness. Our author's main intention is to emphasize the absolute superiority of the blood of the new covenant over that of the old. The purpose of Christ's coming was "to put away sin by the sacrifice of himself" (v. 26 below); and now, "holy, blameless, unstained, separated from sinners, exalted above the heavens" (7:26), he has entered the pure sanctuary above. The blood-shedding and exaltation of him who is our fellow man and our forerunner (2:14; 6:20) have opened the way for mankind into the shrine of God's presence (4:14–16; 9:8; 10:19ff.); and the ultimate effect of the shedding of his blood of the new covenant will be the renewal of the universe, freed at last from sin, and filled with righteousness (12:28; Isa. 65:17; 66:22; 2 Pet. 3:13; Rev.

21:1ff.; Acts 3:21; Rom. 8:21). Such is the measure by which the former sacrifices are judged to have been surpassed by that better sacrifice which was offered once and forever by our great and eternal High Priest.

9:24. For Christ has entered, not into a sanctuary made with hands, a copy of the true one, but into heaven itself, now to appear in the presence of God on our behalf.

The conjunction *For* indicates the close logical connection between this and the preceding verse. In particular, "the heavenly things themselves," as distinct from "the copies of the heavenly things" in verse 23, are seen to be synonymous with "the true sanctuary" which is "heaven itself," as distinct from "a sanctuary made with hands" which is "a copy of the true one" in the present verse. The *true*, or authentic,[33] sanctuary above is the transcendental reality of which the earthly sanctuary, or, more precisely, the holy of holies, is but the *copy*,[34] as, for example, an architect's plan of a building on paper is the representation in two dimensions, but not the substance, of the three-dimensional reality. The negative qualification *not made with hands* has already been explained as meaning "not of this creation" (v. 11 above):[35] that sanctuary which is real and authentic, identified here with *heaven itself*, does not belong to the present worldly order of things. *Christ has entered* this true sanctuary in order that *now*, as our High Priest and Advocate, he may *appear in the presence of God*. In contrast to the levitical high priest who on the Day of Atonement entered alone into the holy of holies, while all others were stringently excluded, Christ's entry into the heavenly holy of holies is the opposite of exclusive; for, as we have seen (4:16; 6:20), his entry is at the same time the opening up of the way for us to follow into the presence of God himself and with confidence to approach the throne of divine grace.

His appearance in the presence of God, moreover, is *on our behalf*. That is to say, he represents us as our High Priest who has offered the perfect sacrifice in satisfaction for our sins and as our Mediator and

---

33. Ἀληθινός.
34. Ἀντίτυπα here is virtually synonymous with ὑποδείγματα in the preceding verse and ὑπόδειγμα in 8:5. In this case, the sense of the term is not the same as is ordinarily understood by "antitype" as that which answers to and fulfils the significance of the "type," but instead the "type" in its faculty of correspondence (ἀντί) with that which it foreshadows. In the only other place where it occurs in the New Testament, 1 Peter 3:21, it has the opposite and familiar sense, baptism being described as the "antitype" (ἀντίτυπον) answering to and fulfilling the type of the waters of the flood through which those in the ark passed to safety. For the use of τύπος in the sense of "type" see Romans 5:14, and cf. also the adverb τυπικῶς in 1 Corinthians 10:11 (though this may mean "by way of example" rather than "in a typical manner").
35. See also Excursus II, pp. 283ff. above.

Advocate constantly intercedes for us (Heb. 7:25; Rom. 8:34; 1 Jn. 2:1).[36] All that the incarnate Son did and does is on our behalf. As Luther observes, "for Christ to have ascended profits us nothing, if he ascended for his own sake. But now our glory and joy is in this, that he went there to our advantage and not to our disadvantage." And he stresses the difference between those who know Christ merely speculatively, and those who know him practically, that is, by personal experience. "The former," he says, "believe that Christ appears before the face of God for others, the latter that Christ appears before the face of God for us"; adding that "that is why a Christian should be certain that it is for him that Christ appears and is a priest before God." During this earthly pilgrimage the Christian, though justified in Christ, is never free from sin and imperfection—he is, as Luther expressed it in a celebrated phrase, at the same time righteous and a sinner (*simul justus et peccator*); hence the necessity of the appearance of Christ above on his behalf and of the continued application of the blood of the covenant which cleanses from all sin (1 Jn. 1:7), that is, the efficacy of the Son's redeeming death, ever available to the covenant people of God.

> *9:25, 26. Nor was it to offer himself repeatedly, as the high priest enters the Holy Place yearly with blood not his own; for then he would have had to suffer repeatedly since the foundation of the world. But as it is, he has appeared once for all at the end of the age to put away sin by the sacrifice of himself.*

Our author now resumes the theme of the uniqueness and perfection of the self-offering of Christ on behalf of sinners. It is a theme which is at the very heart of his instruction concerning the nature and significance of Christ's high-priestly work; consequently, it is repeatedly emphasized (see vv. 11f. above, 7:27, and 10:11–18). Once again, the ceremonial of the Day of Atonement provides the basis of comparison. Under the levitical system *the high priest* entered[37] the holy of holies[38] on this one day only, but nonetheless *repeatedly*, since he did so *yearly*. Year after year the same ritual was repeated, involving not only the entry of the high priest into the sanctuary but also the yearly repetition of the

---

36. See Excursus III, especially pp. 349ff., above, where the significance of Christ's appearance in the presence of God on our behalf is discussed.

37. Our author's use of the present tense, "the high priest *enters*" (εἰσέρχεται), would seem to imply that when he was writing this epistle the Jerusalem temple was still standing and the levitical system still in operation. See Introduction, pp. 30ff.

38. As in verse 12 above, our version (RSV) misguidedly renders τὰ ἅγια here as "the Holy Place" (as also KJV). It was, however, the holy of holies which the high priest, and he alone, entered but once a year. The holy place, with its altar of incense, golden lampstand, and table of showbread, was entered and tended by the levitical priests every morning and evening. On the question of terminology see n. 54, p. 281 and n. 42, p. 309 above.

sacrifice at the altar outside the sanctuary which provided the blood of atonement. By contrast, however, Christ has appeared *once*, and only once, for the purpose of cancelling sin by the single *sacrifice of himself*. Unlike the blood used by the levitical high priest which was the blood of animal victims, *blood not his own*, the blood provided by our High Priest for the atonement of mankind was human blood, and, moreover, his own blood.

In the present passage three "appearings" of Christ receive mention. Verse 24 states that Christ has entered into heaven "now to appear in the presence of God on our behalf"; verse 26, that "he has appeared once for all at the end of the age to put away sin by the sacrifice of himself"; and verse 28, that he "will appear a second time, not to deal with sin but to save those who are eagerly waiting for him." The reference of verse 24 is plainly to Christ's present high-priestly activity in the sanctuary above. Some authors, particularly those who wish to define the heavenly sanctuary as the sphere of our Lord's self-offering or *sacerdotium*, have attempted to interpret the assertion of verse 26 as referring to the same thing. But, apart from any other considerations,[39] the context does not permit such an interpretation. When verse 28, which, as all agree, speaks of the eschatological appearance of Christ, says that he will appear *a second time*, the necessary implication is that there was *a first time* when he appeared, which is defined there as the time when he was "offered to bear the sins of many." It is agreed, moreover, that the "appearance" of verse 28 is an appearance to mankind; and this determines that the first of the two appearances must also have been to mankind, which cannot be postulated of Christ's present "appearance" in heaven, since this takes place "in the presence of God," not of men. The reference, then, of verse 26 is to the incarnation and earthly ministry of the Son, culminating in "the sacrifice of himself" on the cross where he bore the sins of many (cf. 1 Pet. 2:24, "He himself bore our sins in his body on the tree"). Paul speaks to the same effect when he affirms that "he was manifested (or appeared)[40] in the flesh" (1 Tim. 3:16). Thus Westcott comments on the "appearance" mentioned in verse 26: "He, who is our High-priest, hath been manifested, hath entered the visible life of men as man. On the scene of earth, before the eyes of men, He has overcome death."[41]

---

39. See Excursus III, especially pp. 341ff.

40. Note that in this clear reference to the incarnation Paul uses the same verb (ἐφανερώθη) as is used by our author here (πεφανέρωται). Christ was manifested to human eyes. The use of the perfect in our passage indicates that "the fact of the Incarnation is regarded in its abiding consequences" (Westcott; similarly Teodorico, Spicq).

41. It is worthy of remark that a different verb is used for each of the three "appearings" of Christ mentioned in this passage: verse 24, ἐμφανισθῆναι; verse 26, πεφανέρωται; verse 28, ὀφθήσεται.

This first appearance of Christ is described as having taken place *at the end of the age*, or, to translate the Greek more literally, "at the consummation of the ages,"[42] which the NEB renders effectively as "at the climax of history." Our author is saying precisely the same thing Paul says in Galatians 4:4, namely, that "when the fulness of time came God sent forth his Son," and Peter in 1 Peter 1:20: "He was destined before the foundation of the world but was made manifest at the end of the times for your sake."[43] As Moffatt observes, this manifestation of Christ implies "that Christ as the Son of God was eternal and pre-existent" (similarly Spicq). All that preceded the advent of Christ was leading up to this climactic event which is the focal point for the true perspective of all human history. With his coming the long years of desire and expectation are ended and the last, the eschatological, era of the present world is inaugurated (cf. Heb. 1:2). Consequently, we who live since his coming are those "upon whom the end of the age has come" (1 Cor. 10:11). And the supreme purpose of this appearing was *to put away sin*, that is, to deal, root and branch, with the problem of sin which is the very center and core of the human predicament. This Christ does *by the sacrifice of himself;* for it is on the cross, where he dies the sinner's death, that the tyranny of sin is overthrown (Heb. 2:14f.). Its consequences are absorbed by him and thereby removed from us; its force is nullified. This nullification,[44] moreover, is comprehensive: it covers sin in its totality, without qualification, in every form and degree and also in every age of human history, retrospectively as well as prospectively.[45] Were this not so, we would be confronted with the incongruous conclusion that *then he would have had to suffer repeatedly since the foundation of the world.*

Such a conclusion would, of course, be completely irreconcilable with our author's insistence on the once-for-all character of the suffering and sacrifice of Christ. Unless Christ's offering, in contrast to the offerings of old, which because of their imperfection had constantly to be repeated, was perfect and therefore complete and final, it could hardly have been claimed as an advance on the levitical system in that it too would have required repetition. Yet, while it is readily conceivable that a high priest should repeatedly offer up as sacrifices victims other than himself, involving the shedding of blood other than his own, it is not conceivable that a man should offer up *himself* to death more than once.

42. Ἐπὶ συντελείᾳ τῶν αἰώνων.
43. As in 1 Timothy 3:16 (see n. 40 above), so in 1 Peter 1:20 the same verb (φανερωθέντος) is used as in verse 26 here (πεφανέρωται).
44. The significance of the quasi-juridical term ἀθέτησις is "setting aside" or "nullification." The same noun occurs above in 7:18 where it refers to the nullification of the law by which the levitical priesthood was established. See note 30 (p. 264).
45. The implication, says Moffatt, is "that when his sacrifice did take place, it covered sins of the past (see v.¹⁵), the single sacrifice of Christ in our day availing for all sin, past as well as present and future."

For one thing, as verse 27 is about to remind us, "it is appointed for men to die *once.*" For another, the repetition of sacrifices under the former system necessitated a multiplicity of victims for the same reason that no victim was able to suffer and die more than once. Again, even assuming the possibility of Christ's suffering repeatedly, say for each successive generation from the foundation of the world onward, this would have argued for the limited and inadequate effectiveness of his self-offering, which in turn would overthrow the whole argument of this epistle. "He appeared once for all," comments Calvin, "because if he had come a second or third time there would have been a defect in the first sacrifice which would deny this fulness." What was needed, and what the old system cried out for, was a single perfect sacrifice which would deal fully and finally with the sin of the world, throughout the whole course of human history. Hence the proclamation of John the Baptist when Jesus appeared at the beginning of his public ministry: "Behold, the Lamb of God, who takes away the sin of the world" (Jn. 1:29). As Aquinas says, "Christ offered himself for the sins of the whole world, because he became the propitiation for our sins and for those of the whole world (1 Jn. 2:2), and thus if he had been repeatedly offered it would have been necessary for him to have been repeatedly born and repeatedly to have suffered from the beginning of the world, which would have been in the highest degree incongruous." Christ, however, is *unique*, both as priest and as victim. The blood that he sheds is his own, not that of some other and inferior victim. And the infinite holiness of his person ensures the infinite worth of his offering. "The transcendental character of the victim guarantees the eternal value of his sacrifice (cf. verse 14)," writes Spicq. "Here is the nub of the argument: the salvation of mankind has been achieved by a unique sacrifice, that of Christ, who can die but once, and whose offering has a *definitive* character, since it has an infinite value. Once made, it endures for ever. Such is its essential superiority over the expiatory sacrifices of the old law." What he has done for the putting away of sin has been done *once for all*.

9:27, 28. *And just as it is appointed for men to die once, and after that comes judgment, so Christ, having been offered once to bear the sins of many, will appear a second time, not to deal with sin but to save those who are eagerly waiting for him.*

The true humanity of the incarnate Son is exhibited not only in his living but also in his dying. Indeed, the primary object of his coming into our world was that as Man he might die for men or, as our author has already expressed it, "that by the grace of God he might taste death for every one" (2:9, 14). His identification with our humanity is shown, further, by the fact that he died but *once*, for *to die once* is the *appointed* lot of men. The New Testament, it is true, does speak of some who will not experience death (see, for example, 1 Thess. 4:15ff.), but this is an exception to the rule associated with the eschatological moment of the coming of Christ in glory; and the point our author is making is that men when they die do not die more than once. Hence the incongruity of any suggestion of a repetition or multiplicity of deaths for Christ (v. 26). The New Testament, again, does speak of a "second death," but this does not denote the physical death to which our author is referring here, but the ultimate sentence of death that is pronounced on unbelieving and obdurate sinners at the final judgment after this life (Rev. 2:11; 20:6, 14f.; 21:8). It is, in fact, what our author means when he says *and after that* (death) *comes judgment*. In the present argument, then, the particular (the death of Christ which took place once, never to be repeated) is corroborated by an appeal to the general (the common experience of death which comes but once to all men).

The mortality of man has a twofold reference. In the first place, man is mortal by nature. "Death," as Owen says, "was so far natural from the beginning, as that the frame and constitution of our nature were in themselves liable and subject thereunto." Immortality is possessed by God alone (1 Tim. 6:16), and man is totally dependent on God for the gift and the continuance of life. The perfect relationship of love and trust toward his Creator would mean for the creature (and hereafter for the redeemed will mean) an uninterrupted participation in the life that flows from its Source. Left to himself, man will die. Thus, in the second place, man is mortal, not merely potentially but actually mortal, "appointed to die," by reason of the rebellion of sin through which he has wilfully separated himself from the Source of life. Death comes to all because all are sinners; it is the inevitable consequence of turning away from the Life-Giver (Rom. 3:23; 5:12). Hence the connection of death with *judgment*; for while death itself is a judgment that sinful man has brought upon himself, it is not the final judgment which, as something distinct, follows after death.

This judgment, moreover, is inseparably associated with that day when *Christ will appear a second time, not to deal with sin*, [46] for this was the

---

46. The expression χωρὶς ἁμαρτίας, "without sin" or "apart from sin," has already occurred in 4:15. There the reference is to the sinless character of Christ as he overcame every temptation. It is true that when he appears the second time he will still be "without sin" in this sense; but this does not seem to be the point of what our author is saying here, though this is how some of the early interpreters took it. Others have understood the expression to mean "without a sacrifice for sin." Thus, for example, Herveus comments: "that is, without an offering for sin, because then he does not offer a sacrifice for sins, but will condemn

purpose and achievement of his first appearing, when he was *offered once to bear the sins of many*, but *to save*, that is, to receive to the full and consummating enjoyment of their eternal salvation, *those who are eagerly waiting for him*, while for those who neglect such a great salvation (2:3) there can be only a "fearful expectation of judgment" (10:27; cf. 12:25). The man who thrusts from him the word of the gospel thereby judges himself unworthy of eternal life (Acts 13:46). To refuse the cross as the instrument of salvation is to choose it as the instrument of judgment (cf. Jn. 12:48).

The declaration that Christ was "offered to bear the sins of many" is virtually a quotation from Isaiah 53:12, where the prophet affirms, "he bore the sin of many."[47] This is the only plain allusion in our epistle to the Suffering Servant concept of Isaiah, but it is a reminder of the special significance of this concept, and particularly in the 53rd chapter of the prophecy, as applied to and fulfilled in Christ, in the apostolic proclamation of the gospel. From the time of Chrysostom onward there have been numerous interpreters who have explained that, though Christ died for all (see, for example, 2 Cor. 5:15), it is said here that he bore the sins of "many" because in fact not all believe in him. Calvin, however, is more probably correct when he asserts that "many" here is synonymous with "all," as in Romans 5:15. "It is of course certain," he says, "that not all enjoy the fruits of Christ's death, but this happens because their unbelief hinders them. That question is not dealt with here because the apostle is not discussing how few or how many benefit from the death of Christ, but means simply that he died for others, not for himself. He therefore contrasts the many with the one."

The two appearings of Christ (vv. 26 and 28) answer to the pattern of the appearings of the levitical high priest on the Day of Atonement. First the high priest appeared for the purpose of offering the atoning sacrifice on the altar which stood in the courtyard outside the sanctuary. Then he passed from sight as he entered the sanctuary with the blood of atonement, there to make intercession on behalf of the people. Thus Aaron bore the names of the sons of Israel upon his heart and in the sanctuary brought them to continual remembrance before the Lord (Ex. 28:29).

---

those who persevere in sins; for it is a custom of the law that a sacrifice which is offered for sins should be called sin" (cf. the expression περὶ ἁμαρτίας in 10:6 and 8). In the present context, however, the phrase may best be rendered "without reference to sin" or, as our version has it, "not to deal with sin" (similarly JB), for this purpose was achieved at his first coming when he "put away sin by the sacrifice of himself" (v. 26). As Moffatt says, "the striking phrase χωρὶς ἁμαρτίας rests on the idea that the one atonement had been final." "By this second coming," Calvin observes, "he will make clear the efficacy of his death so that sin will have no further power to hurt us."

47. Isaiah 53:12 (LXX): αὐτὸς ἁμαρτίας πολλῶν ἀνήνεγκεν. Hebrews 9:27: εἰς τὸ πολλῶν ἀνενεγκεῖν ἁμαρτίας. Cf. 1 Peter 2:24: ὃς τὰς ἁμαρτίας ἡμῶν αὐτὸς ἀνήνεγκεν.

This done, he came out from the sanctuary and presented himself again to the people, who were assembled in eager expectation of the reappearance of their high priest. So also Christ, our unique High Priest of the order of Melchizedek, who appeared in the precincts of this world in order "to put away sin by the sacrifice of himself" (v. 26), and then passed from sight into the heavenly sanctuary, where he now appears "in the presence of God on our behalf" as our Intercessor and Advocate (v. 24; 7:25; 1 Jn. 2:1), "will appear a second time" to mankind when he comes forth from the true sanctuary to proclaim and to perform the completion of salvation for "those who are eagerly waiting for him" (v. 28). Thus will dawn the morning of the eternal day when those who love his appearing (2 Tim. 4:8) will see him as he is and, being at last fully conformed to his likeness, will be satisfied (1 Jn. 3:2; 2 Cor. 3:18).

10:1–4. *For since the law has but a shadow of the good things to come instead of the true form of these realities, it can never, by the same sacrifices which are continually offered year after year, make perfect those who draw near. Otherwise, would they not have ceased to be offered? If the worshippers had once been cleansed, they would no longer have any consciousness of sin. But in these sacrifices there is a reminder of sin year after year. For it is impossible that the blood of bulls and goats should take away sins.*

In these verses the incompetence of the old levitical order in comparison with the uniquely adequate priesthood of Christ is demonstrated in four particular respects.

(1) *The insubstantial character of the Mosaic system.* The assertion that *the law,* to which the levitical priesthood was closely bound (Heb. 7:11f.), *has but a shadow of the good things to come* is a resumption of what has already been said in 8:5, namely, that the Aaronic priests "serve a copy and shadow of the heavenly sanctuary"; though there the comparison is between the earthly and the heavenly sanctuaries, whereas here it is between the sacrifices offered by the two contrasting orders of priesthood. Héring rightly insists that the primary emphasis is on the gulf that separates the shadow from the reality. There is also, however, a connection, for a shadow, though itself without substance, does not exist apart from a substantial reality, and thus it may be said to presuppose the existence of the reality of which it is the shadow. It is as though, within the perspective of God's antecedent purposes, the reality which is Christ casts its shadow forward over the unfolding drama of the preparation of the gospel, while, historically, that same reality casts a shadow back over those centuries that lead up to the advent of the Savior, a shadow

which received definition in terms of law and priesthood, promise and prophecy. The true source of this shadow is discovered in the person and work of the incarnate Redeemer. Hence our author's description of the shadow as being "of the good things to come." But the shadow, though caused by the reality it portends, is not the same thing as that reality and must not be confused with it. Just as the shadow is other than the substance, so also the regulations of the old covenant (9:1) are distinct from *the true form of these realities,*[48] which are described here as "the good things to come." The form or image of things, says Lefèvre d'Etaples, is "their archetype, their light and truth"; and he explains that "Christ is the light and Christ the truth of things."

(2) *The repetitive nature of the old sacrifices.* The theme of the repetitiveness of the levitical sacrificial system has also received mention earlier in the epistle (7:27; 9:25). Repetition conflicts with finality: an action that is final does not tolerate repetition, and, conversely, an action that is constantly repeated thereby shows itself to be inconclusive. What is inconclusive is imperfect both in itself and in its effect. Hence the argu-

48. In the expression αὐτὴν τὴν εἰκόνα τῶν πραγμάτων the noun εἰκών does not connote a copy or likeness which as such would be other than the reality; if it did, what is said here would be meaningless if not contradictory. Its sense, rather, is the *manifestation* of the reality itself, and this sense is found in both classical and contemporary Greek (see, for example, Plato, *Timaeus* 92c; Philo, *De Spec. Leg.* II.176). Moffatt goes so far as to suggest that our author is actually using a Platonic phrase, since the expression εἰκόνας τῶν πραγμάτων occurs in *Cratylus* 306e. According to H. Kleinknecht, "εἰκών does not imply a weakening or a feeble copy of something," but "the illumination of its inner core and essence" (Kittel, TDNT, II, p. 389); and G. Kittel writes to the same effect: "When Christ is called the εἰκών τοῦ θεοῦ in 2 C. 4:4; Col. 1:15, all the emphasis is on the equality of the εἰκών with the original. Christ is ἐν μορφῇ θεοῦ, in the sense of εἶναι ἴσα θεῷ (Phil. 2:6). In Johannine language His being as εἰκών means: ὁ ἑωρακὼς ἐμὲ ἑώρακεν τὸν πατέρα (Jn. 14:9; 12:45)" (*ibid.*, p. 395). The same is the case with the related expression in 1:3 of our epistle, where the Son is described as χαρακτὴρ τῆς ὑποστάσεως αὐτοῦ, "flawless expression of the nature of God" (Phillips). Delitzsch comments: "We have indeed to understand εἰκών here in accordance with Col. iii.10, τὸν ἀνακαινούμενον κατ᾽ εἰκόνα τοῦ κτίσαντος αὐτόν, with Rom. viii.9, συμμόρφους τῆς εἰκόνος τοῦ υἱοῦ. The meaning in both passages is, not that the new man is only like the image of his Creator, and not like the Creator Himself, but rather that the Creator Himself, the Son of God Himself, is that image or original to which the new man of the resurrection is to be conformed." Thus Bengel explains εἰκόνα here as "imaginem archetypam et primam solidamque." See the interesting contrast in Colossians 2:7 between σκιά, "shadow," and σῶμα, "body." In p⁴⁶ the reading καὶ τὴν εἰκόνα is found instead of οὐκ αὐτὴν τὴν εἰκόνα, giving the sense: "since the law has but a shadow of the good things to come and the image (or copy) of these realities," thus making σκιά and εἰκών virtually synonymous here, an equation that can be matched in Plato (cf. *Meno* 100a with *Republic* 533a; also *Repub.* 510a) and Philo (*Leg. Alleg.* III.96, etc.). Zuntz (*The Text of the Epistles*, pp. 20–23) describes the p⁴⁶ reading as an "ingenious conjecture," but gives adequate reason for its rejection. "Readings attested by p⁴⁶ *solus*," says Tasker, "should not . . . be accepted unless their intrinsic quality stands the severest test" ("The Text of the 'Corpus Paulinum,'" NTS, I, 1954–55, pp. 183f.). Metzger describes it as "an interesting reading, but one which certainly cannot be original, for the construction of the sentence implies a contrast between εἰκών and σκιά" (*A Commentary on the Greek New Testament*, London and New York, 1971, p. 669).

ment in the passage before us. The law, prescribing as it does *the same sacrifices which are continually offered*[49] *year after year,* that is, annually on the Day of Atonement, is unable by means of such sacrifices *to make perfect those who draw near.* This inability to effect perfection, in the radical sense of 9:9 ("gifts and sacrifices are offered which cannot perfect the conscience of the worshipper"), is pressed home by the logic of the question, *Otherwise would they not have ceased to be offered?* Their very repetition argues their inadequacy to bring about a profound and permanent removal of sin and its consequences. The offering, however, of the perfect sacrifice demands thenceforth the cessation of sacrifice. Thus Aquinas observes that "because they did not cease constantly to offer the same sacrifices, it is a sign that they were not being cleansed," and he refers to the saying of Christ in Matthew 9:12: "Those who are well have no need of a physician, but those who are sick." Just as a man who is cured of an illness is no longer aware of being ill, since he no longer has an illness of which to be aware, so our author makes the point that, *if the worshippers had once been cleansed,* or, better, "cleansed once for all"[50] (NEB), *they would no longer have any consciousness of sin*—though what is being spoken of here is more than mere consciousness or awareness (JB): it is the *conscience* or radical knowledge of guilt which places one under the shadow of God's judgment, described as the "evil conscience" in verse 22 below, and which, as we have seen, the blood of Christ alone purifies from dead works to serve the living God (9:14).

(3) *The function of the levitical sacrifices as repeated reminders of sin.* Though, indeed, these sacrifices were concerned with sin and the necessity of its removal, as the ritual of the Day of Atonement clearly showed, the very consideration that they were offered by the high priest *year after year* in itself demonstrated, as has already been explained, that they were neither perfect nor final. The annually recurring Day of Atonement, accordingly, served as a repeated *reminder of sin* and by its repetition pointed to the need for a sacrifice that would be "full, perfect, and sufficient" (Book of Common Prayer) and therefore offered once-for-all, never to be repeated. The people, on whose behalf the sacrifices were offered under the old system, thus had their sinfulness brought to their remembrance, as it were, every time the Day of Atonement came around—not to mention the yet more frequent reminders afforded by

---

49. Literally, "which they continually offer"—the plural is used impersonally. The use of the present tense here (προσφέρουσιν) would seem, again, to indicate that the offering of sacrifices was still taking place in the Jerusalem temple. See Introduction, pp. 30ff. The same implication is present in verse 2 if the inference there is that the levitical sacrifices had still not ceased to be offered; but the meaning may simply be that, if perfect, these sacrifices would not have been repeated.

50. Within the context ἅπαξ means "once for all," and this sense is confirmed by the use of the perfect participle κεκαθαρισμένους which suggests a cleansing that is permanent.

the innumerable other offerings that were made from day to day. It was the Day of Atonement in particular on which their sinfulness and need of forgiveness and reconciliation were brought into focus on a national scale. Moffatt suggests that there may be an echo here of "the offering of remembrance, bringing iniquity to remembrance"[51] mentioned in Numbers 5:15. The resemblance, however, is more apparent than real, for the context of Numbers 5:15 is that of bringing to remembrance in the sense of bringing to light a particular sin committed in secret, the commission of which could not be established by the testimony of witnesses. But it is worthy of notice that the term *reminder*[52] used here by our author is potentially ambivalent, in that the yearly sacrifices not only reminded the people of their own sinfulness but also reminded them that *God remembers sin*. Hence the tremendous impact of the promise of the new covenant already quoted in 8:12, and repeated in verse 17 below, that God "will remember their sins no more." Sins remembered by God are sins for which propitiation has not been made. Sins no longer remembered by God are sins for which full atonement has been freely provided and gratefully received.[53]

(4) *The ineffectiveness of the blood of beasts.* Had the ancient sacrifices been intended as the reality instead of the shadow, there would have been an insuperable incongruity involved in the offering of them, since, as has been remarked earlier in this commentary, a brute beast is by its very nature unqualified to serve as a substitute for man, the crown of God's creation. Lacking both volition and rationality, it is passive and inarticulate and therefore incapable of the spontaneous declaration, "Lo, I have come to do thy will, O God" (v. 7 below). Only man, who is a rational, volitional, articulate, and responsible being, can serve as a proper equivalent and substitute for man: hence the incarnation, whereby the Son of God assumed our humanity, so that as man he might offer himself in the place of our fallen humanity (2:9, 14). Further, only perfect man, himself entirely free from sin, could properly stand in man's place and absorb the punishment due to man's sin (2:14–18; 4:15f.;

---

51. LXX: θυσία μνημοσύνου ἀναμιμνήσκουσα ἁμαρτίαν.

52. Ἀνάμνησις.

53. Philo says, with reference to Numbers 5:15, that the unhallowed sacrifices of ungodly men in fact "call to remembrance (ὑπομιμνήσκουσι) the ignorance and misdeeds of such men" (*De Plantatione* 109) and bring down punishment on them. In such cases the sacrifices, though to outward appearance in order, "effect not remission (λύσις) but remembrance (ὑπόμνησις) of sins" (*De Vita Mosis*, 107). As might be expected, Philo does not question the adequacy of sacrifices offered by good men. "It would be foolish," he writes, "if the effect of sacrifices were remembrance (ὑπόμνησις) instead of forgetting (λήθη) of sins" (*De Spec. Leg.* i.215); for it is the forgetting (ἀμνηστία, the precise opposite of ἀνάμνησις here or Philo's synonym ὑπόμνησις) of past sins that pious men may expect (*Vita Mos.* ii.24; *De Spec. Leg.* i.242), the implication being that it is God who "remembers" and "forgets" sins.

5:8–10; 7:26f.; 9:26). And, finally, only one who by his resurrection from the dead has been vindicated as the Lord of Life, and who lives forevermore, can be our eternal High Priest and the guarantor to us of everlasting salvation (1:2–4; 6:20; 7:16, 24, 25; 8:1; 9:12; 12:2; 13:8). In the light of these necessities, so frequently stressed in our epistle, there is no escape from the conclusion that *it is impossible that the blood of bulls and goats should take away sins* (bulls and goats being specifically mentioned because of the focus of our author's attention on the ceremonial of the annual Day of Atonement).

What, then, it may well be asked, was the justification of the whole sacrificial system connected with the Mosaic law? Was it not a great illusion? Did it not arouse false hopes? The answer to such questions is more implicit than explicit in the content of this epistle. For one thing, the Mosaic system was divinely instituted (3:2ff.; 8:5; 12:18ff.) and accordingly within the scope of God's beneficent purposes for mankind. But it was in nature preparatory, or propaedeutic, showing in particular the seriousness of sin, the reality of the righteousness of God, and the necessity for atonement. For another thing, though itself the shadow and not the substance, and inherently incapable of achieving the reconciliation which it presaged, by its typical forms in association with the promises of the new covenant it pointed forward to the achievement of a full and final expiation through the Lamb which God would provide (7:11ff.; 8:1ff.; 9:11ff.; 10:11ff.). The Old Testament era was one of expectancy rather than arrival, and, as chapter 11 will declare, the godly of that era embraced the promises without seeing their fulfilment. They were not, however, at a disadvantage compared with us, who look back to the completion of the promises in Christ (2 Cor. 1:20), for we and they are made perfect together (Heb. 11:13, 39). The sacrifice offered on the Day of Atonement, says Teodorico, "far from possessing the power to expiate the sins of the past year, served only to dispose their minds to implore in penitence the divine pardon, which was ever accorded in virtue of the future unique sacrifice of Christ." Teodorico observes, further, that the *anamnēsis*, or remembrance, mentioned here by our author was "a reminder, beyond doubt humbling and salutary, but in itself incapable of effecting the removal of the burden which weighed heavily on man's conscience, in the same manner as the law pointed to the evil but did not provide the remedy."

In the present era of grace the proclamation of the cross ever calls to remembrance the sinfulness of mankind, while at the same time it presents the remedy which God has provided in Christ. But Christian faith, too, cannot exist without remembrance, for the whole life of the believer should be the expression of his gratitude as he remembers the infinite cost at which his redemption was purchased. And the Lord of the church has provided a dramatic aid to the declaration of our thankful remembrance by his institution of the sacrament of our redemption, appropriately known as the eucharist (thanksgiving), with the command, "Do this in remembrance (*anamnēsis*) of me." The gospel transforms *anamnēsis* from a remembrance of guilt to a remembrance of grace![54] The teaching of this passage has been excellently expounded by Philip Melanchthon, as follows:

> There was in reality only one propitiatory sacrifice in the world, namely, the death of Christ, as the Epistle to the Hebrews teaches when it says, "It is impossible that the blood of bulls and goats should take away sins." . . . For those levitical sacrifices were only called propitiatory in that they pointed to a future expiation. Accordingly, they were by a certain similitude satisfactions restoring the righteousness of the law, lest those who had sinned should be excluded from the commonwealth. But after the revelation of the Gospel they had to cease, and for this reason, that they were not truly propitiations, since the Gospel was promised for the very purpose that it might provide propitiation.[55]

10:5–10. *Consequently, when Christ came into the world, he said, "Sacrifices and offerings thou hast not desired, but a body hast thou prepared for me; in burnt offerings and sin offerings thou hast taken no pleasure. Then I said, 'Lo, I have come to do thy will, O God,' as it is written of me in the roll of the book." When he said above, "Thou hast neither desired nor taken pleasure in sacrifices and offerings and burnt offerings and sin offerings" (these are offered according to the law), then he added, "Lo, I have come to do thy will." He abolishes the first in order to establish the second. And by that will we have been sanctified through the offering of the body of Jesus Christ once for all.*

Our author takes the words of Psalm 40:6–8 and places them on the lips of Christ at his coming into this world as the apostle of reconciliation. In view of the fact that the Psalmist's immediate concern was to praise God for deliverance and to dedicate himself to the performance of the will of God, this may seem to be a bold procedure. But over and over again the New Testament shows that passages in the Old Testament

---

54. Westcott offers the following comment: "Under the new Covenant God Himself does not remember the sins of His people, still less does He bring them solemnly to their remembrance. The use of the word ἀνάμνησις suggests a contrast between the Jewish sacrifices and the Christian Eucharist. In them there was ἀνάμνησις ἁμαρτιῶν. They were instituted to keep fresh the thought of responsibility: that was instituted, in Christ's words, εἰς τὴν ἐμὴν ἀνάμνησιν (Luke xxii.19; I Cor. xi.24f.), to bring to men's minds the recollection of the redemption which He has accomplished."
55. Philip Melanchthon, *Quid sit sacrificium* . . . , in *Apologia Confessionis Augustanae, Corpus Reformatorum*, XXVII, p. 611.

have a significance and an application beyond and in addition to the original occasion of their composition, and this is especially so with reference to the redemptive work of Christ. If the Psalmist could say, *Lo, I have come to do thy will, O God,* he could do so only falteringly, because of his sinful inadequacy before his Creator. But on the lips of Christ these words are uniquely and preeminently appropriate, first of all because in terms of promise and prophecy he supremely is the Coming One,[56] the messianic deliverer whose advent has been longingly awaited, and, secondly, because the predominant purpose of his coming was to do the Father's will. Hence his declaration: "I have come down from heaven, not to do my own will, but the will of him who sent me" (Jn. 6:38; cf. 4:34). This divine will was the salvation of our sinful humanity. "The saying is sure and worthy of full acceptance," Paul assures Timothy, "that Christ Jesus came into the world to save sinners" (1 Tim. 1:15); and our author is saying the same thing here when he affirms that *by that will we have been sanctified,* for in the terminology of this epistle sanctification, involving the purging away of sin and access into the holy presence of God himself, is synonymous with the whole experience of salvation (see commentary above on 2:11).

For the performance of the Father's will, moreover, the Son required *a body,* since the promised salvation demanded the offering up of himself in the place of sinners. As the Good Shepherd who came to lay down his life for the sheep he announces: "For this reason the Father loves me, because I lay down my life, that I may take it again . . . ; and this charge I have received from my Father" (Jn. 10:11, 15, 17f.). Accordingly, he condescends to our estate in the self-humbling act of incarnation, so that the Psalmist's words, *a body hast thou prepared for me,* receive in him a fulfilment which is ultimate and universal in its evangelical significance. The body prepared for the Son was the body he assumed in the incarnation in which he obeyed the Father's will, even to the death of the cross (Heb. 2:14; 5:8; 12:2; Phil. 2:8). "As the Word who is immortal and the Father's Son it was not possible for him to die," explains Athanasius, "and this is the reason why he assumed a body capable of dying, so that, belonging to the Word who is above all, in dying it might become a sufficient exchange for all. . . . When he offered his own temple and bodily instrument as a substitute for the life of all he fulfilled in death all that was required." Again: "He put on a body so that in the body he might find death and blot it out." Moreover, "he was not limited and confined by the body, but held it under his control so that he

---

56. Cf. εἰσερχόμενος εἰς τὸν κόσμον here with John 6:14, "This is indeed the prophet who is to come into the world" (ὁ ἐρχόμενος εἰς τὸν κόσμον), and John 11:27, "I believe that you are the Christ, the Son of God, he who is coming into the world" (ὁ εἰς τὸν κόσμον ἐρχόμενος).

was both in it and also in all things and outside all created things, reposing in the Father alone; indeed, the wonderful thing is that at one and the same time as man he was living a human life, as Word he was sustaining the life of the universe, and as Son he was in constant union with the Father."[57]

It should be remarked that the statement, "a body hast thou prepared for me," corresponds in meaning with the Greek of the Septuagint, which it is our author's custom to follow when quoting from the Old Testament, but not with the Hebrew of Psalm 40:7, the literal sense of which is, "ears thou hast dug for me" (RSV mg.). It is possible that the translators of the Septuagint version had before them a Hebrew text which read "body" instead of "ears" (though external evidence for any such variant is lacking), or that the discrepancy is due to a copyist's error which became entrenched in the Greek of the Septuagint.[58] Conjectures aside, however, the difference between the Septuagint and the Hebrew is not so great as it might at first appear to be. The former is in fact described by Delitzsch as "a free, generalizing rendering" of the latter.[59] Calvin reminds us that the apostolic authors "were not over-scrupulous in quoting words provided that they did not misuse Scripture for their convenience" and that "we must always look at the purpose for which quotations are made." And Owen contends that we have here an example of synecdoche, that is, the use of a part for the whole, in this instance the ears for the body, "because as it is impossible that anyone should have ears of any use but by virtue of his having a body, so the ears are that part of the body by which alone instruction unto obedience, the thing aimed at, is received."

The context in which the expression is placed makes this all the more apparent. The assertion, "but a body hast thou prepared for me," is preceded by the declaration *sacrifices and offerings thou hast not desired* and followed by the similar declaration *in burnt offerings and sin offerings*

---

57. Athanasius, *De Incarnatione* 9, 44, 17.
58. The LXX rendering, which our author reproduces, is σῶμα δὲ κατηρτίσω μοι. Despite the strong attestation of σῶμα (body), in Vaticanus, Sinaiticus, Alexandrinus, etc., the reading ὠτία (ears) is adopted, surprisingly, by Rahlfs in his edition of the LXX. Bleek and Lünemann have conjectured that the reading σῶμα resulted from the error of a copyist who misread ΣΩΤΙΑ as ΣΩΜΑ (in the text sigma would be the letter immediately preceding ὠτία). If it is asked why כָּרִיתָ is translated by κατηρτίσω ("thou hast prepared") rather than by ὤρυξας or διώρυξας ("thou hast dug"), Delitzsch answers that κατηρτίσω is "by itself an easier and more general rendering of the Hebrew כרית." It is unlikely that, as a number of commentators have supposed, the Psalmist intended an allusion to the rite described in Exodus 21:1–6, in which a slave who voluntarily refused his liberty when it became due to him after six years' service was required to have his ears pierced in token that he had chosen to serve his master for life. The words of Isaiah 50:4f. may be taken as offering an accurate reflection of his meaning: "The Lord God ... wakens my ear to hear as those who are taught. The Lord God has opened my ear, and I was not rebellious."
59. F. Delitzsch, *Biblical Commentary on the Psalms*, II, p. 45.

thou hast taken no pleasure, which in turn is followed by the affirmation, "Lo, I have come to do thy will, O God." This, clearly, is a poetic arrangement. The more prosaic order would be:

> Sacrifices and offerings thou hast not desired,
> in burnt offerings and sin offerings thou hast taken no pleasure,
> but a body hast thou prepared for me.
> Then I said, "Lo, I have come to do thy will, O God."

The Psalmist is stressing the inadequacy and unacceptability of the sacrifices of the levitical system[60] apart from a life of obedience to the will of God. The original form, "ears thou hast dug for me," means simply, "thou hast caused me to hear and obey thy will," or, in other words, to "glorify God in [my] body" (1 Cor. 6:20). The thrust is identical with that of Samuel's admonitory words to Saul: "Has the Lord as great delight in burnt offerings and sacrifices as in obeying the voice of the Lord? Behold, to obey is better than sacrifice, and to hearken than the fat of rams" (1 Sam. 15:22; cf. Isa. 1:11ff.; Amos 5:21f.; Hos. 6:6; Ps. 51:16ff.; Jer. 7:21f.). Thus, as Moffatt comments, "the Greek text meant practically what the original had meant, and it made this interpretation or application possible, namely, that there was a sacrifice which answered to the will of God as no animal sacrifice could."

But this new heart of obedience to the will of God was precisely what the Mosaic covenant was incompetent to provide. Hence the promise of the new covenant: "I will put my laws in their minds, and write them on their hearts, and I will be their God, and they shall be my people" (8:10). It was only, however, by virtue of the body which the Father prepared for the Son, so that in perfect obedience he might taste death for everyone (2:9f.), thus purifying the sinner's conscience from dead works to serve the living God (9:14), that this grace of regeneration became a reality. The body of his incarnation, whereby he identified himself with our humanity and was capacitated to stand in our stead, was essential if the Son was obediently to hear and do the will of the Father for our everlasting redemption.

Moreover, the authenticity of what the Psalmist writes is confirmed by the fact that it is *scriptural.* Thus he claims: *as it is written of me in the roll of the book.*[61] For him, doubtless, "the roll of the book" signified the

---

60. The four designations θυσίαν... προσφοράν... ὁλοκαυτώματα... περὶ ἁμαρτίας cover in effect the whole range of the levitical sacrificial system, representing in order the peace offerings (זְבָחִים or שְׁלָמִים, θυσίαι), the meal offerings (מִנְחוֹת, προσφοραί), the whole burnt offerings (עוֹלוֹת, ὁλοκαυτώματα), and the sin offerings (חַטָּאוֹת, περὶ ἁμαρτίας). In the LXX περὶ ἁμαρτίας is a quasi-technical substantival expression (as in Lev. 14:19, Num. 8:8, and Ps. 40:7, as quoted by our author). It has already been used in 5:3 above and it recurs in verses 8, 18, and 26, and in 13:11 below.
61. The expression "in the roll of the book" reflects the meaning of the original Hebrew, בִּמְגִלַּת־סֵפֶר, rather than the Greek of the LXX which our author reproduces here, ἐν

397

books of Moses (the *Torah*) in which the will of God and the way of obedience were written (particularly perhaps a passage like Dt. 28–30). For our author, who, as we have noticed, places the words of the Psalmist on the lips of Christ, the connotation of "the roll of the book" would have been extended to refer to the Old Testament scriptures in their entirety—Moses indeed, who wrote of Christ (Jn. 5:46), but also, beyond Moses, the prophets and the psalms, in short, "all the scriptures," whose central theme is the coming of Christ into the world to accomplish the redemptive will of God (Lk. 24:27, 45). Once again, however, in the former dispensation the law of God is written externally, "in the roll of the book," whereas in this new dispensation of the gospel it is written internally, in the heart of the new man in Christ (Heb. 8:10; 2 Cor. 3:3).

In verses 8 to 10 our author offers some explanatory comments on the passage he has cited from Psalm 40. He points out, first, that the offer-

---

κεφαλίδι βιβλίου, which would seem to refer literally to the rod (*umbilicus*), or more precisely the top piece of the rod, around which a written document was rolled; but, if this is so, the usage here is that of synecdoche, the whole scroll being intended by the mention of a single part. The noun κεφαλίς means "a little head" (*capitulum*), the "capital" of a column, and so possibly here by deduction the top-piece or knob on the rod at the center of a papyrus roll; but this sense has no confirmation from other sources. It is more probable that κεφαλίς did in fact have a meaning equivalent to the Hebrew *megillah* or scroll. This, at least, is the case in a writing belonging to the fifth century in which, in a passage concerning Ephraim, one of the saints is said to have seen in a vision an angel descending "with a *kephalis* (κεφαλίδα, Latin *volumen*) in his hands, that is, a tome (τόμον, Latin *tomum*) written both within and without" (Migne, PG, LXV, 167–168). Quite possibly, however, this meaning of κεφαλίς was derived from its use here in Hebrews 10:7. Another conjecture is that κεφαλίς acquired this meaning from its similarity in form to the Hebrew root קפל, "to roll"; but this is improbable. The Vulgate translates ἐν κεφαλίδι βιβλίου as *in capite libri*, which some of the Latin fathers understood to mean "in the beginning of the book," that is, the beginning of the Old Testament scriptures, namely, Genesis 1:1, "In the beginning..." (*In principio*), where Beginning (*Principium*) was interpreted as a designation of Christ in whom, as the Beginning, all things were made (Tertullian, Jerome, Hilary, etc.). Owen adopts a similar principle when he contends that the reference is to the first gospel promise of Genesis 3:15: "As the book itself was one roll, so the head of it, the beginning of it, amongst the first things written in it, is this recorded concerning the coming of Christ to do the will of God." In the light of this interpretation it is somewhat surprising that Owen dismisses as "a peculiar conceit" the opinion of the Socinian expositors that a passage like Deuteronomy 17:18f., which could be said to be fulfilled in the Psalmist David, is intended. Others (for example, Alcuin, Peter Lombard, Herveus) have understood the expression as a reference to the beginning of the book of Psalms (Ps. 1:1: "Blessed is the man..."). It is difficult to determine the force of Bengel's view that what is meant is the actual page on which the psalm quoted was written. Aquinas suggests three possible interpretations of *in capite libri scriptum est de me*: (1) "That book is Christ according to his human nature, in whom all things necessary for man's salvation are written"; (2) "The book of life, which is nothing other than the knowledge which God has of the predestination of the saints, who are saved through Christ"; (3) "'In the head of the book', that is, in me according to the divine nature, 'it is written concerning me', according to the human nature, 'that I should do thy will'...." But this is surely to attempt to read too much into what is a generally simple and straightforward assertion.

ings and sacrifices of the levitical system in all their variety *are offered according to the law,* [62] that is, the Mosaic law whose ordinances, as he has shown earlier, have become obsolete as, with the coming of Christ, the order of Melchizedek replaces that of Levi (Heb. 7:11ff.; 8:7, 13). Thus the incarnate Son *abolishes the first,* namely, the sacrifices associated with the Mosaic law, *in order to establish the second,* namely, the will of God involving the offering of himself as the one sacrifice for sins forever. It is *by that will,* and that will alone, that *we have been sanctified,* that is, cleansed from sin and restored to the holy sphere of God's favor—not, of course, that the will of God is intended apart from the action of God in Christ, for, unlike man who, left to himself, finds that to will and to perform are all too often two different things (cf. Rom. 7:15ff.: "I do not do what I will, but I do the very thing that I hate. . . . I do not do the good that I will, but the evil I do not will is what I do"), with God to will and to do go together. The divine will cannot fail of performance. So here, the will of God for our redemption is enacted in *the offering of the body of Jesus Christ once for all* (cf. 2 Cor. 5:19). This offering is "once for all" because, being absolutely adequate, it is absolutely final and determinative forever. The incarnation, then, in which the Son took to himself the body prepared for him, can be understood only in relation to the redemption which he, in accordance with the gracious will of God, achieved for us at Calvary.

10:11-14. *And every priest stands daily at his service, offering repeatedly the same sacrifices, which can never take away sins. But when Christ had offered for all time a single sacrifice for sins, he sat down at the right hand of God, then to wait until his enemies should be made a stool for his feet. For by a single offering he has perfected for all time those who are sanctified.*

The teaching already emphasized in the earlier part of this chapter is now recapitulated, namely, that under the old system there is a ceaseless sequence of sacrifices, involving, indeed, the repetition of *the same sacrifices,* sacrifices, moreover, which, by the logic of the situation, *can never take away sins.* If in verses 1ff. the reference is to the yearly sacrifices offered by the high priest on the Day of Atonement, here it is to the sacrifices offered *daily,* morning and evening, by the priests in general, *every priest*—not, of course, that every priest was occupied every day with the daily ministration, but rather that each took his allotted turn to serve in the ceremonial which was daily performed.

62. The present tense of προσφέρονται, "are being offered," would seem to imply that at the time when this letter was written the temple ritual of the levitical system had not yet ceased to operate. See Introduction, pp. 30ff.

But the contrast between the old order and the new is now enhanced by a consideration which, though implied, has not hitherto been
pressed, namely, that every levitical priest *stands*[63] as he continues to
fulfil the duties of his office, whereas Christ *sat down at the right hand of
God* once he *had offered for all time a single sacrifice for sins.* The priest who
is prosecuting his sacerdotal duties *stands* before the Lord (cf. Dt. 10:8;
17:12; 18:7). The point is that the work of the levitical priesthood is never
finished because both its ministers and its sacrifices are marked by imperfection. Offerings which can never take away sins can only be repeated *ad infinitum.* Such a priesthood is ever "standing," never "seated." Even if the hopes of purist groups like the Dead Sea Sect for the
restoration of a faithful and authentic priesthood had been realized, it
would still have been a "standing" priesthood, continuously offering
inadequate sacrifices. Jesus Christ alone, the unique priest of the order
of Melchizedek, is "seated," and he is so by virtue of the fact that *by a
single offering,* complete in its perfection and therefore never to be repeated, *he has perfected for all time those who are sanctified.* The sacrifice of
himself in our place on the cross was the sacrifice to end all sacrifice (cf.
v. 26 below). The work he came to do is finished (Jn. 17:4; 19:30). Consequently, he who is our great High Priest is no longer "standing" but
"seated" in sovereign glory *at the right hand of God.*

The contrast is, as Spicq points out, highly dramatic: on the one
hand, "the vain zeal, the agitation of these [levitical] sacrificers, always on their feet—the standing position being that of the ministrant
and of action—never at rest, incessantly reproducing the same actions,
offering the same victims, every day starting their task over again, serving without effect, since sin remains"; on the other hand, there is Christ
who "offered but a single sacrifice of absolute worth," so that now "he
has only to rest and be seated, the seated position being synonymous, in
the Orient, with being unoccupied." It would of course be wrong to
infer from this that the glorified Christ is inactive. On the contrary, as
our author has been careful to explain, the exalted Savior is ever at hand
to help and support his people in the hour of trial (2:18; 4:14ff.) and
always lives to make intercession for them within the heavenly

63. The verb ἕστηκεν, though perfect in form, has, as is normal, the force of a present: he
"has taken his stand" and therefore "is standing." Hence ἕστηκα is described as a present
perfect by J. H. Moulton, Blass-Debrunner, and Nigel Turner. Note the significant formation of the verb στήκω (Modern Greek, στέκω), "I stand," from this perfect stem.
Erasmus comments: "'Ιερεὺς ἕστηκε, id est, *Sacerdos stat,* ut verbum verbo reddam."
Note also the present tenses in this same verse: ". . . every priest stands daily at his service
(λειτουργῶν), offering (προσφέρων) repeatedly the same sacrifices, which can (δύνανται)
never take away sins." We have here, then, a further indication that at the time when this
epistle was written the temple ministry had not yet been discontinued. See Introduction,
pp. 30ff.

sanctuary (7:25; 9:24).[64] But his work of sacrifice is done.[65] Its absolute perfection means that it is *a single sacrifice for sins* and that its effectiveness is *for all time*, and thus that it can never be added to or repeated. "A seated priest," says F. F. Bruce, "is the guarantee of a finished work and an accepted sacrifice." And Lefèvre d'Etaples offers the following comment:

> Had there been a multiplication [of Christ's sacrifice] it could not have been truly universal or truly efficacious. But the offering of Christ was truly universal and fully efficacious, and therefore it is one sacrifice and only once offered. For if it had been twice offered the sacrifice on the first occasion would not have been fully universal and absolutely sufficient, or the second sacrifice would have been to no purpose and superfluous.

The theme of Christ's heavenly session, announced here by the statement *he sat down at the right hand of God, then to wait until his enemies should be made a stool for his feet*, echoes and declares the fulfilment of the opening words of Psalm 110, already cited in 1:13 ("Sit at my right hand, till I make thy enemies a stool for thy feet"). The influence of this messianic psalm pervades the whole epistle. Not only is what is said here a resumption of what has already been clearly said (in 1:3, "when he had made purification for sins, he sat down at the right hand of the Majesty on high," and 8:1, "we have such a high priest, one who is seated at the right hand of the throne of the Majesty in heaven"), but it will be insisted on again (in 12:2, "looking to Jesus... who... endured the cross... and is seated at the right hand of the throne of God").[66] Moreover, it is this same psalm which proclaims that the priesthood of Christ is "for ever" and "after the order of Melchizedek," and which thus provides the foundation for the profoundly important doctrine of the priesthood of the new covenant presented in this epistle (5:6, 10; 6:20; 7:1ff.).

---

64. For a fuller discussion of Christ's high-priestly activity in heaven see Excursus III, especially pp. 349ff.

65. This is the clear significance of the aorist participle προσενέγκας: it was *after* he had offered a single sacrifice for sins that he sat down. Accordingly, the present participle *offerens* in the Vulgate version is seriously misleading. As F. F. Bruce remarks, R. A. Knox's translation of the Vg, "he sits for ever at the right hand of God, offering for our sins a sacrifice that is never repeated," is a contradiction in terms. This demonstrates the danger of a translation of a translation. It is only fair to add, however, that Knox does explain in a footnote that the meaning of the Greek text is: "he has taken his seat at the right hand of God after offering sacrifice." For further discussion of the significance of the aorist tenses used by our author in connection with Christ's work on earth and the distinction between his earthly and his heavenly ministry see Excursus III, especially pp. 346ff.

66. Another Old Testament basis for this doctrine has been given in 2:7f., where Psalm 8:5f. is cited: "thou hast crowned him with glory and honor, putting everything in subjection under his feet." The theme is, of course, an important one in the doctrine of the apostles (see, for example, Acts 2:34f.; 3:13, 21; 1 Cor. 15:27f.; Eph. 1:22; Phil. 2:9–11; 1 Pet. 3:22).

In the description of Christ as *waiting* for the subjugation of all his enemies (cf. Heb. 2:8, referring to Ps. 8:6: "we do not yet see everything in subjection to him") there is no shadow of uncertainty regarding the outcome of this period of waiting. The complete defeat of his enemies is assured, for the supreme exaltation by which the redemption he accomplished on earth as the incarnate Son has been crowned spells the doom of every opponent of his authority. Indeed, the coming of the Son into the world is already his overcoming of the world (Jn. 16:33). The cross of Christ is the conquest of Satan (Jn. 12:31; 16:11). That is precisely why it is the place of our salvation. Future judgment is only the application of the final judgment that has already taken place at Calvary. Thus P. T. Forsyth's striking proclamation:

> The absolute ultimate judgment of the world took place in Christ's death. There God spoke His last word—His last endless word. The last moral reality is there, the last standard, the last judgment. The last judgment is behind us. The true judgment-seat of Christ, where we must all appear, is the Cross.... We do not realize that the prince of this world has been finally judged, and that we live in a saved world only because we live in a judged world.... Christ is not Judge merely at some future coming. He is eternal Judge in His great work as the Crucified, a work historic yet timeless and final. In Him the prince of this world has been finally and effectually judged, and the absolute condemnation passed. Satan then fell from his heaven. The absolute and irreversible judgment was passed upon evil. There, too, the judgment of our sins fell once for all on the Holy One and the Just. The judgment Christ exercises stands on the judgment He endured. He assumes judgment because He absorbed it. Salvation and judgment are intertwined....[67]

Why, then, the delay in the subjugation of every enemy? Why, Chrysostom asks, were not Christ's enemies at once placed under his feet; and he answers that it was "for the sake of the faithful that would afterward be born." God is not powerless to perform what he has said he will do. The delay should be seen rather, as the prolongation of the day of grace, and therefore as a token of the mercy and longsuffering of God. "The Lord is not slow about his promise as some count slowness," writes Peter, "but is forbearing toward you, not wishing that any should perish, but that all should reach repentance. But the day of the Lord will come!" (2 Pet. 3:9f.). It is to this effect that Aquinas comments: "This waiting does not suggest any anxiety on Christ's part, as in the case of men, with whom 'hope deferred makes the heart sick' (Proverbs 13:12); but it indicates the desire which God has to be merciful to us: 'the Lord waits to be gracious to you' (Isaiah 30:18)."

---

67. P. T. Forsyth, *Missions in State and Church* (London, 1908), pp. 61f., 72f.

10:15–18. And the Holy Spirit also bears witness to us; for after saying, "This is the covenant that I will make with them after those days, says the Lord: I will put my laws on their hearts, and write them on their minds," then he adds, "I will remember their sins and misdeeds no more." Where there is forgiveness of these, there is no longer any offering for sin.

Our author now cites once more the notable prophecy of Jeremiah concerning the new covenant which he has already quoted at greater length in 8:8ff. The introductory affirmation that *the Holy Spirit also bears witness to us . . . saying* certainly attests his belief in the divine inspiration of Jeremiah's prophecy; indeed, that the Holy Spirit and Yahweh are one is plainly implied by the equation of what the Holy Spirit says with what the Lord (in the Hebrew, Yahweh) says. This teaching coincides with the declaration of 2 Peter 1:21 that the prophets were men moved by the Holy Spirit who spoke from God. At the same time, however, the fact that this quotation does not correspond word for word with Jeremiah 31:33f., or even for that matter with the text of his own quotation in chapter 8 above, demonstrates once again that the sense of the words is of primary importance, not a slavish adherence to each single word (indeed, a wooden literalism in effect rules out the legitimacy and even the possibility of translation and exegesis), and that variations in the quotation of a particular passage do not necessarily suppose variations in loyalty to the original revelation. Moreover, if, as the church has classically believed, our author is writing under the guidance and inspiration of the Holy Spirit, it follows that the Holy Spirit himself is not, so to speak, bound by pedantic notions of verbal punctiliousness but is concerned rather with the understanding and the application of the truth of which he is the source. In brief, our author, writing in harmony with the mind of the Spirit, embraces the truth and authenticity of Jeremiah's prophecy of the new covenant and is intent on emphasizing particular aspects of that prophecy for the benefit of those to whom he is writing, without in any way doing violence to the message of Jeremiah.

The reintroduction of this quotation with the assurance that it is in truth the witness of the Holy Spirit has the effect of clinching and bringing to its conclusion the long argument regarding the nature of Christ's high priesthood and the perfection and finality of his atoning sacrifice, whereby the new covenant is brought to fulfilment. None other than the Holy Spirit testified through Jeremiah both that God would put his laws in the hearts of his people and that he would remember their sins and misdeeds no more; and this is the very essence of the new covenant. The terms of this new covenant make full provision for the past as well as for the future: not only are God's laws implanted in the hearts of the re-deemed, so that they are able at last to glorify him by spontaneous obedience to his will, but also the rebellion of their past unregenerate lives is removed from his remembrance, their guilty consciences purged by virtue of the blood of Christ, who through the eternal spirit offered himself without blemish on their behalf (9:14). For God to remember our sins no more is the same as for him to forgive them; and, obviously, sins effectively dealt with in this way, fully forgiven and put out of sight (so different from the situation under the levitical system), have no need of further propitiation. The all-sufficient propitiation has been made, once and forever (1 Jn. 2:2). At last the longing of the centuries has been satisfied: true forgiveness of sins is provided by Christ's one perfect sacrifice of himself on the cross. The conclusion of the whole argument, then, is that *where there is forgiveness of these,* as by the grace of God there now is in Christ and in him alone, *there is no longer any offering for sin.*

If, as seems to be the case, those to whom this letter is addressed have been swayed by enticements to return to or compromise with a purified type of Judaism, they cannot now, after the full and careful instruction our author has given them, pretend to be ignorant that any reversion to the shadowy forms and sacrifices of the Mosaic law can only mean the negation of the Christian gospel. There follows, appropriately, a prolonged and powerful exhortation to lay firm hold of the blessings of the new covenant which God has made available to them through the mediation of Jesus Christ, our sole Redeemer and Lord.

V. CHRIST SUPERIOR AS THE "NEW AND LIVING WAY" (10:19–12:29)

10:19–22. Therefore, brethren, since we have confidence to enter the sanctuary by the blood of Jesus, by the new and living way which he opened for us through the curtain, that is, through his flesh, and since we have a great priest over the house of God, let us draw near with a true heart in full assurance of faith, with our hearts sprinkled clean from an evil conscience and our bodies washed with pure water.

The conclusion of the central doctrinal section of the epistle is now followed by an earnest exhortation to the readers to apply and practice in their daily living the important truths which have been expounded. This insistence on the interconnection between theology and action is a characteristic mark of the New Testament epistolary method. Doctrine is not mere theory: it must be applied. Faith must be practiced as well as professed. Truth must be lived.

The manner in which our author addresses his readers as *brethren* is particularly appropriate at this juncture as he solemnly urges them to give proof of their faith by acting upon it, for it shows that he admonishes them not as their judge but as their brother or fellow Christian and thus that he is confident that a genuine work of God has taken place in their midst (cf. earlier moments of admonition where he uses comparable appellations: 3:1, "holy brethren"; 3:12, "brethren"; and 6:9, "beloved"). Teodorico sees this as "an indication that our writing is truly a letter, not an abstract doctrinal exposition." The author, moreover, displays an admirable Christian spirit of gentleness and humility by his use of the first-person plural ("let *us* draw near"), thus identifying himself with his readers as he seeks to lead them into the full enjoyment of the blessings of the new covenant. "As we are brothers in the Lord," he is saying in effect, "let us go forward together." Like Paul, he has learned the wisdom of admonishing others "by the meekness and gentleness of Christ" (2 Cor. 10:1).

The possession (*we have*) of *confidence* or boldness *to enter the sanctuary,* that is, the true heavenly sanctuary[1] where our exalted High Priest appears in the presence of God on our behalf (cf. 6:19f.; 8:1f.; 9:11f., 24), should be the logical consequence (*Therefore*) of the careful instruction concerning the high-priestly office of Christ and its significance which precedes this exhortation. The boldness of our entry, far from resting on any supposed merit of our own, is justified and indeed demanded *by the blood of Jesus,* that is to say, within the sphere and on the basis of[2] the incarnate Son's atoning self-offering and thus by virtue alone of his merits. As Westcott points out, the use of the human name *Jesus,* here as elsewhere in the epistle, emphasizes the genuineness of Christ's humanity and hence the authenticity of his vicarious act of redemption on behalf of mankind. The freedom of access into the presence of God guaranteed by the gospel, furthermore, contrasts strikingly with the exclusion of the people from the most holy place where the glory of the Lord rested above the mercy seat—an exclusion which extended to the priests and even to the high priest, with the exception of the one annual occasion when he alone was permitted to enter the inner sanctuary, and then only with the blood of the victims that had been offered, or, in other words, by reason of the sacrifice that had taken place at the altar in the sight of all. The same evangelical note of confident approach to the throne of God's grace has already been sounded in 4:16, where, as here, the ground of the Christian's assurance is the perfection of the reconciling work of our glorified and compassionate High Priest. Similarly, the apostle Paul declares that in Christ Jesus our Lord "we have boldness and confidence of access through our faith in him" (Eph. 3:12).

It is no earthly sanctuary into which the Christian believer is invited to enter, for the Mosaic structure was but an insubstantial shadow of the heavenly reality (Heb. 8:5; 10:1); nor is it by the old way that he now approaches God, through the slaughter of bulls and goats and other animals which, though typologically instructive, was no way at all, as our author has so clearly proved. Rather, it is *by the new and living way,* the way which Christ Jesus has *opened for us* by the offering up of himself in our stead and by his resurrection and triumphant entry into the heavenly shrine as our forerunner (6:19f.). The way is *new* because it is a break with the old, inaugurating the era of the new covenant, and because, as Herveus says, no one before him had walked it. Moreover, it is *ever* new, inasmuch as, unlike the old imperfect way, it never becomes

---

1. The expression τὰ ἅγια designates, once again, the innermost sanctuary of the holy of holies into which, under the old dispensation, the people were forbidden to enter (see n. 54, p. 281 and n. 42, p. 309 above).
2. The preposition ἐν in the phrase ἐν τῷ αἵματι 'Ιησοῦ has a wide range of potentiality. Our version treats it as instrumental.

old and obsolete (cf. 8:13). It is *living*, not only because, as Lefèvre d'Etaples observes, it is the way of eternal life, but still more particularly because it is not, as the old was, a static code or ritual but *a person*, and not just a person of past history, but a person of the present, our risen, dynamic, ever living Redeemer (cf. 7:16, 24, 25, 28): the incarnate, crucified, and exalted Son is himself *the Life* and *the Way* (Jn. 14:6). It follows that our entry into the true sanctuary is *in him* as well as *through him*—indeed, that *his* is the entry, so that our entry is possible and takes place only because by divine grace we are *one with him*. Thus Aquinas, drawing attention to the affirmation of John 3:13 that "no one has ascended into heaven but he who descended from heaven," observes that "therefore he who wishes to ascend must be joined to him as a member is joined to its head." "Believers, exiled and scattered on this earth," writes Spicq, "are invited not only to consider themselves here below as residents in transit, strangers in this world, but to draw near to God. Their life is this approach. They no longer have to ask like the apostle Thomas: how? by what way? They know that Jesus, by passing through the heavens as their forerunner, has opened the way for them to have access. He has inaugurated the 'new way' so that his disciples can follow it, and this way is himself. All that is necessary, then, is to believe in Christ and to hold fast to him in order to find oneself in the presence of God, to receive his light and his life, and even one day to see him face to face (1 Cor. 13:12; 1 Jn. 3:2)."[3]

Our access, further, is *through the curtain*. The allusion is undoubtedly to the curtain which shut off the holy of holies from the holy place in the levitical sanctuary and symbolized the exclusion of sinful mankind from the presence of God. Thanks, however, to the coming of Christ and the completion of his redeeming work, the way that was formerly closed is now open. At the moment of his death on the cross, which was also the moment of our atonement, the menacing and obstructing curtain was rent from top to bottom (Mk. 15:38, par.), indicating that God had acted and the way into his holy presence was open at last.

But what is the meaning of our author's equation of the curtain with the flesh of Christ, when he says that Jesus has opened a new and living way for us through the curtain, *that is, through his flesh*? The patristic and medieval authors generally gave the preposition "through" here an instrumental sense, "by means of," and explained the flesh as the "veil" of his divinity. Chrysostom, for example, says that it was Christ's flesh that pioneered and inaugurated the way for us, and Leo the Great that it was through the veil of his flesh that he passed into the holy of holies

3. *Vie Chrétienne et Pérégrination selon le Nouveau Testament* (1972), p. 76.

above.[4] Calvin retains the concept of Christ's flesh as the veil of his deity, advising us that "his flesh is not to be despised because it conceals like a veil the majesty of God and since it is that which directs us to the enjoyment of all God's benefits." This interpretation is inappropriate, however, because it is the ceremonial of the Day of Atonement which provides the setting and the key to the imagery of the passage now before us. Accordingly, as has already been suggested, the "veil" of which our author is speaking should be interpreted with reference to the curtain through which the high priest had to pass in order to enter the holy of holies once a year.

Westcott follows a different line by taking the mention of Christ's flesh here as a definition of the new and living way rather than as an identification of the curtain. Thus he interprets our author's meaning to be, "a way through the veil, that is, a way consisting in His flesh, His true human nature." To the same effect is the NEB rendering: "the new, living way which he has opened for us through the curtain, the way of his flesh." But the Greek text does not lend itself so naturally to this interpretation.[5] Teodorico suggests the possibility of conceiving the veil "not simply as a means of separation but also as a means of entry"; and F. F. Bruce offers a similar but more imaginative explanation. "The veil," he writes, "which, from one point of view, kept God and man apart, can be thought of, from another point of view, as bringing them together: for it was one and the same veil which on one side was in contact with the glory of God and on the other side with the need of men. So in our Lord Godhead and manhood were brought together; He is the true 'daysman' or umpire who can lay His hand upon both because He shares the nature of both." The line of interpretation proposed by N. A. Dahl is not unrelated. "The 'curtain', through which Christ has consecrated the way, symbolizes the frontier between this world and the heavenly and coming one," he maintains. ". . . The flesh of Jesus is the point where the heavenly and the earthly world meet, but meet in a way which leaves the heavenly world hidden. When Christ left the earthly existence, however, the way to the 'sanctuary' was revealed so that through him we may draw near (7:25). In this double function of hiding the true sanctuary and making the entrance to it possible, the 'flesh of Jesus' is identical with the 'curtain.'"[6]

4. Leo the Great, Sermon LXVIII, 3.
5. In construing ὁδὸν πρόσφατον καὶ ζῶσαν διὰ τοῦ καταπετάσματος, τοῦτ' ἔστιν τῆς σαρκὸς αὐτοῦ the genitive τῆς σαρκὸς αὐτοῦ is more naturally taken as being in apposition to τοῦ καταπετάσματος than as a genitive descriptive of the remotely placed noun ὁδόν.
6. N. A. Dahl, "A New and Living Way: The Approach to God according to Heb. 10:19-25," *Interpretation*, 5 (1951), p. 405. The possibility of a chiastic construction in verse 20 is worthy of attention. This would have the effect of connecting, in the word order of the Greek text, "that is, through his flesh" with "which he opened for us," as follows:

Whether our author intended to allegorize to this extent, however, must be held as doubtful. Given the context, the significance of the curtain would seem rather to be that of a barrier blocking the access of the people into the shrine of God's presence; but a barrier that was removed when, at the time of Christ's blood-shedding, it was torn apart, thus showing that the way into the innermost sanctuary was now open to all. The writer "allegorizes the veil here as the flesh of Christ," comments Moffatt; "this had to be rent before the blood could be shed, which enabled him to enter and open God's presence for the people. It is a daring, poetical touch, and the parallelism is not to be prosaically pressed into any suggestion that the human nature in Jesus hid God from men."[7]

The flesh of Jesus stands here for the incarnation seen in the light of the fulfilment of its purpose in the offering of the perfect and final sacrifice on the cross. This is the perspective already emphasized earlier in the epistle, where we read that the Son "himself likewise partook of the same nature, that through death he might destroy him who has the power of death. . . . Therefore he had to be made like his brethren in every respect, so that he might become a merciful and faithful high priest in the service of God, to make expiation for the sins of the people" (2:14,17). Thus the fact of the incarnation, the partaking by the Son of our human nature, is indissolubly connected with the purpose of the incarnation, the suffering of death for the propitiation of our sins. The significance, then, of the analogy between the curtain of the tabernacle and the flesh of Jesus "is only this," to quote Owen, "that by virtue of

---

ἣν ἐνεκαίνισεν ἡμῖν   ὁδὸν πρόσφατον καὶ ζῶσαν

διὰ τοῦ καταπετάσματος   τοῦτ᾽ ἔστιν τῆς σαρκὸς αὐτοῦ.

One problem with this proposal, which has been made by O. Hofius ("Inkarnation und Opfertod Jesu nach Hebr. 10, 19f.," in Der Ruf Jesu und die Antwort der Gemeinde, ed. by E. Lohse, 1970, pp. 132ff.), is that it requires the understanding of a second (unexpressed) διά, instrumental in sense, to supplement the διά already in the sentence, which is local in sense, and which, whatever else may be said, clearly governs the genitive τῆς σαρκός as well as the genitive τοῦ καταπετάσματος. The single διά has the effect of binding "the curtain" and "his flesh" together, and thus confirms, rather, the interpretation of "that is, his flesh" as being in apposition to and explanatory of "the curtain." This is confirmed by an analytical examination of form and usage, as N. H. Young has shown ("Τοῦτ᾽ ἔστιν τῆς σαρκὸς αὐτοῦ (Heb. x.20): Apposition, Dependent or Explicative?" NTS, 20, 1973, pp. 100ff.). "The grammatical grounds for taking τῆς σαρκὸς αυτοῦ as an appositional explicative to καταπέτασμα are coercive," he concludes (p. 104), while at the same time accepting "a gliding" (F. Gardiner) of the meaning of the preposition διά from a local to an instrumental sense, which, however, on the interpretation we offer is unnecessary. The torn curtain answers to the torn flesh of Christ. The postulation of a chiasmus here is approved by Jeremias, who, however, rightly insists that the "flesh" refers not simply to the incarnation but specifically to the death of Christ, by which the purpose of his incarnation was fulfilled ("Hebräer 10:20 τοῦτ᾽ ἔστιν τῆς σαρκὸς αὐτοῦ," ZNTW, 62, 1971, p. 131).

7. Bengel comments tersely: "carnem suam, quae item scissa est, ut velum."

the sacrifice of Christ, wherein his flesh was torn and rent, we have a full entrance into the holy place [meaning, as the context shows, the most holy place], such as would have been of old upon the rending of the veil."

The confidence of our approach to the throne of God's grace is encouraged by the further consideration that *we have a great priest over the house of God* who is none other than the Redeemer who has opened a new and living way for us into the sanctuary of God's presence. He is a *great* priest because of his dignity as the eternal Son of God, the unique worth of the sacrifice he offered, and the supreme glory to which he has been exalted (1:2–4, etc.). Thus he has already been described as "a great high priest who has passed through the heavens, Jesus, the Son of God."[8] And his superlative greatness is seen in the authority which he wields *over the house of God*—a resumption of what has already been written in 3:6, where the telling contrast is explained between, on the one hand, Moses who was faithful *in* all God's house *as a servant* and, on the other hand, Christ who was faithful *over* God's house *as a son*. The *house*, or household, *of God* over which he rules is the totality of the people of God (3:6, "We are his house. . . .").

Based on the logic of the great truths which have been presented, the earnest exhortation of 4:16 ("Let us then with confidence draw near to the throne of grace") is repeated, but now reinforced by the weight of the intervening argument. The author urges his readers to *draw near*, first of all, *with a true heart*, that is, with genuine singleness of purpose and dedication, secondly, *in full assurance of faith*, that is, with firm and unwavering trust, thirdly, *with our hearts sprinkled from an evil conscience*, and, fourthly, with *our bodies washed with pure water*. The two conditions last mentioned call for further discussion—though in reality these are not so much four separate conditions on which our access to God depends as four aspects, which belong together, of the state of the regenerate man, who alone enjoys this freedom of access. Only a heart that has been "sprinkled from an evil conscience" can be "a true heart" and can know the "full assurance of faith"; and this heart belongs to the person whose humanity has been "washed with pure water." As under the old system the priests drew near in the person of him who was their high priest, so now in the person of our unique High Priest we have priestly access into the sanctuary of God's presence. Thus Peter teaches that Christians constitute "a holy priesthood, to offer spiritual sacrifices acceptable to God through Jesus Christ" (1 Pet. 2:5). And as at their

---

8. The adjective μέγας, "great," in the expression ἱερεὺς μέγας has the same superlative force as it has in 4:14 (ἀρχιερέα μέγαν), so that the expression is significantly more than "a sonorous LXX equivalent for ἀρχιερεύς" (Moffatt) literally rendering the Hebrew כֹּהֵן גָּדוֹל.

consecration the levitical priests were washed with water and sprinkled with the blood of sacrifice (Ex. 29:4, 21), so now sprinkling and washing are obligatory for all who belong to this "holy priesthood." In this connection, the fact that the altar of sacrifice, where the blood of the victims was shed, and the laver, containing the water used for washing by the priests, were closely associated with each other in the court of the tabernacle is particularly significant (see Ex. 40:29–32).

The various ceremonies under the old covenant in which persons were sprinkled with the blood of animal victims effected no more than an external ritual purification, whereas, as our author has pointed out (9:9, 13), the blood of Christ effects the purification of the conscience from dead works, powerfully penetrating to the very root of man's need. From this it follows that "hearts sprinkled clean from an evil conscience" are precisely hearts which have been purged of sin by the blood of Jesus.

In speaking of our bodies as being "washed with pure water," our author must have had in mind the promise of Ezekiel 36:25, which occurs in a passage foretelling the blessings of the new covenant. There the Lord God says to his people: "I will sprinkle clean water upon you, and you shall be clean from all your uncleannesses." Plainly, it is no mere external rite that is intended, but a genuinely radical cleansing, as the continuation of the promise confirms: "A new heart I will give you, and a new spirit I will put within you . . . and I will put my spirit within you, and cause you to walk in my statutes." Paul is saying the same thing when he declares that God saved us "by the washing of regeneration and renewal in the Holy Spirit, which he poured out upon us richly through Jesus Christ our Savior" (Tit. 3:5f.), and, again, when he teaches that Christ has cleansed the church "by the washing of water with the word" (Eph. 5:26), or, better, "in the sphere of the word," that word being the gospel of the grace of God in Christ Jesus. So, too, Christ himself insisted that "unless one is born of water and the Spirit he cannot enter the kingdom of God" (Jn. 3:5). Aquinas, indeed, maintains that "water, because it cleanses, is indicative of the Holy Spirit," citing Titus 3:5, quoted above, where washing and the pouring out of the Holy Spirit upon the believer are conjoined, and the accounts of the descent of the Holy Spirit upon Jesus at his baptism. Calvin and Owen agree with Aquinas in his interpretation of water as a symbol of the Holy Spirit here, but dispute that an association with baptism is intended. The rather clumsy distinction which Owen proposes (and which is suggested in some of the medieval writers) between "the internal and unknown sins of the mind," which require the sprinkling of the heart from an evil conscience, and "the sins that are outwardly acted and perpetrated," which require the washing of the body with pure water, supposes a questionable dichotomy of the human person.

411

But a relationship between Christian baptism and the washing mentioned here is a reasonable conclusion which should not be brushed aside. The outward ceremony of cleansing with water points to the inward reality of the cleansing of the conscience. The apostle Peter, accordingly, is careful to explain that baptism is not the washing away of bodily pollution [that is, surface dirt], but the appeal made to God by a good conscience" (1 Pet. 3:21 NEB). The writer, as Alcuin comments, "is speaking of the water of baptism in this place; for baptism is a cleansing not of the body but of the soul, when faith is present." So here, "our hearts sprinkled clean from an evil conscience" may appropriately be understood as the inner reality of which "our bodies washed with water" is the sign. "The distinctive feature which marked off the Christian washing from all similar ablutions ($6^2 9^{10}$)," says Moffatt, "was that it meant something more than a cleansing of the body; it was part and parcel of an inward cleansing of the heart, effected by the blood of the covenant (v.^{29}). Hence this as the vital element is put first." This is the understanding also of F. F. Bruce, who describes "the outward application of water as the visible sign of the inward and spiritual cleansing wrought by God in those who come to Him through Christ." In other words, baptism is a sacrament of the gospel which, as a visible word (Augustine), proclaims the realization of the covenant promise of Ezekiel 36:25ff. as it points graphically to the central truth that "the blood of Jesus cleanses us from all sin" (1 Jn. 1:7).

Both Delitzsch and Westcott suggest that there is an allusion here to the two Christian sacraments, that is, to the eucharist as well as to baptism, the former being indicated by the heart sprinkled clean (by Christ's blood) from an evil conscience—an allusion which Westcott calls "veiled"—and the latter by the washing of the body with pure water. This, however, must be regarded as a very doubtful interpretation. For one thing, the eucharist is never elsewhere described in terms of sprinkling, but of eating and drinking. For another, the perfect participles employed here[9] denote, as F. F. Bruce observes, "once-for-all and unrepeatable acts with abiding effects," which is a definition appropriate enough for baptism, a sacrament administered once only and symbolizing the regeneration of the one to whom it is administered, but hardly for the eucharist, since participation in this sacrament is frequently repeated. Herveus mentions the view of some commentators that a reference to the eucharist is implicit in the description of Christ's flesh as a curtain. Peter Lombard, for example, after explaining that it is called a curtain because it conceals the deity, adds a second interpretation, namely, that "Christ's flesh, though veiled to every sense, is consumed

9. ʽΡεραντισμένοι, "sprinkled," and λελουσμένοι, "washed."

as a viaticum by the faithful, for it appears to be bread, yet truly is the flesh of Christ." But this understanding is inadmissible, if only because it makes the bread, not the flesh, the veil and leads, not surprisingly, to the confused comment that the veil, which means the flesh, is consumed veiled. This is to reverse what our author is saying by making the flesh the thing that is veiled instead of the thing that veils. Thus to imagine that from this passage support for the teaching of transubstantiation can be elicited is an admonitory example of self-deception.[10]

10:23. *Let us hold fast the confession of our hope without wavering, for he who promised is faithful.*

Our author's appeal here, *Let us hold fast the confession . . .* , is a repetition and reinforcement of the appeal already made in 4:14 ("Let us hold fast our confession"); and this earlier appeal echoes in turn the preceding solemn admonitions of 3:6, "we are his house if we hold fast our confidence and pride in our hope," and 3:14, "we share in Christ, if only we hold our first confidence firm to the end."[11] Now the appeal to the recipients of the letter to *hold fast* is strengthened by adding *without wavering,* and *the confession* is further defined as the confession *of our hope* (cf. again 3:6, quoted above). We might well have expected to read here "the confession of our *faith,*" but the choice of "hope" reminds us that in the writer's mind Christian faith and Christian hope enjoy the closest association. He has already expressed the desire that his readers should show earnestness "in realizing the full assurance of hope until the end" (6:11) and has drawn their attention to the encouragement which is ours, who have found refuge in the promise of God, "to seize the hope set before us . . . a hope that enters into the inner shrine behind the curtain" (6:18f.), and this can be done only by faith. The new and better covenant, moreover, with its unique priest and perfect sacrifice, is the ground of a better hope (7:19, 22). And it is a theme to which he will return, for in 11:1 he carefully defines faith as "the assurance of things hoped for." Hebrews 11, indeed, is a chapter of hope no less than of faith: the patriarchs and saints of old, who did not in their lifetime see the fulfilment

10. The question arises again whether the instruction given here concerning the sprinkling and washing effected under the new covenant is perhaps intended to counteract the teaching and practice of the Dead Sea Sect or some similar movement by which the recipients of our epistle were being enticed to return in effect to the old covenant. See the commentary on 6:2 above and Introduction, pp. 12ff.

11. The verb κρατεῖν which is used here and in 4:14 is synonymous with the verb κατέχειν in 3:6 and 14, the latter being an intensive compound which matches the strong sense of the former, "to hold fast." For the difference between ἔχειν and κατέχειν cf. 2 Corinthians 6:10.

of the promises that had been given to them, died in hope precisely because they died in faith. In the midst of severe testing and adversity they did not waver. The constancy of their faith attested the firmness of their hope (11:13, 39f.). Hope, as Calvin says, is the child of faith and "it is fed and sustained by faith to the end."

It is, of course, a vitally important consideration that the promises in which we have faith and which are the foundation of our hope are the *promises of God,* which as such demand the response of faith that is fully assured (v. 22) and a confession of hope that is *without wavering,* unswerving (NEB). If the promises were to any degree the promises of man, to that degree they would be fallible and uncertain, a questionmark would be placed against their fulfilment, and faith and hope would falter. But of God, and only of God, it can be affirmed as absolutely and everlastingly true that *he who promised is faithful.* And this provides the sole logical basis (*for*) for the Christian's unfaltering confession of hope (cf. 1 Cor. 1:9, 10–13; 1 Thess. 5:24; 2 Thess. 3:3; 1 Pet. 4:19; 1 Jn. 1:9; Rev. 1:5; 3:14; 19:11). The living God has promised, and for this reason Peter speaks of the "living hope" to which, by God's great mercy, we have been born anew through the resurrection of Jesus Christ from the dead (1 Pet. 1:3). Declension from the confession of this hope (the dire consequences of which are described in vv. 26ff. below) is eloquent both of deficiency of personal commitment to our utterly trustworthy God and of deficiency of comprehension regarding the character of God and his unfailing faithfulness.

"The confession of our hope," it should be added, does not mean some detached formula or document, but the vital personal witness of the Christian believer—a witness, in the case of those converted from darkness, first publicly made at their baptism, but also a witness thereafter to be joyfully maintained to the very end of this life (cf. 1 Tim. 6:12, 13). "It is not sufficient to have hope in the heart," says Aquinas, with Romans 10:10 in mind, "but it must also be confessed with the mouth." Similarly Delitzsch, linking what our author writes here to 1 Peter 3:15, declares that "this hope in us, like the faith from which it springs, being full of joyous assurance (ch. vi.12), cannot remain dumb; it must speak, and give a reason both to friends and enemies of its own existence."

10:24, 25. *And let us consider how to stir up one another to love and good works, not neglecting to meet together, as is the habit of some, but encouraging one another, and all the more as you see the Day drawing near.*

This, the third part of what is a threefold exhortation ("let us draw near . . . let us hold fast . . . let us consider . . . "), is an appeal for thoughtful and loving concern both for fellow members of the Christian community and for the integrity of that community. As has frequently been observed, the first appeal (v. 22) is related to faith, the second (v. 23) to hope, and the third (v. 24) to love (cf. 1 Cor. 13:13). Earlier, our author has exhorted his readers to *consider*, [12] that is, to pay thoughtful attention to, Jesus, "the apostle and high priest of our confession" (3:1); now he urges them to give similar consideration to their brethren in the faith, with the purpose that they should *stir up one another to love and good works*. The implication is that there are signs of a weakening of the bonds of Christian fellowship, resulting from a deficiency of that love which should unite them in Christ, and resulting in a falling off of those compassionate deeds by which Christian love expresses itself. Unconcern for the well-being of the body, of which they are members, is symptomatic of self-concern and egocentricity. Selfishness and divisiveness go hand in hand; for self-love breeds the spirit of isolationism. He who does not love his fellow Christians fervently from the heart (1 Pet. 1:22) feels no compelling need to associate himself with them. Indeed, the genuineness of the Christian profession of a man in this state must be seriously suspect, for those who are one in Christ cannot help loving one another. The logic of the love of the brethren derives from God, who is love, and whose love has been freely manifested in the sending of his Son to be the propitiation for our sins: "Beloved, if God so loved us, we also ought to love one another" (1 Jn. 4:7–12).

The failure of love shows itself, then, in selfish individualism, and specifically here in *the habit of some* of *neglecting to meet together*. Such unconcern for one's fellow believers argues unconcern for Christ himself and portends the danger of apostasy, concerning which our author is about to issue another earnest warning (vv. 26ff.). It is important, therefore, that the reality of Christian love should be demonstrated in the personal relationships and mutual concerns of the Christian community. And it will be found that not only does love promote fellowship but also that fellowship stimulates love, because it is by meeting together as a true community that Christians have the opportunity for *encouraging one another* by mutual support, comfort, and exhortation. Chrysostom, with the words of Proverbs 27:17 in mind, observes that "as iron sharpens iron so also fellowship increases love; for if a stone rubbed against a stone sends forth fire, how much more person in contact with person!"[13]

---

12. Κατανοήσατε, 3:1; κατανοῶμεν, here.
13. Chrysostom is taking advantage of an etymological connection between Hebrews 10:24 and Proverbs 27:17. Our author says here, "let us consider one another (κατανοῶμεν ἀλλήλους) in such a way as to lead to (εἰς) a stimulation (παροξυσμόν) of love and good works." The rare noun παροξυσμός, which seems usually to have the less favorable sense of "provocation" (see Acts 15:39; Dt. 29:28; Jer. 39:37; similarly the verb παροξύνειν, see Acts 17:16; 1 Cor. 13:5; Num. 14:11; Dt. 1:34; but the verb is used in a favorable sense by

415

This mutual encouragement should be *all the more* in evidence, the recipients of this letter are advised, as they see *the Day drawing near*. When spoken of in this absolute manner, "the Day" can mean only the last day, that ultimate eschatological day, which is the day of reckoning and judgment, known as the Day of the Lord (cf. 1 Cor. 3:13; Acts 2:20; 1 Thess. 5:2; 2 Thess. 2:2; 2 Pet. 3:10, 12; Mt. 7:22; 10:15; 11:22, 24; 24:36; Mk. 13:32; Lk. 10:12; 17:26, 30, 31; 21:34; Jn. 6:39; Phil. 1:6, 10; 2:16; 1 Cor. 1:8; 5:5; 2 Cor. 1:14; Jude 6; Rev. 6:17). Many have suggested that there may be a more proximate reference by our author to the impending destruction of Jerusalem and with it of the old order of things (A.D. 70), in addition to the eschatological connotation of the term. (Alcuin even suggests that it may be a reference to the day of one's death.) While, however, the events of A.D. 70 were invested with the most portentous significance (cf. Mt. 24), and in the prophetic perspective there could be lesser "days of the Lord" which pointed to the certainty of the ultimate day of judgment, "the Day," without any qualification and therefore emphatic in the absoluteness of its significance, must be the day of Christ's return when this present age will be brought to its conclusion and his everlasting kingdom over the new heaven and the new earth universally established.

But, it may be objected, if the writer of Hebrews and his readers did indeed believe that this Day was drawing near, its non-arrival would seem to have falsified their expectation. Nearly two millennia have now passed and the Day has not come: can it seriously be regarded as other than a mistaken expectation and a non-event? This, however, is not at all a new problem in the church. Even as the first generation of Christians was passing off the scene sceptics were asking, "Where is the promise of his coming? For ever since the fathers fell asleep, all things have continued as they were from the beginning of creation." To this Peter replies that the measure of things is not according to human standards, for "with the Lord one day is as a thousand years, and a thousand years as one day," so that "the Lord is not slow about his promise as some count slowness" (2 Pet. 3:3ff.). Just as the promise of the first coming of Christ, though apparently long delayed in its fulfilment, was proved true by the event, so it will be with the promise concerning the day of his second coming. Meanwhile each generation is challenged to live watchfully in the light of the approaching Day, looking expectantly to Jesus who, when he comes, will both judge the scornful and complete that which he has begun in the redeemed people of

---

Josephus in *Ant.* xvi.125), is a compound based on the same root as ὀξύς, "sharp," and ὀξύνειν, "to sharpen." Both ὀξύνειν and παροξύνειν occur in Proverbs 27:17 in the sense of "to sharpen": "Iron sharpens (ὀξύνει) iron, and one man sharpens (παροξύνει) another." Hence the link which Chrysostom proposes between the mutual "sharpening (παροξυσμός) of love and good works" here and the sharpening of which Proverbs 27:17 speaks.

God (cf. Heb. 12:2). "The period between the first advent of Christ and His parousia is the end-time, the 'last days', the 'last hour,'" writes F. F. Bruce. "Whatever the duration of the period may be, for faith 'the time is at hand' (Rev. 1:3). Each successive Christian generation is called upon to live as the generation of the end-time, if it is to live as a *Christian* generation."

NOTE ON THE MEANING OF ἐπισυναγωγή (10:25)

In the clause, "not neglecting to meet together," which renders μὴ ἐγκαταλείποντες τὴν ἐπισυναγωγὴν ἑαυτῶν (KJV, "not forsaking the assembling of yourselves together"), the significance of the noun ἐπισυναγωγή has been variously interpreted. Aquinas reflects the opinion of many of the Latin fathers when he explains it as meaning the church, which some were deserting under the stress of persecution or because of the subversive influence of false shepherds or through their own arrogance. But, while ἐπισυναγωγή may well be equivalent in meaning to the aggregate of believers which constitutes the local church, there seems to be no justification for treating it as a synonym for the church universal—true though it may be that forsaking the local assembly is a step toward withdrawal from the church in its totality.

Calvin assigns particular significance to the prefix ἐπι, which, he says, "indicates an addition, with the result that ἐπισυναγωγή has the force of a congregation increased by new additions," namely, Gentile believers, who were "a new and unaccustomed addition to the church." Consequently, "many Jews, regarding this as insulting to them, seceded from the church." One must judge, however, not only that this is a questionable interpretation of the term ἐπισυναγωγή, but also that the crisis concerning the acceptability of Gentiles had been faced and resolved a good many years before the writing of Hebrews. Zahn takes this word to mean a separate or additional congregation of Christians; the readers, he says, "who constitute a separate ἐπισυναγωγή (x.25), perhaps with their own officers (xiii.17), are, nevertheless, a part of the collective church of the great city in which they live" (*Introduction to the New Testament*, ii, 1909, p. 350).

Bengel also ascribes special force to the prefix ἐπι, but reaches a different conclusion. Our author, he maintains, is speaking of the Jewish synagogue in relation to which at this time the assembly of Christians was something additional, an "episynagogue" (ἐπι+συναγωγή), so that the sense becomes: "You ought to frequent not only the synagogue, as Jews, which you gladly do, but also the episynagogue, as Christians." The notion has been echoed, though more tentatively, by William Manson, who suggests that the term "episynagogue" designates a "Christian appendage to the Jewish synagogue" composed of Jewish Christians, who, while continuing to attend the services of the synagogue, also met together for Christian worship and fellowship, but

417

who, in the situation which our epistle is designed to correct, because of "stress of one kind or another—opposition, persecution, disappointment," were giving up their Christian meetings and "virtually dissolving back into the general life of the Jewish community." But Manson adds the crippling admission that elsewhere "the word simply means gathering" and that "nothing in the writer's language justifies us in carrying our hypothesis to this extreme" (*The Epistle to the Hebrews*, London, 1951, p. 69).

Moffatt, who denies that it was Jewish Christians to whom our epistle was addressed, supposes that the warning against neglecting to meet together "is directed specially against people who combined Christianity with a number of mystery-cults, patronizing them in turn, or who withdrew from Christian fellowship, feeling that they had exhausted the Christian faith and that it required to be supplemented by some other cult." Spicq also sees in the expression ἐπισυναγωγὴ ἑαυτῶν "an opposition to other assemblies, profane or even heretical"; but, holding that the recipients of our letter were certainly Jewish Christians (which seems to us indisputable—see Introduction, pp. 11ff.), he explains more particularly that "it was not simply that certain converts were slack in frequenting Christian 'churches', but that they were attending the temple or the synagogue and renewing association with their former co-religionists."

The only other occurrence of the noun in the New Testament is in 2 Thessalonians 2:1, where it is used to describe our assembling or gathering together, ἐπισυναγωγή, to meet the Lord at his parousia. The expression ἐπισυναγωγὴ ἐπ' αὐτόν, which we find there, indicates that he is the focal point of this eschatological assemblage of believers and suggests, further, that the prefix, repeated in the preposition ἐπί, adds the idea of gathering together in a certain place. The only occurrence of the noun in the LXX, namely, 2 Maccabees 2:7, which speaks of the gathering together of the people (ἐπισυναγωγὴ τοῦ λαοῦ), confirms this, as does also the frequent construction of the verb ἐπισυνάγειν with ἐπί + the accusative either of the person(s) to whom or the place to which the people come. In the New Testament, the verb occurs only in the Synoptic Gospels, and always with the general sense of gathering together, whether transitive or intransitive (Mt. 23:37; 24:31; Mk. 1:33; 13:37; Lk. 12:1; 13:34).

Here, then, the term ἐπισυναγωγή should be understood as simply the regular gathering together of Christian believers for worship and exhortation in a particular place—a practice that at first took place daily (Acts 2:46), but subsequently weekly, on the first day of the week (Acts 20:7; 1 Cor. 16:2). The JB captures the sense of μὴ ἐγκαταλείποντες τὴν ἐπισυναγωγὴν ἑαυτῶν effectively by rendering it, "Do not stay away from the meetings of the community."

10:26, 27. For if we sin deliberately after receiving the knowledge of the truth, there no longer remains a sacrifice for sins, but a fearful prospect of judgment, and a fury of fire which will consume the adversaries.

The very real danger of apostasy and its dire consequences, against which the most solemn warnings have already been given (2:1ff.; 3:12;

4:1ff.; and especially 6:4ff.), is now stressed once more. Persons who lapse into the irremediable state of apostasy are precisely those members of the Christian fellowship who *sin deliberately after receiving the knowledge of the truth*, in distinction, that is, from those described in 5:2 as "the ignorant and wayward," whose sinning is either inadvertent or not demonstrative of a radical rebellion against the gospel. The distinction, as we have seen (in the commentary above on 5:2), is clearly defined in Numbers 15:27–31, where it is explained that sacrifice and forgiveness are available for the person who sins unwittingly, but that the person who sins with a high hand shall be "utterly cut off" from the covenant people "because he has despised the word of the Lord and has broken his commandment." Such is the person described in Proverbs 2:13f., who "forsakes the paths of uprightness to walk in the ways of darkness" and "rejoices in doing evil and delights in the perverseness of evil." There is an abandonment of the Christian profession and of the way of holiness inseparable from that profession. Such a sinner turns away, of set purpose, from what he knows to be the truth. He rebels against the covenant with whose sign he has been sealed. He sins against the light (Heb. 6:4), showing that he loves darkness rather than light (Jn. 3:19). He repudiates salvation and chooses judgment (cf. Dt. 30:15–20).

For such a person *there no longer remains a sacrifice for sins*. This was true of the deliberate sinner under the old covenant, whose iniquity rested, without expiation, upon his own head (Num. 15:31). It is even more obviously true of the apostate under the new covenant, since, as our author has so carefully explained, the multiplicity of priests and sacrifices of the levitical system has now been superseded by the one priest and the one sacrifice by whose virtue alone we are sanctified and perfected forevermore (vv. 10–14 above). Clearly, then, to reject this sacrifice is to be left with no sacrifice at all. It is important to observe that what is said here is not at all a repetition of the affirmation of verse 18 above, that "there is no longer any offering for sin"; for there the reference is to those who, coming from unbelief to belief in Christ, find full forgiveness on the basis of his all-sufficing sacrifice, so that there can be no question of any additional offering or of any repetition of his one offering, with which all propitiatory offering has come to an end. Here, however, the reference is to those who move from open belief to open unbelief, who, having professed Christ as Savior and Lord, now turn their back on that profession and repudiate Christ's once-for-all sacrifice. For such persons "there no longer remains a sacrifice for sins": they have wilfully cut themselves off from the sole means of forgiveness and reconciliation.

Unfortunately, the rigorist position of the Novatians in the third century who, claiming the support of passages such as this and 6:4ff. above, denied any place for repentance and restoration to those who had lapsed under persecution, influenced, by way of reaction, the interpretation of the patristic authors and those who followed them in the later centuries. Thus, for example, Alcuin contends that the writer "excludes neither repentance nor the propitiation which comes through repentance, and does not repel and cast down the delinquent through desperation, for he is not such an enemy of our salvation." And so the unevangelical doctrine of the necessity of penitential discipline for the purgation of sins committed after baptism was fortified, although it is plainly at variance with the New Testament doctrine of the sole efficacy of the blood of Jesus for the cleansing of all sins, including those committed by baptized Christians (Heb. 9:14, 26; 10:14, 19; and 1 Jn. 1:7 and 2:1f., where it should be noted, the reference is to Christians, baptized persons, who fall into sin). The present passage has nothing to do with the type of rigorism advocated by the Novatians. Our author, as Calvin says, "is directing his attention only to those who desert Christ in their unbelief and so deprive themselves of the benefit of his death." Repentance on the part of those who, through human frailty, have collapsed under persecution is itself clear evidence that they are not guilty of the hardheartedness of apostasy. (For a fuller discussion of this question see the commentary above on 6:4–6.)

If no atoning sacrifice remains for the man who by deliberate apostasy has cut himself off from the grace of God, there does remain *a fearful prospect of judgment*, and this by his own choice, for, in the ultimate perspective, what he has done is to abandon salvation in favor of judgment. As an enemy of the cross of Christ his end is perdition (Phil. 3:18f.), and the anticipation of this end should cause him to tremble with fear, for, as our author remarks a little further on, "it is a fearful thing to fall into the hands of the living God" (v. 31). Here the judgment awaiting him is described as *a fury of fire which will consume the adversaries*. By this language the intensity of the wrath of God "against all ungodliness and wickedness of men who by their wickedness suppress the truth" (Rom. 1:18) is depicted; for, as we shall read in 12:29, "our God is a consuming fire" (cf. Dt. 4:24; 9:3; Isa. 33:14; Ezek. 36:5). Since the "fury of fire" by which the adversaries will be consumed may literally be translated as "zeal of fire," or "fiery zeal,"[14] what is written here is strongly reminiscent of Isaiah 26:11: "Let them see thy zeal for thy people, and be ashamed. Let the fire for thy adversaries consume them," and of Zephaniah 1:18: "In the fire of his jealous wrath[15] all the earth shall be consumed" (repeated in 3:8).

The conclusion of Delitzsch and others that the apostasy of which

14. In the Greek, πυρὸς ζῆλος.
15. LXX, ἐν πυρὶ ζήλου αὐτοῦ, "in the fire of his zeal."

our author is speaking involves a reversion to Judaism is justified by the whole thrust of the argument of this epistle. The lofty ideals of that movement of which the establishment of the Qumran Community was an expression would have proved attractive to those who had once been zealous Jews and were now undiscerning and immature Christians (see 5:11ff.), and especially the expectation of the restoration of the levitical system in a pure form under the leadership of a priestly messiah, if, as Spicq supposes, those to whom this letter was addressed comprised a number of former temple priests, to whom such a prospect would have been particularly alluring, given their insecure grasp of the uniqueness and finality of the priesthood of Christ and his offering.[16] If correct, this reconstruction would certainly give added force to the warning that for him who deliberately departs from the knowledge of the truth, of which the gospel of Jesus Christ is the full and ultimate revelation (1:2ff.), "there no longer remains a sacrifice for sins." Indeed, that the description here of the Christian gospel as "the knowledge of the truth"[17] may be intentionally opposed to the Essene emphasis, so frequent in the Qumran documents, on the possession of the knowledge of the truth,[18] is a possibility worthy of consideration. It would then follow that turning from the Christian gospel to the teaching of Jewish idealism would in fact mean not the attainment but the abandonment of the knowledge of the truth.

10:28, 29. *A man who has violated the law of Moses dies without mercy at the testimony of two or three witnesses. How much worse punishment do you think will be deserved by the man who has spurned the Son of God, and profaned the blood of the covenant by which he was sanctified, and outraged the Spirit of grace?*

Even under the Mosaic system apostasy (as well as various other offenses) was punished with the extreme penalty, which was enforced *without mercy.* To safeguard the justness of the verdict, the corroborating testimony of at least *two or three witnesses* was required. The passage in mind is Deuteronomy 17:2–7, which prescribes the death penalty for any person convicted of "transgressing God's covenant" by the practice of idolatrous worship. Deuteronomy 13:8 affirms the inexorable nature of the sentence passed on the guilty person: "you shall not yield to him or

16. See Introduction, pp. 12f.
17. Ἡ ἐπίγνωσις τῆς ἀληθείας. The reference is to full and authentic knowledge, ἐπίγνωσις being an intensive compound. Thus Westcott observes that "the use of the emphatic ἐπίγνωσις in place of the simple γνῶσις marks the greatness of the fall which is contemplated."
18. See H. Kosmala, *Hebräer-Essener-Christen* (Leiden, 1959), ch. VI.

listen to him, nor shall your eye pity him, nor shall you spare him, nor shall you conceal him." The argument proceeds *a fortiori* by the posing of a rhetorical question (*How much worse punishment . . . will be deserved . . . ?*) and an appeal by the author to his readers' common sense (*do you think?*), the inference being that the treachery of the man who has renounced his allegiance to the new covenant is still more blameworthy than that of *the man who violated the law of Moses*. The reason for this is that the members of the community of the old covenant had the promises but not their fulfilment (cf. Heb. 11:13, 39; 1 Pet. 1:10–12), whereas the members of the community of the new covenant possess both the promises and their fulfilment in Christ, so that theirs is not only the greater privilege but also the greater responsibility, and the wickedness of apostasy is all the more compounded in their case (cf. Mt. 10:15; 11:20ff.; 12:41). The guilt of the apostate from the Christian faith is established on three counts.

(1) He has *spurned the Son of God*, or, more literally, has "trampled under foot the Son of God" (NEB; cf. KJV), that is to say, has treated him with the utmost contempt. What we trample under foot we regard as completely worthless. The designation "Son of God" would seem to indicate that the form of apostasy in view involves a scornful denial of the deity of Christ. This would bring the apostate into line not only with contemporary Jewish officialdom (cf. Mk. 14:61–64; Mt. 26:63–68; Lk. 22:70f.) but also with Judaism as a whole in the diversity of its manifestations. To trample the Son of God under foot implies, within the context of our epistle, the sneering rejection of Jesus as the Son in whom God has spoken and enacted his final redeeming word to mankind, through whom the world was created, and by whose powerful word the universe is sustained and carried forward to its predestined end (1:1–3). It means the rebellious denial of the superiority to the angels of him to whom God has said "Thou art my Son" and "Thy throne, O God, is for ever and ever" and "Sit at my right hand" (1:4–13). It means the supercilious contradiction of the superiority to Moses, a servant in God's house, of him who is over God's house as a Son (3:5f.). It means the callous abandonment of the confession of Jesus as the Son of God and our great High Priest who, infinitely superior to Aaron, has passed through the heavens and through whom we may with confidence draw near to the throne of grace (4:14–16). It means the contemptuous repudiation of him who uniquely is the Son of God, eternal, incarnate, crucified, risen, and glorified, and who, beyond measure greater than Abraham and than all others, has been made perfect forever (7:4ff., 26–28). Such is the apostasy that so totally despises the Son of God as to trample him under foot.

(2) He has *profaned the blood of the covenant by which he was sanctified*. If the former count concerned the divine person of Christ, this one con-

cerns the work of redemption which he accomplished as the incarnate Son. Throughout this epistle *the blood* of Christ is synonymous with his sacrificial death on the cross, where he offered himself as a propitiatory victim in our place. It is the blood *of the covenant* because the Son's sacrifice of himself effected the fulfilment of the promises of the new covenant announced by the prophets centuries before his advent (cf. 8:6–13; 9:15–28; 10:11–18). Accordingly, in 13:20 our author speaks of it as "the blood of the eternal covenant." By this blood-shedding the believer is *sanctified*, that is to say, his defilement is removed and in Christ he is made acceptable to God; his conscience purified from dead works, he is set apart for the holy calling of serving the living God (1:3; 9:14; 10:14). The communion cup, from which we drink in remembrance of our Redeemer, is the new covenant in his blood (1 Cor. 11:25). Week after week the apostate has partaken of the sacrament of the body and blood of Christ, thereby professing to look to Christ for the washing away of sin. But his faith has been simulated, not genuine, and his secession from the community of believers reveals that, far from thankfully trusting in the blood of Jesus for forgiveness, he has *profaned* it, or, literally, counted it as common.[19] The blood which made it possible for him to enter into the sphere of God's holiness he has treated as a thing unholy, thus completely contradicting the profession he had formerly made.

(3) He has *outraged the Spirit of grace:* his rebellion against the gospel is an affront, an insult[20] (cf. NEB, JB), to the Holy Spirit through whose operation the grace of God in Christ Jesus is applied to the human heart. Just as, during his earthly ministry, Christ's opponents wished to ascribe his works of grace to the agency, not of the Spirit of God, but of Satan, the Evil Spirit, so the apostate, in headstrong antagonism to what he knows to be the truth, traitorously denounces the gracious influence of the Holy Spirit, of which he has claimed personal experience, as demonic instead of divine. This outrageous falsification of the Good News, this incredible exchange of the truth about God for a lie (Rom. 1:25), this wilful rejection of grace and light in favor of unbelief and darkness, is the "sin unto death" for which there is no remission (1 Jn.

---

19. The adjective κοινός, "common," which is used here in the expression κοινὸν ἡγησάμενος denotes the opposite of "holy." Cf. 9:13 where the blood of animals offered in sacrifice is said to make holy (ἁγιάζει), in the sense of outward ceremonial cleansing (πρὸς τὴν τῆς σαρκὸς καθαρότητα), those who have become unclean or "common" (τοὺς κεκοινωμένους). Cf. also Mark 7:15, 18, 20, 23 and Acts 21:28, where the verb κοινόω is similarly used in the sense of "defile"; Acts 10:14, 28 and 11:8, where the adjective κοινός is used synonymously with ἀκάθαρτος, "unclean"; and 10:15 and 11:9, where the verb κοινόω is used as the antonym of καθαρίζω, "to make clean."

20. This is the sense conveyed by the Greek term ἐνυβρίσας.

5:16), the eternal and irremissible sin of blasphemy against the Holy Spirit (Mk. 3:22–30).

Chrysostom and some others associate "trampling the Son of God under foot" with unworthy reception of the eucharist. It is true that Paul writes that "whoever eats the bread or drinks the cup of the Lord in an unworthy manner will be guilty of profaning the body and blood of the Lord" and "eats and drinks judgment upon himself" (1 Cor. 11:27, 29); but if particular moments of significance in the experience of one who has closely linked himself to the Christian community are to be sought in the language of verse 29, it would seem preferable to interpret "spurning the Son of God" as equivalent to the repudiation of one's baptism, in which the putting on of Christ (Gal. 3:27) and identification with him in his death, burial, and resurrection is professed (Rom. 6:3–5; Col. 2:12). As already suggested in the commentary above, "profaning the blood of the covenant" would more appropriately be related to the other sacrament of the gospel, in the institution of which Christ gave the cup to his disciples with the words, "This is my blood of the covenant, which is poured out for many" (Mk. 14:23f.). The further suggestion may be offered that in the "outraging of the Spirit of grace" a reference may be discernible to the sovereign distribution of the Holy Spirit of the distinctive spiritual gifts, or charismata,[21] which, like Christ's gracious works of proclamation, healing, and compassion, are signs that God is powerfully active in the midst of his people (cf. Mt. 12:28; Lk. 7:18–23; 1 Cor. 12:4ff.; 2 Cor. 12:12). In the nature of the case, however, interpretations along these lines can at best be only tentative.

10:30, 31. *For we know him who said, "Vengeance is mine, I will repay." And again, "The Lord will judge his people." It is a fearful thing to fall into the hands of the living God.*

That the solemn warning regarding the danger of apostasy and its consequences has not been expressed censoriously by our author is evident from the consistent manner in which he has used the first-person plural in encouraging as well as admonishing his readers (vv. 19ff.: "... let us draw near ... let us hold fast ... for if we sin deliberately ... for we know ..."; cf. the commentary above, p. 405): his identification of himself with them is a mark of his love and concern for them as he earnestly endeavors to head them away from the precipice of apostasy. He refuses to treat them as outsiders, for, perilous though

---

21. The expression τὸ πνεῦμα τῆς χάριτος, "the Spirit of grace (*charis*)," may mean the Spirit who is the source or distributor of the charismata (cf. 1 Cor. 12:4, 9, 10, 28, 30, 31, Greek).

their position is, they have not forsaken the fellowship of grace which is found within the sphere of operation of the new covenant. Hence his appeal to them as those who, with himself, *know* the God who not only bestows grace but who also punishes disobedience. Whatever excuses they may offer for their immaturity, they cannot plead ignorance of him! If they turn their backs on his goodness they are faced with "a fearful prospect of judgment" (v. 27), precisely because this God whom they know is the God who has said, *"Vengeance is mine, I will repay,"* and who has declared that *"The Lord will judge his people."* This God whom they have confessed as the God of grace and mercy is also the God of holiness and justice: faithfulness to his covenant leads to blessing, but rebellion means retribution.

The two utterances cited by our author come from the Song of Moses, the farewell address to the people of Israel in which their aged leader reminds them of God's gracious dealings with them and admonishes them regarding the dire consequences of ingratitude and apostasy. Of the two declarations the first, "Vengeance is mine, I will repay" (Dt. 32:35),[22] applies both to the enemy from outside who refuses to acknowledge Yahweh's sway over him and to the enemy from within the community of the covenant who rebels against the God he previously had professed to honor; while the second, "The Lord will judge his people" (Dt. 32:36), speaks, as originally uttered, of judgment in the sense of vindication (cf. Ps. 135:14)—but, again, those with reference to whom the Lord's people are vindicated are not only the alien adversaries but also the ones who contemptuously desert the fellowship of grace. Vindication by God of his people implies at the same time the judgment of those who have set themselves in opposition to his sovereignty, for, as Westcott says, "the character of God requires that the same act which upholds the righteous should punish the wicked." This is a principle which receives clear enunciation a little later on in Moses' Song, where Yahweh declares, "As I live for ever, if I whet my glittering sword, and my hand takes hold on judgment [vindication], I will take vengeance on my adversaries, and will requite those who hate me" (Dt. 32:40). Calvin, alluding to Psalm 145:20 ("The Lord preserves all who love him; but all the wicked he will destroy"), observes that "God is said to rise to judge his people in the sense that he separates the godly from the hypocrites."

The conclusion to be drawn from such considerations scarcely

22. The form of the quotation here, ἐμοὶ ἐκδίκησις, ἐγὼ ἀνταποδώσω, is identical with Paul's quotation of the same text in Romans 12:19 (where Paul is teaching that it is not for Christians to seek vengeance if they have been wronged, since vengeance is God's prerogative), and is similar to the form found in the Samaritan Pentateuch and the Targum of Onkelos; it is also closer to the Hebrew ("Vengeance is mine, and recompense") than to the LXX ("I will repay in the day of vengeance"). The probability is that our author and Paul are citing a familiar and popular form of the saying.

needs elaboration: *it is a fearful thing to fall into the hands of the living God*—fearful, because he is *God,* the sovereign Judge of all creation, and because, unlike lifeless idols and other false "gods" which, since they are no-gods and non-entities, have no power whatsoever, he is the *living* God, *the* one and only God, who since he lives is able and certain to execute righteous judgment on all. The designation "the living God" has already been used by our author in 3:12 in a similar admonitory context, where he wrote: "Take care, brethren, lest there be in any of you an evil, unbelieving heart, leading you to become apostates from the living God." So far from escaping from God, the apostate falls into the hands of the living God: he abandons God as his Savior only to meet him as his Judge. The fearfulness of the day of God's judgment is graphically depicted in the apocalyptic vision of John: "Then the kings of the earth and the great ones and the generals and the rich and the strong, and every one, slave and free, hid in the caves and among the rocks of the mountains, calling to the mountains and rocks, 'Fall on us and hide us from the face of him who is seated on the throne, and from the wrath of the Lamb; for the great day of their wrath has come, and who can stand before it?' " (Rev. 6:15f.; cf. Hos. 10:8; Lk. 23:30).

> 10:32,33. *But recall the former days when, after you were enlightened, you endured a hard struggle with sufferings, sometimes being publicly exposed to abuse and affliction, and sometimes being partners with those so treated.*

Chrysostom draws attention to the fact that what our author now writes shows him to have been a skilful physician of souls, remarking that "the best physicians, after they have made a deep incision, ... do not go on to make a second, but rather soothe the one that has been made with gentle remedies"; and to the same effect Alcuin comments that our author, "lest he should cause any to despair through excess of fear and be overwhelmed by sadness and hopelessness, now consoles them with praises and encouragements." This is undoubtedly true, but our author displays his skill also by the way in which he affectionately incites them to better things as he suggests the undeniable contrast between the ardor of their first love and the low spiritual level to which they have now declined. Accordingly, he exhorts them to *recall,* and in doing so to learn and be stimulated by the recollection of, *the former days,* the period when they first became Christians or, in other words, were *enlightened.*[23] "Enlightenment" is, indeed, an apt term for the descrip-

---

23. The expression τὰς πρότερον ἡμέρας indicates here a particular period or occasion of the past; because of the weakening of the distinction between comparative and superlative forms in Koine Greek, with the result that a comparative form often bears a superlative

tion of conversion (which is a turning from darkness to light), for the purpose of the coming of Christ is "to give light to those who sit in darkness and in the shadow of death" (Lk. 1:79), and thus the task of the evangelist is to open men's eyes, "that they may turn from darkness to light and from the power of Satan to God" (Acts 26:18).

For the interpretation of the experience of being "enlightened" as a reference to Christian baptism see the commentary above on 6:4. Certainly, baptism, as the sacrament of regeneration, was for the new convert the critical moment when profession of faith was made *in public,* and thus the decisive step and the point of no return. At baptism the new believer declares himself and takes his stand for Christ before the world, and it was to be expected that public baptism would be followed by the endurance of public shame and active antipathy, not least for the Jew converted in the midst of his fellow Jews (N.B. 1 Thess. 2:14). And so, although "enlightenment" is an effect of the inward operation of the Holy Spirit, it was not unnatural for it to become associated with the decisive event of baptism at which the experience of this "enlightenment" was openly professed.

Those, then, to whom this letter is addressed did not keep their "enlightenment" secret but made open confession of their faith, with the result that they *endured a hard struggle with sufferings.* Public witness, in fact, tended to be much more perilous for converts from Judaism than for those of Gentile origin; for non-Jewish society was in general open to and tolerant of the great variety of religious cults of the time in a manner that could not be expected of the adherents of the exclusive faith of Judaism. For a Jew to confess the faith of Christ Crucified brought on him the detestation and obloquy of his compatriots, the ruination of his business, and even expulsion from the family circle. This would particularly be the case in the Jewish homeland, and it goes a long way toward explaining the extreme poverty of the Christian community in Jerusalem, which caused Paul to give such prominence to the collection of relief funds among the Gentile churches. The description in these verses of the severe consequences of embracing Christianity, involving not only physical suffering but also loss of property (v. 34), would well fit a group of converts located in the Jewish milieu of Palestine.[24]

Be that as it may, *sometimes* the recipients of this letter had been *publicly exposed to abuse and affliction,* and at other times, when they themselves escaped being the objects of open demonstrations of hostility, they had been *partners with those so treated,* or, as the NEB more effectively renders it, they had "stood loyally by those who were so

---

sense, a more suitable translation may be "the first days," that is, the time when they first responded to the message of the gospel.

24. See Introduction, pp. 15ff.

treated," and in doing so they had manifested a real and vital appreciation of the unity of the Body of Christ (1 Cor. 12:12ff.). This called both for true courage and for true love, because it meant maintaining their witness in the face of public derision and humiliation. Paul is speaking of a similar experience when he says of himself and his fellow apostles that they have become "a spectacle to the world" (1 Cor. 4:9).[25] Only genuine love of Christ makes it possible willingly to suffer such open shame. Only genuine love of one's brethren in Christ makes it possible to stand boldly in order to support and encourage them in the hour of their trial.

Severe though these afflictions had been, it is evident that these Hebrew Christians had not been called on to seal their profession with the blood of martyrdom, since we learn from 12:4 below that in their struggle against sin they had not yet resisted to the point of shedding their blood. This information indicates that they had not been through the type of organized persecution in which many Christians are put to death, such as occurred in Rome under Nero in A.D. 64; and this accords well with the situation prevailing in Palestine prior to A.D. 70, a situation in which there were no more than a few individual cases of martyrdom (for example, Stephen, Acts 7:54ff., and the apostle James, Acts 12:1f.). The suggestion of F. F. Bruce that the occasion of the affliction mentioned here "could reasonably be interpreted with reference to the circumstances attendant on Claudius' expulsion of the Jews of Rome" is doubtless prompted by his predilection for the view that this letter was addressed to a group of Jewish Christians in Rome. Our author, however, is not concerned here with affliction that overtook Jews as such, which would be beside the point, but with the sufferings which his readers had endured in consequence of their having embraced the Christian faith; in other words, the reference is to antiChristian, not antisemitic, hostility.

10:34. *For you had compassion on the prisoners, and you joyfully accepted the plundering of your property, since you knew that you yourselves had a better possession and an abiding one.*

This verse is explanatory (*For*) of what has just been said. As in the last part of verse 33, so here again in the first part of verse 34 the NEB conveys the force of the original more effectively than does our version

25. Note the similarity of language: θεατριζόμενοι here, θέατρον ἐγενήθημεν in 1 Corinthians 4:9.

(RSV); the affectionate concern to which they had given practical expression by "being partners with" (NEB, "standing loyally by") those who had been subjected to public shame and suffering was particularly displayed in the way in which they had *had compassion on the prisoners* (NEB, "shared the sufferings of the prisoners"). From this it is evident that the public obloquy endured by some of their number had involved the ignominy of being thrown into prison, together with the brutal treatment that inevitably accompanied such an experience. It was an affliction well known to Paul, for whom a great many imprisonments meant a great many beatings, including (up to the time when he wrote 2 Cor.) the suffering of the forty-lashes-less-one at the hands of his fellow Jews on five occasions and of scourgings with rods on three occasions at the hands of the Roman authorities (2 Cor. 11:23–25). Any man who not merely expressed but actually displayed sympathy for persons who had thus been socially condemned and disgraced by seeking to minister to their needs placed himself in peril of a similar fate. This willingness to identify themselves with their imprisoned brethren was in itself a notable manifestation of the spirit of Christ, who by his incarnation identified himself with our unhappy humanity so that he might minister to us in our need (Mk. 10:45), and who, though now our exalted High Priest, still has perfect sympathy and fellow-feeling for his people in all their weaknesses and trials (Heb. 4:15).[26] These Hebrew Christians had given proof that in the Body of Christ "if one member suffers, all suffer together"[27] (1 Cor. 12:26; Rom. 12:5). And as this oneness in the Body is essentially oneness in Christ (Gal. 3:28), so in ministering to their afflicted brethren they were ministering to Christ, in accordance with Christ's own saying: "I was in prison and you came to me. . . . Truly, I say to you, as you did it to one of the least of these my brethren, you did it to me" (Mt. 25:36, 40).

Not that those who showed such compassion had not also themselves passed through affliction and adversity, for, though not thrown into prison, they had suffered *the plundering of their property*. Their possessions and their rights had been snatched from them either by the civil authorities or by their own kinsfolk; but this they had *joyfully accepted*, thereby attesting before all the genuineness and solidity of their Christian profession. Instead of mourning their loss, they had rejoiced because it had happened to them for Christ's sake; and in doing so they had testified that their true treasure was not what this world counts dear but was in heaven, eternally safe with Christ (Mt. 6:19–21; 1 Pet. 1:4; 1

26. It is worthy of remark that in 4:15 the same verb is used of Christ and his fellow-feeling for us (συμπαθῆσαι) as is used here of the fellow-feeling of these Christians (συνεπαθήσατε) for their brethren in prison.

27. It is the same verb again in 1 Corinthians 12:26 (συμπάσχει).

Jn. 2:15–17; Col. 2:3). This joyful acceptance of adversity which overcomes the world is obviously something very different from stoic imper-
turbability. It demonstrates that they were no empty words with which
Christ exhorted his followers, when he said: "Blessed are you when men
revile you and persecute you and utter all kinds of evil against you
falsely on my account. Rejoice and be glad, for your reward is great in
heaven" (Mt. 5:11f.; Lk. 6:22f.). It witnesses to the world that "a man's
life does not consist in the abundance of his possessions" and that it is
fatally possible to be rich in worldly goods but "not rich toward God"
(Lk. 12:16, 21, 33f.). The same triumphant faith enabled the apostles to
rejoice that they were counted worthy to suffer dishonor for the name of
their Lord (Acts 5:41) and caused Paul to encourage the Christians in
Rome to rejoice in their sufferings (Rom. 5:3, as Paul himself was accustomed to do, cf. Acts 16:24f.; also 1 Pet. 4:13) and James to urge his
readers to "count it all joy" (NEB, to "count themselves supremely
happy") when they were called upon to pass through all sorts of trials
(Jas. 1:2). Indeed, Paul's memorable description of himself, "as sorrowful, yet always rejoicing, as poor, yet making many rich, as having
nothing, and yet possessing everything," should be true of every servant of Jesus Christ.

In the same way the joyfulness with which these Hebrew Christians
had endured the deprivation of worldly goods rather than deny the Lord
who had bought them showed that they *knew* that they *had a better
possession and an abiding one*. The surest hope made them confident, says
Herveus, that for the loss of temporal possessions they would gain eternal blessings, for transitory toil eternal rest, and for earthly deprivation
heavenly treasure. Thus, as Calvin observes, "wherever the feeling of
heavenly good things is strong, there is no taste for the world with its
allurements, so that no sense either of poverty or of shame can overwhelm our minds with sorrow." The truth of this can readily be illustrated from every period of the church's history. Eusebius, for example,
quotes from Dionysius' account of the sufferings of Christians in
Alexandria during the Decian persecution in the middle of the third
century. In addition to much more brutal assaults and tortures the following incident is narrated: "Then all with one impulse rushed to the
houses of the pious, and they dragged forth whomsoever any one knew
as a neighbour, and despoiled and plundered them. They took for themselves the more valuable property; but the poorer articles and those
made of wood they scattered about and burned in the streets, so that the
city appeared as if taken by an enemy. But the brethren withdrew and
went away, and 'took joyfully the spoiling of their goods', like those to
whom Paul bore witness"[28] (Paul here, of course, being accepted as the

---

28. Eusebius, *Eccl. Hist.* vi.41.

author of our epistle). In the sixteenth century, John Hooper, despoiled of his worldly possessions and facing a cruel death, writes from his prison that "loss of goods is great, but loss of God's grace and favour is greater," and, further, that "there is neither felicity nor adversity of this world that can appear to be great, if it be weighed with the joys or pains in the world to come."[29]

If there is any substance to Spicq's conjecture that the recipients of this epistle were a company of Jewish priests who had embraced the Christian faith during the early days when there was a spectacular response to the preaching of the gospel in Jerusalem (N.B. Acts 6:7), and who subsequently had left Jerusalem at the time of the great persecution that followed the death of Stephen (Acts 8:1),[30] the hostility shown to them would have been even more intense than that experienced by most other converts from Judaism. In any case, Luke records that Paul, when he was Saul the persecutor, dragged men and women from their homes in Jerusalem and threw them into prison (Acts 8:3), and also, not content with this, set out to hunt down defectors from Judaism and bring them back in chains to Jerusalem (Acts 9:1f.; cf. 22:3–5; 26:9–12). It is not surprising that when he too was converted, Paul, who had been so zealous a persecutor of the Christian church, found himself the target of the fiercest and most violent antipathy from his compatriots (Acts 9:23–25; 14:2, 19; 21:27ff.; 22:22f.; 23:12ff.; 26:21; 2 Cor. 11:23ff., 32f.). Our author makes it plain that those to whom he is writing had endured much in the days following their acceptance of the gospel—sufferings, abuse, affliction, imprisonment, loss of property; and now he is saying to them in effect what Paul found it necessary to say in his letter to the Galatian Christians: "Have you suffered so many things in vain?" (Gal. 3:4 KJV). It would be incomprehensible for them now even to consider the possibility of abandoning the struggle and with it the prize. This is the burden of the appeal that follows.

10:35, 36. *Therefore do not throw away your confidence, which has a great reward. For you have need of endurance, so that you may do the will of God and receive what is promised.*

After joyfully enduring severe afflictions and losses for Christ's sake, to *throw away* their *confidence* as though it were after all something worthless and dispensable would not make sense. Of all desertions apostasy is the most unreasonable, for it means turning one's back on him who has been professed before men as the sole source and ground

29. John Hooper, *Later Writings* (Cambridge, 1852), p. 619.
30. C. Spicq, *L'Epître aux Hébreux*, I (Paris, 1952), pp. 226ff.

of our confidence, and through whose blood we have freedom of access, in full assurance of faith, into the eternal sanctuary of God's presence (vv. 19ff. above; cf. 3:6; 4:16). Discouraged by the perils and hardships of the wilderness, the forefathers of those to whom our letter was sent were moved with a spirit of apostasy when they asked, "Would it not be better for us to go back to Egypt?" (Num. 14:3). These Hebrew Christians of the first century were in danger of following this evil example (cf. 3:12) by "forsaking the God who made them" and "scoffing at the Rock of their salvation" (Dt. 32:15). To do this would be evidence that they had indeed "thrown away their confidence" and returned to the deceptive and impermanent material things of the present world which previously they had professed to "throw away." It would be a tragic failure of "earnestness in realizing the full assurance of hope until the end" (Heb. 6:11).

They are reminded, moreover, that true Christian confidence *has a great reward*, so that to throw away our confidence by abandoning the struggle is also to throw away our reward. That reward is the incomparable glory which awaits all who are faithful to the end (Rom. 8:18), the imperishable inheritance prepared for God's redeemed people (1 Pet. 1:4), the crown of righteousness which the Lord will bestow on all who love his appearing (2 Tim. 4:8). The relationship of the present pilgrimage to the future reward is the relationship of faith to hope, as the quotation which follows teaches (vv. 37 and 38) and the next chapter so amply illustrates. This great reward is a strong encouragement to perseverance; but it is far from being the prize for human merit, as though man's deserving established a claim upon God. The confidence which it crowns is not *self*-confidence, that is, confidence in one's own worth, but precisely confidence *in God*, and this is the exact antithesis of self-merit and self-assurance. The blood of Jesus, that is to say, the perfect atonement provided by the incarnate Son through his sacrifice of himself in our stead, is the whole substance of our confidence (v. 19 above). The only merit in which the Christian trusts is the merit of Christ.

> All that I do and suffer [writes William Tyndale] is but the way to the reward, and not the deserving thereof.... Christ is Lord over all, and whatsoever any man will have of God, he must have it freely given him for Christ's sake. Now to have heaven for mine own deserving is mine own praise and not Christ's. For I cannot have it by favour and grace in Christ and by mine own merits also; for free giving and deserving cannot stand together.[31]

The *need* of these Hebrew Christians, then, was not merit, since the merit necessary for their and our salvation is entirely concentrated in

31. William Tyndale, *Prologue to the Book of Numbers*, in *Works*, I (Cambridge, 1848), pp. 434, 436.

Christ, without whom we can do nothing (Jn. 15:5) but in whom we can do all things (Phil. 4:13). *Endurance* was what they needed, that is to say, faithful perseverance under and in the face of pressure and suffering and discouragement of every kind. To *do the will of God* requires patient continuance. To give up the struggle is also to give up doing the will of God. Disobedience and apostasy are inseparable companions. Patient endurance and faithful performance of the will of God, indeed, are together a true expression of the imitation of Christ, who came to our world specifically to do the will of God (vv. 9f. above; cf. Jn. 4:34), leaving an example of trust and constancy for us to follow, for as Peter points out: "when he was reviled, he did not revile in return; when he suffered, he did not threaten; but he trusted to him who judges justly" (1 Pet. 2:21, 23).

To *receive what is promised*[32] is the consummating joy only of those who, despite all afflictions, persevere trustingly in obedience to the will of God. Accordingly, our great High Priest in glory encourages his struggling followers with the words: "Hold fast until I come," since it is "he who conquers and who keeps my works until the end" that is blessed with the promised reward (Rev. 2:25f.). The men and women of the pre-Christian era, whose heroic endurance is celebrated in the next chapter, did not live to see the fulfilment of the promises in the advent of Christ and the accomplishment of his redeeming work; yet their faith continued firm and their hope undimmed; and their constancy should be an inspiration to us who live in the full light of Calvary and Easter and who, with them, await the final consummation of what is promised, that day without evening of universal restoration which will dawn with the return of Christ in glory (Acts 3:21). Meanwhile we have "need of endurance"; no matter what happens to us, we must hold fast in faith and hope and obedience to the end; for this, in the ultimate issue, is what distinguishes the elect from the reprobate and the wheat from the tares. And the wellspring of this unflinching endurance is the pure love of Jesus, concerning which Thomas à Kempis writes in a famous passage:

> Jesus hath now many lovers of his heavenly kingdom, but few bearers of his cross. He hath many desirous of comfort, but few of tribulation. He findeth many companions of his table, but few of his abstinence. All desire to rejoice with him, but few will suffer anything for him. Many follow Jesus unto the breaking of bread, but few to the drinking of the cup of his passion. Many reverence his miracles, but few follow the ignominy of his

---

32. Literally, "receive the promise." In this epistle there are two expressions in the Greek for receiving the promise: (1) ἐπιτυγχάνειν τῆς ἐπαγγελίας (6:15), which means to receive the word of the promise, that is, in anticipation of its fulfilment, and (2) κομίζεσθαι τὴν ἐπαγγελίαν (here and 11:13 and 39), which means to receive the promise in the actuality of one's own experience, that is, to receive the fulfilment of the promise. In 11:33, however, the verb ἐπιτυγχάνειν probably carries both these meanings, in an ambivalent manner.

cross. Many love Jesus as long as adversities do not happen. Many praise and bless him as long as they receive any comforts from him. But if Jesus hide himself and leave them but a while, they fall either into complaining or into too much dejection of mind. But they that love Jesus for Jesus, and not for some comfort of their own, bless him in all tribulation and anguish of heart as well as in the highest comfort. And although he should never choose to give them comfort, they notwithstanding would ever praise him and always wish to give him thanks. O how powerful is the pure love of Jesus which is mixed with no self-love or self-interest![33]

10:37–39. *"For yet a little while, and the coming one shall come and shall not tarry; but my righteous one shall live by faith, and if he shrinks back, my soul has no pleasure in him." But we are not of those who shrink back and are destroyed, but of those who have faith and keep their souls.*

The need for trustful perseverance which our author has been stressing is now driven home by a citation from the prophet Habakkuk. There is particular appropriateness in the fact that Habakkuk in his day (the latter part of the seventh century B.C.) confronted a situation of national emergency and of severe testing for the people of God. Within the land violence and injustice prevailed, and from outside there was the threat of Chaldean assault and conquest. The passage quoted here is the Lord's response to the anguished inquiry with which the prophecy opens: "O Lord, how long shall I cry for help, and thou wilt not hear?" (1:2). The first words of the quotation, *For yet a little while,* are evidently borrowed from Isaiah 26:20[34] and are fittingly prefixed to the passage from Habakkuk; for the context from which they are taken, and with which the recipients of this letter would doubtless have been familiar, is one in which ultimate deliverance is promised to the people of Judah, though for the present they are sorely pressed by peril and adversity. It is in this situation that they receive the following encouragement: "Come, my people, enter your chambers, and shut your doors behind you; hide yourselves *for a little while* until the wrath is passed. For behold, the Lord is coming forth out of his place to punish the inhabitants of the earth for their iniquity" (Isa. 26:20f.). The affinity between this passage and that cited here from Habakkuk is obvious. As, also, verse 27 above echoes the Septuagint rendering of Isaiah 26:11, it is apparent that this section of Isaiah is very much in our author's mind.

The quotation from Habakkuk 2:3f. also follows the Greek of the

33. Thomas à Kempis, *The Imitation of Christ* II.xi.
34. The phrase μικρὸν ὅσον ὅσον, "for yet a little while," in the LXX of Isaiah 26:20 is exactly reproduced here.

434

Septuagint version rather than the Hebrew of the original text, for the latter refers not, it seems, to a person but to a vision of divine judgment and vindication: "If it seem slow, wait for it; it will surely come, it will not delay"; whereas in the Septuagint the reference is clearly to a *person* who is coming: "If he seems late, wait patiently for him; for he will surely come and he will not delay." "The words seem to belong, in the first instance, to the vision itself," Pusey explains; "but the vision had no other existence or fulfilment than in Him Who was the Object of it, and Who, in it, was foreshadowed to the mind. The coming of the vision was no other than His Coming."[35] Instead of the Septuagint's "he will surely come," our author has *the coming one shall come*[36] (involving no more than the addition of the definite article in the Greek), which, without in any way impairing the note of emphasis and certainty, gives the expression a definite messianic connotation, "the coming one" or "he who is coming" being a familiar description of the Messiah.[37] The interpretation thus implied is perfectly congruous, since it is in relation to Christ that God's purposes, whether of judgment or of salvation, reach their fulfilment (cf. Mt. 3:12; Jn. 3:18f., 36; Acts 4:12; 17:21; Rom. 2:16; 1 Tim. 1:15; 2:5f.; 2 Tim. 4:8). Christ, moreover, is the Coming One in two stages: first, in respect of his coming as Savior to offer himself as an atoning sacrifice for the sins of his people, already fulfilled; and, second, in respect of his coming at the end of the age as Judge and Lord of all, not yet fulfilled (Heb. 9:26–28). To human expectation the latter coming may seem to be long delayed, just as the former seemed to the men of faith of the Old Testament era, but it is no less certain of fulfilment (cf. 2 Pet. 3:3ff.). His coming is ever hastening on, and he *shall not tarry*; when God's predestined hour strikes he will manifest himself. This being so, God's people are to wait patiently and with joyful and confident endurance to persevere in the Christian struggle.[38]

In verse 38, which continues the quotation from Habakkuk, there is a transposition of the two clauses as they appear in the original. Thus Habakkuk 2:4 reads: "Behold, he whose soul is not upright in him is puffed up; but the righteous shall live by his faith"; while as cited here it

---

35. E. B. Pusey, *The Minor Prophets*, VI (London, 1907), p. 74.
36. Ὁ ἐρχόμενος ἥξει. The LXX ἐρχόμενος ἥξει is a Greek rendering of the emphatic Hebrew construction with the infinitive absolute. Cf. the same construction in 6:14 above: εὐλογῶν εὐλογήσω ... πληθύνων πληθυνῶ.
37. Cf. John the Baptist's question: "Are you he who is to come (ὁ ἐρχόμενος), or shall we look for another?" (Mt. 11:3; see p. 395 above). The present participle ("he who is coming") rather than the future participle ("he who will come") effectively preserves the sense of imminence. The rabbinical authors regarded Habakkuk 2:3 as messianic in import.
38. In this section on the necessity of endurance (ὑπομονή, v. 36), it is surprising that our author excludes from his quotation of Habakkuk 2:3 the clause, "if it seem slow, wait for it," that is, "wait patiently," with persistent endurance: ὑπόμεινον. It can hardly be doubted that he had in mind so apposite a connection.

reads: "but my righteous one shall live by faith, and if he shrinks back, my soul has no pleasure in him." This transposition does no violence to the thought of the prophet, and it has the advantage, as F. F. Bruce observes, of allowing "my righteous one" to become the subject of both parts of the verse in a manner particularly suited to the situation which our author is addressing: "If he perseveres in faith he will gain his life; if he shrinks back he will prove himself reprobate." The discrepancy between "he shrinks back"[39] here and "he is puffed up" in the Hebrew of Habakkuk 2:4 is not fundamental, for the man who *shrinks back* is precisely the man who is puffed up with self-sufficiency and is therefore blind to the need of trustful and patient endurance.

The man whom God calls *my righteous one*, that is, the man accounted righteous by God, is, by contrast, the man who *lives by faith*, that is, who has abandoned every pretension to self-sufficiency and whose whole life is one of trust in God (cf. Gal. 2:19f.).[40] To "shrink back" is to renounce the life of faith, and in the man who does this God *has no pleasure*, for, as our author will shortly explain (11:6), "without faith it is impossible to please God." "Faith is now the life of the heart, until he comes who will give life of both soul and body," comments Herveus; "and every just one of mine is justified by faith, not by the works of the law. For he who is justified by the works of the law is not mine, but his own just person, because he is justified not by me but by himself, and he glories not in me but in himself. But he who is justified by faith is my just one, because he is justified by the gift of my grace, and he attributes the fact that he is justified to my grace and not to himself." The central significance of this principle of justification by faith in the theology of the new covenant is apparent throughout the teaching of Christ and his apostles. Paul, who cites Habakkuk 2:4 on two occasions (Rom. 1:17 and Gal. 3:11; cf. Phil. 3:9), makes justification by faith the dominant theme of his epistles to the Romans and to the Galatians; and

39. In accordance with his usual practice, our author follows the LXX here. The divergence of the LXX rendering, "If a man shrinks back, my soul has no pleasure in him," from the Hebrew, "Behold, he whose soul is not upright in him is puffed up," may be explained by supposing either that the Seventy were accurately translating a variant Hebrew text or that they were pursuing the method of *midrash-pesher* or paraphrastic clarification of the text. For a study and discussion of the latter method see E. Earle Ellis, *Paul's Use of the Old Testament* (Edinburgh, 1957).

40. The reading ὁ δὲ δίκαιός μου ἐκ πίστεως ζήσεται, "my righteous one shall live by faith," is found in p⁴⁶, Codex Sinaiticus, Codex Alexandrinus, Old Latin MSS, the Vulgate, Clement, etc., and in Codex Alexandrinus of the LXX. But there is some uncertainty about the position or even the presence of the pronoun μου. Codex Vaticanus (B) of the LXX and a few witnesses in the passage before us read ὁ δὲ δίκαιος ἐκ πίστεώς μου ζήσεται, "the righteous man shall live by his faith in me"—taking μου as an objective genitive; it is less likely to be a subjective genitive with the sense "by my [God's] faithfulness." Numerous witnesses, including p¹³, omit μου, thus giving the sense, "the righteous man shall live by faith"; and this is how Paul cites Habakkuk 2:4 in Romans 1:17 and Galatians 3:11.

the declaration, "my righteous one shall live by faith," provides the *motif* of the great eleventh chapter of our epistle at which we have now arrived.

Our author's confidence that a genuine work of grace has taken place in the hearts of those whom he is addressing is expressed unequivocally in verse 39, and is made all the more appealing by his use once again (cf. v. 26) of the first-person plural, *we*. In view of the signs of God's grace at work in their midst, he is unwilling to believe that, in general, they are not one with him in Christ, even though he finds himself under necessity to warn them of the real and grave danger of apostasy. *We are not of those who shrink back*, he affirms, and who, ultimately and inevitably, *are destroyed*. Destruction is the appointed end of those who desert the faith (cf. Phil. 3:18f.; 2 Pet. 3:7; 1 Jn. 2:19). Those who do draw back in unbelief give proof that they are not "heirs of the righteousness which comes by faith" (Heb. 11:7; cf. 9:15; 1 Pet. 1:4). As in 6:9 above, however, the writer of Hebrews believes "better things that belong to salvation" of his readers: he is confident that they belong to *those who have faith and keep their souls*—those, in other words, in whom God has pleasure. It is faith, gospel faith, that leads to the possession or appropriation of one's existence,[41] which is the very opposite of the destruction that overtakes those who through failure of faith withdraw from the company of believers.

11:1,2. *Now faith is the assurance of things hoped for, the conviction of things not seen. For by it the men of old received divine approval.*

This famous chapter is a sublime and lyrical encomium of faith[42] and of the blessing which comes through trustful confidence in the promises of God and perservering obedience to his word. "There is no renown and honour more enduring," says Lefèvre d'Etaples, "than that which derives from faith."

From himself [he continues] man cannot have his faith; but he who is the fount and infinite source of faithfulness provides it and increases it. This is

---

41. The sense of the Greek, ἡμεῖς ... ἐσμὲν ... πίστεως εἰς περιποίησιν ψυχῆς, is well given by F. F. Bruce: "we maintain our faith and win through to life." The rendering of our version (RSV), "we are ... of those who have faith and keep their souls," is inept because ψυχή here is not the "soul" but the "life" of a person, as in Mark 8:35, Matthew 10:39, Luke 17:33, and John 10:11, 17. The term περιποίησις indicates what one makes one's own, either by keeping or by gaining it; cf. the verb περιποιεῖσθαι, which means "to make one's own" (Acts 20:28; 1 Tim. 3:13). For other occurrences of the noun περιποίησις see Ephesians 1:14, 1 Thessalonians 5:9, 2 Thessalonians 2:14, and 1 Peter 2:9. The NEB renders here: "we have the faith to make life our own."
42. Erasmus describes the chapter as *fidei laudatio*.

why the disciples frequently asked the Lord, "Lord, increase our faith"; because reason does not attain to faith, but grace, which is superior to reason, provides it. What reason provides is, moreover, obscure and weak; whereas what grace affords is clear and strong; and so the trusting man of faith commits himself to God, not to his own reason, to divine truth, not to the possibility of his own cleverness, and his position is spacious, not narrow. He who is unwilling to leave behind the possibility of his own reason encloses himself in a dark and confining prison where the sun of grace does not shine and life-giving faith is not found. O divine faith, wonderful foundation of life, strong support of hope, anchor of devotion, and shining cord extended from heaven, seizing which we climb to him who is above and beyond all altitude!

"We," our author has just said (10:39), "are of those who have faith"; and he now introduces this encomium with a brief definition (vv. 1–3) of the faith which he is about to praise. It is necessary to appreciate the limits of this definition of faith, for it is not exhaustive, and in particular it is placed within the perspective of hope, which in turn is aroused by divine promises—promises as yet unfulfilled in the experience of those men and women of faith who belonged to the age prior to the coming of Christ and whose heroic examples will illustrate our author's theme. For man without faith, hope is cumbered with uncertainty and cramped by unpredictability; it is retarded by the fears as well as spurred by the longings of human subjectivity. For the man of faith, however, hope is something sure and substantial precisely because it is founded on the objective reality of the immutable promises of God, who cannot lie. Indeed, so closely are faith and hope related to each other in the perspective of biblical realism that in our epistle, as we have already noticed, they are virtually interchangeable terms. Thus "the confession of our hope" which, in 10:23, we are exhorted to hold fast without wavering, since "he who promised is faithful," might equally well have been expressed as "the confession of our faith"; and "the full assurance of faith" with which we are encouraged to draw near to the divine presence in 10:22 may be compared with the "full assurance of hope" spoken of in 6:11 and with the "better hope" through which we draw near to God in 7:19. Again, in 6:18, the author urges his readers to "seize the hope" set before them; but seizing, or laying firm hold of, is an act of faith when the object to be grasped is hope, the focus of which is the word of promise still to be fulfilled. Such is the indissoluble bond between faith and hope; and it is apparent in the definition now before us which explains that *faith is the assurance of things hoped for*.

This statement is deceptively simple in appearance, but a question immediately arises concerning the significance of the Greek noun *hypostasis*, which is translated "assurance" in our version. Such knowledge as we have of the term in its biblical usage affords little help, for, although the word *hypostasis* occurs twenty times in the Septuagint, it translates no less than twelve different Hebrew words, while in the New Testament it occurs only five times, twice in 2 Corinthians and three times in our epistle. Accordingly, the context must play an important part in determining the precise meaning which is to be assigned to the term. There are, in the main, four possible connotations from which to choose.

1. *Essence, substance,* in the sense of 1:3 above where our author is speaking of the essential being or *hypostasis* of God. Thus used, it is virtually a technical term of Greek philosophy, and it is not surprising that the Greek fathers interpreted it in this sense here. It seems also to be the sense reflected in the KJV ("faith is the substance of things hoped for") and the NEB ("faith gives substance to our hopes")—that is to say, faith lays hold of what is promised and therefore hoped for, as something real and solid, though as yet unseen.

2. *Foundation, substance,* in the etymological sense of that which "stands under" and thus provides a foundation.[43] Faith, then, is the foundation on which the structure of hope is raised, or the beginning which contains within itself the certainty of completion. This is how Augustine understood it and also Aquinas, who says: "In these words the directing of the act of faith to its end is displayed, because faith is directed towards the things hoped for as a sort of beginning in which the whole is as it were contained in essence, just as conclusions are contained in first principles."

3. *Confident assurance,* in the sense of 3:14 above and of 2 Corinthians 9:4 and 11:17. It is the meaning favored here by Erasmus ("certitude"), the Reformers, and most modern commentators, and reflected in our version ("faith is the assurance of things hoped for") and Phillips ("faith means putting our full confidence in the things we hope for"). Of these three interpretations this is the most satisfactory, but the three are closely interrelated and tend to merge in meaning because of the implications of the context. There is, however, a fourth possibility.

4. *Guarantee, attestation,* a sense which is supported by some papyri where the term *hypostasis* is used of documents which attest or provide evidence of ownership. This consideration inclines Moulton and Milligan to suggest the translation, "faith is the *title-deed* of things hoped for." Spicq comments as follows: "Faith is a guarantee of the heavenly realities for which we hope; not only does it render them certain for us, but it envisages them as rightfully belonging to us; it is, in itself, an objective assurance of our definite enjoyment of them. Consequently, faith 'takes possession by anticipation' of these heavenly blessings and is a genuine commencement of the divine life with the guarantee of its

---

43. Greek ὑπό-στασις, Latin *sub-stantia*.

everlasting permanence." And he adds that "here we bring together the theologies of John, concerning the eternal life already begun here below, and of Paul, concerning the earnest and the firstfruits of the resurrection and of salvation"; for "this is something already accomplished for believers, even though its fulfilment is not yet." This dynamic concept of faith is as important as it is biblical.

The term *hypostasis*, then, is susceptible of a variety of connotations, but, despite the different interpretations proposed, there is in all cases, as Moulton and Milligan point out, "the same central idea of something that *underlies* visible conditions and guarantees a future possession."

To understand faith and fulfilment as cause and effect, and particularly within the framework of merit and reward, as though faith is a meritorious work which will at last be rewarded, as Aquinas suggests, is seriously in conflict with the New Testament concept of man's faith as the response to God's grace. In the apostolic purview faith is essentially non-meritorious, indeed a renunciation of all human merit, since Christian faith is precisely trust in the merits of another, namely, Christ. Certainly, as this chapter will amply demonstrate, faith and works belong together, not, however, in any sense that meritorious works precede faith, or that faith itself is a meritorious work, but that good works spring from faith as their source and provide the evidence of a genuine faith. As our author insists in 12:2 below, it is Jesus "on whom our faith depends from start to finish" (NEB).

Faith is defined, further, as *the conviction of things not seen*. This, it seems, does not so much expand or add to what has already been said as confirm it. The "assurance" or "guarantee" spoken of in the first part of the verse is now termed "conviction" or "persuasion," and the "things hoped for" are precisely the "things not seen." The JB paraphrases it effectively: "Only faith can guarantee the blessings that we hope for, or prove the existence of the realities that at present remain unseen." Though the blessings promised are not yet revealed, the man of faith is *convinced* of their reality. This same conviction caused Paul to make the confident calculation that "the sufferings of this present time are not worth comparing with the glory that is to be revealed to us," and was the ground of his persuasion that nothing whatsoever, not even death, "will be able to separate us from the love of God in Christ Jesus our Lord" (Rom. 8:18, 38f.).

As with the "assurance" in the preceding phrase, so the "conviction" of this phrase has a dynamic quality. It is not a static emotion of complacency but something lively and active, not just a state of immovable dogmatism but a vital certainty which impels the believer to stretch out his hand, as it were, and lay hold of those realities on which his hope is fixed and which, though unseen, are already his in Christ. In striking contrast to the man whose values are entirely those of this present world, the Christian is animated by the conviction that it is the very things which are not (yet) seen, those things which he appropriates by faith, that are real and permanent; he walks by faith, not sight (2 Cor. 4:18; 5:7). Referring to the paradoxical character of a "demonstration of what is invisible," Calvin writes as follows:

> These two things apparently contradict each other, but yet they agree perfectly when we are concerned with faith. The Spirit of God shows us hidden things, the knowledge of which cannot reach our senses. Eternal life is promised to us, but it is promised to the dead; we are told of the resurrection of the blessed, but meantime we are involved in corruption; we are declared to be just, and sin dwells within us; we hear that we are blessed, but meantime we are overwhelmed by untold miseries; we are promised an abundance of all good things, but we are often hungry and thirsty; God proclaims that he will come to us immediately, but seems to be deaf to our cries. What would happen to us if we did not rely on our hope, and if our minds did not emerge above the world out of the midst of darkness through the shining Word of God and his Spirit? Faith is therefore rightly called the substance of things which are still the objects of hope and the evidence of things not seen.

It was *by faith*, faith as just defined and faith as it is illustrated by the examples that follow in this chapter in praise of faith, that *the men of old*,[44] who are synonymous with those described as "our fathers" in 1:1, the believers, namely, of the pre-Christian era, *received divine approval*. For us, as well as for them, faith must be the motivating principle of all our conduct. The literal meaning of the Greek is that they were "approved" or "accorded a good report,"[45] without specifying the source of this approbation. The NEB apparently understands this to mean that the faith of these believers of a former age won for them a place in the Old Testament scriptures ("It is for their faith that the men of old stand on record"). But it is, rather, an instance of a "divine passive," a form of expression common in the New Testament, in which the implication is that the unexpressed agent is God himself. Thus our version correctly renders it "received divine approval."

---

44. Literally, "the elders," οἱ πρεσβύτεροι. Cf. "the tradition of the elders" (Mk. 7:3, 5; Mt. 15:2). Philo observes that Abraham was the first to be designated "elder" in Scripture. The reference is to the LXX rendering of Genesis 24:1, Ἀβραὰμ ἦν πρεσβύτερος, and the corresponding Hebrew term זָקֵן is also used in the Old Testament as a quasi-technical term for "elder." But the sense in Genesis 24:1 is that Abraham was aged or advanced in years. Philo offers the comment that "the true elder is shown not by his length of days but by a laudable and perfect life"; accordingly "he who is enamoured of sound sense and wisdom and faith in God may justly be called an elder" (*De Abrahamo* 46).
45. Ἐμαρτυρήθησαν.

11:3. By faith we understand that the world was created by the word of God, so that what is seen was made out of things which do not appear.

It is arguable that the order of verses 2 and 3 might with some advantage have been transposed, since the mention of "the men of old" in verse 2 would appropriately have been followed by the sequence of exemplary sketches of the heroes of faith belonging to the Old Testament period, which starts with Abel in verse 4. But the traditional order may well be explained by the consideration that the Old Testament begins with the account of the creation, and thus that verse 3, of which creation is the theme, rightly stands at the head of the series and, significantly in this respect, is introduced by the key-phrase "by faith," which recurs as the introductory formula throughout this remarkable panegyric (vv. 3, 4, 5, 7, 8, 9, 11, 17, 20, 21, 22, 23, 24, 27, 28, 29, 30, 31). *The word of God*, moreover, that vital and dynamic force by which *the world was created* and is borne onward to its destined fulfilment (1:3; 4:12), is the reality whose promises evinced the faith and established the hope of the Old Testament believers; for their faith and ours acknowledges God as Creator as well as Redeemer and perceives that the new creation in Christ brings to fulfilment all God's purposes in the original creation of man and the world. For the eye of faith, the future cannot be separated from the past, the origin unfolds into consummation, and the end is already in the beginning. In Christ God reconciles to himself the world he created (2 Cor. 5:19). Faith, then, must embrace creation as well as re-creation; hence the affirmation here that it is *by faith* that "we understand that the world was created by the word of God."

The faith of which our author is speaking is not blind faith, vacuous and unintelligent credulity, but faith that is in the highest sense enlightened and substantial, because the divine word to which it is the response is a word not only of power but also of light (Ps. 119:105). In the biblical purview faith and revelation belong together, and revelation inevitably involves, on the part of the recipient, the activity of the intellective faculty: by faith *we understand*. The origination of all things by the creative word of God is a truth that can be known to us only through revelation, and accordingly its disclosure demands the response of faith. It is an article of faith that recurs throughout the range of Scripture.

The creative power of God's word is apparent, in the first place, in the Genesis account of creation where the formula, "And God said, 'Let there be . . .' And it was so" (or its equivalent) occurs seven times (Gen. 1:3, 6, 9, 11, 14f., 24, 26). The same truth is expressed by the Psalmist when he writes: "By the word of the Lord the heavens were made. . . . Let all the earth fear the Lord. . . . For he spoke, and it came to be; he commanded, and it stood forth" (Ps. 33:6, 9; cf. Isa. 55:11). The evangelist declares, further, that all things were made through him who is preeminently the Word and that "without him was not anything made that was made" (Jn. 1:3). And the apostle explains that the same word of God which effected creation also effects re-creation: "For it is the same God who said, 'Let light shine out of darkness', who has shone in our hearts to give the light of the knowledge of the glory of God in the face of Christ" (2 Cor. 4:6). Peter confirms that it is "through the living and abiding word of God" that we have been born anew (1 Pet. 1:23). Thus Christ the Word is the agent both of creation and of the new creation (2 Cor. 5:17), and the doctrines of creation and re-creation give meaning to each other.

EXCURSUS IV: THE DOCTRINE OF CREATION IN HEBREWS 11:3

The effect of the utterance by God of his creative word, says our author, is "that what is seen was made out of things which do not appear"—εἰς τὸ μὴ ἐκ φαινομένων τὸ βλεπόμενον γεγονέναι. The correctness of this translation (RSV) is questionable, however, for it assumes that μὴ ἐκ φαινομένων is the equivalent of ἐκ μὴ φαινομένων. Admittedly, this interpretation can be matched in classical usage, where the negative may precede the preposition for the sake of emphasis; and it is accepted by some of the Greek fathers and by translators, grammarians, and commentators right up to the present time (thus also NEB, "so that the visible came forth from the invisible"). But our author certainly does not mean that "what is seen was made out of things which do not appear" in the sense, of which this rendering is readily susceptible, that the visible world was made from invisible entities. If the defense is offered that God is the invisible source of the visible universe, this is true enough; but the plural *phenomena* presents a difficulty, for non-phenomena ("things which do not appear") can hardly be intended as a designation of God (the singular, "the invisible," of the NEB is not strictly accurate, though it is less open to misinterpretation). It is preferable, therefore, to take the negative with the verb: εἰς τὸ μὴ ... γεγονέναι, "so that what is seen has not come into being from things which appear." This is, at least, a negation of the notion of pre-existent phenomena as the material from which the world as we now see it was derived; in other words, the visible world is without visible antecedents.

But now the important question arises as to whether invisibility is synonymous here with nonentity. Does the author intend to teach that being came from non-being, the doctrine, that is, of creation out of nothing (*creatio ex nihilo*)? The RSV rendering of the first clause of the verse, "the world was

created by the word of God," may in fact be misleading, for the verb κατη-
τίσθαι is properly used of something which has been "articulated" or "put
together" (cf. KJV "framed," NEB "fashioned"), not of something created out of
nothing. This terminology, some have judged, fits in well with the Genesis
account, according to which the earth, at first formless and void (Gen. 1:2), was
shaped or fashioned by God on the six succeeding days of creation (or, better,
formation). On this interpretation, then, the reference would not be to creation
proper (which would be limited to Gen. 1:1) but to the organization of the matter
already created. But it would then seem inconsistent to add, as our author does,
that "what is seen was not made out of things which appear"—unless possibly
this is taken to refer to the original creative act of Genesis 1:1; for otherwise
presumably the earth, though formless and void, was neither insubstantial nor
invisible (even though no man was present to attest the visibility of this pre-
cosmic state, for the cosmic order which man does witness is, according to
Genesis, of the same substance as the pre-cosmic mass). Nor does the
philosophical distinction between matter and form afford a solution, because
this distinction is an abstraction, like the distinction between substance and
accidents; form does not in reality exist apart from matter nor accidents apart
from substance, and *vice versa*. Accordingly, the contention of Aquinas that
"primary matter" was invisible because it entirely lacked form hardly clarifies
the situation. Indeed, it is not a biblical mode of thought. Genesis 1:2 indicates
simply that as yet the earth lacked organization and arrangement.

Owen's interpretation is along lines not dissimilar from that of Aquinas, for
he defines the primeval matter as "unaspectable" and "unappearing":

> ... all the things which we now behold, in their order, glory, and beauty,
> did arise or were made by the power of God, out of that chaos, or confused
> mass of substance, which was itself first made and produced out of divine
> power. For hereof it is said, that it "was without form and void, and dark-
> ness was upon it," Gen. i.2;—that is, though absolutely, as a material
> substance, it was visible, yet it did not appear conspicuously in any shape
> or form—it was "void and without form"; no such things at all appeared as
> the things which we now behold, that were made out of it by the power of
> God.

As an explanation this is far from satisfactory; indeed, it is involved in contradiction, for to identify the non-phenomenal, as Owen does immediately afterward,
with "that unaspectable, unappearing matter which was first made out of nothing, and covered with darkness until it was disposed into order," and which yet
he has conceded was "absolutely" visible, is hardly compatible with the language of the text and seems near to the confusion by which primeval matter
itself is supposed to have been stultified.

It is interesting that the apocryphal book of Wisdom (11:17) speaks of God's
"all-powerful hand which created the world out of formless matter" (ἡ παν-
τοδύναμός σου χεὶρ κτίσασα τὸν κόσμον ἐξ ἀμόρφου ὕλης); but Luther dismisses
this assertion as having gone a long way toward platonizing. While it is true that
the platonic doctrine of creation involved the reduction of formless matter to a
state of order and comeliness, yet the radical dualism of the platonic system, by its

postulation of the evil character of matter and of the demiurge through whom the "creative" process of transforming chaos into cosmos was achieved, carried it far beyond this point.

Some have supposed that non-appearance is equivalent to non-existence, so that to say (as the RSV renders it) that "what is seen was made out of things which do not appear" is the same as to say that the world was created out of nothing. Thus the gloss of Luther here. It is worth remarking that the Septuagint renders *tohu wabohu* in Jeremiah 4:23 ("I saw the earth, and it was without form and void") by οὐθέν, "nothing," though the prophet is speaking not of creation but of judgment and destruction. K. Rabast is an example of a modern scholar who (in his work *Die Genesis* published in 1951) understands *tohu wabohu* in Genesis 1:2 as signifying a background of indescribable nothingness rather than a formless or chaotic state of primitive matter. G. von Rad, however, in his commentary on Genesis which appeared the following year, takes it to refer to an abyss of formlessness from which all rose and into which all could relapse.[1] These two notions, or notions similar to them, find a kind of dialectical marriage in the thinking of Karl Barth. Rejecting the *tohu wabohu* of Genesis 1:2 as descriptive of "a primal and rudimentary state," Barth explains it as a pointer to "the possibility which God in his creative decision has ignored and despised, like a human builder when he chooses one specific work and rejects and ignores another." It indicates "a world-state over which the Word of God had not been uttered," the "nothing" which is "destroyed by God's creative act," a sphere which is "also real in its absurd way," "a sphere of that which has no existence or essence or goodness." We are assured, nonetheless, that "this ugly realm did exist."[2]

This position, which ascribes reality to nonentity, is one of potential if not actual dualism, as is seen by the fact that Barth finds it convenient to speak of God as having taken upon himself an "undeniable risk" in the venture of creation[3]—a judgment quite alien to the perspective of the biblical writers. It would seem also to approximate to the semantic incoherence of those philosophical schools which have wished to expound the meaning of "nothing" as though it were in fact "something" and by one means or another to find common ground between the unreality of non-existence and the reality of existence.

E. J. Young expounds the meaning of *tohu wabohu* in a manner that is both simpler and saner, as follows:

> To determine the significance of תֹהוּ in Genesis 1:2 is not particularly difficult. In Isaiah 45:18 it is used as a contrast to the phrase "to be inhabited". According to this verse God did not create the earth for desolation, but rather to be inhabited. An earth of תֹהוּ therefore is an earth that cannot be inhabited. Such an earth has not fulfilled the purpose for which it was created; it is an earth created in vain, a desolate earth. If, therefore, we translate as "desolation", we shall probably be doing justice to the word.

1. See E. J. Young, "The Interpretation of Genesis 1:2," *Westminster Theological Journal*, 23 (1961), 151ff.
2. Karl Barth, *Church Dogmatics* III, i (1958), p. 108.
3. *Ibid.*, p. 109.

Likewise, the similar sounding בֹּהוּ apparently signifies something un-
inhabitable, and we may well render it as "waste". Jeremiah uses this
striking combination when describing the land of Palestine after it has been
devastated by the invasion of Nebuchadnezzar's armies. At that time the
land will become what it was at the beginning, a desolation and waste, so
that man will no longer dwell therein. This is stressed in that the prophet
depicts the birds as having flown away, the mountains being removed and
the cities uprooted. On such an earth man cannot live. It is that thought
which is also expressed in Genesis. The earth was in such a condition that
man would have been unable to live thereon.[4]

Young, however, firmly rejects the notion that "desolation" and "waste" are
terms intended to describe a situation that was evil and sinister and that challenged God to overcome it, but interprets them rather as indicating a stage, good
in itself, in the divine work of creation. To quote again:

Were the conditions described in Genesis 1:2, however, such as God
desired them to be? All too often the word "chaos" is applied to this condition, and when we today use that word, we are likely to do so under the
more or less unconscious influence of Milton's *Paradise Lost*. It may be well
to recall his lines,
In the beginning how the heavens and earth
Rose out of chaos...
If then we employ this word "chaos" we must use it only as indicating
the first stage in the formation of the present well-ordered earth and not as
referring to what was confused and out of order, as though to suggest that
the condition described in Genesis 1:2 was somehow out of God's control.
All was well-ordered and precisely as God desired it to be. There is no
reason, so far as one can tell from reading the first chapter of Genesis, why
God might not have pronounced the judgment, "very good", over the
condition described in the second verse. The earth at that time was unin-
habitable, but that same condition appears again during some of the later
days of creation. Genesis 1:2 presents the first stage in the preparation of
the earth for man. It stands out in remarkable contrast with the finished
universe, as that is found in the thirty-first verse of the same chapter. It is
the first picture of the created world that the Bible gives and the purpose of
the remainder of the chapter is to show how God brought this world from
its primitive condition of desolation and waste to become an earth, fully
equipped to receive man and to be his home. The earth was desolation and
waste, but all was in God's hand and under his control; nothing was contrary to his design.[5]

This interpretation is satisfactory because it accords well with the perspective of the biblical writers and is free from extraneous religious or philosophical
presuppositions. There are problems, however, with the doctrine of *creatio ex
nihilo* which, as commonly understood, has no intention of assigning any kind of
reality to the concept of "nothing," and which may be summarized simply as
saying that, where previously there was nothing, now, as a result of God's fiat of

4. *Loc. cit.*, pp. 169f.
5. *Ibid.*, pp. 173f.

creation, there is something. It was only at the Fourth Lateran Council, A.D. 1215, that the doctrine first appeared in the form of a credal article ("We firmly believe and simply confess that there is only one true God... who by his almighty power brought every creature into being from nothing"—*de nihilo condidit*), though its history as a doctrine goes back to the earliest times. The main difficulty with it is the very concept of nothing, or nothingness. By definition, there can be no such thing as nothing, because existence cannot be predicated of nothingness. The problem is apparent in the fact that the statement "nothingness is non-existent" is a contradiction in terms, since what *is* cannot be non-existent, or at best a tautology equivalent to the assertion "non-existence is non-existent." What is more, the concept of nothingness is foreign to Scripture, for it is a concept which, when postulated alongside of existence, necessarily has a limiting effect on existence, the total concept being that of existence *plus* nothingness, as though compounded of two polar opposites, one positive and the other negative—or of *first* nothingness, *then* existence, which amounts to much the same thing.

In the biblical conception of reality there is no place for nothingness or non-existence, precisely because God is both himself pure and eternal existence and the source of all other existence, which is derived from and dependent on his existence, and there can be no limiting concept where God, who is infinite and omnipresent, is concerned, such as would inevitably be introduced by the postulation of a state or sphere of nothingness. God is spoken of, rather, in terms of *fulness*. Alongside "the fulness of him who fills all in all" (Eph. 1:23) there is no room for a concept of nothingness (or, for that matter, of being "alongside"), otherwise one is left with an alien philosophical dualism comprising the two antithetical principles of existence and non-existence, the one ontic, the other meontic (see the discussion of the concept of non-being or nonentity in Plato's *Sophist*, 237ff.).

The ancient postulation of Greek philosophy that "nothing comes into being from nothing" is true in general if it means that "nothing," being non-existent and therefore non-potential, is incapable of producing the effect of existence, of bringing something into being (hence the constant impossibility of speaking in any way positively about "nothing"); and it is true in particular of the phenomenal reality of the cosmic system, in which everything is seen to be the effect of an adequate and existent cause. But to argue from this premise to the conclusion that the material universe is without a beginning leaves one with the non-solution of an infinite regress in which the total effect is without cause (see the second of the five ways of Thomas Aquinas, *Summa Theologiae* 1a.2.3). It seems, for example, to be the view of the Aristotelian philosophy that the world is simply there, necessarily and ingenerately, inferior indeed to the absolute self-generating Thought or Intellect which is above all, but somehow alongside and even independent of it.

The question came to the fore from another angle as the need for a theodicy arose in the face of philosophical objections to the doctrine of creation as an act of God. Do not the decision to create the world and the event of creation itself imply a God who is subject to time and change, and thus with whom there is both a before and an after? Philo of Alexandria addressed himself to the question in the first century, maintaining that in the affirmation of Genesis 1:1 that "in the beginning God made the heaven and the earth" the term "beginning" should not be taken in a chronological sense, "for there was no time before there was a world."

> Time began either simultaneously with the world or after it; for since time is a dimension occasioned by the world's movement, and since movement could not be prior to the moving object, but must of necessity arise either after it or simultaneously with it, it necessarily follows that time is either coeval with or later in origin than the world (*De Opificio Mundi* 7).

Augustine adopted a similar position in discussing the question: What was God doing before he made heaven and earth? After passing by the facetious answer that he was preparing hell for those who poke their noses into mysteries, Augustine responds that before God made heaven and earth he did not make anything at all. If it is objected that the use of the term "before" inevitably involves God in temporality and chance, his rejoinder is that this is not so, since prior to creation there was no time, time being an accompaniment of creation and originating with it, whereas God's existence is that of "the excellence of an ever-present eternity." God's day is one day, without yesterday or tomorrow. It is an unsatisfactory answer, however, for it is shot through with temporal terminology; indeed, it is difficult to see how a really satisfactory answer could be given to a question involving the existence and experience of God in his infinity and eternity when it is possible to express ourselves only in the categories of our human finiteness and temporality. Perhaps all that can be said is that God is not man and is therefore not subject to the frustrations of "no longer" and "not yet."

To some minds, however, a solution seemed to present itself through the postulation of creation as a non-temporal act of God. Could there after all be an affirmative answer to the critical inquiry: If it was the eternal will of God that the creation should be, is not the creation itself also eternal? Thus Augustine refers to those who acknowledge that the world was made by God, "but who wish to ascribe to it a creational rather than a temporal beginning, so that in some scarcely intelligible manner it should always have existed a created world." Such persons, he says, offer an explanation "by which they seem to defend God from fortuitous rashness, lest anyone should imagine that it suddenly occurred to God, as an idea never before entertained, to create the world, and that an innovation of his will took place, although he is altogether unchangeable." The manner of Augustine's refutation of this argument need not detain us here, except to mention that he firmly insists that in creating the world God did not change his eternal purpose and will (see *Confessions* xi.10ff.; *City of God* xi.4).

Boethius, a century later, attempted to combine the Augustinian doctrine of God with the Aristotelian doctrine of the world. Eternity, he maintained, belongs properly to God only, and may be defined as "the perfect possession all at once of an endless life." (This definition, proposed by Boethius in his *De Consolatione Philosophiae*, is discussed by Aquinas in *Summa Theol.* 1a.10.1.) By contrast, "there is nothing placed in time which can embrace all the space of its life at once." The temporal "has not yet attained tomorrow and it has lost yesterday." "Accordingly, whatever suffers the condition of time, even though, as Aristotle thought of the world, it never had a beginning and would never have an end, and its life is continued for an infinity of time, yet it is not such that it should be considered eternal"—that is to say, though everlastingly existent the world is nonetheless a created and temporal entity in such a way that it presents no kind of dualistic threat to the existence of God (*De Consolat. Philos.* v.6).

The question of the "eternity" of creation is carefully discussed by Aquinas. More flexible on this subject, apparently, than his teacher Albert the Great, he argues that the "eternity" of the world can be neither demonstrated nor disproved. Strongly holding to the complete aseity and supremacy of God, he affirms that the existence of the world is not a necessary existence, with the result that its eternal existence cannot be proved.

> There is no need for God to will anything but himself. Therefore there is no necessity for God to will that the world should always have existed. Rather the world exists just so long as God wills it should, since the world's existence depends on his will as its cause. It is not necessary therefore that the world should always have existed, and accordingly this cannot be demonstratively proved.

Aquinas rejects the doctrine of Aristotle that matter and the heavens are ingenerate as having no adequate cause of their coming into being, and also his definition of the void of nothingness as space capable of containing a body but in which no body yet exists, maintaining to the contrary that matter and the heavens are the products of creation and that before the world existed there was no place or space (*Summa Theol.* 1a.46.1).

The discussion is expanded in one of Aquinas' later writings, *On the Eternity of the World*, in which he strenuously repudiates any suggestion of dualism. "If crediting something other than God with eternity means that it was not made by him," he says, "this would be an intolerable error." He contends, however, that the two notions of "having been created by God" and "having always existed" are not necessarily mutually exclusive, on the ground that "there is no need for an efficient cause, which in this case is God, to precede his effects in duration unless he has so willed it." As an illustration he proposes the phenomenon of fire which causes the effect of heat, but in such a manner that cause and effect are simultaneous with each other. But this is an inadmissible analogy, since it is not really possible to distinguish between fire and the heat that belongs to it as though they were two separate entities. In the finite created order of things at least causes are always temporally antecedent to the effects they produce. The fundamental question is whether this is necessarily so when God is the cause and creation the effect. According to Aquinas, a complete cause and its effect are simultaneous, and as no completion is wanting to God's causality, it does not follow that the effect (creation) of which he is the cause must necessarily follow the cause in time. "Could not God have willed that what he has willed always was and never was not?" he asks; and he goes on to affirm that "there is no contradiction in the assertion that an object both has been created by God and has always existed." This being so, the priority of cause over effect is one of meaning, not of temporal sequence. But Aquinas does not positively assert that it is so, only that it could be so without a necessity of contradiction.

This is the kind of speculation which Augustine, as we have seen, dismissed as "scarcely intelligible," involving as it does an illegitimate manipulation of language. The concept of *priority* cannot properly be divorced from temporality, except in the case of symbolical analogy, which does not apply in the discussion of creation and time. One of the dangers of such speculation is that, while designed to safeguard the divine changelessness, it may easily lead to the philosophical conclusion that the existence of God is static, motionless, and uneventful, which would hardly be a scriptural conclusion. Besides, Scripture speaks of a beginning and an end, of destruction as well as of creation. The God who brings into being is also the God who terminates being. Incapable though we are of speaking properly of what is beyond our experience and understanding, it may at least be suggested that the existence of God, so far from being static and uneventful or inert, may guardedly be described in terms of eventfulness (never, of course, in any sense of being *subject* to events but always *sovereign* over the whole of reality), inasmuch as the being of God, like the word of God, which is the expression of his being, is ever *dynamic* and to an absolute degree *vital* and *effective*. Surely creation, incarnation, and judgment may be said to be, within the limitations of our perspective, *eventful* even for God. But for a complete understanding of such mysteries we must await the dawn of that day when at last we shall know fully even as also we are now fully known (1 Cor. 13:12).

Meanwhile our author declares that "by faith we understand that the world was fashioned by the word of God, so that what is seen was not fashioned out of things that are visible," thus insisting on the necessity of the principle of faith as we seek to understand the cosmic system of which we are a part and which must be interpreted as the effect of the utterance by God of his transcendental word. As Scripture consistently testifies, that divine word is not an empty abstraction, not a mere sound that evaporates and is lost as soon as it is spoken, but a personal and indefectible force which is dynamic, vital, effective, and imperishable. Moreover, the word of God that effects creation also precedes creation. God, indeed, whose word it is, is the great and eternal antecedent. Creation, therefore, is not the filling up of a void or vacuum, as though where previously there was nothing now there is something. The basic biblical doctrine is stated in the affirmations "In the beginning God created . . . ," and "In the beginning was the Word . . ." (Gen. 1:1; Jn. 1:1)—that is to say, God who effected the beginning was at the beginning and before the beginning, and no less so the eternal Word who himself is God and through whom all things were made.

The purpose and effect (*so that*) of the word uttered at creation is the bringing into being of *what is seen*, that is, the perceptible order of creation, which is *not* produced from *things that appear*. Now it is not the custom of Scripture to equate invisibility with non-existence; quite the contrary, for, as Paul says, it is precisely the things which are not seen that are eternal (something that cannot be said of nonentity!) and the things which are seen that are impermanent (2 Cor. 4:18). In other words, there are unseen realities as well as seen realities, and the former are more real, because eternally real, than the latter. So, likewise, in this epistle the visible earthly sanctuary is an imperfect and impermanent pointer to the perfect and eternal reality of the invisible heavenly sanctuary (8:5; 9:8ff., 24;

10:19ff.). There are close affinities, further, between what our author says here and the teaching of Paul in Romans 1:20, where he explains that the perceptible created order points plainly to the unseen but ultimate reality of the existence of the sovereign Creator: the invisible facts (τὰ ἀόρατα αὐτοῦ) of his eternal power and deity are, he affirms, clearly seen (καθορᾶται) ever since the creation of the world, for they are rationally perceived (νοούμενα) through the things that he has made (τοῖς ποιήμασιν). Is not our author saying the same thing when he declares that we perceive rationally (νοοῦμεν) that the world was fashioned by the word of God, so that what is seen (τὸ βλεπόμενον—the singular indicating the perceptible creation in its entirety)—did not come into existence from things that are visible (μὴ ἐκ φαινομένων)? The corresponding expressions in the two passages may be juxtaposed as follows:

Hebrews 11:3	Romans 1:20
νοοῦμεν	νοούμενα
τὸ βλεπόμενον	τοῖς ποιήμασιν
μὴ ἐκ φαινομένων	τὰ ἀόρατα αὐτοῦ

Somewhat incongruously Luther, who, as has been mentioned, denounces the notion that the "non-phenomena" should be identified with the supposed primeval chaos of Genesis 1:2 as being too platonic, explains these non-phenomenal things in his gloss as signifying "the divine ideas," which has a strongly platonic ring about it (though apparently what he means is the mind of God, and he does in fact go on to associate them with "the invisible things of God" of Rom. 1:20). Delitzsch holds, more precisely, that "the things which do not appear" (as he interprets the Greek) are specifically the ideas or prototypes of the cosmic creation as they exist in the mind of God, in a manner which he describes as "at once scriptural, and (with certain modifications) Platonic, and Alexandrine." The doctrine of our epistle, that the earthly tabernacle with its functions is "a copy and shadow of the heavenly sanctuary" (8:5), "a copy of the true one" answering to the eternal archetype (9:24), is pressed into use by him as a general principle which applies to "all events in creation and developments in history." He sounds particularly Platonic/Alexandrine when he says that "the divine plan or idea of the universe that is to be, preceded the realization of the universe as it is," so that there is "a world of ideas as well as a world of actualities having the divine Logos for its centre and point of union." Thus he sees the present world as "*anagogical*, ever pointing up to higher things," and affirms that "it is faith, faith only, resting on the revealed creative word, which penetrates through the veil of phenomena to the divine super-sensual ground behind it."

Spicq, though finding it "unnecessary to see here an allusion to the heavenly archetypes of which the visible realities are the copies," offers an interpretation which is otherwise not dissimilar from that of Delitzsch. "It would be more exact," he says, "theologically speaking, to think of the existence of material things, before their creation, *in mente divina*, under the form of exemplary ideas or eternal reasons (St. Thomas)"; and he adds the somewhat fanciful comment that "the inferior world descends from the superior and fecund world, of which it is a disclosure, like a chrysalid emerging from its enveloping membrane." In our judgment, however, opinions of this kind are influenced to an unwarranted degree by the concepts of Greek philosophy. Moffatt seems to us to be right in his conclusion that "our author does not speculate," and that "it is very doubtful if he intends (Windisch, M'Neill) to agree with Philo's idea (in the *de opificio Mundi* 16, *de confus. ling.* 34) of the φαινόμενος οὗτος κόσμος being modelled on the ἀσώματος καὶ νοητός or archetypal ideas, for the language of 8⁵ is insufficient to bear the weight of this inference." It would seem more in harmony with the viewpoint of Scripture simply to speak of creation as conforming to the divine will and purpose.

The unseen reality that lies behind and permeates the whole created order is that of the power and energy of Almighty God—power and energy that are, so to speak, released and organized by God's utterance of his commanding and creative word. This undoubtedly is a deep mystery, beyond the capacities of human reason to comprehend or human language to define—hence the necessity for faith to stimulate our understanding. Yet we are now in a better position than ever to appreciate the truth of this dynamic reality, for modern physics has exposed the fallaciousness of the popular conception of matter as stolid, inert, and passive by its discovery that the basis of material entity is in fact *energy*. The minute nucleus of each atom of matter is a microcosm with its own solar system and a dynamic potential of energy that exceeds all calculation. The substance of the universe is superabundant energy! What is this substratum, or rather all-pervading essence, of energy but a testimony and a sign pointing to the amazingly dynamic character of the Word of God, that principle of infinite power which brought the created order into existence and by which the world is sustained and carried onward to its destined fulfilment (cf. Heb. 1:2, 3)?

Creation, then, is the bringing into being of that which was not previously in existence, namely, the cosmic system in its entirety—not, however, out of nothing in any sense that would imply an area of non-existence alongside of or over against the existence of God prior to creation, and that would thereby impose a limiting factor on the divine existence, any more than the existence of the created order of things implies a limitation of God's existence, as though the world now takes up space formerly occupied by God. The fulness of God, who, personal, dynamic, sovereign, is before all and over all, the supreme and eternal and infinite Reality, is "the fulness of him who fills all in all" (Eph. 1:23). The energy which interpenetrates the whole created order is the energy of the omnipotent word of God.

The biblical doctrine of creation is such that it excludes, on the one hand, dualism and, on the other, pantheism: dualism, because the self-existent God is the sole source and principle of all existence; and pantheism, because God, though infinite and omnipresent, is absolutely other than and above his creation, immanent indeed but also transcendent. It is precisely in his sovereign otherness that he who fills all in all is Creator (else the very idea of creation would be an absurdity), and that he who makes and redeems also judges and destroys.

11:4. *By faith Abel offered to God a more acceptable sacrifice than Cain, through which he received approval as righteous, God bearing witness by accepting his gifts; he died, but through his faith he is still speaking.*

The keynote of this chapter, *by faith*, now introduces the first of a series of illustrations from the personal history of particular individuals who belong to the lineage of men and women of faith during the centuries which preceded the advent of Christ—centuries in which the still future fulfilment of the gospel promises was seen and embraced from afar (v. 13). Those portrayed in this gallery of faith may be classified into four historical periods: (1) antediluvian (vv. 4–7)—Abel, Enoch, Noah; (2) pre-Mosaic (vv. 8–22)—Abraham, Sarah, Isaac, Jacob, Joseph; (3) Mosaic (vv. 23–29)—Moses himself; and (4) post-Mosaic (vv. 30–38)—Rahab and a more general reference to the many other heroes of faith, some named but mostly unnamed, of the succeeding generations.

The earliest in this cavalcade of faith is Abel, the account of whom in Genesis (4:2ff.) is limited, apart from the mere mention of his birth, to the narration of his violent death at the hand of his brother Cain. We are told that "Abel was a keeper of the sheep and Cain a tiller of the ground," that "in course of time" both brought offerings to the Lord, Cain "of the fruit of the ground" and Abel "of the firstlings of his flock and of their fat portions," that "the Lord had regard for Abel and his offering, but for Cain and his offering he had no regard," and that subsequently Cain, enraged and jealous, murdered Abel.

The question naturally arises as to why God should have regarded Abel's sacrifice as *more acceptable*[1] than Cain's—in fact, the one accept-

---

1. The adjective by which the accusative θυσίαν, "sacrifice," is qualified is πλείονα, which means literally "more." It is hardly open to dispute that Abel's sacrifice was superior to Cain's in terms of quality, not quantity—the quality deriving from the disposition of the offerer's heart rather than from the nature of the offering itself. This qualitative sense is confirmed by Matthew 5:20, where πλεῖον is used in comparing the "righteousness" of the Pharisees and that for which God looks; Matthew 6:25, where Jesus assures his disciples that their life is more (πλεῖον) than food; and Mark 12:23, where the widow's mite is praised as more (πλεῖον) than all the much greater sums that had been contributed. A merely quantitative interpretation of such passages would be inappropriate (cf. also Mt. 12:41, πλεῖον Ἰωνᾶ; Lk. 11:31, πλεῖον Σολομῶνος). Westcott, however, interprets πλείονα here in a quantitative manner, as implying that Abel thankfully brought a plentiful offering, whereas Cain grudgingly brought a meager offering. "The narrative in Genesis suggests," he says, "that the deeper gratitude of Abel found an outward expression in a more abundant offering. He brought of the 'firstlings' and did not offer like Cain at 'the end of time', while he also brought 'of the fat' of his flock." This matches closely the explanation given by Philo, who writes that "Cain retained in his own keeping the firstfruits of his husbandry and offered, as we are told, merely the fruits of a later time, although he had beside him a wholesome example," while Abel "brought to the altar the firstborn, not the later-born, thus confessing that even the causes which come higher in the chain of causa-

able, the other unacceptable; and there is a considerable variety of judgment in the answers which have been proposed. Philo, for example, explains that the working of the earth betokens the pursuit of the bad man whose preoccupation is with his earthy body and its pleasures,[2] and, further, that of the two offerings Abel's was living, Cain's lifeless, the one first in age and value, the other later and of secondary worth, the former possessing strength and superior fatness, the latter weak and inferior.[3] Such distinctions, however, are possible only through reading too much into the Genesis account and do not harmonize with the later system of offerings which enjoined the oblation of fruits as well as of animals. It can be granted that the statement of Genesis 4:3f. that Abel brought "of the firstlings of his flock" whereas Cain brought "of the fruit of the ground," without mention of firstfruits, may well be significant of quite different attitudes of heart on the part of the two brothers. This is the view of Delitzsch: "Abel offered his first and best; Cain offered only that which came first to hand. The outward difference betokened also an inward one." F. F. Bruce, however, supposes that just as Abel offered firstlings so also Cain offered firstfruits, and accordingly that it is not Cain's offering as such which was rejected but rather Cain himself—an opinion that is perhaps supported by Genesis 4:7, where the Lord says to Cain, "If you do well, will you not be accepted?" But there is general agreement that it is the inward disposition or motivation which is of first importance. As Gregory the Great says, with reference to Genesis 4:4 ("the Lord had regard for Abel and his offering"), "it is obvious that it was not the offerer who received approval because of the offerings but the offerings because of the offerer."[4] Similarly Aquinas observes that "God first had respect to him who was making the offering rather than to his offering, since an offering is accepted by reason of the goodness of

---

tion owe their existence to the Cause which is highest and first of all" (*De Confusione Linguarum* 124; see also *De Sacrificiis Abelis et Caini* 52). But it is a very questionable inference that whereas Abel brought firstlings Cain brought only a paltry remnant at the end of his harvest, since the Hebrew מִקֵּץ יָמִים means "in course of time" rather than "at the end of time," and in any case would seem to apply to the sacrifices of both Cain and Abel, rather than to Cain's alone.

Zuntz (*The Text of the Epistles*, p. 16) holds that "Cobet's brilliant conjecture HΔEIONA for ΠΛΕΙΟΝΑ restores the required sense, for Abel brought 'more agreeable' offerings and not 'more' in quantity." Moffatt judges that the emendation is favored by Justin Martyr's use of ἥδιον in connection with sacrifices (*Dialogue with Trypho* 29), and remarks that in Demosthenes (*Prooem.* 23) ἥδιον has been corrupted into πλεῖον. It has been contended (by J. D. Maynard in *The Expositor*, 7, 1909, pp. 164ff.) that Justin had Hebrews 11:4 in mind when writing the passage mentioned above. Since, however, the reading πλείονα is solidly attested and πλείονα itself is susceptible of a suitable qualititative sense, there is no necessity for a conjectural emendation of the text here.

2. Philo, *De Agricultura* 22.
3. Philo, *De Sacr. Abelis et Caini* 88.
4. Gregory the Great, Epistle CXXII (Migne, PL, LXXVII, 1053).

the offerer." And Calvin comments that "the sacrifice of Abel was more acceptable than that of his brother only because it was sanctified by faith."

It was his faith *through which*[5] Abel *received approval* from God[6] *as righteous*. The integrity of his heart was what really mattered. Abel, then, is the first example set before us here of the principle propounded at the end of the preceding chapter, "my righteous one shall live by faith" (10:38; Hab. 2:4). He belongs to the number of "those who have faith and keep their life" (Heb. 10:39), even though violently slain by jealous and unrighteous men, that is to say, despite all appearances to the contrary—an important theme of this chapter.

The divine approval of Abel as righteous was demonstrated by the circumstance of *God bearing witness*, or testifying, *by accepting his gifts*. The nature of this attestation is not described, but an ancient Jewish tradition, according to which God's acceptance was shown by the descent of fire from heaven which consumed Abel's but not Cain's offering, became current in the Christian church and also found its way into the Koran. Thus in the second century A.D. Theodotion's Greek version of the Old Testament rendered Genesis 4:4, "the Lord had regard for," as "the Lord sent down fire upon";[7] and, in the fourth century, Jerome asks: "How could Cain know that God had accepted his brother's offerings and rejected his own, unless that interpretation offered by Theodotion is true, 'And the Lord sent down fire on Abel and on his sacrifice, but on Cain and on his sacrifice he did not send down fire'? For it was customary for fire to come from heaven to consume sacrifices."[8] By way of illustration Jerome mentions the dedication of the temple by Solomon (2 Chron. 7:1) and the confrontation of Elijah and the priests of Baal on Mount Carmel (2 Ki. 18:38), both occasions on which a sacrifice was devoured by fire from heaven (cf. also Lev. 9:24). The same view is

---

5. Some commentators, including Ecumenius, Theophylact, Westcott, and Spicq, prefer to take Abel's sacrifice (θυσίαν) rather than his faith (πίστει) as the antecedent of the relative in the expression δι' ἧς, arguing that "the sacrifice was the sign of the righteousness—the true relation to God by faith—which he had inwardly" (Westcott). This, however, does not follow, since the external ceremony does not in itself guarantee the internal grace, as the case of Cain clearly shows. *Faith* is the ruling concept of this verse, and indeed of the whole chapter, as the emphatic position of πίστει at the beginning of the sentence attests, and accordingly πίστει not θυσίαν is the proper antecedent of the relative ἧς, as it is also, by general agreement, the antecedent of the pronoun αὐτῆς in the last clause of the verse. The connection of thought is in fact seen in the sequence πίστει... δι' ἧς... καὶ δι' αὐτῆς....
6. The verb ἐμαρτυρήθη is a "divine passive," implying that it was by God that he was attested as righteous, as the next clause (a genitive absolute construction) confirms, μαρτυροῦντος... τοῦ θεοῦ, "God bearing witness."
7. 'Ενεπύρισεν. See F. Field, *Origenis Hexaplorum quae supersunt* (Oxford, 1875; Hildesheim, 1964), p. 17, in which this rendering is recorded.
8. Jerome, in Migne, PL, XXIII, 992f.

found in Chrysostom and subsequently, among many others, in Herveus, Aquinas, Luther, Owen, Delitzsch, and Spicq. It is, however, a matter on which both Genesis and our epistle are silent.

There is a long line of interpretation which sees in Abel's bringing of the firstlings of his flock an indication that his sacrifice was a sin-offering involving the shedding of blood. Owen, for example, explains that "Cain considered God only as a creator and preserver," but "had no respect unto sin, or the way of deliverance from it revealed in the first promise"; whereas "the faith of Abel was fixed on God, not only as creator, but as redeemer also, as him who, in infinite wisdom and grace, had appointed the way of redemption by sacrifice and atonement." Accordingly, Owen understands Abel's offering as being "by death and blood," the former indicating "the death which himself by reason of sin was obnoxious unto," and the latter "the way of atonement, which was to be by blood, the blood of the promised Seed." Similarly Delitzsch writes that, "inasmuch as the relation between God and man had been disturbed by sin, Abel's faith exhibited itself in recognizing and laying hold of the divine mercy in the midst of wrath and judgment,—an aspect of his personal standing with regard to sacrifice, which had its correlative in his offering being of a life and of blood." Whether or not this is a correct understanding of the situation it is impossible to say. The developed system of blood-sacrifice for sin receives explicit formulation only later in the Old Testament, though it may be assumed that its roots go back to a very early period.

Abel, it is true, *died, but,* our author adds, *through his faith he is still speaking.* In what sense does Abel still speak? One answer given to this question proposes that he does so through or in Scripture (Westcott, Delitzsch, Moffatt), and it is true that but for the biblical record we should have no knowledge of Abel and his faith; but it is unlikely that this is the meaning intended—if it had been, it would doubtless have been expressed in so many words. Another opinion (which may or may not be combined with the foregoing) is that Abel still speaks in the sense that his blood cries out to God for vengeance (Aquinas, Grotius, Owen, Delitzsch, Alford, Héring, F. F. Bruce). This interpretation is influenced by the assertion of Genesis 4:10, "The voice of your brother's blood is crying to me from the ground," which is frequently associated with Revelation 6:9f., where the souls of the martyrs cry out to God for the avenging of their blood; but it belongs with the statement in 12:24 below, that the blood of Jesus "speaks more graciously than the blood of Abel," rather than with the present verse. Spicq understands our author to be saying here that the victim's blood calls not for vengeance but for reconciliation and redemption. "The blood of Abel shed by his brother is," he says, "like a cry directed to the ears of God for the reconciliation of men and the expiation of sin. It is the symbol of guilty humanity expressing its distress and appealing for the blood of redemption."

But the simplest sense remains the best sense, namely, that Abel by his example of faith and righteousness still speaks to us today, even though he has so long been dead. The spectacle of his trustful integrity, even in the face of violence, should inspire us to persevere and to overcome by the same means. His was certainly an example that the faltering readers of this epistle were in need of emulating. The important implication should not be missed, moreover, that Abel, though cruelly slain, nonetheless lives through God. His gaze was firmly fixed on the better country (v. 16). Were it not so, his faith would have terminated in frustration and Cain's example of self-interest would have been the example for subsequent generations to follow. The declaration that Abel "being dead still speaks" means, says Luther, "that he who when he was actually alive could not teach even his only brother by his faith and example, now that he is dead teaches the whole world"—in other words, "he is more alive than ever! So great a thing is faith! It is life in God."

11:5. *By faith Enoch was taken up so that he should not see death; and he was not found, because God had taken him. Now before he was taken he was attested as having pleased God.*

In the Old Testament the sum of what is told of Enoch is found in Genesis 5:18–24, where we read that he was the son of Jared and the father of Methuselah, as well as of other children whose names are not given, that he lived 365 years, and that "he walked with God, and he was not, for God took him." The Septuagint, which our author echoes, has "he pleased God" instead of "he walked with God"; but this is not to say something different, since only he who pleases God walks with God, that is, enjoys a relationship of harmonious fellowship with him. In the New Testament Enoch is mentioned only twice apart from the passage now before us, namely, in the genealogy of Luke 3 (v. 37) and in Jude 14f., where he is introduced ("the seventh from Adam") as a prophet of judgment. Despite the paucity of references in the canonical Scriptures, however, Enoch is a prominent figure in Jewish apocryphal literature, and in the rabbinical tradition he even gained a mediatorial position between God and man on the ground, apparently, of his having lived a perfectly pure life. Thus he is described not only as well-pleasing but also, "because of the righteousness, wherein he was perfect," as the only one whom Noah did not excel (Jub. 10:17; cf. 1 Enoch

71:14). But, on the other hand, he is praised as "an example of repentance to all generations" in Ecclesiasticus (44:16).

Enoch, we are told, *was taken up*, or, more literally "was removed,"[9] and his "removal" was, by implication, from this earthly scene to the presence of God himself, not from one geographical location to another; nor is it a euphemism for his death, as some modern scholars, both Jewish and Christian, have suggested. In the Wisdom of Solomon, where it is said that Enoch was "caught up"[10] and that "being perfected in a short time he fulfilled long years" (4:11, 13), it is not at all clear whether he is intended as an illustration of the truth that "the righteous man, though he die early, will be at rest" (4:7) and that "the righteous man who has died will condemn the ungodly who are living" (4:16). The death of Enoch would have been recorded in the Genesis account just as unequivocally as are the deaths of the other patriarchs, had we been intended to understand that he had died. "His removal from earth," writes H. E. Ryle, "is obviously not to be explained . . . upon the theory of an early death. In the Israelite literature, premature death was never regarded as a mark of Divine favour; and, if Enoch had thus died in early life, we should have expected the use of the same phrase, 'And he died', which occurs in the mention of the other Patriarchs. The ordinary interpretation is certainly the correct one of the words, 'He was not, for God took him.'"[11]

There is, of course, no uncertainty about our author's understanding of the removal of Enoch, for he explains quite unambiguously that he was taken up *so that he should not see death*. (To "see" death is to experience or to pass through death. The same idiom is used in Lk. 2:26, where the evangelist narrates that it had been revealed to Simeon by the Holy Spirit "that he should not see death [that is, die] before he had seen the Lord's Christ.") It is in the light of this explanation that the statement which follows immediately, *and he was not found, because God had taken him*,[12] must be interpreted: suddenly and supernaturally removed from this earthly existence, he was not anywhere to be found, thus providing evidence of the power of God to exalt a man without his first passing through the experience of death.[13] Enoch, indeed, may be

9. Greek, μετετέθη. The verb indicates a change of place, a removal from one location to another, and does not in itself imply an "upward" direction, though the context, as here, may point to it (cf. the paraphrases of Phillips, "was promoted to the eternal world," and NEB, "was carried away to another life").
10. Greek, ἡρπάγη—a stronger verb than μετετέθη, meaning "was snatched away."
11. H. E. Ryle, "The Early Narratives of Genesis," *The Expository Times*, 3 (1891/2), p. 355.
12. Greek, μετέθηκεν, the same verb as is used in the first part of the verse (μετετέθη). Our author is in fact quoting from the LXX of Genesis 5:24, which corresponds exactly with καὶ οὐχ ηὑρίσκετο διότι μετέθηκεν αὐτὸν ὁ θεός.
13. To quote one of Bengel's memorable epigrams: "Ex mortalitate sine morte in immortalitatem traductus est."

seen as a sort of prototype (together with Elijah at a later period) of the men and women of faith who will be living at the moment of Christ's return—an occasion of surpassing glory—and who, too, will be caught up to be with Christ without passing through the experience of death (see 1 Thess. 4:15–17).

The belief is found early on in some of the patristic writings that Enoch and Elijah would return to earth in the last days as the two witnesses mentioned in Revelation 11, who were to be slain and then raised to life and taken up into heaven. Thus Tertullian writes: "Enoch was translated, and also Elijah; nor is there any record of their death, since it was postponed; for they are kept in reserve for the suffering of death so that they may destroy Antichrist by their blood."[14] Influenced, no doubt, by a particular interpretation of John 21:22, Hippolytus with a strange inconsistency adds a third witness, John the Evangelist.[15] It is well known that the Jews looked for the reappearance of Elijah, but in some circles at least there seems to have been the expectation that Enoch would appear with him. In 2 Esdras 6:26, for example, we find the following prophecy concerning the end of the age: "They shall see the men who were taken up, who from their birth have not tasted death; and the heart of the earth's inhabitants shall be changed and converted to a different spirit." Aquinas speaks of Enoch as having been "caught away to an earthly paradise" (by which he evidently means the paradise from which Adam was expelled) "where, it is believed, he is living with Elijah until the coming of Antichrist."[16] But the author of our epistle avoids every kind of speculation, and also, it is worth noting, the allegorizing method of Philo which enables the latter to explain the narrative concerning Enoch as a parable of the man who is "removed" from the love of pleasures and other harmful distractions, and who is "not found" because he withdraws from the crowd and cultivates a life of solitude and contemplation.[17]

The concluding sentence of the verse, *Now before he was taken*[18] *he was attested as having pleased God*, is an explanatory comment on the *faith* of Enoch, mentioned in the opening phrase, which was the determining factor in the wonderful experience granted to him. Admittedly, it is not specifically stated in Genesis (or elsewhere) that Enoch was a man of faith, but this goes without saying in the light of the attestation that he pleased God and walked with him[19] in sacred spiritual communion.

---

14. Tertullian, *De Anima* 50.
15. Hippolytus, *De Consummatione Mundi* 21; Migne, PG, X, 921f. This, however, is among the works doubtfully attributed to Hippolytus.
16. Aquinas, *Summa Theol.* 3a.49.5.
17. Philo, *De Praemiis et Poenis* 16f.; *De Abrahamo* 17ff.
18. Literally, "before his removal," πρὸ γὰρ τῆς μεταθέσεως.
19. Spicq is caught nodding when he affirms that it is not said of any other patriarch that

This could be true only of one whose life was lived in trust and obedience toward his Creator. Hence the logical sequence here: "By faith Enoch . . . for he pleased God," and the opening declaration of the next verse, that "without faith it is impossible to please him."

> 11:6. *And without faith it is impossible to please him. For whoever would draw near to God must believe that he exists and that he rewards those who seek him.*

The particular example of Enoch illustrates the general principle now propounded, that *without faith it is impossible to please God*. Faith, indeed, is the disposition which should be characteristic of the creature in relation to his Creator; for faith is that trustful reliance which finds expression in willing obedience and submission to the sovereign word of God, in grateful acknowledgment of the unmixed goodness of all his works, and in confident recognition of the complete trustworthiness of his promises. As the account of the fall in Genesis 3 shows, the failure of faith manifests itself in rebellion against God's authority, questioning of his goodness, and denial of the truth of his word. To abandon faith is to behave as though God were not there. The man without faith is the man who wickedly attempts to suppress the truth about God (Rom. 1:18ff.). He cannot possibly be included in the number of those who please God. To repudiate faith is to sever the lifeline which links the creature to his Creator and is thus to lose the very meaning and purpose of one's existence. It is to be without God and therefore without hope in the world (Eph. 2:12).

Whoever would draw near to God, then, *must*, before all else, *believe*, have faith, *that he exists*—for faith must have an object, and God is the supreme and eternal object of all true faith. And there is necessity, further, to believe that God *rewards those who seek him*—to have faith, in other words, that God is personal and responds to the cry of his creatures by graciously providing mercy and forgiveness for those who repent and put their trust in him. For when he speaks of reward our author is not encouraging a mercenary attitude. On the contrary, what he means is that the approach and relationship of faith involves commitment to the truth that the self-existent God is at the same time a

---

he walked with God, for it is in fact said of Noah (Gen. 6:9) and of Levi (Mal. 2:6), though perhaps the designation "patriarch" does not apply to the latter. F. F. Bruce draws attention to the fact that the expression "to walk before God" is rendered "to be well pleasing before God" in the Septuagint, and is used of Abraham (Gen. 17:1; 24:40), of Abraham and Isaac (Gen. 48:15), and of the pious Israelite (Ps. 56:13; 116:9).

personal God, and therefore a just and holy God who has a loving concern for his creatures. Thus Aquinas says, referring to Isaiah 40:10 ("Behold, the Lord God comes... ; behold, his reward is with him"): "This reward is nothing other than God himself, because man ought not to seek anything apart from him—Gen. 15:1: 'I am your protector and your exceeding great reward'—for God gives nothing other than his own self." To imagine that faith is in itself meritorious or establishes a claim on God and his rewards is to do violence to the very concept of faith, which is the response of total dependence on the grace and goodness of God. "It is sheer profanity," insists Lefèvre d'Etaples in a remarkable passage which anticipates Luther and the other Reformers,

> to speak of the merit of works, especially in the presence of God. For plainly merit does not ask a favour but demands what is due; and to attribute merit to works is virtually to share the opinion of those who believe that we can be justified by works, an error for which the Jews are most of all condemned. So let us be silent about the merit of our works, which amounts to very little or rather nothing at all, and let us magnify the grace of God which is everything. He who defends merit respects man; but he who defends grace respects God.... If merit is to be attributed to anyone, it is properly and completely attributed to Christ, who has merited everything for us, while we, confessing that before God we deserve nothing, look to him for grace.[20]

This conclusion is implicit in the assertion of our text that God rewards those who seek *him*, not those who seek his rewards or imagine that they have earned them, which would be something very different.

The Reformed understanding of the New Testament doctrine of rewards is well presented by Martin Bucer, who writes: "That the Lord rewards his people for their good works is not on the grounds of their righteousness, but purely from his free grace and for the sake of his dear Son (Rom. 11:6), in whom he chose us for eternal life before the foundation of the world (Eph. 1:4), and created us for good works (Eph. 2:10) which through him he effects in us (Jn. 15:5) and rewards so generously (Rom. 8:10–14, 26–30)." Consequently, "when God rewards our good works he is rewarding his works and gifts in us, rather than our own works." Moreover, while the faith we exercise and the good works we perform proceed from our own free will, "nevertheless it is he who produces this good will and action in us, impelling us by his Holy Spirit (Phil. 2:13)"; thus "all the good that God does to us and the eternal life that he gives us still remain the results of his grace alone, so that no one should boast of himself, but only of the Lord (Phil. 2:13; Rom. 6:23;

20. Lefèvre d'Etaples, Commentary on 1 Corinthians (8:8), *Commentariorum in Epistolas Beatissimi Pauli Apostoli...* (1512).

11:5f., 36; 1 Cor. 1:29f.)."[21] That this teaching coincides with that of the apostles had of course been recognized long before by Augustine, with whose writings Lefèvre d'Etaples and the Reformers were familiar. Referring to passages such as 2 Corinthians 4:7 ("What have you that you did not receive? If then you received it, why do you boast as if it were not a gift?") and James 1:17 ("Every good and perfect gift is from above"), Augustine affirms that "it is his own gifts that God crowns, not our merits, even though we regard these as our own acts," and that "if they are good, they are God's gifts"—"not," he explains, "that the apostle meant to deny good works or to empty them of their value, because he says that God renders to every man according to his works; but he would have works proceed from faith, and not faith from works." Thus "we have even our good works from God, from whom likewise our faith and our love come,"[22] and God gives what he commands.[23]

The drawing near to God of which this verse speaks should not be understood in the limited sense of drawing near only at times of worship, but in the comprehensive sense of drawing near to God at all times, in our daily occupations as well as in our church-going, in prosperity as well as in adversity—the nearness, that is to say, of uninterrupted communion with him of the kind that Enoch enjoyed, so that it could be said of him that "he walked with God."

It should be noticed that our author does not attempt to offer arguments and proofs for the existence of God. Throughout the whole of Scripture the existence of God is never a matter of doubt or debate. Such reasonings as are found (for example, Ps. 19:1ff.; Rom. 1:19ff.) always start from assurance, never from uncertainty. God is not a metaphysical concept for questioning and discussion. He is the supreme reality, and the foundation and source of all created being. Hence when the reader is advised that to draw near to God he *must believe that he exists* he is not being invited to take a step in the dark but to turn to the light; he is not being encouraged to work up a blind faith but to entrust the whole of his being to him who is himself truth and light and life. The offering of ourselves to God is indeed our "reasonable service" (Rom. 12:1), for, as Delitzsch comments, the verb "must" here "expresses not so much a moral obligation as a logical necessity." This is not to deny, however, that refusal to acknowledge the existence of God is as immoral as it is irrational.

---

21. Martin Bucer, *A Brief Summary of Christian Doctrine*, 10 (1548); see *The Common Places of Martin Bucer*, trans. and ed. by D. F. Wright (Abingdon, 1972), p. 82.
22. Augustine, *De Gratia et Libero Arbitrio* 15, 17.
23. *De Gratia* 29. Cf. *Confessions* XI.xiii.34: "Whoever recounts his true merits to thee, what is it that he recounts to thee but thine own gifts?" See also the commentary above on 6:10 and 10:35.

11:7. By faith Noah, being warned by God concerning events as yet unseen, took heed and constructed an ark for the saving of his household; by this he condemned the world and became an heir of the righteousness which comes by faith.

The third example of victorious faith in the period leading up to the flood is Noah, whose story, unlike that of Abel and Enoch, is narrated at some length in the book of Genesis (5:28–9:29), where he is spoken of as "a righteous man, blameless in his generation," who "walked with God" (6:9)—that is to say, his life, like Enoch's, was blessed by a harmonious relationship of communion with God. Ezekiel (14:14) also specifically mentions the righteousness of Noah, which, being righteousness before God, was not self-righteousness but, as our author explains, *the righteousness which comes by faith.* In the New Testament he is described as a preacher or herald of righteousness (2 Pet. 2:5), for his memory was revered down through the centuries because of the boldness with which he challenged the unrighteous generation of his day to repent and put their faith in God and warned them that if they continued obdurate divine judgment would overtake them. Accordingly, in 1 Peter 3:19f. the years during which the ark was being built are seen as the period of God's patience and the opportunity for repentance. The situation in which Noah labored and preached is graphically depicted in the Genesis account, which states that "the Lord saw that the wickedness of man was great in the earth, and that every imagination of the thoughts of his heart was only evil continually," and, again, that "the earth was corrupt in God's sight . . . and filled with violence" (Gen. 6:5, 11). This was the background against which Noah's faith was tested and prevailed.

It was by the building of the ark that the faith of Noah was most dramatically demonstrated. The reason for this undertaking was that he had been *warned by God concerning events as yet unseen*, the coming events, namely, of the destruction of the flood by which the unrepentant would be judged and of the deliverance of himself and of those who would join him in the ark. The conduct of Noah illustrates and confirms the definition of faith given in verse 1 as "the assurance of things hoped for" (his own salvation) and "the conviction of things not seen"[24] (the judgment of the flood), founded as it was on his confidence in the word which he had received from God. Thus it was *by faith* that he *took heed*[25]

---

24. The Greek here, περὶ τῶν μηδέπω βλεπομένων, corresponds closely to πραγμάτων ἔλεγχος οὐ βλεπομένων in verse 1.

25. The careful attentiveness signified by the participle εὐλαβηθείς is exercised in particular within the setting of the pious or religious life. Thus the noun εὐλάβεια found in our epistle at 5:7 and 12:28 (and not elsewhere in the New Testament) means attentiveness to the divine will or godly reverence; and the adjective εὐλαβής, which occurs in Luke 2:25 and Acts 2:5 and 8:2, applies especially to devout or pious persons.

and constructed an ark, an enterprise which must have appeared ludicrous to his contemporaries, especially as it was carried through at an inland location far from sea or ocean. The scene is dramatized in Book I of the Sibylline Oracles, where Noah, who is described as most righteous and most faithful, is commanded by God to proclaim repentance so that all may be saved, while warning them that if his message is not heeded the whole generation will be destroyed by a great flood of waters. The following address is then placed on his lips:

> Faithless men, maddened by passion, do not forget the great things God has done; for the immortal all-provident Saviour knows all things, and he has commanded me to be a messenger to you, lest you be destroyed by your madness. Sober yourselves, cease from your evil practices and from your murderous violence against each other, soaking the earth with human blood. Reverence, my fellow mortals, the supreme and unassailable Creator in heaven, the imperishable God who dwells on high. Call upon him, all of you (for he is good) to be merciful to you all. For this whole vast world of men will be destroyed with water and you will then utter cries of terror. Suddenly the elements will turn against you and the wrath of Almighty God will come upon you from heaven. . . .[26]

The Sibylline versifier goes on to recount how they all treated Noah with contempt, calling him a raving madman. Thereupon Noah resumes his denunciation of their viciousness and warns them again of the cataclysmic judgment by which they will all perish.

But Noah persevered in faith, and it was *by faith* that he *condemned the world,* its mocking laughter forever silenced when all came to pass exactly as he had forewarned; and by this same faith he *became an heir of the righteousness which comes by faith*—the righteousness which, as Paul insists, is derived not from human works and deservings, but is bestowed by God on the man of faith (Eph. 2:8f.; Phil. 3:9).[27] It is the heir who becomes the possessor, and the inheritance of righteousness into the possession of which Noah entered was the inheritance that God has provided in Christ; for, as Aquinas affirms, no one in any age is saved except through faith in Christ and on the basis, either anticipated or fulfilled, of his mediatorial work. Christ, indeed, is supremely and uniquely the Heir: he it is, and none other, whom the Father has "appointed the heir of all things." Noah and every other heir of righteousness is so only by virtue of having been made one with Christ, the sole Heir, by faith (see commentary above on 1:2). If Christ is the heir of all things, there is no inheritance remaining for others unless they are

26. Sibylline Oracles i.125ff.
27. Teodorico comments that in the phrase ἡ κατὰ πίστιν δικαιοσύνη the qualification "κατὰ πίστιν indicates the way or the condition by which righteousness is realized, or by which God bestows it: its norm or measure."

united with him. Thus in giving us Christ God gives us all things (Rom. 8:17, 32). "So let no one boast of men," says the Apostle, "For all things are yours, . . . and you are Christ's, and Christ is God's" (1 Cor. 3:21ff.).

The story of Noah demonstrates, finally, the simultaneousness of judgment and salvation; for *the saving of his household* and the condemnation of the unbelieving world took place at the same time and by the same means. What was a means of salvation was also a means of destruction: the water which overwhelmed the scornful also supported the ark and those who were in it. In the hour of judgment there is security for those whose life is hid with Christ in God (Col. 3:3). Thus the eight persons in the ark were "saved through water" (1 Pet. 3:20). The sacrament of the eucharist was ordained by Christ as a means of grace, but to the unworthy recipient, who profanes the body and blood of the Lord, it becomes instead a means of condemnation, so that "he eats and drinks judgment upon himself" (1 Cor. 11:27ff.). The day of Christ's parousia will be not only the consummating moment of salvation for those who are his but also the moment of final judgment for those who persist in unbelief. Of this the world has been forewarned by the flood of Noah's day, as Christ himself taught: "As were the days of Noah, so will be the coming of the Son of man. For as in those days before the flood they were eating and drinking, marrying and giving in marriage," and their faithless and unheeding attitude persisted "until the day when Noah entered into the ark," and then, that same day, "the flood came and swept them all away," so, Christ warns—"will be the coming of the Son of man" (Mt. 24:37ff.; cf. 17:26f.; 2 Pet. 2:4ff.; 3:6f.). Those who will not have God as Savior will meet him as Judge.

11:8. *By faith Abraham obeyed when he was called to go out to a place which he was to receive as an inheritance; and he went out, not knowing where he was to go.*

Though the line of faith stretches back beyond Abraham through Noah, Enoch, and Abel to the very earliest of times, it is not surprising that Abraham, the progenitor of the Hebrew nation who was commonly regarded as the father of the faithful, is more fully portrayed than anyone else in this gallery of heroes of faith. The keynote of Abraham's life and conduct is sounded in Genesis 15:6, where it is said that "he believed the Lord; and he reckoned it to him as righteousness"; and this note is taken up by Paul, who explains, with reference to Abraham's example, that "to one who does not work but trusts in him who justifies the ungodly, his faith is reckoned as righteousness" (Rom. 4:5). By virtue, then, of the indomitable intensity of his faith in the face of the severest trials and afflictions, Abraham is honored as the father of all who believe (Rom. 4:11f.,16). All, in every age, "who are men of faith are blessed with Abraham who had faith" (Gal. 3:9), and the true and eternal posterity promised to him by God comprises all who, like Abraham, have faith in Christ. These, as Paul affirms, are "Abraham's offspring" and "heirs according to the promise" (Gal. 3:29). Conversely, refusal to believe in Christ nullifies any claim to belong to the posterity of Abraham (Jn. 8:31ff.). Justification is not by physical pedigree but by faith, and it is inward renewal not external lineage that constitutes one a member of the true Israel of God (Heb. 10:38; Rom. 2:29; 5:1; Gal. 6:15f.; Jn. 3:18, 36).

Abraham's example teaches us, further, that true faith always leads to decisive action, that trust must manifest itself in obedience, indeed that works are the evidence of faith. This is what James means when he says, with specific reference to Abraham, that faith apart from works is barren and dead (Jas. 2:14ff.). So, too, our author says that by faith *Abraham obeyed when he was called:* the word of God calls not merely for faith but also for action which springs from faith in that word. When Christ demands of his disciples that they should follow him, he is demanding not some kind of abstract contemplative pursuit but that following which displays itself decisively in the act of rising, forsaking all, and daily taking up the cross (Mt. 4:18ff.; 9:9; 10:38f.; 19:27ff.). Likewise Abraham, when he heard the call, arose and without hesitation[28] *went out* from Ur of the Chaldees, thus demonstrating to the world the genuineness of his faith. "Abraham departed the moment he was bidden... ," writes Philo. "Taking no thought for anything, either for his fellow-clansmen, or wardsmen, or schoolmates, or blood relations on father's or mother's side, or country, or ancestral customs, or community of nurture or home life, all of them ties possessing a power to allure and attract which it is hard to throw off, he followed a free and unfettered impulse and departed with all speed from Chaldea, a land at that time blessed by fortune and at the height of its prosperity."[29]

But the call which Abraham received was not only a command for him to obey; it was also a promise for him to lay hold of, the promise of an inheritance on which he should fix his hope: *he was called to go out to a place which he was to receive as an inheritance.* Yet he was ignorant when he left home and fatherland what or where this place was; accordingly, *he went out not knowing where he was to go,* and, as Calvin observes, "it is no

---

28. The immediateness of his response is suggested by the coupling of the present participle καλούμενος with the aorist of the main verb ὑπήκουσεν: as he was being called he obeyed. "He obeyed the call," Westcott comments, "while (so to say) it was still sounding in his ears." Similarly, Delitzsch and Spicq.
29. Philo, *De Abrahamo* 66f.

ordinary trial of faith to give up what we have in hand in order to seek what is afar off and unknown to us." Here, again, we have a striking illustration of "the assurance of things hoped for" combined with "the conviction of things not seen," the two components of faith as defined in the opening verse of this chapter. Abraham set out in faith, his destination unrevealed, but he also set out in hope, firmly grasping the promise of an inheritance. The bare word of God was sufficient warrant for his going. "But," says Luther in a characteristic passage,

> this is the glory of faith, simply not to know: not to know where you are going, not to know what you are doing, not to know what you must suffer, and with sense and intellect, virtue and will, all alike made captive, to follow the naked voice of God.... Abraham with this obedience of faith shows the highest example of the evangelical life, because he left all and followed the Lord, preferring the word of God to everything else and loving it above all things; of his own free will a pilgrim, and subject to the perils of life and death every hour of the day and night.

11:9, 10. *By faith he sojourned in the land of promise, as in a foreign land, living in tents with Isaac and Jacob, heirs with him of the same promise. For he looked forward to the city which has foundations, whose builder and maker is God.*

The faith of Abraham was all the more remarkable because he lacked any of those helps and advantages which his posterity, physical as well as spiritual, would later enjoy as a rich heritage (cf. Rom. 9:4f.). He did not have the example of godly men to stir him to emulation, as Chrysostom points out; indeed, his father was a heathen and an idolater (see Josh. 24:2); nor did he have the teaching of prophets to instruct him. Moreover, *the land of promise* to which God brought him was not for him a land of possession as it later became for the nation of which he was the progenitor. How strange that when he arrived in this land of promise, designated as the "place which he was to receive as an inheritance" (v. 8), he should only have *sojourned* there, like an alien or transient *in a foreign land!* In what sense could he be said to have received this land as an inheritance when it was a territory in which he led no settled existence and to which he had no claim of ownership? God, as Stephen reminded his accusers, "gave him no inheritance in it, not even a foot's length"; furthermore, he came to it aged and childless (Acts 7:5). Even when a line of posterity was provided (see vv. 11 and 12), and *Isaac and Jacob* became associated with him as the visible beginnings of the line of promise, Abraham's temporal insecurity and lack of tenure were thrown into relief by the way in which he continued *living in tents* with them. On the death of his wife Sarah, many years after his coming to the land, he had to purchase from the inhabitants a piece of land in which to bury her, by reason of his being "a stranger and a sojourner" in their midst (Gen. 23:4). The manner of his existence was altogether that of one who did not belong in the land, a migrant rather than a permanent inhabitant.[30]

The solution of the apparent paradox involved in this strange combination of entry and yet non-possession is the solution that sounds forth again and again throughout this chapter in the brief but radical explanation: *by faith*. All unremittingly from beginning to end is by faith. He who begins by faith must continue by faith, for faith is the principle not only of initiation but also of perseverance. The life of faith did not cease for Abraham when he left Ur of the Chaldees behind him or when at length he set foot on the territory toward which he had directed his steps. Indeed, the situation into which he moved on his arrival in the land of promise was a more severe trial of his faith than was the call to leave home and kindred, and it was easier for him to live by faith as he journeyed toward a goal as yet unseen than to do so upon reaching this goal and finding that the fulness of all that had been promised was "not yet." To live like an alien, with no better or more permanent shelter than the insecure covering of tents, in the very land with which the promise was associated—an existence which, by all worldly standards, contrasted far from favorably with the stability he had enjoyed in the civilization of Chaldea—demanded an outstanding degree of faith on the part of Abraham.

It was by faith that Abraham learned to look beyond this present fleeting scene to the unseen and eternal blessings which God has prepared for those who love him (1 Cor. 2:9) and to account the sufferings

---

30. This temporal or this-worldly insecurity is clearly indicated in the Greek by the verb παρῴκησεν, since παροικεῖν (Lk. 24:18 as well as here), together with the cognate nouns παροικία (Acts 13:17; 1 Pet. 1:17) and πάροικος (Acts 7:6, 29; Eph. 2:19; 1 Pet. 2:11), implies the transitory residence of strangers or outsiders, whether in an actual or a spiritual sense. The concept of the Christian as an impermanent sojourner on earth who is on his way to his true home that lies beyond the present scene is derived from the experience of Abraham and the terminology by which it is described. Thus in the LXX of Genesis 23:4 Abraham speaks of himself as πάροικος καὶ παρεπίδημος among the inhabitants of the land (cf. Ps. 39:12). In verse 13 of the present chapter it is said that Abraham and his fellow patriarchs acknowledged that they were ξένοι καὶ παρεπίδημοι on the earth, ξένοι being here a synonym for πάροικοι. And Christians are called πάροικοι καὶ παρεπίδημοι by Peter (1 Pet. 2:11; cf. 1:1, 17). For them, this earth is not their homeland, but rather, as Abraham found the land of promise, foreign territory: παρῴκησεν εἰς γῆν τῆς ἐπαγγελίας ὡς ἀλλοτρίαν. Cf. the similar terminology of the Jewish composition known as the Psalms of Solomon, which is generally assigned to the first century B.C.: πάροικος καὶ ἀλλογενὴς οὐ παροικήσει αὐτοῖς ἔτι. The spiritual sense has from the apostolic period on been part of the idiom of Christianity. It might benefit the modern church to be reminded of the spiritual significance of the familiar term "parish" ("parochial"), which is directly derived from the Greek term παροικία.

of this present time as unworthy of comparison with the glory that was to be revealed to him (Rom.8:18). Accordingly, he realized that the attainment of this earthly territory was not the completion of his pilgrimage and perceived that this land of promise, so unpromising in itself, was in fact a pointer to a further and more solid reality. The testing circumstances of his sojourn within its boundaries were a daily witness to him that fulfilment was not here and not yet. And so the land became to him a sacrament, or rather an element which, linked as it was with the word of the promise, was invested with sacramental significance, and which, as such, pointed beyond itself to a more excellent consummation. It was with this farsighted perspective, then, that Abraham *looked forward to the city which has foundations, whose builder and maker is God*. The glory of this prospect was all the more enhanced by the striking contrast of his tent-dwelling which dramatically testified to the fact that the foundations of his life were not in this present world. Abraham, Isaac, and Jacob, writes Lefèvre d'Etaples, "were figures of all believers, and the land promised to them was a figure of the heavenly habitation. Their pilgrimage was a figure that the present life is nothing other than a kind of pilgrimage whose destination is the heavenly city which has been made by the hands not of men but of God." This great truth is admirably summed up, again in the words of Lefèvre d'Etaples (commenting on 8:6): "to be with Christ is to be in the land promised to the fathers."

For Abraham, who had left behind him the comparative solidity of the Chaldean civilization, to have sought security in similar foundations and cities in the land of Canaan would have made no sense (cf. v. 15 below). His tent-dwelling was precisely a dwelling without foundations in this world, a dwelling which, though it offered scant protection against elemental and hostile forces of every kind, he was content to endure because as a man of faith he looked forward with certainty[31] to the eventual attainment of *the city*—not any city, but the one and only city—of which alone it is ultimately and eternally true that it has foundations,[32] in that its designer and constructor is God himself.[33] As the

---

31. Ἐξεδέχετο may well be intensive in force. Spicq, for example, understands it to mean, "he expected with an absolute confidence" (cf. Jas. 5:7).

32. Note the definite article in the phrase τὴν τοὺς θεμελίους ἔχουσαν πόλιν.

33. The description of God as τεχνίτης καὶ δημιουργός, translated "builder and maker" in our version, is interesting. This is in fact the only place in the New Testament where the two nouns occur. Τεχνίτης is properly a craftsman. The application of the term to God as the "craftsman" of creation is found in the *Wisdom of Solomon*, which, it is generally agreed, is the composition of an Alexandrian Jew of the first century B.C.; but it is not classical. In later Christian literature τεχνίτης is often used to designate God as the creator-architect of the universe. Sometimes, however, it signifies a mere shaper who gives form to matter as distinct from the creator who brings things into existence (κτίστης, ποιητής, or δημιουργός). Athanasius, for example, writes: "If God is not the cause of matter, but entirely makes (ποιεῖ) all things from preexistent matter (ἐξ ὑποκειμένης ὕλης), he is shown to be weak,

city of God it is not the achievement of the civilizing efforts of man, nor is it a city of this present age, but a city, indeed *the* city, of the everlasting age to come. Of that city Abraham was already, through his faith, a citizen; for it is, as Augustine says in the preface to *The City of God*, "a city surpassingly glorious, whether we view it as it still lives by faith in this fleeting course of time, and sojourns as a stranger in the midst of the ungodly, or as it shall dwell in the fixed stability of its eternal seat, which it now with patience waits for, expecting until 'righteousness shall return unto judgment', and it obtain, by virtue of its excellence, final victory and perfect peace."

The rapture of Enoch from this earth (v. 5 above) was in itself an event which pointed significantly to a reality beyond that of this present life; and this awareness of an existence of transcendental glory was depicted in the traditional Jewish distinction between the Jerusalem here below and the Jerusalem which is above. According to the *Apocalypse of Baruch* (4:1ff.), for instance, the heavenly city was shown to Adam before he sinned and lost by him together with paradise at the fall, and was shown also to Abraham and to Moses, and now together with paradise is kept by God. God, our author says, has prepared a city for his saints (v. 16 below), "the heavenly Jerusalem" (12:22), "the city which is to come" (13:14). Paul, too, distinguishes between "the present Jerusalem" and "the Jerusalem which is above" (Gal. 4:25f.). The latter, he adds, "is our mother," that is to say, this city with foundations for which Abraham looked is the true *metropolis* or mother-city;[34] and this, again, is

---

since he is unable apart from matter to have achieved (ἐργάσασθαι) any of the things that have come into being.... How, then, may he still be called creator and maker (ποιητής καὶ δημιουργός) when he is obliged to create (ποιεῖν) from something else, I mean from matter? This being so, God will be, according to those who hold this view, only a craftsman (τεχνίτης) and not a creator (κτίστης)" (*De Incarn.* 24). The particular view which Athanasius, himself an Alexandrian, is opposing is the dualistic Pythagorean notion of matter as an eternal uncreated principle. In the neo-platonic soil of Alexandria this view flourished and in its association with gnosticism seriously threatened the Christian gospel. The connotation of the term δημιουργός, "demiurge," as an inferior deity responsible for the "creation" of the world through the molding or ordering of chaotic matter is familiar in Plato and is retained in this sense by the gnostic authors. But in Philo and in the patristic authors it is used to specify the Creator, in the orthodox biblical sense of the term. Here, of course, our author uses the expression τεχνίτης καὶ δημιουργός to designate God as the "builder and maker" of the eschatological city: God who created all things also re-creates all things in Christ, thus bringing to fulfilment all his purposes in creating the universe.

34. The notion of a "mother-city" or metropolis (μητρόπολις)—as in Galatians 4:26, ἥτις ἐστὶν μήτηρ ἡμῶν—is classical. Philo also uses it, but in a thoroughly mystical and platonic fashion. Thus he speaks, in connection with Abraham, of "a city good and large and very prosperous," a city, however, which the mind attains "when, in all matters turning away from what is base and from all that draws it to things mortal, it soars aloft and spends its time in contemplation of the universe; when, mounting yet higher, it explores the Deity and his nature, urged by an ineffable love of knowledge" (*Leg. Alleg.* iii.83f.); and he speaks similarly of man's reasoning faculty which "forsook its heavenly abode and came

spoken of in the Apocalypse as "the city of my God, the new Jerusalem which comes down from my God out of heaven" (Rev. 3:12), "the holy city" with twelve foundations, the splendor and beauty of which are described in terms of twelve precious jewels (Rev. 21:2, 19f.).

11:11, 12. *By faith Sarah herself received power to conceive, even when she was past the age, since she considered him faithful who had promised. Therefore from one man, and him as good as dead, were born descendants as many as the stars of heaven and as the innumerable grains of sand by the seashore.*

There is much debate as to whether Sarah is the proper subject of verse 11. The section comprising verses 8 to 10 is certainly a section about Abraham, and some scholars have felt that the interposition of Sarah as the subject of verse 11 interrupts the flow of the argument. Abraham, admittedly, is as obviously the subject of verse 12, although his name is not repeated there, as he is of verses 8 to 10, for in the Greek both the pronoun "one" and the qualifying participle translated "as good as dead" are in the masculine gender.[35] There is, however, every justification for the introduction of Sarah at this point, since she, as Abraham's wife, had an essential part to play in the realization of the promise concerning a numerous posterity, and it is difficult to see how our author's mention of her interferes with the theme he is developing.

Another, and more plausible, objection is that the commonly accepted translation, by which the author is understood to mean that "Sarah received power to conceive seed," is inaccurate and unacceptable because the terminology of the Greek text denotes not the reception of seed by a woman but the communication of seed by a man.[36] If this is so, the subject of verse 11 cannot be Sarah and the meaning is that Abraham received power to communicate seed, that is, to beget offspring through Sarah. But, if this is accepted, it still remains to explain the precise sense in which the reference to Sarah is intended. It is beside the point to draw attention to the notion found in some ancient writers, pagan, rabbinical, and Christian, that the woman also produces seed

---

into the body as into a foreign land," and on which God "will take pity and loose its chains and escort it in freedom and safety to its mother-city"—ἄχρι τῆς μητροπόλεως (*De Somn.* I.180f.).

35. Ἀφ᾽ ἑνός... νενεκρωμένου.

36. The text reads δύναμιν εἰς καταβολὴν σπέρματος ἔλαβεν, and the expression καταβολὴ σπέρματος can certainly mean the contribution of semen by the man, whereas an expression like ὑποδοχὴ σπέρματος or σύλληψις σπέρματος would be appropriate for the reception of semen by the woman.

which mingles with the seed of the man,[37] for this is no more than a matter of terminology: the woman does indeed produce and contribute ova, which in themselves are a kind of seed; but it may confidently be asserted that no such thing was intended by our author here. No more acceptable is the solution proposed by those who contend that the mention of Sarah ("Sarah herself")[38] must be ruthlessly excised on the ground that it must be a gloss or interpolation which had no place in the letter as originally written.[39] External evidence for such a conclusion is entirely lacking and it is impossible to accept this as a legitimate way in which to overcome the difficulty.

A much more reasonable proposal is that the expression "and Sarah herself" should be regarded as a parenthetical extension of the subject, so that the sense is as follows: "By faith he [Abraham]—and this means Sarah too—received power to beget offspring."[40] Alternatively, the problem may be solved by taking the case of the phrase "Sarah herself" in the Greek text to be dative instead of nominative, with the result that the difficulty of having to understand Sarah as the subject of the sentence is removed.[41] This solution has been favored by a number

37. Lactantius, writing at the beginning of the fourth century, cites Varro and Aristotle for the view that "non tantum maribus inesse semen, verum etiam foeminis" (De Opificio Dei 12), and Erasmus mentions the statement of Theophylact (11th century) that there were some who held this opinion. Bonsirven points out that in rabbinic Hebrew the verb seminare is used of the woman as well as of the man.

38. The words, namely, καὶ αὐτὴ Σάρρα, with or without the addition of στεῖρα, "barren"—the evidence for the inclusion or omission of the adjective is rather evenly balanced.

39. This is the judgment, for example, of Windisch. Zuntz unreservedly dismisses the phrase as a gloss, "which," he says, "is condemned by a welter of converging objections: (1) Sarah is less suited than most to serve as a model of unfailing trust; (2) καὶ αὐτή makes a poor connexion (it is typical of 'Scholiasten-Griechisch'): 'likewise' is the only admissible translation. This makes nonsense of the context: who else had been said to have received, through faith, δύναμιν εἰς καταβολὴν σπέρματος? (3) the latter phrase refers to a male, and (4) so do the following masculines ἀφ᾽ ἑνός and νενεκρωμένου" (ut supra, p. 16, n. 4). The insistence that "likewise" is "the only admissible translation" of καί here is an unnecessary piece of dogmatism, since the words may perfectly well be rendered "even Sarah herself," barren and aged as she was and incredulous as she had at first been. The other objections raised by Zuntz are discussed in the body of the commentary.

40. Delitzsch observes that the phrase καὶ αὐτός, or, as here, καὶ αὐτή, has "often merely the office of extending the predicate of a former sentence to a second subject," so that "here it associates with the great forefather the honoured foremother of the chosen people." Another suggestion, posited on the inclusion of the adjective στεῖρα, is that καὶ αὐτὴ Σάρρα στεῖρα should be treated as a Hebraic circumstantial clause, giving the sense: "by faith, even though Sarah was barren, he [Abraham] received power to beget..." (A Textual Commentary on the Greek New Testament, ed. by B. Metzger, London, 1973, ad loc.). This would be an attractive solution if there were no uncertainty regarding the authenticity of στεῖρα.

41. The omission of iotas subscript in the Greek MSS means that αὐτὴ Σάρρα could be read as αὐτῇ Σάρρα. Westcott and Hort give the latter as a marginal alternative, and this evokes the cantankerous comment from Zuntz (loc. cit.) that "one does a disservice to the memory of Westcott and Hort by recalling the device by which they thought it possible to settle these difficulties." The reading of the dative is approved by Nigel Turner (J. H. Moulton, Grammar of New Testament Greek, III, p. 220). It could be described as a dative of

of modern scholars, including Rendall, Hort, Riggenbach, Michel, Lenski, and most recently F. F. Bruce. "It is not necessary," says Bruce, "to cut out 'Sarah herself' from the text; all that is required is to construe the words in the dative case instead of the nominative, and the verse then runs: 'By faith he [Abraham] also, together with Sarah, received power to beget a child when he was past age, since he counted him faithful who had promised'—and verse 12 follows on very naturally." These proposals are not unattractive, but they come up against the considerable obstacle that there is no evidence to indicate that the verse was construed along these lines by any of the ancient authors, including, significantly, the Greek fathers. If the author had intended Abraham as the subject of verse 11 it is most improbable that this would not have been reflected, at least partially, in the interpretation of the post-apostolic centuries.

Taking everything into consideration, it remains the most natural construction to accept Sarah as the subject of the sentence. Granted that the Greek terminology does not properly mean that she received power to conceive seed (though this is how such modern versions as the RSV, NEB, and JB still render it) and that the appropriate meaning of communication by the male is unsuitable when Sarah is the subject, a solution to these difficulties is in fact available in a different but completely suitable understanding of verse 11, namely, that the writer is speaking, not of the receiving of seed by the woman from the man nor of the transmission of seed by the man to the woman, but of the founding or establishing of a seed or posterity. In Scripture it is very common for the noun "seed" to be used in the sense of "posterity"—as is the case in verse 18 of this chapter and in 2:16 above (cf. also, for example, Gal. 3:16, 19, 29), and indeed the very first mention of the term is of the seed or offspring *of a woman* (Gen. 3:15; note also Rev. 12:17). Moreover, when we read, literally, that "Sarah received power for the *katabolē* of seed," it is of particular interest that this Greek noun *katabolē* means "foundation" or "establishment" in each of the ten places where it occurs elsewhere in the New Testament (two of them in our epistle, namely, 4:3 and 9:26). Those who advocate interpreting the term in this sense here include De Wette, Bleek, Lünemann, Teodorico, and Spicq, who draws attention to a rabbinic tradition according to which Sarah was the mother of believers just as Abraham was their father. We take the original to mean, therefore, that "by faith Sarah herself received power for the founding of a posterity,[42] even though she was [sterile and] past the age of child-bearing."

---

association or accompaniment. This option is recognized also by Metzger (reference as in preceding note).

42. Εἰς καταβολὴν σπέρματος. N.B. also the use of the verb καταβάλλεσθαι in 6:1, where our author is speaking of laying down a foundation (θεμέλιον καταβαλλόμενοι).

There is the further consideration that the circumstance of being *past age* applies much more fittingly to Sarah than to Abraham, both because it describes the condition of a woman who has reached the menopause and because Abraham, though himself aged, had evidently not lost his virility, since he took another wife and became the father of more children after the death of Sarah (Gen. 25:1ff.). As Augustine explains, both Abraham and Sarah were old, "but she was also barren and had ceased to menstruate, so that she could no longer bear children even if she had not been barren."[42a]

The entire naturalness with which Abraham and Sarah are closely associated with each other means that the resumption of Abraham as the subject of verse 12, without his being named, is free from any awkwardness. There is in fact nothing unusual or forced in the linking of Abraham and Sarah in these verses, as the ancient prophetic exhortation serves to remind us: "Look to the rock from which you were hewn, and to the quarry from which you were digged. Look to Abraham your father and to Sarah who bore you" (Isa. 51:2). Similarly our author has an appreciation of the significance of Sarah—a significance which is well summarized by Owen, who, calling in the support of Paul and Peter, comments as follows: "As Abraham was the father of the faithful, or the church, so she was the mother of it, so as that the distinct mention of her faith was necessary. She was the free-woman from whence the church sprang, Gal. 4:22, 23. And all believing women are her daughters, 1 Pet. 3:6."

There is, however, still another difficulty that has been alleged concerning the mention of Sarah here, namely, the inappropriateness of citing her as a paragon of faith. The narrative in Genesis describes how Sarah laughed to herself incredulously when she overheard the announcement to Abraham that she was to become the mother of a son (Gen. 18:9ff.). Where is the justification, some have asked, for asserting that her conduct was governed *by faith* and that she was blessed *since she considered him faithful who had promised?* Should she not rather serve as an example of unbelief? But this is to build too much on a single incident in her history. Her incredulous laughter is, humanly speaking, readily understandable in view both of her barrenness and of her advanced age. But it does not *ipso facto* stamp her as one who was devoid of faith. Immediately after laughing she heard the Lord say to Abraham: "Why did Sarah laugh and say, 'Shall I indeed bear a child now that I am old?' Is anything too hard for the Lord? At the appointed time I will return to

---

42a. Augustine, *Civ. Dei* xvi.28. Cf. Josephus' description of a woman as having "passed the age," i.e. time of childbearing: γύναιον τι τὴν ἡλικίαν ἤδη προβεβηκός (*Ant.* vii.182), and the expression used by our author here: παρὰ καιρὸν ἡλικίας.

you, in the spring, and Sarah shall have a son." It is more reasonable to conclude that this admonition, together with the repetition of the promise, dispelled any unbelief that had arisen in her heart; and that she then denied her laughter, awed by what she had heard, may well indicate, as Chrysostom suggests, an attempt to correct her former attitude of incredulity. For Sarah, we must remember, had proved herself to be a woman of faith by her willingness to identify herself completely with Abraham's great venture of faith, from the time of the departure from Ur and throughout the long years of danger and hardship in the land of promise.

Abraham, too, had laughed some time previously when the promise was first communicated to him (Gen. 17:17). His laughter, however, as Aquinas comments, was the laughter not of doubt but of wonder—"no distrust made him waver concerning the promise of God," writes Paul, "but he grew strong in his faith as he gave glory to God, fully convinced that God was able to do what he had promised" (Rom. 4:20f.)—whereas Sarah, who, though essentially a woman of faith, had at first doubted the promise, afterward believed on being reminded of the omnipotence of God. Due weight must be given, further, to the consideration, stressed by Aquinas, that every miraculous conception in the Old Testament was "as it were a figure of that supreme miracle which took place in the incarnation of Christ; for it was desirable," Aquinas adds, "that his birth of a virgin should be in some way prefigured, so that men's minds might be prepared to believe—not that it could be prefigured by the exact equivalent, because necessarily a figure falls short of what is figured; and so Scripture portends the virgin birth by the childbearing of barren women, namely, Sarah, Hannah, and Elizabeth"; and he might have added the mother of Samson to the list.

The conjunction *Therefore*, with which verse 12 begins, points to the logic of faith which opens the door to the experience of miraculous results. The miracle is seen, first, in that one who was *as good as dead* should have become the parent of a son and the progenitor of a nation. While the "one" referred to here is plainly Abraham, since the pronoun in the Greek text is masculine in gender (hence the rendering "one man"), Sarah continues to be an important, indeed indispensable, factor, for it was through her union, her "one flesh" relationship, with Abraham that the birth of Isaac came about.[43] Our author might well

43. Westcott's interpretation keeps Sarah in the forefront, as follows: "*Wherefore also* children *were born* through her *from one, and that* from one *as good as dead.* . . . Though Sarah is lost, so to speak, in Abraham with whom she was united (ἀφ' ἑνός), yet her act of Faith completing his Faith is made the reason of the fulfilment of the promise (διό)." Aquinas, in company with Peter Lombard and other medieval commentators, takes the "one" here to refer to Sarah's womb which was already dead ("ab uno, scilicet utero Sarae, iam emor-

have spoken of Sarah's body, rather than Abraham's, as being *as good as dead*, if only because, as we have already observed, after Sarah's death Abraham married again and became the father of more children; but the same expression is used by Paul of Abraham's body in a similar context (Rom. 4:19). The expression "as good as dead" undoubtedly relates to Abraham's great age (as Rom. 4:19 explains), even though he had not lost his virile power, but particularly, in the circumstances, within the sphere of his marriage to Sarah. As Teodorico remarks, the deadness may be spoken of as threefold, applying not only to Abraham's senility but also his wife's barrenness and to the circumstance of her being past the age of childbearing.

And the miracle is seen, second, in that *from one man*, of whom it was least to be expected, *were born descendants* so great in multitude that they are said to be *as many as the stars of heaven and as the innumerable grains of sand by the seashore*. When the promise reiterated in Genesis 15:5, 22:17, 26:4, and 32:12 is compared with passages such as Deuteronomy 1:10, 10:22, 26:5, 28:62, Numbers 23:10, 1 Kings 3:8, 4:20, 2 Chronicles 1:9, and Nehemiah 9:23, it is evident that this promise was regarded as having been literally fulfilled in the multiplication of the *physical* posterity of Abraham. But the New Testament makes it plain that there is a further and ultimate fulfilment which is manifested in the *spiritual* lineage of Abraham; and it is in this respect that the deepest truth of the promise is to be discerned. As Paul teaches, the focus of the promise is precisely Christ, who is the seed of Abraham in whom and through whom all nations are blessed, and the seed of Abraham in its multiple sense is composed of those who are united to Christ the Seed (Gal. 3:7–9, 16, 29). These it is who, within the eternal perspective, constitute the innumerable multitude of the redeemed, "from every nation, from all tribes and peoples and tongues," who "have washed their robes and made them white in the blood of the Lamb" (Rev. 7:9, 14).

It is unlikely that, as many of the medieval commentators supposed, the double description of Abraham's descendants has a twofold significance, the stars of heaven referring, on the one hand, to the "heavenly" posterity of the elect, and the sand by the seashore, on the other hand, to the reprobate who are "earthbound." The point, rather, is single, namely, the contrast between the one unlikely progenitor and the numberless multitude of his offspring.

---

tuo"), linking it, surprisingly, with the mention of the deadness of Sarah's womb (τὴν νέκρωσιν τῆς μήτρας Σάρρας, "emortuam vulvam Sarae") in Romans 4:19 (where neither μήτρα in the Greek text nor "vulva" in the Vulgate offers a suitable link with ἀφ' ἑνός or "ab uno" in Heb. 11:12, since they are feminine nouns), instead of with the mention in the same verse of Abraham's body "which was as good as dead" (τὸ ἑαυτοῦ σῶμα ἤδη νενεκρωμένον, "corpus suum emortuum," corresponding closely with ἀφ' ἑνός ... καὶ ταῦτα νενεκρωμένου, "ab uno ... et hoc emortuo," here).

11:13, 14. *These all died in faith, not having received what was promised, but having seen it and greeted it from afar, and having acknowledged that they were strangers and exiles on the earth. For people who speak thus make it clear that they are seeking a homeland.*

Obviously, as Héring observes, our author is not saying here that it was by virtue of faith that the patriarchs *died*, but that *these all* (meaning either the patriarchs in general—with the exception, naturally, of Enoch who did not see death—or Abraham, Isaac, and Jacob who were so closely associated with the reception and outworking of the promises) died *in faith*, that is, in accordance with the principle of faith.[44] Death, with terrible finality, disintegrates man as a person, obliterating his faculties and frustrating his ambitions; but faith, which triumphs over the vicissitudes of life, transcends also the negation of death. If this were not so, the principle of faith would be completely nullified. But the hour of death in particular is the hour of the victory of faith. "It is especially in the case of those who are dying that faith prevails (verses 20ff.)," writes Bengel, "and in death that hope in things which are future and invisible shines most brightly."

Although these men and women of faith had been brought into the land of promise and the hereditary line of the promise had become a reality, yet they are described as *not having received what was promised;*[45] for had their hopes been fixed merely on earthly property and physical lineage death would have made a mockery of their faith and the promise

44. The Greek here is κατὰ πίστιν, placed, like πίστει elsewhere, emphatically at the beginning of the sentence. F. F. Bruce and others hold that the change from the simple dative πίστει to the phrase κατὰ πίστιν is no more than a literary variation. There is, however, more to the change than this. In the first 31 verses of the chapter the dative πίστει occurs no less than 18 times, while κατὰ πίστιν occurs here only. Had our author been concerned to relieve the monotony of repetition he would surely have rung the changes more frequently than just this once. Though κατὰ πίστιν might appropriately have been used throughout, the simple dative πίστει effectively marks the decisiveness of the faith by which these patriarchs lived and acted; whereas κατὰ πίστιν indicates that it was in accordance with the principle of faith that they faced the moment of death, that is, the end of their living and acting on earth. A man's death is not his act or his decision, and therefore the simple dative would have been less suitable here. These believers of the past did not allow the crisis of death to invalidate the principle of faith.

45. Μὴ κομισάμενοι τὰς ἐπαγγελίας. On the difference between κομίζεσθαι and ἐπιτυγχά-νειν see note 32, p. 433, above. Some MSS, including p[46] and D as well as the Textus Receptus, on which the KJV is based, read λάβοντες, which F. W. Beare (JBL, 63, 1944, p. 394) and F. F. Bruce favor as the correct reading, regarding the reading κομισάμενοι, attested by Sinaiticus, etc., as having been influenced by the occurrence of the same verb in 10:36 and 11:39. The reading λάβοντες, however, may equally well have been influenced by τὴν ἐπαγγελίαν λάβωσιν in 9:15. The important witness Vaticanus (B) is unfortunately deficient from 9:14 onward. Up to that point, a count reveals that the agreements between p[46] and B outnumber the disagreements by a ratio of four to one (139 to 36); but this does not allow us to conclude, as Beare is disposed to do (*loc. cit.*, pp. 379f.), that p[46] and B would have been found to coincide here at 11:13. Whichever reading is preferred, the sense, determined here by the context, is not affected.

of an *everlasting* possession would have been rendered an absurdity (Gen. 17:8). Their faith, accordingly, met the challenge to penetrate beyond death and beyond this present world, for the promise of an everlasting possession and universal blessing portended far more than the rights to a piece of geographical territory and a privileged posterity. Hence, as we have seen (vv. 9f.), the land of promise was as a foreign land to them and their hope was concentrated on an eternal and transcendental realm in which they themselves as well as the succeeding generations of those who belonged to the line of the promise would be everlastingly blessed.

This is why our author speaks of them here as *having seen* the promised reality *and greeted it from afar*. They perceived that the fulfilment was not yet, and indeed the crisis of death confirmed them in this conviction, assured as they were that the word of God was true and could not fail. And so, once again, we see the principle illustrated that "faith is the assurance of things hoped for, the conviction of things not seen" (v. 1); for the seeing from afar of which we read here is the inward seeing of faith, not the outward faculty of physical sight. Christ himself spoke to precisely the same effect when he said: "Abraham rejoiced that he was to see my day; he saw it and was glad" (Jn. 8:56). So real were God's promises to him that their fulfilment, though not yet, was as certain to him as something already and inalienably possessed. Thus the existential power of faith made the distant hope a present reality, and these believers of the ancient world "saw" and "greeted" the promised consummation, even, and indeed especially, in the hour of death, as though already face to face with it.

Moreover, the victory of their faith at the moment of death was the culminating acknowledgment of what they had confessed in a life of pilgrimage, namely, *that they were strangers and exiles on the earth*, that is to say, that this present world system was not their true home and ultimate destination. And this is the perspective of all men of faith in every age. David, for example, at a time when Israel was settled in the promised land, could describe himself, no less than Abraham, as "a stranger and an exile" in the land.[46] Not that this perspective is unearthly, but, rather, more than earthly, encompassing the restoration of the whole creation to that perfect harmony of purpose and function for which it was created. It is "worldliness" with which the vision of faith is impatient as, transcending all present limitations, it penetrates to that

---

46. Regarding the expression "strangers and exiles" see note 30, p. 468, above. The statement ξένοι καὶ παρεπίδημοί εἰσιν ἐπὶ τῆς γῆς echoes David's declaration, πάροικος ἐγώ εἰμι ἐν τῇ γῇ καὶ παρεπίδημος (Ps. 38:12 LXX), which in turn echoes—note the explanation "like all my fathers" which David adds—the words of Abraham, πάροικος καὶ παρεπίδημος ἐγώ εἰμι μεθ' ὑμῶν (Gen. 23:4).

limitless glory which is its true destiny. Abraham, says Chrysostom, "was accustomed to yield the first place to others, to expose himself to dangers, to endure numberless afflictions; he built no splendid houses, he enjoyed no luxuries, he had no care about dress, which all belong to the things of this world; but he lived in all respects as one whose home is in the City which is yonder."

It follows that *people who speak thus,* that is, who confess by word and life and by the manner of their dying that this present existence on earth is one of sojourning and exile away from their true and eternal home, *make it clear,* leaving no possible room for doubt or misunderstanding, *that they are seeking a homeland.* They are citizens, with us, of the new heaven and the new earth (Phil. 3:20; Rev. 21:1ff.; cf. Isa. 65:17; 66:22).

11:15, 16. *If they had been thinking of that land from which they had gone out, they would have had opportunity to return. But as it is, they desire a better country, that is, a heavenly one. Therefore God is not ashamed to be called their God, for he has prepared for them a city.*

The expatriate, feeling unsettled and estranged in an environment to which he does not belong, has a longing for his own country. The man of faith is the spiritual expatriate who has left behind him one country in order that he may commit himself to the promise of a better one, but who, like the recipients of this letter, is tempted to turn back because of the hardships and afflictions of his pilgrimage. For him, however, blessing is to be found not in going back but in going forward. It was of the Israelites who, discouraged by the unfriendly wilderness which lay between them and their destination, wished to turn back to Egypt instead of going on that God said: "They shall never enter my rest" (Heb. 3:18f.; 4:3). Our author endeavors to put new spirit into his readers, some of whom are near to abandoning the struggle, both by warning them of the dire consequences of imitating the example of those apostate Israelites and reminding them that "grace to help in time of need" is ever available to them through our great High Priest who himself had first to travel the way of suffering and humiliation before he was "crowned with glory and honor" (2:9, 18; 4:15f.; 6:1; 12:2f., 12f.): had he turned back, we would have been without a Redeemer and High Priest. He assures them, moreover, of his persuasion that they "are not of those who shrink back" (10:39).

Abraham and those who accompanied him provide a magnificent example of that spirit of faith and perseverance which overcomes the world (1 Jn. 5:4). As expatriates they sought a homeland (v. 14). *If they had been thinking of that land from which they had gone out* there was ample *opportunity* for them *to return*. Indeed, if this were the manner of their thinking, the question would inevitably arise as to why they should have left Chaldea at all, or, once having left it, they did not retrace their steps, pleading as an excuse the rigors of life in the inhospitable land to which they had come. But to have gone back would have been the reversal of the principle of faith and the turning of their backs on the hope that had been set before them. By their steadfast endurance and perseverance in the midst of every kind of adversity, however, they make it plain that they *desire a better country*, altogether other and beyond any country past or present of this fallen world, in other words, *a heavenly one*, unmarred by any imperfection, glorious forevermore.

Therefore, because of this unwavering intensity of purpose, *God is not ashamed* (the figure of speech is a litotes, as in 2:11, the negative implying that, positively, God is willing and happy) *to be called their God*. This was so not only while they were still living on earth but also after they had died, so that the God of Israel became known as "the God of Abraham, the God of Isaac, and the God of Jacob" (Gen. 28:13; 31:5; 39:9; Ex. 3:6; 4:5). Of particular significance is the manner in which Christ himself admonished the Sadducees, who denied the resurrection, that God "is not the God of the dead, but of the living," with the consequence that Abraham, Isaac, and Jacob must be accepted, not as dead and done with, but as still living and awaiting the consummation for which their faith had caused them to hope (Mt. 22:31f.). Our author's use of the present tense in verse 16 should be noticed: they desire—even now—that better country, and God is not ashamed—even now—to be called their God.

Moreover, it is no metaphysical mirage that they are pursuing, for God *has prepared for them a city*, a real city, which, as we have already been advised (v. 10), has foundations.[47] This is the homeland toward which the man of faith presses on. It is the same goal as that on which Christ urged his disciples to fix their gaze when, encouraging them to persevere in faith, he assured them that he was going to prepare[48] a place for them, and would come again to take them to be with him in that blissful abode (Jn. 14:1–3). It is the same goal toward which the

47. In verses 9 and 10 the concepts of a land (γῆ) and a city (πόλις) are combined; and now in the present passage (vv. 14–16) the concepts of homeland or fatherland (πατρίς) and city (πόλις) are also brought together. As F. F. Bruce observes, "there is, of course, no difference between the heavenly country and the city of God." Teodorico remarks that "the equivalence of the terms πατρίς and πόλις suggests the idea of a perfectly ordered fatherland in which freedom, security, and well-being reign, in accordance with the ideal Greek conception of the πόλις."
48. The verb ἑτοιμάζειν is used both in John 14:2f. and here in Hebrews.

apostle Paul, unhindered by present afflictions, pressed on, "forgetting what lies behind and straining forward to what lies ahead," in the conviction that "our citizenship is in heaven" where at last we shall be fully transformed into the likeness of our glorified Redeemer (Phil. 3:12f., 20f.); and toward which we who are Christian believers hasten as we "run with perseverance the race that is set before us, looking to Jesus the pioneer and perfecter of our faith" (Heb. 12:1f.). In such single-minded commitment there can be no thought of turning back.

11:17–19. *By faith Abraham, when he was tested, offered up Isaac, and he who had received the promises was ready to offer up his only son, of whom it was said, "Through Isaac shall your descendants be named." He considered that God was able to raise men even from the dead; hence, figuratively speaking, he did receive him back.*

These verses recall the most severe and unexpected trial of Abraham's faith, so much so that it was by this trial more than by any other that the rocklike firmness of his faith was confirmed and established. *When he was tested*, that is, by God[49] (the account is given in Gen. 22:1ff.), by being commanded to do something which in itself seemed altogether outrageous and destructive of the very promise he had embraced, he demonstrated his complete trust in God by obeying without calling into question the divine wisdom or goodness. Chrysostom draws attention to the apparent opposition between the command and the promise: God, he says, "made demands which were contradictory of the promises, and yet even so this righteous man was not staggered, nor did he say that he had been deceived."

Ought Abraham to have asked God to justify so preposterous a command? And was it right of God to test his servant with a trial which involved such anguish? No doubt facing such questions was part and parcel of Abraham's testing. Because, however, he enjoyed a proper relationship with God Abraham knew that God is altogether holy and just and loving and that he cannot be untrue to himself; and he realized that it was not for him, a sinful, finite creature, to query the word of his infinite Creator, indeed that to query the word of God is to query the goodness of God. This trial, in fact, so far from shaking Abraham's faith, actually served to establish it, for through it the unchangeable character of God's purpose and the impossibility that God should prove false to

49. The passive participle πειραζόμενος is a "divine" passive, which is another way of saying, as in Genesis 22:1, echoed here, that "God tested Abraham" (ὁ θεὸς ἐπείραζεν τὸν Ἀβραάμ, LXX).

his promise became more than ever the great motivating realities to him as he pressed forward on his pilgrimage. Moreover, as we have already been reminded, this triumph of Abraham's faith gives us "strong encouragement to seize the hope set before us," whatever may be the trials that assail us (6:13–18).

Our restricted human horizons incapacitate us for passing judgment on the thoughts and the ways of God (cf. Isa. 55:8f.). God in any case is the God of the humanly impossible—hence the corrective question in response to Sarah's incredulity when the birth of Isaac was promised: "Is anything too hard for the Lord?" (Gen. 18:14), and the assurance given to Mary at the annunciation that she was to be the mother of the long-awaited Messiah: "For with God nothing will be impossible" (Lk. 1:37)—and it is folly where he is active to judge solely by appearances. The focus on God's purposes of blessing was specifically concentrated on Isaac, since, even before the birth of Isaac, the promise was given to Abraham: "I will establish my covenant with Isaac" (Gen. 17:21). For God to command the offering of a human sacrifice seemed in itself savage and immoral, but to require that Isaac should be the victim seemed also to overthrow the very heart of the promise and the covenant and to cast a cloud over the trustworthiness of God. For the man of faith, however, whose whole life is committed to God and his truthfulness, conclusions of this sort are unthinkable. Furthermore, obedience to this mysterious word of God proved in due course that God is not wicked and that his promise is not false. An animal substitute was provided for Isaac and the line of promise was not cut off. And for Abraham the victory of obedience, which was at the same time the victory over the temptation to question the integrity of God, was also the vindication of God's faithfulness.

When it is said that Abraham *offered up Isaac*[50] the meaning is that in purpose and intention he did so, and would in fact have done so had not God at the last moment stayed his hand and provided a substitute. Hence the additional statement that *he was ready to offer up*[51] Isaac: he was actually in process of performing the deed when God intervened. The dramatic poignancy of the situation is increased by the considera-

50. Προσενήνοχεν 'Αβραὰμ τὸν 'Ισαάκ. The perfect tense is generally explained as denoting Abraham's full intention to do as God had bidden him: his obedience was such that the deed was as good as done. "It indicates," says Spicq, "the sacrifice perfectly accepted and as it were already completed in the heart of Abraham." Moffatt, however, thinks "it is more likely to be aoristic"; but even so a similar explanation would be required for an aoristic perfect.
51. The phrase translates the simple imperfect προσέφερεν. This may be explained as a conative (Héring) or inceptive imperfect—"he was on the point of offering up" (F. F. Bruce)—or, in a somewhat more "linear" sense, "he was in process of offering up." "The first verb [προσενήνοχεν] expresses the permanent result of the offering completed by Abraham in will," says Westcott; "the second [προσέφερεν] his actual readiness in preparing the sacrifice which was not literally carried into effect."

tion that the one who was preparing to sacrifice his son was none other than *he who had received the promises,* that is to say, he who by faith had responsibly appropriated the promises entrusted to him.[52] It is true that Abraham depended on God, but there is a sense also in which God depended on him; he had done his part, so to speak, and now it seemed that all that had been so wonderfully achieved was to be cruelly snatched away from him. It would be difficult to exaggerate the intensity of his trial.

The most severe aspect of this trial of Abraham's faith is seen in the demand that he should be willing to offer up *his only son,* the very one *of whom it was said, "Through Isaac shall your descendants be named"* (the quotation is from Gen. 21:12). The sentence of death pronounced upon Isaac while still an immature youth seemed in effect the sentence of death, also, upon God's promise itself. Not that Abraham was the begetter of no other sons, for he was the father of Ishmael by Hagar and was to be the father of other sons by Keturah; yet there was but one son of the covenant, namely, Isaac, who, contrary to human possibility but in accordance with the power of the promise, was born to Sarah. Within the perspective of God's infallible purposes he was the *only son* (cf. Gen. 17:18f., where God rejects the appeal that Ishmael might become the fulfilment of the promise, and 22:2). "Isaac," comments Calvin, "is not to be thought of as simply one of the common company of men, but as one who contained Christ in himself."

Abraham, however, as a man of faith, held tenaciously to the conviction that what appeared to him to be an insoluble problem was for God no problem at all. Though everything else was obscure, one thing was clear to him, namely, that God, whose word was unshakably true, had a way of resolving the problem which was as yet unrevealed. Like the apostle Paul in a later age, Abraham was assured that it is precisely the powerlessness of man which provides the opportunity for the triumphant manifestation of the omnipotence of God. It was on this certainty that he counted: taking into account the fact of God and his power and goodness, *he considered,* or better "he reckoned" (NEB),[53] *that God was able to raise men even from the dead,* that is, that God was able to

---

52. The verb ἀναδέχεσθαι, here in the form of the aorist participle ἀναδεξάμενος, means more than merely "to receive." It may well be an intensive compound meaning "to receive with confidence," which would give good sense here; but it is also susceptible of the meaning "to take upon oneself," and thus to appropriate in the sense of assuming responsibility for what has been accepted. Thus Moulton and Milligan (*sub voc.*) suggest that "the statement that Abraham had 'undertaken', 'assumed the responsibility of' the promises, would not perhaps be alien to the thought."

53. The Greek term λογισάμενος "explains why he had the courage to sacrifice Isaac," writes Moffatt, "although the action seemed certain to wreck the fulfilment of what God had promised him." The verb λογίζεσθαι is used by Paul in this sense of to calculate or reckon up on the basis of firm evidence (cf. Rom. 6:11; 8:18). "It denotes inward conviction, persuasion," says Teodorico, "not a more or less reliable opinion."

perform the greatest of all miracles if this was necessary for the preserva-
tion of his promise. This conviction of Abraham's is not mentioned in
the Genesis account, but it is implied in his words to the servants who
had accompanied him and Isaac, as he and Isaac left them to go to the
place of sacrifice: "I and the lad will go yonder and worship, and come
again to you" (Gen. 22:5)—so certain was he that this was not to be the
end of Isaac and of the promise associated with him. Indeed, Isaac
himself was a constant witness to the power of God to give life where
before there was the equivalent of death because of the remarkable
nature of his birth (see vv. 11f. above). This was not something Abraham
was likely to forget. "He considered," observes Herveus, "that he who
had made it possible for Isaac, when he was not in existence, to be born
of aged parents was able also to restore him from death; for he believed
that God would either deliver him from sacrifice or would raise him up
forthwith after he had been sacrificed, and so would fulfil the promise
concerning his future posterity in him."

The striking comment is now added that, *figuratively speaking*, that
is, in the form of a parable or analogy,[54] *he did receive him back* from the
dead.[55] So dramatic was the sequence of events that it was as though
Isaac really had died and had been raised up to life again. It is not
surprising that from the earliest times this event has been seen by the
church as parabolic or typical of the death and resurrection of Christ.
This analogy may well have been in our author's mind here and also in
the mind of Paul when, speaking in a manner that is strongly reminiscent of the Genesis narrative, he speaks of God as "he who did not spare
his own Son but gave him up for us all" (Rom. 8:32). Before the end of
the first century, the writing known as the *Epistle of Barnabas* mentions
"the type established in Isaac when he was offered upon the altar" as

---

54. Ἐν παραβολῇ. The sense of παραβολή here is similar to that of its only other occurrence in this epistle, at 9:9. Westcott (among others) suggests that ὅθεν αὐτὸν καὶ ἐν
παραβολῇ ἐκομίσατο may refer back to the circumstances of the birth of Isaac, when
Abraham received him as it were a life from the dead, but it is hardly possible that this is
the meaning intended here. Less satisfactory still is the interpretation of Lünemann and
some others by which παραβολή is given the sense of an act of risking, so that the meaning
becomes: Abraham received Isaac back in the very act of imperilling his life. Not only,
however, is this a rare sense of παραβολή, but it is also a sense never found elsewhere in
Scripture, or for that matter among the patristic authors; it is most improbable that it is the
sense of the term here. The traditional interpretation of παραβολή as signifying an analogy
or similitude is in any case much more natural.
55. Commentators are divided as to whether ὅθεν is here a causal conjunction, "therefore,"
which is its connotation in the five other places where it occurs in our epistle (2:17; 3:1;
7:25; 8:3; 9:18), or a relative adverb, "whence," "from where" (as in Mt. 12:44; Lk. 11:24;
Acts 14:26), signifying "from the dead," as the NEB renders it. The former interpretation is
favored by Spicq, Teodorico, Moffatt ("in return for his superb faith"), etc.; the latter,
which is also the traditional interpretation, by F. F. Bruce, Delitzsch, Westcott, Grotius,
Calvin, etc. According to Strack-Billerbeck, a late rabbinical tradition held that Isaac actually died and then was restored to life.

having been fulfilled in the sacrifice of Christ at Calvary.[56] Clement of Alexandria (150-215) expands the parallel: like Isaac, Christ was the only Son led to the place of sacrifice; as Isaac carried the wood of the sacrifice (Gen. 22:6), so Christ carried the wood of the cross (Jn. 19:17); Isaac, it is true, was not slain, but in this there is "an intimation of the divinity of the Lord . . . for Jesus rose again after his burial, having suffered no harm, like Isaac released from sacrifice."[57] In his homilies on Genesis Clement's pupil Origen (185–254) develops much more extensively the typical significance of Isaac, maintaining that here we have the commencement of belief in resurrection, on the understanding that "Abraham hoped for the resurrection of Isaac and also believed that what had not hitherto happened would take place." He, too, saw Isaac as a figure of Christ in his act of carrying wood to the place of sacrifice, and taught that the assurance given by Abraham to Isaac that God would provide himself a lamb (Gen. 22:8) had its ultimate fulfilment in God's provision of a Lamb in the person of Christ (cf. Jn. 1:29). The lamb, in fact, is seen as a symbol of Christ's human nature which suffered and died, Isaac as a symbol of his impassible divine nature.[58] Similarly Athanasius (ca. 296–373) writes that Abraham, "when restrained from sacrificing Isaac, saw the Messiah in the ram, which was offered up instead as a sacrifice to God."[59] Augustine (354–430) concurs with this interpretation; indeed, it became part of the mainstream of Christian typological exegesis. Aquinas, for example, comments as follows in the twelfth century: "This was a *parable*, that is, a figure of Christ to come; for the lamb caught by its horns in the thicket is the humanity nailed to the cross which suffered, while Isaac, that is, the divinity, escaped when Christ truly died and was buried." And in the sixteenth century we find Lefèvre d'Etaples explaining that "Isaac, the only son whom Abraham loved, figures Christ our Lord, the only Son whom the Father loves; . . . the mountain shown, the place of calvary; the sacrifice of Isaac commanded by God, the true sacrifice of Christ; the receiving back of Isaac from the sacrifice that had been ordered, the true resurrection of Christ"; while Luther observes that "the hidden sense[60] is that just as Isaac was led away to be sacrificed but in the end was saved and a ram caught in the thorns was sacrificed in his stead, so the Son of God, since he was both mortal and immortal in one and the same person, was sacrificed, but only his flesh, that is, his humanity, was slain."[61]

---

56. Epistle of Barnabas, ch. VII.
57. Clement of Alexandria, *Paedagogus* I.v.
58. Origen, *In Genesim Homilia VIII.*
59. Athanasius, Festal Letter VI (334).
60. That is, the sense indicated by the expression ἐν παραβολῇ.
61. Moffatt explains ἐν παραβολῇ as meaning "in a way that prefigured the resurrection (κρείττονος ἀναστάσεως, v.³⁵)."

The story of Abraham and Isaac made a deep impression on Theodore Beza. His verse drama *Abraham Sacrifiant* was first published in 1550, and the following extracts help to depict, imaginatively, both the anguish and the faith of Abraham as he passed through this great trial:

> (740) Because, O God, this is thy pleasure, it is sure
> That it is right, and so I shall obey.
> But in obeying shall I not make God
> A liar, for he promised this to me,
> That from my son Isaac there would come forth
> A mighty nation who would fill this land?
> With Isaac dead the covenant dies too!
>
> . . . .
>
> (805) If then to borrow Isaac is thy will,
> Wherefore should I complain at thy command?
> For he is thine: he was received from thee;
> And then when thou hast taken him again
> Rather wilt thou arouse him from the dead
> Than that thy promise should not come to pass.
> Yet, Lord, thou knowest that I am but man,
> Incompetent to do or think what's good;
> But thanks to thine unconquerable power
> He who believes knows all is possible.
> Away with flesh! Away with sentiment!
> All human passions now withdraw yourselves:
> Nothing is right for me, and nothing good,
> But what is pleasing to the Lord himself.
>
> . . . .
>
> (O heaven . . . and thou the land of promise . . .)
> (923) Bear witness now that faithful Abraham
> Has by God's grace such persevering faith
> That notwithstanding every human thought
> God never speaks a single word in vain.[62]

11:20–22. *By faith Isaac invoked future blessings on Jacob and Esau. By faith Jacob, when dying, blessed each of the sons of Joseph, bowing in worship over the head of his staff. By faith Joseph, at the end of his life, made mention of the exodus of the Israelites and gave directions concerning his burial.*

The portraiture of the men of faith of the patriarchal era is continued with these brief illustrations, each one exemplifying the constancy of faith at the very point of death of the chief figures in the line of succession of the three generations after Abraham, namely, Isaac, Jacob, and Joseph. It might have been expected that their lives as well as their

---

62. For the French text see *Abraham Sacrifiant*, ed. by K. Cameron, K. M. Hall, and F. Higman (Geneva, 1967). The translation is mine.

deaths would be praised here, if only because their histories, like that of Abraham, are so fully recounted in the book of Genesis. But our author evidently felt that what he had already said about Abraham as an example of constancy was sufficiently instructive regarding the principles and the practice of the life of faith during this period when the foundations of Israel were being laid, and that, as one generation succeeded another and the promises still awaited fulfilment, his purpose was effectively served by pointing to the triumph of faith in the face of death, the last and darkest trial of all. As a witness to the reality of faith as "the assurance of things hoped for, the conviction of things not seen" (v. 1), the death of faith is, if anything, even more remarkable than the life of faith (see commentary on vv. 13f. above).

It was *by faith*, then, that *Isaac invoked future blessings* on his sons *Jacob and Esau* (see Gen. 27:28ff.). This was in accordance with the custom whereby a father, when he came to the end of his days, would pronounce a paternal blessing over his children, who were regarded by him as a guarantee of the future. But for Isaac this was something more than the insubstantial hope that his name would be kept alive in a physical posterity, for his children were the guarantee of *his own* future, inasmuch as his faith was focussed on *the line of the promise*, and this promise, as we have seen, belonged to him and to his father Abraham no less than to his posterity. Far from being the end for him, his death was but a milestone along the way to that "better country" on which his hope was fixed.

The fact that here the younger son, Jacob, is mentioned first is also of special significance. Normally, in the affairs of men, the chief blessing and the major part of the inheritance belong, by right of primogeniture, to the firstborn son. But the promises of God and their blessings are not subject to human standards and conventions. Constantly we need reminding that God's ways are not our ways (Isa. 55:8f.) and that the divine Spirit is free and sovereign (Jn. 3:8). The will of God cannot be forced into conformity with human patterns and preconceptions. His power manifests itself precisely within the sphere of human weakness (2 Cor. 12:9). And so it has been from the beginning: it was not the older and stronger Cain but the younger and weaker Abel who found favor with God; not Ishmael but Isaac is the son of the promise; and now again, when the hour has come for Isaac to give his blessing, it is Jacob, the younger and weaker son, who obtains the blessing of the firstborn and Esau who receives the lesser inheritance. The message is clear: the line of the promise is not the line of the flesh but the line of faith; the true heir is not the outward heir but the inward heir; "not all who are descended from Israel belong to Israel, and not all are children of Abraham because they are his descendants" (Rom. 2:28f.; 9:6ff.); for, in the ultimate perspective, they who are one by faith with Christ, and only they, are "Abraham's offspring, heirs according to promise" (Gal. 3:29)— that community of believers, in other words, who are born, "not of blood nor of the will of the flesh nor of the will of man, but of God" (Jn. 1:12f.).

We see the same principle in operation in Jacob's blessing of Ephraim and Manasseh, *the sons of Joseph*, which is mentioned next (see Gen. 48). As his father lay dying, Joseph brought the two boys in to receive his patriarchal benediction, and, in accordance with custom, placed the elder, Manasseh, by Jacob's right hand, the hand with which the chief blessing was conveyed to the firstborn, and the younger, Ephraim, by his left hand. But Jacob deliberately crossed his hands, so that the right was placed on Ephraim and the left on Manasseh, despite the expostulation of Joseph: "and thus he put Ephraim before Manasseh" (Gen. 48:20). The crossed arms of Jacob have been understood, by Lefèvre d'Etaples for instance, as signifying "the cross of Christ from which every blessing has been poured upon us"; but this is to allow too much rein to the imagination.

Our version (RSV) makes it appear that Jacob blessed his grandsons while *bowing in worship over the head of his staff*, but in the Genesis narrative the act of worship belongs to the earlier occasion when Jacob required Joseph to swear that he would bury him, not in Egypt, but with his fathers in the land of promise (Gen. 47:29–31); and here the Greek text, which may literally be rendered, "Jacob . . . blessed each of the sons of Joseph *and* bowed in worship over the head of his staff" (as in the KJV and NEB), is best taken to refer to two separate actions, blessing and worship, performed by Jacob from his death-bed. That our author mentions the earlier action (worship) after the later (blessing) presents no particular problem, since both belong to the end of his life, and a similar inversion of order, equally without significance, may be pointed to in 7:6 above, where our author says that Melchizedek "received tithes from Abraham and blessed him," though in Genesis 14:19f. the blessing comes first and then the reception of tithes.

There is another difference, however, which does require some discussion: our author asserts that Jacob bowed in worship over the head *of his staff*, whereas in Genesis 47:31 it is said that he did so upon the head *of his bed*. In itself, indeed, this discrepancy would be of minimal consequence, for the important thing in both cases is that Jacob bowed himself in worship, that is, he acknowledged his trust in God who had blessed him in life and who would continue to bless him in and beyond death. Such is the constancy, the confidence, and the conquest of faith. Moreover, the origin of the discrepancy is not difficult to trace. The adding of points or vowel signs to the consonantal Hebrew text of the Old Testament was carried out by the Massoretic scholars only between the sixth and eighth centuries A.D. The Hebrew noun in question is composed of the consonants MTH.[63] If this is pointed to read *maṭṭeh*[64] it means "staff"; but if it is pointed to read *miṭṭāh*[65] it means "bed." A choice, then, has to be made in accordance with the requirements of the context; but in this instance it seems that either understanding of the term would fit the context well. The Massoretes read the noun as *miṭṭāh*, "bed"; hence the rendering of Genesis 47:31 in our English versions. But the Septuagint version, which antedates the Massoretic pointing by some nine centuries, interprets it as *matteh*, "staff," and our epistle coincides with this text here as elsewhere.[66] In the Latin Vulgate version of the fourth century Jerome has "bed" in Genesis 47:31[67] and, in conformity with the Old Latin version, "staff" here in Hebrews 11:21.[68] Owen's attempt to conflate the two meanings—"addressing himself unto the solemn adoration of God, he so bowed himself towards the bed's head as that he supported himself with his staff"—is unnecessary and can hardly be, as he imagines, "the true solution of this difficulty,"[69] even though it is quite possible that he did both. A decision still has to be made, and the probability is that the significance of the Hebrew text of Genesis 47:31 is "staff" rather than "bed," and that this has been preserved in the Septuagint rendering.

The meaning of the Vulgate version here, in fact, is that Jacob "worshipped the top of his staff." This, however, is not a possible rendering of the Greek,[70] though it is one to which Roman Catholics have hitherto been bound because of the authority with which the Vulgate translation is officially invested for them.[71] In general, however, it has not been their practice to understand it literalistically.[72] The comments of

63. מטה.
64. מַטֶּה
65. מִטָּה.
66. There is an exact correspondence between the Greek of 11:21 and that of the LXX text: προσεκύνησεν ἐπὶ τὸ ἄκρον τῆς ῥάβδου αὐτοῦ.
67. "... adoravit Israel Deum, conversus ad lectuli caput."
68. "... adoravit fastigium virgae eius."
69. F. F. Bruce seems to incline to a similar view: "The picture of the patriarch sitting on his bed and leaning on his staff is convincing enough." There is of course no difficulty in the concept of a person "bowing himself upon the head of his bed," as is shown by reference to 1 Kings 1:47, where it is said that David "bowed himself upon the bed"; but because a different term for bed (*mishkāb*) is used there this consideration cannot be allowed to determine the translation of Genesis 47:31.
70. The expression προσκυνεῖν ἐπί with the accusative means to worship on or over something, and the text here cannot mean "he worshipped the top of his staff"—*adoravit fastigium virgae eius*. The implied object of the verb "worshipped" is "God," as in the NEB: "... and worshipped God, leaning on the top of his staff."
71. Cf. Ronald Knox's translation: "Jacob made reverence to the top of Joseph's staff."
72. The movement away from the tyranny of the Vulgate version is well represented in the rendering of the JB: "By faith Jacob, when he was dying, blessed each of Joseph's sons,

Aquinas, based on the Vulgate text, are characteristic of the explanations offered by the scholastic authors. Jacob was an old man, he says, "and so carried a staff, or took Joseph's sceptre until he had sworn, and before he returned it to him he worshipped, not the staff or Joseph, as some have mistakenly thought, but God himself." The notion that Jacob did obeisance to Joseph as the one now about to succeed him as the head of the Israelites is found as early as Chrysostom, who connects it, apparently, with Joseph's dream when a boy that his father and mother and brothers would bow down to him (Gen. 37:5–11) and sees Jacob's obeisance as symbolical of the obeisance of the whole people to Joseph.

The identification of the "staff" mentioned here with Joseph's sceptre became current in the interpretation of this passage. Primasius, for example, in the sixth century, writes that, "inspired by the spirit of prophecy, Jacob knew that by Joseph's rod the reign of Christ was designated, and by the top or highest point of the rod the power and honour of Christ's reign," and he cites the words of Psalm 45:6: "Your royal sceptre[73] is a sceptre of equity" (quoted by our author in 1:8 above). Aquinas adds a similar interpretation when he writes that Jacob was moved to this act of worship "by consideration of the power of Christ which was prefigured in Joseph, for as prefect of Egypt he carried the sceptre, in token of the power of Christ," and he cites Psalm 2:9, which speaks of the Messiah as ruling with a rod of iron. He covers himself, further, by explaining that if Jacob did worship the head of the staff, "the sense is the same, because he worshipped Christ who was signified by that staff, just as we worship the crucifix and the cross by reason of Christ who suffered on it; though it is not properly the cross that we worship but Christ crucified on it." Erasmus remarks likewise that "it was not Joseph's rod that he worshipped but the kingship of Christ which he understood that sceptre to signify." Lefèvre d'Etaples regards the staff on which Jacob leaned as a symbol of the wood of the

leaning on the end of his stick as though bowing to pray." Cf. also the comment of Teodorico, that "προσκυνεῖν ἐπί indicates the place or the object over which he bowed himself, not the object of his worship." A New Catholic Commentary on Holy Scripture (London, 1969) frankly declares that "both the Vg's adoravit fastigium virgae eius and CV's 'bowed in worship towards the top of his staff' are mistranslations" (CV = Confraternity Version; cf. Knox's rendering given in the preceding note). According to rabbinical tradition the staff was created on the evening of the sixth day of creation and entrusted to Adam in paradise; it was then handed down in turn from Adam to Enoch, from Enoch to Noah, from Noah to Shem, from Shem to Abraham, from Abraham to Isaac, from Isaac to Jacob, and from Jacob to Joseph, on whose death it found its way into Pharaoh's palace, whence in course of time Jethro took it and planted it in his garden, where Moses saw it and said: "This will rescue the Israelites from Egypt!" (Strack-Billerbeck, ad loc.); and it was ultimately to be wielded by the Messiah.

73. In Psalm 45:6 (LXX) ῥάβδος, the same noun as occurs here in 11:21, is used—Vg, virga.

cross; and Zwingli proposes another allegorical variant according to which the staff represents the genealogical tree and the head of the staff is Christ who was to be born of this nation. Our author, however, has no place for these and other flights of symbolical interpretation by which hidden significances are displayed which were never intended and which very easily divert attention from the main thrust of his argument. He is saying simply that Jacob, triumphant in faith even at the approach of death, bowed over his own staff (rather than Joseph's sceptre) in submission to the divine will and acknowledgment of the divine goodness, and showed his confidence in the reality of all that God had promised by placing his hands on the heads of his grandchildren and affirming the certainty of a future of boundless blessing.

Joseph, in like manner, *at the end of his life* demonstrated the unshakable nature of his faith when he *made mention of the exodus of the Israelites,* which in fact would not take place until another century and a half had passed, but which he foresaw with assurance because of his trust in God and his promises, *and gave directions concerning his burial*—literally, concerning his bones. From the age of seventeen, when the envy of his brothers caused them to sell him into slavery (Gen. 37:2ff.), Joseph had been an exile in Egypt where, after at first enduring hardship and injustice, he had risen to a commanding position of influence. But he did not forget his native land and the promises associated with it. Prosperity did not dim the flame of his faith. Hence the expression of these last wishes from his death-bed to his kinsmen who with his father had settled in Egypt under his patronage. "I am about to die," he told them; "but God will visit you, and bring you up out of this land to the land which he swore to Abraham, to Isaac, and to Jacob"; and then he enjoined that they should carry up his bones with them (Gen. 50:24f.). In due course this injunction was honored by Moses, who "took the bones of Joseph with him" as the Israelites turned their backs on Egypt and marched toward the promised land (Ex. 13:19); and the procedure was completed by Joshua who, following Moses' death, led them into Canaan: "The bones of Joseph which the people of Israel brought up from Egypt, were buried at Shechem, in the portion of ground which Jacob bought from the sons of Hamor. . . ; it became an inheritance of the descendants of Joseph" (Josh. 24:32). Thus Joseph, after a long interval, followed his father Jacob whose body, in accordance with his final instructions, was taken back to Canaan and "buried in the cave of the field at Machpelah, to the east of Mamre, which Abraham bought with the field from Ephron the Hittite, to possess as a burying place" (Gen. 47:29ff.; 50:4ff.). We are to note, then, that even by the circumstances of their burial these patriarchs declared that they awaited the fulfilment of the covenant promises and eternal life beyond the grave, and, as Calvin says, "sharpened the desire of the people so that they would look more earnestly for their redemption."

11:23. *By faith Moses, when he was born, was hid for three months by his parents, because they saw that the child was beautiful; and they were not afraid of the king's edict.*

Turning now to Moses, our author leaves behind the book of Genesis and its patriarchs and comes to the period of the Exodus and the entry of the Israelites into the land of promise (vv. 23–31). Moses shares with Abraham the distinction of having his accomplishments as a man of faith recounted at some length compared with the brief notice accorded to the other persons who are mentioned. The present verse shows that, in the true spirit of the covenant whose promises embrace believers together with their children, even in infancy Moses was surrounded by the pure atmosphere of faith. Here we are simply told that it was *by faith* that the new-born child *was hid for three months by his parents*,[74] without any explanation of the precise content of that faith respecting God's will for him. The information that *they saw that the child was beautiful*[75] may well imply more than the naturally affectionate and protective impulse of those who have become the parents of a fine child; for faith penetrates to a level deeper than that of physical attractiveness.[76] Chrysostom observes that the sight of their child's fairness drew them on to faith by which they perceived that in a way which was more than natural he was the object of God's grace; and Peter Lombard says that because of his exceptional beauty they believed that God intended to do some great thing through him.

Certainly we may assume that Moses' God-fearing parents were driven by an inner conviction that their child had a role to play within the divine purposes and that it was because they were sustained by this conviction that *they were not afraid of the king's edict*, which required every

---

74. The account in Exodus (2:2) speaks of the hiding of Moses as the action of his mother, but there is no reason to doubt that this was done with the approval and cooperation of the father.

75. The adjective ἀστεῖος, translated "beautiful" here, is used of the infant Moses in the LXX (Ex. 2:2) and also by Stephen (Acts 7:20). It describes an attractiveness or comeliness that is uncommonly striking. Philo says that immediately upon birth the appearance of Moses was more than usually beautiful—ἀστειοτέραν (*Vita Mos.* i.9).

76. Josephus reproduces the tradition that Moses' father Amram was assured by God in a dream and, in answer to his prayers, that his son would be preserved and would become the deliverer of the Hebrew people from the bondage of Egypt; and he narrates, further, that when the infant was placed among the bulrushes Amram believed that God would in some way ensure the child's safety (*Ant.* ii.210ff.; cf. Philo, *Vita Mos.* i.9).

male child born to the Hebrews to be destroyed—just as Moses himself, when he had grown to manhood, by virtue of the firmness of his faith was not afraid of the anger of the king (v. 27 below). The great risk which Amram and Jochebed took in secretly keeping their infant son despite Pharaoh's cruel command was in itself evidence of the reality of their faith. But their faith was still more severely tested when it became impossible for them to conceal him any longer in their home and they adopted the perilous device of placing him in a specially prepared basket among the reeds by the bank of the river, while his sister kept watch from a safe distance—for here, too (*pace* Calvin who interprets this procedure as indicating the collapse of their faith), it is apparent that they continued to believe that in some way God would preserve their child. Little did they expect that he would be found by no less a personage than Pharaoh's daughter and be brought up by her in the royal palace as her own son, with his own mother as his nurse, thanks to the alertness of his sister (Ex. 2:1–10). Yet, due no doubt to the instruction he received from his mother, he grew up conscious both of his own nationality and of his divine vocation, for, as Stephen tells his audience in Acts 7:25, on the occasion when he first attempted to identify himself with the Hebrews and their cause, "he supposed that his brethren understood that God was giving them deliverance by his hand, but they did not understand."

In 3:2ff. above our author draws a comparison between Moses and Christ in terms of the faithfulness of each. That Moses prefigured Christ is made plain in the messianic promise given him by God, that he would raise up a prophet like him from his brethren and put his words in his mouth (Dt. 15:15, 18; Acts 7:37). This relates to Moses not only as the one through whom God's law was communicated to the people but also as a notable type of Christ in his role of deliverer, who led the chosen people from the bondage of Egypt to the borders of the promised land. So, in fulfilment of this type, Christ is the pioneer of our salvation who, not ashamed to call us brethren, delivers God's people from lifelong bondage and brings them to the promised rest (Heb. 2:10, 11, 15; 3:14ff.; 4:3; 12:2). But even the events of Moses' infancy foreshadow the experience of him who is greater than Moses (Heb. 3:3), for the life of the infant Jesus was threatened by the edict of a despotic monarch ordering the slaughter of all male children under the age of two years, and by their faith and obedience Joseph and Mary were enabled to preserve the child by taking refuge in the very country where Moses was preserved (Mt. 2:13ff.). "It is wonderful how similar the first experiences of the newborn Moses were to the infancy of Christ," exclaims Lefèvre d'Etaples; and Spicq is surely right in suggesting that our author saw in what happened to Moses a figure of the childhood of Jesus.

493

11:24–26. By faith Moses, when he was grown up, refused to be called the son of Pharaoh's daughter, choosing rather to share ill-treatment with the people of God than to enjoy the fleeting pleasures of sin. He considered abuse suffered for the Christ greater wealth than the treasures of Egypt, for he looked to the reward.

It was *by faith,* again, that *Moses,* now *grown up* to the maturity and the responsibility of manhood, faced the critical decision which was to determine the whole direction of his life from that time on. A personage of the highest dignity, prince of the great Egyptian nation, "instructed in all the wisdom of the Egyptians" and "mighty in his words and deeds," he had now reached the age of forty (Acts 7:22f.). Like his illustrious predecessor and fellow Hebrew Joseph, Moses was identified with the palace and the ruling dynasty. Unlike him, he turned his back on this position of power and privilege, and is commended for doing so. Yet Joseph, who retained his elevated status among the Egyptians to his dying day, was in no way censured for failing to break away from this alien people. How is this difference to be explained? Quite simply, as follows: under Joseph's exalted authority the family of Jacob was enabled to find refuge, survival, and prosperity in Egypt, whereas in Moses' day, when the family had become a nation and was now meeting not with favor but with hostility and oppression from the Egyptian overlords, the time was ripe for the Israelites to move out of Egypt and to possess the land that had been promised to Abraham's posterity. The divine purposes were served equally, given the differing circumstances, by Joseph's remaining in high office and by Moses' renunciation of this privilege. Joseph was God's man to preserve the little band of his kinsfolk in Egypt. Moses was God's man to lead the people of Israel from Egypt to Canaan.

Accordingly, realizing that his destiny under God was different from Joseph's, Moses *refused to be called the son of Pharaoh's daughter.* He left behind him the power and prestige of the palace, *choosing rather to share ill-treatment with the people of God,* who were now a people hated and sorely afflicted, *than to enjoy the fleeting pleasures of sin.* Moses might well have argued that, like Joseph, he could serve God and help his own people by remaining in power; but his calling was to relinquish his position of privilege and in faith to take up the challenge of obedience to the will of God, which required him to cast aside the earthly security he had known for so long and in the face of incalculable dangers to lead an undisciplined crowd across the wilderness from bondage to freedom. The great sin for Moses would have been to disobey his heavenly calling (cf. Heb. 2:1; Acts 26:19) and to choose instead the fleeting pleasures of the ease and affluence of the palace. Obedience to the call demanded determination of faith and concentration of purpose in pressing toward an eternal goal that was still afar off. It demanded, further, the *calculation of faith* by which it becomes obvious that the values and allurements of this world are not comparable with those everlasting blessings which are guaranteed by the promises of God. In the true succession of faith from Abraham, Moses *considered,* he reckoned (cf. v. 19 above),[77] *abuse suffered for the Christ greater wealth than the treasures of Egypt,* which, phenomenal both in quality and quantity, were freely available to him. The apostle Paul made precisely the same calculation when he declared that "this slight momentary affliction is preparing for us an eternal weight of glory beyond all comparison" (2 Cor. 4:17f.; Rom. 8:18).

The title *Christ,* which is the Greek equivalent of the Hebrew term *Messiah,* signifies simply one who has been anointed; but in the New Testament it becomes the specific designation of Jesus, the incarnate Son, who in a unique and transcendental sense is God's Anointed One. In the Old Testament period, as is well known, kings, priests, and prophets were anointed for service in their respective vocations and as "God's anointed ones" typologically prefigured the threefold office of him who is the Christ *par excellence* (see p. 49 above). The term, further, was applied to the people of God. Thus in the psalm of thanksgiving which David appointed to be sung on the occasion of the restoration of the ark of the covenant to Jerusalem the providential care and faithfulness of God in dealing with his people, "his anointed ones," to whom the promises belong, is extolled:

He is mindful of his covenant for ever,
    of the word that he commanded, for a thousand generations,
the covenant which he made with Abraham,
    his sworn promise to Isaac,
which he confirmed as a statute to Jacob,
    as an everlasting covenant to Israel,
saying, "To you I will give the land of Canaan,
    as your portion for an inheritance."
When they were few in number,
    and of little account, and sojourners in it,
wandering from nation to nation,
    from one kingdom to another people,
he allowed no one to oppress them;
    he rebuked kings on their account,
saying, "Touch not my anointed ones!"[78]
        (1 Chr. 16:15-22; Ps. 105:8-15)

The term may be used in the plural, as here, or in the singular of the people collectively (see, for example, Ps. 28:8; Hab. 3:13). Our author's

77. Λογισάμενος used of Abraham in verse 19 is the exact equivalent of ἡγησάμενος used of Moses here.
78. Μὴ ἅψησθε τῶν χριστῶν μου, "Touch not my christs."

language, indeed, is reminiscent of Psalm 89:50f.: "Remember, Lord, the reproach of thy servants . . . wherewith thine enemies have reproached, O Lord, have reproached the footsteps of thine anointed" (KJV). [79]

It may be said, then, as many commentators have pointed out, that in renouncing the treasures of Egypt and choosing instead to identify himself with the Israelite nation, which, despite the contempt and hostility of the world, as a unit was "God's anointed," Moses was in this sense deliberately sharing the reproach of the Lord's anointed (cf. NEB, "the stigma that rests on God's Anointed"). But our author undoubtedly means more than a mere association with the children of Israel; for when, within the context of the New Testament, he speaks of "the Christ" here, he is speaking specifically of the single messianic person of the Redeemer. As this chapter shows so clearly, for the man of faith the way of obedience is also the way of suffering, and in choosing this way Moses was conforming to the pattern which was to have its perfect exemplification in the obedience and suffering of him who in a unique and ultimate sense is God's Anointed One (cf. Heb. 2:10). The servant-songs of Isaiah speak of Israel in terms of obedience and suffering, not, however, in an absolute sense, for commingled with the faithful were many covenant-breakers, but with respect to the indefectible purpose of God in accordance with which this nation had been chosen as the vehicle of the promise pointing forward to perfection and fulfilment in the One who was coming. Hence the insistence of the New Testament writers on the completion of the servant-songs, and especially Isaiah 53, in the divine-human person of him who in an absolute sense is God's Anointed One. Christ himself, as our author repeatedly stresses, chose the way of obedience, even though it led to humiliation and suffering and death, for this was the cost of our redemption; but always there is the fuller perspective by which it is discerned as the way leading also to resurrection and glory (1:3f.; 2:9, 14f.; 4:14f.; 5:7–9; 9:11f.; 10:10, 12f.; 12:2f.).

Moses, like the believing men and women who preceded and followed him, was animated by this perspective of faith which penetrates beyond the trials and afflictions of the present time to the glory that lies ahead: *for he looked to the reward*—or, as the next verse explains, "he endured as seeing him who is invisible," just as the recipients of this letter will shortly be exhorted to endure and persevere by "looking to Jesus"[80] (12:1f.). For Moses, then, "abuse suffered for the Christ," or, as the KJV renders it, "the reproach of Christ," was not simply the re-

---

79. Compare τὸν ὀνειδισμὸν τοῦ Χριστοῦ here with Psalm 89:50f. (LXX): μνήσθητι, κύριε, τοῦ ὀνειδισμοῦ τῶν δούλων σου . . . οὗ ὠνείδισαν οἱ ἐχθροί σου, κύριε, οὗ ὠνείδισαν τὸ ἀντάλλαγμα τοῦ χριστοῦ σου.
80. Ἀφορῶντες in 12:2 is the exact equivalent of ἀπέβλεπεν here. Both verbs mean to "look away," that is, within this context, from present suffering to future reward.

proach accepted by identifying himself with the people of God but, more precisely, the reproach of the coming Messiah with whom he was united by faith. Hence (as Stephen reminded his accusers) his assurance to the Israelites: "God will raise up for you a prophet from your brethren as he raised me up" (Acts 7:37); and hence, also, the rebuke of Jesus Christ to his adversaries: "If you believed Moses, you would believe me, for he wrote of me" (Jn. 5:46).

And so the man of faith chooses the way of obedience and suffering, not by constraint, but willingly and joyfully, knowing that the goal is a glorious one. This had been the case with the Hebrew Christians to whom our author is writing; but now some of them are daunted and discouraged, and therefore have already been admonished: "Do not throw away your confidence, which has great reward. For you have need of endurance, so that you may do the will of God and receive what is promised" (10:35f.; on the connotation of the term "reward" see the commentary there and on 6:10 and v. 6 of this chapter). Christ's followers must be prepared to follow him in suffering, for theirs too is the way of the cross (Mt. 10:24f., 38; Jn. 15:18ff.); but with the constant certainty that their sorrow will turn to joy (Jn. 16:20). And this is the way of blessing, even as Christ himself taught: "Blessed are you when men revile you and persecute you and utter all kinds of evil against you falsely on my account. Rejoice and be glad, for your reward is great in heaven" (Mt. 5:11f.). Those who are Christ's, says Aquinas, "looking to the ultimate goal of eternal happiness on which their hope is fixed, choose afflictions and poverty rather than riches and pleasures, because the latter hinder their pursuit of the hoped-for goal." That goal or reward is summed up in Christ, for whom, and to attain to whom, the apostle Paul gladly suffered the loss of all things (Phil. 3:7f.), and to whom we are urged to look, not only as the source but also as the objective of our faith (Heb. 12:2). Thus the Psalmist could protest at a time when his faith was being sorely tested: "Whom have I in heaven but thee? And there is nothing upon earth that I desire besides thee" (Ps. 73:25).

11:27–29. *By faith he left Egypt, not being afraid of the anger of the king; for he endured as seeing him who is invisible. By faith he kept the Passover and sprinkled the blood, so that the Destroyer of the first-born might not touch them. By faith the people crossed the Red Sea as if on dry land; but the Egyptians, when they attempted to do the same, were drowned.*

When Moses *left Egypt*, our author continues, he did this too *by faith*. Until comparatively modern times this departure of Moses from

Egypt has been understood to refer to his flight to Midian in the Sinai peninsula when, following his killing of an Egyptian who had been beating a Hebrew, he learned that Pharaoh intended to put him to death. Many commentators, however, from Calvin onward, have considered that the exodus proper, when Moses led the people out of Egypt, is intended here, arguing that Moses' earlier flight as an individual is difficult to reconcile with our author's assertion that he departed *not being afraid of the anger of the king*, since Exodus 2:14f. speaks of Moses as being afraid and fleeing from Pharaoh. Owen, for example, states emphatically that "it is not likely, nay, it is not true, that the apostle intends that first departure out of Egypt," and praises the fearlessness of Moses in his confrontations with Pharaoh which immediately preceded the exodus of the Israelites from Egypt. This interpretation is clearly not lacking in cogency. Even though it means that our author places the exodus before the passover, it can be argued that the sequence of events commonly associated with the exodus includes the passover itself and Moses' encounters with Pharaoh which it followed.

But the case presented by Owen against the opinion that verse 27 designates the earlier and private departure of Moses is far from strong. The three points of his argument are: (1) that in Exodus 2 it is said that Moses "fled from the face of Pharaoh," which, he says, indicates a hasty and fearful action, whereas here it is said that he "left Egypt," which, he maintains, "expresseth a sedate act of his mind"—a tendentious conclusion, because the verb "to leave" expresses nothing in itself concerning the state or disposition of a person's mind and may equally well denote actions both precipitate and sedate; (2) that no mention is made in Exodus 2 of Moses' faith in leaving the country, but only of his fear—the implication being, apparently, that it was a faithless act and also, presumably, that his forty years of isolation in Midian were not years lived by faith, a conclusion that begs the question, especially as the rejoinder is possible that neither is there any specific mention of his faith in the narrative of the exodus proper; and (3) that our author closely connects this departure from Egypt with the keeping of the passover—another tendentious conclusion, however, for by the same logic it can equally be affirmed that the crossing of the Red Sea (v. 29) is closely connected by our author with the fall of Jericho (v. 30), since the one is mentioned immediately after the other, whereas in fact there was an interval of forty years between the two events, as there was also between Moses' flight and the institution of the passover.

The bare assertion that "he left Egypt," without any reference to the people of Israel, describes more appropriately the action of Moses as a single individual (even granting that it could mean his leaving at the head of the Israelites), and the observation which is added, that *he endured as seeing him who is invisible*, while certainly applicable to the life of Moses as a whole, would be particularly apposite here as a reference to the forty years of obscurity and inactivity (from the point of view of his vocation to national leadership), which were also years of testing and preparation for the final forty years as the deliverer of his people. This prolonged interval was indeed a period which called for great faith and endurance if he was to overcome the temptation to frustration and discouragement. It is worth noticing that in the not dissimilar historical survey which is the foundation of his defense Stephen devotes a considerable section to the flight of Moses into Midian (Acts 7:23–34) before he gives an account of the exodus.

How, then, is the statement here that Moses was not afraid of Pharaoh's anger compatible with the declaration of Exodus 2:14f. that he was afraid and fled from Pharaoh? The answer to this question is that it was not personal fear of Pharaoh but the awareness of his destiny as the deliverer of the covenant people that caused him to take flight. Had he remained, at that juncture, this destiny would have been thwarted, humanly speaking, by his execution; and so, impelled by faith in the divine purpose for his life, Moses took refuge in Midian. That he was a man of courage rather than of fear is shown by the risk he took in coming to the help of his compatriots who were being ill treated and in the boldness of his return at God's command after the lapse of forty years to withstand the Egyptian king face to face and demand the release of his people. Thus Chrysostom insists that even Moses' flight was an act of faith and that for him to have stayed in Egypt at that time would not only have been foolish and senseless but would also have been in a devilish manner, contrary to faith, to put God to the test (alluding to Mt. 4:5–7). Peter Lombard and Aquinas comment to the same effect. Indeed, as there is a time for every matter (Eccl. 3:1ff.), so there is a time for flight and a time for confrontation, as Moses' life illustrates, and as we see above all in the conduct of Christ himself who on more than one occasion disengaged himself from those who were about to put him to death "because his hour had not yet come" (see Jn. 7:30; 8:20, 59; 10:31–39), but who, when the hour arrived in which the purpose of his coming into the world was to be fulfilled, faced without flinching his cruel accusers and the agony of the cross (see Jn. 12:27; Mk. 8:31; 10:33f., par.).

Moses, too, knew that in God's good time his hour would come; otherwise the long years of his exile would have been altogether intolerable. But the constancy of his trust in God enabled him to endure "as seeing him who is invisible" (cf. Jn. 1:18; 1 Tim. 1:17; 6:16; Col. 1:15; 1 Jn. 4:20). In other words, the governing impulse of his flight from Egypt was faith, not fear, as is neatly suggested by the NEB translation: "By faith he left Egypt, and not because he feared the king's anger." It was

499

not with the physical eye but with the eye of faith that Moses saw him
who is invisible.[81] Some have supposed that there is a reference here to
the encounter at the burning bush. There is, however, little justification
for such a connection. "As for Moses' endurance, 'seeing him who is
invisible,'" comments F. F. Bruce, "this need not be taken as a specific
allusion to the burning bush, but to the fact that Moses paid more
attention to the Invisible King of kings than to the king of Egypt. If faith
is 'a conviction of things not seen', it is first and foremost a conviction
regarding the unseen God, as has been emphasized already in the affirmation that he who comes to God must believe that He is (verse 6)."

When Moses, on the eve of the departure of the Israelites from
Egypt, *kept the passover*[82] and sprinkled the blood, this, too, was an act of
faith and not just a piece of religious ceremonialism, for it was a response of obedience to God's command and of trust in his promise that
the Destroyer of the first-born would *not touch them*, but would pass over
those houses whose doorposts and lintels were sprinkled with the blood
of the paschal lamb (Ex. 12:1ff.). The typological importance of the
passover and its ceremonial is obvious in the New Testament, for as the
passover lamb was required to be perfect and unblemished and its sacrifice was the moment of the people's moving from bondage to liberty,
so Christ is the fulfilment of all that was symbolized by this event: he is
"the Lamb of God" (Jn. 1:29, 36), "our paschal Lamb" (1 Cor. 5:7),
whose precious redeeming blood is "like that of a lamb without blemish
or spot" (1 Pet. 1:19), and who through his death has destroyed the
power of the devil, our spiritual Pharaoh, and delivered us from lifelong
bondage (Heb. 2:14f.). "If the blood of a lamb then preserved the Jews

---

81. "The words ὡς ὁρῶν are in themselves ambiguous. They may mean either 'as though
he saw' or 'inasmuch as he saw'. The peculiar gift of Moses determines that the latter is the
sense here" (Westcott). "He had as certain a persuasion as if he had seen God working
with him and for him by his bodily eyes" (Owen). These two quotations show how a
forceful meaning can be given to either understanding of ὡς ὁρῶν—"as in fact seeing" or
"as though seeing."
82. "Kept the Passover" translates πεποίηκεν τὸ πάσχα. Spicq comments that "the single
perfect, in the midst of the aorists, suggests that this celebration was the inauguration of a
definitive institution" (similarly F. F. Bruce, Westcott, Delitzsch, etc.). Moffatt, however,
explains it as an aoristic perfect. The expression ποιῆσαι τὸ πάσχα is taken from the LXX of
Exodus 12:48, and it is not without significance that this same verb is used of the institution of the eucharist, which in the New Testament may be said to correspond to and to
replace the passover. Thus in Matthew 26:18 Christ speaks of his intention to keep the
passover (ποιῶ τὸ πάσχα) with his disciples, and then, in the midst of the passover
observance, he inaugurates the sacrament of the Lord's Supper, with the injunction: "Do
this (τοῦτο ποιεῖτε) in remembrance of me" (see also Lk. 22:19 and 1 Cor. 11:24, 25; the
present imperative implies the continued observance of this institution), thereby indicating the new observance which is to take the place of the old—for, as our epistle makes
abundantly plain, after the shedding of Christ's blood there is no place for any further
blood-shedding.

unhurt in the midst of the Egyptians and in the presence of so great a destruction, much more will the blood of Christ save us, for whom it has been sprinkled not on our doorposts but in our souls," proclaims Chrysostom. "For even now the destroyer is still moving around in the depth of night; but let us be armed with Christ's sacrifice, since God has brought us out from Egypt, from darkness and from idolatry."

Scarcely, indeed, had the Israelites turned their backs on Pharaoh and set out on their journey to the land of promise than they found themselves in a situation which tested their faith to the limit. In front of them was the apparently insuperable barrier of the Red Sea and behind them the fearsomely pursuing army of Pharaoh, who had had a change of heart regarding their departure. Unless God should prove himself the God of the impossible, there was no chance of survival for so weak and ill ordered a multitude. And it was Moses, the man of faith, who rallied the despairing people with the exhortation: "Fear not, stand firm, and see the salvation of the Lord, which he will work for you today; for the Egyptians whom you see today, you shall never see again. The Lord will fight for you, and you have only to be still" (Ex. 14:10ff.). Thereupon, and entirely by the power of Almighty God, so that faith in his word alone was fully vindicated, a way was opened up before them through the waters of the Red Sea. It was *by faith*, therefore, that *the people crossed the Red Sea as if on dry land*. The fact that *the Egyptians, when they attempted to do the same, were drowned*[83] illustrates the truth that what is for the believer the way of life is for the unbeliever the way of death. "See," exclaims Lefèvre d'Etaples, "how the same waters of baptism are for the salvation of the regenerate and for the destruction of the forces of evil!"[84] As we have seen (v. 7 above), the waters of the flood which bore up the ark and those sheltering in it were at the same time the waters which destroyed all who had scornfully rejected the preaching of Noah. Thus the gospel is to one "a fragrance from death to death," but to another "a fragrance from life to life" (2 Cor. 2:16); Christ is set for the fall as well as for the rising of many (Lk. 2:34); he is the chosen cornerstone, so that "he who believes in him will not be put to shame," whereas to the unbeliever he becomes a rock of stumbling 1 Pet. 2:6–8; Isa. 28:16; 8:14f.). The crucial importance of faith could hardly be more dramatically emphasized than by the opposite fortunes of the Israelites and the Egyptians at the Red Sea.

---

83. Κατεπόθησαν, an intensive compound: "they were totally engulfed," "overwhelmed."

84. See the commentary on 4:12 above. "Duo cum faciunt idem, non est idem," is Bengel's laconic observation. In 1 Corinthians 10:1f. Paul speaks of the passage through the Red Sea as an experience of baptism. The relationship between faith and baptism in the New Testament needs no elaboration here.

11:30, 31. By faith the walls of Jericho fell down after they had been encircled for seven days. By faith Rahab the harlot did not perish with those who were disobedient, because she had given friendly welcome to the spies.

The crossing of the Red Sea was followed by the forty years of wandering in the wilderness. Even when, under the leadership of Joshua, the promised land was at last entered there were still daunting obstacles in the path of the Israelites. The first of these, after the Jordan had been crossed, was the walled city of Jericho, which must have appeared impregnable to Joshua's ill-equipped company. But Joshua, like Moses whom he had succeeded, was a man of faith. Ringing in his ears were the words with which he had been divinely commissioned: "Be strong and of good courage; be not frightened; neither be dismayed; for the Lord your God is with you wherever you go" (Josh. 1:9). His faith was now tested by a command that must have seemed strange and indeed incomprehensible, namely, that the people were to march around the city in a prescribed order, the vanguard comprising the armed men, then following them seven priests blowing on trumpets of rams' horns, then the ark of the covenant, and in the rear the rest of the community. The city was to be encircled once on each of the first six days and seven times on the seventh day, while no word was to be spoken by any person; but at the end of the seventh circuit on the seventh day a long blast on the rams' horns was to be the signal for all the people to "shout with a great shout." Upon the completion of this unusual procedure, *the walls of Jericho fell down* and the Israelites marched straight in and took the city (Josh. 6:1ff.). And this was achieved *by faith*, for, as Chrysostom remarks, "assuredly the sound of trumpets is unable to cast down stones, though one blow for ten thousand years, but faith can do all things." Faith indeed, as Spicq explains, "is not concerned with means; it achieves its objective because God intervenes for its vindication." And F. F. Bruce rightly points out that "archaeology can throw much light on the collapse of ancient cities," but that "the forces that operate in the unseen realm, such as the power of faith, cannot be dug up by the excavator's spade."

Closely associated with the account of the fall of Jericho is the story of *Rahab*. The inclusion of Rahab in this recital of heroic examples of faith is of particular interest. In the first place, Rahab was a woman, and indeed is the only woman specifically mentioned by our author in this chapter, apart from Sarah (v. 11), who not surprisingly was introduced in close association with Abraham. The introduction of Rahab as an independent woman may be taken to illustrate the principle that, though the differentiation between man and woman in physical functions and social relationships is as proper as it is inevitable, in the sphere of faith there is neither male nor female (Gal. 3:28)—and of course there are other women of faith whom our author might suitably have cited from the Old Testament period had his method been comprehensive rather than selective.

Secondly, Rahab was known, and continued to be known, as *the harlot* (a designation which is found also in Jas. 2:25 and 1 Clem. 12 as well as in the Old Testament). This, however, is a description of Rahab as she was before she came to faith and identified herself with the people of God—just as Matthew continued to be known as "the tax collector" (Mt. 10:3) and Simon as "the zealot" (Lk. 6:15; Acts 1:13) even after they had deserted their former occupations and joined the apostolic band. There is not the slightest need to seek some means of toning down the description of Rahab as a harlot, as though it were inappropriate for one so designated to be included in a catalogue of believers.[85] In fact, as Calvin says, the designation "harlot" heightens the grace of God. Grace, together with the faith it evokes, is for sinners, and it was precisely sinners, not the self-righteous who blind themselves to their sin and their need, whom Christ came to call to repentance (Lk. 5:32). Significantly, therefore, Christ rebuked the religious leaders of the day with these words: "Truly, I say to you, the tax collectors and the harlots go into the kingdom of God before you. For John came to you in the way of righteousness, and you did not believe him, but the tax collectors and the harlots believed him; and even when you saw it, you did not afterward repent and believe him" (Mt. 21:31f.). Rahab, in her day, was a harlot who believed and who in consequence is justly commemorated here as one who *by faith . . . did not perish with those who were*

---

85. The attempt to soften the description of Rahab as "the harlot" probably goes back to pre-Christian times. In the first century A.D. the Jewish author Josephus speaks of her as the keeper of an inn where the spies hid themselves (ἐν τῷ τῆς 'Ραάβης καταγωγίῳ, *Ant.* v.8). This is also the way in which the Targum interprets the Hebrew term זוֹנָה, *zonah,* explaining it as the equivalent of פונדקיתא, a Grecism transliterated from πανδοκεύτρια, a female innkeeper or hostess. The justification for this interpretation is discussed by D. J. Wiseman, "Rahab of Jericho," *Tyndale House Bulletin* (Cambridge, June 1964), pp. 8ff. Nicholas of Lyra in the fourteenth century and Cornelius à Lapide in the seventeenth century are Christian scholars who explain the Hebrew term as meaning *caupona,* a female innkeeper. The first hand of Codex Sinaiticus (fourth century) reads here in 11:31 ἡ ἐπιλεγομένη πόρνη, "the so-called harlot" (a reading reflected in the Harclean Syriac and also found as a variant reading in 1 Clem. 12), which is clearly another attempt at ameliorating the designation "harlot." But whatever possibility there may be for a more favorable interpretation of the Hebrew term זוֹנָה, the Greek πόρνη, which is also the rendering of the LXX, can mean only one thing. Aquinas comments as follows: "She was a harlot whom the spies visited, not for the purpose of sinning, but to find a hiding-place. For the houses of such women are open, especially at night-time; and it was during the night that they came. Her house also was joined to the wall. Harlots, moreover, always receive their guests without discrimination, and for this reason it was all the easier for them to be hidden on her premises."

disobedient—disobedience being synonymous with unbelief (as in 3:18 above; see also Jn. 3:36; Acts 14:2, Gk.; 19:9, Gk.; Rom. 2:8; 10:21; 11:30f.; 15:31, Gk.). Her faith was outwardly expressed in the manner in which she gave *friendly welcome to the spies*, entertaining them and sheltering them, literally, "in peace"[86] instead of treating them as intruders and enemies, for she had heard of the wonderful things that Yahweh had done for the Israelites and believed that he was indeed the true God. "I know," she said, "that the Lord has given you the land..." (Josh. 2:1ff.). The unbelieving defiance of the people of Jericho showed itself in their shutting up of the city in the expectation that it would prove impregnable to any assault by the Israelites (Josh. 6:1). In a later period of Jewish history Judas Maccabeus, when confronted with a fortified town, is said to have invoked "the great Sovereign of the world who, without battering-rams and instruments of war, laid Jericho low in the days of Joshua" (2 Macc. 12:15).

Thirdly, Rahab was, from the viewpoint of the Israelites, a foreigner. She did not belong to the chosen people; but through faith she was accepted into their company and enjoyed the privileges and blessings from which formerly she had been excluded. In this she was an exemplification of the truth of the covenant promise that in the seed of Abraham all the nations of the earth would be blessed (Gen. 22:18; Gal. 3:8f.). Especially interesting is the fact that, once incorporated into the people of God, she even won an honored place in the line that led to the fulfilment of the divine promises in the birth of Christ. Thus, according to the genealogy at the beginning of Matthew's Gospel, Rahab married Salmon and became the mother of Boaz, who in turn also married an alien woman, Ruth the Moabitess, who became the mother of Obed, David's grandfather (Mt. 1:5f.).[87]

In Rahab, then, the church has discerned a type of the ingathering of the Gentiles and a confirmation both of the universal scope of the gospel and of the depth of God's grace as extending even to the most degraded of sinners;[88] while the destruction of Jericho has been regarded as symbolic of the overthrow of worldly opposition to God by the preaching of the gospel. The following passage from a sermon by the

---

86. Μετ' εἰρήνης, "peaceably."
87. "Even Jewish priests were proud to trace their descent from Rahab," writes Moffatt; "her reputation stood high in later tradition, owing to the life which followed this initial act of faith."
88. Even before the close of the first century we find Clement of Rome explaining that the scarlet cord, which was placed in the window of Rahab's house and ensured the salvation of Rahab and her kinsfolk when Jericho fell (Josh. 2:18; 6:22f.), was a symbol which "showed beforehand that through the blood of the Lord there would be redemption to all them who believe and hope in God." "You see, dearly beloved," Clement adds, "not only faith but also prophecy is found in this woman" (*Ep. ad Cor.* 12).

celebrated preacher Caesarius of Arles (ca. 470–542) will serve to illustrate the manner in which spiritual lessons were drawn from the story of Jericho and Rahab:

> Jericho, dearest brothers, was a type of this world; for just as its walls fell at the sound of the trumpets, so also now the city of the world, that is, human arrogance with its towers, namely, greed, envy, and luxury, together with its population, that is, all evil lusts, must be destroyed and must perish by the unremitting preaching of priests. For priests must not be silent in the church, but must hear the Lord saying, "Cry aloud, do not cease, lift up your voice like a trumpet and denounce the sins of my people" [Isa. 58:1]. . . . There is no doubt that all these things were done in a figurative manner: for what else do we think the priestly trumpets of that time prefigured than the priestly preaching of this time, by which preachers do not cease to proclaim with terrible note severe judgment to sinners? . . .

Caesarius goes on, appropriately, to cite Paul's words in 2 Corinthians 10:4f.: "The weapons of our warfare are not worldly but have divine power to destroy strongholds, destroying arguments and every proud obstacle to the knowledge of God, and taking every thought captive to obey Christ." In Rahab Caesarius sees a picture of the church:

> This harlot, dearest brothers, was a figure of the church, which before Christ's advent used to commit fornication with many idols. But when Christ came he not only delivered her from fornication but also by a great miracle made her a virgin; for the apostle says concerning the church: "I betrothed you to one husband to present you as a pure virgin to Christ" [2 Cor. 11:2].[89]

The derivation of spiritual lessons of this kind from the narratives of the Old Testament was widely practiced from the earliest days. Aquinas, for example, gives an exposition very similar to that of Caesarius, adding that "the liberation of Rahab as a result of her reception of the spies signifies that those who receive preachers of the Gospel are liberated from eternal death."

11:32. *And what more shall I say? For time would fail me to tell of Gideon, Barak, Samson, Jephthah, of David and Samuel and the prophets.*

Having carried his survey to the period of the entry of the Israelites into the promised land, our author, doubtless realizing that to continue as he has begun would involve him in the writing of a lengthy treatise, and that sufficient examples have been given for the illustration of his theme, now breaks off from the more specifically biographical enumera-

89. Caesarius of Arles, *Sermones* (Turnholti, 1953), I, pp. 480ff.

tion of the conquests of faith and concludes this section of the epistle with a general summary of the triumphant faith of God's people in the face of every kind of cruel opposition. The implication of the rhetorical question *And what more shall I say?* is that there is no need for further elaboration: the accuracy of the postulate with which he started, namely, that "faith" is the assurance of things hoped for, the conviction of things not seen" (v. 1), has been amply established; and in a comparatively brief communication of the kind he is writing *time would fail ... to tell* of all the other notable men and women of faith of the former dispensation, such as *Gideon, Barak, Samson, Jephthah, ... David and Samuel and the prophets*—names which, it is evident, are no more than a random sampling of the many deserving of mention. The periods suggested by these names are those of the history of Israel subsequent to the time of Joshua, that is to say, the periods of the judges (Gideon, Barak, Samson, Jephthah), the kings (David and Samuel), and the prophets. So random, indeed, is this list that the order of the names as given is not even chronological. The correct order, had this been the author's concern, would have been: Barak (Judg. 4–5), Gideon (6–8), Jephthah (11–12), Samson (12–16), Samuel (1 Sam. 1ff.),[90] and David (1 Sam. 16ff.). The prophets are cited as a separate category, without the mention of individual names.

Barak was the military leader who, at the summons of Deborah, led the Israelite army against Sisera the Canaanite and his chariots, completely routing them in a celebrated battle—a victory immortalized in the Song of Deborah and Barak (Judg. 5). Barak's exploit was manifestly an act of faith inasmuch as he and his "infantry" overcame the "mechanized" force of Sisera. The spirit in which it was undertaken is revealed in Deborah's exhortation to Barak: "Up! For this is the day in which the Lord has given Sisera into your hand. Does not the Lord go out before you?" (Judg. 4:14). Even more remarkable was *Gideon's* maneuver whereby the hosts of Midian were ignominiously defeated by the three hundred selected men whom he led against them. Under *Jephthah's* leadership the Israelites overthrew the armies of the Amorites and the Ammonites; while Samson was the great champion of Israel against the Philistines. These conquests illustrate the truth that God is able to save by

90. In 1 Samuel 12:11, Jerubbaal (another name for Gideon, cf. Judg. 6:32; 7:1), Barak, Jephthah, and Samuel are mentioned together in that order. On the basis mainly of intrinsic probability, one is disposed to accept the reading of the Syriac Peshitta, in which Samson is substituted for Samuel. The reading is in fact adopted in the NEB. It seems somewhat incongruous for Samuel, who is speaking, to cite himself as one of Israel's deliverers. The Peshitta also adds the name of Deborah to the list, between Gideon and Barak. Assuming that Samson is the correct reading, there is every likelihood that our author had this passage in mind. The order is not identical (Gideon, Barak, Jephthah, Samson as compared with Gideon, Barak, Samson, Jephthah), but it is no more chronological in 1 Samuel than it is in Hebrews—a consideration of some interest!

many or by few (cf. 1 Sam. 14:6). F. F. Bruce observes that "on three of these four—Gideon (Judg. 6:34), Jephthah (Judg. 11:29), and Samson (Judg. 13:25, etc.)—the Spirit of Yahweh is said to have come, and this could be taken as conclusive evidence of their faith."

Much space is devoted in the Old Testament to the deeds and words of Samuel and David. Of these two, Samuel, whose life was distinguished by the integrity and intensity of his faith, may be seen as a bridge-figure linking the period of the judges to that of the kings of Israel, and David, his serious faults notwithstanding, as the outstanding representative of the monarchy and the kingly type of the Messiah, "great David's greater Son."

There is an echo of the verse now before us in the encyclical letter written by Athanasius in A.D. 356 to the bishops of Egypt and Libya who were facing great dangers, spiritual as well as physical—at a time, moreover, when he himself had been driven from his diocese of Alexandria by the enemies of the apostolic faith.

> The patriarch Abraham [he reminds them] received the crown, not because he suffered death, but because he was faithful to God; and the other saints who are mentioned, Gideon, Barak, Samson, Jephthah, David, and Samuel, and the rest, were not made perfect by the shedding of their blood, but were justified by faith; and to this day they are the objects of our admiration as men ready even to suffer death because of their devotion to the Lord. . . . Therefore, considering that this struggle is for our all, and that the choice is now before us either to deny or to preserve the faith, let us also make it our earnest care and aim to guard what we have received, taking as our instruction the confession drawn up at Nicea.[91]

One further point of interest that arises from this verse is the indication that the author of our epistle was a man and not, as some have supposed, a woman.[92] This is not apparent in the English translation, but in the Greek text the pronoun "me" is qualified by a participle in the masculine gender.[93]

11:33, 34. *Who through faith conquered kingdoms, enforced justice, received promises, stopped the mouths of lions, quenched raging fire, escaped the edge of the sword, won strength out of weakness, became mighty in war, put foreign armies to flight.*

These heroic contenders for the truth, both named and unnamed, overcame every imaginable type of adversity *through faith*. Some (for

91. Athanasius, *Ad Episcopos Aegypti etc.* 21.
92. See Introduction, pp. 25f.
93. In the Greek: με . . . διηγούμενον.

507

example, Westcott, Teodorico) are of the opinion that the nine classifications of these two verses fall naturally into three triads. Symmetries of this kind, however, are unlikely and unnecessary to the purpose of our author, whose manner of writing here is spontaneous and unstudied. Be that as it may, it is not only in splendid achievements such as those listed in these verses that faith is victorious, but also in the suffering of tortures, imprisonments, and brutal deaths, as described in the verses which follow (35–38), that faith displays its unconquerable character, so that we see, once again, how inseparably constancy of faith and certainty of hope are bound together. Through faith, then, these contestants of the pre-Christian era accomplished the following things.

They *conquered kingdoms*. This would apply to the judges mentioned in the preceding verse and to David[94] and other great leaders who gained celebrated victories over formidable enemy nations and overthrew proud and ambitious potentates.

They *enforced justice*—or, better, "ruled in justice" (Phillips) or "established justice" (NEB).[95] The expression is used of doing what is right with reference to personal integrity, as in Psalm 15:2 and Acts 10:35 (cf. JB), but it is better understood here in the sense of setting up just government. Samuel, for example, when an old man, received acknowledgment of the justness of his leadership in the following exchange with the people of Israel:

> "Here I am; testify against me before the Lord and before his anointed. Whose ox have I taken? Or whose ass have I taken? Or whom have I defrauded? Whom have I oppressed? Or from whose hand have I taken a bribe to blind my eyes with it? Testify against me and I will restore it to you." They said, "You have not defrauded us or oppressed us or taken anything from any man's hand." And he said to them, "The Lord is witness against you, and his anointed is witness this day, that you have not found anything in my hand." And they said, "He is witness" (1 Sam. 12:3–5).

The name of David was also honored because as king he "administered justice and equity to all his people" (2 Sam. 8:15; 1 Chr. 18:14).[96] To the same effect were the words of the queen of Sheba to Solomon: "Because the Lord loved Israel for ever, he has made you king, that you may execute justice and righteousness" (1 Ki. 10:9). This, too, is typological, for the messianic kingdom over which the Son of David will rule forever

---

94. Josephus uses the same verb as is used here, καταγωνίζεσθαι, of David's defeat of the Philistines: the leaders of the Israelites, he says, "declared that God had enabled him to save the land of the Hebrews by conquering the Philistines"—καταγωνισαμένῳ Παλαιστίνους (*Ant.* vii.53).

95. Ἐργάζεσθαι δικαιοσύνην is to practice justice. Thus in Psalm 15:2 (LXX) the upright man is described as ἐργαζόμενος δικαιοσύνην (see also Acts 10:35).

96. Καὶ ἦν Δαυὶδ ποιῶν κρίμα καὶ δικαιοσύνην (LXX), where ποιεῖν δικαιοσύνην is the same as ἐργαζέσθαι δικαιοσύνην in Hebrews 11:33.

will be distinguished to a preeminent degree by everlasting justice and righteousness (Isa. 9:7; cf. 1:8f. in our epistle).

They *received promises,* and these promises called forth their faith as they were given and vindicated their faith insofar as they were fulfilled. This would be true of the messianic promises whose fulfilment they did not see in their time and of the many other promises of divine aid whose fulfilment they did experience.[97] In Joshua 21:43ff., for instance, it is acknowledged that "the Lord gave to Israel all the land which he swore to give to their fathers. . . . Not one of all the good promises which the Lord had made to the house of Israel had failed; all came to pass" (cf. Ex. 23:31; Josh. 1:4; 1 Ki. 4:20–25; Neh. 9:7–9, 23–25). David, too, gave thanks because of the faithfulness of God's covenant promises (1 Chr. 16:15ff.; Ps. 105:8ff., 42). It was on the strength of God's promises of victory that Gideon led his small band against the Midianite army (Judg. 6:14; 7:7). In accordance with specific divine promises Elijah was sustained in the transjordanian desert and after that by the widow in Zarephath, and the drought of three years was broken (1 Ki. 17:1ff., 8ff.; 18:1, 41ff.). These cases are typical of the many persons who in the Old Testament period were blessed by the reception of promises.

They *stopped the mouths of lions.* The incident most readily recalled by this statement is the deliverance of Daniel when he was in the lions' den. "My God sent his angel," Daniel testified to king Darius, "and shut the lions' mouths, and they have not hurt me" (Dan. 6:22). Samson, David, and Benaiah, one of David's "mighty men," could also be said to have stopped the mouths of lions (Judg. 14:5f.; 1 Sam. 17:34ff.; 2 Sam. 23:20), but these were feats of physical prowess rather than exploits of faith.

They *quenched raging fire.* This would apply with particular appropriateness to the ordeal and deliverance of the three Hebrew youths, Shadrach, Meshach, and Abednego, Daniel's companions and compatriots, from the blazing furnace into which Nebuchadnezzar had ordered them to be thrown. The firmness of their faith was shown in the boldness with which they confronted the king, whose image they had refused to worship: "Our God whom we serve is able to deliver us from the burning fiery furnace" (Dan. 3:17). And in the midst of their ordeal the presence of a fourth Person was seen to be with them (v. 25). So the promise made to Joshua (Josh. 1:5) and repeated by our author in 13:5

---

97. Moffatt prefers to limit the reference to the latter: "Such was their faith, too, that they had promises of God's help realized in their experience." Similarly Owen interprets these promises of "the things which were peculiarly promised unto them in their occasions." The expression ἐπέτυχον ἐπαγγελίας here is matched by the statement in 6:15 that Abraham obtained the promise, ἐπέτυχεν τῆς ἐπαγγελίας. On the special force of the verb κομίζεσθαι, which is used in verses 13 and 39 of this chapter and in 10:36, see note 32, p. 433, above.

below, "I will never fail you or forsake you," became a glorious reality to them in the hour of their trial.

They *escaped the edge of the sword*. This is reminiscent of the experience of David on a number of occasions during the period when he was a fugitive from the homicidal jealousy of Saul, of Elijah when he fled for his life from the enraged Jezebel, of Elisha when the king of Syria sent an armed force to destroy him, and of other men of faith whose lives were imperilled because they remained loyal to God and his truth.

They *won strength out of weakness*. To everyone who has been mentioned above and who will be mentioned below this declaration is applicable, for faith is the response of all who are conscious of their own weakness and accordingly look to God for strength. This principle is illustrated many times over in the records of Scripture. It is seen in Samson's last great exploit when out of weakness and in dependence on God he prayed for just one more accession of strength and was enabled to bring the temple of Dagon down upon the mocking assembly of Philistines (Judg. 16:23ff.). David's slaying of Goliath and Esther's courageous advocacy of her fellow Jews are other instances of the weak becoming strong through faith. The apostle Paul speaks of the same reality when he recounts how, denied release from the weakness of his own personal affliction, he was given the assurance by the Lord: "My grace is sufficient for you, for my strength is made perfect in weakness"; with the result that, now made aware that human weakness is precisely the opportunity for the manifestation of divine power, he declares: "I will the more gladly boast of my weaknesses, that the power of Christ may rest upon me. For the sake of Christ, then, I am content with weaknesses, insults, hardships, persecutions, and calamities; for when I am weak, then I am strong" (2 Cor. 12:8–10).

They *became mighty in war*. The words of the Psalmist provide the best commentary on this assertion, the truth of which is attested on many occasions in the history of Israel:

> They came upon me in the day of my calamity;
>   but the Lord was my stay.
> He brought me forth into a broad place;
>   he delivered me because he delighted in me.
> . . . .
> Yea, by thee I can crush a troop;
>   and by my God I can leap over a wall.
> . . . .
> He trains my hands for war,
>   so that my arms can bend a bow of bronze.
> Thou hast given me the shield of thy salvation,
>   and thy right hand supported me,
>   and thy help made me great.
> . . . .

> For thou didst gird me with strength for the battle;
>   thou didst make my assailants sink under me.
> . . . .
> The Lord lives; and blessed be my rock,
>   and exalted be the God of my salvation,
> . . . .
> who delivered me from my enemies;
>   yea, thou didst exalt me above my adversaries,
>   thou didst deliver me from men of violence.
>   (Ps. 18:18f., 29, 34f., 39, 46–48)

They *put foreign armies to flight*. This affirmation belongs closely with the preceding clause, and its truth is repeatedly shown in the history of the faithful judges and kings of Israel. But it may well be that our author, when writing that these champions of faith "became mighty in war" and "put foreign armies to flight," is moving on to a later period of the history of Israel and had particularly in mind the heroic deeds of the Maccabean resistance to the brutal tyranny of Antiochus Epiphanes, as narrated in the first two books of Maccabees. Some commentators, in fact (for example, Delitzsch), refer not only these two clauses but also the two that precede them to the Maccabean period; others (for example, Moffatt, F. F. Bruce) the last three clauses of the verse. The exploits recorded by our author are, as we have shown, for the most part widely applicable through the course of Israelite history; but if a general chronological progression is intended and the fourth and fifth clauses (which speak of stopping the mouths of lions and quenching raging fire) recall events described in the book of Daniel, it is not improbable that the heroism of the Maccabean resistance is in mind in some or all of the last four clauses.[98]

11:35, 36. *Women received their dead by resurrection. Some were tortured, refusing to accept release, that they might rise again to a better life. Others suffered mocking and scourging, and even chains and imprisonment.*

As the history of the Maccabees contains no account of *women* who *received their dead by resurrection*, though otherwise these verses are strongly reminiscent of the persecutions endured by the faithful Jews in that period, we may suppose that our author introduced this particular clause at this point in order to emphasize, by way of contrast, that those

---

98. The fact that the terms παρεμβολή and ἀλλότριοι, which our author uses here (παρεμβολὰς ἔκλιναν ἀλλοτρίων), are found in 1 Maccabees, the former frequently, is not in itself necessarily significant (*pace* Delitzsch and Moffatt) since their occurrence is also frequent in the canonical books of the Old Testament (LXX).

who did not receive back their dead by resurrection but had their hope fixed on a glorious future resurrection were no less impelled by faith than those who did. We have already seen that Abraham "considered that God was able to raise men even from the dead" (v. 19), and there are two occasions in the scriptural record on which women had their dead restored to life, namely, the raising up by the prayer of Elijah of the son of the widow of Zarephath (1 Ki. 17:17ff.) and the similar act of Elisha who brought back to life the son of the Shunammite woman (2 Ki. 4:8ff.).[99] It is of interest that even in the New Testament it is women for the most part, rather than men, whose dead are restored to life, as the widow of Nain had her son given back to her from death (Lk. 7:11ff.), Martha and Mary their brother Lazarus (Jn. 11:1ff.), and the widows of Joppa their friend Dorcas (Acts 9:36ff.).

But if the faith of God's people could boast of spectacular achievements in the form of famous military exploits, remarkable deliverances, and even the raising of the dead to life, it was no less triumphant in the willing endurance by others of barbarous tortures and cruel deaths. Accordingly, mention is now made of *some who were tortured, refusing to accept release, that they might rise again to a better life,* that is to say, that they might experience a resurrection better than a reprieve from death at the hand of their tormentors and in this sense the restoration to life which was offered them if they would deny their faith in God. One such hero of the faith in the Maccabean period was Eleazar, an aged scribe, who, refusing release at the cost of compromising his profession, "welcomed death with renown rather than life with pollution" and "of his own accord advanced to the instrument of torture" (2 Macc. 6:18ff.).[100] The account of Eleazar's death is followed by that of the martyrdom of seven brothers and their mother. The brutal tortures they chose to endure rather than renounce the truth and defile themselves by eating swine's flesh in order to gain their release included tearing out the tongue, scalping, mutilation, and frying over the flames (2 Macc. 7:4ff.), and the instruments used by their interrogators in the attempt to break the spirit of these and other indomitable martyrs were, the chronicler tells us, wheels, joint-dislocators, racks, bone-crushers, catapults, cauldrons, braziers, thumbscrews, iron claws, wedges, and branding irons

---

99. The language of 2 Kings 4:37 (LXX), ἔλαβεν τὸν υἱὸν αὐτῆς, and of the author of Hebrews, ἔλαβον ... τοὺς νεκροὺς αὐτῶν, is noticeably similar.

100. The instrument of torture in this case was the τύμπανον (tympanum or drum), which corresponds to the verb ἐτυμπανίσθησαν in verse 35 here, meaning, if used precisely, that some were tortured on or with the τύμπανον. This was probably a form of rack or wheel on which the victims were stretched and at the same time beaten until they died. Thus 2 Maccabees 6:30 speaks also of the blows which Eleazar received. The account of the same incident in 4 Maccabees mentions torture-wheels (τροχοί) as well as brutal scourging (5:32; 6:3ff.).

(4 Macc. 7:12). Their expectation of a better resurrection was expressed in the words uttered by one of the brothers: "The King of the universe will raise us up to an everlasting renewal of life, because we have died for his laws," and in the manner in which the mother exhorted her sons to suffer and die without flinching: "The Creator of the world, who shaped the beginning of man and devised the origin of all things, will in his mercy give life and breath back to you again" (2 Macc. 7:9, 23). So also the youngest brother, when his turn came to suffer and die, confidently testified to Antiochus the king that his brothers, now dead, "after enduring their brief pain, now drink of ever-flowing life, by virtue of God's covenant" (2 Macc. 7:36 JB).

Such dauntless fortitude, fed by an unquenchable flame of faith and hope, is incomprehensible to the man who lacks faith and who consequently has no hope of a better resurrection. This serene perspective is poetically portrayed in the words of another apocryphal writing, as follows:

> The souls of the righteous are in the hand of God,
> and no torment will ever touch them.
> In the eyes of the foolish they seemed to have died,
> and their departure was thought to be an affliction,
> and their going from us to be their destruction;
> but they are at peace.
> For though in the sight of men they were punished,
> their hope is full of immortality.
>
> (Wisdom of Solomon 3:1–4)

Those who took part in the Maccabean resistance could certainly claim a place among those *others* who *suffered mocking and scourging, and even chains and imprisonment;* but this has been the experience of God's faithful witnesses in every generation—apostles, prophets, martyrs, reformers, and innumerable disciples whose names, though unknown to men, are well known to God (2 Cor. 6:9). Thus, because he boldly declared the word of the Lord, Jeremiah was beaten and exposed to public obloquy in the stocks. "I have become a laughingstock all the day; every one mocks me," he cried. ". . . For the word of the Lord has become for me a reproach and derision all day long." Again, on a later occasion, he was falsely accused, beaten, and thrown into prison, and afterward lowered into the mud of an empty cistern, where he would have died had not Ebed-Melech the Ethiopian rescued him (Jer. 20:1ff., 7, 8; 37:13–15; 38:5ff.). Yet, intense though the suffering of God's faithful servants is, it is as nothing compared with the sufferings of the Savior of mankind who is the object of our faith, and who for our sakes "endured the cross, despising the shame" (12:2). In him the words were fulfilled of another prophet, who wrote: "He was despised and rejected by men; a man of sorrows, and acquainted with grief. . . . Surely he has borne our griefs and carried our sorrows. . . . He was wounded for our transgressions, he was bruised for our iniquities; . . . and the Lord has laid on him the iniquity of us all" (Isa. 53:3–6). He is our Master, and it is enough for the servant that he should be like his master (Mt. 10:25). The servant has the assurance, moreover, that if he endures he will also reign with his Master (2 Tim. 2:12).

11:37, 38. *They were stoned, they were sawn in two, they were killed with the sword; they went about in skins of sheep and goats, destitute, afflicted, ill-treated—of whom the world was not worthy—wandering over deserts and mountains and in dens and caves of the earth.*

In these verses the catalogue of the sufferings of God's faithful witnesses is continued. Christ himself lamented the fact that Jerusalem had killed the prophets and *stoned* the messengers sent by God (Mt. 23:21), and it is recorded that stoning was the fate of Zechariah, the priest who pronounced a dreadful judgment upon his compatriots for their wilful transgression of God's commandments: "Because you have forsaken the Lord, he has forsaken you" (2 Chr. 24:20f.; cf. Lk. 11:49–51). According to a widely accepted tradition, which a number of the patristic authors repeat, the prophet Jeremiah was stoned to death in Egypt by his fellow Jews.[101] The tradition that the prophet Isaiah suffered death by being *sawn in two* with a wooden saw is also found in the patristic writings,[102] as well as in the Talmudic books[103] and in the pseudepigraphic Jewish work *The Martyrdom of Isaiah* in which it is recounted that during this terrible ordeal "Isaiah neither cried aloud nor wept, but his lips spoke with the Holy Spirit until he was sawn in two."[104]

---

101. Tertullian, *Scorpiace* 8; Hippolytus, *De Christo et Antichristo* 31; Jerome, *Adversus Jovinianum* ii.37.
102. Justin Martyr, *Dialogue with Trypho* 120; Tertullian, *De Patientia* 14; *Scorpiace* 8; Origen, *Epistola ad Africanum* 9; Hippolytus, *De Christo et Antichristo* 30; Jerome, *In Isaiam* xv.57.
103. See, for example, *Yebamoth* 49b, *Sanhedrin* 103b.
104. In the Textus Receptus ἐπειράσθησαν, "they were tempted," is added between ἐπρίσθησαν, "they were sawn in two," and ἐν φόνῳ μαχαίρης ἀπέθανον, "they were killed with the sword," but this is rightly rejected as being weak and out of place in this context. Erasmus remarks on its incongruity and notices that there is no mention of it in Chrysostom and Theophylact; and he expresses his suspicion that it was added to the text from the marginal gloss of some pretentious meddler who felt that ἐπρίσθησαν should be changed to ἐπειράσθησαν. This is as good an explanation as any. Other possibilities are that it resulted from an attempt to adjust an early scribal repetition of ἐπρίσθησαν (dittography) or that it is a corruption of a more appropriate verb such as ἐπρήσθησαν, "they were

The remaining afflictions of God's people which receive mention here—their being *killed with the sword*, their having no better covering than the *skins of sheep and goats*, their being *destitute, afflicted, ill-treated*, their *wandering over deserts and mountains, and in dens and caves of the earth*—were experienced (and have continued to be experienced) by so many individuals and communities from one century to another that to point to specific instances is needless. The language is vividly descriptive of the savage indignities and severe hardships which men and women of faith have been willing to endure rather than deny the truth by which they have been liberated. It depicts, moreover, the fierce hatred of the unbelieving world in its guilty hostility to the truth as it ruthlessly hunts and assaults those whose trust is in the immutability of the divine promises. Rejecting the world they are ejected by the world. For their refusal to conform to this world's fallen standards the world attempts to eliminate them and their witness. But it is precisely these hunted heroes of the faith *of whom* (as our author declares in a resounding parenthesis) *the world was not worthy*. Their nobility and their integrity shine forth all the more brilliantly against the world's dark hatred; for in a world darkened and degraded by sin they truly are the light, and theirs is the true blessedness and the everlasting reward (Mt. 5:10–13). As those whose gaze is fixed on a better world they endure and by their faith they overcome, knowing as they do (and as the world refuses to know) that "the world passes away," but that "he who does the will of God abides for ever" (1 Jn. 2:17; 5:4).

With the present verses in mind, Ambrose wrote to the church of Vercellae as follows:

> They were found most strong when thought to be most weak, and they did not shrink from the mockings of men because they looked for heavenly rewards; they, on whom the beauty of eternal light was shining, did not dread the darkness of the dungeon. . . . Fed to the full by fasting, they did not seek to be diverted by pleasure; refreshed by the hope of eternal grace, the burning heat of summer did not parch them, nor did the cold of icy regions break their spirit; for the warm breath of devotion invigorated them; they did not fear the bonds of men, for Jesus had set them free; they did not desire to be rescued from death, for they looked forward to being raised to life by Christ.[105]

---

burned" (a reading which is found in one minuscule MS, but in association with ἐπειράσθησαν; cf. Philo, *Ad Flaccum* 20, where ἐνεπρήσθησαν is used of the persecutions of the Jews, also 2 Maccabees 6:11 and 7:4, where, however, different verbs are used), or, to mention another conjecture, ἐπηρώθησαν, "they were mutilated." It is certainly worthy of remark that ἐπειράσθησαν is not present in our earliest textual witness, the Chester Beatty papyrus p⁴⁶—information, of course, that was not available to Erasmus—as well as the Syriac Peshitta, the Sahidic Coptic, some Ethiopic MSS, some of the minuscule and lectionary readings, and in the citations of some of the patristic authors.

105. Ambrose, Letter LXIII.67, 69.

11:39, 40. *And all these, though well attested by their faith, did not receive what was promised, since God had foreseen something better for us, that apart from us they should not be made perfect.*

All these, that is, the whole succession of men and women of faith, named and unnamed, who witnessed and endured in the centuries leading up to the coming of Christ, persons *well attested by their faith* in that their faith, so far from being extinguished, was constant and prevailed in the face of the severest testing and opposition and thus declared the genuineness of their profession—all these *did not receive what was promised;* for though they received and set their hope on the divinely given promises, yet during their earthly pilgrimage they did not see the glorious fulfilment of those promises, since it was in Christ that they were to be brought to reality (2 Cor. 1:20). But, having seen, with the penetrating eye of faith, and greeted the fulfilment from afar, they lived in faith and they died in faith (see vv. 13ff., 21, 22 above, and cf. Jn. 8:56). "If those on whom the great light of grace had not yet shone showed such surpassing constancy in bearing their ills, what effect ought the full glory of the gospel to have on us?" asks Calvin. "A tiny spark of light led them to heaven, but now that the Sun of righteousness shines on us what excuse shall we offer if we still cling to the earth?"

There is no suggestion that these believers of the pre-Christian era were in any sense barred from the full enjoyment of the promised reality. Quite the contrary, for when our author asserts that *God,* who cannot fail to perform what he has promised, *had foreseen something better for us*—or, as the NEB has more effectively rendered the Greek, "with us in mind, God had made a better plan"—he immediately explains this as meaning *that apart from us they should not be made perfect,* "us" being the believers of the Christian era. It is not that God had one plan for them and another for us, for in anticipation and faith they looked forward to the introduction of this better plan which would involve a High Priest superior to those of the levitical order (7:7), a sacrifice superior to that of bulls and goats (9:23), a covenant superior to that of the Mosaic dispensation (7:22), and a country superior to any earthly territory (11:16). As Owen observes, "God's prevision is his provision," and so it was graciously ordained that they should experience the substantiation of their hope not in separation from but in union with us. This plan was put into operation by the coming of Christ and the performance of his perfect work of atonement. The apostle Paul is speaking of the same thing when he writes of "the mystery of God's will, according to his purpose which he set forth in Christ as a plan for the fulness of time, to unite all things in him, things in heaven and things on earth" (Eph. 1:9f.).

Accordingly, the Old Testament believers do indeed attain the promised perfection, but not apart from us. They with us belong to the many sons who, thanks to the pioneer of our (and their) salvation, are brought to glory. Nor is their perfection attributable, any more than ours, to their own suffering but solely to the suffering of Christ for us all, whereby all who are designated his brethren are sanctified, that is, made perfect before God (Heb. 2:9–11, 14f.). This perfection, to quote Moffatt, "is entirely wrought out through Christ, and wrought out for all. It covers all God's people, for now the Promise has been fulfilled to these earlier saints." Our author's teaching here, then, clearly implies the continuity and the unity, in Christ, of all believers of both Old and New Testaments.

Ours is therefore the era of fulfilment. And yet it is still an era of faith. That is one of the main emphases of this epistle. The faith of those who belonged to the former era is set before us as an example to emulate. For the Christian era is compounded of both the "now" and the "not yet" of fulfilment. God has indeed achieved every purpose of blessing in the mediatorial work of his Son and our High Priest Jesus Christ. In him the blessings of the new covenant are a reality here and now. With him the believer is raised to newness of life and experiences the exaltation of heavenly bliss (Eph. 2:6; Col. 3:1ff.). At the cross our redemption has been accomplished once for all. But there is still an interval between this fulfilment and the final consummation. We still await the renewal of all creation, the redemption of our bodies (Rom. 8:21–25), the swallowing up of what is mortal by life (2 Cor. 5:1–4; 1 Cor. 15:42ff.), the disclosure of the new heaven and the new earth in which righteousness is unchallenged (2 Pet. 3:13; Rev. 21:1–5). And so, in our pilgrimage through this still groaning world (Rom. 8:22f.), it is inevitable that we too should endure suffering and hardship and required that we too should overcome by faith, our gaze fixed intently on him who is the goal and prize of our ultimate and eternal perfection. This is precisely the lesson which our author is now about to press home: as in faith we persevere and endure, our inspiration, to a degree far surpassing that of the heroic witnesses of old, is preeminently Jesus himself, who was known to the former believers only by expectation but is known to us in fulfilment (12:1ff.) Our greater privilege is also our greater responsibility.

The following lines from one of Bishop Christopher Wordsworth's hymns fittingly draw together the thoughts which constitute the theme of this great chapter:

> Hark the sound of holy voices, chanting at the crystal sea
> Hallelujah! Hallelujah! Hallelujah! Lord to thee.

Multitude, which none can number, like the stars, in glory stands
Clothed in white apparel, holding palms of victory in their hands.

Patriarch, and holy prophet, who prepared the way of Christ,
King, apostle, saint, confessor, martyr, and evangelist,
Saintly maiden, godly matron, widows who have watched to prayer,
Joined in holy concert, singing to the Lord of all, are there.

They have come from tribulation, and have washed their robes in blood,
Washed them in the blood of Jesus; tried they were, and firm they stood;
Mocked, imprisoned, stoned, tormented, sawn asunder, slain with sword,
They have conquered death and Satan, by the might of Christ the Lord.

Now they reign in heavenly glory, now they walk in golden light,
Now they drink, as from a river, holy bliss, yea infinite;
Love and peace they taste for ever; and all truth and knowledge see
In the beatific vision of the blessed Trinity!

God of God, the One-begotten, Light of light, Emmanuel,
In whose body joined together all the saints for ever dwell,
Pour upon us of thy fulness, that we may for evermore
God the Father, God the Son, and God the Holy Ghost adore!

12:1. *Therefore, since we are surrounded by so great a cloud of witnesses, let us also lay aside every weight, and sin which clings so closely, and let us run with perseverance the race that is set before us.*

Our author now applies to his readers, with whom he, like a wise and loving pastor, associates himself (*Therefore... let us*), the lesson which is to be learned from the example set by those whose faith triumphantly prevailed over every testing circumstance of life and death during the centuries prior to the advent of Christ. In doing this he effectively uses the dramatic imagery of an athletic contest in which the competitors down in the arena are surrounded by the crowded tiers of an amphitheatre. The analogy, which was natural enough in an empire where athletic games provided an entertaining spectacle for the populace in many different cities, is found in the classical literature of Greece and, at the time of our epistle, in Philo who says, somewhat anachronistically, of Abraham that, "taking the good runners as his example," he finished the race of life without stumbling and was rewarded with crowns and prizes.[106] Another contemporary writing speaks of the Maccabean heroes Eleazar and the seven brothers and their mother (see above, pp. 512f.) as having "hastened to death by torture as if running on the track to immortality" (4 Macc. 14:5), their

106. Philo, *De Migratione Abrahami* 133.

virtue and endurance gaining for them the imperishable prize of ever-lasting life, with "the tyrant as their adversary and the world and the life of men as the spectators" (4 Macc. 17:11ff.). The analogy clearly had a strong appeal to the apostle Paul, who frequently depicts the Christian as an athlete, self-disciplined and concentrated, as he strives to gain a glorious and unfading crown (see 1 Cor. 9:24–27; Gal. 2:2; Phil. 1:29f.; 2:16; Col. 1:29; 2:1; 1 Tim. 6:12; 2:5; Acts 20:24; cf. 2 Cor. 10:13ff.), and who, as he himself faces the ordeal of his own martyrdom in the world's arena, movingly testifies: "I have fought the good fight, I have finished the race, I have kept the faith. Henceforth there is laid up for me the crown of righteousness, which the Lord, the righteous judge, will award to me on that Day, and not only to me but also to all who have loved his appearing" (2 Tim. 4:6–8).

Thus our author pictures himself and his readers as competitors who, as they contend for the faith in the arena of life, are *surrounded by so great a cloud of witnesses,* namely, those champions of faith and persever-ance of earlier generations, crowded as it were row upon row within the encircling amphitheatre. If these are witnesses in the sense of spec-tators, as the imagery implies, it is even more important to understand that they are witnesses in the sense of those who have proved them-selves to be unflinching professors of the faith and have overcome by the word of their testimony (see Rev. 12:11). They are "the glorious com-pany of martyrs,"[107] faithful in their witness both in life and even unto death. (Though the term *martyr* does not in the New Testament have the particular meaning of one who has sealed his witness with his blood that it later came to have, many of those in this cloud of witnesses were, as we have noticed above, martyrs in this later sense.)[108] They have trium-phantly completed their course, and we who are now contestants in the arena should be inspired by their example to give of our utmost in the struggle. Like them we *also* must be prepared to *lay aside every weight,* that is, everything that would hinder us and hold us back ("every en-cumbrance," NEB). As the athlete whose name is entered for the games strips for action, both by the removal of superfluous flesh through rigor-ous training[109] and by the removal of all unnecessary garments and

---

107. Μάρτυρες ("martyrs") is the Greek noun for "witnesses." In itself it does not mean spectators (θεαταί): any such implication is derived from the idea of a surrounding com-pany in an amphitheatre.
108. Moffatt judges, from the context, that "μάρτυς is already, as in Rev. 2^{13} etc., begin-ning to shade off into the red sense of 'martyr,'" and F. F. Bruce concurs, saying that "this is one of the early examples of the beginning of the semantic change by which the ordinary Greek word for 'witness' acquired its distinctive Christian sense of 'martyr.'"
109. Ὄγκος, found only here in biblical Greek, means properly "bulk" or "mass" and could be used to denote excessive bodily weight. It also came to be used in the sense of "pride," which it is given here in the Sahidic Coptic version and by Bengel. But such a

adornments at the time of the contest itself (the Greek custom in fact required the competitors to be stripped naked), so the Christian should discipline himself (1 Cor. 9:25, 27) and shun every excess which would hamper or incapacitate him as a participant in the greatest of all contests.

More specifically, the Christian contestant needs to divest himself of *sin which clings so closely*, an expression which seems best understood as a clarification of what is meant by the weight or encumbrance of every kind which must be laid aside.[110] It is precisely sin, of whatever kind, that impedes or slows down the Christian in the spiritual race, and conversely, anything, however innocent in itself, which impedes or slows down the Christian in the spiritual race is for that reason sinful and must, with God's help, be discarded. Indeed, self-discipline is itself an integral part of the daily spiritual contest, for "the desires of the flesh are against the Spirit, and the desires of the Spirit are against the flesh"; the two are "opposed to each other, to prevent you from doing what you would," and only through "living by the Spirit" will this conflict be won (Gal. 5:16–25; cf. Rom. 7:14–25).[111]

The unencumbered Christian is the one who is fit and ready to *run the race that is set before us* and to do so *with perseverance*. One of the chief problems with the Hebrew Christians to whom this letter is addressed is that they have set out on the race but, after a good start (10:32–34), are now slackening in the will to persevere: their effort is decreasing (2:1), sin is holding them back (3:17–4:1), they need to recover their intensity

---

special sense is inappropriate, since our author speaks of *every* (= every kind of) weight, that is, any and every encumbrance by which one might be weighed down. Philo uses the term in a manner which reflects the presuppositions of hellenistic dualism when, also within the framework of an athletic similitude, he speaks of the weight of the body (σωματικὸς ὄγκος) as a hindrance in the contest for the winning of virtue and the ascent to higher things (*Quod Deterius Potiori Insidiari Soleat* 27. N.B. also *De Legibus Allegoricis* iii.47).
110. So Delitzsch: " . . . we may interpret εὐπερίστατον ἁμαρτίαν here as more precisely defining the vague ὄγκον πάντα"; also Teodorico: "le due espressioni ne formano, in effetto, una sola, complessa."
111. Note should be taken of the variant reading εὐπερίσπαστος, with the sense probably of "easily distracting," which is found instead of εὐπερίστατος in p⁴⁶, one minuscule (1739), and possibly some Old Latin witnesses. Zuntz (*The Text of the Epistles*, pp. 25–29) argues for its authenticity, contending that "the meanings which can be attached to the rival reading are so far inferior to this as to make it justifiable, nay necessary, to regard the reading of p⁴⁶ as original." The p⁴⁶ reading is reflected in the alternative rendering of the NEB mg, "the sin which all too readily distracts us." However, if this reading is both original and so clearly superior it is astonishing that it has virtually disappeared from sight. Moulton and Milligan find support, *via* Deissmann (*Bible Studies*, p. 150), for Theophylact's explanation of εὐπερίστατος as meaning here "because of which one easily falls into distresses." The commonly accepted sense, however, is still the best, as it is given, for example, by Erasmus: "εὐπερίστατον, id est, quod facile circumsistat, et haereat atque amplectatur, quasi nolens abjici." The unfamiliarity of the adjective has given rise to various other proposals for its interpretation which do not require discussion here. We may at least assume that the term was readily comprehensible to the recipients of this letter. It is hardly likely that, as Spicq supposes, the adjective was coined by our author.

of purpose (4:11), to shake off the sluggish mood into which they have fallen (6:11f.), to regain their confidence (10:35, 39) and their competitive spirit (12:12). The consideration that they are performing, as it were, in the presence and with the example of the veterans of the faith who courageously bore testimony in the centuries leading up to Christ's advent should remind them that they are engaging in a contest of the utmost seriousness and that their goal belongs not to the realm of time but of eternity. But there is Someone Else, infinitely more illustrious, who has run this race before them and on whom above all others their gaze should constantly be fixed, so that by the grace that flows from him they may be strong to persevere and to prevail. It is to him that the writer of our epistle now directs his readers' attention. With this passage in mind (though actually preaching on 8:13) Chrysostom exhorts his audience as follows:

> Many of you have many times been spectators at the Olympic games, and not only spectators but also enthusiastic partisans and admirers of the competitors. You know then that both during the days of the contests and also all night long the herald thinks of nothing else and has no other care than that the combatant should not disgrace himself when he goes forth.... If therefore he who is about to engage in a contest before men uses such great forethought, much more will it befit us to be continually thoughtful and earnest, since our whole life is a contest. Let every night then be a night of devotion, and let us be careful that when we go out in the day we do not make ourselves ridiculous. And would that it were only making ourselves ridiculous. But the Judge of the contest is seated at the right hand of the Father, diligently hearkening lest we utter any false note, anything out of tune. For he is not the Judge of actions only, but of words also. Let us watch through the night, beloved: we also have those who are eager for our success if we are willing.... Therefore I exhort you: let us lay aside all things and look to One only, as we strive to obtain the prize and to be crowned with the chaplet. Let us do all that will enable us to attain to the promised blessings. May we all attain them in Christ Jesus our Lord, to whom with the Father and the Holy Spirit be glory, might, and honour now and for ever and world without end. Amen.

12:2. *Looking to Jesus the pioneer and perfecter of our faith, who for the joy that was set before him endured the cross, despising the shame, and is seated at the right hand of the throne of God.*

As the athlete concentrates all his energies on winning the victor's prize, so the participant in the Christian race is urged not only to divest himself of every encumbrance and to compete with unflagging determination but also to do this *looking to Jesus,* that is, like Stephen in the hour of his martyrdom (Acts 7:55f.), to be so totally involved that, with singleness of purpose and undistracted by all that is going on around him, his gaze is firmly fixed on him who is both the goal and the prize.[112] Thus the apostle Paul could testify that he had suffered the loss of all things which this world counts dear, regarding them as refuse, in order that he might win Christ (Phil. 3:8). This same intensity of purpose was characteristic of the victors of faith who had competed prior to Christ's coming. Moses, for example, as we have been reminded (11:26f.), considered the agonies of the race greater wealth than the treasures of Egypt precisely because he looked away from present sufferings and fixed his attention on[113] him who is the reward, for "he endured as seeing him who is invisible."

Further, as this is the race of faith, what could be more necessary than to keep constantly before our eyes him who is *the pioneer and perfecter of our faith?* Apart from him in whom all the promises of God find their fulfilment fallen mankind would have neither ground nor object of faith. It is on him, as we have seen, that in every age the gaze of faith is focused. He alone evokes and stimulates faith; and it is because he is the pioneer of our salvation (Heb. 2:10) that he is the author of our faith. Our faith, moreover, is initiated and sustained by him because he has prayed the Father that we may come to faith (Jn. 17:20f.) and that our faith may not fail (Lk. 22:31f.). Thus we look to him as "the apostle and high priest of our confession" (Heb. 3:1), and we have the assurance that he who has begun a good work in us will bring it to completion (Phil. 1:6).

But, in addition to all this, the incarnate Son is himself the man of faith *par excellence,* and this seems to be the primary sense intended by the Greek original of the expression, which reads literally, "the pioneer and perfecter of faith,"[114] faith, that is, absolutely and without qualification. His whole earthly life is the very embodiment of trust in God (Heb. 2:13). It is marked from start to finish by total dependence on the Father and complete attunement to his will (10:7–10). His faith expresses itself, necessarily, in prayer (5:7; Jn. 17; Mk. 1:35, etc.), and is completely victorious as, surmounting all temptations and afflictions, he is made perfect through suffering (Heb. 2:10; 4:15),[115] thus becoming "the source

112. Ἀφορῶντες, "looking away from," εἰς Ἰησοῦν, "looking to, focusing attention on, Jesus," and, as the present participle indicates, doing so, "not only at the first moment, but constantly during the whole struggle" (Westcott). Similar language is used of the scribe Eleazar and of the mother and her seven sons (see the commentary on 11:35 above) who, looking away from their immediate afflictions and keeping their gaze fixed on God—εἰς θεὸν ἀφορῶντες—willingly endured torture and death (4 Macc. 17:9f.).
113. Ἀπέβλεπεν εἰς in 11:26 corresponds exactly to ἀφορῶντες εἰς here. Thus Moffatt observes that "ἀφορᾶν implies the same concentrated attention as ἀποβλέπειν: 'with no eyes for any one or anything except Jesus.'"
114. Τὸν τῆς πίστεως ἀρχηγὸν καὶ τελειωτήν.
115. In 2:10 ἀρχηγός is associated with the verb τελειῶσαι; here, comparably, with the noun τελειωτής. Though this noun is not found elsewhere, except in later Christian writers, it is not necessary to conclude, with Moffatt, that the term was coined by our

of eternal salvation to all who obey him" (5:8f.). In looking to Jesus, then, we are looking to him who is the supreme exponent of faith, the one who, beyond all others, not only set out on the course of faith but also pursued it without wavering to the end. He, accordingly, is uniquely qualified to be the supplier and sustainer of the faith of his followers. But the faith of all others, patriarchs, apostles, and martyrs though they may be, is marred by sin and imperfection. Of none of them can it be said that he is the pioneer and perfecter of faith. Their lives are indeed stirring illustrations of the wonderful power of faith (ch. 11); but the one above all others on whom the Christian athlete's attention must incessantly be concentrated is Jesus, our only Mediator, who is not ashamed to call us brethren (2:11) and who, when our faith is being tested, not only shines as an example for us to follow but also supplies the grace for us to do so, and in doing so to overcome (2:17f.; 4:15f.).

We should consider, too, the utter loneliness of Jesus on his earthly course. We run together, he ran alone; for he came to do what no one else was competent to achieve. His course led him to the terrible forsakenness of the cross, whereas we run toward the prize of everlasting salvation and glory which he won for us through his death on the cross. But he too, in his unique and solitary struggle, had a goal on which his attention was inflexibly fixed, namely, *the joy that was set before him*,[116] the joy, that is, of completing the work of reconciliation he had come to perform for our eternal benefit and to the glory of the Father's name (cf. Jn. 12:28), thus bringing to fruition all the purposes of God's creation and all the promises of his covenant. His joy, which is indeed the fulness of joy (Ps. 16:11), is the joy also of his elect; for it is his will that his own joy should dwell in them so that their joy, like his, may be full, and it was his prayer that they might have his joy fulfilled in themselves (Jn. 15:11; 17:13). His joy is the joy of heaven over every sinner who repents and returns to the Father's home, over every lost sheep that is found, over every son that was dead and is alive again (Lk. 15:6f., 24, 32).

It was *for*, that is, "for the sake of" (NEB),[117] this joy with which his

---

author. The virtual interchangeability of the concepts of faith and obedience in our epistle has already been remarked, and this applies equally to the incarnate Son (cf. 3:18f., where "those who were disobedient" are the ones who "were unable to enter in because of unbelief").

116. Ἡ προκειμένη αὐτῷ χαρά: this is still the terminology of the athletic contests. In verse 1 ὁ προκείμενος ἡμῖν ἀγών is the race itself that lies before us, while here it is the conclusion of the race with its joy of victory and achievement that lies before Jesus, as the finish line and crowning ceremony lie ahead of the athlete.

117. Ἀντί. Some have wished to take this preposition in the substitutionary sense of "instead of," thus giving the meaning: "instead of the joy that was set before him he endured the cross"—a rendering that is reflected in the Syriac Peshitta and in the NEB mg. Cyril of Alexandria, for example, explains that, though the Son was free to enjoy the dignity and glory of his divine nature, yet he exchanged this for the humiliation of the

victory was to be crowned that Jesus *endured the cross*—a statement which confirms that in our author's mind the death of Christ on the cross was absolutely central in the purpose of his coming to earth, or, in other words, that Calvary is the explanation of Bethlehem. The road to the joy ahead was the way of the cross. The incarnate Son, accordingly, set his face to go to Jerusalem, knowing full well that this meant arrest, false accusation, and unjust condemnation, and the extremes of suffering and death, but also thereby and thereafter resurrection, exaltation, and joy (Mk. 8:31; 9:12, 31; 10:33f.; Lk. 9:22, 44; 17:25; 18:31ff.).

The implication of what is said here is, as Chrysostom observes, that "it was in his power, if he so willed, not to suffer at all" (cf. Jn. 10:17f.), with the following corollary for us who profess to be his followers: "If then he who was under no necessity of being crucified was crucified for our sake, how much more is it right that we should endure all things courageously!" Moreover, his determination to endure the cross meant *despising the shame*, since nothing more disgraceful could happen to any man than to suffer public crucifixion, a fate designed for the basest of criminals and the lowest of social outcasts. There was no lower depth of ignominy or humiliation. It was indeed a punishment so degrading that no Roman citizen might be subjected to it. Cicero's most damning charge against Gaius Verres, the notorious governor of Sicily, was that he had actually dared to crucify a man who claimed to be a Roman citizen and who had never previously even set eyes on an object so accursed as a cross, and that the victim's protestations had failed to make Verres hesitate or delay before inflicting this "most brutal and horrifying torture."[118] The cross assures us that Christ, in suffering, the

---

incarnation (Migne, PG, LXXIV, 993). This interpretation is clearly related to what Paul says in Philippians 2:6ff. It has the support of Gregory of Nazianzus and, among the moderns, Wettstein, Von Soden, Goodspeed, and Delitzsch. The last named in fact connects it explicitly with Philippians 2:6, as follows: "This προκειμένη χαρά is the same thing as that of which the apostle speaks at Phil. ii.6 (ἴσα εἶναι τῷ θεῷ) as the being in a like condition to God. . . . here he willingly endures a cross of shame in order to obtain the dignity of divine co-session as the promised reward." There is much, however, that is unsatisfactory about this interpretation, especially the awkward notion that instead of glory he sought glory, albeit by way of suffering. Chrysostom (Migne, PG, LXIII, 193) and Theophylact (Migne, PG, CXXV, 369) take the expression to mean that instead of living a life free from suffering, as was the right of one free from all sin, Christ chose the cross and its shame. Somewhat similarly, Calvin comments that instead of every kind of enjoyment of which he could have availed himself had he so pleased, Christ preferred to suffer. Aquinas explains the expression with reference to John 6:15: "The joy referred to was that earthly joy for which he was sought by the crowd he had fed in order that they might make him king, but for which he showed his contempt by withdrawing to the mountain." But the context is much better served by understanding ἀντί here to mean "for the sake of," "because of," which is not only a good classical sense (Sophocles, Plato, Aristotle) but also the sense of the preposition in some other passages of the New Testament (for example, Eph. 5:31; Mt. 17:27). It may also be the sense in verse 16 of the present chapter, where Esau is said to have sold his birthright ἀντί—either "for the sake of" or "in exchange for"—a single meal.

118. Cicero, *Contra Verrem* II.v.62–64: "crudelissimi taeterrimique supplicii."

Righteous for the unrighteous (1 Pet. 3:18), plumbed the furthest depths of human shame and that, consequently, there is no person, however debased by sin and guilt, who is beyond the reach of his pardon and grace. Paul, himself a Roman citizen, had to learn not to be ashamed of the gospel of a crucified Savior, a gospel against which he had at first poured forth the full fury of his persecuting and blasphemous zeal (Acts 8:3; 9:1; 1 Tim. 1:13); for he discovered, thanks to the grace of God, that the message of the cross, foolishness though it is to those who are perishing, is the power of God unto salvation to all who believe (Rom. 1:16; 1 Cor. 1:18, 24; 1 Tim. 1:14f.). Hence his determination, as a messenger of the gospel, to know nothing except "Jesus Christ and him crucified" (1 Cor. 2:2; NEB, "Jesus Christ—Christ nailed to the cross").

It is important to recognize that the shame of the cross, where Christ bore the sins of the world, is something infinitely more intense than the pain of the cross. Others have suffered the pain of crucifixion, but he alone has endured the shame of human depravity in all its foulness and degradation.

But the cross is the gateway to joy, his joy and ours; for Jesus, who endured the cross, despising its shame, *is now seated at the right hand of the throne of God.* (On the significance of such language see the commentary above on 1:3.) The theme recurs throughout our epistle (1:3; 2:9; 4:14; 5:5, 8f.; 6:19f.; 7:26; 8:1; 9:12, 24, 28; 10:12; 13:20), and has momentous consequences for the believer who, while sharing in "the fellowship of Christ's sufferings," is always in association with the experience of "the power of his resurrection" (Phil. 3:10), and is one with his Redeemer also in his exaltation to glory (Eph. 2:6; Col. 3:1ff.). Sealed with the promised Holy Spirit, we have "the guarantee of our inheritance until we acquire possession of it" (Eph. 1:13f.) and the constant assurance that "if we endure, we shall also reign with him" who is enthroned on high (2 Tim. 2:12).

12:3, 4. *Consider him who endured from sinners such hostility against himself, so that you may not grow weary or fainthearted. In your struggle against sin you have not yet resisted to the point of shedding your blood.*

It is a matter of concern to our author that the Hebrew Christians whom he is addressing are now, after an enthusiastic start, showing signs of growing *weary* and *fainthearted.* The mental picture is still that of the race track. Their perseverance is faltering. Some, it may well be, feel the allurement of withdrawal from the world and its antipathy and of a more "respectable" judaizing theology which would ease the pressure of hardship suffered for Christ's sake, after the pattern of the Qumran community. Some are even tempted to give up the struggle altogether (cf. 2:1; 3:12, 14; 4:1, 11, 16; 6:4–6, 11; 10:23, 26ff., 35f., 39); but to do so would demonstrate that they are not of the true line of those who by faith surmount every opposition and victoriously endure to the end (ch. 11). More seriously still, it means that they are taking their eyes off Jesus (v. 2), who is supremely their source of strength and inspiration and who is waiting to welcome them at the end of the course with a crown of righteousness (2 Tim. 4:7f.). They are urged, accordingly, to *consider him*—that is, to make a careful reckoning by comparing[119] him and the extremity of his suffering with themselves and the limited extent of their suffering—*who endured,* and to whose unfaltering endurance they owe their eternal salvation,[120] *from sinners,* rejecters of Christ and his redemption and therefore rejecters of those who profess to be his followers and witnesses, *such hostility*[121] *against himself,*[122] the hostility, namely, which reached its climax in the cross (v. 2), where all the forces of evil were concentrated in an attempt to destroy him who is the Holy and Righteous One and the Author of life (Acts 3:14f.; cf. 4:27).

The reminder is now gently added that their experience of affliction has in fact been lighter also than that of so many other contestants, both

---

119. Ἀναλογίσασθε, "reckon up."

120. The perfect participle ὑπομεμενηκότα suggests the abiding effect of Christ's redemptive suffering.

121. Ἀντιλογία, which by etymology has the sense of "speaking against," has a much broader sense here, as the RSV, "hostility," and the NEB and JB, "opposition," recognize. The KJV, "contradiction" (cf. Vg, "contradictio"), and Phillips, "all that sinful men could say against him" reflect the etymology but are inappropriate for the context: what Christ endured was far more than words, though he was indeed subjected to much contrary speaking and reviling. The concentrated hostility of evil, which is summed up in the single term "the cross," with all the suffering, spiritual and physical, that this implied for Christ, is intended here. Cf. John 19:12, "every one who makes himself a king sets himself against (ἀντιλέγει) Caesar," where ἀντιλέγει clearly means much more than "speaks against."

122. Our version (RSV) reflects the reading εἰς ἑαυτόν, "against himself," as attested in Codex Alexandrinus and many later MSS, including the Textus Receptus. The attestation of the alternative reading εἰς ἑαυτούς (or αὑτούς), "against themselves," is much more impressive and includes the following early witnesses: p⁴⁶ p¹³ ℵ D*ᵍʳ Origen. Indeed, on the external evidence there could be little question about accepting the latter reading. But it fits ill with the internal requirements of the context. As Zuntz says, "the singular is the only imaginable reading that fits the context" (*op. cit.,* p. 120); so also F. F. Bruce: "εἰς ἑαυτόν yields the only tolerable sense in the context." Westcott, who accepts the plural, εἰς ἑαυτούς, suggests a parallel usage in Numbers 16:38, and others, including Spicq, have added Proverbs 8:36 and a few other texts from the Old Testament and Philo. But it is difficult to see how these passages provide a true parallel. In any case, if the meaning had been, "Consider him who endured such hostility from those who sinned against themselves," a participial expression, ὑπὸ τῶν ἁμαρτησάντων εἰς ἑαυτούς, would have been expected, rather than ὑπὸ τῶν ἁμαρτωλῶν εἰς ἑαυτούς. "Besides," to quote Bruce again, "the phrase εἰς ἑαυτούς or εἰς ἑαυτόν is placed here in the attributive position and therefore is to be taken closely with ἀντιλογίαν." It seems right to conclude, therefore, that the plural reading ἑαυτούς represents an early corruption of the text (Moffatt, Zuntz, *et al.*).

past and present, for *in the struggle against sin* (the metaphor is still that of the athletic contests, but now shifts from the race track to the boxing ring,[123] with sin personified as the opponent) they *have not yet resisted to the point of shedding* their *blood*. In the days following their reception of the gospel, as we have seen (10:32–34), they had "endured a hard struggle with sufferings," involving public abuse, the plundering of their property, and imprisonment for some, but so far they have not been tested with the challenge of laying down their lives for the faith they profess (which is the implication of the shedding of blood mentioned here). This suggests a striking contrast between such affliction as they had passed through and the manner in which Christ came with the express purpose of shedding his blood on the cross for their redemption. It is true, of course, that the sufferings of Christ's followers, however severe they may be, are always incomparably slight when weighed against the sufferings of the Master himself. But the point here seems to be that these Hebrew Christians are now shrinking back, and even thinking of abandoning the race, as the possibility of further and perhaps more painful persecution presents itself. Well do they know that their consciences have been purified from dead works and their eternal redemption procured by the shedding of the blood of Jesus (9:12, 14; cf. 10:29): how willingly, then, should they be prepared to persevere and to suffer, even to the point of shedding their lifeblood, in gratitude to him who gave his all for them and in loyalty to so wonderful a gospel! The contest continues and the sabbath rest for the people of God is not now but hereafter (3:9f.). "There is no reason for us to seek our discharge from the Lord, whatever service we have performed," says Calvin, "because Christ does not have any discharged soldiers except those who have conquered death itself."

12:5–8. *And have you forgotten the exhortation which addresses you as sons?—"My son, do not regard lightly the discipline of the Lord, nor lose courage when you are punished by him. For the Lord disciplines him whom he loves, and chastises every son whom he receives." It is for discipline that you have to endure. God is treating you as sons; for what son is there whom his father does not discipline? If you are left without discipline, in which all have participated, then you are illegitimate children and not sons.*

The discouragement of the recipients of this letter is attributable, at least in part, to a false reading of the situation in which they find them-

123. For a similar shift see 1 Corinthians 9:24–26: "I do not run aimlessly, I do not box as one beating the air." Contestants in the pentathlon engaged in five different competitions.

selves. Such hardship and affliction as they have had to endure in consequence of their Christian profession does not mean, as some seem to
have assumed, that God is unconcerned for their welfare and has left
them without his aid and support. On the contrary, as they have already
been assured more than once, he is constantly at hand and his gracious
help is ever available to them (2:18; 4:15f.; 7:25; 10:19ff.). And there is
another consideration which they have *forgotten*, or are in danger of
forgetting, namely, that anything they suffer for the gospel should encourage them to recognize that God, so far from neglecting them, is
showing himself to be a true Father to them by treating them as truly his
sons. They are referred to *the exhortation* in the book of Proverbs (3:11f.)
which addresses you as sons. As Westcott says, "the utterance of Scripture
is treated as the voice of God conversing with men," and, we may add,
conversing with men in every age—hence its relevance and applicability
to the situation our author is addressing. The reality of the filial relationship of which this exhortation speaks is attested specifically by the experience of *discipline*, for discipline is the mark not of a harsh and heart-
less father but of a father who is deeply and lovingly concerned for the
well-being of his son. Indeed, paternal love and discipline belong together; and if this is true of earthly fathers (*for what son is there whom his
father does not discipline?*), how much more is it true of him who is our
Heavenly Father (cf. Mt. 7:11)! "See," exclaims Chrysostom, "it is those
very things in which they suppose they have been deserted by God that
should make them confident that they have not been deserted." Thus, if
only they will heed this important truth, that *the Lord disciplines him
whom he loves,* they will *not regard lightly the discipline of the Lord,* nor will
they *lose courage* when the going is hard and painful, but rather take
courage and press on in the Christian contest. The hostility of ungodly
men is always difficult to endure, but it is overruled and turned to our
advantage by God and it should be accepted, even gratefully, as chastisement from the hand of the Heavenly Father intended for the correction
and benefit of those whom he receives as sons.

It is *for*, or with a view to, *discipline*, then, that they are called upon
to *endure* afflictions; and so whenever their testimony meets with the
response of persecution they should have this assurance ringing in their
ears: *God is treating you as sons!*[124] On the other hand, if they are *left
without discipline*, then, since discipline is the common experience of
sons (*in which all*—that is, all who are sons by reason of faith, as ch. 11
illustrates—*have participated*), by the same logic they have cause to regard

---

124. Spicq observes that even the etymology of παιδεία, "discipline," points to this truth,
since the term derives from παῖς, "child" or "son," and means, strictly, the rearing or
training of a child. "Sonship and fatherly discipline are correlative," he writes. Whether our
author had this association in mind is, however, another question—probably not, seeing
that the noun he uses for "son" is υἱός, not παῖς.

themselves as *illegitimate children*, bastards who do not truly belong to the family with its privileges, or, to use the language of verse 23 below, who are excluded from "the assembly of the first-born enrolled in heaven."[125] This same principle is insisted on in another passage from Proverbs: "He who spares the rod hates his son, but he who loves him is diligent to discipline him" (Prov. 13:24; cf. 22:15; 23:13ff.);[126] and the exhortation of the writer of 2 Maccabees is very much to the point when he beseeches his readers not to be discouraged by the calamities he is relating, "but to reflect that our people were being punished by way of chastening and not for their destruction" (2 Macc. 6:12).

Discipline, indeed, as the Latin *disciplina* implies, is a process of learning or schooling, and in every generation there are believers who pass through the school of suffering and who in doing so find blessing and learn to rejoice, as, like gold, they are tested and refined in the fiery ordeal. "Rejoice in so far as you share Christ's sufferings," Peter writes, "that you may also rejoice and be glad when his glory is revealed. If you are reproached for the name of Christ, you are blessed, because the spirit of glory and of God rests upon you" (1 Pet. 4:12–14). The triumphant joy of those who are brought into this school is well exemplified by the spirit in which five young students, imprisoned in Lyon in 1552 and shortly to suffer martyrdom, write to the church in Geneva: "We testify that this is the true school of the children of God in which they learn more than the disciples of the philosophers ever did in their universities," they say, and they praise God for giving them by his grace "not only the theory of his Word but also the practice of it."[127] This is the spirit of genuine sonship!

> 12:9, 10. *Besides this, we have had earthly fathers to discipline us and we respected them. Shall we not much more be subject to the Father of spirits and live? For they disciplined us for a short time at their pleasure, but he disciplines us for our good, that we may share his holiness.*

The argument is from the lesser, human relationship, in which it is customary for *earthly fathers* to *discipline* their sons, to the greater,

---

125. "Νόθοι must be taken in its ancient juridical sense, as strictly opposed to γνήσιοι," comments Spicq; "legitimate children alone had the right of inheriting their father's property, whereas the νόθος could never be ἐπίκληρος nor even participate with the paternal family in the acts of public worship (ἱερά), for the reason that he had never been presented to the members of the φρατρία and had not been inscribed in the register of citizens (cf. ἀπογεγραμμένων, v. 23)."

126. "It is fathers who have hope that chastise their sons," comments Herveus. "Those whom they see to be entirely beyond hope and intractable they leave to do as they wish.... The son whom they chastise is the one for whom they keep the inheritance."

127. *The Register of the Company of Pastors of Geneva in the Time of Calvin*, ed. and trans. by P. E. Hughes (1966), pp. 191f.

spiritual relationship, in which the one who administers discipline is none other than God himself, *the Father of spirits*. If, as is taken for granted, *we respected* the former, *shall we not much more be subject to* the latter? Thus the logic proceeds *a fortiori*, with respect both to the contrast between the natures of the two fathers, earthly and heavenly, and to the contrast between the manner and worth of the discipline received from each: our earthly fathers *disciplined us* only *for a short time*, while we were boys growing to manhood, and *at their pleasure*, that is to say, subject to the fallibility of human judgment, sometimes immoderately, sometimes capriciously, sometimes swayed by favoritism, though presumably always with the best of intentions; whereas our heavenly Father *disciplines us for our good*, ever and unfailingly with full knowledge of our persons and of the situation in which we are placed and in accordance with what is beneficial to us not simply now but forever, since there can be no higher or more desirable good than that we should *share in his holiness*, which is to be admitted to the everlasting glory and enjoyment of his presence.

Some commentators have mistakenly sought support from the designation of God here as "the Father of spirits" for a particular metaphysical theory concerning the origin of the spirit or soul in man. Contrasting this expression with "the fathers of our flesh"[128] (which is the literal rendering of the Greek phrase rendered "earthly fathers" in our version), they wish to maintain that the body or flesh comes into being as the result of human generation, but that the soul of each man is newly and immediately created by God and infused into the body—a notion which is more Greek than Christian. Aquinas, for example, writes that "man generates man so far as the body is concerned, not so far as the soul is concerned, which comes into being through creation and is not inherited." Likewise Owen asserts that "the soul is immediately created and infused, having no other father but God himself"; and Delitzsch declares: "I cannot doubt, for my own part, that the sacred writer meant what he here says of God as 'the Father of spirits' in a creationist sense." It is a strange dichotomy, however, which divides the fatherhood of our humanity between man and God. We should affirm rather, with Calvin, that "God is the Father both of soul and body, and properly speaking the only one." The description of God here as "the Father of spirits" is evidently identical in meaning with the description of him in Numbers 16:22 and 27:16 as "the God of the spirits of all flesh."[129] Keil and Delitzsch explain there that "the Creator and Pre-

<hr>

128. The Greek reads: τοὺς μὲν τῆς σαρκὸς ἡμῶν πατέρας ... τῷ πατρὶ τῶν πνευμάτων.
129. The comparable expression "the Lord of spirits" occurs frequently in the Similitudes or Parables of 1 Enoch (chs. 37ff.). Cf. also "the Sovereign of spirits and of all authority" in 2 Maccabees 3:24.

server of all being, who has given and still gives life and breath to all flesh, is God of the spirits of all flesh."[130] Consistently with this interpretation, we might have expected Delitzsch to understand "the Father of spirits" here to signify that God is the source of all life and perhaps more particularly, within the economy of redemption, the source of new life in Christ. The contrast then is a simple one, between our mortal earthly fathers and our spiritual or heavenly Father. Thus John Brown understands "the Father of spirits" to mean "our spiritual Father, as opposed to our natural fathers—he to whom we are indebted for spiritual and eternal life." Moffatt rightly says that "the expression is quite intelligible as an expression of practical religion, and is only rendered ambiguous when we read into it later ideas about traducianism and creationism, which were not in the writer's mind." As F. F. Bruce says, "to try to trace metaphysical implications in the phrase is unwarranted."

To *be subject* to the Father who is the source of all life is indeed to *live*. To turn away from him is to turn away from life. To make the discipline of hardship and affliction an excuse for dropping out of the Christian race is to cast doubt on one's filial relationship to the heavenly Father and on the seriousness of one's desire to "share his holiness." The sphere of redemption is indeed the sphere of holiness. "God has not called us for uncleanness," Paul admonishes the Thessalonian Christians, "but in holiness" (1 Thess. 4:7). Thus, as we have seen, our author describes God as "he who sanctifies" and his redeemed as "those who are sanctified" or set apart for holiness (2:11; cf. 10:10, 14; Acts 20:32); and he will soon say (v. 14) that apart from holiness no man will see the Lord, that is, stand before him and enjoy the inexpressible favor of his loving presence. How easily the desire for holiness is set aside when our worldly affairs are proceeding smoothly and comfortably! And how needful, then, is God's fatherly discipline which, when rightly received, teaches us not to rely on ourselves or to seek earthly security but to look trustingly and gratefully to him alone for help and blessing! The strong Christian is the disciplined Christian. "Women who are brought up in the country," Chrysostom quaintly says, "are stronger than men who live in towns." Hugh Latimer speaks, in characteristic fashion, of the Christian's sufferings as "sauces" which give us a relish for Christ:

> For like as sauces make lusty the stomach to receive meat, so affliction stirreth up in us a desire to Christ. For when we be in quietness we are not hungry, we care not for Christ; but when we be in tribulation, and cast into prison, then we have a desire to him; then we learn to call upon him; then

130. C. F. Keil and F. Delitzsch, *Biblical Commentary on the Pentateuch*, III (1881), p. 109.

we hunger and thirst after him; then we are desirous to feed upon him. As long as we be in health and prosperity we care not for him; we be slothful, we have no stomach at all; and therefore these sauces are very necessary for us. . . . Therefore it cometh of the goodness of God when we be put to taste the sauce of tribulation: for then he doth it to a good end, namely, that we should not be condemned with this wicked world. For these sauces are very good for us; for they make us more hungry and lusty to come to Christ and to feed upon him. [131]

"Before I was afflicted I went astray," the Psalmist testifies; "but now I keep thy word. . . . It is good for me that I was afflicted, that I might learn thy statutes" (Ps. 119:67, 71).

12:11. *For the moment all discipline seems painful rather than pleasant; but later it yields the peaceful fruit of righteousness to those who have been trained by it.*

It is the nature of *all discipline* to seem *painful rather than pleasant,* otherwise it would fail of its purpose, which is to head one away from what is unprofitable for holiness. But it seems to be so only *for the moment,* that is, at the time when it is experienced; for he who benefits from discipline invariably finds that the pain of it is followed by joy, and to this consummation of bliss the man of faith looks forward with eager anticipation. Thus in the midst of all that he suffered as a messenger of the gospel Paul was certain that "this slight momentary affliction is preparing for us an eternal weight of glory beyond all comparison" (2 Cor. 4:17). The period of discipline is our present earthly pilgrimage, and its hardships are as nothing either in duration or in quantity when contrasted with the eternity and the infinity of the glory that awaits us (Rom. 8:18). *Later,* that is, once our earthly course is run, the discipline imposed by our heavenly Father *yields* a rich harvest, here described as *the peaceful fruit of righteousness,* but only *to those who have been trained by it.* To lose spirit and give up the struggle because the way is hard is to break training and to forfeit the harvest.

The notion of the beneficial fruitfulness of discipline is an ethical commonplace. Aristotle, for example, is cited by Diogenes Laertius (V. 18) as having said that "the roots of discipline are bitter, but its fruit is sweet"; and Aquinas observes that "outwardly discipline holds sorrow as it is endured, but inwardly it holds sweetness because of the good end that is intended." For the Christian, the seed of divine chastisement proves to be wonderfully productive. When our author describes the

131. Hugh Latimer, *Works,* I (1844), pp. 463ff. Cf. also the comment of Aquinas: "Because our senses and our thoughts are prone to evil, as Gen. 8:21 says, therefore the Lord disciplines us, so that he may draw us back from evil."

harvest it produces as "peaceful" the metaphor is still that of the athletic contest, for the adjective bespeaks the rest and relaxation enjoyed by the victorious contestant once the conflict is over.[132] The "fruit of righteousness," moreover, may be equated with the "crown of righteousness," which the apostle Paul, as he approached the end of his course, saw ahead, awaiting him in the glory of his Master's presence (2 Tim. 4:9).[133] Righteousness and peace had long since been associated with each other in the vision of the prophet, when he proclaimed: "The effect of righteousness will be peace, and the result of righteousness, quietness and trust for ever" (Isa. 32:17; cf. also 9:7, where righteousness and peace are marks of the everlasting kingdom of Christ). The righteousness produced by discipline is that perfect righteousness which, imputed in justification and striven for in the Christian race, is fully imparted when at last the victor stands before his exalted Lord face to face (1 Jn. 3:2); for it is indeed nothing other than the unblemished righteousness of Christ himself. This, too, is the perspective of Peter when he speaks of our "living hope" which is firmly fixed on "an inheritance imperishable, undefiled, and unfading, kept in heaven for us," adding that this causes us to rejoice, even though now for a little while we have to endure a variety of trials. These trials, in fact, are intended for the purifying of our faith, even as gold is tested and purified by fire (1 Pet. 1:3ff.). So also James pronounces that man blessed "who endures trial, for when he has stood the test he will receive the crown of life which God has promised to those who love him" (Jas. 1:12). Enduring the trial and standing the test of disciplinary affliction is precisely the "training" of which our author is speaking here. It is the perspective of faith which explains the "unutterable and exalted joy" of the Christian athlete as, willingly enduring all things, he fixes his gaze on the glorious Person of him who is the object of his faith and his love (v. 2 above; 1 Pet. 3:8).

12:12, 13. *Therefore lift your drooping hands and strengthen your weak knees, and make straight paths for your feet, so that what is lame may not be put out of joint but rather be healed.*

The practical logic (*Therefore*) of the argument that has preceded is now applied to the readers in a prolonged and diversified exhortation,

132. Thus Delitzsch (following Tholuck and others) says that the epithet εἰρηνικός, "peaceful," "implies a previous ἀγών, conflict"—a judgment that is confirmed by the association between εἰρηνικός and γεγυμνασμένοις, "trained," that is, through participation in the contest. Spicq comments to the same effect.
133. We have explained the yielding by discipline of the peaceful fruit of righteousness in terms of an eschatological harvest; but this does not rule out what is indeed a fact of

which continues virtually to the end of the epistle. In these two verses the imagery of the athletic contest is retained: the severity of the conflict with its continuous discipline is such that the competitor who lacks determination allows his hands to hang down and feels his knees to be weakened; and, giving way to discouragement, he easily falters in the race and fails to keep a straight course. The essential thing, however, is to press on and to continue competing. The struggle is serious, and on its outcome eternal issues depend. Present trials are the way to the greatest prize. Those to whom this letter is sent are, like us, not the only contestants, nor are they the first contestants (ch. 11!). Paul and Barnabas, as they blazed a trail for the gospel, learned the fierceness and the fatigue of the struggle; not only, however, did they themselves joyfully and undauntedly persevere, but they also "strengthened the souls" of their converts, "exhorting them to continue in the faith, and saying that through many tribulations we must enter the kingdom of God" (Acts 14:22).

Our author encourages his readers here with words borrowed from Isaiah 35:3, which reads: "Strengthen the weak hands, and make firm the feeble knees," and in the next verse continues (showing once again the contextual appropriateness of our author's use of quotations from the Old Testament): "Say to those who are of a fearful heart, 'Be strong, fear not! Behold, your God . . . will come and save you.'" The expression "drooping hands and weak knees" seems, indeed, to have been somewhat of an idiom or stereotype. It is found, for example, in the apocryphal book of Sirach (25:23),[134] which belongs to the second century B.C.; and in Job 4:3f. Eliphaz reminds Job that in the past he has encouraged weak hands and made feeble knees firm (though the terminology of the Septuagint does not correspond exactly with that of our text, the concept is identical); and Philo, in a manner very appropriate to the present theme, likens the Israelites in the wilderness who want to give up the

---

Christian experience, namely, that it has a fruitful and beneficial effect in the course of our earthly life as it increasingly attunes us to the will and the holiness of God. It is along these lines that F. F. Bruce interprets the language here: "The man who accepts discipline at the hand of God as something designed by his heavenly Father for his good," he says, "will cease to feel resentful and rebellious; he has 'stilled and quieted' his soul (cf. Ps. 131:2), which thus provides fertile soil for the cultivation of a righteous life, responsive to the will of God."

134. The terminology of Sirach 25:23 corresponds exactly with that of our text, χεῖρες παρειμέναι καὶ γόνατα παραλελυμένα, and Isaiah 35:3 (LXX) is practically identical, the only difference being that of a prefix, ἀνειμέναι instead of παρειμέναι. Sirach 2:12 speaks, suitably, of "drooping hands" in association with "cowardly hearts." In the LXX of Deuteronomy 32:36 the two participles occur together in a context where God encourages his servants when they are enfeebled (παραλελυμένους) and dejected (παρειμένους). Cf. also Zephaniah 3:16, "Be of good courage, Zion, do not let your hands droop!"

struggle and return to Egypt to weary athletes who drop their hands through weakness.[135]

The second part of the exhortation, namely, *make straight paths for your feet, so that what is lame may not be put out of joint but rather be healed*, echoes the admonition of Proverbs 4:26: "Make straight paths for your feet[136] and order your ways aright. Do not swerve to the right or to the left; turn away your foot from the way of evil." The Christian athlete must keep to the "running-lane"[137] which has been assigned to him; he must keep his steps from wavering (NEB), swerving neither to the right nor to the left. Otherwise lameness, instead of being healed, may lead to dislocation, that is, total incapacitation. This seems to be the sense of our version (RSV), "put out of joint," and it is the interpretation favored by the JB, the NEB, and most of the modern commentators, including F. F. Bruce, Bonsirven, Moffatt, Westcott, and Grotius. But the rendering of the KJV, "turned out of the way," approved by the older writers and also by Spicq, is to be preferred.[138] The objection of Bruce, Westcott, and others that healing has no connection with straying is readily answered by observing that this is beside the point since it has a perfectly appropriate connection with lameness. Besides, as Delitzsch remarks, "that which is lame already does not need to be further 'put out of joint' in order to stumble or make no progress." The danger threatening these Hebrew Christians is, as has been apparent time and again, precisely that of turning aside from the true path, and thus committing themselves to the irremediable sin of apostasy.

The note of concern and responsibility for others seems to be implicit in the admonition: by holding a straight course himself the Christian sets an example of constancy which will help those who are lame or faltering to do the same and thus to be healed and restored to the contest. In the spirit of 10:23-25 above, by holding fast the confession of our hope without wavering not only will we prove the faithfulness of all

---

135. Philo, *De Congressu* 164.
136. The close verbal correspondence should be noticed:
Hebrews 12:13, τροχιὰς ὀρθὰς ποιεῖτε τοῖς ποσὶν ὑμῶν
Proverbs 4:26 LXX, ὀρθὰς τροχιὰς ποίει σοῖς ποσίν.
137. The rare noun τροχιά I have taken here to mean a "running-lane," by reason both of the athletic imagery of the context and of the term's etymological association with the verb τρέχειν, "to run." Héring approves this sense (French, *piste*). Erasmus cites Theophylact, who says that the noun means either a wheel-track or the track made by the feet of the runners.
138. The usual sense of ἐκτρέπειν is "to turn aside," and this is its meaning elsewhere in the New Testament (cf. 1 Tim. 1:6; 5:15; 6:20; 2 Tim. 4:4), such turning aside being coterminous with apostasy (with the exception of 1 Tim. 6:20) and thus particularly appropriate to the situation our author is addressing. The sense "to put out of joint" or "to dislocate" is found in the medical treatises of Hippocrates (*De Offic. Med.* 14) and others.

that God has promised but others also will be encouraged and freed from the crippling spirit of despondency and self-pity.

12:14. *Strive for peace with all men, and for the holiness without which no one will see the Lord.*

Since God is the God of peace (Heb. 13:20) who through our Melchizedek, the King of peace (Heb. 7:2), has brought us from disharmony to peace and from alienation to reconciliation (Col. 1:20; 2 Cor. 5:18ff.), we, in our daily dealings and relationships, are to *strive for peace with all men* (see Paul's similar exhortation in Rom. 12:18). This we are to do not merely so that we ourselves may enjoy a peaceful existence, but so that the blessing of God's peace may flow through us into the lives of others. The effect of the gospel should be felt in society as a whole. Our author seems to have in mind the injunction of Psalm 34:14 to "seek peace and pursue it"[139] (cf. 1 Pet. 3:11 where this occurs in a more extensive quotation from Ps. 34); but what he says here may be seen also as an echo of the admonition of Jesus to his disciples to "be at peace with one another" (Mk. 9:50).

The pursuit of peace with others is coupled with the pursuit of holiness, and particularly *the* (that kind of) *holiness without which no one will see the Lord.* That it is possible, and indeed all too common, for men to pursue a spurious kind of "holiness" is plain from Christ's condemnation of the "holiness" of those religious hypocrites whose sanctimonious piety is a public display of self-esteem, manifested in the calculated ostentation of their devotional exercises and almsgiving, "that they may be praised by men." True holiness, however, is inward and private, between a man and his God, and the good deeds which are its fruit are performed as secretly as possible as an expression of loving concern and with an aversion for all fanfare and publicity (Mt. 6:1–18). This kind of holiness, which reflects the pure goodness of God, springs from single-minded love of God, not from love of human applause, and is consistent with a longing to see the Lord, who is all-holy, not with a lust to be seen by men. "Those who are not holy and pure in heart will not see God," writes Lefèvre d'Etaples, "and this is the most tragic loss of all and the ultimate evil of all." Moreover, as John assures us, to see the Lord is to be like him, and this is the perfection of all holiness, and at the same time the great incentive to the pursuit of holiness, for "every

---

139. Hebrews 12:14, εἰρήνην διώκετε
Psalm 34:14 (LXX, 33:15), ζήτησον εἰρήνην καὶ δίωξον αὐτήν.

one who thus hopes in him purifies himself as he is pure" (1 Jn. 3:2f.). Holiness is the essential requirement if we are to be admitted to his holy presence. The logic of this, unvarying from age to age, has been precisely formulated in 1 Peter 1:15f.: "As he who called you is holy, be holy yourselves in all your conduct; since it is written, 'You shall be holy, for I am holy'" (cf. Lev. 11:44f.; 19:2; 20:7, 26; Mt. 5:48). And our holiness is achieved in Christ Jesus, whom God has made our sanctification (1 Cor. 1:30).

This incitement to the pursuit of peace and holiness is matched by the manner in which Paul urges Timothy to "pursue[140] righteousness, faith, love, and peace, along with those who call upon the Lord from a pure heart" (2 Tim. 2:22); and it is reminiscent, further, of the two contiguous beatitudes in which Christ declares the blessedness of the pure in heart (a truly holy state) and the peacemakers (Mt. 5:8f.). Indeed, what is stated negatively here—"holiness, without which no one will see the Lord"—is stated positively there—"blessed are the pure in heart, for they shall see God." Nothing unclean can enter the city of God's glorious presence, "nor any one who practices abomination or falsehood, but only those who are written in the Lamb's book of life" (Rev. 21:27; 22:15), only those who have been "washed . . . sanctified . . . justified in the name of the Lord Jesus Christ and in the Spirit of our God" (1 Cor. 6:9–11; cf. Rev. 7:9–17). For such, who as yet see but indistinctly, there is the glorious and assured prospect of seeing their King and High Priest face to face when their course is done (1 Cor. 13:12)—a hope which spurs them manfully to persevere as they look away to him who is both the start and the prize of the Christian race (v. 2 above).

12:15. See to it that no one fail to obtain the grace of God; that no "root of bitterness" spring up and cause trouble, and by it the many become defiled.

The peace and the holiness of which the preceding verse speaks belong together: the holy man is a man of peace. The lack of peace, individually, socially, and internationally, in our world is the inevitable consequence of the unholiness which flourishes when the relationship with God who is the Holy One is severed through the rebellion of sin. But the Lord of peace gives peace which the world cannot give, and he who, through faith in Christ, is at peace with God is *ipso facto* at peace

---

140. The influence of Psalm 34 is doubtless present here also. The same verb, διώκειν, is used: δίωκε . . . εἰρήνην. Cf. 1 Timothy 6:11: "Pursue (δίωκε) righteousness, godliness, faith, love, steadfastness, gentleness."

with himself and with his fellow men (2 Thess. 3:16; Jn. 14:27; Rom. 5:1; 1 Cor. 7:15). His life and his witness together proclaim reconciliation. The Christian community, then, should be a living example of harmony and holiness. Where disharmony and disaffection appear it is a sure sign of the presence of unholiness within the fraternity. Our author is concerned that the integrity of the fellowship should be preserved, being well aware that bitterness even in one person can disrupt the harmony of all, and that unholiness in one can defile the whole group (cf. 1 Cor. 5:6).

The readers are admonished, therefore, to *see to it*,[141] to show practical concern, *that no one fail to obtain the grace of God*, or, rather, that none of their fellow contestants fall behind in the race and turn away from[142] the prize that is before them. As we have repeatedly seen, the danger by which they are threatened is that of apostasy: in 3:12 they have been warned to take care lest in any of them an evil, unbelieving heart should cause them to desert the living God; in 4:1 they have been advised to fear lest any of them be judged to have failed to reach God's rest; in 6:4–6 they have been told of the impossibility of restoration for any who wilfully abandon the blessings of the gospel; and in 10:26–31 they have been cautioned again regarding the irremissibility of the sin of deliberately profaning the blood of the covenant. Similarly here it is once more the peril of apostasy, of dropping out of the race, of "rejecting him who warns from heaven" (vv. 25–29 below), against which they are being warned. Our author, then, is not speaking of some relatively serious deficiency in the Christian life, but of the absolutely disastrous eventuality of cutting oneself off from the grace of God. Where there are symptoms that such a situation may be developing, earnest attentiveness and searching self-scrutiny on the part both of the community and of the individuals of which it is composed are an urgent necessity.

The interpretation given above is corroborated by the warning of Deuteronomy 29:18 of which our author's words here are virtually a

---

141. The connection with what precedes is unmistakable in the Greek, where verse 15 is introduced, not with a main verb (imperative), but with a participle, ἐπισκοποῦντες, and the punctuation at the end of verse 14 is, accordingly, a comma, not a full stop. This structure is preserved in the KJV: "Follow peace... and holiness... looking diligently lest...." "See to it" (RSV, NEB) is perhaps too weak a rendering of ἐπισκοποῦντες, a term which, as Westcott says, "expresses the careful regard of those who occupy a position of responsibility"—not, however, here in any official sense, but with the implication, as Westcott adds, that "each shares this in due degree."

142. The idiom here is ὑστερεῖν ἀπό, to fall behind to the extent of cutting oneself off from the contest. NEB, "forfeit," is an improvement on RSV, "fail to obtain," which seems to betray a misunderstanding of the meaning intended.

quotation. Moses, addressing the assembly of God's covenant people, utters this solemn caution against the sin of apostasy: "Beware lest there be any among you . . . whose heart turns away this day from the Lord our God to go and serve the gods of those nations; lest there be among you a root bearing poisonous and bitter fruit" (cf. the passage in its entirety, Dt. 29:1–28). So, too, the recipients of our epistle are urged to avoid the sin of unfaithfulness by ensuring *that no root of bitterness spring up and cause trouble.* [143] Evidently a person rather than a motive is intended by the expression a "root of bitterness," as in Deuteronomy 29:18f.: " . . . a root . . . , one who, when he hears the words of this sworn covenant, blesses himself in his heart, saying, 'I shall be safe, though I walk in the stubbornness of my heart.' " [144] The implication is that one embittered and rebellious person in their midst can have a disastrous effect on the community as a whole, so that *the many are defiled*—just as one noxious root can poison a whole crop, leading, in the words of Moses, to "the sweeping away of moist and dry alike" (Dt. 29:19). One person in whom discouragement because of the hardships of the contest has hardened into a bitter and rebellious spirit and caused him to abandon the race could by his apostasy cause incalculable damage. Such a "root of bitterness" was Esau, whose story, of which they are now to be reminded, should be a caution and a deterrent to them all.

---

143. Our author would at first sight seem to be following the Alexandrinus reading in the LXX of Deuteronomy 29:18, namely: μὴ τίς ἐστιν ἐν ὑμῖν ῥίζα ἄνω φύουσα πικρίας ἐνοχλῇ καὶ πικρία, which corresponds exactly with the text of Hebrews 12:15, except that in the latter πικρίας follows immediately after ῥίζα and the awkward and redundant words καὶ πικρία are omitted. The much more acceptable LXX reading (which is also closer to the Hebrew) is μὴ τίς ἐστιν ἐν ὑμῖν ῥίζα ἄνω φύουσα ἐν χολῇ καὶ πικρία, "lest any root spring up among you in irascibility and bitterness," the Greek terms χολή and πικρία answering to the Hebrew terms רֹאשׁ and לַעֲנָה, "gall" and "wormwood" ("poisonous and bitter fruit," RSV). The probability is that the Alexandrinus reading has been influenced by and "corrected" from the reading of Hebrews 12:15, rather than *vice versa*, and that in the text of our epistle, by a visual error or some other scribal lapse, the letters of ἐν χολῇ have been transposed to form ἐνοχλῇ. On the basis then of this conjectural emendation our text would mean, "that there be no root of bitterness springing up in anger" (the verb "to be" being understood). The association of χολή and πικρία is found again in the LXX of Lamentations 3:19, πικρία καὶ χολή μου μνησθήσεται, "my wormwood and gall will be remembered," and in Acts 8:23, εἰς γὰρ χολὴν πικρίας . . . ὁρῶ σε ὄντα, "For I see that you are in the gall of bitterness." The verb ἐνοχλεῖν occurs elsewhere in the New Testament only in Luke 6:18, of those who are afflicted with unclean spirits; but ὀχλεῖν, without the prefix, in Acts 5:16 has exactly the same meaning, and in Acts 15:19 παρενοχλεῖν means to trouble or harass.

144. For another instance of the application of the term "root" to a person in a bad sense see 1 Maccabees 1:18, where Antiochus Epiphanes is called ῥίζα ἁμαρτωλός, "a sinful root." In a good sense it is found in the messianic prophecies of Isaiah 11:10 and 53:2; cf. Revelation 5:5 and 22:16.

12:16, 17. That no one be immoral or irreligious like Esau, who sold his birthright for a single meal. For you know that afterward, when he desired to inherit the blessing, he was rejected, for he found no chance to repent, though he sought it with tears.

Our author sets the example of *Esau* before his readers as that of a man who despised and profaned the blessing that belonged to him and whose loss proved to be irrecoverable. Some commentators (including Chrysostom, Owen, Lünemann, Westcott, and F. F. Bruce) have questioned the propriety of calling Esau an *immoral* man, literally a fornicator,[145] contending that he is not portrayed in this light in the Old Testament. Accordingly they have wished to apply to him only the second of the two terms used here, namely, *irreligious*. The sense would then be: "that no one be a fornicator or, like Esau, a profaner of sacred things." Given the structure of the language here, however, it is much more natural to understand both adjectives as referring to Esau. It has been pointed out (by Aquinas, Delitzsch, Spicq, and others) that Esau's act in taking two foreign women as wives, who "made life bitter for Isaac and Rebekah," must have been regarded by his parents as immoral and tantamount of the commission of fornication (Gen. 26:34f.; 27:46). Certainly, the tradition current among the Jews depicted Esau as a man of sensuous passions, and this would have been well known to the Hebrew recipients of this epistle.[146] It is unlikely also that the mention of fornication is intended only in a metaphorical sense of spiritual impurity, as, for example, in James 4:4 and of course frequently in the Old Testament, where such unfaithfulness is synonymous with apostasy. That there were actual cases of fornication and adultery among those to whom our author was writing is suggested a little further on in the epistle, when to the commendation of marriage the warning is added that God will judge fornicators and adulterers (13:4). This makes it all the more probable that the word "fornicator" is intended literally here. Licentiousness is the destroyer of holiness; hence the clear apostolic admonition: "Among you there must be not even a mention of fornication or impurity in any of its forms, or promiscuity: this would hardly

---

145. Πόρνος.
146. See, for example, Philo, *Legum Allegoriae* iii.2; *Quaestiones et solutiones in Genesin* iv.201; *De Virtutibus* 208; *De Ebrietate* 9; *De Fuga et Inventione* 39; also, in the rabbinic literature, *Genesis Rabba* 65, 70, 72 and *Exodus Rabba* 116. Cf. also Strack-Billerbeck, *in loc.* Of particular interest in view of the terminology used by our author is Jubilees 25:1ff. (second century B.C.), where Rachel advises Jacob: "My son, do not take thee a wife of the daughters of Canaan, as Esau, thy brother, who took him two wives of the daughters of Canaan, and they have embittered my soul with all their unclean deeds: for all their deeds are fornication and lust"; and Jacob says to Rebekah: "I have guarded myself in my spirit against sinning or being corrupted in all my ways throughout all the days of my life; for with regard to lust and fornication Abraham, my father, gave me many commands."

become the saints!... For you can be quite certain that nobody who actually indulges in fornication or impurity or promiscuity—which is worshipping a false god—can inherit anything of the kingdom of God" (Eph. 5:3, 5 JB).

Esau was also "irreligious," that is to say, a man who profanely and contemptuously tramples under foot that which is sacred, as the recipients of our epistle were in danger of doing (10:29). He squandered *for a single meal*, for something so fleeting and unprofitable as the gratification of his carnal appetite of the moment, the precious privilege of *his birthright*, thus despising what he should have treasured as a holy trust (Gen. 25:29ff.). These Hebrew Christians will be guilty of a much greater act of profanity if, disheartened by the difficulties of the contest, they barter not an earthly but a heavenly birthright for a short period of worldly ease and prosperity.

Moreover, being well versed in the Old Testament, they *know* the tragic outcome of Esau's profane deed, how *afterward, when he desired to inherit the blessing, he was rejected*. The moment of contempt for his birthright had consequences which could not be reversed. He lost, irretrievably, the blessing of the firstborn in an earthly lineage; but those whom our author is addressing are in danger of forfeiting their place in "the assembly of the firstborn who are enrolled in heaven" (v. 23 below). Esau found no way of escape from the judgment he had so wantonly brought upon himself, and in his rejection *he found no chance to repent,*[147] *though he sought it*[148] *with tears.* His weeping was of no avail and he became an embittered man (see Gen. 27), for his was not the "godly grief" which produces "repentance that leads to salvation," but the "worldly grief" which produces death (2 Cor. 7:10). It was his loss, not his profanity, that he mourned. How much less will there be escape from judgment for those who are contemptuous of the great salvation they have tasted in Christ Jesus (Heb. 2:1–3)! Esau continues as a cautionary example of the impossibility of restoring again to repentance those who have rebelliously sinned against the light (cf. Heb. 6:4ff.).

147. All the ancient writers and the majority of modern commentators take μετανοίας γὰρ τόπον οὐχ εὗρεν to mean that Esau found no place or opportunity of repentance for himself. A number of scholars, however (including Beza, Owen, Lünemann, Teodorico, Spicq, and Héring), have understood the sense to be that he found no means of inducing a change of mind on the part of his father Isaac. But had this been the meaning, an expression like μετανοίας τοῦ πατρός would have been required, as Delitzsch and Moffatt point out. Otherwise, to render the Greek in this way is, to quote Westcott, "equally against the language and the argument."

148. Opinion is divided as to whether "it," αὐτήν, refers to "the blessing," τὴν εὐλογίαν, or to "repentance," μετανοίας. Owen remarks that "it is all one whether we refer αὐτήν... unto the remote antecedent, 'the blessing', or unto the next, which is 'repentance'; for that which he sought for in repentance... was the blessing also."

12:18–21. *For you have not come to what may be touched, a blazing fire, and*
darkness, and gloom, and a tempest, and the sound of a trumpet, and a voice whose
words made the hearers entreat that no further messages be spoken to them. For they
could not endure the order that was given, "If even a beast touches the mountain, it
shall be stoned." Indeed, so terrifying was the sight that Moses said, "I tremble
with fear."

The theme is now resumed of the definitive contrast between the
old and the new which permeates this epistle—the contrast between the
imperfect and the perfect, the temporary and the permanent, the law
and the gospel (cf. 2:1–3; 3:5f.; 7:11ff.; 8:1ff.; 9:11ff.; 10:1ff., 11ff.).
Throughout, also, our author emphasizes that the greater the privilege
the greater too is the responsibility. Those who, since the advent of
Christ, are blessed with the clear light of God's day of grace are for that
very reason all the more solemnly accountable for their use or neglect of
this blessing. If disobedience to the message communicated through
angels at Sinai received just punishment, much less shall we escape if
we ignore the salvation communicated through him who is the Son
(1:1–3; 2:2f.). The bodies of that disobedient generation which fell in the
wilderness are a warning to us that through unfaithfulness we may fail
to enter into a rest far more splendid than that of the land of Canaan
(3:16–4:1, 11). Death was the penalty for the violation of the law of
Moses: a much worse punishment awaits whoever tramples under
foot the blood of the eternal covenant and treats with contempt the grace
of God in Christ Jesus (10:28f.; 13:20). So here our author defines the
contrast once again, as he leads up to the solemn admonition of verse 25:
"If they did not escape when they refused him who warned them on
earth [at Sinai], much less shall we escape if we reject him who warns
from heaven"; and he does so by way of a graphic comparison between
the significance of Mount Sinai, the locus of the old covenant, and
Mount Zion, the locus of the new covenant.

Sinai is not mentioned by name, but there is no question that it is to
this mountain, and in particular the giving of the law associated with it,
that these verses refer. The language employed reproduces that of
Exodus 19:12ff. and Deuteronomy 4:11ff. Even the word "mountain"
does not appear in verse 18[149] (though it does occur in v. 20); but "For
you have not come to what may be touched..." (v. 18) is balanced by
"But you have come to Mount Zion" in verse 22.

The assertion *you have not come* implies, by way of contrast, "as the
Israelites came" (cf. Dt. 4:11, "you came and stood at the foot of the

---

149. The evidence for the inclusion of ὄρει ("mountain"), though considerable in quantity,
is inferior in quality. The participle ψηλαφωμένῳ alone, without ὄρει, is attested by p⁴⁶
אAC, the Old Latin MSS, and the Syriac, Coptic, and Ethiopic versions.

mountain"), *to what* (that is, to a mountain that) *may be touched* (cf. Ex. 19:12, "whoever touches the mountain shall be put to death"), to *a blazing fire* (cf. Dt. 4:11, "the mountain burned with fire"), to *darkness, and gloom, and a tempest* (cf. Dt. 4:11, "darkness, cloud, and tempest"), and to *the sound of a trumpet* (cf. Ex. 19:16, "the loud blast of a trumpet sounded"; also 19:19 and 20:18), *and a voice,* literally, "a voice (or sound) of words," that is, a voice uttering words (cf. Dt. 4:12, "the Lord spoke to you out of the midst of the fire; you heard the sound of words..."; also Ex. 19:19, "God answered him [Moses] with a voice"), so awesome in itself as to make *the hearers entreat that no further messages be spoken to them* (cf. Ex. 20:19, the people "said to Moses, 'You speak to us, and we will hear; but let not God speak to us lest we die'"; also Dt. 5:25–27). Their fear was intensified by the prohibition, which applied to both man and beast, against approaching and touching the mountain while God's presence was being manifested there. Any infraction of this command was to be punished with death by stoning or by javelin, that is, from a distance, as no one was permitted to set foot on and thus desecrate what was holy ground (cf. Ex. 19:12f.).

Moses, however, was allowed to approach and ascend the mountain (Ex. 19:20; and also Aaron, according to Ex. 19:24); but *so terrifying was the sight,* that is, the manifestation of the divine power and majesty, that he said, *"I tremble with fear."* This statement is not found in the pentateuchal accounts of the law-giving at Sinai, and its inclusion here probably reflects a haggadic tradition to this effect. Moses who drew near to the divine presence within the fiery cloud must have been inspired with awe beyond the rest of the people who remained below. It is a statement, moreover, which is consonant with the earlier confrontation at the burning bush, when "Moses hid his face, for he was afraid to look at God" (Ex. 3:6), or, in the words of Stephen, "Moses trembled and did not dare to look" (Acts 7:32). Sinai, where there were "thunders and lightnings" and "a thick cloud" and "very loud trumpet blast" and "the whole mountain quaked greatly" (Ex. 19:16ff.), must have been an even more terrifying experience for him.

Such were the terrors of Sinai, the mount of God's law, where because of their sinfulness the people were unable to draw near to God's presence. How different are the circumstances of Zion, the mount of God's grace, where, thanks to the perfect law-keeping and the all-sufficient sacrifice of himself offered by the incarnate Son in our stead, we are invited to draw near with boldness into the heavenly holy of holies (Heb. 10:19ff.)! Yet those to whom this letter is addressed are in danger of going back to Moses and Sinai, of preferring the shadow to the substance, and the incompetent sacrificial system of tabernacle and temple to the finality and perfection of Christ's one sacrifice, of deserting the gospel of grace for the futility of legalism—influenced, as we have supposed, by teachings and expectations similar to those of the Dead Sea Sect.[150]

12:22–24. *But you have come to Mount Zion and to the city of the living God, the heavenly Jerusalem, and to innumerable angels in festal gathering, and to the assembly of the first-born who are enrolled in heaven, and to a judge who is God of all, and to the spirits of just men made perfect, and to Jesus, the mediator of a new covenant, and to the sprinkled blood that speaks more graciously than the blood of Abel.*

Mount Sinai, coming at the very beginning of the years spent in the wilderness, symbolizes not only the Mosaic law-giving and the institution of the Aaronic priesthood but also the wanderings, the non-arrival, of that generation which was under a cloud of condemnation because of its infidelity and ingratitude and which perished in the wilderness; whereas Mount Zion symbolizes the establishment of the unique and everlasting priesthood of Christ, the fulfilment in him of all the promises of the new covenant, the end of wandering, and the entry into the eternal rest prepared for the people of God.

The author's assertion, *But you have come to Mount Zion, etc.,* is in itself indicative of his confidence that a genuine work of the gospel has been experienced among those to whom he is writing, however much some of them may be in danger of falling away into apostasy. This confidence has already been expressed, as we have seen, in those places where he has warned them most solemnly: in 6:9, for example, he has said, "Though we speak thus, yet in your case, beloved, we feel sure of better things that belong to salvation," and in 10:39, "We are not of those who shrink back . . . but of those who have faith." Where God is active he is indefectibly active. Those who depart into apostasy have never truly belonged to the people of God, though it may for a time have appeared otherwise. Thus it is said of the "antichrists" who had been in the membership of the apostolic church: "They went out from us, but they were not of us; for if they had been of us, they would have continued with us; but they went out, that it might be plain that they all are not of us" (1 Jn. 2:18f.).

The significance of the various entities or designations set down by our author to describe the superior reality to which Christian believers have come must now be discussed.

150. See Introduction, pp. 12ff.

544

... *to Mount Zion.* Just as Mount Sinai (though not actually named) comprehends all that is written in verses 18 to 21, so also "Mount Zion" may be treated as a general heading which covers all that is said in these three verses: the people of the old covenant came to Mount Sinai; the people of the new have come to Mount Zion. Each passage has seven subsections:

MOUNT SINAI: 1. "What may be touched"
                2. "a blazing fire"
                3. "darkness"
                4. "gloom"
                5. "a tempest"
                6. "the sound of a trumpet"
                7. "a voice ..."
MOUNT ZION: 1. "the city of the living God, the heavenly Jerusalem"
                2. "innumerable angels in festal gathering"
                3. "the assembly of the first-born ..."
                4. "a judge who is God of all"
                5. "the spirits of just men made perfect"
                6. "Jesus, the mediator of a new covenant"
                7. "the sprinkled blood ..."

If there is any degree of symmetry it is unstudied; and it is impossible to agree with Bengel and Delitzsch who imagine they can discern in the former passage a series of seven "earthly" entities which is nicely balanced in an antithetical manner by the series of "heavenly" entities in the latter. The two lists are so categorically incompatible as to rule out any correspondence of this kind. The basic comparison is that of the two different mountains and the significance of what takes place at each.

... *and to the city of the living God, the heavenly Jerusalem.* It would perhaps be better to translate the Greek copula[151] here as "even" rather than "and," as introducing the explanation of what is meant by "Mount Zion." Some commentators wish to treat Zion and Jerusalem as two separate entities, but there is no doubt that they were so closely associated with each other in the Hebrew mind as to be to all intents and purposes synonymous.[152] Thus in the account of David's capture of Jerusalem from the Jebusites the explanation is given that Jerusalem is "the stronghold of Zion, that is, the city of David" (2 Sam. 5:6–8). The Psalmist is addressing one place, not two, when he sings: "Praise the Lord, O Jerusalem! Praise your God, O Zion! For he strengthens the bars

---

151. Καί.
152. See the extensive article on "Zion-Jerusalem" (Σιών, Ἰερουσαλήμ, κτλ.) by Georg Fohrer and Eduard Lohse in Kittel, TDNT.

of your gates; he blesses your sons within you" (Ps. 147:12f.). Similarly Amos proclaims: "The Lord roars from Zion, and utters his voice from Jerusalem" (Amos 1:2); and Micah prophesies: "Out of Zion shall go forth the law, and the word of the Lord from Jerusalem" (Mic. 4:2). The divine judgment recognized in the destruction of Jerusalem gave rise to the expectation of a restored and more glorious city in the coming age: "for the Lord of hosts will reign on Mount Zion and in Jerusalem" (Isa. 24:23; cf. Mic. 4:7; Zeph. 3:14–20; Zech. 1:16; Jer. 31:38; Joel 3:17, etc.).

Paul's allegory in Galatians 4:25f. associates Mount Sinai and "the present Jerusalem"—thus providing a perfect contrast to Mount Zion and "the heavenly Jerusalem" here—and distinguishes between the two Jerusalem concepts (present or below and above or heavenly) as representing bondage and freedom respectively. "The city of the living God, the heavenly Jerusalem," is in essence the same city to which Abraham in faith looked forward, that is, "the city which has foundations, whose builder and maker is God" (Heb. 11:10), as it is "the city which is to come," sought in this age by the people of God, who have no lasting city here (Heb. 13:14), and whose true citizenship is in heaven (Phil. 3:20). It is "the holy city, new Jerusalem," the capital city of the new heaven and the new earth, in which, in fulfilment of his covenant promise, God dwells with men, and they are eternally his people, and all the former things with their sorrows and imperfections have passed away (Rev. 21:1–4). Indeed, the citizens are themselves the city, because, as Peter Lombard suggests, God, who gives them life, dwells in them. The presence of God is what constitutes the new Jerusalem.

If the recipients of this letter were being enticed by expectations akin to those professed by the Dead Sea Sect to look for the restoration of an earthly city and priesthood patterned on the Sinaitic legislation, our author's insistence here that the Jerusalem of the living God is a *heavenly* city serves as yet another corrective to misconceptions of this kind.[153] As it always has been (ch. 11), so the perspective of the man of faith must always be the opposite of this-worldly, penetrating beyond the imperfections of the present scene to that eternal reality which is still hidden from our eyes.

. . . and to innumerable angels in festal gathering. The angels are exalted spiritual beings, "mighty ones" who in perpetual service of God perform his will, "hearkening unto the voice of his word" (Ps. 103:20), and, as we have been reminded in the early part of the epistle, "ministering spirits sent forth to serve, for the sake of those who are to obtain salvation" (1:14). The eternal Son, who, to procure our redemption, "for a little while was made lower than the angels," is now "crowned with

---

153. See Introduction, pp. 12ff.

glory and honor," high above all angels (2:9). Before him, in the heavenly city, "myriads of myriads and thousands of thousands," that is to say, an *innumerable*[154] company, of angels adore him by singing: "Worthy is the Lamb who was slain, to receive power and wealth and wisdom and might and honor and glory and blessing" (Rev. 5:11f.). This scene of joyful praise and celebration in the heavenly Jerusalem is what is meant by their being *in festal gathering*,[155] an expression which, as Moffatt explains, "describes the angelic hosts thronging with glad worship round the living God." To their worship the adoration and thanksgiving of the countless multitude of those whom Christ has redeemed is added (Rev. 7:9ff.). A contrast may well be implied between the "ten thousands of holy ones" (angels) who were in attendance at the awesome event of Mount Sinai (Dt. 33:2; see commentary above on 2:2) and the "ten thousands of angels" now described as united "in festal gathering" to celebrate the glorious triumph of Mount Zion.

. . . *and to the assembly of the first-born who are enrolled in heaven.* Once again there is an implicit contrast between Mount Sinai and Mount Zion: the *assembly,* or "church" (*ecclesia*),[156] mentioned here is the counterpart of the congregation or "church" of the Israelites assembled under the leadership of Moses at Sinai. Thus Stephen says of Moses: "This is he who was in the congregation (*ecclesia*) in the wilderness with the angel who spoke to him at Mount Sinai" (Acts 7:38). In fact, this awe-inspiring occasion is referred to in Deuteronomy (4:10; 9:10; 18:16) as "the day of the *ecclesia*" (Septuagint). Furthermore, the people of Israel were regarded by God as his *first-born.* Moses, accordingly, is commanded to say to Pharaoh, "Israel is my first-born son. . . . Let my son go that he

---

154. The expression μυριάσιν ἀγγέλων, meaning literally "to myriads, or tens of thousands, of angels," indicates a number that cannot be counted; hence the rendering of our version, "to innumerable angels." Cf. the "ten thousands of holy ones" of Deuteronomy 33:2, the "thousand thousands . . . and ten thousand times ten thousand" of Daniel 7:10, and the "thousands of thousands and ten thousand times ten thousand" of 1 Enoch 40:1.

155. Πανηγύρει. The term πανήγυρις designated the gathering of the populace in celebration of a festival or cultic occasion. "In Israel," Spicq writes, "the word evokes the observance of celebrations and pilgrimages (Ez. 46:11; Hos. 9:5; Amos 5:21) and especially the happiness they arouse (Hos. 2:13; cf. Is. 46:10): people would gather in great numbers at Passover, at Pentecost, and at the Feast of Tabernacles with fervour and exultation in the expectation of 'seeing the face of God' in his temple (Rev. 21:2–4, 22–27). Outside of Palestine *panegyris* conveys the notion of good fortune and victory; but it also involves the offering of sacrifices and retains a religious character, as is the case in this passage" (*Vie Chrétienne et Pérégrination selon le Nouveau Testament,* p. 211). For a discussion of the question whether πανηγύρει should be connected with what precedes or with what follows, see the Note on the Varieties of Interpretation of Hebrews 12:22ff. below, pp. 552ff.

156. The noun ἐκκλησία is used throughout the LXX version of the Old Testament to translate the Hebrew קָהָל, which signified the assembly or congregation of the people of Israel (cf., for example, Dt. 31:30).

may serve me" (Ex. 4:22f.). Consequently, "the assembly, or *ecclesia*, of the first-born" is a designation which was applicable to the Israelites under Moses. Now, however, it is transferred and belongs to the people of God in this age of the new covenant. The term *ecclesia* is used by Christ to denote the membership of his kingdom (Mt. 16:18) and by the apostolic authors constantly as a description of the company of believers, who together, both locally and universally, constitute the church of God, the *ecclesia* of the first-born. Thus they are through the agency of the gospel the company of the reborn (Jn. 3:3, 7; Eph. 2:1), who by God's great mercy "have been born anew to a living hope through the resurrection of Jesus Christ from the dead" (1 Pet. 1:3), brought forth, as James puts it, by the word of truth to be as it were "first fruits" of God's creatures (Jas. 1:18)—where "first fruits" corresponds in significance to "first-born" here (under the old covenant both first fruits and first-born were dedicated to God; Ex. 13:2, 12ff.; 23:19, etc.). As first-born, moreover, the members of Christ's body the church are heirs of all things, "heirs of God and fellow heirs with Christ" (Rom. 8:17)—that is to say, through union with him who is the only Son (see the commentary on 1:2 above). It would be incredible foolishness for those whom our author is addressing, or any others for that matter, even to contemplate the possibility of following the tragic example of Esau (v. 16 above) by bartering their far more precious birthright[157] for a brief period of worldly security, gained, it may be, by attempting to return to the provisional and now obsolete system of the old covenant.

Yet another point of comparison with the Sinaitic dispensation is suggested by the description of the first-born as *enrolled in heaven*. Moses in his day was instructed to register or enrol by name "all the first-born males of the people of Israel" (Num. 3:40ff.). This of course was an enrolment on earth, and our author contrastingly speaks of an enrolment of the first-born in heaven—a conception which accords well with Christ's encouragement to his disciples to rejoice because their names were written in heaven (Lk. 10:20). Similarly, Paul refers to his fellow workers as those "whose names are in the book of life" (Phil. 4:3), that register above which is mentioned again in the book of Revelation (3:5; 13:8; 17:8; 20:12, 15). As well as contrast, however, there is continuity, for Moses, as a man of faith (Heb. 11:23ff.), looked beyond the earthly to the heavenly enrolment in that book which God keeps (Ex. 32:32f.) and which is mentioned again in Psalm 69:28 and Daniel 12:1. This enrolment in heaven is permanent: the names inscribed in God's book are inscribed for eternity and will never be removed.[158] They include the

---

157. Πρωτοτόκια (v. 16), the right of the first-born, οἱ πρωτότοκοι (here).
158. This is the force of the perfect participle ἀπογεγραμμένων, which, as Spicq says, "emphasizes the indelible permanence of this inscription."

believers of the age before the advent who did not in their lifetime see the fulfilment of the promises they had received (ch. 11), as well as those of our age whose faith is in the finished work of Christ: all, in short, from the very beginning who belong to that line of faith which constitutes "the Israel of God" (Gal. 6:16; cf. 3:7, 9, 14, 29). "Who would not wish to enjoy the high companionship of these!" exclaims Athanasius. "Who would not desire to be enrolled with these, that he may hear with them, 'Come, ye blessed of my Father, inherit the kingdom prepared for you from the foundation of the world!'" (Mt. 25:34).[159]

... *and to a judge who is God of all.* The *judge* before whom we have to stand is none other than he who is *God of all.* This is by implication a monotheistic statement: if he is the God *of all,* then there can be no other God; he is the one and only God. And he is the God of all, first, because he is the Creator of all; and, second, because he is the Sustainer of all created existence (cf. Rev. 4:11; Jn. 1:3; Ps. 104:24ff.; Heb. 1:3). It follows that the one supreme God is also the Judge of all, before whom no creature is hidden, and to whom all must give an account (Heb. 4:13; 10:30f.; 2 Cor. 5:10; Mt. 16:27; Rev. 6:15ff.; 20:11ff.). The consideration that the judge to whom we have come is he who is the God of all is immensely solemn; but for the believer it is also immensely reassuring, for this Judge is also the God of our Lord Jesus Christ (Eph. 1:3) whose perfect sacrifice is, as this epistle so clearly shows, the firm ground of our acceptance and justification. In coming to him, therefore, we come to one who is both just and merciful and who, as the Father of our Lord Jesus Christ, is also our Father in heaven and the champion and vindicator of all his people. To him the Christian believer comes gladly and with confidence, knowing that what is for others a throne of judgment is for him a throne of grace (Heb. 4:16; 10:22).

... *and to the spirits of just men made perfect.* The term "spirits" here is, as Spicq explains, "a current designation of the souls of men separated from their bodies, prior to the resurrection" (cf. 1 Enoch 22:3, 9; 41:8; 103:3; Rev. 6:9).[160] The expression has been understood by some (including Cornelius à Lapide, Moffatt, and F. F. Bruce) as referring to the

---

159. Athanasius, Letter 43.

160. The first hand of Codex Claromontanus (6th century) and the Sixtine Vulgate have the singular πνεύματι, *(ad) spiritum,* instead of the plural πνεύμασι, *(ad) spiritus. Spiritum* is accepted by Aquinas who understands it to mean the Holy Spirit, influenced, it seems, by the desire to see a trinitarian structure here—the "judge who is God of all" being the First Person, the "Spirit of just men made perfect" being the Third Person, and "Jesus the mediator of a new covenant" being the Second Person of the Holy Trinity. He explains: "You have come to the Holy Spirit, who makes you perfect in righteousness... for all righteousness and perfection is from the Holy Spirit." But the weight of the textual evidence is such as to make the singular inadmissible. The singular reading may originally have been due to the error of a copyist (it is only a single letter that is involved) or to a predisposition on the part of someone to find a trinitarian structure in this passage.

believers of the Old Testament period whose faith looked for the fulfilment of the promises entrusted to them. Friedrich Loofs, for example, relates it to the declaration of Hebrews 11:39f. that these believers before Christ's coming, "though well attested by their faith, did not receive what was promised," since, in accordance with the better purpose of God, they were not to be "made perfect" apart from those who are believers in this age inaugurated by Christ's coming; and he sees these "spirits of just men made perfect" as balancing and complementing the previously mentioned "church of the first-born," which he interprets as meaning the "apostles and other believers of the first generation." He points out, further, that it was only when Christ came that the way into the true sanctuary was opened up for the Old Testament saints (9:8), so that their perfecting had to await his advent.[161]

Others, however (including Grotius, Bengel, and Lünemann), understand the reference here to be to the believers of the New Testament period who have fallen asleep in Christ and are now existing as disembodied "spirits" in the intermediate state between death and resurrection. Héring limits it more narrowly to those who have suffered Christian martyrdom (cf. Rev. 6:9). Commentators who hold that it is Christians who have died that are in view also appeal to Hebrews 11:40, arguing that the situation of the Old Testament saints was imperfect in comparison with that of the New Testament saints who have been "made perfect" by Christ's single offering of himself (10:14).

But the point of 11:40 is that the Old Testament saints, imperfect though their situation formerly was, now share with us the perfection which has been procured by the incarnate Son's all-sufficient sacrifice, the effect of which reaches back to include them no less than it reaches forward to include us who belong to the post-advent era. It was "for every one," them as well as us, that Christ tasted death, so that he might deliver "all those" (them as well as us) "who through fear of death were subject to lifelong bondage" (2:9, 15). It is preferable, therefore (with Owen, Delitzsch, Alford, Westcott, Teodorico, etc.), to understand "the spirits of just men made perfect" as an inclusive designation, comprehending all who through faith have been accounted righteous by God (10:38) from the beginning of the world onward (ch. 11) and who now, their earthly pilgrimage completed, have experienced for themselves that Jesus is not only the pioneer but also the perfecter of their faith (12:2). Absent from the body, they are at home with their Lord (2 Cor. 5:8; Phil. 1:21, 23). It is true that they await the culminating moment of the resurrection and the clothing of their spirits with glorified bodies; yet, as Westcott observes, they are essentially "made perfect,"

161. F. Loofs, *Encyclopedia of Religion and Ethics*, IV, p. 662.

since "they have realized the end for which they were created in virtue of the completed work of Christ." Their union with Christ means that they are now one with him in the perfection of his exaltation, so that it is truly said of them: "Blessed are the dead who die in the Lord!" (Rev. 14:13).

. . . *and unto Jesus, the mediator of a new covenant.* Christ has already been described as the mediator of a new covenant (9:15) which is also a better covenant (8:6). It is unnecessary to repeat or add to the comments which have been offered in those places. The announcement by the prophets who themselves lived in the period of the old covenant that God would establish a new covenant clearly implied the inadequacy and impermanence of the old (see Jer. 31:31ff.; Ezek. 11:19f.; Heb. 8:8ff., 13).[162] *Jesus,* the name of the incarnate Son, declaring as it does the saving work of God on our behalf (Mt. 1:21), is appropriately used here of him whose mediation of the new covenant was by means of the shedding of his own blood, and whose blood accordingly is designated "the blood of the eternal covenant" (Heb. 13:20); for, unlike the old, the new covenant is fully adequate and everlasting in its efficacy. It is the blood of Jesus which completes the sequence of evangelical realities to which those who belong to the community of the new covenant have come.

. . . *and to the sprinkled blood that speaks more graciously than the blood of Abel.* The blood of Jesus stands in contrast both to the blood of the animal victims sacrificed by the levitical priests, which under the former system was sprinkled for the purification of almost all things (9:18-22), but which could never take away sins (10:4, 11), and also, and more particularly here, to the blood of Abel, which was the first human blood to be shed by man. This horrifying violence of fratricide in which, impelled by hatred, brother sheds the blood of brother, and which displays the depravity and enormity of sin and its consequences for society, is offset and nullified by the terrible violence of Christ's death in which, impelled by sheer love, he of his own will sheds his blood for us whom he is not ashamed to call his brothers (2:11, 14). The notion of Abel's

---

162. This is the only place where the adjective νέος is used of the new covenant. Elsewhere the adjective is καινός (Heb. 8:8, 13; 9:15; Lk. 22:20; 1 Cor. 11:25; 2 Cor. 3:6). In the Greek of the first century the two terms are interchangeable and it is unnecessary to propose a semantic distinction along classical lines here, as Alford, Westcott, and others prior to the modern era of linguistic investigation have done. See, for example, Ephesians 4:24 where καινὸς ἄνθρωπος is identical with νέος ἄνθρωπος in Colossians 3:10. Moffatt cites the *Testament of Dan* 5:12 and the *Testament of Levi* 8:14. Whether any semantic distinction is intended in Luke 5:36-39, a favorite passage with the old nuance advocates, must be regarded as very questionable—all the more so if the words were originally spoken by Christ in Aramaic, for then there follows the difficult task of postulating corresponding terms which would convey the same fine distinction of meaning in that language.

blood as *speaking* derives from Genesis 4:10, where God says to Cain; "The voice of your brother's blood is crying to me from the ground." Abel's blood, wickedly shed, cries out for justice and retribution (cf. Jub. 4:3; 1 Enoch 22:6f.), and a curse is placed on Cain (Gen. 4:11). But the blood of Jesus, as it is the blood of a better covenant, speaks to us who, like Cain, are guilty sinners something better [163] (*more graciously*) than the vengeance demanded by Abel's murder. It speaks eternal redemption to us (Heb. 9:12) instead of condemnation, the final putting away of sins (9:26), the purging of evil consciences (10:22), the perfecting and sanctification of all to whom it is applied (10:10, 14); it speaks of acceptance instead of rejection (10:19), of blessing instead of cursing; for it is uniquely this blood which cleanses us from all sin (1 Jn. 1:7). Abel's blood cried out for judgment; but Christ's blood cries out for mercy and pardon. To this precious blood of Jesus the citizen of the heavenly Jerusalem has come, and though faith in the atoning blood of his High Priest's perfect sacrifice the accusing voice of his past wickedness is silenced forever as the blood of the cross of Jesus speaks peace to his heart (Col. 1:20).

NOTE ON THE VARIETIES OF INTERPRETATION OF HEBREWS 12:22FF.

There has been a wide diversity of opinion among scholars regarding the interpretation of the section translated in our version as "to innumerable angels in festal gathering, and to the assembly of the first-born who are enrolled in heaven." The grammatical construction of the sentence which extends from verse 22 to verse 24 is simply that of the main verb προσεληλύθατε with the dative case, "you have come to...." The lack of unanimity is occasioned both by the different possibilities of punctuation and by the noun πανηγύρει, "festal gathering," in the dative case, which may be connected either with what precedes or with what follows, or may stand on its own in the sequence of datives governed by the main verb. The interpretations which have been proposed may be listed as follows:

(1) "To a festal gathering comprising myriads of angels." In the expression μυριάσιν ἀγγέλων πανηγύρει, which is taken as a unity, πανηγύρει is treated as a dative governed by προσεληλύθατε, while μυριάσιν is treated as a dative descriptive of the festal gathering. This is the sense of the Vulgate rendering, "mul-

---

163. The Greek term, translated "more graciously" in our version, is κρεῖττον. See note 1, p. 50 above.

torum millium angelorum frequentiam," where the genitive "multorum millium" corresponds to the variant μυρίων of D*, which may be regarded as preserving the attempt by an early scribe to clarify the sense.

(2) "To myriads of angels in festal gathering." In this case μυριάσιν is treated as the dative governed by προσεληλύθατε and πανηγύρει as a dative descriptive of the myriads of angels. It is the interpretation favored by Chrysostom, Moffatt, Westcott, Héring, RSV, etc.

(3) "To myriads, to a festal gathering of angels and to the church of the first-born." Μυριάσιν is treated as a dative on its own, while the genitive ἀγγέλων is linked with πανηγύρει, and the datives πανηγύρει and ἐκκλησίᾳ are in apposition to μυριάσιν, so that the "myriads" are defined in terms both of elect angels and of redeemed mankind—a view supported by Bengel, Lachmann, Bleek, Delitzsch, etc.

(4) "To myriads, to a festal gathering of angels, and to the church of the first-born," where the difference from (3) is that of a comma placed after πανηγύρει, which is taken as being in apposition to μυριάσιν, while ἐκκλησίᾳ is understood as a dative governed by προσεληλύθατε, giving the sense, "you have come to myriads, namely, a festal gathering of angels, and to the church of the first-born." This interpretation is advocated by Griesbach, Bisping, etc.

(5) "To myriads of angels, to a festal gathering, and to the church of the first-born." Here all three datives, μυριάσιν, πανηγύρει, and ἐκκλησίᾳ, are regarded as governed by προσεληλύθατε, so that syntactically πανηγύρει stands on its own, though understood as descriptive of the preceding phrase "myriads of angels." Thus there is an affinity of meaning with (1) and (2). This accords with the view of Ecumenius, Theophylact, Grotius, Weiss, Bonsirven, etc.

(6) "To myriads of angels, to the festal gathering and church of the first-born." In this case πανηγύρει is treated as a dative governed by προσεληλύθατε and is closely linked in sense with what follows, so that the "festal gathering" is not of angels but of the first-born—an interpretation which has the approval of Beza, Lünemann, Windisch, KJV, Von Soden, Westcott and Hort, Souter, NEB ("the full concourse and assembly of the first-born citizens of heaven"), and the Bible Societies' Edition of the Greek New Testament.

It would seem, however, that a clue at least to the punctuation of the sentence covered by verses 22–24 is ready to hand in the use of the copula καί, "and," which occurs seven times, so that the structure is then as follows:

You have come to Mount Zion

and (or, as suggested in the commentary above, *even*, on the understanding that all that follows is explanatory of what coming to Mount Zion means) to the city of the living God, the heavenly Jerusalem

and to innumerable angels in festal gathering

and to the assembly of the first-born who are enrolled in heaven

and to a judge who is God of all

and to the spirits of just men made perfect

and to Jesus the mediator of a new covenant

and to the sprinkled blood that speaks more graciously than the blood of Abel.

If this is a correct understanding of the basic structure of this passage, then the interpretations numbered (3) and (6) above would suffer disqualification.

There is another interpretation, not yet mentioned, according to which not only the "innumerable angels in festal gathering" but also "the assembly of the first-born who are enrolled in heaven" is understood as a reference to the elect angels (cf. 1 Tim. 5:21). Spicq is numbered among its more recent advocates; but his claim that it has the support of the Greek fathers is an exaggeration. He cites Psalm 89:5, where he takes "the assembly (*ecclesia*) of the holy ones" to be a designation of the angels; the *Shepherd* of Hermas (Vision III.iv.1), which speaks of "the holy angels of God" as those "who were first created and to whom the Lord handed over his whole creation"; and the Extracts of Theodotus (xxvii.3f.), in which the highest angels are called "first-created" (πρωτόκτιστοι). This is meager evidence, however, on which to conclude that our author is describing angels when he writes "the assembly of the first-born who are enrolled in heaven." Joachim Jeremias grants, when discussing the significance of the term ἐκκλησία, that "at Qumran the Hebrew ʿēdā, used *in bonam partem*, occasionally designates the angels as the heavenly host," but he adds that it "most often refers to the Essene community as the community of the members of the people of salvation (in contrast to the *massa perditionis* which refuses to repent)."[164]

Not only the structure of the sentence but also the general tenor of Scripture would seem to be incompatible with this interpretation to which Spicq has lent the weight of his reputation. Indeed, in the judgment of Westcott "the word πρωτότοκοι appears to be wholly inapplicable to angels, nor could they be described as 'enrolled in heaven.'" Spicq actually acknowledges that it accords with the constant usage of Scripture to relate the "heavenly enrolment" to men; but he asks, "How could Christians 'come to' Christians?" This, however, is a strangely unsubstantial difficulty, since it is precisely by becoming Christians that persons leave behind the old existence and "come to" the company of those whose names are written in the book of life. This is their new identity, for it is true of every Christian that he has joined or "come to" the assembly of those who are henceforth his fellow Christians. Nor do the differences of opinion regarding the precise significance of "the assembly of the first-born" (see next paragraph) on the part of those who accept the expression as a reference to men invalidate its application to human beings, as Spicq maintains. For one thing, the divergence of interpretation concerns the connotation of the phrase "the first-born" (which in turn, of course, affects the understanding of the expression as a whole); and for another, while they may disagree over this question, they do not disagree over the conclusion that it is men who are intended here.

The question concerning the interpretation of πρωτότοκοι here comes down to this: does the designation "first-born" imply some kind of priority in a temporal sense, and if so, to what group of Christians does it apply? or is it a general description which denotes the company of the redeemed in its entirety? Of those who hold that the term indicates a particular class or section of redeemed humanity some have explained it as referring to the believers of the Old Testament

164. J. Jeremias, *New Testament Theology* (1971), p. 168.

period, who are regarded as "first-born" because they preceded the believers of the Christian era; others as referring to those who were the original converts to Christianity in New Testament times; others as referring to the apostles, who, in the view of Aquinas and other medieval writers, were the first to receive the gifts of grace and through whom these gifts were passed on to those that followed them; others as referring to those Christians who had already died and entered into rest; others as referring more particularly to those who had suffered martyrdom; while others have wished to understand it of those Christians who are still alive and who together constitute the church on earth.

Far more satisfactory is the understanding of the term "first-born" as signifying the totality of redeemed mankind, the people of God from every age of human history. As F. F. Bruce says, "all the people of Christ are the 'firstborn' children of God, through their union with him who is The Firstborn *par excellence.*" Within the biblical purview, the first-born is the heir; hence the tragedy of Esau who bartered the blessing of his inheritance as the first-born for a single meal (v. 16). Christ, who is uniquely the First-born (Heb. 1:6) is accordingly "the heir of all things" (1:3), and our first-born status in him is the guarantee of our eternal inheritance with him (cf. Rom. 8:17). Moreover, in the eschatological perspective of the Apocalypse, it is at the end of this age, and specifically on the day of judgment, that the books will be opened, and that those whose names are not found written in the book of life will be eternally judged (Rev. 20:11-15). This indicates that the book of life contains the names of all the redeemed, and consequently the appropriateness of an inclusive understanding of "the assembly of the first-born who are enrolled in heaven" as referring to the totality of believers is apparent.

12:25. See that you do not refuse him who is speaking. For if they did not escape when they refused him who warned them on earth, much less shall we escape if we reject him who warns from heaven.

The language of the first clause of this admonition links it in terminology as well as in thought to what has already been said. The mention of *him who is speaking* takes up, in the first place, the assertion of the immediately preceding verse that the sprinkled blood of Jesus *speaks* to us, which is the same as saying that God speaks to us by virtue of the redemption he has freely provided in Christ our High Priest. And, in the second place, it takes up what was said at the very beginning of the epistle, namely, that "in these last days God has spoken to us by a Son" (1:2). To *refuse* him who is speaking is, for those who, like the recipients of this letter, have been associated with the believing community, to trample under foot the blood of the covenant (10:29), or, what is the same thing, to treat with contempt the goodness of God's word of grace (6:5f.), or, again, to rebel against the living God (3:12).

The refusal against which our author is warning is linked, moreover, with what he wrote in verse 19 above about the entreaty of the
Israelites "that no further messages be spoken to them"—indeed, in the
Greek original this is all the more evident because the same verb is used
in both places.[165] The Hebrew Christians whom he is addressing were in
danger, like their forebears under Moses, of stopping their ears against
the voice of God himself. While it is true that in the Old Testament
accounts (Ex. 20:19 and Dt. 5:25–27) the motivation is fear rather than
rebelliousness, the writer of Hebrews doubtless has in mind the unhappy history of the people of Israel in the wilderness which was repeatedly marred by ingratitude and disobedience, and so sees in their
request at Sinai that God should no longer speak to them a parable of
the hardness of their hearts—much in the same way as the apostle Paul
finds an allegory of their unreceptive attitude in the necessity for Moses
to veil his face on coming down from Sinai because of their inability to
look on the glory that shone from his face (2 Cor. 3:13ff.; Ex. 34:29ff.).

There is a difference of opinion concerning the identity of *him who
warned on earth* and him who warns from heaven: is it two different
persons that are meant or one and the same person? Theophylact,
Luther, Moffatt, Héring, and Montefiore are among the many scholars
who understand two different speakers to be intended, maintaining that
the former refers to Moses, the earthly and merely human mediator of
the law, and the latter to Christ, the Mediator from heaven of the new
covenant. In the view of Aquinas and some others a contrast is intended
between the angelic mediation at Sinai and the mediation of Christ (cf.
2:2 above and Acts 7:38). Many others, however, including Chrysostom,
Owen, Bengel, Westcott, Spicq, and F. F. Bruce, contend that God is the
sole speaker intended. Thus Teodorico insists that what we have here is
not a diversity of persons but simply a diversity of circumstances, expressed by the phrases "on earth" and "from heaven." The correctness
of this judgment is confirmed by the statement in the next verse: "His
voice then shook the earth; but now he has promised . . . ," from which it
plainly follows that God is the sole speaker; for it was the voice of
Yahweh, certainly not of Moses or an angel, that shook the earth at
Sinai, and it is Yahweh again who promises yet one further shaking in
Haggai 2:6f. We have here, in fact, the same kind of statement as is
found in the opening words of the epistle, where God who "spoke of
old to our fathers" is one and the same with him who has spoken to us
"in these last days by a Son" (1:1f.). Furthermore, the Greek verb translated here "to warn"[165a] is used by our author of the utterances or revelations that come from God; cf. 8:5, "Moses . . . was instructed by God";[166]

165. Χρηματίζειν.
165a. Verse 19, παρητήσαντο; verse 25, παραιτήσησθε.
166. Κεχρημάτισται.

and 11:7, "Noah, being warned by God...."[167] It was the Lord God who spoke "on earth" when he met with Moses on Mount Sinai (Ex. 19:18ff.), and it is significant for the interpretation of the verse before us that Moses later reminded the people of Israel of this occasion in the following words: "The Lord spoke with you face to face at the mountain, out of the midst of the fire, while I stood between the Lord and you at that time, to declare to you the word of the Lord" (Dt. 5:4f.).

The Israelites under the old covenant *did not escape* condign punishment when they turned a deaf ear to the word spoken to them by God, but were prevented by their unbelief from entering into the promised rest (Heb. 3:19; 4:1). This being so when God warned them on earth, *much less shall we escape,* or, the argument being in fact *a fortiori,* much more shall we not escape,[168] *if we reject,* that is, if, in an act of apostasy, we turn away from,[169] him who warns from heaven. The admonition here is in effect a repetition of that already issued at 2:2f., where, in the light of the retribution which overtook those who defiantly dishonored the Sinaitic covenant, the question is asked how we can expect to escape if we despise a salvaton so incomparably great and wonderful as is ours in Christ—one of the leading themes of this epistle being the superiority, the perfection, and the finality of the redemption procured by Christ's self-offering in contrast to the imperfection and inconclusiveness of the levitical system and its sacrifices, to which the recipients of this letter are being enticed to return. The warning against apostasy under the old covenant of law was terrible enough; more terrible still is the warning of the consequences which will overwhelm those who defect from the new covenant of grace.

12:26, 27. *His voice then shook the earth; but now he has promised, "Yet once more I will shake not only the earth but also the heaven." This phrase, "Yet once more," indicates the removal of what is shaken, as of what has been made, in order that what cannot be shaken may remain.*

Then, at Mount Sinai, the *voice* of God *shook the earth* in such a way that "the whole mountain quaked greatly" (Ex. 19:18; cf. Judg. 5:5; Ps.

---

167. Χρηματισθείς. Both this and κεχρημάτισται (preceding note) are "divine" passives, as is plain from the context in each case. It is surprising to find Moffatt affirming, with reference to the use of χρηματίζειν here in 12:25, that our author "deliberately writes τὸν χρηματίζοντα of Moses, keeping τὸν λαλοῦντα as usual for God."

168. This is evident from the expression πολὺ μᾶλλον in the Greek, which reads: εἰ ἐκεῖνοι οὐκ ἐξέφυγον... πολὺ μᾶλλον ἡμεῖς..., leaving the apodosis, οὐκ ἐκφευξόμεθα, unexpressed.

169. The verb ἀποστρέφειν which is used here (ἀποστρεφόμενοι is), says Spicq, "the verb of apostasy" (cf. Tit. 1:14; 2 Tim. 4:4).

68:7f.). This awesome moment when God communicated his law before which our fallen and disobedient world stood condemned, portended the much greater terror of the last judgment when, in the words borrowed from Haggai 2:6, God *will shake not only the earth but also the heaven,* that is to say, the whole created order (as in Gen. 1:1, where "heaven and earth" stand for the totality of creation; Haggai in fact adds "and the sea and the dry land," thus emphasizing the comprehensiveness of this final shaking). But, terrifying though such a prospect is, it is also good news for those who are God's faithful people, for the final shaking, which is the completion of judgment, is also the completion of salvation. Hence this prophecy is set within the framework of an exhortation by God to his people to take courage because he is with them, and not to fear because his Spirit abides among them, and a promise that the future glory of God's house will exceed all that has been known hitherto.

Our author adds the explanation that the expression *"Yet once more"* points clearly to *the removal of what is shaken,* and therefore of what is shakable and as such unreliable and impermanent, by which the created order in its fallenness is intended (*as of what has been made*). This accords well with the passage from Psalm 102 cited earlier in the epistle (1:10–12), which declares that earth and heaven, the work of God's hands, will perish, that is, as they are presently known to us, and will be changed, whereas God remains eternally the same (cf. Heb. 13:8). The purpose of this ultimate shaking is *in order that what cannot be shaken may remain.* For the people of God, who belong to the order of things which are unshakable, the removal of all that is insecure and imperfect is something to be eagerly anticipated; for this final shaking of both heaven and earth is necessary for the purging and eradication from the universe of all that is hostile to God and his will, for the establishment of all that, being in harmony with the divine mind, is permanent, and for the inauguration of the new heaven and the new earth, that is, the renewed or "changed" creation, in which all God's purposes in creation are brought to everlasting fulfilment at the consummation of the redemption procured in and by Christ (Rev. 21:1ff.; 2 Pet. 3:10–13); and this will take place with the return of Christ in glory and majesty (Rev. 19:11ff.). Thus Gregory of Nazianzus explains that "this last shaking is none other than the second coming of Christ, when the universe will be transformed and changed to a condition of stability which cannot be shaken."[170]

Among those things which are shaken are the sacrifices of the old levitical system and the impermanent order of things instituted through the mediation of Moses, which have been surpassed and superseded by

170. Gregory of Nazianzus, Oration xxi.25 (On the Great Athanasius).

the one perfect sacrifice of Jesus Christ, our great High Priest. This unique sacrifice, unshakable in its efficacy, is itself the foundation of that unblemished new order that abides forever (Rev. 5:11ff.; 7:13ff.). Our author is concerned lest those to whom he is writing should forsake the unshakable realities of the gospel for the outmoded system they have professed to abandon.[171]

12:28, 29. *Therefore let us be grateful for receiving a kingdom that cannot be shaken, and thus let us offer to God acceptable worship, with reverence and awe; for our God is a consuming fire.*

Those things *that cannot be shaken* are all summed up in the single concept of *a kingdom*, that is to say, an ordered and harmonious society governed by him who is the Sovereign Lord of all (Rev. 19:16), that realm described above (v. 22) as "the city of the living God, the heavenly Jerusalem," where God eternally dwells with his people and righteousness reigns (Rev. 21:1ff.) and whose light is the glory of God and the Lamb (Rev. 21:23). It is an unshakable kingdom because it is a purified kingdom from which every shakable thing, or, in other words, everything stained by defilement and corruption, has been excluded, and in which there is a perfect and unfailing unison of goodness and justice and joy. The manifestation of this kingdom in the fulness of its imperishable splendor awaits the glorious appearance of Christ; but even so it is already a reality: Jesus is already enthroned at the right hand of the Majesty on high (v. 2 above; 1:3); the people of God have already come to it (v. 22); it is a kingdom of which Christ's followers are even now the recipients, *receiving* it by faith in their hearts, in the centrality of their being, as first-born sons who, one with him who is the only Son, are even now enjoying the blessings of that kingdom which is their everlasting inheritance.

This being so, it is no wonder that our author exhorts his readers to *be grateful*. As ingratitude lies at the very root of all sin and rebellion against God (Rom. 1:21), so gratitude is the pulsating heartbeat of every positive response to the gospel, gratitude which spontaneously bursts forth in the apostle's exclamation: "Thanks be to God for his inexpressible gift!" (2 Cor. 9:15). Whatever his circumstances, whatever he does or suffers, "always and for everything" the Christian should be "giving thanks in the name of our Lord Jesus Christ to God the Father" (Eph. 5:20; Col. 3:17; 1 Thess. 5:18). His whole life should be one con-

171. See Introduction, pp. 10ff.

stant expression of gratitude. With complete appropriateness, therefore, the whole section of the Heidelberg Catechism on the theme of the Christian life is headed with the single word "Gratitude" (*Dankbarkeit*). So, too, the last words of the aged Chrysostom, mercilessly driven to death on hostile soil by his persecutors, were, "Glory to God for all things!" This, once more, is the triumph of faith in the sovereign goodness and faithfulness of God, with the assurance that the gratitude of which this present life is an expression is but the beginning of that thanksgiving which the redeemed multitude will express eternally in the heavenly kingdom.

Gratefulness, moreover, is the impulse, the motive force, which constrains us, as a holy priesthood belonging to the unshakable kingdom (Rev. 5:10), to *offer to God acceptable worship* by presenting ourselves, thankfully, as a living sacrifice in his service (Rom. 12:1; cf. 14:17f.) and by declaring the wonderful deeds of him who called us out of darkness into his marvellous light (1 Pet. 2:5, 9). Such worship flows from and is a manifestation of the response of our love. All self-esteem and self-righteousness renounced, it is centered entirely on him who is our sovereign Redeemer and Lord. Moreover, remembering our own insignificance and unworthiness and the infinite majesty of him before whom we serve, it is offered *with reverence and awe. For,* our author adds, *our God is a consuming fire*—an echo of the admonitory words of Moses to the Israelites in the wilderness (Dt. 4:24), and thus a reminder that the God of Sinai is the same as the God of Zion: just as the people then needed the solemn warning, "Take heed to yourselves, lest you forget the covenant of the Lord your God, which he made with you. . . . for the Lord your God is a devouring fire," so now those to whom this letter is addressed need to be warned of the dreadful consequences of abandoning the new covenant procured and sealed by the blood of Christ, lest they too, like their ancestors under Moses, should be consumed by the fire of the divine wrath. Apostasy, as they have already been told, can mean only one thing: "a fearful prospect of judgment, and a fury of fire which will consume the adversaries" (10:27).

VI. CONCLUDING EXHORTATIONS, REQUESTS, AND GREETINGS (13:1–25)

13:1–3. Let brotherly love continue. Do not neglect to show hospitality to strangers, for thereby some have entertained angels unawares. Remember those who are in prison, as though in prison with them; and those who are ill-treated, since you also are in the body.

Chapter 13 forms a postscript to the main body of the epistle. In it our author loosely strings together an assortment of practical and social exhortations and doctrinal admonitions (vv. 1 17), followed by a request for their prayers on his behalf (vv. 18f.), his own prayer for God's blessing on them (vv. 20f.), and a final appeal and salutation (vv. 22–25). The authenticity of this chapter has been questioned, on the grounds of style and content, by some who hold that it fits ill with the solid theological homily contained in the twelve preceding chapters. It has been suggested that the hand and vocabulary of Paul can be detected in this final chapter. Others suppose it to be an addendum by the same author. Héring offers the hypothesis that it was written as a covering letter when he sent a copy of his homily to a particular parish or church. More satisfactory is the view of Montefiore that "the distinctive style and content of chapter xiii are sufficiently explained by the author's adaptation of his original homily to the needs of an epistle." In Montefiore's judgment, "if the vocabulary, linguistic usage and literary construction of chapter xiii are examined, and if its thought and argument are analysed, it will appear extremely improbable either that Paul could ever have written it, or that it is constructed out of earlier chapters of the Epistle." His conclusion is that "the whole of the Epistle to the Hebrews comes from the same hand." There is in fact no necessity at all to see this thirteenth chapter as an awkward appendage or afterthought, for it is plain that all that precedes is addressed to a particular group of persons who are in need of the specific instruction and reproof given by the author and well known and loved by him, and whom he accordingly addresses in a personal manner as "brethren" and "holy brethren" and "beloved" (3:1, 12; 6:9; 10:19). It is only natural, therefore, that he should

561

bring what he writes to conclusion in epistolary fashion, with exhortations and prayers and greetings.

The *brotherly love* (*philadelphia*) which he encourages his readers to cultivate is that love which should prevail between those who as fellow believers are brothers in Christ (NEB, "fellow Christians"). The term is used in the same sense by Paul (Rom. 12:10; 1 Thess. 4:9) and Peter (1 Pet. 1:22; 2 Pet. 1:7); and it reflects the custom in the apostolic church for Christians to look on and address each other as brothers—a designation which recurs frequently in the New Testament, including, as we have noticed, our own epistle. Indeed, our author has provided the key to the correct theological understanding of this brotherly relationship in an important passage (2:11ff.), where it becomes plain that the brotherhood enjoyed among Christians derives from Christ himself, first of all by his incarnation through which he became one with us as a fellow human being, and second by our becoming one with him through our experience of the redemption which he has accomplished for us. Christian brotherhood, therefore, is essentially *brotherhood in Christ*; for as he is the only Son (1:2, 5ff., etc.) so, as has already been stressed, it is through union with him that we participate in the grace of his sonship, and in him are accepted as the sons of God and, as sons, brothers and fellow heirs with him who is the heir of all things (1:2; Rom. 8:14–17; Eph. 1:5–7, 11–14; Jn. 1:13).

If our brotherhood derives from Christ, so also does our *love* as brothers. His infinite love for us is the source and stimulus of our love for each other. Hence the precept given by the Master in the upper room: "This is my commandment, that you love one another as I have loved you" (Jn. 13:34; cf. 15:12, 17; 2 Jn. 5; 1 Jn. 3:11, 14, 16–18; 4:7–12). Paul writes to the members of the Thessalonian church: "Concerning the love of the brethren (*philadelphia*) you have no need to have any one write to you, for you yourselves have been taught by God to love one another" (1 Thess. 4:9). Seeing that as fellow Christians we all participate in the blessing of the supreme love of God in Christ, how is it conceivable that we should not love one another? Yet too seldom is the love of God in Christ Jesus our Lord, from which nothing whatsoever can separate us (Rom. 8:38f.), triumphantly manifested in what should be the loving fellowship of Christ's church. Too often we need to hear the reminder, which comes also as a rebuke: "Beloved"—a term which should naturally describe those who are "brothers"—"Beloved, if God so loved us, we also ought to love one another" (1 Jn. 4:11).

The Hebrew Christians to whom this letter is addressed are flagging, it seems, not only in their zeal for the race on which they have set out (12:1, 12) but also in the ardor of their love for each other. Our author has already urged them to "recall the former days" when they were wonderfully united by the bonds of love and compassion (10:32–34); and he now admonishes them to *continue* in brotherly love. They have become slack, too, in their friendliness toward strangers—strangers in general, no doubt, but in particular fellow Christians coming from elsewhere and hitherto unknown to them. Accordingly they are exhorted that they should *not neglect*, as they have been doing,[1] *to show hospitality to strangers* (literally, "love of strangers").[2] Christian hospitality is a matter of faithfulness and loyalty to that love by which we have been redeemed and which unites us to all who are our brothers in Christ. Thus Gaius is commended: "Beloved, it is a loyal thing you do when you render any service to the brethren, especially to strangers, who have testified to your love before the church" (3 Jn. 5). True hospitality springs from the limitless fountain of the divine love manifested to us while we were still estranged sinners (Rom. 5:8), and it must likewise be spontaneous, unforced, and free from reluctance. Christians, as Peter urges, should reach out in love to each other[3] and should "practice hospitality ungrudgingly" (1 Pet. 4:8, 9).

That special blessing attends the practice of Christian hospitality is suggested by the reminder that *thereby some have entertained angels unawares*. The allusion is undoubtedly to the hospitality so willingly shown by Abraham to the three strangers whom he entertained and who, unknown to him, were God's angels or messengers (Gen. 18:1ff.)—one of them, indeed, is designated and addressed by him as Yahweh ("Lord," Gen. 18:17, 20, 22, 26ff.), so that the occasion is evidently intended to be understood as a theophany, or, more specifically, an appearance of the Second Person of the Godhead together with two angels (Gen. 19:1). To these two angels, when they came unexpectedly to Sodom, Lot in turn displayed the spontaneous generosity of his heart by immediately making the hospitality of his home available to them (Gen. 19:2). Another instance of the same kind is the appearance of the angel of the Lord to Manoah and his wife and the unhesitating extension of hospitality to him by Manoah (Judg. 13:3, 9, 13, 15). Clement of Rome ascribes the blessing of the birth of Isaac to the faith and hospitality of Abraham, the rescue of Lot from Sodom to his hospitality and godliness, and the deliverance of Rahab when Jericho was overthrown to her faith and hospitality[4]—and he does this in order to incite the members of the Corinthian church to whom he is writing, and who formerly had been

---

1. The construction is μή with the present imperative: μὴ ἐπιλανθάνεσθε, "do not go on being unmindful" of hospitality.
2. Φιλοξενία.
3. Their love is to be ἐκτενής, "at full stretch," without any slackening.
4. Clement of Rome, *Ep. ad Cor.* 10–12.

renowned for their hospitality,[5] to give attention to this Christian grace, now in need of restoration.[6]

Of course, the open-heartedness of Christian hospitality is liable to invite abuse on the part of unprincipled persons who regard it as an opportunity for eating and lodging at the expense of others. In the sub-apostolic period, for example, instructions are given in the writing known as the *Didache* (or "Teaching of the Twelve Apostles") that every stranger who came in the name of the Lord, that is, professing to be a fellow Christian, should be received, but that his profession should afterward be put to the test, and, if a wayfarer, his stay should be for only two or three days. Still more problematical was the appearance of men who falsely, but often persuasively, claimed to be Christian teachers, apostles, and prophets. Anyone whose teaching was contrary to the doctrine these early Christians had received was, naturally, to be rejected; but also anyone who stayed for more than two days or who asked for money was to be dismissed as an impostor and a parasite.[7] The second-century satirist Lucian speaks scornfully of the devotion with which the Christians cared for the bogus prophet Proteus Peregrinus when he was in prison, and relates how, after his release and the resumption of his activity as an itinerant preacher, he had "ample source of funds in the Christians, through whose ministrations he lived in unalloyed prosperity." Their founder, he explains, "persuaded them that they were all brothers of one another . . . so that if any charlatan and trickster who knows how to turn things to his own advantage comes among them he quickly acquires sudden wealth by imposing on simple folk."[8] This may be sarcastic testimony to Christian gullibility, but it is also, ironically, evidence of the spirit of brotherly love and liberality displayed in Christian circles. The vulnerability that goes with the truly hospitable nature is never fully obviated by the adoption of precautionary measures; nonetheless, Christians should continue to be of all people the most hospitable.

Brotherly love extends also to those fellow believers who are in prison and who therefore are in no position to enjoy the hospitality of the Christian home. Such persons the recipients of this epistle are exhorted to *remember*, by praying for them and by ministering as far as possible to them in their need; for fellow feeling that is genuine must find means of practical expression—*as though in prison with them*, so close are the bonds of faith and love which unite them—just as in "the

---

5. *Ep. ad Cor.* 1.
6. *Ep. ad Cor.* 35, where Clement exhorts the Corinthians to cast off from themselves inhospitality, ἀφιλοξενία, together with other vices.
7. *Didache* 11, 12.
8. Lucian, *The Passing of Peregrinus* 12, 13, 16.

former days" they had "had compassion on the prisoners" (10:34; cf. Mt. 25:35f.). Thus Paul gratefully commended Onesiphorus who, he says, "often refreshed me" and "was not ashamed of my chains" (2 Tim. 1:16). Our author encourages his readers to remember also *those who are ill-treated*, that is, those who are enduring indignities and afflictions other than imprisonment because of their Christian witness, adding the important reminder that they *also are in the body*—by which he means, not, as Calvin and others suppose, that they are fellow members of the one Body of Christ, so that "if one member suffers, all suffer together" (1 Cor. 12:26), true and appropriate though this consideration is, but rather that, as they themselves are leading a bodily existence,[9] the bodily hardships now being experienced by some of their fellow believers could equally well, and perhaps will, be experienced by them too,[10] as indeed, again in "the former days," they had "endured a hard struggle with sufferings," having at times been "publicly exposed to abuse and affliction" (10:32f.). The impostor and the hypocrite betray themselves by their lack of brotherly love and compassion. "Faith and love are all in all, and nothing is preferred before them," Ignatius writes to the Christians in Smyrna, pointing out how "contrary to the mind of God" are those who come with "strange doctrine touching the grace of Jesus Christ." Such persons, he says, "have no care for love, none for the widow, none for the orphan, none for the afflicted, none for the prisoner, none for the hungry or thirsty."[11] True faith, which springs into being from the love of God, must itself blossom out into love for our fellow men. Brotherly love is the hallmark of the genuine Christian.

13:4. *Let marriage be held in honor among all, and let the marriage bed be undefiled; for God will judge the immoral and adulterous.*

That the church was being troubled in the apostolic period by advocates of extreme asceticism who regarded marriage as defiling and insisted on celibacy for the attainment of sanctity is evident, for example, from 1 Timothy 4:3ff., where Paul warns against those "who forbid marriage" and adds the explanation that "everything created by God is good, and nothing is to be rejected if it is received with thanksgiving, for

9. Moffatt comments that "ἐν σώματι refers to the physical condition of liability to similar ill-usage."
10. Cf. the similar terminology of 2 Corinthians 5:6–11, where to be "at home in the body" is to be leading this present physical existence, and the deeds done "in the body," for which each must give an account, refer to what we have done in and with this earthly existence.
11. Ignatius, *Ep. ad Smyrn.* 6.

then it is consecrated by the word of God and prayer." In the post-apostolic centuries the emphasis on virginity as belonging to the state of Christian perfection was promoted by the Montanist movement, which attracted a large following, and by the development of monasticism, which became widely accepted as a superior way of meritorious living. Indeed, as Moffatt observes, "prejudices born of the later passion for celibacy led to the suppression of the inconvenient *among all,*" which has been omitted in some manuscripts and by a number of the patristic writers.

It is possible that the Hebrew Christians to whom this letter was sent were being influenced by Essene doctrines of asceticism involving the denunciation of marriage as a state detrimental to the attainment of godliness. Or it may be that they were situated in a social environment in which the marriage bond was lightly esteemed or even regarded as unnecessary and sexual license of every kind condoned, and which therefore was in conflict with the Christian ideal of marriage and chastity. In either case the construction should be treated as hortatory rather than declaratory. (As there is no verb in the Greek, a verb has to be supplied. The KJV understands an indicative, and thus renders it as a statement or affirmation: "Marriage is honourable in all, and the bed undefiled." But this fits ill both with the admonition introduced by the conjunction *for* which follows and with the context which is compounded of a sequence of exhortations: in fact the two at the beginning of the next verse, which are certainly exhortations, also have no verb in the Greek.) The sense then is: "Let marriage be held in honour among all and let the marriage bed be held as undefiled," or, as in the RSV, "let the marriage bed be undefiled," that is to say, by promiscuity and unfaithfulness. The latter provides the better antecedent to the ensuing warning: "for God will judge the immoral and adulterous."

The description *immoral*[12] designates those persons who indulge in sexual relationships outside the marriage bond, both heterosexual and homosexual, while *adulterous*[13] indicates those who are unfaithful to their marriage vows; thus the two adjectives cover all who licentiously engage in forbidden practices. Such persons *God will judge* (cf. Heb. 10:30). It is because of immorality and impurity, says Paul, that "the wrath of God comes upon the sons of disobedience" (Eph. 5:5f.; cf. Rom. 1:26ff.), cutting them off from the divine blessing, as our author has warned by citing the example of Esau (12:16f.). Similarly, again, Paul admonishes the members of the Thessalonian church: "This is the will of

12. Πόρνοι.
13. Μοιχοί.

God, your sanctification: that you abstain from immorality . . . because the Lord is an avenger of all these things, as we solemnly forewarned you. For God has not called us for uncleanness, but in holiness" (1 Thess. 4:4–7). Marriage, since it is an ordinance of God, is neither defiling nor is it to be defiled. Lefèvre d'Etaples observes that "marriage ought indeed to be honourable, seeing that Christ found it worthy of honour; for, although he was born of a virgin, yet he wished her to be betrothed in marriage, and he honoured marriage in the presence of his virgin mother by the miraculous performance of the first of his signs" (see Jn. 2:1ff.).

13:5, 6. Keep your life free from love of money, and be content with what you have; for he has said, "I will never fail you nor forsake you." Hence we can confidently say, "The Lord is my helper, I will not be afraid; what can man do to me?"

We may assume that *love of money* was another temptation to which the recipients of this letter were showing signs of giving in. Many commentators have remarked on the close connection that exists in the New Testament between immorality (see v. 4) and covetousness. Spicq draws attention to the sequence of the sixth and seventh commandments. Immorality and greed are named together in 1 Corinthians 5:11, Ephesians 5:3, and Colossians 3:5, and adulterers and thieves in 1 Corinthians 6:9f. As Moffatt says, "the love of luxury and the desire for wealth open up opportunities of sensual indulgence." Paul, indeed, warns Timothy that "the love of money is the root of all evils" and that because of this craving "some have wandered away from the faith and pierced their hearts with many pangs"; for, as he has just explained, "those who desire to be rich fall into temptation, into a snare, into many senseless and hurtful desires that plunge men into ruin and destruction"; whereas, on the other hand, "there is great gain in godliness with contentment" (1 Tim. 6:6–10). And this accords perfectly with the injunction now added by our author: *be content with what you have.* The avaricious man is never content: ungenerous and grasping, he always wants more and is always afraid of losing what he has. How different from the serenity of the true Christian who knows that, having Christ, he lacks nothing that is essential for his well-being (cf. Ps. 23:1). Paul, destitute of worldly possessions, sublimely speaks of himself "as having nothing, and yet possessing everything" (2 Cor. 6:10). "I have learned," he assures his friends in Philippi, "in whatever state I am, to be content" (Phil. 4:11). His is the true imitation of the Master, who on earth had no place of his own where he might rest his head (Mt. 8:20), who taught that "a man's life does not consist in the abundance of his possessions" (Lk. 12:15), and who advised his disciples to lay up treasure for themselves in heaven rather than on earth (Mt. 6:19f.)—in other words, though poor in the eyes of men, to be "rich toward God" (Lk. 12:21). We are made rich, indeed, by the poverty which he embraced for our sakes in the incarnation and at the cross (2 Cor. 8:9), and having the assurance that our God will supply our every need "according to his riches in glory in Christ Jesus" we can find no excuse for discontent (Phil. 4:19).

It seems, however, that those to whom this letter was sent are forgetful of the manner in which, in "the former days," they had joyfully accepted the plundering of their property, knowing that they had "a better possession and an abiding one" (10:34). They are faithlessly assailed, it seems, with doubt and anxiety regarding the ability of their heavenly Father to care for them (cf. Mt. 6:25–34). Consequently, our author finds it necessary to remind them of God's promise, tried and proved through the centuries: *"I will never fail you nor forsake you"*—a promise given to Joshua at a critical hour (Josh. 1:5) and in substance to many other servants of the Lord (cf., for example, 1 Chr. 28:20; Dt. 31:6; Gen. 28:15).[14] With this promise, no matter how limited our earthly resources may be, *we can say* with the Psalmist, and we can do so *confidently: "The Lord is my helper"*–and having his help no other help is needed!—*"I will not be afraid"*—for having been freed from the greatest of all fears (Heb. 2:14f.) there is no room for lesser fears!—*"what can man do to me?"*—he may deprive me of my belongings and even kill my body (Mt. 10:28), but he cannot so much as touch the eternal life and wealth that are mine in Christ Jesus my Lord: indeed all things are mine, and I am Christ's, and Christ is God's (1 Cor. 3:21f.)! The quotation is from Psalm 118 (v. 6), a hymn expressing joy and confidence in God which was sung at the great festivals of the Jewish people. The same joy and confidence should be ours who are Christians, for ours is the same God, known to us in his grace and power as the God and Father of our Lord Jesus Christ.

---

14. Compare the following texts:
Hebrews 13:5, οὐ μή σε ἀνῶ οὐδ' οὐ μή σε ἐγκαταλίπω
Joshua 1:5 (LXX), οὐκ ἐγκαταλείψω σε οὐδὲ ὑπερόψομαί σε
1 Chronicles 28:20 (LXX), οὐκ ἀνήσει σε καὶ οὐ μή σε ἐγκαταλίπη
Deuteronomy 31:6 (LXX), οὐ μή σε ἀνῇ οὔτε μή σε ἐγκαταλίπη
Genesis 28:15 (LXX), οὐ μή σε ἐγκαταλίπω.
The quotation is found in precisely the same form as in our text in Philo (*De Confus. Ling.* 166), though in a different context. It does not necessarily follow, as Moffatt and others have concluded, that our author owes the quotation in this form to Philo. More probably, it is a version of Joshua 1:5, or one of the other verses given above, then current and familiar both to Philo and to our author, which possibly, as Delitzsch suggests, was a "liturgical or homiletical usage of the Hellenistic synagogues."

13:7. *Remember your leaders, those who spoke to you the word of God; consider the*
outcome of their life, and imitate their faith.

The leaders mentioned in verses 17 and 24 below, whom the recipients of this letter are told to respect and to whom our author sends his
greetings, are clearly the present leaders of the congregation or community. But the *leaders* spoken of here are the original leaders, now dead—
hence the exhortation to *remember*[15] them. They are described as *those*
who spoke to you the word of God, that is, who brought the Good News to
them after first receiving it from the Lord (2:3), or possibly who, as
instructors rather than evangelists (if such a distinction obtains), taught
them "the first principles of God's word" (6:12). Our author is, in effect,
making a further appeal to his readers to "recall the former days" (10:32)
when they had given earnest and enthusiastic attention to the teaching
of these leaders.

They are urged to *consider,* to look back carefully on,[16] *the outcome of*
their life, or, more accurately, "the outcome of their conduct,"[17] an expression which probably does not mean "the glorious finale of their
witness in martyrdom," as many commentators have understood it
(Teodorico, Spicq, Moffatt, Westcott, Theophylact, and most of the
Latin authors), but rather the "sum total" or "achievement"[18] of their
day-to-day behavior, manifested in a whole life. Thus Chrysostom explains "the outcome" as signifying the manifestation by these original
leaders of a pure life. This "achievement" of their daily living included,
no doubt, and was completed by the triumph of faith in the closing
scene of death, whether peaceful or painful. The "accomplishment" of
the men and women of faith of the former age is apparent from the

---

15. Cf. 1 Corinthians 11:24f., "Do this in remembrance of me." The aorist tense of the
participle in the clause οἵτινες ἐλάλησαν κτλ., "those who spoke... ," "brings together
the whole duration of this ministry of the word" (Spicq).
16. This seems to be the force of ἀναθεωροῦντες; cf. Moffatt, "scanning closely, looking
back (ἀνα-) on."
17. Τὴν ἔκβασιν τῆς ἀναστροφῆς. The noun ἀναστροφή means daily conduct.
18. Moffatt interprets ἔκβασις here as a metaphor for death, like ἔξοδος in Luke 9:31 and
2 Peter 1:15. "This proves," he says, "that the allusion in 12:4 does not exclude some
martyrdoms in the past history of the community," adding, however, the proviso, "unless
the reference here is supposed to mean no more than that they died as they had lived κατὰ
πίστιν (11:13), without giving up their faith." But it must be doubted whether ἔκβασις is
intended as a synonym for death here. The only other occurrence of the noun in the New
Testament is in 1 Corinthians 10:13, where it means a "way out" (NEB) or "way of escape"
(RSV) from temptation. True, in Wisdom 2:17 it is used of a person's departure in death—
the only instance of its use in this sense given by Liddell and Scott. Lampe (*A Patristic*
Greek Lexicon, s.v.) finds only one instance of the use of ἔκβασις in the church fathers,
namely, Basil of Caesarea, *Hom. in Ps. 1.* Otherwise it is found with the senses of "going
away," "leaving behind," "issue," "result," "accomplishment," "completion," "fulfilment" (of prophecy), "emanation," and "deviation."

consideration of their living as well as their dying, as chapter 11 above demonstrates. If these individuals of a bygone era set a splendid example of faith for the recipients of this letter to emulate, so also did those who first instructed them in the word of God and whom, therefore, they had actually known in person: hence our author's appeal to *imitate their faith*. The recollection of the victorious witness of these persons who had first led them in the way of faith, of their joyful living to the glory of God, and of their untroubled dying in the assured hope of resurrection, should inspire them to follow their lead still and to put away all unworthy thoughts of giving up the struggle.

13:8. *Jesus Christ is the same yesterday and today and for ever.*

This affirmation has been a source of strength and encouragement to Christian believers in every generation. It has rightly been understood as expressing the unfailing reliability of him who is our Savior rather than as an ontological definition, and its aphoristic terseness suggests, says Montefiore, "a semi-credal liturgical formula." But while it is a truth which applies to all ages and generations, it is not a statement in isolation; it belongs to the context in which it appears, and accordingly we must first seek its significance within this particular setting. The point would seem to be that, in the case of the original recipients of this letter, he who *yesterday* was the source and object of the triumphant faith of those leaders who instructed them in the word of God (see the preceding verse) is still *today* the same all-sufficient and all-powerful Redeemer and Lord, and will continue so *for ever*. Thus Herveus comments: "The same Christ who was with them is with you, and will be with those who come after us, even to the end of the age. Yesterday he was with the fathers; today he is with you; and he will be with your posterity for evermore." Peter Lombard proposes a connection with the promise cited in verse 5 above: "I will never fail you nor forsake you"; so that our author is in effect inviting his readers to conclude that he who "yesterday" did not fail to help Joshua, as he had promised, "today" helps them, and will continue to help his faithful people "for ever," without cessation.

The understanding of the present verse along the lines suggested above brings out well the connection with what has just been said. Nor does the immediate application of this great affirmation to the particular circumstances of those to whom the letter is addressed involve, as Owen fears, a narrowing or impoverishment of its comprehensive scope; on the contrary, the glory of this and other great truths of the Christian faith is precisely this, that, so far from being mere abstractions, they belong and apply to any and every concrete situation in which the people of God may happen at any time and in any place to find themselves. Moreover, as many commentators have pointed out, the contextual connection is not only with what precedes but also with what follows; for, if Jesus Christ is unchanging, so also is the truth concerning him, with the consequence that there can be no place for differing and discordant doctrines (see next verse). In him we have the completion as well as the source of our faith (v. 2 above). The constancy of Jesus Christ, already announced in the opening section of the epistle (1:11f.), implied throughout, and now reaffirmed here, is inseparable from the constancy of his word.

Less defensible, though understandable in the light of the christological debates of the period, is the interpretation of this verse by the fathers of the fourth and fifth centuries in an ontological manner. Origen had prepared the way by supposing that our author was speaking of the immutability of Jesus Christ in the age that is past ("yesterday"), in the present age ("today"), and in the endless age that is to come ("for ever").[19] Athanasius argues, against the Arians, that the immutability of the Son, as expressed here, implies his consubstantiality with the Father.[20] Gregory of Nazianzus goes further, however, in that he understands the verse to indicate a distinction of the natures in Christ by referring "yesterday" and "today" to his humanity and "for ever" to his deity.[21] This line of interpretation is adopted also by Cyril of Alexandria and Theodoret. But it is difficult to believe that any differentiation of this kind was in the mind of the author of the epistle.

13:9. Do not be led away by diverse and strange teachings; for it is well that the heart be strengthened by grace, not by foods, which have not benefited their adherents.

The fact that those to whom this letter is addressed are allowing themselves to be enticed and beguiled by doctrines alien to the gospel is indicative both of their own immaturity and instability (cf. Heb. 5:11f.) and of their need to be reminded of the perfect constancy of Jesus Christ, whose followers they profess to be (see preceding verse). Hence this

19. Origen, *De Oratione* 27.
20. Athanasius, *Letters to Bishop Serapion* ii.3; *Deposition of Arius* 3; *Three Orations against the Arians* i.36, 48; ii.10; Letter 59 to Epictetus, 5.
21. Gregory of Nazianzus, *Fourth Theological Oration, ad fin.*

admonition to cease being *led away*, or carried off course,[22] by *teachings* that are *diverse*, that is, which offer the specious attraction of variety but which by the same token are shifting and unreliable,[23] and *strange*, that is to say, alien to and incompatible with the truth. History bears ample testimony to the astonishing fecundity of the heretical mentality. But it is evidently one particular element of these erroneous doctrines which is of primary concern to our author at this point, namely, observances involving *foods* which are in fact unedifying and unevangelical.

It has been supposed that the mention of "foods" here relates either to abstinence in conformity with the ascetic practices currently observed in Essene circles, or to the prohibition of particular foods associated with the gnostic syncretism of the Colossian heresy ("do not handle, do not taste, do not touch," Col. 2:16–23),[24] or to teaching of the kind denounced by Paul in 1 Timothy 4:3, which enjoined "abstinence from foods which God created to be received with thanksgiving by those who believe and know the truth."But the difficulty with interpretations of this kind is that our author does not appear to be speaking of abstention from food. When he says that the heart is strengthened not by foods but by grace, he plainly means that a person experiences spiritual strength by the reception of grace, not the reception of certain foods; and as "grace" cannot possibly mean "abstention from grace" so also "foods" here cannot mean "abstention from foods." Paul appears to be saying something similar when he asserts that "the kingdom of God does not mean food and drink but righteousness and peace and joy in the Holy Spirit" (Rom. 14:17).

A clue to the sort of "foods" intended here is found in the verses that immediately follow (11ff.), which speak of a Christian altar from

---

22. The force of the present imperative in the prohibition μὴ παραφέρεσθε is, "do not go on being led astray"; that is, they are to put a stop to what is already taking place.

23. In the expression διδαχαῖς ποικίλαις the adjective carries the pejorative sense of that which is at variance with the truth; cf. the sense "changeable," "unstable," and the phrase ποικίλως ἔχειν, "to be different from" or "other than," found in the classical authors. There is, of course, no implication that Christian doctrine is dull and limited; in Ephesians 3:10, indeed, the wisdom of God is described as πολυποίκιλος, "many faceted," inexhaustible in its variety. In Delitzsch's view, "the epithet ποικίλαι, implying a complex of precepts and doctrines leading away from the plain and simple truth, refers evidently to the subtle casuistry of the Jewish doctors, which, as we know, found a congenial sphere in discussions concerning lawful and unlawful meats."

24. F. F. Bruce, for example, suggests that "the strange teaching which laid such insistence on food was probably some form of syncretistic gnosis, perhaps with Essene or quasi-Essene affinities"; and T. W. Manson finds support in this verse for his theory that our epistle was written to the churches of the Lycus valley, where Colossae was located: 'The reference in both Hebrews and Colossians," he says, "may well be the same whether we take the dietary restrictions to be Jewish food laws or pagan mystical asceticism" (*Studies in the Gospels and Epistles*, Manchester, 1962, p. 254). Cf. the commentary above on 1:4.

which those who conduct the ministry of the tent, that is, the levitical priests, have no right to eat. This suggests that the "foods" in question were connected with some form or forms of sacrificial ceremony. There is absolutely no indication, however, that our author has in mind the issue of eating food that has been offered to idols on pagan altars to which Paul addresses himself in 1 Corinthians 8. Nor is it probable that, as Moffatt supposes, the reference is to a literalistic interpretation of the eucharistic eating and drinking, which takes participation in the Lord's Supper to imply "an actual eating of the sacrificial body of the Lord," as though our author were arguing that as on the Day of Atonement, under the old system, there was no eating of the flesh of the sacrificial victim, which was completely burned, so the flesh of Christ "cannot be literally eaten, as these neosacramentarians allege." But if this were the reference, the singular "food" would seem to be required rather than the plural "foods," which implies a number or variety of foods. Moreover, there is no evidence of any such "sacerdotalist" or "neo-sacramentarian" interpretation of the eucharist, which would include the description of the Lord's table as an altar, for a hundred years after the writing of this epistle, and it was not until the third century that such an interpretation was given developed expression.[25]

It may more appropriately be concluded that, just as the recipients of this letter, allured by the now obsolete Judaistic practices and expectations, appear to have been in danger of fatally compromising if not abandoning the Christian faith, so here our author is referring to participation in the eating of certain foods within a Judaistic setting. "The allusion must envisage," in Spicq's judgment, "the partaking of Jewish sacrifices, such as the eating of the passover lamb and other victims under the law" (cf. Ex. 12:8f.; Lev. 19:5f.; 22:29f.). Owen explains it of "the religious distinction of meats among the Jews," a distinction, he points out, which "arose from the altar." "And hence," he says, "we may see the reason why the Jews laid so much weight on these meats, namely, because the taking of them away, the distinction about them and the privilege of them, did declare that their altar, which was the life

25. The noun βρῶμα is not used in the New Testament for the sacramental bread. Severian (d. ca. 408), alluding to this passage (vv. 9 and 10), writes: "Today we have an altar (θυσιαστήριον) of which the faithful partake," and goes on to speak of its "life-giving food" (βρῶμα ζωοποιόν) (De Mundi Creatione, Oratio VI, Migne, PG, 56, 488), intending, it would seem, a reference to the eucharist. In the sixth century this passage is cited by Cosmas Indicopleustes, though he writes: "Today we have a food that saves" (βρῶμα σωτήριον instead of θυσιαστήριον), ". . . a life-giving food" (βρῶμα ζωοποιόν) (Topographia Christiana, 10, Migne, PG, 88, 425). There is no other instance of the use of βρῶμα in this connection among the patristic authors. The use of the singular, βρῶμα, should be noticed, for, as we have remarked, the plural, βρώματα, in our text is inappropriate when applied to the eucharist.

and centre of their religion, was of no more use." An understanding of
the text along these lines would, of course, be all the more compelling if
Spicq's hypothesis is correct that those to whom this letter was sent had
formerly served as priests of the Jerusalem temple.[26] Whether this is so
or not, they were mistaken in imagining that *the heart* could be
strengthened by partaking of *foods which,* in reality, *have not benefited their
adherents.* The admonition given here is virtually a repetition of what has
already been said in 9:9f. above, where our author has insisted that the
gifts and sacrifices offered under the levitical system "cannot perfect the
conscience of the worshipper," since they are no more than temporary
"regulations for the body" which "deal only with food and drink and
various ablutions." The same principle is tersely formulated by the apostle Paul when he writes (though in a different context): "Food will not
commend us to God" (1 Cor. 8:8).

Food goes into the stomach for the strengthening of the body; but
only *grace* strengthens *the heart,* that is, the vital center of man's being
and personality and the source of his conduct and character. "The good
man out of the good treasure of his heart produces good," Christ himself
taught, "and the evil man out of his evil treasure produces evil; for out of
the abundance of the heart his mouth speaks" (Lk. 6:45; cf. Mk. 7:18–23).
These Hebrew Christians are being enticed to follow the tragic example
of Esau, who bartered his birthright for a single meal (12:16). But, as
Delitzsch observes, "judaizing doctrine and precepts about meats and
the grace of the new covenant mutually exclude one another." Not in
conformity to outward and outmoded observances, but only at the
throne of God's grace to which we have free access by virtue of the
reconciling work of Christ will we find help and strength in the hour of
need (4:16). The grace that strengthens the heart flows from the death
which Jesus tasted for everyone (2:9).

13:10, 11. *We have an altar from which those who serve the tent have no right to eat.
For the bodies of those animals whose blood is brought into the sanctuary by the
high priest as a sacrifice for sin are burned outside the camp.*

Under the Mosaic dispensation the priests were entitled to retain as
food for themselves the flesh of certain animal sacrifices and also the
cereal offerings that were presented (as explained, for example, in Lev.
7); but there were other sacrifices of which they were not permitted to
eat, such as the sin offering described in Leviticus 4:1ff. and—a consid-

26. See Introduction, pp. 12ff.

eration of special significance in our understanding of the present passage—the great annual sacrifices for sin offered on the Day of Atonement (Lev. 16). The close association of the altar with the sacrifice that is offered on it, and of the eater with both, is evident from the question addressed by Paul to the Christians in Corinth: "Consider the practice of Israel; are not those who eat the sacrifices partakers in the altar?" (1 Cor. 10:18; cf. also the question, posed in a different context, of 1 Cor. 9:13: "Do you not know that those who are employed in the temple service get their food from the temple, and those who serve at the altar share in the sacrificial offerings?"). The particular ritual which our author has in view here is, once again, that of the Day of Atonement, when, on this day of the year alone, the blood of the victim slain on the altar *is brought*[27] *into the sanctuary*, that is, the holy of holies, *by the high priest*. Yet *those who serve the tent*, namely, the priests of the levitical order, *have no right to eat* of this, the most portentous of all the Jewish sacrifices; for on this day *the bodies* of the sacrificial animals are totally *burned outside the camp*.

Now, as our author has so carefully explained (in chs. 9 and 10), the typology of the ceremonial enacted on the Day of Atonement has its fulfilment in Christ's unique offering of himself once-for-all on the cross for the sins of the world and in his entry into the heavenly sanctuary, whereby also he has opened the way for us into the very presence of God. Some, it would seem, had been shaking the confidence of the Hebrew Christians to whom this letter was sent by alleging that Christianity compared unfavorably with Judaism because it had no altar. This evokes the rejoinder from our author that *we have an altar*, namely, the cross on which the sacrifice of the Son took place, and that this is the reality which answers to the shadow of the high-priestly offering on Israel's Day of Atonement; and, further, that there is this significant distinction, in addition to the important differences mentioned earlier in the epistle, that whereas the levitical priests have no right to eat of their sin offerings, we Christians, who together constitute a holy priesthood (1 Pet. 2:5), enjoy the privilege of partaking of Christ's sacrifice, which is the true and perfect *sacrifice for sin*.[28] This privilege does not belong to the levitical priests, though it can be theirs also if they transfer their trust to Christ and his sacrifice. At the same time, it is a privilege which the recipients of this epistle will forfeit if, senselessly, they turn back from the new to the old covenant and trample under foot the blood of their

---

27. The present tenses here (εἰσφέρεται, "is brought," and κατακαίεται, "are burned") and also in verse 10 (λατρεύοντες, "serve," and ἔχουσιν, "have") should be noticed as indicators that the levitical system was still functioning and therefore that the Jerusalem temple was still standing when this epistle was written. See Introduction, pp. 30ff.
28. The phrase περὶ ἁμαρτίας denotes the "sin offering." See note 60, p. 397, above.

sanctification (cf. Heb. 10:29). The sacrifices of which those Aaronic priests partook imperfectly prefigured the all-availing sacrifice of him who is the Lamb of God and were incapable of effecting more than a ceremonial and external cleansing; whereas the one sacrifice of which we partake purifies us inwardly from all sin (Heb. 9:9f., 13f., 26; 10:1–4, 10–14; cf. 1 Jn. 1:7, 9). Their eating was physical; ours is spiritual. Their eating, further, was partial, and it was limited, because there could be no eating of their sin offerings, which were incompetent to convey what they portended since the brutish victims were unfitted to take the place of sinful mankind, and it was only with the provision by God of the totally sufficient sin offering of his incarnate Son that such eating at last became a possibility and a reality. Our eating, by contrast, is total and unrestricted. We, as John Brown observes, "are permitted to feast on the whole sacrifice of Jesus Christ. We not only eat his flesh, but we do what none of the priests durst do with regard to any of the sacrifices, we drink his blood. We enjoy the full measure of benefit which his sacrifice was designed to secure. We are allowed to feed freely upon the highest and holiest of all sacrifices. Our reconciliation with God is complete, our fellowship with him intimate and delightful."

Unlike the levitical priests, then, who were forbidden to eat the flesh of their sin offerings, and indeed were unable to do so because the bodies of the animals offered in such sacrifices were completely burned outside the camp, the Christian is both permitted and commanded to feed on him who is his Sin Offering. His feeding, in short, is on the *crucified* Christ. This is plainly declared in Jesus' great discourse on the Bread of Life in John 6: "I am the living bread which came down from heaven," he says; "if any one eats of this bread, he will live for ever; and the bread which I shall give for the life of the world is my flesh" (Jn. 6:51). To the perplexity of his hearers as to how he could give them himself to eat (for any notion of a literal eating of his flesh or drinking of his blood would have been abhorrent to them, and in any case his flesh, if intended literalistically, would have been quite inadequate to feed the multitude surrounding him, let alone the whole world) he solemnly responds: "Truly, truly, I say to you, unless you eat the flesh of the Son of man and drink his blood, you have no life in you; he who eats my flesh and drinks my blood has eternal life, and I will raise him up at the last day. For my flesh is food indeed, and my blood is drink indeed" (Jn. 6:52–55).

The question *how* is in fact clearly answered in verse 35 of the same chapter, where Jesus says that whoever comes to him will not hunger and whoever believes in him will never thirst, which is the same as saying that it is by coming to Christ that we eat his flesh and by believing in him that we drink his blood. But this is one, not two things; for to come to Christ is the same as to believe in him (cf. Jn. 1:12; 3:36; 5:40): accordingly, it is by committing ourselves in faith to him who is both our High Priest and the Victim offered in our stead that we eat his flesh and drink his blood. Christ himself, as Paul affirms, is our sacrificial Paschal Lamb, our passover feast (1 Cor. 5:7). This, too, is the central significance of the eucharist, in which the Christian believer partakes of Christ's flesh and blood—or, in the words of the Book of Common Prayer, feeds upon him in his heart by faith with thanksgiving; for the act of communion in obedience to the Lord's command to "eat" and "drink" is essentially a coming to him in faith and a means appointed by him of receiving the benefits of his atoning passion and death. That Eusebius, Chrysostom, and Cyril of Alexandria should have spoken of the Lord's Supper as the "food"[29] of Christians is understandable, though there is no indication in the passage before us that the author had this sacrament particularly in mind.

It is true that from medieval times on a considerable number of commentators, and especially, as might be expected, those of "catholic" persuasion, have interpreted the statement "We have an altar" as a reference to the sacrament of the eucharist. Significantly, however, the term "altar" is nowhere in the New Testament associated with the institution or the observance of the Lord's Supper, nor is it found as a synonym for the eucharistic table—indeed, it is perfectly plain that no altar was present when Christ inaugurated this sacrament in the upper room. And it is evident throughout this epistle that the author is not concerned to speak about the eucharist, though he might effectively have done so, had he so wished. He might well, for example, have expounded the connection and the contrast between the eucharist and the annual feast of the passover, but he prefers to concentrate his attention on the ceremonial of the annual Day of Atonement and its relationship to the high-priestly work of Christ. We must conclude that the eucharist was not a matter at issue between the author and those to whom he was writing.

The term "altar" as used here is a sort of shorthand, or synecdoche, for the whole sacrificial action of Christ, as the context plainly shows. Spicq, himself a Roman Catholic, insists that the word "altar" "is in rigorous antithesis with the 'tent' and can only designate the centre of the new cult, Jesus Christ, more precisely Christ as sacrificed." He is mistaken, however, in affirming that the interpretation of "altar" here as an allusion to the eucharist is unknown to the medieval scholars (it is found, for example, in Ecumenius, Lanfranc, Peter Lombard, Theophylact, and Aimone d'Auxerres). In the post-apostolic period the

29. Βρῶσις; cf. βρώματα in verse 9 above.

word is employed in a symbolical sense by Ignatius and Polycarp, and later by Clement of Alexandria and Tertullian, but it is only with Cyprian, in the third century, that it begins to be used as a synonym for the Lord's table. Teodorico proposes the assertion of Ignatius that "there is one altar"[30] as a clear reference to the altar on which the eucharistic sacrifice is offered; but, as Lightfoot has said, "it would be an anachronism to suppose that Ignatius by the 'altar' here means the 'Lord's table.'"[31] It is certainly interesting to find Thomas Aquinas stating that "this altar is either the cross of Christ, on which Christ was sacrificed for us, or Christ himself, in whom and through whom we offer our prayers." Somewhat similarly, Calvin, Owen, Westcott, Bonsirven, Spicq, and Montefiore explain this "altar" in terms of the sacrifice of Christ at Calvary, and Bengel, Lünemann, Delitzsch, and many others understand it to mean more specifically the cross on which Christ offered himself—though of course the cross necessarily implies all that took place there for our eternal redemption.[32]

13:12–14. *So Jesus also suffered outside the gate in order to sanctify the people through his own blood. Therefore let us go forth to him outside the camp, bearing abuse for him. For here we have no lasting city, but we seek the city which is to come.*

As we have just been reminded, the carcasses of the beasts slaughtered at the altar on the Day of Atonement were carried forth

---

30. Ignatius, *Philad.* 4.
31. J. B. Lightfoot, *The Apostolic Fathers*, II, ii (1889), p. 258. Cf. J. M. Creed: "It need scarcely be said that when the writer speaks thus of a Christian altar he does not refer to any actual concrete object. . . . It is not until a much later date . . . that the Holy Table of the Eucharist is spoken of as an 'altar'" ("Great Texts Reconsidered," *Expository Times,* 50, 1938/39, p. 13).
32. The wish of some (for example, Zahn, Windisch, Moffatt) to understand "those who serve the tent" as referring not to the priests of the levitical order but to Christians of the new order, the "tent" then being explained as meaning the heavenly sanctuary, is misconceived. For one thing, the term "tent" when used by itself designates the earthly sanctuary in our epistle (see 8:5; 9:2, 3, 21; and cf. 9:6, 8); whereas the heavenly sanctuary is described as "the true tent" (8:2) or "the greater and more perfect tent" (9:11). For another, the change from the first person—"we have an altar"—to the third person—"from which those who serve the tent have no right to eat"—indicates a change of subject; otherwise the first person would have been retained throughout. Moffatt's explanation, moreover, that our author's "point is simply this, that the Christian sacrifice, on which all our relationship to God depends, is not one that involves or allows any connection with a meal" is one that strangely ignores Christ's instruction concerning the necessity of eating his flesh and drinking his blood and his institution of the eucharistic meal. J. M. Creed, in the article cited in the preceding note, favors Moffatt's interpretation; for a rejoinder, see James P. Wilson, "The Interpretation of Hebrews xiii.10," *ibid.,* pp. 380f. As Delitzsch

outside the camp, in accordance with the prescription of Leviticus 16:27, and completely burned. The camp ground was holy ground, but the ground outside the camp was unholy ground; consequently, ceremonial cleansing was required before a man could return to the camp from outside (as we see from Lev. 16:26 and 28). Our author finds it particularly significant that *Jesus also suffered outside the gate*—that is, the gate of the city of Jerusalem which, bounded by its walls, corresponds to the holy ground of the wilderness camp with its boundaries—making there, on that unholy ground, a total sacrifice of himself. How extraordinary, indeed shocking, to the Hebrew mind, to be told that he did this *in order to sanctify the people through his own blood*, precisely on this unsanctified territory! The very concept must have seemed self-contradictory. The location of Calvary was one of defilement, not sanctification. But the presence of God's Holy One (Heb. 7:26; Acts 2:27) made holy what was previously unholy and introduced a completely new perspective. "The Levitical passage describes the holy camp of the wilderness people," writes Helmut Koester. "To leave this camp, even in the performance of holy duties, rendered a man unclean and excluded him from the holy fellowship. The writer of Hebrews, however, insists that the sacrifice of Jesus was performed *outside* of the holy place, and it is this sacrifice which sanctifies his people. This act of sanctification marks the abolition of the necessity of holy places for sanctification."[33]

By suffering outside the gate, moreover, Jesus identifies himself with the world in its unholiness. While we are unable to draw near to God because of our sin, God draws near to us in the person of his Holy One who on our unholy ground makes his holiness available to us in exchange for our sin which he bears and for which he atones on the cross. Through the shedding of his blood outside the gate he *sanctifies* his people: he makes them holy—the concept of sanctification here, as elsewhere in the epistle, being that of rendering acceptable to God, through the removal of defilement and guilt, and thereby of setting apart as holy unto the Lord, those who by their disobedience and ingratitude have alienated themselves from their Creator (cf. Heb. 2:11; 9:13f.; 10:10, 14).

The demands which Christ makes of his followers are total, and logically so, first, because the salvation he provides is total, redeeming and restoring man in the wholeness of his being, body as well as mind and spirit, and, second, because the procuring of this salvation was by

---

points out, "the positive truth indirectly implied in this negative sentence is, that the sacrifice once offered on the altar of the cross is one of which, as Christians, we are permitted to partake, and that it far excels in virtue all other βρώματα."

33. Helmut Koester, "'Outside the Camp': Hebrews 13:9–14," *Harvard Theological Review*, 55 (1962), pp. 300f.

way of his own total self-sacrifice (cf. Rom. 8:32; 12:1). "The cross," observes Teodorico, "is the symbol of total separation and dedication." And, more than a symbol, the cross is also the way of Christ's followers. Hence the Master's admonition to the Twelve: "A disciple is not above his teacher, nor a servant above his master; it is enough for the disciple to be like his teacher, and the servant like his master... and he who does not take his cross and follow me is not worthy of me" (Mt. 10:24f., 38). This following of Christ inescapably involves going *outside the camp* where the cross, too shameful to be placed inside the camp, is located. It means not only separation *from* but also separation *to*—separation from the old unregenerate life which seeks the acceptance of men in the camp, and separation to Christ (*let us go forth to him*) who, despised and rejected, was crucified outside the gate. Doing this, we shall indeed discover the meaning of *bearing abuse for him*—or, as the KJV more accurately translates, "bearing his reproach," that is, associating ourselves with his shame (cf. NEB, "bearing the stigma that he bore"), and yet, like Moses of old, "esteeming the reproach of Christ greater riches than the treasures in Egypt" (Heb. 11:26 KJV). For the Christian there must be a real identification with Christ and his shame; he must enter into a genuine "fellowship of Christ's sufferings" (Phil. 3:10), and be willing even, like the first martyr Stephen, to lay down his life for his Lord and Savior "outside the city" (Acts 7:58). The recipients of this letter had gone forth "outside the camp" to associate themselves with Christ and his cross; but now their resolve is weakening and they are being tempted to turn back in the hope of finding an easier and more respectable existence "inside the camp."

"Going forth" to Christ "outside the camp" certainly meant for these original readers, as it does for us, separation from the fallen values of unregenerate society, but in their case it meant also departure from the old Jewish order of their upbringing, from dependence on the levitical priesthood with its feasts and sacrifices, and also, it may well be, from the expectation of the restoration of a purified Judaism such as was entertained by the adherents of the Dead Sea Sect. Moses had been summoned to leave behind Egypt and its civilization; now they are urged to turn their backs on Sinai and the earthly Jerusalem. They are "now called upon," as Westcott comments, "to withdraw from Judaism even in its first and purest shape. It had been designed by God as a provisional system, and its work was done."

In any case, the security of earthly cities, establishments, and institutions, however religious they may be, is illusory. The history of Judaism had already shown that even Jerusalem, the city of God, and its magnificent temple dedicated to the glory and worship of God, were destructible; and soon it would prove again, with the approach of A.D.

70, the transitoriness of the restored city and temple. It is imperative, therefore, that these Hebrew Christians, tempted as they are to insulate themselves from the reproach and the reality of the cross "outside the gate" by retreating to the traditional respectability and apparent solidity of a system which Christ's coming has rendered obsolete, should learn that *here*, in this present world order, *we have no lasting city*.

Yet in going forth we are not left without a city, *for we seek the city which is to come*—not some hypothetical indefinite city, the product of a vague optimism, but *the* city, one, that is to say, which is real and assured. We do this not in uncertainty but with all the confidence of that faith which is "the conviction of things not seen" (Heb. 11:1). Thus in joining Christ crucified "outside the gate" we are not separating ourselves *from* reality but *to* that reality which alone is ultimate and eternal. This indeed, as we have seen, unites us in spirit with the men and women of authentic faith who lived in the centuries before the coming of Christ, for they too, instead of staying, or returning, moved out from their worldly strongholds since they, no less, "looked forward to the city which has foundations, whose builder and maker is God"; they too, like us, were "seeking a homeland" and "a better country, that is, a heavenly one" (11:10, 14, 16).

Of special interest in connection with the passage before us is the account (in Ex. 33:7ff.) of how, after the incident of the golden calf (Ex. 32) but prior to the setting up of the tabernacle proper (Ex. 40), Moses took a tent and pitched it outside the camp, at a sufficient distance to make it quite separate from the camp, and called it "the tent of meeting." This served as a temporary sanctuary upon which the pillar of cloud descended when God spoke with Moses there. Moses, by this action, effectively emphasized the fact that the people's sin of apostasy had separated them from their God and had defiled the holy ground of the camp, with the result that it was now necessary for anyone who sought the Lord to go forth outside the camp. Thus the normal situation in which all territory outside the camp was regarded as unholy and the man who left the camp *ipso facto* became unclean was at this time reversed. Sin had rendered the camp unholy and Moses' withdrawal in order to establish a holy location outside the camp prefigured the setting up of the Christian altar, Christ's cross, outside the gate and the necessity for God's people to join Christ there.

It is significant, further, that Christ not only suffered but also ascended in glory "outside the gate" (Acts 1:12), for this carries the implication that those who are united with Christ in his shame are also united with him in his exaltation. In every respect the Christian's life is "hid with Christ in God" (Col. 3:3): his baptism symbolizes not only his dying and burial with Christ but also his rising with Christ to newness of life

(Rom. 6:3ff.), and his ascension and enthronement with Christ (Eph. 2:6).

Did our author have some special reason for exhorting his readers to go forth to Jesus "outside the camp" rather than "outside the gate"? Considering that the wilderness experience of the Israelites belonged to ancient history, and that the rôle of tabernacle and camp had become that of temple and city, the latter expression might have seemed more appropriate, in the same way that it is used of the suffering of Jesus at Calvary. But the writer reverts to the former expression, urging these Hebrew Christians to take up their position "outside the camp"—a change which has every appearance of being deliberate. We need only remark here that if indeed the recipients of this letter were being adversely influenced in one way or another by the teachings of a perfectionist Jewish sect like that of Qumran, whose aim was the detailed reproduction of the camp organization of the Israelites in the wilderness pending the reinstitution of what they considered the authentic levitical system in Jerusalem, then clearly the exhortation to go forth "outside the camp" would have come to them with particular force.[34] Be that as it may, they are urged to turn their backs resolutely on the observances and ordinances of the old system and to ally themselves unreservedly with Christ who has brought in the new and eternal order. Christ is our only sanctuary, and everyone who seeks God must go forth to find him in and through Jesus outside the camp. As F. F. Bruce explains, "what was formerly sacred was now unhallowed, because Jesus had been expelled from it," and "what was formerly unhallowed was now sacred, because Jesus was there." And Leo the Great preaches that

> when Christ offered himself to the Father a new and true sacrifice of reconciliation, he was crucified not in the temple, whose worship was now at an end, and not within the confines of the city, which for its sin was doomed to be destroyed, but outside, "outside the camp", so that, on the cessation of the old symbolic sacrifices, a new Victim might be placed on a new altar, and the cross of Christ might be the altar not of the temple but of the world.[35]

May we not say, too, that the Son who invites us to join him "outside the camp" himself first left the "camp" of heaven, which is the true and abiding camp and to which he returned in triumph; and that he came to our unholy ground for the purpose of removing the defilement of his people and for the consecration and renewal of the whole creation, so that in the eternity of his glorious kingdom all will be one "camp," one "city," without blemish and without bounds, because there will no

---

34. See Introduction, pp. 12ff.
35. Leo the Great, Sermon LIX.5.

longer be any such thing as unholy territory, and the harmony of heaven and earth, of God and man, will be established forevermore?

13:15, 16. Through him then let us continually offer up a sacrifice of praise to God, that is, the fruit of lips that acknowledge his name. Do not neglect to do good and to share what you have, for such sacrifices are pleasing to God.

By virtue of his sacrifice of himself as a ransom for sinners (Heb. 9:15; 1 Tim. 2:5f.) Jesus Christ is our sole Mediator, and it is accordingly *through him* (emphatically placed at the beginning of the sentence in the Greek as well as in our version)—not through the priestly ritual of an outmoded order or any other person or system—that we *offer up* sacrifices to God; for the members of the Christian church constitute "a holy priesthood" whose duty is "to offer spiritual sacrifices acceptable to God through Jesus Christ" (1 Pet. 2:5). These spiritual sacrifices are defined here as, first, *praise to God* and, second, compassionate service of one's fellow men: *such sacrifices,* our author declares, *are pleasing to God.*

The offering up of praise is not just a matter of the singing of hymns. As the General Thanksgiving of the Book of Common Prayer reminds us, it is "not only with our lips, but in our lives" that we are to show forth God's praise. Our spiritual, or logical, worship, says Paul, is to present our bodies "as a living sacrifice, holy and acceptable to God" (Rom. 12:1). This sacrifice of praise and thanksgiving affects our being in its entirety and therefore is to be offered to God *continually,* at all times and under all circumstances—not occasionally or even at regular intervals, as with the sacrifices of old, but uninterruptedly. (For further discussion of the nature of Christian gratitude see the commentary above on 12:28.)[36]

The gratitude which is the motive force of the whole life of a Christian cannot fail to burst forth from his lips. Hence the description of the "sacrifice of praise to God" as *the fruit of lips that acknowledge his name.* Unlike the thank offerings of the levitical system, this sacrifice requires no presentation or eating of foods (cf. v. 9 above; Lev. 7:11ff.); it is regulated by no outward ceremonial, but rather breaks forth spontaneously from within through the lips. Such praise cannot be silenced by threatenings and persecutions (cf. Acts 4:20; 16:23–25).

The expression "the fruit of the lips" is evidently borrowed from

---

36. Of interest in this connection is the rabbinical teaching that all the Mosaic sacrifices would have an end except the thank offering, and that all prayers would cease except the prayer of thanksgiving (see Strack-Billerbeck, I, p. 246; cf. Jer. 33:11)

Hosea 14:2, "we will render the fruit of our lips," where the Septuagint version corresponds with the Greek of our text. The Hebrew original, however, is generally taken to mean "we will render the bullocks of our lips." The question at issue is, in fact, that of the word-division of the Hebrew rather than of a choice between different readings,[37] and it does not necessarily follow, as Moffatt affirms, that the Septuagint rendering (and therefore that also of our text) is a mistranslation of Hosea 14:2. More probably, the Septuagint represents the understanding of this passage in the second century B.C. (and our text likewise of the first century A.D.), in which case the Massoretic text has been erroneously divided. In either case, however, the sense is clear, namely, that praise and acknowledgment of his name are the sacrifices desired by God, the "bullocks" for which he looks, not mere conformity to outward ceremonies; or, alternatively, that the sacrifice of praise which is the "fruit of lips" is the natural harvest borne by the root of loving faith. The celebrated passage which occurs earlier in the same prophecy is to the same effect: "I desire steadfast love and not sacrifice, the knowledge of God, rather than burnt offerings" (Hos. 6:6). Thus also God declares through the Psalmist: "He who brings thanksgiving as his sacrifice honors me" (Ps. 50:23).

Just as sanctimonious participation in the outward forms of worship is no substitute for a heart that is right with God and a life lived totally to his praise, so also it is no substitute for a compassionate concern for one's fellow men. This is the burden of the memorable utterance of another ancient prophet: "Will the Lord be pleased with thousands of rams, with ten thousands of rivers of oil?... He has showed you, O man, what is good; and what does the Lord require of you but to do justice and to love kindness, and to walk humbly with your God?" (Mic. 6:7f.). The commandments of God are summed up in the two great requirements, to love God with all one's being (as in v. 15 here) and to love one's fellow man as oneself (as in v. 16 here), and these two belong inseparably together. The Hebrew Christians whom our author is addressing were faltering in their fulfilment of both these requirements. Hence the appeal to them not only to praise God continually but also *not to neglect to do good* to their fellow men *and to share*, sacrificially, such

---

37. The Hebrew of Hosea 14:2 may be divided and vocalized either as *pārīm sephāthēnū*, "bullocks of our lips," or as *perī missephāthēnū*, "fruit of our lips." Of particular interest is the discovery of the expression "the fruit of the lips" in the Qumran literature (*Hymns* I.28), while the expression "the oblation of the lips" is also found (*The Community Rule* IX.4; cf. 26). This would seem to indicate that the Qumran understanding of Hosea 14:2 agreed with that of the Septuagint, and thus to confirm the correctness of our author's language when he speaks of a "sacrifice" which is "the fruit of lips."

things as they have with others who are in need. "Let us not grow weary in well-doing," Paul urges the Christians in Galatia, "for in due season we shall reap, if we do not lose heart. So, then, as we have opportunity, let us do good to all men, and especially to those who are of the household of faith" (Gal. 6:9f.). This, too, belongs to our service of sacrifice, which, because it springs from a loving and compassionate heart, is *pleasing to God*. Indeed, it is part of the true imitation of Christ whose love and compassion for mankind were the motive not only for the good that he did on earth, ministering to the afflicted and binding up the heartbroken, but also for his redeeming sacrifice of himself in our stead on the cross of Calvary. "Beloved," says John, "if God so loved us, we ought also to love one another" (1 Jn. 4:11). With Hosea 6:6 as well as the verses now before us in mind, Augustine writes:

> That which in common speech is called sacrifice is only the symbol of the true sacrifice. Now mercy is the true sacrifice, and therefore it is said, "Such sacrifices are pleasing to God". All the divine ordinances, therefore, which we read concerning the sacrifices in the service of the tabernacle or the temple, we are to relate to the love of God and our neighbour. "For on these two commandments", as it is written, "hang all the law and the prophets."[38]

13:17. Obey your leaders and submit to them; for they are keeping watch over your souls, as men who will have to give account. Let them do this joyfully, and not sadly, for that would be of no advantage to you.

The recipients of this letter, who have already been exhorted to remember and to imitate the faith of their former leaders already dead (v. 7), are now enjoined to *obey* their present *leaders*. Such an admonition implies the author's confidence in the ability and genuineness of this leadership, and it suggests that the community to whom he is writing is not as a whole giving these leaders the respect that is their due. It may perhaps be that the occasion of this epistle was the reception by its author of a report, either in writing or in person, from these leaders of the potentially serious situation which was developing among those over whom they had been placed. Christian leadership is intended for the *advantage* of all, not just for the advantage of those who hold positions of authority, and good and successful leadership is to a considerable degree dependent on the willing response of obedience and submission on the part of those who are under authority. "Anarchy," says Chrysostom, "is an evil, the occasion of many calamities, and the source

---

38. Augustine, *Civ. Dei* X.6.

of disorder and confusion"; moreover, "a people that does not obey a ruler is like one that has none, and perhaps even worse." We can well understand, then, Paul's appeal to the members of the Thessalonian church: "We beseech you, brethren, to respect those who labor among you and are over you in the Lord and admonish you, and to esteem them very highly in love because of their work" (1 Thess. 5:12f.).

The authority our author is commending must not be confused with authoritarianism. These leaders are thoroughly deserving of obedience and respect: they are men, he tells his readers, who *are keeping watch*, unceasingly and without regard to themselves,[39] *over your souls,*[40] or, as the NEB renders it, "they are tireless in their concern for you." This in itself is indicative of the conscientious and selfless manner in which they discharged their duties. Our author's concern is, then, as Calvin observes, "only with those who faithfully exercise their office"; for "those who have nothing except the title, and indeed those who abuse the title of pastor to destroy the Church, deserve little reverence and even less trust." The authority of Christian leaders, moreover, is exercised in the light of eternity since eternal issues are involved—in particular the eternal destiny of the flock over which they have been appointed and the outcome for good or ill of their ministry. They are *men who will have to give account to God,* and this solemn consideration should affect not only the quality of their leadership but also the quality of the obedience with which the Christian community responds to that leadership.

Aquinas cites the shepherds in the nativity story who were "keeping watch over their flock by night" (Lk. 2:8) as an example of unremitting care for Christian pastors to follow; and Hugh Latimer, the great preacher of the English Reformation, expounds this text to the same purpose, in the following words:

> Now these shepherds, I say, they watch the whole night, they attend upon their vocation, they do according to their calling, they keep their sheep, they run not hither and thither, spending the time in vain and neglecting their office and calling. . . . Here, by these shepherds, all men may learn to attend upon their offices and callings. I would wish that clergymen—the curates, parsons, and vicars, the bishops, and all other spiritual persons—would learn this lesson by these poor shepherds; which is this, to

39. The verb ἀγρυπνεῖν which is used here means "to pass sleepless nights" and then "to watch ceaselessly," as in Christ's exhortation to be constantly watchful in readiness for the coming of the Son of man (Mk. 13:33; Lk. 21:36). The cognate noun ἀγρυπνία is used by Paul of his own watchful concern as a leader of the church (2 Cor. 6:5; 11:27).

40. The noun ψυχαί, "souls" in our version, is better rendered by the personal pronoun "you" in the NEB. It is frequently used in the New Testament for individuals or persons (see, for example, Acts 2:41, 43; 3:23; 7:14; 27:37; 1 Pet. 3:20) and to translate it "souls" in such cases can easily lead to misunderstanding. The Christian pastor's concern is not merely for the "souls" of those entrusted to his care but for their human existence in its entirety.

abide by their flocks and by their sheep, to tarry amongst them, to be careful over them, not to run hither and thither after their own pleasure, but to tarry by their benefices and feed their sheep with the food of God's Word, and to keep hospitality, and so to feed them both soul and body.[41]

Accountability to God attaches not only to the pastors but also to the members of those flocks which are blessed with earnest and faithful leaders. Let your leaders give an account to God *joyfully,* our author counsels his readers, *and not sadly;* in other words, enable them, when the day of reckoning comes, to present a joyful report of blessing, thanks to your willing obedience and cooperation. A sad report of disharmony and spiritual decline, occasioned by an ungracious and recalcitrant spirit on your part, will *be of no advantage to you,* he warns. The faithful watchman, as Ezekiel's prophecy (3:17ff.) had long since admonished, is not answerable for the disobedient community, but the community that disregards the warnings of the faithful watchman will have to answer for their disobedience—to their, not his, disadvantage! On the other hand, the joy of a faithful pastor is precisely that of a flock which is responsive to his leading. Thus Paul tells the Philippian Christians that they are his "joy and crown" (Phil. 4:1), and John writes: "No greater joy can I have than this, to hear that my children follow the truth" (3 Jn. 4).

13:18, 19. *Pray for us, for we are sure that we have a clear conscience, desiring to act honorably in all things. I urge you the more earnestly to do this in order that I may be restored to you the sooner.*

The request for prayer by the writer of our epistle says much for his confidence in his readers as genuine fellow believers and reassures them of the warmth and humility of his attitude toward them. He can hardly ask them to pray for him if he has decided that they are already in a state of apostasy (cf. Heb. 6:4–6, 9 and 10:26–29, 39). It is true that, *desiring to act honorably in all things,* as a genuine Christian friend and mentor should do, he has spoken very frankly of the perils by which he sees their spiritual well-being to be threatened; and he is *sure* that he has a *clear conscience,* that is, that his conduct in relation to them can stand the scrutiny both of man and of God. But the impulse behind the stern admonitory character of much of this letter has not been hostility or an authoritarian desire to inflate his own importance at their expense. That he has spoken the truth in love and compassion is confirmed by this appeal to them to pray for him. In a similar manner Paul besought the

41. Hugh Latimer, *Works,* II (Cambridge, 1845), pp. 119f.

Corinthian Christians for their prayers on his behalf (and this in an epistle in which he had the painful necessity of firmly asserting his apostolic authority): "You must help us by prayer," he writes. ". . . For our boast is this, the testimony of our conscience that we have behaved in the world, and still more toward you, with holiness and godly sincerity. . . . We have renounced disgraceful, underhanded ways; we refuse to practice cunning or to tamper with God's word, but by the open statement of the truth we would commend ourselves to every man's conscience in the sight of God" (2 Cor. 1:11f.; 4:2).

I urge you the more earnestly, or especially,[42] *to do this*, that is, to pray for me, our author adds, *in order that*, by God's response to your petitions, *I may be restored to you sooner*, or in the near future.[43] This appeal can only increase the assurance of the genuineness of his love for those to whom he is writing: not only does he desire their prayers as it were at a distance but he longs to be united in person with them again, no longer separated from them by miles or suspicions. The implications of this brief request are, first, that the writer had previously been associated with those he is addressing, perhaps as one of their leaders, second, that he is now in a different location, presumably in a different country, and, third, that he is for the present prevented from coming to them, though he hopes to be able to do so soon.

13:20, 21. *Now may the God of peace who brought again from the dead our Lord Jesus, the great shepherd of the sheep, by the blood of the eternal covenant, equip you with everything good that you may do his will, working in you that which is pleasing in his sight, through Jesus Christ; to whom be glory for ever and ever. Amen.*

This invocation forms the proper conclusion of the epistle. What follows in verses 22–25 is to all intents and purposes a postscript. While it is far from being stereotyped or a mere formality, this invocation has certain affinities with comparable passages in the concluding sections of some of Paul's letters, notably 1 Thessalonians 5:23, 2 Thessalonians 3:16, and Romans 15:33, in which prayer for blessing from *the God of peace* is expressed. (For other mentions of "the God of peace" at or near the ends

---

42. The adverb περισσοτέρως, though comparative in form, is probably elative in force, without any comparison being intended, as also in 2:1 and 6:17 (περισσότερον).

43. As with περισσοτέρως (preceding note), so with τάχιον it is unlikely that a comparative sense is intended. In the case of τάχιον here the force is probably positive, as it seems certainly to be in verse 23 below. What our author is saying, then, is, "Pray especially that I may be restored to you soon," rather than "The more earnestly you pray the sooner I will be restored to you."

of letters see Philippians 4:9 and Romans 16:20, and cf. Ephesians 6:23.) It is unlikely that the appellation "the God of peace" is used here with the specific purpose of promoting loving harmony among the members of the community our author is addressing, whom it has been necessary to exhort to show brotherly love to one another and obedience to their leaders (vv. 1 and 17 above), as Delitzsch, Westcott, and F. F. Bruce suppose, or of encouraging a composed attitude on the part of those whose faith is wavering in the face of opposition and affliction (see, for example, 10:24f., 35f.; 12:12), as Spicq and Teodorico suggest, though the implications of this appellation are obviously highly relevant to their situation. The *peace* here of which God is the author is primarily the peace of the gospel (Eph. 6:15), the peace which has been established, or re-established, between man and his Creator by the blood of Christ's cross (Col. 1:20), the peace of God in Christ Jesus which passes all understanding (Phil. 4:7), peace, in short, in its deepest and fullest sense. It is the God of this peace, which speaks forgiveness and acceptance to man at the very heart of his being and which should permeate the whole of his existence in all its relationships and vicissitudes, whom our author invokes here.

The ground of this transcendental peace which has God as its source is in effect defined in the affirmation that it was *by*, on the basis *of, the blood of the eternal covenant* that *our Lord Jesus* was *brought again from the dead*. To put it in words used earlier in the epistle, he was "crowned with glory and honor because of the suffering of death" (2:9; see the commentary there). The price of our peace was the blood of Jesus, that is, the sacrifice of the incarnate Son on the cross. The proof of the acceptance of this sacrifice on our behalf is his resurrection from the grave and his exaltation to the right hand of the Majesty on high (Heb. 1:3; 12:2), whereby he is declared to be Lord of all (Phil. 2:8–10). Had he not shed his blood for us he could not be our Savior. Had he not been brought again from the dead he could be neither Savior nor Lord. His dying would have been just one more in the long sequence of sacrifices which cannot take away sins (Heb. 10:11f.). Death would have had the final word. But the resurrection manifested his glory as the prince of life and conqueror of death and confirmed that his blood is the seal of a *covenant* that is *eternal* and that by this single offering of himself "he has perfected for all time those who are sanctified" (10:14).

In all that he has done and does our Lord Jesus displays himself as *the great shepherd of the sheep*—great, that is, in comparison with all other shepherds, who beside him pale into insignificance, and therefore unique; just as he is also our great and unique High Priest (Heb. 4:14; 7:23f.). He, and he alone, is the Good Shepherd, who laid down his life for the sheep, but who laid down his life in order that he might take it

589

again; for he, the Lord, had power to lay down his life and power to take it again (Jn. 10:11–18; Ps. 23:1). In accordance with his eternal covenant, he gives his sheep eternal life, and neither man nor devil can snatch them out of his hand (Jn. 10:28f.). The provision of "the blood of the eternal covenant" fulfils the prophecies of Zechariah 9:11, where God speaks of "the blood of my covenant," and Ezekiel 37:26, where the God of peace promises: "I will make a covenant of peace with them; it shall be an everlasting covenant with them" (cf. Isa. 55:3; Jer. 31:31ff.; 8:8ff. above). We have already seen that Christ is the mediator of this new covenant, the purpose of which is "that those who are called may receive the promised eternal inheritance" (9:15), and that there is no hope for the person who has "profaned the blood of the covenant by which he was sanctified" (10:29). Thus the blood of the incarnate Son is eternally powerful; for, as Calvin writes, "God raised up his Son in such a way that his blood once shed in death has power to ratify the eternal covenant after his resurrection and brings forth its fruit as though it were always flowing."

It is against this rich redemptive background that our author prays that God may *equip you with everything good*—an inelegant translation; NEB, "make you perfect in all goodness,"[44] is much better—*that you may do his will*. The new man in Christ is a man restored to the harmonious integrity of his humanity.[45] The new creation is at the same time the re-creation; for redemption means reintegration and reconciliation (2 Cor. 5:17ff.). And just as being cannot be divorced from doing, so the creature is redeemed not only to *be* a new man but also to *do* the works that spring from and make manifest the new nature, which means specifically to do God's will, for the performance of the divine will is the proper function of every creature. Yet this "doing" is not the doing of the creature only, but at the same time the doing of the Creator; for it is the God of peace who is said here to be *working*, or doing,[46] *in you that which is pleasing in his sight*. That is to say, the harmony which is restored to man derives from the fact that, thanks to the mediation of our divine-human High Priest—hence the addition, *through Jesus Christ* (cf. 2 Cor. 5:19)—there is a restoration of harmony between man and God. The union of the divine will and the human will is the true harmony of creation. This is by no means the eclipse of the human will but, on the

---

44. Καταρτίσαι ὑμᾶς ἐν παντὶ ἀγαθῷ. Many late MSS have added ἔργῳ to ἀγαθῷ and this is reflected in the TR and the KJV. The reading of Alexandrinus, παντὶ ἔργῳ καὶ λόγῳ ἀγαθῷ, looks like a borrowing from 2 Thessalonians 2:17.

45. The verb καταρτίζειν means to re-articulate what has been dislocated, to restore to a state of functional perfection.

46. The verb both for God's and for our action is ποιεῖν: ... εἰς τὸ ποιῆσαι ... ποιῶν ἐν ὑμῖν.

contrary, its fulness and its perfection. God working in us enables us to work with him and thus to perform the purpose of his will. "This is the will of God," Aquinas comments, "that we should will what God wills; for otherwise we have no good will. But God's will is our good." What could be more sublimely satisfying than humanity so dignified as to be united with the will and the work of God? Accordingly, Paul urges the Philippians to "work out," that is, to give practical expression to, the salvation that is theirs, but to do so with the assurance that "God is at work in them, both to will and to work for his good pleasure" (Phil. 2:12f.); and he reminds the Ephesians that "we are his workmanship, created in Christ Jesus for good works, which God prepared beforehand, that we should walk in them" (Eph. 2:10). The Christian's service of God, therefore, is not passive submission but willing, joyful, and cooperative obedience. Thus in Christ the lifeline which connects the creature to the Creator and his eternal purposes is restored.

This, too, is the way of genuine Christ-likeness; it is the true following of the Master. For when the Son came into the world it was with the affirmation, "Lo, I have come to do thy will, O God" (Heb. 10:7). His testimony was, "I always do what is pleasing to him" (Jn. 8:29). And it is by virtue of that divine will that "we have been sanctified through the offering of the body of Jesus Christ once for all" (Heb. 10:10). No wonder our author breaks into the doxology: *to whom be glory for ever and ever!*— for the spontaneous glorification of our Redeemer God is itself an evidence of the union of the will of man with the will of his Creator.

13:22. *I appeal to you, brethren, bear with my word of exhortation, for I have written to you briefly.*

A short postscript, verses 22 to 25, is added, perhaps in the author's own handwriting if he has been using the services of an amanuensis. He appeals to those to whom this document is addressed to *bear with* his *word*, or instruction, which is intended as an *exhortation*. In insisting on the uniqueness of the Christian gospel and its claims he has spoken plainly of the outmoded character of the levitical system and has sternly warned them of the extreme peril of apostasy from single-minded devotion to Jesus Christ; but his aim all through has been their strengthening and encouragement and his attitude has not been coldly censorious. So, too, when using some severity in writing to the Corinthians, Paul gives them the affectionate assurance: "It is in the sight of God that we have been speaking in Christ, and all for your upbuilding, beloved" (2 Cor. 12:10; cf. 10:8; 13:10). The way in which our author addresses his readers as *brethren* here and elsewhere (3:1, 12; 10:19) and as "beloved" (6:9) and his mention of Timothy in the next verse as "our brother" is proof of the love and devotion he feels for them. Moreover, he has not written at inordinate length, but *briefly;* for there is much more teaching that he could have given (cf. 9:5), and perhaps intends to give in person when he comes to them. Certainly, the missive is full of solid doctrine concerning important issues, but, as Moffatt and Montefiore point out, it could all be read aloud in an hour.

The description of what he has written as a *word of exhortation* may perhaps indicate the form as well as the purpose of this document, suggesting that it is intended as a homily, *written,*[47] however, like a letter to friends, as this postscript shows. This consideration could explain the abrupt commencement without an epistolary introduction identifying the writer and designating the recipients. It may well correspond with another "word of exhortation"[48] or homily spoken, not written, by the apostle Paul in the synagogue at Pisidian Antioch (Acts 13:15ff.). In view, however, of the epistolary conclusion, this composition may be described as both homiletic and epistolary; and there is nothing unusual in this, for the main purpose of the letters of the New Testament is homiletic and hortatory. A "word of exhortation" is then, as F. F. Bruce remarks, "a very suitable description for this epistle, which is a homily in written form, with some personal remarks added at the end."

13:23. *You should understand that our brother Timothy has been released, with whom I shall see you if he comes soon.*

It must be assumed that the *Timothy* mentioned here is the same person whom we meet frequently elsewhere in the New Testament as Paul's younger companion or emissary. Our author's description of him as *our brother* suggests that he is well known to those to whom this letter is addressed, and the impression given by this brief communication

---

47. The verb ἐπέστειλα, "I have written," implies the writing of a letter, ἐπιστολή—the noun and the verb ἐπιστέλλειν being cognate. L. P. Trudinger, however, takes the verb to mean "enjoin" or "instruct" here, without any epistolary connotation, and the brief "word of exhortation" to refer only to a few instructions given in this thirteenth chapter. ("KAI ΓΑΡ ΔΙΑ ΒΡΑΧΕΩΝ ΕΠΕΣΤΕΙΛΑ ΥΜΙΝ: A Note on Hebrews XIII.22," JTS, N.S. 23, 1972, pp. 128ff.). He claims the support of Moulton and Milligan for this meaning, but even so a letter or missive is implied as the vehicle by which the instruction is conveyed; for, as Moulton and Milligan also affirm, "the general use of the verb... is in connexion with sending a letter or other written communication" (*sub voc.*).

48. The same Greek expression, λόγος παρακλήσεως, is used both here and in Acts 13:15.

regarding his release is that it will be welcome news to them[49] (NEB, "I have news for you," conveys the spirit more effectively than our version's *you should understand that*).[50] Timothy, apparently, has been in custody of some kind, presumably on account of his Christian profession, but now he *has been released*.[51] Evidently, at the time of writing, he is not in the same place as our author, though not too far distant, since the hope is expressed that, depending on his joining the author *soon*, they will be able to visit the readers together.

13:24, 25. *Greet all your leaders and all the saints. Those who come from Italy send you greetings. Grace be with all of you. Amen.*

The laconic brevity of this concluding salutation raises some interesting questions to which no certain answer is available. The request, *Greet*, on the author's behalf, *all your leaders*, is unmatched elsewhere in the New Testament. It would seem, incidentally, to confirm the authenticity and authority of these leaders, to whom the readers have been admonished to be obedient and respectful (v. 17). If "all" is emphatic the implication may be that they had been cooperative with some but insubordinate to others of their leaders. The designation "all" does not necessarily indicate a great number, but possibly just four or five. That a local church or district might at this time have a number of leaders is demonstrated by Paul's invitation to the elders of the Ephesian church to come to him at Miletus (Acts 20:17ff.; note how in v. 25 Paul addresses them as "you all,"[52] though how many there were is not stated). It does not follow, as, for example, Zahn and Moffatt conclude, that our epistle is addressed to a particular section, perhaps a household congregation, of a larger local church; nor need it be supposed that the communication was sent to the members as distinct from the leaders, which surely is far from probable. The missive, rather, is intended for all: thus they are asked to greet not only all their leaders but also *all the saints*. Our author sends his salutations to everybody in the community.

Greetings are added from *those who come from Italy*—though the Greek text is hardly so clear as this rendering might suggest. Literally,

---

49. Cf. Bengel: "*scitote* cum gaudio"; Phillips: "You will be glad to know."
50. The Greek text simply has γινώσκετε, which should be taken as imperative, not indicative.
51. Ἀπολελυμένον. The verb ἀπολύειν has a wide range of meaning. It is used, for example, of releasing Paul and Barnabas for missionary work (Acts 13:3; cf. 15:30, 33), but its most frequent sense in the New Testament is that of releasing from custody persons who are under arrest or in prison.
52. Ὑμεῖς πάντες.

the meaning is "those who are from or of Italy,"[53] an ambiguous expression which could mean either those from Italy who are now in a different country or those who are of Italy and still in Italy.[54] If it is a greeting from Italians living outside Italy then it is not unreasonable to conclude that this epistle was written in the place where they were resident and sent to a group of Hebrew Christians in Italy. But if it is a salutation from Italians in Italy then the implication would seem to be that the epistle originated in Italy and that those whom it addresses were resident in some other country. There is also the possibility that neither of these inferences is correct. No dogmatism is justifiable on the basis of the cryptic statement before us, and F. F. Bruce wisely counsels that "it is best to render the ambiguous Greek by an ambiguous English phrase." The NEB does this well: "Greetings to you from our Italian friends."

The final short benediction, identical with that of Titus 3:15 (cf. 2 Tim. 4:22), is a prayer that *grace*, that is, the grace of God which is mediated through Jesus Christ (who by the grace of God tasted death for everyone, Heb. 2:9) in the fellowship of the Holy Spirit, in other words, *Christian* grace, may be with them all. This grace, says Spicq, "is a stream of living water flowing through the desert, a power which enables us to withstand every adversity and to reach the promised land, the place of our rest, the heavenly Jerusalem." The source of this grace is the throne of grace where divine assistance is ever available to us in the hour of necessity (Heb. 4:16) and strength to enable us to overcome every assault of the enemy and to persevere to the end (Heb. 13:9; cf. 2 Cor. 12:9f.).

---

53. Οἱ ἀπὸ τῆς Ἰταλίας.
54. Both meanings are found elsewhere in the New Testament, the former in Acts 10:23 (τινες τῶν ἀδελφῶν τῶν ἀπὸ Ἰόππης) and 38 (Ἰησοῦν τὸν ἀπὸ Ναζαρέθ), and 21:27 (οἱ ἀπὸ τῆς Ἀσίας Ἰουδαῖοι), the latter in Acts 17:13 (οἱ ἀπὸ τῆς Θεσσαλονίκης Ἰουδαῖοι—cf. 12:1). Moffatt cites the contemporary Oxyrhynchus papyri (i.81) in which τῶν ἀπ' Ὀξυρύγχων means "the inhabitants of Oxyrhynchus." See also John 11:1, where Lazarus is described as ἀπὸ Βηθανίας, "of Bethany": he was certainly not "away from" Bethany.

INDEX OF SUBJECTS

INDEX OF NAMES

INDEX OF SCRIPTURE REFERENCES

2:14f.	499	30:7f.	312, 319	15:29f.	378	
3:2	62	30:10	313	Ch. 16	176, 277, 376,	
3:6	480, 543	30:18ff.	201		575	
4:5	480	30:29	309	16:2	309, 316	
4:22f.	548	31:13	103	16:3	309	
6:7	301	Ch. 32	581	16:4	201, 324	
12:1ff.	500	32:13	230	16:6	276	
12:5	290	32:19	315	16:11	276	
12:8f.	573	32:32f.	548	16:12	311	
13:2	59, 548	33:7	282, 581	16:14ff.	316, 377	
13:12ff.	548	33:9ff.	42	16:15	276	
13:19	491	34:29	556	16:16	176, 309	
14:10ff.	501	Ch. 40	581	16:17	309	
14:31	134	40:5	310, 312	16:17ff.	313	
16:32–34	315	40:9ff.	377	16:18	310	
17:1ff.	142	40:22, 24	312	16:20	309	
Chs. 19–20	75	40:26	310	16:23	309	
19:12	543	40:29–32	411	16:24	201	
19:12ff.	542	40:34ff.	316	16:25	177	
19:16	543			16:26	201, 579	
19:16ff.	543	*Leviticus*		16:27	309, 579	
19:18	557	2:1ff.	277	16:28	201, 324, 579	
19:19	543	2:3	309	16:29	319	
19:20	543	2:10	309	17:10f.	335	
19:24	543	Ch. 4	178, 277	18:5	76, 296	
20:18	543	4:1f.	321	19:2	537	
20:19	543, 556	4:1ff.	574	19:5f.	573	
21:1–6	396	4:3ff.	277	20:7	537	
22:29	59	4:13ff.	277	20:8	103	
23:19	548	5:6f.	378	20:26	537	
23:31	367, 509	5:11ff.	378	21:1ff.	273	
Ch. 24	374, 375, 376	5:17ff.	321	21:16ff.	273	
24:3ff.	366, 374	6:14ff.	276f.	22:6	201	
24:5	374, 375	6:17	309	22:29f.	573	
24:7	376	6:25	309	22:32	103	
24:8	354, 376	6:27	201	23:13	241	
24:15ff.	42	6:29	309	23:18	241	
25:10–15	315	Ch. 7	574	24:28f.	319	
25:16	315	7:1	309	26:12	301	
25:17ff.	316	7:6	309			
25:22	316	7:11ff.	583	*Numbers*		
25:31ff.	318	7:13	241	3:5ff.	252	
25:40	293	8:10f.	377	3:12f.	59	
26:1ff.	309	8:30	354, 377	3:40ff.	548	
26:31	312	9:22f.	350	5:15	392	
26:33	309	9:24	455	6:2ff.	324	
26:35	312	10:8ff.	324	6:22ff.	350	
27:20f.	319	11:1–47	324	8:5ff.	324	
28:1	175	11:28	324	8:6	175	
28:1ff.	179	11:40	324	8:8	397	
28:29	388	11:44f.	537	11:11	134	
29:4	411	13:54	201	12:7	130, 134, 137	
29:10ff.	377	14:1ff.	324, 375	14:3	432	
29:21	354, 411	14:19	397	14:11	415	
29:45f.	301	Ch. 15	378	14:22f.	143	
30:1	312	15:1ff.	324	14:26ff.	154	
30:6	309f.	15:14f.	378	15:27ff.	178